A History of

CHRISTIAN THOUGHT

•

Volume II

A History

of

CHRISTIAN THOUGHT

by

Otto W. Heick

VOLUME II

FORTRESS PRESS PHILADELPHIA

Library of Congress Catalog Card Number LC-65-23839

2902C66 Printed in U.S.A. UB9

TABLE OF CONTENTS

Book Four

THE DISINTEGRATION OF CONFESSIONAL THEOLOGY

Book Five

EUROPEAN THOUGHT SINCE THE NINETEENTH CENTURY

SECTION ONE—CONTINENTAL THOUGHT

SECTION TWO—THEOLOGICAL THOUGHT IN GREAT BRITAIN

Book Six

THEOLOGICAL THOUGHT IN AMERICA

Book Four

THE DISINTEGRATION OF CONFESSIONAL THEOLOGY

Introduction

The developments to be discussed comprise two groups. The one is comparatively conservative, the other is radical. The conservative movements are: (1) the theology of the radical Reformers and its influence on the established churches through pietism and Wesleyanism; (2) Arminianism in Holland, issuing into (3) latitudinarianism in England. The radical developments include: (1) English deism, (2) French naturalism, (3) German rationalism, and (4) Unitarianism in Europe and America. The Roman Catholic church experienced both a strengthening and a deterioration of its position during this period.

CHAPTER I

THEOLOGIES IN CONFLICT WITH THE CONSERVATIVE REFORMATION

The Radical Reformation on the Continent

Both Luther and Zwingli included the institutional aspect in their concept of the Church. They considered the organized Church an essential element for the propagation of the gospel and the religious education of the people. In this respect, Lutheranism and Zwinglianism (later to be superseded by Calvinism) maintained a historical continuity with medieval Catholicism and its theory of a Universal Church dominating the whole of Western civilization.

Side by side with the medieval unity of Church and civilization, sectarian and mystical movements had always arisen, for example, the Waldensian movement and others, which repeatedly challenged the idea of a Christian civilization. Such movements had occurred from the time of the Montanists, Novatians, and Donatists in the early Church. The same trend continued both within and alongside Protestantism. Protestantism, too, developed what Troeltsch has called the "sectarian and mystic" type of Christianity.[1] The movement was represented by a veritable medley of men whom Roland Bainton and others have designated as the "left-wing Reformers." Others have called the movement the "radical Reformation." [2] More recently we

[1] Cf. Ernst Troeltsch, *The Social Teaching of the Christian Churches* (London: George Allen & Unwin, Ltd., 1931).

[2] Cf. *Library of Christian Classics*, eds. John Baillie, John T. McNeill, and Henry P. Van Dusen (Philadelphia: Westminster Press, 1953 ff.), hereinafter referred to as *LCC*, XXV, 20. H. Kurtz, *Church History*, dismissed the whole movement as a "deformation of the Church." In the first edition of the present volume the movement was called "The Theology of the Inner Light." This caption has been discarded because of the more inclusive character of the discussion offered here.

have come to appreciate the significance of these Reformers in the rise of modern, especially American, Christianity.

Among the dissenters on the Continent three main groups may be distinguished: the Anabaptists, the Spiritualists, and the Rationalists. The Anabaptists looked upon Scripture as the only norm of faith and practice and at times espoused a legalistic interpretation of the Bible. The Spiritualists believed in immediate illumination by the Holy Spirit and established themselves on strictly supernatural grounds. The third group in the radical Reformation, the Rationalists, represented the spirit of reform in the countries of southern and eastern Europe which had remained pre-eminently Roman Catholic. George H. Williams has called them "evangelical Rationalists." [3] Their main concern was a natural piety. They recognized reason as a source of authority alongside Scripture and, as in the case of the Socinians, felt the urge to establish disciplined congregations on the New Testament pattern.

A person difficult to classify is David Joris.[4] Born in Holland about 1501, Joris was an eccentric mystic who befriended Castellio and wrote a defense of Servetus. He stood with the Mennonites in rejecting armed resistance. He held that baptism with water is of no avail without the Spirit and that Scripture is nebulous because the truth resides in the inner Word. Joris regarded himself as the Third David, at times exalting himself above Christ. He was ordained a bishop by Obbe Philips. Menno Simons, however, dissociated himself from the Davidians or Davidists as Joris's followers were called. When persecution threatened the Anabaptists in 1543, Joris went to Basel, announcing himself as Jan van Brugge, a fugitive for the sake of the gospel. The deception was not discovered until three years after his death in 1556. In May, 1559, he was solemnly declared a heretic and his remains were unearthed and burned.[5]

Williams divides Anabaptism and Spiritualism into three main sub-

[3] *LCC,* XXV, 23-24.

[4] George H. Williams did not include Joris in his survey of the Reformers in *LCC* (written with Mergal) but does mention Joris several times in *The Radical Reformation* (Philadelphia: Westminster Press, 1962).

[5] Williams, *op. cit.,* pp. 380 ff. Menno Simons has several references to the Davidians; see the index in *Complete Works of Menno Simons,* ed. John C. Wenger, trans. Leonard Verdouin (Scottsdale, Pa.: Herald Press, 1956), hereinafter referred to as *Works,* p. 1076. Cf. also R. H. Bainton, "The Heretic as Hypocrite" in *The Travail of Religious Liberty* (1951), pp. 125 ff.

divisions: evangelical, revolutionary, and contemplative Anabaptists; evangelical, revolutionary, and rational Spiritualists.

The evangelical Anabaptists were oriented toward the past. They sought to find their image and blueprint for church life in the New Testament and in the martyr church of the pre-Constantinian period. They organized local congregations, stressed personal experience and witness by adult baptism, and exercised corporate discipline (the ban and shunning). They were or soon became distrustful of Spirit possession and the vagaries of prophecy. The life and teachings of the historic Jesus, especially the Sermon on the Mount, were normative for these Anabaptists. This evangelical group includes the Swiss Brethren (Conrad Grebel, George Blaurock, George Mantz, *et al.*), Jacob Hutter and Ulrich Stadler in Austria and Moravia, and later Menno Simons in the Netherlands.

The revolutionary Anabaptists stressed possession of the Spirit. They leaned heavily on the Old Testament and conceived of the Church as God's Israel to be established in their own times. These ideas eventually led to their violent and polygamous theocracy in Muenster. Their first prophet was Melchior Hofmann, a layman whose mind was steeped in millennial and eschatological fancies.

The most important contemplative Anabaptists include John Denck and Louis Haetzer. Although Denck presided over a body of evangelical Anabaptists in southern Germany for a while, he had an entirely different spirit. Neo-Platonic and medieval mysticism constituted a major strand in his work. His chief interest was in the inward Christ, whom he identified with the inner Word common to all mankind. Consequently he has been regarded by some modern writers as a Quaker, by others as a Unitarian or humanist.

In contradistinction to the Anabaptists, the Spiritualists gazed mostly into the future. They were distrustful of all contemporary Reformers, holding that none of them were called by God. They despaired of all attempts to establish the true Church and instead comforted themselves with the fellowship of the invisible Church of the Spirit. The Spirit, they taught, defines the Word; the Bible does not define and interpret the Spirit. The Spirit is regarded as an impersonal, divine energy. Redemption involves a deification of nature through the healing and restorative ministry of the Spirit. Scripture is primarily a guide and confirmation of one's own personal religious experience.

Prominent among the evangelical Spiritualists was Kaspar von Schwenckfeld, a Silesian nobleman. He sought to hold a position which mediated between Luther and Zwingli, but succeeded in standing midway between the Anabaptists and the Spiritualists. Like the former, he founded religious conventicles and rejected infant baptism, but he did not practice believers' baptism. The only baptism he could admit was the baptism of the Holy Spirit. Baptism with water was of no consequence. In 1525 he endeavored to mediate between the Lutherans and the Zwinglians. Following a personal interview with Schwenckfeld, Luther denounced him as the "third head of the destructive sacramentarian sect" (Karlstadt and Zwingli were the other two). Schwenckfeld's view of the Lord's Supper is spiritualistic-dynamic and approximates the teaching of Calvin. While Luther's doctrine of the ubiquity of the body of Christ was not repulsive to Schwenckfeld, he declined to believe that an earthly element could convey the spiritual. Rather, he regarded the Supper, symbolic of the humanity and divinity of Christ, as a means of spiritual nourishment without any direct relation of the body and blood of Christ to the bread and wine.[6]

The revolutionary Spiritualists deviated to some extent from the purely spiritualistic concept of the Church. They felt called to defeat the ungodly and to establish a theocratic order of society—by military force, if necessary. The Zwickau prophets whom Luther called *Schwärmer*, Andreas Karlstadt and Thomas Muentzer, belong to this group. On the surface there seems to be little if any difference between the revolutionary Anabaptists, or Muensterites, and the revolutionary Spiritualists, or Muentzerites, except that to the latter, water baptism of any kind is meaningless.

The theology of the rational Spiritualists is grounded more in the spirit of man than in the Spirit of God. Stress is laid on the universal aspect of Christianity. Christian theology is turned into a philosophy of religion by men like Sebastian Franck, Valentine Weigel, and Theobald Thamer.

The majority of the radical Reformers were men with university training, among them Conrad Grebel, Philip Manz, and Kaspar von Schwenckfeld. A goodly number of them, like Luther and Zwingli,

[6] Cf. in *Corpus Schwenckfeldianorum* (Leipzig), II, 439 ff.

were ordained to the Roman Catholic priesthood. Among these were Thomas Muentzer, Andreas Karlstadt, Balthasar Hubmaier, George Blaurock, and Menno Simons. Others, especially the revolutionary leaders, were lay people without formal education. Nicholas Storch, one of the Zwickau prophets, was a cloth manufacturer; Hans Hut, a carpenter; Peter Rideman, a shoemaker; Melchior Hofmann, a furrier; Jan Matthys, a baker; Jan van Leyden, a tailor.

After the Peasant Revolt, its leaders and followers alike were subjected to a ruthless suppression by both Catholic and Protestant authorities who could see in them nothing but a seditious, licentious element destructive to the well-being of society. The Protestant Reformers, Luther, Melanchthon, Zwingli, and Calvin, fully concurred in this sentiment. In fairness to the conservative Reformers it must be admitted that it was not always easy to draw a line of demarcation between the nonresistant group and the revolutionaries. The Radicals themselves recognized a kind of solidarity which bound them together. The Swiss Brethren addressed Thomas Muentzer in a letter as a "dearly beloved brother" and "true proclaimer of the Gospel." [7] Obbe Philips was ordained an elder in the Melchior group and in turn was baptized by Menno Simons.[8]

A Brief Resume of Radical Thought

The following aberrations from the traditional orthodoxy of both Roman Catholicism and the conservative Reformation were common to the leaders of the radical Reformation.[9]

(1) The radical Reformers rejected the sacramental character of baptism and the Eucharist. These two rites, they held, were not sacraments at all. They were to be interpreted as ordinances of the Lord.[10] Baptism was a covenantal action by which a penitent person would become a member of the righteous remnant, the true Church. Hofmann spoke of baptism in the emotional language of the sacrament of marriage. In baptism the penitent man bound and betrothed himself in

[7] *LCC,* XXV, 73-74.

[8] The Muensterites were the spiritual followers of Melchior Hofmann. Obbe Philips later defected and denounced the self-styled leaders in no uncertain terms. Cf. *LCC,* XXV, 206 ff.

[9] For a discussion of the evangelical Rationalists cf. our Chapter VIII.

[10] Cf. Melchior Hofmann, "The Ordinances of God," *LCC,* XXV, 182 ff.

complete surrender to Christ as his Lord, King, and Bridegroom.[11] Hofmann conceived of the Anabaptists collectively as the Bride being led and driven through the Spirit and will of God and the anointed Savior to spend, like Christ, forty days and forty nights in the wilderness. This Bride would fight to the end and conquer.[12] To Schwenckfeld, the Lord's Supper was a sacramental recollection of the Last Supper and of one's own experience of receiving mystically the celestial flesh of Christ.[13]

(2) The Nicene doctrine of the Trinity was rejected by the evangelical Radicals and even posed a problem for the biblical Radicals. Menno Simons, for example, had to defend the Nicene faith against one of his own brotherhood, Roelof Martens, better known as Adam Pastor, whom he had ordained a bishop about 1542.[14]

(3) Another aberration from the orthodox faith is to be seen in the Radicals' doctrine of Christ, which ranged all the way from an insistence on an exclusively human nature of Christ, as on the part of the Unitarians, to an insistence on an exclusively divine nature commonly known as the teaching of the celestial flesh or body of Christ. Clemens Ziegler of Strassburg taught that the Son was born within the Trinity before the foundations of the world were laid, brought his translucent body with him from heaven, and acquired visibility from Mary.[15] Hofmann, going even further than Ziegler, held a strictly monophysitic view: The Logos did not take flesh upon himself, but transformed himself into flesh for our salvation.[16] Schwenckfeld, on the other hand, replied to Luther that he was not a Eutychian or Monophysite. He said that Mary was the true mother of Jesus Christ, but denied any creatureliness in Christ. Instead, Almighty God brought uncreated flesh out of the Holy Virgin.[17]

The doctrine of the celestial flesh of Christ, reviving ancient Gnostic and monophysitic Christology, was an abortive effort on the part of the radical Reformers to strike at the very root of Nicene Christianity

[11] *Ibid.*, p. 187.
[12] *Ibid.*, p. 190.
[13] Schwenckfeld, *op. cit.*, pp. 161 ff.
[14] See Menno's tract, "Confession of the Triune God" (1550), *Works*, pp. 488 ff.
[15] For reference see Williams, *op. cit.*, pp. 328-29.
[16] *LCC*, XXV, 198; cf. also Williams, *op. cit.*, pp. 329 ff.
[17] *LCC*, XXV, 179 ff.; Williams, *op. cit.*, pp. 332 ff.

as developed under the tutelage of the state. This Christology was augmented by the Aristotelian-Thomistic view according to which only the male sperm is formative in the process of procreation.[18] This observation is especially borne out by the Radicals' mystical-covenantal concept of marriage as a spiritual wedlock. The spiritual relation as brother and sister in the Lord often took precedence over the natural relation as husband and wife. Conversely, man's relation to God was described as a betrothal (Melchior Hofmann). In keeping with these tendencies Peter Rideman says that first of all marriage is a relationship of God with the soul, second a relationship of the spirit with the body, and third that of one body with another, "the last and lowest grade." [19] Consequently, a man should not follow "his flesh" but ask the elders of the Church "that God might show him through them what He has appointed for him." [20] The Radicals followed a *via media* between the sacramental view of the Catholic church and the creaturely concept of Luther and Calvin. Because marriage was a covenant to the Radicals, as their relationship with Christ was a betrothal, Williams remarks, "they found a basis for greater personal loyalty within the covenantal bond than in sacramental Catholicism, and for greater freedom of divorce and remarriage." [21]

(4) The bondage of the will in things spiritual, salvation *sola gratia* and *sola fide*, which had constituted the center of Luther's Reformation, was in the eyes of the radical Reformers only a half-truth, "an angelic form to cover over all the license of the flesh." [22] The moral condition in the churches that had separated from the Roman community seemed to bear out this contention. Hence the Radicals stressed the freedom of the will. Man, they taught, is capable of making a decision for or against Christ. They also stressed progressive sanctification through the imitation of Christ, over against the forensic view of justification through faith in the redemptive work of Christ. In mystical union with Christ, whose body is celestial flesh, the human nature of believers is progressively deified. Melchior Hofmann maintained that men put on Christ through faith and in baptism: "The

[18] Cf. A. C. Pegis, *Basic Writings of St. Thomas*, I (1945), 932.

[19] Peter Rideman, *Account of Our Religion, Doctrine and Faith* (London: Hodder & Stoughton, Ltd., 1950), p. 98.

[20] *Ibid.*, p. 100.

[21] Williams, *op. cit.*, p. 507.

[22] Hubmaier, *LCC*, XXV, 114-15.

Law cannot make them guilty nor, like a mirror, show up blemishes and spots, because they are pure. They have been found unpunishable before the judgment seat of God." [23] Holiness, therefore, is an empirical quality, a state discernible to the human eye. Inasmuch as the law cannot condemn the regenerate, they no longer need to pray for the forgiveness of sins. Progress in holiness renders the fifth petition of the Lord's Prayer meaningless in the lives of the regenerate.

Menno Simons

Menno Simons remained much closer to Luther's position than the other radical Reformers. It is true that he believed in personal holiness and strict discipline and that his writings abound in a description of the fruit of regeneration, which he felt was lacking in both Catholic and Protestant churches, but he did not teach perfectionism. Like Luther, he said that faith is not an accomplishment of man but rather a gift of God, and that man is righteous by the imputation of the righteousness of Christ.[24] "In and by yourself," he wrote in a beautiful letter of consolation to his sister-in-law, "you are a poor sinner . . . but in and through Christ you are justified and pleasing unto God and adopted by Him in eternal grace as a daughter and child." [25] This statement echoes Luther's understanding of the Christian life as *simul justus et peccator*. In themselves the saints are unclean. "All our righteousness is as filthy rags." [26] The saints "daily sigh and lament over their poor, unsatisfactory evil flesh, over the manifest errors and faults of their weak lives." [27] To be sure, Menno was much concerned with the fact that faith cannot be barren, that it works ceaselessly in love.[28] In this respect Menno did not deviate from the position of the Wittenberg Reformation, for Luther was no less emphatic on faith as active in love. Luther's understanding of faith as expressed, for example, in his preface to Romans is almost identical with Menno's.[29]

[23] *LCC,* XXV, 188.
[24] *Works,* pp. 116, 342, 1053.
[25] *Ibid.,* p. 1053.
[26] *Loc. cit.*
[27] *Ibid.,* p. 95.
[28] *Ibid.,* p. 116.
[29] *Works of Martin Luther* (Philadelphia: Holman and Muhlenberg, 1915-1943), hereinafter called *PE,* VI, 447 ff.

Although basically in agreement with Luther, Menno was absorbed with a different concept of holiness. He spent much time and effort to describe and make the Church a community of "visible saints." To Menno, holiness is a mark discernible to the eye of man. It is not so much believed in as experienced. If a man's life is not fully in conformity with his faith it is evident that he is not actually "born again." The moral conduct of man is, in Menno's eyes, a dependable criterion of regeneration. Cornelius Krahn has stated, "Menno could only with a kind of modification accept Luther's dictum of *simul justus et peccator*." [30] To Menno works were a third "mark" of the Church, where the Augsburg Confession, in Articles VII and VIII acknowledged only two: the proclamation of the gospel and the administration of the sacraments according to the institution of the Lord. "Good works" in themselves are deceptive. It is not for man to know whether or not they proceed from love or from a selfish motive. The natural man may wear the garb of a saint and yet be "nothing" as the Apostle says (I Cor. 13:1 ff.). To borrow an expression of Kierkegaard, "the knight of faith" is often indistinguishable from other respected burghers, whose lusty singing in the choir on Sundays proves only that they have healthy voices. However, both Luther and Menno were agreed on the primacy of faith as well as on the necessity of good works.

The difference between Luther and Menno Simons was a matter of emphasis, probably psychologically conditioned. Luther discovered the gospel as a power liberating him from anguish and despair when he was trying desperately to please God in a life of holiness. Menno, on the other hand, said that he had spent his life as a priest emptily in playing cards with two other priests, drinking, and in diversions "as alas, is the fashion of such useless people." [31] He had never read the Scriptures. Intellectual doubts concerning the doctrine of transubstantiation started him on the road that led him out of Rome. Next he began to question the validity of infant baptism. Finally he was moved by the plight of the people misled by the Muensterites; this led him to preach true repentance and the narrow path of holiness.[32]

[30] Cornelius Krahn, *Menno Simons* (Karlsruhe, 1936), p. 124.

[31] *Works*, p. 668.

[32] Cf. Menno's "Conversion, Call, and Testimony," *ibid.*, pp. 668 ff.

Menno was a Bible theologian. "The Word of the Lord," he wrote, "is the only doctrine by which our souls can live forever." [33] Moses and Isaiah, Matthew, Mark, Luke and John, Paul, Peter and James, and the other writers of the Bible are, he said, the most able doctors of the church and are received by him and his beloved brethren "in every word of doctrine." [34]

As Luther waged a twofold war for the whole of Protestantism, a war against both Roman traditionalism and the theology of the "inner light," so Menno stood opposed not only to the unscriptural traditions of the Roman communion, but also to the vagaries of inner light theology. He purged the Anabaptist movement from the chiliastic fantasies of the Melchiorites which were, in the last analysis, responsible for the cataclysmic disaster at Muenster. From Menno's point of view, the infallible Word needed no new revelations or heavenly inspiration. Scripture is complete and perfect. He prefaced every treatise by quoting I Corinthians 3:11, "For other foundation can no man lay than that is laid, which is Jesus Christ." [35] He solemnly implored his erring brethren, "I am no Enoch, I am no Elias, I am not one who sees visions, I am no prophet who can teach and prophesy otherwise than what is written in the Word of God and understood in the Spirit." [36]

Scripture was to Menno an organic unity; the key to both Testaments was Christ. If rightly explained, according to the intent of Christ and his Apostles, both Testaments are profitable for doctrine, for reproof, etc. (II Tim. 3:16).[37] Because of this christocentric approach, the New Testament definitely takes precedence over the Old. The Mount of the Beatitudes overshadows Mount Sinai,[38] as is evident from Menno's aversion to the law of retaliation in every form. Yet, to Menno as to Calvin, God is always the demanding Lord. For this reason, Luther's reference to James as a "strawy epistle" seems to Menno a frivolous and vain doctrine which throws wide the gate

[33] *Ibid.*, p. 165.

[34] *Ibid.*, p. 233.

[35] Cf. "Foundation of Christian Doctrine," especially Section D, "To the Corrupt Spirits," *ibid.*, pp. 215 ff.

[36] *Ibid.*, p. 310.

[37] *Ibid.*, p. 312.

[38] Cf. Krahn, *op. cit.*, p. 108.

to such an ungodly and abominable life among Lutherans as is found among Turks and Tartars.[39] Revelation and Scripture, especially revelation and the New Testament, Menno considers identical. His interpretation of Scripture is frequently literalistic and legalistic. His main argument against infant baptism is that the New Testament does not explicitly state that children are to be baptized or were in fact baptized in apostolic times. His theological argument against infant baptism is that original sin is not damnatory in children; that they cannot have saving faith is merely subsidiary.[40]

Concerning the extent of the Old Testament canon, Menno treated the Apocrypha as if they possessed the same authority as the books of the Hebrew canon. He quoted, for example, II Maccabees,[41] Tobit,[42] Ecclesiasticus,[43] Wisdom of Solomon,[44] and others.

On the fundamental doctrines of the Christian faith as expressed in the ecumenical creeds there was no significant difference between Menno and the other Reformers. Like Luther, Menno accepted the Nicene theology, confessing the one God who exists within himself as Father, Son and Holy Spirit.

Menno was confronted with the anti-trinitarian tendencies current in some circles of the radical Reformation in the person and teaching of Adam Pastor, who had been ordained a bishop about 1542 by Menno himself and his associate Dirk Philips. Pastor began to deny the true deity of Christ, and some other Anabaptist bishops labored in vain to lead him to the orthodox view of Christ. He was excommunicated by Menno and Dirk in 1547. In 1550, to counteract the influence of Pastor, Menno wrote "A Solemn Confession of the Triune Eternal and True God and Father, Son and Holy Ghost."[45] This treatise was a simple statement of the biblical truth that the one, eternal God exists in three persons, Father, Son and Holy Spirit. It called God "omnipotent, incomprehensible, invisible, ineffable, and indescribable," language reminiscent of the Athanasian Creed and of the discussion of God in Scholastic theology.

[39] *Works,* pp. 333-34.
[40] *Ibid.,* pp. 130 ff.
[41] *Ibid.,* pp. 337, 591, 620.
[42] *Ibid.,* p. 389.
[43] *Ibid.,* pp. 46, 239, 241, 431.
[44] *Ibid.,* pp. 610, 617, 789, 850.
[45] *Ibid.,* pp. 488 ff.

Although in agreement with the Nicene doctrine of God, Menno could not accept the Chalcedonian interpretation of the person of Christ. His view on the subject was a peculiar type of Monophysitism. The doctrine of the two natures, he maintained, inevitably leads to the view of two persons. We dare not divide Christ, "but confess Him entirely to be the true Son of the true and living God."[46] His flesh came down from heaven.[47] If Christ had been born "of" Mary he would have sprung from the sinful flesh of Adam.[48] In that case, Mary would have been saved through her own flesh and Adam would have been reconciled through his own flesh. Then the justice of God would have been broken and our condemnation, curse, and death dissolved and requited through a flesh condemned, cursed, and guilty of death.[49] Christ was not born "of" Mary but rather "by" or "through" Mary.[50]

Christ was not only conceived of the Holy Ghost but also made of the Holy Ghost. The eternal Logos became flesh, was conceived and descended from the Holy Spirit, but was nourished in Mary.[51] If the Church is to be without spot or blemish, its Head must be pure and undefiled. Christ's pure nature guarantees man's redemption. As may be seen, the soteriological concern for the full deity of Christ in the teachings of Athanasius is carried to its extreme in this view of the incarnation, which Menno shared with some of the less orthodox leaders of the radical Reformation. In the eyes of Menno, this view of the incarnation is supported by the process of natural procreation, for he held the notion current in his day that the father is the real origin of his child, while the mother is simply the "prepared field." God ordained man to be the sower and the woman a receptive field.[52]

Menno also dealt with questions of Church and state. For Luther, reorganization of the empirical Church remained subject to his interest in the proclamation of the gospel; his primary concern was the *sola gratia* which was denied full expression in the Roman communion.

[46] *Ibid.,* p. 800.
[47] *Ibid.,* p. 796.
[48] *Ibid.,* p. 797.
[49] *Ibid.,* p. 805.
[50] *Ibid.,* p. 768.
[51] *Ibid.,* p. 436.
[52] *Ibid.,* p. 768.

Calvin went a step further. Displaying a genuine interest not only in "faith" but also in "order," he considered the pattern of the Church of the Apostolic Age normative for all ages. Calvin's theocratic ideal, which was rooted in the Old Testament concept of the kingdom, made him, like the Catholic church, an ardent supporter of the idea of a Christian civilization. Sharing Calvin's interest in "order," both ecclesiastical and moral, but taking his cue from the New Testament, Menno disavowed the concept of the Church as coexistent with the civic community, influenced though it may be by Christian ideals.

Menno's break with the past is much more radical than that of Luther, Zwingli, or Calvin. For him "the Church's one foundation is Jesus Christ alone," "not the twelve articles" (i.e., the Apostles' Creed). If a person reflects on articles, then "regeneration, repentance, baptism, the Holy Supper, expulsion, etc. must be counted among those articles on which true Christians must agree." [53]

The community of God, or the Church of Christ, in Menno's own words, "is an assembly of the pious and a community of the saints." [54] The saints are the penitent who are born by the Spirit of God and follow the example of Christ.[55] They are flesh of His flesh and bone of His bone.[56] As repentant people, the Church can come into being only through repentant preachers, for "it has never from the beginning been God's usage to preach repentance through the impenitent." [57] The Church is not a mixed society where good and evil persons may exist side by side. Since the Lutherans and Zwinglians (as well as the Catholics) admit and tolerate impenitent persons and dispense the sacraments to them, they are the church of Anti-Christ.[58]

According to Menno there are six marks of the true Church of Christ: (1) unadulterated, pure doctrine; (2) a scriptural use of the sacraments; (3) obedience to the Word; (4) unfeigned, brotherly love; (5) a bold confession of God and Christ; and (6) oppression and tribulation for the sake of the Lord's Word.[59] The student of Church history

[53] *Ibid.*, p. 761.
[54] *Ibid.*, p. 734.
[55] *Ibid.*, pp. 94, 234, 734.
[56] *Ibid.*, p. 645.
[57] *Ibid.*, p. 660.
[58] *Ibid.*, p. 661.
[59] *Ibid.*, p. 743. Cf. Luther's seven marks of the Church: The Word, baptism, the Supper, absolution, the ministry, prayer, and tribulation (*PE*, V, 131 ff.).

will note that Menno's view of the Church bears a strong resemblance to that of the Novatians and Donatists in the ancient Church who also took the position that the Church must be a communion of regenerate saints and that its bishops must be holy men. In Luther's view, the Church was holy by virtue of the imputation of Christ's righteousness; in Menno's, the holiness of the Church was a matter of disciplined discipleship. For Luther, holiness was an object of faith; for Menno, an object of sight.

In order to preserve the purity of the Church Menno put great emphasis on excommunication or the ban.[60] As a real ordinance of Christ (Matt. 18:17), the ban was to Menno primarily an expression of brotherly love, meant to raise the fallen brother "by gentle admonition and brotherly instruction." [61] The unrepentant must be "shunned," whether he be father or mother, brother or sister, man or wife, son or daughter.[62] One must not eat with such a person, not even at a table in an inn.[63] Nor should one have *commertium,* social intercourse, with him. One must not "have an apostate as a regular buyer or partner. . . . But when trading is conducted without such social intercourse, then it is a different manner." [64] The ban is a counterpart to baptism. As baptism is the ordinance by which the reborn are received into the Church, the ban is the sign by which the apostate are cut off from the body of Christ.

As may be surmised, the teaching of the ban and of shunning caused strife and divisions among the followers of Menno. In his *Clear Account of Excommunication* (1550), Menno reported "that for some time now much strife has been occasioned" among the members of his brotherhood. He wrote that some wanted to avoid and shun, not the excommunicated persons "but only their false doctrines and offensive lives." Others failed to put the ban into practice, "some, I suppose, out of lassitude, some for the sake of carnal favor and the love which they feel toward the apostate ones, or because they are neighbours or

[60] Menno has dealt with the ban primarily in three treatises: "A Kind Admonition on Church Discipline" (1541); "A Clear Account of Excommunication" (1550); and his "Instruction on Excommunication" (1558). They are found in *Works,* pp. 407 ff., 455 ff., and 959 ff., respectively.

[61] *Ibid.,* p. 412.

[62] *Ibid.,* pp. 412, 478-79.

[63] *Ibid.,* p. 482.

[64] *Loc. cit.*

friends, etc." [65] Menno failed to restore unanimity in practice and the principle of the ban has proved to be a divisive factor throughout Mennonite history.

According to Menno, there are only two sacraments: baptism and the Lord's Supper.[66] His understanding of them is essentially that of Zwingli. They are outward symbols of a spiritual reality and signs by which the believer bears witness to his faith and distinguishes himself from the world. The sacraments do not mediate or offer the grace of God. The Holy Spirit works immediately on the soul of man. Christ's blood is the only remedy for sins; neither baptism nor the Lord's Supper is a source of salvation.

In contending against sacramentalism, Menno misinterpreted not only Luther but in part also the teaching of Rome. In Catholic thought a man in a state of mortal sin does not benefit from participating in a sacrament, as Menno assumed, and Luther quite plainly stated that without faith baptism does not save. Menno, however, was right insofar as the position which he attacked is a frequent abuse of the sacraments on the part of the people in both Catholic and Lutheran churches. Undoubtedly he was forced into his position by his spiritualistic principle of the immediacy of the Holy Spirit's operation. Consequently he was unable to appreciate Luther's distinction between the historic work of Christ, by which he obtained our salvation, and the means by which the fruit of his death is offered to man. His blood is the only source of our redemption. The Supper is not a sacrifice implementing the cross. Instead, the Supper, like baptism and the Word, is a means by which redemption is proclaimed and offered on the condition of repentance and faith.

Baptism, Menno maintained, is neither a sign of grace[67] nor a seal of the covenant of grace.[68] It is only for people who have been instructed in the Christian faith and who are rationally able to be instructed. Since children "have less sense at birth than do irrational creatures," [69] infant baptism is idolatrous, useless and vain.[70] Infants

[65] *Ibid.*, p. 457.
[66] *Ibid.*, pp. 238, 302.
[67] *Ibid.*, p. 125.
[68] *Ibid.*, pp. 685, 686.
[69] *Ibid.*, p. 240.
[70] *Ibid.*, p. 238.

need no ceremonies to be saved.[71] They are innocent from conception. If they die before coming to years of discretion, they die under the promise of God.[72] "Faith does not follow from baptism but baptism follows from faith." [73] Menno's religious concern is evident. He does not want to consider baptism a substitute for personal conversion. On the other hand, it is evident that he is toning down the impact of original sin. Contrary to Article II of the Augsburg Confession, he held that original sin is not damnatory in children. It was in keeping with these presuppositions that Menno steered away from the doctrine of double predestination.[74] His repeated admonitions and exhortations to repent reflected implicitly his belief in the moral responsibility of man.

The Lord's Supper is a high-water mark in the life of the Church. It is the Christian marriage commanded and ordained by the Lord himself.[75] It is neither sacrificial nor sacramental, but rather a memorial of the Lord's love, manifested in His death, exhorting us to strive for Christian unity, love, and peace. Menno dismisses the doctrine of the real presence as "contrary to nature, reason, and Scripture; an open blasphemy of the Son of God; an abomination and idolatry." Bread and wine are not actually the flesh and blood of Christ; they are signs signifying the reality of Christ's sinless sacrifice.[76]

Menno does not include footwashing as a sign of the Church, since for him it is a symbol of a spiritual cleansing. "We must be prepared to wash the defiled feet of our human tendencies and affections in the spiritual basin of Jesus Christ, with the water of His Holy Spirit." [77] But he also regarded footwashing as an expression of Christian humility and service.[78] It was never an established custom in his brotherhood.

Lutheran Pietism

The age of the Reformation dismissed the concern of the radical Reformers for a disciplined congregation as subversive to doctrine

[71] *Ibid.*, pp. 120, 130.
[72] *Loc. cit.*
[73] *Ibid.*, p. 120.
[74] *Ibid.*, p. 75.
[75] *Ibid.*, p. 48.
[76] *Ibid.*, p. 143.
[77] *Ibid.*, p. 1063.
[78] *Ibid.*, p. 417.

and life. Though recognizing in principle the desirablity of a disciplined congregation, Luther regarded such an order impractical: "I have not yet the persons necessary to accomplish it; nor do I observe many who strongly urge it." [79] It took a century and a half until a serious attempt was made to put Luther's ideas into practice by Spener and the Pietists in general.

Albrecht Ritschl thought of the pietistic movement as an intrusion of medieval mysticism into Protestantism mediated by Dutch and Rhenish mystics. Emanuel Hirsch, on the other hand, considers pietism to be germane to Luther's Reformation. It is, he says, "a tendency which was already at work during the infant years of the Reformation, integrated into the life of the Lutheran church." [80] According to Hirsch, Schwenckfeld was the most distinguished forerunner of pietism and Jacob Boehme was the man who transmitted and interpreted Schwenckfeld's theology to Spener and especially to the radical swing of pietism.[81]

As in the case of the radical Reformation, it is also necessary in pietism to distinguish between a biblical evangelical group and a speculative spiritualistic wing. The father of biblical evangelical pietism was Spener. After Spener, pietism had its two main centers in Halle and Württemberg. Among the leaders of the speculative spiritualistic wing were Gottfried Arnold, Johann Conrad Dippel, Johann Wilhelm Petersen and his wife, Johanna Eleonora, and others. Zinzendorf and his Moravian Brotherhood held a mediating position.

Conservative pietism was moulded and guided by Philip Jacob Spener.[82] He was born in Alsace, in 1635, and died in Berlin in 1705. In 1675 he published his famous *Pia Desideria*,[83] the celebrated program of his reformatory movement. It contains six proposals for a reformation of the Church: (1) a more diligent study of the Bible; (2) a more serious application of Luther's doctrine of the general

[79] *PE,* VI, 173.

[80] Emanuel Hirsch, *Lutherstudien,* II (1954), 67.

[81] Hirsch, *Geschichte der neueren evangelischen Theologie,* II, 208 ff.

[82] The most exhaustive study of Spener is by Paul Gruenberg, *Philip Jacob Spener,* 3 vols. (1893 ff.).

[83] Translated, edited, and with introduction by Theodore G. Tappert (Philadelphia: Fortress Press, 1964). Cf. also John T. McNeill, *Modern Christian Movements* (Philadelphia: Westminster Press, 1954).

priesthood of all believers; (3) confession of Christ by deed rather than a fruitless search after theological knowledge; (4) prayer for unbelievers and erring Christians rather than useless dogmatic disputations; (5) reform of the theological curriculum with emphasis on personal piety; (6) devotional arrangement of sermons instead of formal arrangement after the manner of rhetoric.

In the Halle university, pietism was represented by August Hermann Francke (d. 1727), founder of the Halle Orphanage and other institutions, Joachim Lange (d. 1744), and others. The most renowned representative in Württemberg was Johann Albrecht Bengel (d. 1752), editor of a new critical edition of the Greek New Testament (1734) and of the *Gnomon Novi Testamenti* (1742), a much-used commentary on the New Testament.

A few general characteristics of the Pietists must suffice. First of all, they turned from dogmatics to a study of Scripture. Though recognizing in principle the inferior authority of the Book of Concord, the Orthodox had practically put the symbolical writings on the same level as the Bible. They would not admit any flaws or errors in either volume. This equation of Scripture and the Book of Concord called forth the criticism of the Pietists and gave rise to allusions to "the papacy of the Book of Concord." As indicated above, Spener emphasized the study of Scripture for both the clergy and the laity, for the academic world and the congregation. In Halle the faculty expected a student to read through the whole Greek New Testament twice a year, and the Hebrew text of the Old Testament once a year. Johann Heinrich Michealis edited a critical edition of the Massoretic text of the Old Testament. Bengel produced a critical edition of the New Testament.

By and large, the conservative Pietists remained faithful to the dogma of the past. Their dogmatics was that of the Orthodox, but trimmed of its excesses. Like the Orthodox, they believed in the literal infallibility of the Scriptures and upheld the satisfaction theory of the atonement. They were less interested in some of the fine distinctions made by the Orthodox dogmaticians. Spener was the first Lutheran theologian to include theological errors among those covered by the forgiveness of sin. Though a man errs in the intellectual apprehension of revealed truth, Spener asserted, he may possess a genuine faith. An upright and sincere *fides qua* may be hidden beneath a false *fides quae creditur*.[84] A diversity of dogma does not necessarily imply a diversity of faith. This attitude provided an opportunity for a rapprochement of the Lutherans and the German Reformed. In fact, Spener was the first "union theologian."

For Spener the two churches were separated by only three fundamental doctrines: the doctrine of predestination, of the incarnation and of the Lord's Supper. Concerning the person of Christ, he believed the multivolipresence[85] of Melanchthon possessed the same validity as the teaching of the ubiquity of the Christ's body of the stricter Lutheran party. With respect to the Lutheran teaching of the *manducatio oralis*, he held that such a view was not essential for Church unity. The teaching of a *manducatio spiritualis* was sufficient. In other words, he recognized not Zwingli's but Calvin's teaching as orthodox. The Calvinistic doctrine of predestination, however, was a real offense to Spener. He was happy to observe that this particular doctrine was practically unknown in the German Reformed churches. His own Reformed sovereign, the Great Elector of Brandenburg, and his son, who later became the first King of Prussia, had openly disavowed it. In this matter Luther himself had been closer to Calvin than to the Lutheranism of the Formula of Concord. Spener maintained that the doctrinal difference between the two churches of the Reformation, the Lutheran and the Reformed, was such that it should no longer exclude a mutual recognition in the faith. In this manner Spener and the Pietists in general did the spade work for the church unions of the nineteenth century.

The heart of the Pietists' concern is to be seen in their insistence on personal holiness. Spener distinguished between a historical knowledge of the Bible and a spiritual apprehension of divine truth. As a conservative Lutheran he used a term from Luther's explanation of the Third Article to designate the basic work of the Holy Spirit in man: He (the Spirit) enlightens me with his gifts. According to the order of God, illumination, conversion, regeneration, and renovation belong together intrinsically. Though not denying the forensic nature of

[84] *Fides qua creditur* is the faith by which a Christian lays hold of Christ; *fides quae creditur* is the objective content of the Christian faith.

[85] This term designates the real presence as contingent upon the gracious will of the Savior.

justification, the Pietists revealed a predilection for describing the work of the Holy Spirit in terms of regeneration and renovation. While Orthodoxy conceived of regeneration objectively as coinciding with baptism, pietism equated regeneration with conversion, conceiving of it as a subjective change in man. The doctrine of baptismal regeneration, ardently defended by the Orthodox theologians, was rejected by the Pietists. Regeneration is not complete, they taught, until the baptized responds to the promise of God with repentance and faith. Divine sonship is contingent upon conversion; only believers are sons of God.

Though basically Orthodox in doctrine, Spener nevertheless became the connecting link between the evangelical piety of the seventeenth century and that of rationalism in the eighteenth. Faith in forgiveness of sins gradually gave way to faith in divine providence. Luther's quest of a gracious God lost much of its significance. In the Age of Reason, the quest for a gracious God was replaced by a concern for practical Christianity. Spener himself was responsible for this shift in emphasis, though unintentionally, by his preoccupation with the practical fruit of faith. Two instances may serve as an illustration.

The first instance is Spener's teaching of Christian perfection. In Article XII, the Augsburg Confession rejects those who teach that some believers may attain perfection in this life and therefore cannot sin. Spener does not deny this. He does not expect the believer to be able to lead a sinless life, but undeterred by its traditional abuses, he makes a distinction between "having" and "committing" sin, "keeping" and "fulfilling" the law. Though not able to "fulfill" the law, a believer has power to "keep" the law; while still "having" sin, he will not "commit" sin, for he is no longer under the dominion of sin but under the lordship of Christ. Only a faith active in life has the promise of salvation. This view proved to be a stimulus to a Christian activity unknown in Orthodox Lutheran piety. Halle became the cradle of Lutheran social and foreign missions, of Christian education and diaspora work. This view also gave rise to an ascetic attitude toward life. Francke, more than Spener, rejected card playing, dancing, visiting theatres, etc., as incompatible with Christian holiness. The Pietists tried in retrospect to measure their progress in holiness. But "to fix the reflection upon holiness achieved is as dangerous as to fix it upon the permanency of sin,"[86] the danger of Spener's Orthodox opponents. Shorn of its supernatural features, this type of piety issued into the moralistic religion of the Rationalists.

The second influence of Spener was to invert the relationship between faith and piety. Luther, like Paul, began with faith. Although faith, of necessity, will be active in love, the primary concern of both was faith in God who justifies the ungodly. Spener, on the other hand, like James, concentrated on piety as a proof of faith. Man is justified because by faith he walks in love. In the background lurks the Catholic and rationalistic idea of the meritoriousness of the Christian life. The just, not the sinner, is justified before God.[87]

Two peculiar doctrinal tenets of pietism should be mentioned in passing. Spener and his followers looked favorably upon a kind of subtle chiliasm.[88] They expected a more glorious revelation of God in the future through the power of his Spirit. Johann Albrecht Bengel spent much time and effort to unlock the mystery of the Book of Revelation. He toyed with the idea of a "restoration of all." He also developed in detail a doctrine of the blood of Christ. The body of Christ, he taught, was totally drained of blood on the cross. In the resurrection it was not reunited with the body, but is retained in heaven as the precious ransom of man's sin. In the act of justification the believer is sprinkled in a mysterious manner with the blood of Christ and thus cleansed from his sin. This emphasis on the blood of the Savior played a very important part in the theology of Zinzendorf.[89]

Pietism made two important contributions to the culture of the eighteenth century. Francke in Halle gave a prominent place to the study of natural sciences in the curriculum of his educational institutions. The period of pietism was also the silver age of the Lutheran chorale before the cold wave of rationalism nipped the flower of evangelical poetry in its bud. The current hymnal for the Christian

[86] Franz Hildebrandt, *From Luther to Wesley* (London: Lutterworth Press, 1951), p. 88.

[87] Cf. Hirsch, *op. cit.*, II, 148 ff.

[88] Cf. Spener, *op. cit.*

[89] Cf. William Cowper's well-known hymn "There Is a Fountain Filled with Blood."

youth movement in Germany, *Wachet auf* (1952), contains some ninety-five hymns written during this period. Prominent among the writers were K. H. von Bogatzki, whose hymn, "Wach auf, du Geist der ersten Zeugen" ("Awake, Thou Spirit of the Watchmen!") is the first missionary hymn in the German language; Gottfried Arnold, "O Durchbrecher aller Bande" ("Thou Who Breakest Every Fetter"); J. D. Herrnschmidt, "Lobe den Herren, O meine Seele," a metrical version of Psalm 146; P. F. Hiller, "Jesus Christus herrscht als König" ("Jesus Christ as Lord He Reigneth"); Benjamin Schmolck, "Tut mir auf die schöne Pforte" ("Open Now Thy Gates of Beauty"), and "Himmelan geht unsere Bahn" ("Heavenward Still Our Pathway Tends"); J. H. Schroeder, "Eins ist not, ach Herr, dies Eine" ("One Thing's Needful, Then, Lord Jesus!"); Erdmann Neumeister, "Jesus nimmt die Sünder an" ("Sinners Jesus Will Receive"); J. J. Rambach, "Ich bin getauft auf deinen Namen" ("Father, Son, and Holy Spirit, I'm Baptized in Thy Dear Name"); J. A. Rothe, "Ich habe nun den Grund gefunden" ("Now Have I Found the Sure Foundation"); Johann E. Schmidt, "Fahre fort, fahre fort" ("Zion Rise! Zion Rise!"), a hymn based on the Seven Letters of Revelation; and J. J. Winckler, "Ringe recht, wenn Gottes Gnade" ("Strive When Thou Art Called of God").

Another prolific hymn writer was E. G. Woltersdorf. Like Francke at Halle, Woltersdorf helped to found an Orphan's Home of which he became the first superintendent (1758). Very few of his hymns, however, are included in the official hymnals of the Lutheran churches. They are practically unknown in English.[90] The same must be said about the numerous hymns written by Zinzendorf. Very few are used today outside his Moravian church. The best-known Moravian hymns are his "Jesu, geh voran" ("Jesus, Still Lead On") and "Herz und Herz vereint zusammen" ("Heart and Heart in Love United"), written by his son, Christian Renatus (1727-1752). Prominent among the Rhenish Reformed Pietists are Joachim Neander and Gerhard Tersteegen. From the pen of the former we have "Sieh hier bin ich, Ehrenkönig" ("Here Behold Me as I Cast Me") and "Lobe den Herren, den mächtigen König der Ehren" ("Praise to the Lord, the Almighty, the King of Creation"). Tersteegen's best-known hymns in English

[90] John Julian, *Dictionary of Hymnology* (New York: Charles Scribner's Sons, 1891), has only a brief reference to Woltersdorf, p. 417.

are "God Himself Is Present" and "God Calling Yet, Shall I Not Hear?"[91]

Swedish pietism produced the hymnal *Mose og Lambsens visor* ("Hymns of Moses and the Lamb") with Jacob Frese and Karl Rutstroem as its most important contributors. The most distinguished Danish hymn writer of the pietistic school was Hans Adolph Brorson. The Lutheran *Service Book and Hymnal* (1958) contains two of his hymns in translation: the Christmas hymn, "Thy Little Ones, Dear Lord, Are We," and the hymn commemorating the departed, "Behold a Host like Mountains Bright."

The radical wing of pietism bears a strong resemblance to the spiritualistic group of the radical Reformers. Like the latter, it developed a heterodox theology, tended to organize its followers in separate religious communities, and contributed to a separation of Church and state, religion and public morality. Boehme was the forerunner of radical pietism.

Jacob Boehme, the "Teuton Philosopher," was born in 1575; he died in Görlitz, a city on the German-Polish border, in 1624. By profession he was a shoemaker. He received no formal education, but men like Hegel, Schelling, and others acknowledged their dependence on the written *Works* of the shoemaker of Görlitz.[92]

Boehme's system is a hodgepodge of theology, philosophy, chemistry, and astrology. His interest is both speculative and practical. His teaching of the origin of the world reminds the reader of the cosmogenic speculations of the ancient Gnostics. He conceives of the world as an emanation from the inner being of God, the "abyss," the nothing. He describes this with a multitude of alchemistic terms which he probably learned from Paracelsus. God and nature are the main objects of his speculation. He wants to penetrate into the spiritual letter of Scripture, into the very essence of nature. He is concerned neither with Hebrew nor Greek; neither with the external letters of the Bible nor with what we call natural sciences. In fact, he rejects the academic way of knowledge. All knowledge, he holds, is by the intuitive faculties of the soul. It is given by revelation. These

[91] Cf. the articles on these writers in *ibid.*

[92] The edition by Will-Erich Peuckert, *Jacob Boehme, Sämmtliche Schriften,* hereinafter referred to as *Works,* is a facsimile reprint of the 1730 edition, 11 vols., 1955 ff. Cf. Hirsch, *op. cit.,* II, 208 ff.

ideas are most fully developed in his early writing *Aurora oder Morgenröthe im Aufgang, das ist die Wurzel oder Mutter der Philosophie, Atrologiae und Theologiae.*[93]

Though not a pantheist, strictly speaking, Boehme established a close correlation between God and nature. A trinitarian structure, he holds, underlies the being of both God and the cosmos.[94] As Father, God includes the whole of the Deity. The Son and the Spirit exist personally in the one God. Though he follows the Nicene theology in speaking of the person of the Father, Son, and Spirit, Boehme interprets the word "person" as will or energy. As "abyss," God dwells in bitter darkness but reveals himself in the world as a consuming fire. The Son is within the Father as the light, heart, and mercy. In God there are wrath and love, hell and heaven, evil and good.[95] In Christ we know that God is love while apart from Christ, God is a consuming fire.[96] The Spirit proceeding from the Father and the Son is the gurgling, bubbling element in God. He is God in action.[97] All things in the cosmos participate in this trinitarian structure: darkness, light, and the material world.[98] The angels, however, are an exception. They represent only the first two principles, darkness and light. Despising this order, Lucifer fell from the second principle (light, love), but remained captive within the first, that is, fire deprived of light, and hence in darkness.

Man replaced Lucifer as ruler of the external world. Man alone of all creatures participates in both worlds, the spiritual and material. In the original state, his body was formed of crystalline, translucent material because the inner was almost absorbed by the outer form. God created only one man, who combined within himself the male and female principles. In this state sex organs were missing. Man ate with his mouth but was in need neither of teeth nor of a stomach nor of

[93] "Dawn or Daybreak as the Root or Mother of Philosophy, Astrology and Theology" (1612), *Works,* Vol. I.

[94] *Works,* I, 471. God is the being of all beings. He is the ground of being; IV, 9.

[95] "Von der Menschwerdung Christi," *ibid.,* IV, 140 ff.

[96] Cf. Theodosius Harnack's interpretation of Luther's theology as man apart from Christ under the wrath of God and in Christ, reconciled to God. *Luther's Theologie,* I (1862), 253 ff.

[97] *Works,* I, 47.

[98] Cf. "De tribus principiis oder Beschreibung der Drey Principien Göttlichen Wesens," *ibid.,* Vol. II.

intestines.[99] Tempted by Lucifer to reach out for the things of the coarse, material world, Adam lost his heavenly nature.[100] He fell asleep in the heavenly world and woke up in the earthly world.[101] During this sleep Jesus effected the separation of the male and female principles in Adam. Now the respective organs appeared in Adam and Eve as a sign of their animal, earthly nature. Jesus formed his own celestial flesh of the heavenly female principle, and later he formed his earthly body of Mary. In this way Boehme tried to harmonize the Church's doctrine of the incarnation with the view of a celestial body of the Savior as held by the radical Reformers. In a way, sexuality in man is a sign of his fall. The first fall produced the second when both Adam and Eve transgressed the commandment of the Creator and ate of the forbidden tree.[102]

The eternal Son of God was made man in order to reveal the true nature of the original man and to restore the lost image of God. He is the one who liberates man from the fetters of his earthly, sinful existence. Though not denying the forensic view of justification nor Luther's doctrine *simul justus et peccator*,[103] Boehme concentrates his interest on the necessity of the spiritual renewal of man. Unless Christ is born in man, church membership with all its implications is absolutely useless. Since the great majority of Lutherans, no less than Roman Catholics, are unregenerate church members, the Lutheran church is no more the Church of Christ than is the Catholic church; it too is the Babel of the Book of Revelation. Luther's dictum that the true Church is hidden Boehme applies with great consistency to the empirical Lutheran church.[104]

Influenced by Boehme's mystical religion, some of the fundamental principles of the conservative Reformation suffered severely at the hands of the radical Pietists, as follows.

(1) The *sola Scriptura* of the Reformation was toned down. The "inner word" was now vying with the authority of Scriptures. Possession of the Spirit by the regenerate competed with the Bible as given

[99] "Von der Menschwerdung," *ibid.*, IV, 30.
[100] *Ibid.*, IV, 32 ff.
[101] *Ibid.*, IV, 50.
[102] *Ibid.*, IV, 32 ff.; "Weg zu Christo," IV, 114 ff.
[103] *Ibid.*, IV, 136.
[104] *Ibid.*, IV, 136 ff.

by the inspiration of the Holy Spirit. Luther had rejected the allegorical interpretation of the past. Now allegory was often the use of the Scriptures in defense of one's own fanciful theological vagaries.

(2) The Church's doctrine of the Trinity and of Christ was restated in terms rejected by the ancient Church. Boehme's own view of the Trinity was a kind of modified Sabellianism, and his teaching of the celestial body of Christ an example of extreme Monophysitism.

(3) Both the satisfaction theory of the atonement and the forensic view of justification were repugnant to most of these men. For Conrad Dippel the former reflected a view of God which turned the Deity into "a veritable envious devil." [105] Emphasis on regeneration as a thorough spiritual and ethical renewal of man replaced Luther's concern for the justification of sinful man by the imputation of Christ's righteousness.

(4) The teaching of chiliasm was widely current and the resolute rejection of predestination at times issued into the doctrine of the "restoration of all." [106]

As stated above, the Radicals' view of the Church as a community of dedicated regenerate people contributed to the principle of separation of Church and state with the resultant idea of a secularized state whose center of coherence was to be found, not in religion, but rather in ethics. As a rational being, man knows the good and is free to put his knowledge into action. These ideas fully matured in the Age of Reason that was to come.

Another cultural contribution along similar lines must be mentioned. In 1699, J. G. Arnold published his epoch-making work *Unparteiische Kirche-und-Ketzerhistorie* ("An Impartial History of the Churches and Sects"). In this work the author stressed the principle of impartiality in the treatment of Church history, but went to the other extreme of practically becoming the apologist for the heretical movements of the past. As to method, Arnold presented his matter in the form of biographies of saints and their antagonists. This was the inception of the pragmatic-moralistic approach to Church history by the Rationalists, the veneration of personality by the Romanticists, and

[105] Hirsch, *op. cit.*, II, 285.

[106] J. W. Petersen, *Das ewige Evangelium der allgemeinen Wiederbringung aller Creaturen* (1700). Cf. Hirsch, *op. cit.*, II, 232 ff.

of the composition of biographies, autobiographies and, in fact, of the modern novel.

Emanuel Swedenborg (1688-1772) may also be included among the radical Pietists. His pietistic leanings are modified by a strong religious rationalism. Faith, he holds, is something to be apprehended and seen. The faith of the Church is a "faith of the night." From such a false faith flow many paradoxes: the personal concept of Father, Son and Holy Ghost; the orthodox doctrine of the atonement; the moral depravity of man; the imputation of Christ's righteousness; that faith alone without the works of the law, and not formed from charity, is saving, etc.[107] Scripture, like nature, is a divine symbol. Besides the literal sense adapted to men, Scripture contains a spiritual sense adapted to angels. These two senses are connected by the "science of correspondence."[108] The mundane sun, for example, has its counterpart in the "divine wisdom" of the spiritual world. The clouds of heaven mentioned in Matthew 24:30 denote physical clouds, but applying the science of correspondence they also mean those theologians who have obscured the sun of divine wisdom by believing in a personal return of Christ. The Trinity is not of persons but of great essences, Father, Son, and Spirit representing respectively divine love, wisdom, and operation. Sin is a moral disease; it is contrary to divine order. Immersed in selfishness, sinful men became devils. In order to restore order in the universe, the Infinite assumed human nature and victoriously withstanding the many temptations of the devils, he brought men and angels back to the original order.[109]

The followers of Swedenborg organized the Church of the New Jerusalem in London in 1787. The first New Church society in America was founded in Baltimore in 1792. Perpetuated by this small denomination—it has about six thousand members—radical pietism is still a living force today.[110]

Count Nicholas von Zinzendorf (1700-1760) held a position midway between the conservative and the radical Pietists. He was educated

[107] Cf. Emanuel Swedenborg, *Miscellaneous Theological Works* (New York: Swedenborg Foundation, 1959), pp. 215 ff.

[108] *Ibid.*, p. 377.

[109] George Trowbridge, *Swedenborg: Life and Teaching* (New York: Swedenborg Foundation, 1955), pp. 151 ff.

[110] The Swedenborg Foundation, New York, has published a revised English edition of Swedenborg's *Apocalypse and Arcana Celestia* (12 vol., 1949 ff.).

at Halle and Wittenberg, where he studied law. While traveling in Western Europe he established contact with Reformed Pietists and even with Noailles, Cardinal of Paris. Inspired with the idea of gathering into one fold all true lovers of the Savior, he became involved in a grand scheme of Church union. However, at the request of his family, he accepted a position in the service of the Electoral government at Dresden (1721-1727). During this period he edited *Le Socrate de Dresde*, a weekly which anticipated Schleiermacher's *Discourses on Religion*, to win back the despisers of religion among the cultured. In 1722 he settled a group of persecuted Moravians in a village on his estates in Saxony. From 1727 he identified himself with this group and thus became the founder of the *Unitas Fratrum*, the Moravian Brethren.

The refugees who settled at Herrnhut, as the village was called, were a segment of radical Pietists. Like-minded people from Germany came and an association was formed in which the religious ideas of Zinzendorf and those of the Moravians were combined. The Augsburg Confession was accepted as an ecumenical creed of biblical Christianity. A distinct order and discipline, perpetuating elements of the old Moravian church, was established. Zinzendorf was ordained a Lutheran minister in 1734, and was consecrated a Moravian bishop three years later by Daniel Jablonski. The Moravian episcopate was thus transferred to the new association. On this basis the group was recognized in Germany as affiliated with the Lutheran church and was granted legal status in Great Britain as an episcopally constituted church body by an Act of Parliament in 1749. Declining to proselytize among the members of the established churches of Europe, it limited its work to evangelization and to cultivating fellowships and conventicles in the spirit of Spener. In America, on the other hand, Zinzendorf tried to gather all true believers into one fold regardless of their confessional backgrounds. In these endeavors he was opposed in Pennsylvania by Henry Melchior Muhlenberg, himself a Halle Pietist who wanted to perpetuate the Lutheran church in the colonies. In America, Zinzendorf preferred to be known in public as "Mr. von Thurnstein," though he posed as a Lutheran pastor among the Germans in Pennsylvania.[111]

[111] Cf. *The Journals of H. M. Muhlenberg,* trans. Theodore G. Tappert and John W. Doberstein (Philadelphia: Muhlenberg Press, 1943), I, 80-81.

In opposition to the religious intellectualism of the Orthodox theologians Zinzendorf established himself on what he called a theology of the heart, with Jesus as the center of his religious devotion. He regarded Jesus as the "special father of His children." In his thought the Second Article of the Creed swallows the First and also the Third. God the Father is our father only because he is the father of Jesus. We are related to him as to a father-in-law or grandfather. Combining John 14:16 ff. with Isaiah 66:13, Zinzendorf called the Holy Spirit our Mother. God is known in Christ only. Christianity is "Jesuanity." In such a case the truth of the First Article is in acute danger of being lost. As is frequently the case in pietism, we are faced "with an atheism concealed by Jesu-latry." [112]

The Church, Zinzendorf said, originated in the wounds of Christ; it was born of the wound in the Savior's side (John 19:34). Zinzendorf's "Christ cult" issued into devotion to the pierced side of the Savior or *Seitenhöhle*, and the very abbreviation SH became a special object of religious devotion for him. He conceded to Dippel that the Orthodox view of the wrath of God which Christ came to appease was an overstatement. In Gethsemane and on the cross Christ rendered a perfect repentance. As the perfectly penitent one, Christ bore vicariously the penalty of sin. Faith is kindled by a mystic contemplation of the wounds of Christ. The way to the precious knowledge of forgiveness is by the contemplation of Christ's wounds. In the Supper we participate mystically in the blood of Christ reserved in heaven. Together with justification the penitent receives the gift of sanctification. Zinzendorf's view of the Christian life was less puritanical than that of the Halle Pietists and more quietistic than was acceptable to Wesley. Zinzendorf allowed no other motive for sanctification "than a grateful love, proceeding from the experience of the heart of a pardoned sinner." [113] Francke's and Wesley's concept of sanctification was, in the eyes of Zinzendorf, too legalistic. On the other hand, Zinzendorf's predilection for describing the Christian life in terms of an amorous devotion to Christ was highly objectionable to the men of Halle and also to John Wesley. To some extent this fact accounts for

[112] Cf. Hildebrandt, *op. cit.*, p. 160.

[113] David Benham, *Memoirs of Hutton* (1856), p. 112; cited in Umphrey Lee, *Wesley and Modern Religion* (Nashville: Cokesbury Press, 1936), p. 169.

the friction that developed between Halle and Herrnhut as well as for the separation of the Methodists from the (Moravian) Fetter Lane Society in London.[114] In addition, the Moravian teaching of "stillness," that is, abstaining from the means of grace in case of doubt and uncertainty and waiting passively for the Spirit's work, was a serious distortion of Spiritual truth in the eyes of Wesley. The Moravians regarded critically the emotionalism displayed in the meetings of the Methodists.

For Zinzendorf the existing denominations were means of training men in Christianity. In his own communion the Lutherans, Reformed, and Moravians (episcopal) were equally recognized. I have only one passion, he said, that is Christ, who died "to gather together in one the children of God that were scattered abroad" (John 11:52). His Brethren church was a union church within Lutheranism, anticipating the Prussian Union by almost a century.

The Radical Reformation in England

Like the Continent, the British Isles experienced the impact of the radical ideas. As the Continental movement was pre-figured by the Waldensian reform, so Lollardry was the background of Puritanism and of the sectarian movements in England.[115] German and Dutch Anabaptists who had fled to England were exiled or put to death during the years 1535-1539, but again became especially numerous under Edward VI (1547-1553). During the reign of Elizabeth I an Anabaptist congregation existed in London. The Anabaptists were charged with "most damnable and detestable heresies" such as the teaching of the celestial flesh of Christ, the denial of infant baptism, and that a Christian man cannot be a magistrate, bear the sword, or take an oath. Among those martyred were Joan Boucher (Joan of Kent), John Wielmaker, and Henry Terwoort. Unmolested by Cromwell, the Anabaptists were again severely persecuted after the Restoration. The most famous of their confessors was John Bunyan.[116] The chiliastic and revolutionary fervor, as revealed in the Muenster tragedy,

[114] Cf. p. 39.

[115] This view has recently been supported, for instance, by E. Gordon Rupp and K. B. MacFarlane.

[116] Cf. Alfred C. Underwood, *A History of the English Baptists* (London: Kingsgate Press, 1947).

was focused in the regiment of Robert Harrison during the English Civil War. These Radicals looked for the coming of Christ, for the establishment of the kingdom of the "Saints" without priest or sacrament, king, law or government, and for the complete anarchy of Christian love.[117]

The Family of Love (*familia caritatis*) or Familists was another group which wanted to base social life entirely on the law of love. Its founder was Henry Niclaes, born in Muenster about 1501. He was a follower of David Joris.[118] Like Joris, he referred to himself as the "prophet of the last days." His system is a blend of Anabaptist and Roman Catholic ideas. Following the example of the former he wanted to establish a pure community, the New Jerusalem; following the example of Catholicism, this community ought to be governed by a holy priesthood. Membership in the priesthood could be obtained only by "an inner election." These ideas spread, especially along the Rhine, from Holland to Switzerland, but also far and wide in England. Troeltsch says that in England almost all fanatical phenomena can be traced back to the Familists. John Bunyan transformed the mystical and allegorical journeys of Niclaes the Prophet into his *Pilgrim's Progress*. The so-called "Ranters," a very eccentric, spiritualistic group, are supposed to have derived their ideas from the Familists.[119]

After the dissolution of the Short Parliament the Levellers made their appearance. Their leader was John Lilburn (d. 1657). They did not insist on equality of material possessions but on full equality before the law and the Christians' real share in the affairs of the government. They felt that Jesus had been the first leveller. During the Protectorate they encouraged active resistance and attempted assassinations until they were suppressed. Their leader finally found refuge among the Quakers. The premises of their theology were religious. The law of nature as it was before the fall, of God, and of Christ, allows no compromise with social institutions corrupted by sin. The whole social structure must be brought into harmony with the Christian political and social ideal.

Differing from the Levellers were the Diggers, the socialists and

[117] Cf. Troeltsch, *op. cit.,* II, 708-709.

[118] Cf. p. 6.

[119] Troeltsch, *op. cit.,* II, 772.

communists of the revolution. They represented the rural proletariat. They blended the spiritualism of Hans Denck and Sebastian Franck with the social aspirations of Thomas Muentzer. Their leader was Gerard Winstantley. His "Law of Freedom," a pamphlet dedicated to Cromwell, contains a program of Christian social reform. According to Winstantley, Christ, the inner light, and reason, all mean the same thing. Through John Bellers, a Quaker, and Robert Owen there is a direct connection between Winstantley and modern British socialism. Disillusioned in the same way as Lilburn, Winstantley and many of his followers found a home in the Quaker community.[120] All the varying ideas of the Continental Radicals have their counterpart in the teachings of their English spiritual kinsmen: complete separation of Church and state as well as the theocratic ideal of the rule of the saints; the ushering in of the kingdom by a supernatural act of God as well as by a forceful incentive of men; emphasis on Scripture as well as reliance on the inner light, on Christ, and on reason.

As Menno finally gathered the disillusioned Muensterites into a pacifistic brotherhood, so many of the English Radicals found a haven of refuge among the "plain people" of George Fox (d. 1690), the Quakers. However, while Menno Simons was a Bible theologian, George Fox was a mystic and religious individualist. God communicates directly with every spirit he has made. Order and organization are matters of subordinate interest to Fox. They must not be allowed to limit the freedom of the individual. The sacraments are nonessential; what counts is the baptism of the Spirit and the spiritual communion with Christ (Schwenckfeld).

The teachings of these Radicals had their roots in Continental thought. Nonetheless, the rise of Congregationalism was a strictly English phenomenon.

Calvin had been concerned with a disciplined Church. He tried hard to turn Geneva into a "holy city of God." English Puritanism owed much to Calvin. Both tried to realize the ideal of a formal, national Church, coterminous with the civic community. Even the non-elect were to conform to a Christian standard of life. Yet the Puritan ideal met with little success. A new party made its appearance demanding that the Reformation should proceed without concur-

[120] *Ibid.*, II, 710 ff.

rence of the civil power. The early leader of the Separatists (or Congregationalists or Independents) was Robert Browne (d. 1630), a clergyman of the Anglican Establishment. Among his followers were Henry Barrow, John Robinson, and Henry Ainsworth. In his *Catechism* (1582) Browne defines the Church as a company of believers "which by a willing covenant made with their God as under the government of God and Christ, and keep His laws in an holy communion." [121] Apart from this concept of the Church as a local group of believers, administering its own affairs and responsible to Christ alone, the Brownists were orthodox Calvinists. Browne even agreed that a prince should have the right "after the example of the good kings of Judah" not to force the people to embrace the true Church but when they had received it, "to keep them to it and even to put them to death if they fall away." [122] Congregationalism then is a "middle way" between an Establishment and complete religious independence.[123] In fact, the Congregationalists became a ruling and religious power in England during the protectorate of Cromwell, and later in New England.

Early in its history the Separatist movement was divided over the issue of infant baptism, a practice retained by the Congregationalists. In 1606, John Smyth, a former Anglican divine, together with a small band of followers, settled in Amsterdam. He introduced the practice of adult baptism and joined the Mennonites. A fraction of his church under the leadership of Thomas Helwys, a jurist, returned to England in 1611. The following year Helwys was burned at the stake as an Anabaptist heretic. Theologically he was an Arminian and his followers became known as the General Baptists. Independently of these, the Particular Baptists came into existence. They had their origin in Congregational churches in which the issue of adult versus infant baptism was hotly debated. Doctrinally the Particular Baptists were Calvinists. Both groups followed the congregational pattern of Church

[121] Quoted from James Hastings (ed.), *Encyclopedia of Religion and Ethics* (New York: Charles Scribner's Sons, 1913), II, 876.

[122] *Loc. cit.*

[123] R. H. Bainton, "Congregationalism, the Middle Way," *Christendom,* a quarterly published by Blackwell, Oxford, V, 345 ff.

government and both were opposed to the cultural and political exclusiveness of the Mennonites.[124]

The Wesleyan Revival

Methodism is the "Oxford movement of the eighteenth century." It started when the two brothers, John and Charles Wesley, George Whitfield and others began to meet at Oxford for religious exercises. These friends became known as the Holy Club. John Wesley (1703-91) was the real founder and guide of the movement while Charles (1707-80) excelled as the hymn writer of Methodism.

John and Charles were the sons of Samuel Wesley, an Anglican high churchman. Their mother, Susannah, was the daughter of a Nonconformist preacher, but she concurred fully in the religious and Tory political sentiments of her husband. In her religious duties she was methodical to the extreme. Hence she has often been called the "mother of Methodism."

John Wesley entered Anglican orders at the age of twenty-two. The next year he came across Jeremy Taylor's treatises, *Holy Living and Holy Dying*.[125] The reading of this book affected Wesley exceedingly. He resolved instantly to dedicate his life to God. In 1725 he referred to this event as the beginning of Methodism.[126] Next he began to read Thomas à Kempis' *Imitation of Christ* and William Law's *Christian Perfection* (1726) and *A Serious Call to a Devout and Holy Life* (1728).[127] These writings convinced Wesley more than ever of

[124] Cf. for example, R. G. Torbert, *A History of the Baptists* (Philadelphia: Judson Press, 1950); E. A. Payne, *The Fellowship of Believers: Baptist Thought and Practice Yesterday and Today* (London: Kingsgate Press, 1945).

[125] The treatises were published in 1650 and 1651 respectively, and in numerous later editions. Taylor was an Anglican bishop who has been called "the Shakespeare of English prose."

[126] Thomas Jackson (ed.), *Wesley's Works* (Grand Rapids: Zondervan Publishing House, n.d.), VII, 421.

[127] John W. Meister prepared a new and abridged edition, *A Serious Call to a Devout and Christian Life,* 1962. Inspired by German pietism, "religious societies" had come into being in the second half of the seventeenth century which promoted an ascetic type of piety within the established Church. This movement gained momentum through the writings of William Law, a Non-Juror Anglican. Because of his impact on Wesley some have called him the "grandfather of Methodism." Wesley later broke with Law when his writings evidenced a tinge of the mysticism of Jacob Boehme.

"the impossibility of being half a Christian." [128] "From this time on Wesley sought nothing less than Christian Perfection." [129] Wesley at this time was a ritualistic, high Anglican who emphasized fasting on Wednesdays and Fridays, weekly, or preferably daily communion, and tradition as a source of religious authority, etc.

In the fall of 1735 the Wesleys set out for Georgia. On this long and weary trip they came in contact with some Moravian missionaries. From these men the Wesleys learned what they were lacking: humility, peace of mind in the midst of danger, and assurance of salvation. John Wesley's stay in Georgia proved to be a miserable failure. His high church rigor got him nowhere. In addition, he became involved in a love affair. When he hesitated to marry the girl and she married another gentleman, he refused to admit her to Holy Communion, was arrested and tried in court, but fled from Savannah by night.[130] He arrived back in England on February 1, 1738. In London he renewed his contact with the Moravians and joined the Fetter Lane Society founded by Peter Boehler. Among these friends Wesley experienced, on May 24, 1738, what has usually been considered the beginning of Methodism. We shall let Wesley speak for himself:

> In the evening I went very unwillingly to a society in Aldersgate Street, where one was reading Luther's preface to the Epistle to the Romans.[131] About a quarter before nine, while he was describing the change which God works in the heart through faith in Christ, I felt my heart strangely warmed. I felt I did trust in Christ, Christ alone, for salvation; and an assurance was given me that He had taken away my sins, even mine, and saved me from the law of sin and death.
>
> I began to pray with all my might for those who had in a more special manner despitefully used me and persecuted me. I then testified openly to all there what I now first felt in my heart. But it was not long before the enemy suggested "This cannot be faith; for where is thy joy?" Then was I taught that peace and victory over sin are essential to faith in the Captain of our salvation; but that as to the transports of joy that usually attend the beginning of it, especially in those who have mourned deeply,

[128] Jackson, *op. cit.,* XI, 367.

[129] Lee, *op. cit.,* pp. 59 ff. The author analyzes Law's concept of perfection as a new birth resulting in perfection of the heart and a "habit of the mind."

[130] At the age of forty-eight Wesley married a widow with four children. But the couple became alienated and finally separated. Wesley was not present at her death or burial.

[131] *PE,* VI, 447 ff.

God sometimes giveth, some times withholdeth them, according to His own will.

After my return home I was much buffeted with temptations, but cried out, and they fled away. They returned again and again. I as often lifted up my eyes, and He sent me help from His holy place. And herein I found the difference between this and my former state chiefly consisted. I was striving—yea, fighting with all my might under the law, as well as under grace; but then I was sometimes, if not often, conquered; now I was always conquered.[132]

This Aldersgate experience marked a stage in Wesley's religious development, and an important one at that; but it was neither the beginning nor the end of his Christian life. For about fifteen years he had been seeking Christian perfection and he continued to search for a fuller understanding of the will of God. His religious experience was nearer to that of Augustine than to that of Luther. With Wesley the central idea of Christianity is the love of God in the heart of man, which is the indwelling of the Holy Spirit. The enjoyment of God is the happiness of a Christian born again.[133] "Use the world, and enjoy God." [134] But love is holiness. "It is impossible for any that have it to conceal the religion of Jesus Christ. Your holiness makes you as conspicuous as the sun in the midst of heaven." [135] But Wesley's concept of salvation was not only concerned with the emotional state of the believer. From his earliest days in college he had clung to the conviction that "without holiness no one can see the Lord." For him Christian joy is obedience: "joy in loving God, and keeping his commandments." [136] "Nothing is higher than this, but Christian love; the love of our neighbour flowing from the love of God." [137]

With this emphasis on love, what becomes of the *articulus stantis et cadentis ecclesiae*[138] of the Reformation, the doctrine of justification by faith? Theoretically, Wesley clung to the definition of justification

[132] From Wesley's *Journal,* reprinted in *Christian Advocate,* May 19, 1938, p. 464.

[133] Robert W. Burtner and Robert E. Chiles, *A Compend of Wesley's Theology* (New York: Abingdon-Cokesbury Press, 1954), p. 170.

[134] *Ibid.,* p. 204. Cf. Nygren's discussion of Augustine in *Agape and Eros* (Philadelphia: Westminster Press, 1953), pp. 449 ff.

[135] Burtner and Chiles, *op. cit.,* p. 23.

[136] *Ibid.,* p. 227.

[137] Herbert Welch, *Selections from The Writings of the Rev. John Wesley, A.M.,* p. 129. Cf. "Treatise on Charity," *ibid.,* pp. 122 ff.

[138] "The article by which the Church stands or falls."

as stated by the Reformers. To him justification means pardon, the forgiveness of all sins of the past.[139] Wesley is careful to keep the concept of faith pure of the idea of merit. Faith is not a psychological condition which deserves the grace of God; it justifies because it embraces the promises of God.[140] Without faith man cannot be saved; "for we cannot rightly serve God unless we love Him." [141] Wesley makes a clear-cut distinction between justification and sanctification. Justification is the first act of God by which we are saved from the guilt of sin; sanctification is a distinct and totally different gift of God by which we are saved from the power of sin.[142] In emphasizing this distinction, Wesley moved in the direction of Lutheran Orthodoxy. Luther and Melanchthon had a more unified view of the redemptive work of God in man. Justification, then, is only the initial step toward full salvation. This explains Wesley's doctrine of "perfect sanctification" on the one hand, and on the other, his readiness to concede salvation also to a person who denies the article of justification by faith. "It is a high time," he says, "to return to the plain word, 'He that feareth God and worketh righteousness is accepted of Him.' " [143]

The heart of Wesley's theology is expressed above all in two distinctive doctrines: the teaching of universal salvation and of Christian perfection.

(1) *Universal salvation.* Over against Calvinism with its teaching of a limited atonement, Arminianism taught that Christ died for all men, not only for the elect. Salvation is universal in its intention. Wesley went a step further, holding that salvation is actually offered to all men, regardless of whether or not they hear the gospel proclaimed. No man, Wesley says, is in a state of mere nature or without some "preventing grace." The image of God is both natural and moral. While the latter was lost in the fall, the former is only impaired through sin. Man is still capable of God; the inferior creatures are not.[144] All men have in common a spiritual nature and possess a degree

[139] Burtner and Chiles, *op. cit.*, p. 164.

[140] *Ibid.*, p. 166. Cf. Melanchthon's thorough discussion of the problem under consideration in his Apology to the Augsburg Confession, Art. IV.

[141] Lee, *op. cit.*, p. 152.

[142] *Ibid.*, pp. 140, 162 ff.

[143] *Ibid.*, p. 161.

[144] Burtner and Chiles, *op. cit.*, p. 111.

of liberty, and all that which is "vulgarly called natural conscience." [145] Man is a responsible, free agent.

John Fletcher (d. 1785), who next to Wesley was the ablest defender of Methodism, distinguished three dispensations in the economy of grace. The Father's dispensation, which is the most extensive one, embraces all men. In this kingdom men are guided by the light of the natural knowledge of God. The dispensation of the Son embraces those who live within the limits of Christendom and who will be judged by the Christian law.[146] They are people living a moral life and attending the ordinances of God. They are justified but fail to walk "in the more excellent way." [147] People who "walk the more excellent way" belong to the realm of the Spirit. They are those who have an experiential knowledge of the regenerating and sanctifying power of the Spirit. Hence there are two kinds of Christians, the one kind living as servants in the house of God, the other, as children.

Needless to say, if salvation is free and universal, there is no place for the doctrine of predestination in the theology of Wesley. As far as Wesley is concerned Calvin's doctrine is full of blasphemy; it makes preaching and the sacraments irrelevant and destroys the comfort of religion and the zeal for good works.[148]

(2) *Christian perfection.* The distinction between ordinary Christians and those who walk the more excellent way leads to the second distinctive mark of Methodism, the doctrine of "perfect holiness." Schaff puts it very aptly, saying: "Calvin's ideal Christian is a servant of God, Luther's, a child of God, Wesley's, a perfect man in the full stature of Christ." [149] The doctrine has its root in Catholic piety with its distinction between those who obey the commandments of God and those who, in addition, follow the "evangelical counsels" of chastity, poverty and obedience. For Wesley the doctrine of the perfected man was the very heart and core of the gospel. Since his training in the Epworth parsonage he had been concerned with holiness. The admonition of Scripture, "Follow . . . holiness without which no one

[145] *Ibid.*, pp. 150-51.
[146] *Ibid.*, p. 229.
[147] Cf. Lee, *op. cit.*, pp. 210-11.
[148] *Ibid.*, pp. 51 ff.
[149] Philip Schaff, *Creeds of Christendom* (New York: Harper & Bros., 1877), I, 892.

shall see the Lord" (Heb. 12:14) is a recurrent theme in his writings.

Wesley defines perfection as a "habitual dispensation of the soul, its essence is love to God and neighbour." In an article originally published in the *Arminian Magazine* in 1787,[150] Wesley reiterates the distinction between the two orders of Christians as having existed from the beginning of the Church, the one order living an innocent life and attending the ordinances of God, the other "walking the more excellent way" and "sparing no pains to arrive at the summit of Christian holiness."[151] Wesley says he does not want to affirm "that all who do not walk in this way are on the high road to hell. But . . . they will not have so high a place in heaven as they would have had if they had chosen the better part."[152] He adds a few particulars illustrative of the "more excellent way." People walking this way will not spend more than six to seven hours in bed, for this is all that health requires. (In the case of women Wesley allows one more hour.) They will not rely on the same form of prayer but rather suit their devotions to the needs of the day. They will transact their daily business not only with diligence and justice, but do everything in the spirit of sacrifice. They will be moderate as to the quantity of food. Their conversation will focus on things divine. They will shun the theatre, dancing and playing cards. For diversion they will spend their time in the open air, read useful books, visit their neighbors and the sick. They will spend their money in a way which God will certainly reward, for every pound given to the poor is put into the bank of heaven and will bring glorious interest.[153]

Little wonder that Wesley regarded Luther as woefully lacking in the conditions of salvation. Commenting on Luther's (shorter) *Commentary on Galatians*, he wrote in his journal, "How blasphemously does he speak of good works, and of the law of God—coupling the law with sin, death, hell or the devil; and teaching that Christ delivers us from them all alike."[154] Lee remarks, "It is significant that Wesley never included any writings of either Luther or Calvin in his numerous

[150] Reprinted in Jackson, *op. cit.*, II, 266-73, and in Welch, *op. cit.*, pp. 92 ff.
[151] Welch, *op. cit.*, p. 94.
[152] *Ibid.*, p. 95.
[153] *Ibid.*, pp. 95 ff.
[154] Lee, *op. cit.*, p. 164.

reprints for Methodists. . . . As far as Wesley could go was to include two short biographies of the Reformers in his Christian Library."[155]

Speaking about "entire sanctification" did Wesley teach "sinless perfection"? Did he mean that sin is totally eradicated in the believer? The proper answer depends upon Wesley's understanding of sin. Wesley realizes that the Adamic nature of man remains in the believer. His righteousness is not that of Adam before the fall, nor does a believer share in the nature of angels. The carnal mind remains even in them that are regenerate. Man is still subject to faulty knowledge, mistakes of judgment, etc., for as long as he lives his soul is connected with his body and cannot think but by the help of the imperfect organs of the body. "Therefore, all may have need to say daily, 'Forgive us our trespasses.'"[156] However, this state, conditioned by our somatic nature, is not sin. Properly speaking, nothing is sin "but a voluntary transgression of a known law of God. Therefore every voluntary breach of the law of love is sin; and nothing else, if we speak properly."[157] Christian perfection, then, may be said to be instant and entire; but it is also a progressive experience of the Christian life. Cautiously Wesley remarks that the greater part of those he has known "were not sanctified throughout, not made perfect in love, till a little before death."[158]

As may be seen from this brief discussion, Wesleyanism was not a revival of the Calvinistic Puritan piety of the seventeenth century. It could originate only in a denomination whose teaching was shot through with Arminian tendencies.[159] Wesleyanism may be called a Protestant version of Franciscan-Jesuit theology. Like Lutheran pietism, Wesleyanism became a driving force of religious individualism stressing personal experience rather than the objective biblical content of the Christian faith. Because of the strong ethical concern of Wesley, Methodism was also susceptible to the moralistic, humanitarian understanding of the kingdom as "humanity organized according to the

[155] *Ibid.*, p. 165.

[156] Burtner and Chiles, *op. cit.*, p. 177.

[157] *Loc. cit.*

[158] *Ibid.*, pp. 182-83.

[159] See the Thirty-nine Articles of the Church of England, Art. IX. According to this Article, man is not "dead in trespasses and sins" (Eph. 2:1), but only "very far gone from original righteousness."

principle of love" (Albrecht Ritschl). On the other hand, the doctrine which in Wesley's opinion formed the heart of the gospel, the perfect sanctification of the individual, was later disavowed by the Methodist church. The official rejection is classically expressed in the revision of Charles Wesley's famous hymn, "Love Divine All Loves Excelling." In the Methodist hymnal, the second stanza now reads "Let us find the promised rest," instead of the original "that second rest," that is, the second work of grace or entire sanctification. This doctrinal defection of the Methodist church has occasioned several schisms resulting in the Holiness Movement in America.

BIBLIOGRAPHY

BAUMGART, P. *Zinzendorf als Wegbereiter historischen Denkens.* 1960.
BEYREUTHER, ERICH. *Der junge Zinzendorf.* 1957.
———. *Zinzendorf und die sich allhier beisammen finden.* 1959.
———. *Zinzendorf und die Christenheit.* 1960.
———. *Studien zur Theologie Zinzendorfs.* 1962.
——— and MEYER, G. (eds.). *Zinzendorf's Hauptschriften.*
BLANKE, F. *Zinzendorf und die Einheit der Kinder Gottes.* 1960.
BORNKAMM, H. *Mystik, Spiritualismus und die Anfänge des Pietismus.* 1926.
BURRAGE, CHAMPLIN. *The Early English Dissenters in the Light of Recent Research.* 2 vols. Cambridge: The University Press, 1912.
BURTNER, ROBERT W. and CHILES, ROBERT E. *A Compend of Wesley's Theology.* New York: Abingdon-Cokesbury Press, 1954.
CANNON, W. R. *The Theology of John Wesley.* New York: Abingdon-Cokesbury Press, 1946.
CELL, G. C. *The Rediscovery of John Wesley.* New York: Henry Holt & Company, Inc., 1935.
CLARK, HENRY W. *History of English Nonconformity from Wyclif to the Close of the 19th Century.* 2 vols. London: Chapman & Hall, Ltd., 1911–1913.
DESCHNER, JOHN. *Wesley's Christology, an Interpretation.* Dallas: Southern Methodist University Press, 1960.
EBERHARD, S. *Theologie und Sprache bei Zinzendorf.* 1937.
ELLIOT-BINNS, L. E. *The Early Evangelicals.* Greenwich: Seabury Press, 1953.
GAIRDNER, JAMES. *Lollardry and the Reformation in England.* 4 vols. London: Macmillan & Co., Ltd., 1908-1913.
GREEN, J. B. *John Wesley and William Law.* London: Epworth Press, 1945.
GRIMM, HAROLD J. *The Reformation Era.* New York: Macmillan Co., 1954.
HILDEBRANDT, FRANZ. *From Luther to Wesley.* London: Lutterworth Press, 1951.

HIRSCH, EMANUEL. *Geschichte der neueren evangelischen Theologie.* Vol. II. 1951.

HOEK, GOESTA. *Zinzendorfs Begriff der Religion.* 1948.

JACKSON, THOMAS. *Wesley's Works.* 3rd, ed. 14 vols. London, 1829-31.

KANTZENBACH, F. W. "Das Bild des Grafen," *Lutherische Monatshefte.* August, 1962.

LEE, UMPHREY. *John Wesley and Modern Religion.* Nashville: Cokesbury Press, 1936.

LEWIS, A. J. *Zinzendorf, the Ecumenical Pioneer.* London: SCM Press, 1962.

LINDSTROEM, HARALD. *Wesley and Sanctification.* Stockholm, 1946.

LITTELL, FRANKLIN H. *The Anabaptist View of the Church.* Boston: Starr King Press, 1958.

LOANE, M. L. *Masters of the English Reformation.* London: Church Book Room Press, 1954.

MACFARLANE, K. B. *John Wycliffe and the Beginnings of English Nonconformity.* London: English Universities Press, 1952.

MAIER, PAUL L. *Caspar Schwenckfeld on the Person of Christ.* Essen, 1959.

NAGLER, A. W. *Pietism and Methodism.* Nashville: Smith & Lamar, 1918.

NIELSEN, SIGURD. *Intoleranz und Toleranz bei Zinzendorf.* 3 vols. 1952.

PFISTER, OSKAR. *Die Frömmigkeit des Grafen Ludwig von Zinzendorf; ein Psychoanalytischer Beitrag.* 1910. 2nd ed. 1925.

RAGSDALE, WILLIAM. *The Theology of Wesley with Special Reference to the Doctrine of Justification.* Nashville: Cokesbury Press, 1946.

REICHEL, GERHARD. *Zinzendorfs Frömmigkeit im Lichte der Psychoanalyse.* 1911.

RITSCHL, ALBRECHT. *Geschichte des Pietismus.* 3 vols. 1880 ff.

ROUTLEY, ERIK. *English Religious Dissent.* Cambridge: University Press, 1960.

RUPP, E. GORDON. *Six Makers of English Religion.* London, Hodder & Stoughton, Ltd., 1957.

________. *Studies in the Making of the English Tradition.* Cambridge: University Press, 1949.

SCOTT, PERCY. *John Wesley's Lehre von der Heiligung verglichen mit einem lutherisch-pietistischen Beispiel.* 1939.

SMITH, J. W. and JAMISON, A. L. (eds.). *Religion in American Life.* IV, 76 ff. Princeton: University Press, 1961.

UTTENDORFER, OTTO. *Zinzendorf und die Mystik.* 1951.

WEINLICK, J. R. *Count Zinzendorf.* Nashville: Abingdon Press, 1956.

WELCH, HERBERT. *Selections from the Writings of the Rev. John Wesley, A.M.* Rev. ed. 1918.

WENGER, JOHN C. (ed.). *The Complete Works of Menno Simons.* Translated by Leonard Verdouin. Scottsdale, Pa.: Herald Press, 1956.

WILLIAMS, GEORGE H. *The Radical Reformation.* Philadelphia: Westminster Press, 1962.

________ and MERGAL, ANGEL M. *Spiritual and Anabaptist Writers.* ("Library of Christian Classics," Vol. XXV. Philadelphia: Westminster Press, 1957.

CHAPTER II

GEORGE CALIXTUS AND SYNCRETISM

George Calixtus

In order to grasp the principles involved in the syncretistic controversy we must understand the training and development of this irenical theologian. He was a student in the University of Helmstedt for six years, and then was professor in that same school for forty-two years, 1614-1656.

Helmstedt, in the Duchy of Brunswick, was different from the other universities of seventeenth-century Lutheranism. This institution was opposed to the Formula of Concord, and served as a place of refuge for those Melanchthonians who were uprooted by the Crypto-Calvinistic controversies in electoral Saxony. Among the professors in this school were such ardent advocates of humanism as the learned John Casselius and the brilliant Cornelius Martini of Antwerp. History, the ancient classics, and philosophy were studied intensely, not to support biblical doctrine, but for their own sake. These Helmstedt professors were not hostile to theology. Reason was not exalted to a position of opposition to theology. However, they did oppose the "barbarism of polemics" as practiced between the churches, and they held that education in the classics, ancient philosophy, and history would make theology more palatable.

Helmstedt was Melanchthonian in character. The father of Calixtus, who opposed Flacius and afterwards the Formula of Concord, had been a pupil of Melanchthon in Wittenberg after Luther's death. In the Melanchthonian-humanistic atmosphere of Helmstedt, young Calixtus received a broad education, spending four of the six years in a study of the humanities. He was a brilliant student and upon graduation was selected as a candidate for professorship. His chief interest was the history of the ancient Church, an interest clearly manifested in his later writings.[1] Humanism, when dissatisfied with the present, flees into antiquity to discover there correctives for the misdevelopment of the centuries.

Following his graduation and before undertaking his professorship, Calixtus traveled extensively. He visited many German universities and traveled in Belgium, Holland, England, and France, making a close study of the churches, particularly their creeds.

Calixtus on Fundamentals and Nonfundamentals

Calixtus appealed for mutual recognition and co-operation between the churches on the basis of existing agreement in the fundamentals of Christianity. As to organic union, he was open-minded enough to see that there ought to be agreement also on some nonfundamentals. On this subject there had been definite expression by the Lutheran Nicholas Hunnius and others.[2] In our next two chapters on Arminianism in Holland and in Great Britain we shall see that tolerance and mutual recognition on the basis of a distinction between fundamentals and nonfundamentals were widely advocated.[3] It was a sentiment that had developed as a reaction against the confessional polemics in the seventeenth century.

Calixtus defined a fundamental doctrine as follows: It is a doctrine that is necessary to be believed for salvation; a doctrine which no one, be he layman or theologian, can ignore without endangering his salvation. He included as fundamental doctrines belief in eternal life, resurrection of the body and soul, that eternal life will be a life with God, and that salvation comes only through Christ, through the work of the Holy Spirit in the Christian Church. Following Bonaventura, he classified the Church's teaching into three divisions: (1) *Antecedentia:* religious matters which man, without the aid of revelation, can know by his own reasoning—for example, the facts of providence, the immortal-

[1] Cf. his *Apparatus Theologicus,* 1628, his *Orationes Selectae,* 1659, and various books on the history of ancient dogmas.

[2] See the thorough review of this situation by Otto Ritschl, *Dogmengeschichte des Protestantismus,* IV (1927), 231 ff.

[3] We refer to Jacob Acontius and the Confession of the Arminians by Episcopius in Holland, to Edward Stillingfleet in England, and to John Dury in Scotland.

ity of the soul, knowledge of the Scriptures. (2) *Constituentia:* real matters of faith, the objects of revelation for the salvation of man, man's sinfulness and God's grace in the acts of redemption. For Calixtus these were the real fundamentals. (3) *Consequentia:* more or less theological doctrines derived from fundamentals and incorporated into the creeds—for example, predestination, personal union of the two natures of Christ, and the doctrine of the Supper.[4]

Appeal to Tradition and to the Apostles' Creed

As to confessional standards for the fundamentals necessary to be believed for salvation, Calixtus appealed to the doctrinal tradition of the early Church of about the first five centuries, to the *consensus quinquesaecularis.* Though Calixtus held that the Scriptures are the sole source of salvation, he insisted that the teaching of the early Church constituted a real criterion of fundamental truth. Abraham Calovius (1612-86) of Wittenberg University was an outstanding opponent of Calixtus who had many supporters among the Lutheran theologians. He attacked Calixtus on his theory of tradition as a secondary standard of truth and insisted that the Scriptures are the only infallible norm of true doctrine.[5]

Thereafter Calixtus spoke less of tradition, and settled on the Apostles' Creed as representative of what was fundamental in the teaching of the early Church. He argued that the ancient Church in its earliest form certainly possessed all the truth needed for salvation. We must remember that Calixtus appealed to antiquity mainly to support his claim of fundamental unity (*communio interna*) among the churches. On this point Calixtus again found in Calovius a ready opponent. Calovius rejected the claim that the Apostles' Creed represents a complete doctrinal norm of truth for all time and that it contains the fundamentals of the Scriptures in such a way that nothing needs to be added, amplified, or defined.

Before proceeding further we want to interpose a few relevant critical remarks about this point of view. While the Apostles' Creed represents an admirable expression of the rudiments of Christian truth,

[4] Cf. the thorough investigation based on original sources in Heinrich Schmid, *Geschichte der synkretistischen Streitigkeiten,* pp. 156 ff.

[5] *Consideratio novae theologiae,* 1649; *Syncretismus Calixtinus,* 1653, and other works. Cf. Schmid, *op. cit.,* p. 237.

it is only a general outline upon which the individual parts of Christian faith, the *fides quae creditur*, were erected. This growth took place through the process of progressive doctrinal experience, chiefly in conflict with error. The Apostles' Creed, as it developed out of the baptismal formula, represents the formulation of the first doctrinal experience of the Church. Later developments could be expected naturally. To demand of the Church after the Reformation that it should limit its public confession to the statements of the Apostles' Creed would be equivalent to reducing a full-grown man to the status of a child. Besides, the churches of the Reformation Age were not divided over the validity of the Nicene and Chalcedonian theology; the conflict was over the doctrine of justification with its many ramifications.

The Apostles' Creed and Later Creeds

Baur, the founder of the Tübingen school, once said that Calixtus undertook to lead the church back from theology to religion. His attempt to put the Apostles' Creed into contrast with the other creeds of Christendom was an endeavor to establish religion and theology as opposites.

As has been pointed out, Calixtus had established himself upon a distinction between fundamentals and nonfundamentals. Fundamental, he said, is what is necessary to be known and to be believed for salvation. To the plain statements of the Apostles' Creed nothing of a fundamental nature can be added. The later, more elaborate creeds contain fundamentals only where the substance of that creed is repeated in a practically identical form; wherever the later creeds offer interpretation and qualification of the Apostles' Creed, there they no longer express fundamentals. Such interpretive and supplementary matter, which was necessitated by the activity of heretics, has no significance for the ordinary Christian; it is material for teachers only, to guide them in their work.[6]

Many of the Church's teachers, Calixtus continued, made the mistake of delving too deeply into such mysteries as the Trinity, the two natures of Christ, original sin, the relation of God's grace to man's will in conversion, and other matters. They should have contented

[6] Schmid, *op. cit.*, pp. 143 ff.

themselves with simply teaching what is clearly revealed and needs to be known for salvation. So Calixtus, as an irenic, argued in his zeal for bridging the chasms between the churches and tried to make the differences appear to be of minor consideration. He did not deny that occasions might arise when a teacher would be compelled to go beyond the clearly revealed statements of Scripture. But this, he said, should be done only in theological discussion, with much reticence and with the awareness that man will always be denied a full insight into the mysteries of the Christian faith. He insisted that such doctrinal differences are not fundamental to salvation and, therefore, do not affect the underlying unity among the churches.

Regarding the later, more theological creeds, Calixtus made a distinction between the creeds of the first five centuries and the confessions of the Reformation age. He looked upon the former as confessional testimonies of the fundamental period of the Church's life, but held that they are theological in character and for that reason their acceptance is not necessary for salvation. As to the confessions of the Reformation, he would again say: Either they repeat the plain statements of the Apostles' Creed, and in such part they are fundamental for salvation; or they interpret that creed and deduce additional doctrines from it (*per consequentiam*), in which cases they constitute no articles of faith, but are intended to serve only the teachers of the church. He even went so far as to call the doctrinal differences between the churches *appendices quaedam et quaestiones annatae* ("a kind of appendages and attached questions").

Calovius, Huelsemann, Dannhauer, and also John Musaeus, opponents of Calixtus, had a different appreciation of the more theological creeds of Christendom, and it cannot be denied that they were more correct in their positions. To them the Apostles' Creed was merely a general outline of the Church's faith, a first attempt to state the essentials of Christian truth. The Creed's statements gave a seminal expression of the Christian faith which was in need of development and further unfolding.

The leading objections of Calovius were as follows: The Apostles' Creed was not formulated for the purpose of giving to believers of all ages a really complete summary of the Christian faith. The later creeds of the ancient Church were not intended to interpret or to supplement the Apostles' Creed; they were simply written to meet the errorists of the age, such as Arius, who denied the full divinity of Christ, the Macedonians who denied the personality and the divinity of the Spirit, and the Nestorians and Monophysites who held fundamental errors regarding the person and natures of Christ. In meeting these teachers[7] the Church found itself called upon to state other features of revealed truth which were essential and fundamental, but which had so far not been generally recognized. Calovius took the position that all revealed truth is fundamental for salvation in one way or another, and that in the later creeds of the first five centuries, as also in those of the Reformation, we have new and needed statements of scriptural truths. These, he insisted, have their significance not merely for the teachers of the Church, but for every soul. It is for this reason that the confessions of Lutheranism contain articles of faith which must also be counted among the fundamentals.

Calovius pointed to the undeniable fact that the various errors which had been the occasion for the development of the creeds constituted temptations and dangers for the life of the Church. He held further that the rejection of these errors in the creeds had much to do with the faith of the Church, and for this reason the creeds offer important messages for the common Christian, even if it is the special duty of the teacher to interpret those messages.[8]

On the basis of his theory of fundamentals and nonfundamentals and his distinction between Apostles' Creed and later creeds, Calixtus declared that there was a virtual union between Lutherans and Reformed, and even Rome, that needed only to be recognized. He admitted that an outward union was not possible as long as these churches were wrongfully charging each other with fundamental errors. He felt that the doctrine of the Lord's Supper was a serious obstacle to an external union between Lutherans and Reformed, but not because of the doctrinal difference in itself—for it is not a fundamental doctrine—but because of the place of this sacrament in the *cultus* of the Church and because of the tenacity with which the churches hold to their differing opinions.

The Lutherans admitted that they had much in common with the

[7] *Ibid.*, p. 209.
[8] *Ibid.*, pp. 237 ff.

Reformed. They did not seriously regard the Reformed as Jews and heathen, nor even as a sect like the Anabaptists and Socinians. They regarded them as a church. But the Lutherans denied the existence of a real union in the faith. For Lutherans the differences were differences in the faith. Calixtus insisted upon distinguishing in every doctrine between the "what" (*quid*) and the "how" (*quomodo*)—that is, between the substance of a doctrine and the manner of teaching it. The Lutherans answered: It is not enough to know that Christ is the Savior, it is also necessary to know how he saves. The teachings on the way of salvation, on the means of grace and on man's attitude are by no means nonfundamental matters. It is in the conflicts on these very important doctrines that the differences on commonly accepted doctrines appear. Dannhauer declared: The churches accept the words of the Creed, but they disagree as to their meaning, and this shows that the assumption of an existing union is, after all, a deception.[9]

The Lutherans refused to distinguish between fundamentals and nonfundamentals according to the theory of Calixtus. Their arguments were as follows: The Scriptures speak of no such distinction and draw no line. Truth is an organism. In this organism there are parts of seemingly minor importance, but even these cannot be removed without injuring the whole. Dannhauer declared it to be a mistake to call articles of faith only those doctrines which must be believed for salvation. He held that many doctrines of Scripture, which are not fundamental in that sense, are nevertheless articles of faith because of the help and comfort they give to the seeking sinner and to the Christian. As such he mentions the doctrine of the real presence of Christ's body and blood in the Supper.

Calixtus took the position that no church could call itself the true Church because all churches, Rome included, have the fundamentals of the Apostles' Creed. He regarded the Lutheran church as the purest in theology, but in matters necessary for salvation he could see no difference. The greater or lesser purity, he said, was concerned not with the religion but merely with the theology of the churches.

It was in connection with the problem of an existing virtual union between the churches that the question was asked: Who is a heretic and what is a heresy? Here Calixtus had to express himself. Consistent

[9] *Ibid.*, pp. 290 ff.

with his leading views, he said: We must distinguish between error and heresy. Departure from the statements of the Apostles' Creed constitutes a heresy, and a heretic, in this sense, is not in the union of faith with other Christians. But departure from the teaching of the later creeds and from the doctrinal matters derived from the Apostles' Creed *per consequentiam* merely constitutes an error which does not affect the faith. A heretic, then, in the proper sense of that term, is only the person who rejects an article of faith as it is plainly expressed in the Apostles' Creed.[10] Furthermore, a heretic is one who rejects that article of faith consciously and who intentionally makes himself the cause of a schism, not one who by providence finds himself in a schismatic communion. As has been said, the Lutherans objected in this discussion to the distinction between the Apostles' Creed and later creeds. Calovius declared that such a definition of heresy was certainly opposed to the practice of the church which demanded subscription to the later creeds as proof of orthodoxy. He further reminded Calixtus that if only acceptance of the Apostles' Creed is sufficient as evidence of orthodoxy, then even the Arians, Socinians, Arminians and Anabaptists could not be charged with heresy.[11]

As we have seen, Calixtus did not demand an organic union of the churches as long as serious theological difficulties stood in the way, but he pleaded for the recognition of an existing union (*communio virtualis*) based on the fundamentals of the Apostles' Creed. On this basis he demanded that the churches mutually recognize each other as true churches, all being orthodox in the fundamentals of the faith. The Lutherans declared that if there were a real inner union in the matters pertaining to salvation, then the obstacle to an external union would be removed and a full union should be consummated. Lutherans, however, denied the existence of such an inner union, and therefore declared that the recognition which Calixtus advocated would be infidelity to truth.

Even the mediating Musaeus of Jena took this position.[12] Rejecting the theory of Calixtus regarding the fundamentals, the Jena theologians declared that the Church is steward not merely of all revealed truth

[10] *Ibid.*, pp. 172 ff.
[11] *Ibid.*, p. 263.
[12] *Ibid.*, pp. 397 ff.

that is helpful in leading souls in the way of salvation. They argued that if the Lutheran church is serious in her particular confession and does appeal to the Scriptures with good conscience, it cannot recognize the opposing churches as orthodox and evangelical, but is in duty bound to testify against their errors. To do otherwise the Lutheran church would be espousing the principle that one conception of religion is as good as another.[13] The Jena theologians recognized, with the Formula of Concord, that in other churches there are many true Christians who err innocently. These, they said, can be regarded as brethren. They added that it is not always possible to know the inner attitude of such individuals; therefore, the rule will have to be that individuals must be judged by their public confession in the church of which they are members. As to recognizing other churches as true churches, the position was taken that this could not be done consistently when these other churches were confessionally established in positions which were subversive to the creed of the church from which recognition was expected.

An Evaluation of Calixtus and of the Lutheranism of His Age

The distinction between fundamentals and nonfundamentals, when applied to the question of mutual recognition in the hope of union, cannot be made by asking: What is indispensable for the individual to know and to believe in order to be saved? Calixtus failed to distinguish between Church and individual.

Regarding the individual, salvation depends upon an attitude of the soul to Christ, not upon the knowledge and acceptance of a fixed number of doctrines. It is also true that by having faith in Christ the intellect is not altogether passive. The gospel which is accepted calls for a doctrinal expression even in the mind of the ordinary believer. No comprehensive rule can be made as to the details of such doctrinal expression. For an individual with little religious training, when it comes to the last struggle, it may be only one thought centering about Christ as the Savior from sin, consequently much less than is contained in the Apostles' Creed. In another individual who grew up in a Christian environment under careful instruction in scriptural truth, a much

[13] Report of the Jena faculty, published in Calovius' *Historia Syncretismi*, pp. 999 ff.

larger insight into divine truth would be natural, so that elements of even the later creeds would be embraced in his confession. Again, it is one thing not to know or not to have a clear conception of fundamental truth, and quite another to reject such truth with purpose and against one's conscience. It should also not be denied that a larger religious knowledge is helpful to the soul in finding the way of salvation.

The question is an altogether different one when the object in view is the mutual recognition of the churches and when the aim is to prepare the way for Church union. The Lutherans were right when they took the position that all scriptural truth is fundamental which aids the Church in its work of winning souls for Christ and of leading the congregation of believers into all truth.[14]

Calixtus demanded that churches of different creeds should recognize each other as "true" churches. To support his demand he asked his Lutheran opponents: Cannot the members of other churches be saved? God himself adopts his children, and we must recognize them as brethren in the faith.[15]

Such argument sounded well and was bound to make the position of Calixtus popular. His argument forced the question by cutting the knot of the problem which he was unable to solve theologically. He was too persistent in ignoring the difference of Church and individual in the discussion of this question. His argument was based too much upon the presuppostion that one church is as good as another, and he failed to see that church membership is, or ought to be, a matter of conviction and of conscience. The Lutherans expected the other churches, as most of them actually did, to refuse them full recognition and actual union so long as there was no agreement in matters of faith.[16]

It is true, however, that the Lutherans of the age of Calixtus were inclined to make Christianity and the salvation of the individual depend too much upon orthodoxy of faith. Many of them overlooked the

[14] See the discussion of F. J. Stahl, *Die lutherische Kirche und die Union* (1859), pp. 339 ff.

[15] Schmid, *op. cit.*, pp. 173 ff.

[16] For a complete discussion of the problems see the interpretation of Article VII of the Augsburg Confession in J. L. Neve, *The Augsburg Confession* (Philadelphia: The Lutheran Publication Society, 1914), pp. 92 ff., and in *Introduction to the Symbolical Books of the Lutheran Church* (Columbus, O.: Lutheran Book Concern, 1926), pp. 181-91.

fact that a sincere Christian can live in doctrinal errors and may even defend them. They said: When a Christian has been sufficiently instructed, then the responsibility for doctrinal correctness devolves upon him. Considering the tenacity of prejudices, the natural fidelity to the church into which an individual was born, and the influence of environment, seventeenth-century Lutherans were not right when they took the position that "sufficient instruction" is bound to convert the lover of truth. They were defective in their psychology. They were right in stating that in the relation of one church to another, the recognition of an existing internal union and public fellowship in the faith must be regulated by the public profession.

From the standpoint of conservative Lutheranism, the positions of Calixtus cannot be accepted. This was the practically unanimous verdict of the Lutherans of his own age, including the more liberal Jena school, of the great Lutheran theologians who wrote in the second third of the nineteenth century, and of Lutheranism in America.[17] Ferdinand Kattenbusch, in his article on symbolics,[18] offers the following severe judgment which weighs heavily if we consider his decidedly liberal theological position: "The Syncretism of the seventeenth century deserves no sympathy. He who really knows George Calixtus cannot judge him with any special appreciation; neither as man nor theologian does he stand upon a higher level than his much-scolded opponent Abraham Calovius."

It cannot be denied that in the age of Calixtus Lutheranism was in need of correctives. Orthodoxy had degenerated into orthodoxism. The continuous controversies between Lutheranism and Calvinism had led to an intellectualism and to a preaching of pure theology in the pulpits which yielded little bread to gospel-hungry souls. Ubiquity was a favorite subject for discussion in the sermons. The appeal to the congregation was of such a nature that the layman was hardly regarded a full Christian unless he was a theologian. With it all went a polemics that in most cases was out of place in the pulpit.

The Lutherans of the seventeenth century went too far in identifying religious truth with the theological and dialectical formulation of that

[17] Cf. the article "Georg Calixt" in Meusel, *Kirchliches Handlexikon,* I, 632 ff.

[18] *Realencyklopädie für protestantische Theologie und Kirche,* ed. Albert Hauck (Leipzig, 1896), hereinafter referred to as *PRE,* XIX, 204.

truth. In the practical life of the Church there are situations where, in the application, a distinction between religion and theology must be observed. In denominational problems it has not always been easy to distinguish properly between the *fides qua* and the *fides quae creditur*, that is, the subjective and the objective faith. In the distinction of Calixtus between the simple facts of the Apostles' Creed and the later creeds of a more theological nature we have the reaction against the intellectualism of seventeenth-century Lutheranism. But the theory of Calixtus was not acceptable. His distinction between religion and theology was too mechanical. It must never be forgotten that to a certain degree true scriptural theology will always have to be the form of the objective faith without which a healthy subjective faith cannot be cultivated in the Church.

Calixtus' assertion of a practically existing internal union could be made only by an almost complete abstraction from the objective faith. Common recognition of the Apostles' Creed did not mean much because the differences appeared in the interpretation of that creed. Internal union has a certain degree of reality only when recognition is given to the *fides qua creditur*, that is, to the relation and attitude of the heart to God and His Son as Savior from sin.

Pietists, especially the newly converted among them, are always unionists when it comes to denominational problems. The profound impression of their religious experience leads them to regard all who have had a like experience as brethren in the faith. If the spiritual development and growth of such a newly converted individual is normal, then the time is bound to come when he feels the need of linking his religious experience with the doctrinal experiences of the historic Church which is crystallized in the creeds. Thus pietistic Christians develop into confessional Christians with denominational interests.

Calixtus failed to appreciate the Reformation.

Paul Tschackert, an advocate of irenics on the subject of the relation between the Lutherans and the Reformed who was opposed to seventeenth-century Lutheranism and sympathetic with Calixtus, has said:

> As regards his irenics, we shall acknowledge and highly appreciate his good intention. But in taking the position that the Apostles' Creed and the *consensus quinquesaecularis* are the best representation of Christianity, he proved that he did not have the proper appreciation of the reli-

gious content of the Reformation. From the standpoint of Calixtus the historic reformation of Luther loses its specific value. The natural consequence was indifferentism towards the confessions of the church which, in a number of cases, evidenced itself in the conversion of Lutheran princes and princesses to Roman Catholicism.[19]

Dannhauer remarked correctly that in following Calixtus, the Lutheran church would have to cease praising Luther and his Reformation and apologize for the schism that had been caused in Protestantism. Characteristic of Calixtus' position was the answer he gave to Duke Anton Ulrich of Brunswick, who had asked him whether a Protestant princess could marry a Roman Catholic king with good conscience and embrace his faith. He answered: (1) The Roman Catholic church does not err in the foundation of faith and the matter of salvation. (2) Consequently the changing of one's church relationship from Protestantism to Roman Catholicism is permissible.[20]

The humanistic trait in Calixtus had much to do with his liberal views in dealing with denominational problems. Baur remarked that Calixtus favored a line of development leading from the purely Christian to the generally human. Perhaps this was the real root of his conflict with Lutheranism. In the introduction to this chapter we have acknowledged that humanism could have had a beneficial influence upon seventeenth-century Lutherans. By that we meant with respect to form, method, and temper. Humanism makes the theologian freer and more scientific, and helps him to draw conclusions from history and psychology. But humanism also inclines to a criticism of the foundations. The hand of God in history is ignored. The Reformation is looked upon as a misdevelopment.

Syncretism as a Movement

The term syncretism came into frequent use as a charge against Calixtus and his followers. It stigmatizes the endeavor to combine opposing confessions of faith into one church. The term is wrongly derived from *synkerannymi*, "to mix together." It is perhaps more correct to think of the *synkretismon* by which the old Cretans,

[19] *PRE*, III, 647.

[20] The inquiry concerned the Duke's daughter, Princess Elizabeth Christine. She married Emperor Karl VI and became the mother of Empress Marie Therese.

who were at odds with one another, meant (according to Plutarch) that they should always be united against a common foe. In this sense it had been suggested by Zwingli, Bucer, Melanchthon that they should form a *synkretismon,* meaning by that a united front against Rome, even if a full doctrinal union could not be realized.[21]

The University of Wittenberg took the lead in opposing the Syncretists. Abraham Calovius proposed a new confession, the *Consensus repetitus fidei vere Lutheranae,* 1664.[22] This new symbol went far beyond the Formula of Concord in rendering decisions on theological problems. Following the order of the Augsburg Confession, there are eighty-eight sections. First the true doctrine is presented, introduced by a *profitemur;* then follows a *rejicimus,* the rejected error; finally there is a proof quotation from the writings of the Helmstedters, Calixtus, Hornejus, Latermann, and Dreier. Among the things rejected as heresies are the following: that the article of the Trinity is not clearly revealed in the Old Testament, and that the believers of the Old Testament should not have known this doctrine; that the Angel of Jehovah is not Christ; that the Old Testament believers did not know and believe the doctrine of Christ's person and office; that creationism is not a heresy; that the existence of God does not need to be proved by theology; that newly born children have no real faith; that John 6 speaks of the Lord's Supper; that Romanists and Calvinists can belong to the true Church; that they can have a hope of salvation and are not to be condemned to eternal death. Consent to these matters was required for church fellowship. It was the intention of this confession to exclude the Helmstedters from the Lutheran church. Calovius published one work after the other to prepare the church for an adoption of his symbol.

But Wittenberg no longer truly represented the Lutheran church. John Musaeus, along with the faculty of the Jena University, stepped in as a regulating factor and rendered a valuable service to Lutheranism. He criticized the Wittenberg theologians in their controversy with Calixtus for not sufficiently distinguishing between necessary articles of faith and matters in which there may be disagreement without

[21] For references to Erasmus, Zwingli, Bucer, Melanchthon, *et al.,* see *PRE,* XIX, 239 ff.

[22] See Schaff, *op. cit.,* I, 349 ff.

injury to the Christian faith. He demanded the recognition of "open questions." [23]

A characteristic passage from the Jena circle may be quoted:

> In the detailed and thorough discussion of necessary articles of faith, in the interpretation of difficult passages of Scripture, in the dealing with philosophical questions relative to their bearing upon necessary articles of faith, in the method of polemics and in like matters, even orthodox and doctrinally pure theologians cannot always be expected to agree. This is especially true of the men at the schools of higher learning, for they have not been called to lecture before their audiences without further thought of what they have learned of their teachers or read of other theologians; but they are to consider carefully special difficulties and should aim as much as possible to elucidate and to interpret. If this be done, then it cannot be otherwise but that sometimes there will be dissensions in the manner of teaching, in formulating and defending the doctrines of faith, . . .

In evaluating the theological situation, the Jena circle called attention to the fact that in matters of knowledge, convictions mature gradually, and that it is often necessary for men to make judgments before all the facts are known. For such ventilation of thought, it was said, there must be toleration in the Church. Progress should not be barred by too much insistence upon conformity to detail.[24]

The Jena theologians were far from agreeing with Calixtus in his manner of distinguishing between fundamentals and nonfundamentals. On this point they were in entire harmony with Wittenberg. To the honor of seventeenth-century Lutherans it can be reported that the *Consensus repetitus* was never adopted. The large work of Calovius, his *Historia syncretistica* (1682) was practically confiscated by the government of Lutheran Saxony.[25]

Besides the theologians mentioned above, the controversy involved three personages whose memories are still alive in Protestant circles. The first is Paul Gerhardt, the famous hymnist of the Lutheran church. His sovereign, Friedrich Wilhelm of Brandenburg, was a Calvinist and thoroughly sympathetic to Calixtus. He issued a decree restricting freedom of speech in matters of controversy between the Lutherans

[23] Wilhelm Gass, *Georg Calixt und der Synkretismus,* pp. 113 ff.; Schmid, *op. cit.,* pp. 410-11.

[24] Schmid, *op. cit.,* pp. 405 ff.

[25] *PRE,* XIX, 261.

and the Calvinists. Though of an irenical disposition, Paul Gerhardt refused to sign the pledge required of the clergy and was consequently deposed from his pastoral office in Berlin, 1666.

In Hanover the ideas of Calixtus were warmly endorsed by the philosopher Leibnitz and his friend Gerhard Walther Molanus. Both men approved of the conversion of Princess Elizabeth Christine to Roman Catholicism referred to above. As Director of the Consistory of Hanover and Abbot of Loccum, Molanus wielded a great influence on the churches in Lower Saxony, inculcating the pastors under his jurisdiction with the tenets of Calixtinian theology.

Though Leibnitz never joined the Roman communion, he regarded the central concern of the Reformation, that is, justification by faith over against the Roman doctrine of works, as "a kind of bickering in the course of which the ill-advised statements of some and the exaggerated notions of others played into the hands of the Roman party."[26] He also was ready to approve and recommend the Roman view of the seven sacraments, the doctrine of the mass, the veneration of saints and relics, etc. To expedite reunion with Rome, both Molanus and Leibnitz entered into negotiations with representatives of Rome. In addition, the political clime at the court of Hanover was very favorable to such endeavors. Linked by marriage to the Catholic house of Hapsburg and the Reformed dynasty of the Hohenzollerns, Electress Sophia, herself of Calvinist training, became the heir apparent to the throne of Great Britain by Act of Parliament. Her son George I ascended the British throne in 1714. Because of his dual reign he was head of the Lutheran church of Hanover, of the Anglican church in England, and of the Presbyterian establishment in Scotland.

The aim of this chapter has been to review critically the positions taken by George Calixtus in which the theology of the Reformation was for the first time toned down to a level of mild interdenominationalism and to positions later occupied by the union movements. As a reaction against seventeenth-century Lutheran theology Calixtus' views contained the seeds of liberalism which were not yet noticed. The syncretistic movement was crushed for the time being. Union

[26] Quoted by Otto Ritschl, *op. cit.,* IV (1927), p. 27. Leibnitz' *Systema theologicum* was published in Latin and in a German translation by C. Haas, 1860.

movements of succeeding ages revived Calixtinian tendencies of irenics, for example, the Moravian movement and the Prussian Church Union. The syncretism of Calixtus addressed itself to the Lutheran wing of Protestantism. The following two chapters show how the same tendencies asserted themselves in domains of the Reformed churches, in Holland and in England.

BIBLIOGRAPHY

CALIXTUS, FRIEDRICH ULRICH. *Catalogus Operum Calixitini.*

DOWDLING, WILLIAM C. *German Theology During the Thirty Years War: Life and Correspondence of George Calixtus.* Oxford: J. Henry & J. Parker, 1863.

GASS, WILHELM. *Georg Calixt und der Synkretismus.* 1846.

HENKE, E. L. T. *Die Universität Helmstedt im sechzehnten Jahrhundert.* 1833.

———. (ed.). *Georg Calixtus Briefwechsel.* 1833, 1835, 1840.

———. (ed.). *Georg Calixtus und seine Zeit.* 2 vols. 1853-54.

LEUBE, H. *Die Reformideen in der deutschen lutherischen Kirche zur Zeit der Orthodoxie.* 1924.

———. *Kalvinismus und Luthertum.* Vol. I. 1928.

NEVE, J. L. *Lutherans in the Movement for Church Union.* Philadelphia: United Lutheran Publication House, 1921.

RITSCHL, OTTO. *Dogmengeschichte des Protestantismus.* Vol. IV. 1927.

SCHMID, HEINRICH. *Geschichte der synkretistischen Streitigkeiten.* 1846.

SCHUESSLER, H. *Georg Calixtus, Theologie und Kirchenpolitik.* 1954.

CHAPTER III

ARMINIANISM IN HOLLAND

Arminianism cannot be understood unless the entire historical background of the controversy is considered. The syncretism of George Calixtus had a Lutheran background, but it should not be overlooked that similar tendencies were afoot in Holland and in England where the background was Calvinism or Arminianism as its counterpart.

The Arminian movement began with a controversy over predestination, but this was only the starting point of the conflict. The discussion will look first at this starting point and then at the further development of Arminianism.

The Origins of Arminianism

The immediate cause of the conflict was Calvin's teaching of double predestination in the form of supralapsarianism as contrasted with infralapsarianism. After the death of Calvin Reformed theologians used these two terms to refer to the logical order of the decrees in discussing predestination. Charles Hodge wrote on the meaning of supralapsarianism as follows:

> According to this view, God, in order to manifest His grace and justice, selected from creatable men (from men to be created) a certain number to be vessels of mercy, and certain others to be vessels of wrath. In the order of thought, election and reprobation precede the purpose to create and to permit the Fall. Creation is in order to redemption.[1]

Continuing, Hodge spoke of infralapsarianism:

> God, with the design to reveal his own glory, that is, the perfections of his own nature, determined to create the world; secondly to permit the fall of man; thirdly, to elect from the mass of fallen men a multitude whom no man can number as vessels of mercy, . . .

Calvin and Beza did not always express themselves consistently on this matter. The burden of their teaching was the supralapsarian conception of predestination.

[1] *Systematic Theology* (New York: Scribner, Armstrong & Co., 1874), II, 316.

D. V. Koornheert, a scholarly layman, wrote against this teaching. He gathered a following, which demanded a revision of the Belgic Confession. Jacob Arminius, known for dialectical skill and for loyalty to Calvinism, was asked to reply to him. On closer study of this problem Arminius turned against Beza and all the strict predestinarians. He soon was in conflict with his fellow professor at the University of Leyden (1603), Francis Gomarus, a rigid Calvinist. The historical cause of this conflict must be seen against the background of strict adherence to Calvinistic principles and emphasis upon the doctrine of predestination on the one hand, and of an anti-Calvinist party, inclined toward rationalism, which wished to be rid of every vestige of the biblical doctrine of predestination on the other.

The conflict resulted in a schism which affected the whole of the Reformed church in Holland. Arminius died in 1609. The scholarly and able Simon Episcopius became his successor in the university and the spokesman for his followers. It was he especially who systematized and developed the "Arminian" views. In 1610 the Arminians expressed their position in their Five Articles under the title *Articuli Arminiani sive Remonstrantiae*, which gave them the name "Remonstrants." The adherents of the official church issued a *Counter-Remonstrance*. All endeavors to reach an agreement were to no avail. The question came before the famous Synod of Dort, which convened from November 13, 1618 until till May 9, 1619, during which time 154 formal sessions and a large number of conferences were held.[2] The whole Dutch delegation, consisting of 84 clerical and 18 secular commissioners, was orthodox. There were 28 foreign delegates of the Reformed churches in England, Scotland, the Palatinate, Hesse, Nassau, East Friesland, and Bremen. King James had instructed the English delegates to "mitigate the heat of both sides." [3] Some of the German delegates were urging the same thing, but such voices were ignored. The representatives of Arminianism, 13 in all, were treated as persons under indictment and were excluded from participation in the proceedings. The result was the condemnation of the Five Articles of the *Remonstrance* and the

[2] On the composition and history of this synod, which was representative of the whole of Reformed Protestantism, see Schaff, *op. cit.,* I, 512 ff. Schaff gives the Latin text of the canons (*ibid.,* III, 550 ff.) followed by an English abridgment adopted by the Reformed (Dutch) Church in America.

[3] *Ibid.,* I, 513.

drafting of five decidedly Calvinistic canons. The Belgic Confession and the Heidelberg Catechism were formally adopted.

The Doctrine of Predestination in the Discussion of the Synod

The general situation is characterized by Schaff: "The Arminian controversy is the most important which took place within the Reformed Church. It corresponds to the Pelagian and the Jansenist controversies in the Catholic Church. It involves the problem of the ages, which again and again has baffled the ken of theologians and philosophers, and will do so to the end of time: the relation of divine sovereignty and human responsibility." [4]

The particular tenets of the Remonstrants are contained in the Five Articles mentioned above.[5] The document is first negative, then positive. The doctrines rejected by the Articles are: double, supralapsarian predestination; atonement limited to the elect; grace working irresistibly in conversion and that a man thus converted can never totally and finally lose it.

On the positive side, the Articles maintain (1) that election and condemnation are conditioned by divine foreknowledge and dependent on the foreseen faith or unbelief in man; (2) that Christ "died for all men and for every man"; (3) that man in his fallen state is unable "to think, will, or do anything that is really good" unless he be born again of God in Christ through the Holy Spirit; (4) that the grace of God is the beginning, continuance, and accomplishment of all good, but that the working of divine grace is not irresistible; (5) that it has not been proved from Scripture that grace, once given, may not be lost through negligence on the part of the regenerated.

Underlying these statements is the idea that the divine call is always seriously considered—there is no calling of the reprobates merely for the purpose of hardening them—and that the moral power of man is a positive factor in the process of salvation. The *Canons of Dort* are the reply of the Synod to the Five Articles of the Remonstrants. They state first, positively, what has become known as the "Five Points of High Calvinism," and then negatively reject the "errors" of the Armin-

[4] *Ibid.*, I, 509.

[5] The Arminian Articles are given in Dutch, Latin and English in *ibid.*, III, 545 ff.

ians. Each "Head of Doctrine" is subdivided into a number of articles.

The First Head deals with divine predestination. The issue of supra-lapsarianism versus infralapsarianism is evaded. The tenor of the argument, however, favors the latter view, for the starting point is the fact of the universality of sin issuing from the disobedience of Adam. Because of the fall, God would have done no injustice by leaving all men to perish and delivering them over to condemnation (Art. I), but as a God of love, he sent his "only-begotten Son, that whosoever believeth in Him should not perish, but have everlasting life" (Art. II). In order that men may believe, God sends his messengers to whom he will (Art. III). By faith man is delivered from the wrath of God which remains with those who do not believe the gospel (Art. IV). The cause of unbelief and all sin, however, is "nowise in God, but in man himself; whereas faith in Jesus Christ . . . is the free gift of God" (Art. V). The reason that some receive the gift of faith and others do not receive it is to be seen in God's eternal decree. This decree is double; it includes election as well as reprobation (Art. VI). In addition, this decree is unchangeable. Election includes a fixed number of persons (Art. VII). The elect cannot "be cast away, nor their number diminished" (Art. XI). The elect may attain, "though in various degrees and in different measures," the assurance of their eternal and unchangeable election "by observing in themselves, with a spiritual joy and holy pleasure, the infallible fruits of election . . . such as a true faith in Christ, filial fear, a godly sorrow for sin, a hungering and thirsting after righteousness, etc." (Art. XII). Godly parents have no reason to doubt that their children who died in infancy belong to the elect of God "by virtue of the covenant of grace" (Art. XVII). As to the reprobate, God has decreed to pass them by, and to leave them in the misery of sin "into which they have wilfully plunged themselves." This decree of reprobation declares God "to be an awful, irreprehensible, and righteous judge and avenger" (Art. XV).

To these articles of the First Head the Synod attached a "rejection of errors" in nine paragraphs. Among these was this, that the whole of predestination is simply the general truth that God will save all who believe and persevere (Art. I); also that this predestination is conditioned upon the right use of the "light of nature" (which would be Pelagian), and upon the foreseen attitude of man in repentance, faith, and perseverance (Arts. IV, V); also that the elect may be lost, which would be in conflict with the immutability of God (Arts. VI, VII); that God cannot have decreed to condemn anybody (VIII); finally that the evangelization of some peoples is to be explained by merits that these had before others (IX).

The Second Head or Chapter of Doctrine discusses the meaning of the atonement. Since "God is not only supremely merciful but also supremely just," satisfaction had to be made to the divine justice (Art. I). This was accomplished by Christ (Arts. II-IV). Though He expiated the sin of the whole world, "the quickening and saving efficacy" of Christ's death extends to the elect only (Art. VII).

The rejectory paragraphs are directed against the teaching that Christ had suffered without regard to special persons (Art. I); that Christ, by his satisfaction, had merely opened the way for the Father to offer salvation under new conditions to be met by man in the use of his free will (Art. III); that a federation of grace had been established in which God had declared himself satisfied with faith and with an obedience which, while it is imperfect, is yet worthy of eternal life (Art. IV); that all men must be regarded as having been adopted into that federation of grace so that nobody is under condemnation because of original sin (Art. V); that in reality the death of Christ was not necessary for those who love God and are his elect (Art. VII).

The doctrines of sin and grace are discussed jointly in the Head or Chapter III. Man, through a false use of his freedom, and under temptation by the devil, sank into the state of the fall: "entailing on himself blindness of mind, horrible darkness, vanity and perverseness of judgment." He "became wicked, rebellious, and obdurate in heart and will, and impure in his affections" (Art. I). His children and "all the posterity of Adam, Christ only excepted, have derived corruption by their original parent, not by imitation, as the Pelagians of old asserted, but by the propagation of a vicious nature in consequence of a just judgment of God" (Art. II). Man, therefore, is under God's wrath, "incapable of any saving good, prone to evil, dead in sin, and in bondage thereto; and, without the regenerating grace of the Holy Spirit men are neither able nor willing to return to God, to reform the depravity of their nature, nor to dispose themselves to reformation" (Art. III). However, there is "in man, since the Fall, the glimmerings of a natural light whereby he retains some knowledge of God, of natural things, and of the difference between good and evil, and discovers some regard for virtue, good order in society, and for maintaining an orderly external deportment. But so far is this light of nature from being sufficient to bring him to a saving knowledge of God, and to true conversion, that he is incapable of using it aright even in things natural and civil" (Art. IV). Not even "the law of the decalogue" can bring salvation. "For though it discovers the greatness of sin, and more and more convinces man thereof, yet as it neither points out a remedy, nor imparts strength to extricate him from misery, and thus being weak through the flesh, leaves the transgressor under the curse, man cannot by this law obtain saving grace" (Art. V).[6]

"What, therefore, neither the light of nature nor the Law could do, that God performs by the operation of His Holy Spirit through the Word or ministry of reconciliation" (Art. VI). This call is not feigned, but serious (Art. VIII).

If there are those who neither accept the call nor persevere, then "the fault lies in themselves" as also in those who, "though they receive it, suffer it not to make a lasting impression on their heart. Therefore, their joy, arising only from a temporary faith, soon vanishes and they fall away . . ." (Art. IX). The accepting of the call by others is not to be ascribed to the proper exercise of a free will, but to God's eternal election; it is this election that makes the call efficient (Arts. X, XI).

Regeneration does not come about through teaching or moral persuasion (which would lead into Pelagian conceptions), but through a supernatural work of God. After this divine work has taken place and man is renewed, then the will itself becomes active (Art. XII). Faith is to be considered "the gift of God" (Art. XIV). In all this, the "grace of regeneration does not treat men as senseless stocks and blocks, nor take away their will and its properties, neither does violence thereto; but spiritually quickens, heals, corrects . . . that where carnal rebellion and resistance formerly prevailed a ready and sincere spiritual obedience begins to reign" (Art. XVI). The last article emphasizes the need of the means of grace: "the sacred precepts of the gospel, in

[6] With regard to the proper relation of original sin and freedom of the will, this Chapter is a Calvinist counterpart to Articles I and II of the Lutheran Formula of Concord.

the exercise of the Word, the sacraments and discipline" (Art XVII).

The doctrine of the total depravity of human nature and the teaching of the irresistibility of divine grace are not meant to eliminate the psychic functions of man as a rational and volitional being nor the faithful use of the means of grace. The communication of grace is considered as being intimately connected with the proper use of the Word, the sacraments and Church discipline.

To these articles a number of very interesting rejectory paragraphs were attached.[7] The synod rejected the teaching that original sin in itself was not sufficient to merit temporal and eternal punishments for the whole race (Art. I); that spiritual gifts and virtues, such as goodness, holiness and justness in the will, cannot have been present in the first man and that for this reason he cannot have fallen from them (Art. II); that in man's spiritual death the spiritual gifts cannot be separated from his will, because this will was never depraved, but was merely hindered through the darkness of mind and irregularity of passions, so that after the removal of these hindrances man again is free and can choose in his own free powers as he wills (Art. III); that the unregenerate is not entirely dead in his sins, but can hunger and thirst after righteousness (Art. IV); that man in his depraved and natural condition is able to use the general grace which he has in the natural light . . . so correctly that in this way he can gradually attain to a larger evangelical saving grace (Art. V).

Regarding the communication of grace, the following sentences are rejected: that in a true conversion God cannot infuse into the will new qualities, ways (*habitus*) or gifts, and that, therefore, the faith of conversion is no divinely infused quality or gift, but an act of man (Art. VI); that the grace of conversion is nothing but a persuading which produces the consent of the will (Art. VII); that man can resist grace and that it is in his power to become regenerated or not (Art. VIII); that the cause of conversion must be seen in the co-operation between grace and free-will, and that grace does nothing until man's will first has moved and made the decision (Art. IX).

Chapter V deals with the perseverance of the saints. God has liber-

[7] In reading them we must keep in mind the Socinian influences which we shall have occasion to point out below as having contributed to the historical background of developing Arminianism.

ated the regenerated from the dominion and service of sin though not yet altogether from the body of sin and the infirmities of the flesh. Daily sins of infirmity are a constant cause for humiliation before God, for flying for refuge to Christ, for mortifying the flesh and for pressing forward to perfection. If left to their own strength the converted could not persevere in grace. They are not always so influenced and actuated by the Spirit of God that they are not led into temptation and do not fall into grave sins—"sometimes by the righteous permission of God." "By such enormous sins, however, they very highly offend God, incur a deadly guilt, grieve the Holy Spirit, interrupt the exercise of faith, very grievously wound their consciences, and sometimes lose the sense of God's favor, for a time, until on their returning into the right way by serious repentance, the light of God's fatherly countenance again shines upon them" (Arts. I-V).

God, ". . . according to His unchangeable purpose of election, does not wholly withdraw the Holy Spirit from His own people; . . . nor suffer them to proceed so far as to lose the grace of adoption and to forfeit the state of justification, or to commit the sin unto death. He preserves in the elect 'the incorruptible seed of regeneration' from perishing and by His Word and Spirit effectually renews them to repentance so that they may again experience the favor of a reconciled God" (Arts. VI, VII).

The cause for this is seen in "God's free mercy," not " in their own merits and strength." "With respect to God, it is utterly impossible . . . that they should totally fall from faith and grace . . . and perish in their backslidings . . . since His counsel cannot be changed, nor His promise fail, neither can the call according to His purpose be revoked, nor the merit, intercession and preservation of Christ be rendered ineffectual, nor the sealing of the Holy Spirit be frustrated or obliterated" (Art. VIII). The assurance for this preservation of the elect the true believers find "according to the measure of their faith" in the "Word of God," in the "testimony of the Holy Spirit" and "in a serious and holy desire to preserve a good conscience, and to perform good works" (Arts. IX-XI). "This certainty of perseverance" will not excite in believers a "spirit of pride" nor make them "carnally secure"; it is, on the contrary, "a real source of humility." "Neither does renewed confidence of persevering produce licentiousness . . . , but it renders them much more careful . . . lest by abusing His fatherly kindness, God should turn away" (Arts. XII-XIII).

On this fifth point the Synod added the following rejections of opposed errors: that the perseverance of believers is not the effect of election, but a necessary condition for man to comply with of his own free will (Art. I); that while God furnishes the needed strength for perseverance, it is dependent upon man's will whether he wants to persevere or not (Art. II); that believers and elect can definitely fall from grace and commit the sin against the Holy Spirit (Arts. III, IV).

Regarding the assurance of salvation the following sentences are rejected: that a special revelation alone could give such an assurance (Art. V); that the teaching of such a guarantee of salvation would furnish a comfort for the flesh and be detrimental to the religious and ethical life (Art. VI); that the difference between those who believe only for a time and those with permanent, justifying, and saving faith consists merely in the element of duration (Art. VII).

The Development of Arminianism

Although the Remonstrants had been very cautious and guarded in their Five Articles, it seems clear that they had had more on their minds than what they had expressed. That this was the case is discernible in the rejectory statements attached to the canons of the Synod of Dort. Further indication that this was so can also be seen in the *Confessio Remonstratia* which Episcopius prepared for the Remonstrants in 1622.[8]

In Holland certain influences were at work which foreshadowed the theological liberalism of later Arminianism. There a confluence of humanistic and practical mystical tendencies developed which looked unfavorably upon fixed doctrines and set forms of polity. The spirit of the day called for tolerance, adherence to the simple teachings of the Bible, and a universal religion fit to promote and foster morality. The Bible alone was to be authoritative. Binding confessions were to be rejected.

[8] This document of a considerable length appeared in Holland first in Dutch (1621), then in Latin (1622) as *Confessio sive declaratio sententiae pastorum, qui in foederato Belgio Remonstrantes vocantur.* It was also printed in Latin in the works of Episcopius, *Opera Episcopii* (2nd ed.; London, 1678), II, 75-94.

The teachings of two men, Jacob Acontius and D. Koornheert, illustrate this whole peculiar situation. Acontius represents the mild humanistic views of Erasmus. His book, *Stratagemata Satanae* (1565), went through twelve editions and was widely read in Holland and England. Christianity was reduced to certain basic and essential teachings. He demanded tolerance and the abolition of the death penalty for heresy. Koornheert was less conservative than Acontius. He delighted in criticizing the Church, but regarded the Scriptures as authoritative in matters of faith. Traces of Socinian rationalization are observable in his thought. He suggested modifications of doctrine in a number of respects. Scripture, he declared, knows nothing of original sin. The idea of imputation in connection with the doctrine of justification is to be rejected. Redemption through Christ consists of making man righteous. The teaching of predestination in the sense of Calvin is a fundamental error because it makes God the author of sin.[9]

In Jacob Arminius the traits of the movement can be seen as a whole. In his first pastorate he won distinction as a preacher and pastor of an irenic spirit. The change of conviction regarding predestination, which drove him to a study of the Scriptures, developed into differences with the official Church on other matters as well. More than once he was accused of defection from Reformed orthodoxy. For instance, he had critically rejected the statement that "the righteousness of Christ is imputed as righteousness," for, as he said, strictly speaking, righteousness which is imputed is not righteousness. Arminius admitted that the saying, "the righteousness of Christ is imputed" is found in Scripture (Rom. 4:3). But it is unscriptural, he pointed out, to teach that it is imputed as righteousness. To illustrate by way of example: if someone owes a person one hundred dollars and then repays the whole amount, the creditor may not truthfully say, "I reckon this payment to you as righteousness." Yet if the debtor pays him only ten dollars while the creditor remits the debtor the rest of his debts, then the creditor may rightfully say, "I reckon these ten dollars as a full payment." This would be an act of grace which the debtor had to acknowledge. Arminius, then, considered faith not primarily as the

[9] The literary sources for these statements are given by Seeberg, *Lehrbuch der Dogmengeschichte,* IV (1920), 672 ff.

instrument by which man accepts the grace of God, but rather as the *first cause* of justification. The faith which resides in man as a potential quality is what is imputed to the sinner as righteousness. It is the "ten per cent of the debt" which man has to render to God. Thus, man is justified on account of faith. Justification, in the eyes of Arminius, is an "analytic judgment." This view flatly contradicts what Melanchthon said in the Apology to the Augsburg Confession, "For faith does not justify or save because it is a good work in itself, but only because it accepts the promised mercy." [10] Otto Ritschl's verdict that "the Apostate of supralapsarianism" (i.e. Arminius) was totally out of touch with the religious concern of the Reformation will stand. The Reformers' teaching of justification by an "alien righteousness" had no place in his system.[11]

The theological leaders of the movement after the death of Arminius (1609) helped to develop its real genius. The following names must be mentioned: Uytenbogaert (d. 1644), Vorstius (d. 1622), Episcopius (d. 1643), Grotius (d. 1645), Curcellaeus (d. 1659), and van Limborch (d. 1712).[12] With regard to the theological positions that were taken the following should be mentioned:

Uytenbogaert, the close friend of Arminius, who functioned as leader in 1610 when the *Remonstrance* was drafted, was opposed to making the Church a school of theologians. With Arminius he emphasized the devotional import of religion. The Bible was to be the authority; confessions and catechism were not to have binding force.

Vorstius, having cultivated a relationship with the Socinians, had fundamental antipathies toward the theology of the Reformed church, especially against the traditional concept of the atonement. This position naturally affected his attitude toward other doctrines, especially predestination and justification. He protested against a dogma in conflict with reason.

Grotius contributed the much discussed "governmental" theory of the atonement.[13] Starting from the idea that God's relation to the sinner should not be thought of as that of an offended individual

[10] IV, 56.

[11] Cf. Ritschl, *op. cit.*, III, 332 ff.

[12] Cf. *ibid.*, III, 339 ff.

[13] On Grotius cf. *ibid.*, III, 343 ff.; also Hirsch, *Geschichte der neueren evangelischen Theologie,* I, 221 ff.

demanding satisfaction, he taught that God was to be regarded as a great moral ruler. The death of Christ, therefore, "was not a payment for man's sin—which is freely forgiven—but a tribute to the sanctity of the divine government, showing that while God remits the penalty, he vindicates the majesty of his divine government." Grotius aimed to meet the objection of the Socinians against the Anselmic theory. This "theatrical" explanation of the atonement, however, was not followed by the Arminians. Men like Episcopius, Curcellaeus and Limborch followed their teacher Arminius and developed ideas which led in the direction of Socinianism or into lines of thought which formerly had been dwelt upon by the Franciscans against the Dominicans.[14]

Episcopius, their spokesman, covered all the characteristic tenets of Arminianism in a well-balanced way. Curcellaeus was a relentless critic of traditional dogmas. He made positive contributions to the teaching of the Arminians, especially with respect to subordinationism in their concept of the Trinity.

Limborch, the only one of the Arminian theologians to leave us a complete system of dogmatics including ethics, called attention to the distinction between fundamentals and nonfundamentals. His theology was later called "rational supernaturalism." Like Vorstius, he rejected in Scripture what is not agreeable with reason. He was a subordinationist, taught the freedom of the will, spoke of faith as an act of obedience, favored a moralistic Christianity, and tried to avoid the traditional terminology of dogmatics. In him we see a flexibility of theology that is characteristic of Arminianism.[15]

Karl Meusel, a conservative, sums up the doctrinal tenets of later Arminianism thus:

> According to its whole genius it gradually made dogma second to ethics; it saw in Christ pre-eminently a new lawgiver, not the redeemer. In the dogma of the Trinity it inclined to the subordination of the Son and the Holy Spirit to the Father. Original sin was taken as an inborn weakness. The image of God in man was not seen in a righteousness and holiness given him at the creation, but was understood as consisting merely in the dominion over the creatures, as the Socinians held. In the receiving of divine grace (in conversion) there was a co-operation of

[14] Grotius, *loc. cit.*

[15] Cf. Ritschl, *op. cit.*, III, 339 ff. for a more thorough treatment of these theologians.

man by virtue of an inborn moral freedom. The substitutionary atonement of Christ and His fulfillment of the Law was denied to have been sufficient in itself, but was merely a free act of love which was accepted as sufficient. For this reason there can be no justification of the sinner by an imputation of Christ's merit in the sense of a forensic justification. The sacraments have only a ceremonial significance. Baptism is the ceremony of an admission of believers into the church. Infant baptism has little favor, because children cannot believe. The Lord's Supper offers only a moral strengthening of faith and love.[16]

Standards of Faith

In the confession which was prepared by Episcopius and published by the Remonstrants after their excommunication and banishment, they took occasion to express themselves on standards of faith. Their leaders had been writing against confessions. Now the Remonstrants themselves published a confession. This forced them to give a long and very interesting discussion of creeds and confessions in the introduction.[17] They say that conditions can arise in the Church which make confessional statements a matter of necessity. Confession is a means of defending truth against error, of pointing out fundamentals in distinction from nonfundamentals. Nonetheless, confessions must not become decrees of what is to be believed; they are not norms and rules of faith, by which truth and error are to be judged. The purpose of confessions is to indicate what the writers of these confessions believed regarding religion in order to aid the less informed and the careless. Confessions must not be put on a level with the Scriptures. They are not tests of truth, not even in the sense of being entitled to render a decision where the meaning of Scripture is doubtful. Nobody is bound to the view of the confession if he becomes convinced in his conscience that it does not agree with Scripture.[18]

With all the truth in these statements, the document of the Arminians did not take into consideration that in critical and decisive moments the confession of the Church must serve as a bond of union. There are moments in the Church's life when believers will need to know who is a fellow-believer and who is not. Episcopius also over-

[16] Karl Meusel, article on Arminianism in *Kirchliches Handlexikon.*

[17] The text is given in Episcopius, *op. cit.,* II, 71 ff.

[18] Cf. E. G. A. Boeckel, *Die Bekenntnisschriften der evangelisch reformierten Kirchen* (1847), especially pp. 506-507.

looked the fact that the confessions can claim to represent stages of religious experience in the life of the Church, and on that account they are bound to have at least a derived authority that cannot, as a rule, be attributed to other religious literature.[19]

In reading the Confession of Episcopius one is impressed by the energy with which he stressed the authority of Scripture. He held that this authority does not rest upon decrees of the Church, ancient or modern; the Word has its authenticity in itself, is established upon God's veracity and is in need of no official interpreter because it addresses itself to the individual Christian. The Remonstrants spoke of the authority of Scripture as merely "directive." They had a less rigid concept of the inspiration of Scripture than the Calvinists, especially with respect to the historical books of the Bible.[20]

Summary Evaluations

John Tulloch, a representative Presbyterian theologian, wrote: "Arminianism was a great deal more than a dogmatic theory. It was also, or at least it rapidly became, a method of religious inquiry. . . . The method alone has given to it enduring significance in the history of Christian thought. It revived the suppressed rational side of the original Protestant movement, and, for the first time, organized it into a definite power and assigned to it its due place both in theology and the Church."[21]

Schaff wrote: "Calvinism represented the consistent, logical conservative orthodoxy; Arminianism an elastic, progressive, changing liberalism."[22] He continues: "Their literary and religious influence has gone far beyond their organization. Their eminent scholars . . . have enriched exegetical and critical learning and liberalized theological opinions, especially on religious toleration and the salvation of unbaptized infants. Arminianism in some of its advocates had a leaning towards Socinianism, and prepared the way for rationalism. Many

[19] Cf. J. L. Neve, *Introduction to the Symbolical Books of the Lutheran Church* (Philadelphia: United Lutheran Publication House, 1927), pp. 31 ff.; and *Lutherans in the Movements for Church Union* (Philadelphia: United Lutheran Publication House, 1921), pp. 153 ff.

[20] John Tulloch, *Rational Theology and Christian Philosophy in England in the Seventeenth Century* (1874), I, 28.

[21] *Ibid.*, I, 19.

[22] Schaff, *op. cit.*, I, 509.

Arminians adhered to the original position of a moderated semi-Pelagianism." [23]

Troeltsch remarks that the Arminians, in opposition to the confessionally governed churches "widened the sphere of the natural." [24] It was here that the idea of Hugo Grotius of a natural law, of a state emancipated from the dominion of the Church, of an ethics independent of the motives derived from the Christian religion, first found a place. The conservative Protestant churches of today recognize an independent philosophy, and with this an ethics such as the Reformation had spoken of under the term *justitia civilis*.[25] But the danger for religion came when, under the sway of deism and its successors, the Church itself was tempted to turn away from theological ethics, and when psychological analysis alone furnished and exhibited the motives for doing good. In the last analysis it was this new emphasis on ethics that stimulated the "Arminian" attitude to predestination and synergism in England. The impulses for this movement came from the new philosophy of Montaigne, Charron, Spinoza, and Hobbes. The English empiricists took up the problem in their development of an analytical psychology. It is in the light of these philosophical undercurrents that we must see the further development of Arminianism and its influence in England.

BIBLIOGRAPHY

ARMINIUS. *Opera Theologica.* 1629. English translation by JOHN NICHOLS, 2 vols., 1825 ff. Reprinted in 3 vols., Buffalo: Parby Miller & Orton, 1853.

CURTIUS, G. L. *Arminianism in History.* Cincinnati, 1894.

GIRARDEAU, J. L. *Calvinism and Evangelical Arminianism Compared.* New York: Baker & Taylor Co., 1890.

HODGE, CHARLES. *Systematic Theology.* Vol. II. New York: Scribner, Armstrong & Co., 1874.

NICHOLS, JOHN. *The Life of Arminius.* 1843.

[23] *Ibid.,* I, 516.

[24] Troeltsch, "English Moralists" in *PRE,* XIII, 441.

[25] Cf. the Augsburg Confession, Art. XVIII.

CHAPTER IV

ARMINIANISM IN ENGLAND

Two things must be kept in view when speaking of the influence of Arminianism upon England: (1) The liberalistic trend of that movement led to rationalism; and (2) the emphasis upon the more practical aspects of religion produced a Church life which viewed Christianity primarily as a force for moral transformation.

Beginning with the first of these two influences of Arminianism, we must think of that wide sphere of theological interests which we have described in the preceding chapter. The conflict at Dort was not merely over predestination. Arminianism was not really a faith but, as Tulloch put it, "a method of religious inquiry," which "revived the suppressed rational side of the original Protestant movement,"[1] or, as Schaff said: "It liberalized theological opinions."[2] We should guard against insisting that Arminianism of necessity leads to rationalism. We are not justified in sayng more than Schaff when he added: "In some of its advocates it had a leaning toward Socianism, and prepared the way for Rationalism." But with the coming of Arminianism to England we soon see in that country a gradual rationalizing of its Calvinistic theology in ever widening circles. It progressed to such an extent that "latitudinarianism" became a general characteristic of England's theology. Together with other influences, especially philosophical, Arminianism created an atmosphere favorable to the propagation of the radical rationalism that appeared in the English Deists and in the Unitarians of England and America.

The second influence of Arminianism in England and America to which we must refer is the emphasis upon a practical type of Christianity such as appeared in Methodism and later became a strong religious influence in America. When we speak of Arminianism in

[1] Tulloch, *op. cit.*, p. 19.

[2] Schaff, *op. cit.*, I, 516.

connecton with the Methodist and other churches we do not think especially of the liberalizing trait in Arminianism, which we analyzed in our presentation of developments in Holland and shall treat further in this chapter. Rather we mean the strongly synergistic trait of Methodism discernible in its evangelistic practice. We see this trait in the fundamental aversion to the doctrine of predestination; in materially modifying conceptions in that strong emphasis upon the unimpaired spiritual powers of man before his conversion, in which he is urged to lay hold of saving grace; and in the stress that is put upon man's action in general.

We shall now see how Arminianism gradually began to find favor in England, where it was to have even greater influence than in Holland.

Calvin's Influence in England

Calvinistic voices advocating strict emphasis upon predestination had been heard in England. Indeed, this emphasis was characteristic of English and Scottish Calvinism after James I (1603-1625). After the temporary abolition of the Prayer Book and the overthrow of Archbishop Laud, the Westminster Assembly was convened (1643-47). The Assembly issued the famous Westminster Confession with "larger" and "shorter" Catechisms. These documents stressed the two aspects of Calvinistic predestination: salvation and reprobation. William Prynne's *Anti-Arminianism* urged bishops to extirpate the "Arminian thieves and robbers." Bishop Davenant denied the universality of divine love on the ground that this obscures God's unique and special love for the elect.

John Tulloch, a Scottish Presbyterian, has characterized the Calvinism of the Puritans as follows:

> Dogmas are rigorously carried out to their consequences. The letter of Scripture is itself turned into logic, and the divine idea, living and shapely in its original form, is drawn out into hard and unyielding propositions. Nothing is more singular, nor in a sense more impressive, than the daring alliance thus forced between logic and Scripture. The thought and the letter, the argument and the fact, are inwrought. This identification of Scripture with its own forms of thinking was the very essence of Puritanism and gives it something of its marvelous success in an age when argument was strong and criticism weak. However, to do justice to Puritanism, it must be admitted that it did not only bring its ideas to

Scripture, but supposed that it found them here. . . . Calvinism was Chrisianity reduced to a system. . . . Calvinistic speculation has always this true element of sublimity in it. It soars directly to the throne of God, and seeks to chain all its deductions to that supreme height. But it fails to realize how far men's best thoughts are below this height and how much human weakness and error must mingle in the loftiest efforts to compass and set forth divine truth. . . . It barely recognizes even now in the sphere of theology that truth is not all on one side. It still looks with jealousy on that more tolerant spirit, both of faith and of criticism, which labors to distinguish the essential from the accidental, and so to penetrate and sift all systems as to lay bare the multiplied influences of time, place, and character, which have mingled in their production, and stamped and colored them with their own impress and hue.[3]

Among the leaders of the Independents there were some representatives of the strictest kind of Calvinism. Cromwell complained in Parliament that Bishop Neile of Winchester gave countenance to divines who preached Arminianism.[4] John Owen, a strong Congregationalist, defended Calvinism in emphatic terms: God had settled the fate of the reprobates from all eternity, without regard either to their unbelief or their impenitence. To say that Christ died for all means in reality that he died for none. An atonement as a price for all, and yet effectively applied to none, is a price not paid. One of the worst heresies of Arminianism, Owen pointed out, was the belief that even pagans who had never heard the gospel might be saved. He admitted, however, that pagans who strove to live an upright life had their reward here, in outward prosperity or peace of mind. They may also have a reward hereafter in a diminution of the degrees of their torments. But they cannot escape torments entirely, for by nature they were corrupt and from all eternity they were children of wrath.[5]

Early Steps Toward Arminianism

In the latter part of his reign James I grew indifferent toward the specific points of emphasis in strict Calvinism. The Calvinistic insistence that the temporal ruler cannot be the head of the Church made the kings of England suspicious of high Calvinism. It was this political opposition to Calvinism that opened the gate for Arminian entry into

[3] Tulloch, *op. cit.*, I, 66 ff.
[4] John Hunt, *Religious Thought in England* (1870 ff.), I, 149.
[5] "Display of Arminianism" in John Owen, *Collected Works* (London, 1721).

England. Richard Montague defended Arminianism in two books which he wrote against those who believed that faith, once possessed, can never be lost.[6] Montague's idea was strongly opposed, especially by Carleton, a delegate to Dort, who would not admit that the denial of Peter had been a real fall: "A Christian cannot fall totally and finally." He cited Augustine as having distinguished between those who are regenerated and justified only sacramentally, and those who have had this experience according to God's election.[7]

Arminianism soon gained ground. The story is told that when Bishop Morley was asked what (opinions) the Arminians held, he answered that "they held all the best bishoprics and deaneries in England." [8]

Even a high churchman like Archbishop Laud combined the doctrines of Arminius with his theories of the episcopacy.[9] It may seem strange that Laud, as head of the Anglican church, should have created a gateway through which Arminianism came in and was strengthened in England. The immediate cause was, as has already been suggested, his opposition and that of the crown to the orthodox Presbyterians. It was this turn in the political development of England which gave the theology of the Episcopal church in that early day a liberal tendency. Laud promoted his cause by favoring anti-Calvinists, and by passing injunctions forbidding the clergy to preach on subjects connected with predestination. On the surface this seemed to be only a political measure. But Laud was a consistent Arminian. On the Bible, for instance, he offered this thought, which had been defended so strongly by the followers of Arminius in Holland: "We must distinguish between the Word of God and the Scriptures. Before Scripture was written—that is before it was Scripture—it was God's Word." [10]

In the controversy with some of the Independents over the article on baptism, to be incorporated in the Westminster Confession, the Arminians did not hesitate to express themselves in favor of baptizing

[6] *A Gagg for the New Gospel* and *Apello Caesarem.* Cf. Hunt, *op. cit.,* I, 151.
[7] For details, see Hunt, *op. cit.,* I, 154.
[8] Tulloch, *op. cit.,* I, 124.
[9] Schaff remarks: "The distinctive Arminian doctrines of sin and grace, free will and predestination, have been extensively adopted by the Episcopal Church since the reign of Charles I" (*op. cit.,* I, 516). Cf. Tulloch's brilliant review of Anglicanism, *op. cit.,* I, 37 ff.
[10] Cf. Hunt, *op. cit.,* I, 169 f.; II, 141.

infants. They took the position that all are redeemed, and therefore, that children also should receive the seal of the covenant of redemption. If they did not keep the conditions of the covenant, the blame rested with them. This was in harmony with what the Arminians in Holland had been emphasizing.

John Goodwin (d. 1665), an Independent, renounced the specific dogmas of Calvinism decidedly. The problem of scriptural interpretation was uppermost with him. He wanted to stand upon the Scriptures, but he insisted that in many of the Calvinistic points of emphasis the Scriptures were misinterpreted: for instance, the Presbyterians' assertion that their form of government was taught in the Bible, or the interpretation of the Scriptures as commanding that heretics, blasphemers, and idolators be put to death; or the doctrine of the Trinity spoken of as expressly taught in Scripture or by the Word of God without further qualification of that term. Hunt quotes Goodwin as follows: "The true and proper foundation is not ink and paper, not any book or books, not writing or writings, whatsoever, whether translations or originals, but that substance of matter, those glorious counsels of God concerning the salvation of the world by Jesus Christ which are indeed represented and declared both in the translations and the originals, but are distinct from both. . . . The Word of God had a beginning and was extant in the world, nay, in the hearts and consciences of men before there was any copy of the Word extant in writing, either in the one language or the other." "Moses," he continued, "was the first penman of the Scriptures, but the Word was from the beginning. . . . Matthew, the first penman of the New Testament, did not write till eight years after the ascension, but the foundations of the Christian Religion were long before that." In *Sion College Visited*, he said, "that Jesus Christ and not the Scriptures, was the foundation of the Christian Religion." [11]

The question as to whether pagans may be saved was much discussed in that day. Goodwin expressed himself on this in a paper, the *Pagan's Debt and Dowry*, in these words: "The Scriptures intimate that there is a capacity in all men, by the light of nature to know that some atonement has been made for sin. St. Paul declares that they have heard the Gospel who have heard that sound which goes out day and

[11] *Ibid.*, I, 263.

night from the heavens unto the end of the world. In all ages there have been grains of seeds of piety in men's hearts. What men have actually known in the light of nature is considerable, but not to be measured by what they might know."[12] Expressions like these are interesting because they show that a mildly liberalized theology had entered the Church of England. They also illustrate that Arminianism was not just a dogmatic theory on the doctrine of predestination, but that it was a state of mind and a method of religious inquiry. Many Arminians have been known to foster biblical criticism and unbiased exegesis.

In the study of the rise of Arminianism in England the name and theology of Richard Baxter (1615-1691) ought not be passed by, although he was not really an Arminian. However, there was the unconscious tendency toward the Arminian attitude in Baxter's independence of theological inquiry. We know him as a theologian of fervent piety, especially as the author of *The Saints' Everlasting Rest* (1649) and of much devotional literature.[13] Baxter was a man of great learning and ingenuity. He had developed a mediating system of theology which came to be known as "Baxterianism." It was a theology which—much like pietism in Germany—furnished foundations for a type of ardent piety, but which after him, through independence of inquiry and attitude of mind, contributed to a breakdown of the forms of doctrine and polity by which conservative theology in England aimed to preserve the positive contents of Christian teaching. Under the influence of Socinianism and deism, the Presbyterian congregations of England during the eighteenth century which had come under the influence of Baxter followed anti-trinitarian lines of thought and, after 1800, even began to call themselves Unitarian.

There was nothing in the theology of Baxter that would not do honor to his piety and that was not consistent with the ardor of his religious interest. His motto was that familiar and attractive remark of the Lutheran divine Rupert Meldenius, a friend of John Arndt: "In essentials, unity; in non-essentials, liberty; in everything, charity."

[12] The statements are quoted from the article on Goodwin in the *Dictionary of National Biography*, Vol. XXII. Cf. Hunt, *op. cit.*, I, 259 ff.

[13] Baxter's practical *Works* have been edited by W. Orme, 23 vols. (1830); republished by H. Rogers, 4 vols. (1868). Cf. Isolde Jeremias, *Richard Baxter's Catholic Theology* (Göttingen, 1956).

Among the essentials in which there should be unity in the Church Baxter reckoned the recognition of the supernatural. In his writing on the evidences for the truth of Christianity he pointed to the testimony of Scripture concerning miracles and the fulfillment of prophecy. At the same time he emphasized that man should not rely only upon the illumination of the Spirit but also accept reason as the gift of God, even if reason has to be rectified, purified and illuminated. Baxter excluded the idea of implicit trust without proper evidence from his concept of faith. The truth of Christianity, in the end, must rest upon an "objective cause" which we have in the evidence as contained in the Scriptures. To see properly, however, the Spirit's illumination is needed. A great part of our sanctification consists in the rectifying of our reason. The grace which we have received may be measured by the degree of sanctified reason which we possess.

It was only natural that a prolific writer such as Baxter should have dealt also with the Calvinistic doctrine of predestination. He reconciled himself to the decrees of the Synod of Dort because of their statements that Christ died for all men. He thought that this statement relieved him of preaching divine reprobation. At the same time he and his followers claimed certain fruits of the death of Christ exclusively for the elect; the grace of a true faith, repentance and the higher Christian life, the peace of conscience, inner affiliation with the Church as the congregation of believers, the hope and assurance of eternal life, justification on the day of judgment, and glorification of soul and body in the resurrection. Baxter and his followers believed that the beneficiaries of these fruits of the death of Christ were few in number. As to the rest of mankind, he and his followers would speak of divine reprobation only because of the unbelief and impenitence foreseen by God. This position, if it meant anything at all, was a subversion of the first principles of Calvinism.[14]

The Rationalizing Trait of Arminianism

Bishop Jeremy Taylor (d. 1667) was an outspoken Arminian.[15] "There are but few doctrines on which Taylor's views would not

[14] See Baxter's tract "The Denominational Reason," *Works*.

[15] See the complete sketch of his life and work by Tulloch, *op. cit.*, I, 344-410. Cf. Hunt *op. cit.*, I, 334-360 and George Park Fisher, *Bibliotheca Sacra*, IX, 364.

exclude him from the common pale of the orthodox in the judgment of the majority of Christians, of whatever sect or party." [16] Strictly speaking, he was not a member of the "rational theology" group, since he lived before their time.

In his *Liberty of Prophesying* (1647) Taylor advocated tolerance. He was opposed to the sharp theological definitions in the Nicene and the Athanasian Creeds, especially to the anathematizing phrases of the latter. He insisted that errors of understanding are not heresy. Heresy is a matter of the will and not of the intellect. He speaks of the "Catholics" as a party, who took it upon themselves to determine what was heresy and what was not. It was the general councils which created heretics, he said, but councils are not infallible; they have contradicted one another. The uncertainty of the meaning of the Scriptures should make men tolerant. He, with many others, voiced the growing feeling of his age in reacting against the persecuting methods of the state under influence of the ruling church parties. The history of England in the seventeenth century is marked by a widespread discussion of the liberty of conscience.[17]

It was especially in his expression on such subjects as original sin, regeneration, grace and good works, that he revealed himself as an advocate of Arminian opinions. On these subjects he was out of harmony with the Thirty-nine Articles of the Church of England. He was an outspoken opponent of Augustine as well as of Calvin. Although a bishop of the Anglican church, he did not hesitate to say that we can rely neither upon apostolic nor upon later traditions as infallible. The moralistic trait is conspicuous in his writings. "He sets a higher value on a good life than on an orthodox creed. He evaluated every doctrine by its capacity to do men good. Religion was meant to make us more just and more merciful, and it is a sufficient reason for the rejection of any doctrine if it does not serve that object. We may then conclude that it is not sound." [18]

John Milton (d. 1674), the friend of Hugo Grotius, and many of the original thinkers of that day, were of an Arminian disposition. In the *Apology* Milton defended the Remonstrants against *Smectymnus*.[19]

[16] Hunt, *op. cit.*, I, 334.
[17] Tulloch, *op. cit.*, I, 372 ff.
[18] Hunt, *op. cit.*, I, 341.
[19] This peculiar title for a book was a word formed from the initial letters of

His intellectual independence appeared when he was a student in Cambridge about 1625. In a tract on education, 1644, he denounced the traditional scholastic methods as "an asinine feast of sow-thistles and brambles." There was reason for such language when we learn that themes such as the following were discussed: "The music of the spheres," "whether day or night is more excellent," "whether there are not partial forms of an animal in addition to the whole," "how many angels can find place on the point of a needle." He was a relentless opponent of force in matters of religion. On subjects such as the Trinity, the relation of Christ to the Father, the personality of the Holy Spirit, and predestination, he favored Arminian expressions and often spoke as if he were in harmony with Unitarians and Arians. Nonetheless, he held to biblical revelation as the source of religious knowledge.[20]

The "Calixtian" Trait of Arminianism

A study of the later development of Arminianism in Holland shows the general interest of the seventeenth century in the distinction between fundamental and nonfundamental articles of Christian belief. The so-called "syncretistic controversies" in Germany, which were treated in Chapter II, revolved about that distinction.

A man of Arminian tendencies who produced a work in England on syncretism was Edward Stillingfleet (later Bishop of Worcester, d. 1699). We may condense the long title of his writing into the words of his biographer, John Tulloch,[21] and call it *The Irenicum of a Comprehensive Church.* The book, which appeared on the eve of the Restoration (1659) and was reprinted three years later (1662), the year in which the Act of Uniformity was passed, was an appeal for confessional peace. He explains Christianity "as a religion of peace and tolerance." The design of Christ was "to ease men of their former burdens and not to lay on more." "What possible reason can be assigned or given why such things should not be sufficient for com-

the names of the authors: Stephen Marshall, Edmund Calamy, Thomas Young, Matthew Newcommer, and William Spurtstow.

[20] Cf. E. M. W. Tillyard, *Studies in Milton* (London: Chatto and Windus, 1951); A. Baker, *Milton and the Puritan Dilemma* (Toronto: University Press, 1952).

[21] Tulloch, *op. cit.*, I, 411 ff.; cf. Hunt, *op. cit.*, I, 135 ff.

munion with a church, which are sufficient for eternal salvation?" "What ground can there be why Christians should not stand upon the same terms now which they did in the time of Christ and His apostles? Was not religion sufficiently guarded and fenced in by Him? The great commission with which the Apostles were sent out was only to teach what Christ had commanded them—not the least intimation of any power given them to impose or to require any thing beyond what He himself had spoken to them or they were directed to by the immediate guidance of the Spirit of God."

In these utterances of Stillingfleet we must distinguish between the differences touching doctrine and those regarding Church polity. Both are not of the same significance for the life of the Church. On the Church polity question the whole situation in England (conflict between Episcopalians, Presbyterians, and Independents; between Conformists and Nonconformists) added a difficulty that did not exist on the Continent. Stillingfleet refers to this when he remarks on "an unhappy controversy to us in England, if ever there were any in the world." [22]

As far as matters of doctrine are concerned it must be remarked that much in this *Irenicum* of Stillingfleet reminds us of the positions of Calixtus in his distinction between fundamentals and nonfundamentals. It must be admitted that the intolerance of that age, coupled with endless persecution, as had been the case in England up to the Toleration Act of 1689, justified the plea for an *Irenicum*. As to the correctness of Stillingfleet's argument for Church union on the basis of recognizing the fundamentals and ignoring nonfundamentals, much is to be considered that does not lie on the surface of his proposition. Is it always possible to force a mutual recognition of doctrinally differing churches or tendencies in the Church by dismissing the matters of disagreement as nonfundamental and nonessential? While lying on the periphery they may nevertheless have a determining and qualifying

[22] In England the question of Church government became an especially aggravated problem because over against the watchword of the Anglican church, "No bishop, no king," the Puritans and Independents established themselves upon the principle that the Church of Christ can recognize only a spiritual rulership. There is a large literature in England on the subject. For an exhaustive study of the problem see Henry W. Clark, *History of English Nonconformity from Wycliffe to the Close of the 19th Century*, 2 vols. (London: Chapman & Hall, Ltd., 1911-1913).

effect on the things in the center. Stillingfleet asks: "What ground can there be why Christians should not stand upon the same terms now which they did in the time of Christ and His Apostles?" Has the Church not learned very essential things since the days of Christ and his Apostles? Calixtus wanted to unite all churches upon the Apostles' Creed. Schaff remarked: "It must be admitted that the very simplicity and brevity of this creed, which so admirably adapts it for all classes of Christians and for public worship, makes it insufficient as a regulator of public doctrine for a more advanced stage of theological knowledge." [23] Truly, the Church has grown in the understanding of the Scriptures. A creed, to be sufficient today, must contain statements on matters about which the phrases of the Apostles' Creed have received different interpretations by the various denominations of Christendom.[24]

Rational Theology

Rational theology is the name given to the common endeavors of a group of men who, about the time of the English Civil War, stressed the importance of reason in matters of religion. Usually three men are mentioned who were close friends: Lord Falkland, John Hales, and William Chillingworth.

Lord Falkland (d. 1643), who stood in the center, professed that he was open to every reasonable influence. Yet he did not intend, he said, to exclude the grace of God which is as much necessary to salvation as rational instruction. He only wanted to fix the mind of his contemporaries upon a broader and more tolerant view of religion.[25]

John Hales (d. 1656) had been at the Synod of Dort and was greatly impressed by the address of Episcopius and offended over the treatment accorded the Remonstrants. Still it cannot be proven that he actually turned against Calvinism at that time.[26] However, he argued vigorously for the claims of reason in the interpretation of

[23] Schaff, *op. cit.*, I, 16.

[24] John Dury (Duraeus), a Scot (d. 1680), spent fifty years of untiring activity in England and Germany in the futile task of reconciling in Calixtine fashion the difference of opinion between the Syncretists and the confessional Lutherans.

[25] Tulloch, *op. cit.*, I, 76 ff.

[26] The remark: "I did bid John Calvin goodnight," attributed to Hales (when he heard Episcopius address the Synod at Dort), is not sufficiently established. Cf. Fisher, *op. cit.*, p. 363, and Tulloch, *op. cit.*, I, 223.

Scripture and the criticism of dogma. He insisted on the distinction between dogmatic and religious differences. This took him into the argument of fundamentals and into deliveries on "heresy" and "schisms" in which he expressed himself like Calixtus, the Arminians in Holland, and like Stillingfleet.[27]

William Chillingworth (d. 1644), the most prominent theologian in this group, was a moderate and liberal churchman. He affirmed Scripture as the basis of belief. The truth of Scripture is established by just reasoning, with the full right of private judgment. Charity must be used with regard to those who differ.[28] These men and others were opposed to party strife, to Anglican narrowness with regard to ritual, and to Puritan dogmatism. All may be called Arminians. They marked a revival of the freedom of inquiry which characterized early Protestantism. They favored comprehensiveness and inclusiveness and stressed the inner, spiritual side of Christianity as contrasted with conformity to outward institutions. They were liberal, but not radical. Many of these men did their part in clipping the wings of the overbearing Deists and Freethinkers.

LATITUDINARIANS

The Latitudinarians, partly identical with the men of rational theology and supported also by theologians of the "Cambridge school,"[29] should be mentioned. The term "men of latitude" was fastened upon all of a broad and mediating type who were opposed to the Church polity of the Laudian school and the doctrinal strictness of the Puritans. Even the Socinians (Unitarians), Deists and Atheists were frequently called by that term.

The Latitudinarians, with their liberal views of varying degree, were not radicals as a rule. They were Arminians. Against the strict Calvinism they preached the freedom of the will and the universality of redemption through Christ. They were rationalists in that they were convinced that nothing can be true in theology which is false in

[27] See Tulloch, *op. cit.*, I, 170 ff.

[28] Born an Anglican, Chillingworth embraced Roman Catholicism but was later reconverted to the Church of England. His principal work is *The Religion of Protestants: A Safe Way to Salvation.* Cf. Tulloch, *op. cit.*, I, 261 ff.

[29] Cf. William R. Inge, *The Platonic Tradition in English Religious Thought,* 1926.

philosophy; that the results of science must be recognized; that theology must co-operate with philosophy; and that the masses must be held in the Church by policies of accommodation.

The Latitudinarians had a practical way of preaching. Such was the comment on them by Bishop Burnet, himself a Latitudinarian: "This set of men contributed more than can well be imagined to reforming the way of preaching, which among the divines of England before them was overrun with pedantry, a great mixture of quotations from the Fathers and ancient writers . . . full of many sayings of different languages." Of the new preachers, he says: "Their style was clear, plain, and short. They gave a short paraphrase of their text, unless where great difficulties required a more copious enlargement: but even then they cut off unnecessary shows of learning and applied themselves to the matter in which they opened the nature and reasons of things so fully, and with that simplicity that their hearers felt an instruction of another sort than had commonly been observed before, so that they became very much followed. . . ."[30]

As prominent representatives, the following names are mentioned: Burnet, Tillotson, Whiston, Spencer; also Norris, Gale and Cumberland. Archbishop John Tillotson (d. 1694), who was prominent as a preacher, may be taken as representative of the English Latitudinarians. They represented a remarkable blending of conservatism with rationalism.[31] Some lost themselves in radicalism, as, for instance, Bury, who declared that all Christian doctrines outside of repentance and faith are nonessentials.[32]

The aim of the Latitudinarians, especially during the years 1689 and 1699, had been to mediate between and to unite the Episcopalians and the Presbyterians who stood face to face in hopeless discord, but they failed and were crushed between the two extremes. Latitudinarianism, as like movements on the Continent, soon lost itself in indifferentism and thus became unproductive in theology. In a general way, it may be said that the whole movement, including all the liberal tendencies that we have presented in this chapter, together with the Cambridge

[30] Quoted by Fisher, *op. cit.*, p. 367.

[31] See quotations from Tillotson's sermons by A. C. McGiffert, *Protestant Thought before Kant* (New York: Charles Scribner's Sons, 1911), pp. 194 ff.

[32] Cf. his *Naked Gospel*, 1690; followed by his *Latitudinarius Orthodoxus*, 1697.

school, must be looked upon as precursory to the broad church movement of the mid-nineteenth century which was represented by such men as Coleridge, Arnold, Hare, Maurice, Kingsley, the authors of the *Essays and Reviews*, Conybeare, and Colenso.

BIBLIOGRAPHY

BAKER, A. *Milton and the Puritan Dilemma.* Toronto: University Press, 1952.

CLARK, HENRY W. *History of English Nonconformity from Wyclif to the Close of the 19th Century.* 2 vols. London: Chapman & Hill, Ltd., 1911-1913.

HUNT, JOHN. *Religious Thought in England.* 3 vols. 1870 ff.

INGE, WILLIAM R. *The Platonic Tradition in English Religious Thought.* New York: Longmans, Green & Co., 1926.

JEREMIAS, ISOLDE. *Richard Baxter's Catholic Theology.* Göttingen, 1956.

TILLYARD, E. M. W. *Studies in Milton.* London: Chatto & Windus, 1951.

TULLOCH, JOHN. *Rational Theology and Christian Philosophy in England in the Seventeenth Century.* 2 vols. 1874.

CHAPTER V

THE ENGLISH DEISTS

The preceding chapters of this section have outlined the first influences leading to the confessional disintegration of Reformation theology. The next three chapters trace the first steps in radical liberalism: the English Deists, the French Naturalists, and the German Rationalists. These three connected movements aimed at the complete overthrow of the faith of the Reformation. Upon this follows a review of the Unitarian movements.

We often hear that the German universities were the foundation of theological liberalism. Tulloch is correct when he says that "the home of rational thought was certainly not in Germany in the earlier times of Protestantism."[1] Holland was in a special sense the starting point for the radical liberalism in the seventeenth century. There Descartes came and laid the foundations of modern philosophical rationalism; there Spinoza constructed the greatest of all rational systems; there Bayle published his famous *Dictionary*. From Holland the new influences spread first to her neighbors to the south and to the west. France had the first of her "Naturalists" and England her "Deists" before Germany had her Age of Reason.

The beginnings of theological liberalism were in England. Freedom of the press was declared in 1693, and this principle invited the liberals of that early time to publish their views. The philosophy of John Locke, which made reasonableness the criterion of truth, dominated the age. Alexander Pope, "the prince of rhyme and the grand poet of reason," wrote his "Essay on Man" (1732-34) in which he declared:

> For modes of faith let graceless zealots fight.
> His can't be wrong, whose life is in the right.
> On faith and hope the world will disagree,
> But all mankind's concern is charity.

[1] Tulloch, *op. cit.,* I, 8. Cf. A. V. G. Allen, *The Continuity of Christian Thought* (Boston: Houghton Mifflin Company, 1894), p. 357.

The books of the English Freethinkers were widely read in Germany. Baumgarten reviewed them in his *Nachrichten von merkwürdigen Büchern* (Halle, 1752-58). Thorschmidt published a *Versuch einer vollständigen engelländischen Freidenker-Bibliothek* (Halle, 1765-67).

The tardiness of the Germans in responding to the liberalizing tendencies of the age was due to the conservative principles of the Lutheran Reformation with its strong emphasis upon the objective side of religion, and particularly to the definiteness with which Luther rejected humanism, certain spiritualistic positions of Zwingli, and the ideas of the Spiritualists. A further reason may be seen in the devastating effect of the Thirty Years War. The spiritual progress of the nation was arrested. In comparison with Western Europe, Germany was an undeveloped country during the century following that cataclysmic event.

The deistic movement was an expression of aversion to the positive and historical forms of religion. The individual, in his insistence upon absolute freedom of thought, emancipated himself from all external authority. In the term of Anthony Collins in 1713, he wanted to be a freethinker.

There were many causes for the resentful attitude of thoughtful observers to the established forms of religion. Reference may be made to the manner in which the confessional controversies were fought in that day, to the unhistorical use of Scripture on the dogmatic points of difference between churches and individuals, to the excessive claims of the churchmen backed by political power, to the tyrannical abuse of royal prerogatives so completely in contrast to the ever growing spirit of political and religious liberty. All these things contributed to making the official forms of religion objectionable. In their protest against these the Deists were unable to be conservative reformers; in history they will always be known as the group which took the first steps toward inculcating radicalism into Christian theology.

The aim of the Deists was to find a religion that all men would want to recognize—a "natural religion" that might serve as a common ground for the critical examination of supernaturalism of any form. With the strong emphasis upon dogmatics in theology, this natural religion felt it had to present itself in the form of a system. The theory of knowledge to be employed was empiristic-sensualistic, and the system to be constructed was to be mechanistic. The practical interest was in the moral elements of religion. This theology was in reality nothing but a theory of morality. The natural law of the old Stoics (*lex naturae*) was studied a great deal. The movement was a criticism of supernaturalism. Since this criticism had to be conducted with constant reference to statements of the dogmaticians of supernaturalism, it became a religious philosophy. Deism aimed at a religion in harmony with scientific thought, a religion liberated from the supernatural and from a special interest in a world and life beyond the present, and at the same time in which the confessional differences would be looked upon as the natural variations of an historical situation.

The name Deist which was applied to these men needs qualification. The term deism as employed by present-day theology refers to the idea of a transcendent God who created the world, but who, by withholding His immanence, left the world to take care of itself. This was the conception of the universe built upon the basis of Newtonian observations. As yet it was not the developed system which it later became when philosophy and theology came to distinguish between deism, pantheism, and theism. The English Deists were not concerned with a deism as opposed to theism. They called themselves deists because they were opposed to atheism. The content of their belief in God, in which Christ as redeemer and mediator had no place, did not go beyond a personal "first cause" that had established a realm of law in which the world moved in an unchangeable mechanical order. The more fitting name, therefore, was the one claimed by Collins, Freethinkers.

English deism was a product of a reasoning spirit stimulated by political events. It ran a course parallel to the gradual emancipation of the individual from the all-embracing power of absolute government in the state. It was a movement that covered a century and a half (from Herbert of Cherbury, d. 1648, to David Hume, d. 1776), was in essential harmony with naturalism in France, and anticipated practically all the positions of German rationalism. It had a period of youth (Herbert, Hobbes, Blount), a period of maturity (Toland, Collins, Tindal, Morgan, Annet, Middleton), and a time of old age (Shaftesbury, Mandeville, Dodwell, Bolingbroke, Hume). Arising during the reign of Charles I, it flourished in the period extending from the revolution of 1688, and decayed toward the close of the reign of George II and thereafter.

Philosophical Background

In a study of the English Deists a brief review of the philosophical outlook of that age is useful, for their theology was nothing but a system of philosophy, as all natural theology must be. The significance of the English Deists lies in their having become the founders of our modern philosophy of religion.

Catholic as well as orthodox Protestant theologians regarded the natural sciences, and philosophy in general, as handmaidens of theology. Science points to God as the primary cause of all things, to a God who is wise and benevolent in relation to his creatures. All things happen for the ultimate good of man. In any predicament the faithful will turn to God in prayer, and God, in turn, will come to their rescue —if necessary, through a miracle. He will reward the pious with eternal bliss in heaven.

This view was seriously challenged by a galaxy of scholars in the age under discussion. Two emphases appeared. The first of these was the mathematical emphasis (Copernicus, Kepler, Giordano Bruno, Descartes, Galileo, Spinoza); the second was the empirical, the emphasis on verification by experience (Bacon, Hobbes, Locke, Newton, Hume, and Kant).[2]

The Bible, literally interpreted, and Aristotelian physics were the two pillars on which theologians built their understanding of the universe. Both now came under attack. Copernicus (d. 1543) had taught the heliocentric view of the cosmos, and Kepler (d. 1630) put his theory on a scientific basis. Galileo (d. 1642) was brought to trial for teaching the Copernican system. His teaching was condemned by the Roman authorities as contrary to the Bible. Mathematical science, Galileo held, furnishes man with a certainty that is intensive and consequently akin to the knowledge of God. He discarded Aristotelian physics as a blind and unreasonable system. He was seconded by Descartes (Cartesius, d. 1650) who rejected the Aristotelian method

[2] E. A. Burtt, *Types of Religious Philosophy* (New York: Harper, 1951), pp. 171 ff.

of explaining physical phenomena by means of final causes, and insisted that everything takes place mechanically. Animals too, in his view, are nothing but machines. The world consists of two substances: spirit or thinking substance, and matter or extended substance. In a somewhat novel manner Descartes restated the old ontological proof for the existence of God: We conceive God as the most perfect being. It is evident that such a being must exist, for if he did not exist he would lack one important aspect of perfection. (This argument was torn to shreds by Kant.) Doubting was his method of arriving at certainty: *Cogito ergo sum!* The system of Descartes contains in embryo three elements which were to come to the fore in the next century: an emphasis on the *Ego*, which produced German idealism; his principle of doubt, which issued in agnosticism; and the concept of mechanism, which resulted in determinism and naturalism.

Spinoza (d. 1677) was a younger contemporary of Descartes and a careful student of his philosophy. He accepted Descartes' position that mathematics furnishes man with a universally valid type of science, but rejected the idea that the spiritual and the physical are two different substances; they are only two different modes of one ultimate reality. According to Spinoza God and nature are one: *Deus sive natura*, "God or nature," not God and nature. God is not transcendent, existing apart from nature, but He is nature itself as an active self-determining process. God is *natura naturans* while the effect of the process is *natura naturata*. This impersonal God acts without purpose, and has no emotions or passions like men. The one, infinite substance or God has an infinite number of attributes, but is known to man solely through the attributes of thought and extension. Every idea is an expression of the attribute of thought and every physical object a mode of extension. Although there is no interaction there is an exact correspondence between the modes of thought and extension. This is Spinoza's teaching of the "parallelism of mind and body." Man is a part of nature, he forms no kingdom within a kingdom. His actions are as determined as lines, planes, and solids. To attain freedom, it is necessary to recognize the bondage of the self, the fixed determination of man's desires and emotions through natural law. Knowledge is the way to salvation. Through knowledge it is possible to liberate man from the bondage of his emotions. Intuition, the insight that all things are conditioned by God, the one, infinite substance, is the highest kind of knowledge. To see all things, not as a series of events in time, but in their logical relation to God, is what Spinoza calls "viewing the world under the form of eternity" (*sub specie aeternitatis*).

Spinoza had been preceded in his pantheism by Giordano Bruno (d. as heretic February 16, 1600) who defined God as *monadum monas* (supreme active substance), the immanent cause of nature. It is evident that there is no place in the system of Spinoza for the biblical view of special revelation, miracle, and prayer.

The second group of scholars mentioned above represent the empiricists of the day. The first to be considered is Francis Bacon (d. 1626). His special interest lay in the tangible matters of the natural sciences, that is, in the things observable by sense-experience. Descartes also aimed at certainty, with this difference, that he sought it in the intellectual utterance of consciousness. Herein is the early indication of the development of two differing types of theology: the theology following the philosophy of English empiricism with Francis Bacon, Thomas Hobbes, and John Locke as first guides, and the Continental (German) theology of idealism following Leibnitz and his successors.

The special points of interest in the philosophy of Bacon which influenced the religion of the English Deists are as follows: (1) Bacon rejected the syllogistic-demonstrative method of Scholasticism upon which theology had been relying. In his inquiry for a reliable method of finding truth he opposed deduction from a general principle except when this principle or hypothesis was identical with an actual experience. Bacon insisted that all thinking must be established upon experience arrived at by induction. (2) Among the misleading conceptions or prejudices ("idols") which must be discarded in pursuing this method he names the "idols of the tribe," concepts peculiar to man's constitution, among which Bacon counted the teleological view of things. This was a mistaken notion because it ignores the mechanistic character of causality. (3) As a child of the age when philosophy and science were passing out of the hands of the theologian, he drew a sharp line between the work of science and that of theology. Philosophy was to be secularized. His optimism, as expressed in the *New Atlantis*, was for the future of science, the mastery of nature ("knowledge is power"). He had no intention to discredit religion or to deny to theology its legitimate sphere. He warned against an unreasonable confounding of the divine with the human. Mediating causes, if they are not known, must not be traced to the working of God, because this would result in a conviction not resting on truth. The findings of science are not to be feared because, properly considered, they will support faith and discredit superstition. The source of theology must be seen in the divine revelation through the word of God, not in the natural light nor in the dictates of reason. This must be done even when the testimony of God runs counter to reason. Still, the "natural light" in man, if this is taken as the remnant of an original purity and insight in the human race, should be looked upon as sufficient to yield some reliable information on matters of the moral law, even though it is not perfect. "Natural theology," as a part of philosophy, furnishes proof against atheism, but it is not sufficient to establish religion on a positive basis. The boundaries between sacred theology and the natural theology of philosophy are not to be confused.

The Deists went beyond these last-mentioned suggestions of Bacon. To them the "natural light" in man was sufficient to establish the real, the true, the "natural religion." It is interesting to follow the evolution of Bacon's term "natural theology" to that of "natural religion," first used by Arthur Bury in the English literature of that day.

More of a real pioneer of English deism was Lord Herbert of Cherbury (d. 1648). This man of attractive personality was in a special sense the father of English deism.[3] He had been stimulated to thought on the problems of religion by visits to France and by direct or indirect contact with the liberals of the age. Toward the close of his life he published the following writings: (1) *De veritate*, to which he appended two shorter treatises–*De causis errorum*, and *De religione laici*– and (2) *De religione gentilium*. The first of these offers a theory of the laws of knowledge; the second is built upon the first and presents a critique of faith or religion.

A few leading thoughts of his writings as a whole may be presented. The test of true religion, he said, lies in its universality. There are common religious conceptions among all men of every race. In these we have the essentials of religion. True religion has its foundations in

[3] Cf. the excellent discussion of Lord Herbert in Hunt, *op. cit.*, I, 441 ff. There are also many references to him in Vol. II.

the natural instincts, in truths which are intuitively perceived. He enumerates five such truths that are common to all religions: (1) The being of God; (2) the duty to worship him; (3) the practical-moral character of divine worship; (4) the duty to repent of sins and to forsake them; (5) divine retribution, partly here and partly hereafter. These have frequently been styled the "five points of deism." The position is taken that this "religion of nature or reason" is innate in man. There are no atheists; atheism is an abnormality. The priests of the various religions added to these innate religious ideas a multiplicity of deities to be worshiped through ceremonies, oracles which the priests alone could interpret, and means of expiation which they alone could dispense. Christianity returned to an emphasis of the above-mentioned essentials of religion. But in the process of doctrinal development the true religion was soon overlaid with the divisiveness and sectarianism of religious conceptions which characterized the age of the writer.

Supernatural revelation is not spoken of as impossible, but its probability in individual cases is tied to conditions which make it practically superfluous. Reason is the real authority in matters of truth and error; revelation is uncertain, although it may be admitted that there can be things beyond reason. In the heathen religions, as in Christianity with its Bible, we must try to find the real truth, the real word of God.

The significance of Lord Herbert in the history of theological liberalism lies in his predication of subjective reason as the principle of religious truth. In this respect he was on common ground with Descartes, Spinoza and many of the advanced thinkers of the age. In England the points of conflict between churchmen and Puritans had ceased to attract attention and the appeal was to the powers and prerogatives of reason. It was the age of reason in all countries, an age in which freedom of political and religious thought was demanded. In religion and ethics the thinkers went back behind the Scriptures to the standards of philosophical thought.

Thomas Hobbes (1588-1679) continued the warfare against the Church. He took psychology out of the hands of the theologians. Interest shifted from theological ethics to civil or social ethics. Hobbes had his predecessors in men like Hugo Grotius who laid down the principle of the independence of the state from the Church. The

Arminians had labored to widen the sphere of the purely natural.

Hobbes received his stimulus from conditions in England after the revolution (1642-49) which had brought about the dissolution of the existing society. Cromwell, at the head of the army of the Independents, established a commonwealth in which an unsettling spiritualism and puritanism kept society in a state of restlessness. He had been forced to establish a dictatorship, which he had to maintain with an iron hand against the threatening influence of extremists and restless Spiritualists. It was during this time that Hobbes published his *Leviathan* (1651). He felt the necessity of establishing a modern theory of absolute monarchy in contrast to the democratic revolutionists as well as to the completely antiquated divine right theories such as Filmer expressed in his *Patriarcha*. This monarchical government was to rest upon the basis of purely secular or human ethics, derived from man's natural conceptions of right and wrong. Starting with the Aristotelian conception of an original state in which there was a war of all against all, Hobbes attributed to man's reason and sense of self-preservation the desire to end this anarchic and chaotic state of affairs by establishing an organized society through the transfer of supreme authority from this society to a governor. This is done in the form of a contract. Organized society through its spokesman, the king, adopts an official religion, and has the absolute right to do so, for the purpose of securing the happiness of all.

The question then arises: What is the most natural and beneficial system of ethics to be adopted by the state? It was this question that created a special interest in an analytical psychology, and on this Hobbes set the English thinkers of the seventeenth and eighteenth centuries to work. This new psychology was empirical in character. It ignored the metaphysical teachings of Bible and Church concerning the nature of the soul, the influence of divine grace upon the natural faculties of man and the impulses bound to be received from a divinely revealed destiny. It sought the laws for ethical action in the natural functions of the mind and in an immanent psychological analysis of them. While the decisive step in this direction was taken by Hobbes, he had his predecessors, the French Naturalists, such as Montaigne and Charron who, following the old Stoics, endeavored to record the psychological laws underlying the motions of feeling and will.

It is especially the mechanistic character of the psychology of Hobbes to which we must call attention. In his struggle for a new theory of knowledge he arrived at the two statements: "All that exists is body," and "All that occurs is motion." All knowledge and all willing are traced to impressions upon the brain received through the nerve senses from external objects.[4]

The fundamental principle of Hobbes' philosophy was the mechanical conception of the physical world. Hobbes extended its application to the mental sphere and the psychology described was the result. Upon the basis of his mechanistic psychology he theorized that the idea of deities was originally produced by the fear of hostile beings thought of, though mistakenly, as having an incorporeal existence. Man investigates the causes of interference with his welfare and discovers something which he conceives of, mistakenly, as spirit. A similar faith of many individuals leads to organized religion and to the worship of a deity. Since the outstanding trait of the English Deists was the naturalization of religion, it is clear what influence the philosophy of Hobbes must have had upon them.

What is the criterion or norm with regard to the claims of revelation? What is the relation of revelation to natural religion? On these problems in which the deistic movement was vitally interested John Locke (1632-1704) first expressed himself in his "Essay on Human Understanding" (1689). The claims of revelation by pagans, sectarians and dogmatists, must stand the test of reason applied to the external situation and an inner credence (conviction). The truths of divine revelation which, according to Locke, we cannot have by innate ideas, must commend themselves to reasonable metaphysics and ethics, to a knowledge arrived at by perception in the way of experience.[5] If in such a way the reliability of the truth of revelation has been established then we may allow *a posteriori* a favorable prejudice with regard to some mysterious details. If we ignore this criterion of reasonableness in the foundations of Christianity, then the most absurd matters might be introduced as revelation. The central teachings of Christianity should be derived exclusively from the Gospels and Acts which

[4] Thomas Hobbes, *Leviathan* (1651), Part I.

[5] On the difference between Lord Herbert and Locke regarding the "inner ideas," see Hunt, *op. cit.*, I, 452, who is of the opinion that "both seem to mean much the same thing."

stress the moral demands for participation in the messianic kingdom and are identical with the laws of natural religion. The Christian religion, different from all pagan religions and philosophies, presents natural religion in its purity, perfection, and with authority. With this fundamental position Locke combined a certain belief in miracles and in the inspiration of Scripture.

These supernatural features made his teaching on the relation between the religion of nature and that of revelation somewhat acceptable to many of the moderate conservatives. This class of clergymen, mostly Latitudinarians, would have expressed the situation with the following words of M. Pattison: "Christianity is a resume of the knowledge of God already attained by reason, and a disclosure of further truths. These further truths could not have been comprehended by reason. When divinely communicated, however, they approve themselves to the same reason which has already put us in possession of so much." [6]

The Deists were encouraged by Locke in emphasizing the practical identity between natural and revealed religion, making natural religion the norm and criterion of the revealed. Thus the question has arisen whether Locke was the "father of deism." Considering the fact that the Deists as freethinkers took a fundamentally different attitude toward religion than was the case with the serious-minded and religiously inclined Locke, it would not be correct to put him with the Deists.

Charles Blount, in his first writing, *Anima Mundi* (1679), emphasized the relative perfection of natural religion among the non-Christians. In the translation of Philostratus' *Life of Apollonius of Tyana*, he evidently desired to discredit the supernatural character of Christ by paralleling His miracles with those attributed to non-Christians.

His friend Charles Gildon, who later retracted, published the *Oracles of Reason*, which contained articles by himself, Blount and others.[7] It was suppressed by the authorities as the "worst calumny of Christianity."

The Earl of Shaftesbury (d. 1713) left as his chief work three

[6] Mark Pattison, "Tendencies of Religious Thought in England, 1688-1750," *Essays and Reviews* (1860), p. 297. For further discussion see the account of Archbishop Tillotson by McGiffert, *op. cit.*, pp. 194 ff.

[7] The contents are described by A. S. Farrar, *A Critical History of Free Thought* (London: John Murray, 1862), pp. 174-75.

volumes on *Characters of Men, Manners, Opinions, Times* (2d ed., 1714). His significance lies in tracing the ethical to the conscience, which is autonomous; it must not be sought in an external authority. The sense for the ethical is born in us as an instinct, the same as the sense for beauty. The selfish and the social instincts are in our nature. It is the pleasure in beholding the harmony of these that constitutes virtue, which produces happiness. While pedagogically helpful and needed because of human depravity, it is wrong in principle to promote virtue by praise or punishment and by promise of rewards, as preachers do on the basis of the Bible. Love is the driving motive of Christianity.

While reason should not be taken as an outward authority, true revelation will be in agreement with reason; otherwise it is deceptive, even if it should be attested by miracles. The excrescences of religion can best be met by ridicule and irony. Shaftesbury's practice of just this kind of writing provoked books of protest from the camp of the conservatives.[8]

The Warfare against the Supernatural

In the general attack upon the supernatural, John Toland (d. 1722) published a book entitled *Christianity Not Mysterious, or a Treatise showing that there is nothing in the Gospel contrary to Reason nor above it, and that no Christian doctrine can be properly called a Mystery* (1696). This book had several editions. Pressing the question of authority in matters of religion, he rejected tradition and the authority of the Church and Scripture as it was usually interpreted. Reason is proclaimed as the only principle of authority. Even the divine source of Scripture can be established only by reason. He admits that the use of reason can suffer perversion; it should then be restored to its original power. The criterion of unimpaired reason must be sought in the force of evidence. There may be revelation as a means of information, but the teachings of revelation must satisfy man's reason. From this standpoint he draws the conclusion that in Christianity there can be nothing mysterious. There cannot be even the appearance of a conflict between reason and the gospel. In this statement Toland goes beyond the position of Spinoza, Herbert, and Hobbes, who admitted that in

[8] Cf. Hunt, *op. cit.*, II, 343-44.

Christianity and Scripture there may be something beyond the faculty of reason. The statement of Toland was made in order to prove that the essence of the Christian religion is found in that "natural religion" which all peoples and races are alleged to have in common. Christianity is something "sectarian," to use the present-day term, a special branch of the real religion.

In his denial of the mysterious element in Christianity Toland asks whether the very concept of faith does not demand a supernatural object. He denies this by pointing to the reasons for faith in Scripture: We must satisfy ourselves that the biblical writings are genuine as to authority, and we must be convinced that the contents of the writings are worthy of God. Hunt notes that this is right in so far as it goes, but that Toland overlooks the fact that the believer finds something in the Scriptures which lies beyond the intellectually demonstrable, something that is seen and felt only by the intuitive vision of the spiritually minded reader.[9]

Among the attacks on the supernatural there was a publication by Anthony Collins (d. 1729) on the concept of the Old Testament prophecies, their bearing on the New Testament reports, and the results derived from this consideration for the proper estimate of Christianity. This work bears the title *A Discourse of the Grounds and Reasons of the Christian Religion* (1724). The Christian religion is viewed as an allegorized Judaism, a "mystical Judaism," a religion of reason, developed and perfected by the allegorization of the Jewish religion of reason.[10]

The conflict was continued by Thomas Woolston (d. 1731) as spokesman for Collins in his *Discourse on the Miracles of Our Saviour* (eight treatises, 1727-30). In overbearing and very offensive language he ridiculed the literal understanding of the biblical records. A severe controversy resulted from the publication of this book. In the battle between the natural religion of the Deists and the supernatural religion of Christianity the Church was cut to the quick. This gave a strong stimulus to the development of Christian apologetics, and many schol-

[9] *Ibid.*, II, 236-51.

[10] G. V. Lechler gives a very complete and lucid report, *Geschichte des Englischen Deismus* (1841), pp. 266-88. See also Hunt, *op. cit.*, II, 369-99.

ars came forward to defend the Bible. Lechler, in writing on this conflict, speaks of some sixty publications which appeared.[11]

Later, Peter Annet (d. 1768), in his desire to reply to the defenders of miracles who had been pointing to the biblical eyewitnesses, undertook to tear down this part of the bulwark. He wrote *The Resurrection of Jesus Considered in Answer to the Trial of Witnesses* (1744), suggesting that Christ may not have been really dead after his burial. He spoke of Paul as the founder of a new religion and questioned the genuineness of his writings. All supernaturalism was rejected.

Conyers Middleton (d. 1750) also fought the inspiration of the Bible, the possibility of miracles, etc., and aimed to wipe out all difference between sacred and profane history. Middleton was the first in England to point out that the historical conditions of a movement must be considered before its significance can be understood.

The Deist Concept of Religion

Several of the Deists devoted themselves to a constructive statement of the tenets of deism. Tindal's and Chubb's ideas will serve as examples.[12]

Matthew Tindal (d. 1733) published the book *Christianity as Old as the Creation, or the Gospel a Republication of the Religion of Nature* (1730). The leading ideas are as follows: Reasonable living, which leads to happiness in life, is religion and constitutes the morally good. A follower of John Locke, Tindal admits no innate ideas in men, but to this rule he makes an exception—the desire for happiness. This he calls the only innate principle of the mind. Religion is essentially a reasonable way of living. Fundamental to all religions is the recognition of the law of nature which is always perfect, plain, simple, and universal. The divisions in religions deal with the non-fundamentals, with matters not truly religious. The criterion of true religion is the universality of natural religion. From the identity of the Christian religion with natural religion Tindal argues that Chris-

[11] Lechler, *op. cit.*, pp. 298-323. Cf. Hunt, *op. cit.*, II, 400 ff.

[12] Bolingbroke might have claim to a review at this place if we consider his general aims. But he was more brilliant than solid; therefore we prefer to consider the untutored Chubb, a man of much moral earnestness. As to the views of Lord Bolingbroke see Hunt, *op. cit.*, III, 148 ff.

tianity can have no articles of faith which are not in agreement with reason. Those who object to this, he says, try to explain religion with the aid of reason. Many things in the Bible must be rationalized in order to make them acceptable. Tindal overlooks the fact that there is a difference between using reason in the interpretation of Scripture and the laying down of a rule that there can be nothing mysterious and miraculous in revelation. The misleading thought of Tindal is seen in the demand that underlay the title of his writing: Christianity must be identical with natural religion, otherwise it cannot be true. If Christianity teaches more than is contained in natural religion, then such additions belong to the realm of superstition or to the corruption of true religion. This was the real position of the Deists. The views of Tindal, together with those of Chubb, are representative of the views of deism on religion as a whole.

Thomas Chubb (d. 1747) was a common workman who by a remarkable interest in theological controversies trained himself to present his thought clearly in writing. In his book, *The True Gospel of Jesus Christ* (1738), and in a defense of that book, *The True Gospel of Jesus Christ Vindicated* (1739), he aimed to show that Christ simply wanted to teach the moral law, the "law of reason," the "law of nature." Christianity is the religion of obeying the moral law or the dictates of the conscience. If this law has been violated, then there must be repentance and reform, which will be followed by divine forgiveness. This is the whole doctrine of salvation. There can be no inclusion of doctrines and opinions in this gospel of Christ. Such matters as Christ's divinity have nothing to do with man's salvation. Christ was not really the Son of God; he was man, and as such he is our example. The doctrine of the imputation of Christ's righteousness is harmful because it deprives men of the incentive to rely entirely on the moral law for their salvation. Chubb anticipated in an especially clear and simple way the rationalism which was soon to flourish, particularly in Germany.

Evaluation of the Deists

In addition to the few critical remarks of a general nature which were expressed above, we offer a few further statements regarding the significance of the English Deists. (1) While it is true that the French

Deists (Naturalists) were more radical than some of the English writers (Tindal, Toland, Chubb), yet most of the latter were men who took the first step into radical liberalism. They remind us of that type of criticism which in the history of Christian thought was further cultivated by Voltaire, Frederick the Great, Joseph II, Benjamin Franklin, Thomas Jefferson, Thomas Paine, and later by Robert Ingersoll. (2) Not counting such philosophers as Herbert and Hume, who strictly speaking did not belong to this group, they were throughout small men in the field of literature. Troeltsch characterizes them as second- and third-rate men who had the real intelligentsia of England against them.[13] (3) Most of them bear the marks of laymen who undertake the discussion of philosophy and religion without having the requisite training for such a task. This was one reason why their work was purely negative and non-constructive. (4) In making human reason the criterion of revelation in the sense of religious philosophy, they failed to appreciate the appeal which the Holy Scriptures have always had to the soul of man; and therefore they did not feel the need of crediting any special significance for the life of the Church to the Bible. This applies more to the French than to the English Deists. In discussing the relation between natural religion and revelation, the chief interest of the English Deists was in such subjects as the probability or improbability of the prophecies and miracles. It did not occur to them—nor, for that matter, to their conservative opponents—that the much-discussed special revelation might be viewed as a history of redemption. (5) The Deists had no interest in the so-called Arian or Unitarian controversy concerning the person of Christ which was going on in England at that time. A. V. G. Allen remarks: "As there had been no special message, there was no necessity for a supernatural messenger." [14] (6) It cannot be denied that the assaults of the Deists upon the faith of the Church served to call attention to matters in theology which needed to be rectified. (7) Finally, we must note the fact that the whole deistic inquiry, taken together with the philosophical influences surrounding the movement, created the "philosophy of religion" which serves as an auxiliary branch of systematic theology today.

[13] See his article on Deism in *PRE,* IV, 546.

[14] *Op. cit.,* p. 364.

Conservative Reaction

It is impossible in this chapter to present, to classify, and to give a critical review of all the writings which proceeded from the conservative quarters of the Church against the Deists. They were numerous. All we can do is to mention the outstanding replies and characterize the methods of refuting the foe.

Against Lord Herbert came a reply from Thomas Halyburton: *Natural Reason Insufficient*, and from Richard Baxter, *More Reasons for the Christian Religion and No Reason Against It.* Charles Leslie wrote his *Short and Easy Method with the Deists* against Blount. This book brought Charles Gildon, who had been siding with the liberals, into the conservative camp. As a retraction he wrote *The Deists' Manual.* Other works by Leslie include: *The Growth of Deism, The Five Crowns of the Church*, and *The Growth of Error.* John Toland's book, *Christianity Not Mysterious*, drew forth many replies: Stephen Nye wrote *Historical Account of the New Testament;* John Richardson, *The Canon of the New Testament Vindicated;* and Jeremiah Jones, *A New and Full Method of Settling the Canonical Authority of the New Testament.* Thomas Mangey, Thomas Brett, and James Paterson replied to Toland's *Nazarenus, or Jewish, Gentile, Mahometan Christianity.* John Brown, John Balguy and others criticized the derisive method of the Earl of Shaftesbury. The writings of Anthony Collins (*Discourse of Free-Thinking* and *Grounds and Reasons of the Christian Religion*) engaged the whole Church in controversy. Among his opponents were: William Carroll, objecting to a place for reason in theology; Richard Bentley in *Eleutherius Lipsiensis;* Francis Hare in *A Clergyman's Thanks for Eleutherius Lipsiensis;* Daniel Williams in *A Letter to the Author of Free-thinking;* John Addicombe; Edward Chandler in the area of Old Testament prophecy; Samuel Clarke in *A Discourse Concerning the Connection of the Prophecies of the Old Testament and Their Application to Christ.* Thomas Woolston, who also had written against Collins, was later severely criticized for his allegorical interpretation of Scripture and especially of the miracle stories by Nathanael Lardner, Simon Brown and Richard Smalbroke. Several replies were published against Matthew Tindal's *Christianity as Old as Creation.* We mention: John Conybeare, *Defense of Revealed Religion;* John Leland, *An Answer to Tindal;* John Jackson,

Remarks on Christianity as Old as Creation. Against Chubb's *The True Gospel of Jesus Christ* there came a reply from J. Hallet, and another from G. Benson. Against Lord Bolingbroke there were writings by Leland and Warburton.[15]

The conservatives admitted a natural religion in addition to the revealed. They denied, however, that the two are identical, or that the latter came as the culmination of the former. They protested especially against the endeavor of the Deists to make natural religion the norm and criterion of the revealed. Whereas the Deists sought to naturalize religion, the conservatives strove to supernaturalize it. They emphasized special revelation. Against the "five points" of Lord Herbert, Thomas Halyburton advanced the following objections: (1) The five points cannot be regarded as being generally acknowledged; (2) The element of truth in the Gentile religions is not a matter of independent discovery, but is a remnant of the original divine revelation; (3) Purely natural religion is insufficient for salvation because of the weakened condition of sinful man. It was upon these statements that many of the replies to the later Deists were based. These objections reiterated that religion in its depths cannot be comprehended by the reasoning mind; that even natural religion presents points of difficulty to pure reason; and that the noblest of heathen philosophers had altogether mistaken notions about God and immortality. It goes without saying that in many respects the conservatives of that day used methods and emphasized points which sound unnatural to the conservative theologian of today who has learned to view revelation as a history of redemption.

Among the above-mentioned writers against the Deists there was one whose book was so extraordinary that we must devote a special paragraph to it. It was *The Analogy of Religion Natural and Revealed to the Constitution and Course of Nature* by Joseph Butler, Bishop of Durham (d. 1752). This work was the most complete and best answer given to the Deists' objections to a revealed religion. It was destined to hold a distinct place in English literature for a long time. Published in 1736, it was remarkable in that no opponent ventured to risk a reply. Butler disconcerted the Deists by admitting that an absolute proof for the facts of revealed religion cannot always be

[15] Cf. the detailed analysis of these writings in Hunt, *op. cit.*, II, 98-462.

given. But from man's experience regarding the present world-order he drew conclusions for the reasonableness and probability of a higher order. The difficulties of revelation, admittedly embarrassing in themselves, cannot be counted as destructive to religious belief, inasmuch as difficulties of a similar nature beset the recognition of nature as a coherent and systematic whole. The course of nature, according to Butler, suggests not only the conclusions which the Deists admitted, of the existence of God and of man's duty to worship him, but also, upon closer examination, natural laws and occurrences seem to furnish evidence for the doctrines of revealed religion which the Deists discarded and rejected. Prophecy and miracles held a prominent place among the doctrines of the Church rejected by the Deists. To this charge Butler points out that the unintelligibleness of prophecies does not invalidate the proof of foresight because, in part, they have been fulfilled in the past. Things are to be judged by the interpretation that can be given to the known parts, rather than to be rejected *in toto* because some parts are still wanting in explanation. Divine revelation is historical and "prophecy is nothing but the history of events before they come to pass." [16] Miracles, Butler maintains, are an integral part of the historical tradition related in the Bible. Their reports must be accepted in the same way as the other events that seem natural to us. They may be different from what we know today. But that does not make them incredible. They have been necessitated by the moral condition of a previous age. To argue for their incredibility we must be acquainted with parallel instances in our own world or at least in a world similar to ours. But this means of verification is denied us.

Butler also addressed himself to the problem of ethics. Against Hobbes, who had said that moral distinctions are merely conventional and rest upon the authority of the state, Butler maintains that conscience is the supreme authoritative principle to which both self love and benevolence are subordinate. Man is a law unto himself. If conscience had strength and power, it would rule the world. Its authority is absolute as a principle of human nature. Anticipating Kant by several decades Butler, then, affirmed the absolute authority of conscience as a principle of the moral nature of man. His *Analogy*, together with Hume's *Dialogues on Natural Religion* (to be discussed

[16] *The Analogy of Religion,* ed. Howard Malcolm (1873), p. 281.

below), served to undermine the rationalistic basis of natural religion before Kant's systematic criticism. It should be noted, however, that Butler did not profess to furnish proofs for the doctrines of revealed religion. He only wanted to show their probability by pointing out their analogy with the course of nature. Reason cannot establish the truth of revealed religion for it does not know of the depth of true religion. Probability is the very guide of life.[17]

The Cambridge School

Although Arminian and latitudinarian in their advocacy of the freedom of inquiry, in their aversion to confessional controversies, in their defense of toleration, and in their emphasis upon religious life as opposed to form, the men of the Cambridge school nevertheless represented a theology which contributed to the overthrow of deism. Ralph Cudworth (d. 1688), in his work, *The True Intelligent System of the Universe* (1678), particularly endeavored to refute deism. To him the God of the Deists was a God of fatalism. Such a conception was bound to be of serious consequence to the clear distinction between good and evil as well as to man's freedom. Bishop Chandler added a posthumous treatise to Cudworth's book under the title: *A Treatise Concerning Eternal and Immutable Morality* (1731). A century later another admirer published Cudworth's *A Discourse on Moral Good and Evil* (1838). This rational type of theology, which argued from the foundations of Neo-Platonism, had a speculative depth which stood as a formidable witness against the shallowness of the deistic writings. McGiffert gives a fitting characterization of the men of this school, when he speaks of "their emphasis upon reason as a faculty by which we may enjoy a direct vision of spiritual realities hidden from the senses and inaccessible by the ordinary processes of discursive reason." [18]

The Significance of Hume's Skepticism

David Hume's philosophy of skepticism (1711) was a logical development of the philosophy of the English empiricists. All of these had spoken of experience as the foundation of knowledge. Bacon sought

[17] William J. Norton, *Bishop Butler, Moralist and Divine* (New Brunswick: Rutgers University Press, 1940), pp. 305 ff.

[18] McGiffert, *op. cit.*, p. 192.

to arrive at facts by observation and experiment. Hobbes traced all knowledge to sense-perceptions. Locke explained the acquired ideas in man by pointing to experience, either external or by sensation or reflection. Then came Hume who said: If nothing can be reality but that which is traceable to real experience, then there are two things which must be entirely eliminated, namely substance and causality. Substance, as existing back of qualities, conditions and actions, has never been really observed. Its reality for man is not in its materiality but in the sensations. It is just an idea, an imagination, a fiction. All matter, as far as we know it, is only a mental condition, a mental habit. It is not a conception based upon real experience, but consists only of isolated impressions and ideas. In this he agreed with Berkeley. Causality is also ruled out. Upon the basis of "laws," outside of strict mathematics, it cannot really be proved that one thing necessarily follows another in the relation of cause and effect. We cannot trust deductions which are not mathematically verified. Since all deductions under consideration are neither mathematical nor experimental, we know nothing of realities outside of ourselves. Berkeley (1684-1753) had denied the reality of matter ("things") before Hume. Hume agreed that we have no certainty with regard to the existence of matter. He went beyond Berkeley by carrying his skepticism to the question of the certainty of the mind. Will Durant has summarized Hume's position in these words: "We know the mind," said Hume, "only as we know matter; by perception, though it be in this case internal. Never do we perceive such entity as the 'mind'; we perceive merely separate ideas, memories, feelings, etc. The mind is not a substance, an organ that has ideas; it is only an abstract name for the series of ideas; the perceptions, memories and feelings are the mind; there is no observable 'soul' behind the processes of thought." [19] This was skepticism carried to such an extent that all grounds for certainty in matters of religion seemed to disappear.

We must now consider what effects this skeptical philosophy had upon the tenets of deism.

The Deists, following Locke, had made reason the criterion in matters of religion. Now Hume denied reason the right to create and derive truth from itself, because this would mean speaking of things

[19] *The Story of Philosophy* (Toronto: Irwin & Gordon, 1927), p. 281.

of which there can be no real experience. So the Deists, along with the conservatives, lost the foundation upon which they had been building.

Furthermore, by ruling out cause and effect, the customary deistic arguments for the existence of God were lost. Hume argued that on the basis of real experience we know nothing of God as the creator of the world. The teleological proof falls, because we cannot draw any analogy between a human intelligence which creates small things and a divine intelligence which created the universe. By doing this we should overlook the fact that the world is finite and that creation is beset with many imperfections. The cosmological proof falls with the admission that there is no necessity in causality. In addition to this the following question would be in order: Why may not the world, like God, have its cause in itself? Neither can there be anything in the moral proof which claims that the presence of evil in the world necessarily calls for a just and omnipotent God who will right the wrongs which we behold. We might just as well conclude that there is a God who is evil or unjust or powerless or who exists as a blind force.

Another dogma of the Deists was the immortality of the soul. The Deists taught that the injustices of this life demand an equalization by a just God in a future life. But, said Hume, we do not know that there is a God; and if there should be one, how do we know that there will be such an equalization? Eternal punishments for temporal transgressions are in themselves a gross injustice. According to experience, the soul is more likely to be mortal than immortal, when we consider how all things in this world fade and pass away, and especially when we observe how the soul is affected by the weaknesses and aging of the body.

Concerning miracles, Hume was more on common ground with the Deists, at least in his aversion to admitting the reality of alleged "supernatural" happenings. Though regarding experience as the source of all knowledge, he admitted that all effects do not follow from their supposed causes with like certainty. A wise man, therefore, restricts his belief to the evidence. The evidence presented in religion never exceeds what we would call probability. Hence "no testimony is sufficient to establish a miracle, unless the testimony be of such a kind, that its falsehood would be more miraculous than the fact which it endeavors to establish." In case of a report that a dead man was restored to life, he would immediately consider "whether it would be more probable that this person should either deceive or be deceived, or that the fact which he relates should really have happened." Hume adds four reasons against the probability of the reality of miracles reported in any religion: (1) no miracle was ever attested by a sufficient number of educated men; (2) since a report of the unusual arouses in man the passion of surprise and wonder, "being an agreeable emotion," man is easily swayed to believe the report for reasons of emotional satisfaction; (3) people who claim to have observed miracles were chiefly among barbarous and ignorant nations, or if civilized people believe, then, they have received them from their barbarous ancestors; (4) since prodigies are reported in all religions, we cannot dismiss these stories as falsehoods without destroying faith in events on which Christians have built in the past.[20]

Finally, Hume contributed to the dissolution of deism by overthrowing its fundamental presupposition: namely, that the "religion of reason" had been monotheistic in origin and that gradually it had been adulterated by priests into polytheism until it was finally restored to its pristine purity by Christianity. Beginning with the crudest factors of experience, Hume insisted that religion did not originate in reason, but in the feelings of primitive man, and that therefore polytheism was the primary form of religion. Assuming that there has been a gradual evolution from the lower to the higher, he traced the development of religious systems, ethics and philosophy in an ascending scale throughout the ages, and claimed that under the influence of powerful natural events it came to pass that monotheism superseded polytheism.

With regard to his personal attitude toward religion the books of Hume offer conflicting reports. In his *Natural History of Religion* he declares himself on the side of theism and professes to arrive at it by reasoning. On other occasions, he finds "ignorance the mother of devotion," and loses himself in skepticism.

However, the effects of Hume's critique of deism were not seen immediately, for his writings were comprehended only gradually. For

[20] David Hume, *Concerning Human Understanding* (Chicago: The Open Court Publishing Company, 1926), pp. 114 ff.

the moment his ideas—so far as their general influence was concerned—were considered in line with the ideas of Voltaire in France. It is evident that the English people had grown tired of the Freethinkers. The decay of interest in the topic was marked by the fact that the opinions of Hume failed to stimulate curiosity or antagonism. Yet it is of the greatest importance to keep in mind that the fundamental philosophical ideas of Hume had a profound influence upon Kant and through him upon the final development of German rationalism.

BIBLIOGRAPHY

Allen, A. V. G. *The Continuity of Christian Thought.* Boston: Houghton Mifflin Company, 1894.

Burtt, E. A. *Types of Religious Philosophy.* New York: Harper & Bros., 1951.

Colie, R. L. *Light and Enlightenment.* London: Cambridge University Press, 1957.

Cragg, G. R. *From Puritanism to the Age of Reason.* London: Cambridge University Press, 1950.

Durant, Will. *The Story of Philosophy.* Toronto: Irwin & Gordon, 1927.

Farrar, Adam S. *A Critical History of Free Thought.* London: John Murray, 1862.

Heffelbower, S. G. *The Relation of John Locke to English Deism.* 1918.

Hirsch, Emanuel. *Geschichte der neueren evangelischen Theologie.* Vol. I, 1949. Vol. III, 1951.

Hunt, John. *Religious Thought in England.* 3 vols. 1870 ff.

Lechler, G. V. *Geschichte des englischen Deismus.* 1841.

Leland, John. *A View of the Principal Deistical Writers,* 1754. 3rd ed. London: Longman, Hurst, Rees, 1839.

McGiffert, A. C. *Protestant Thought before Kant.* New York: Charles Scribner's Sons, 1911.

Pattison, Mark. "Tendencies of Religious Thought in England, 1688-1750," *Essays and Reviews,* 1860.

Simon, T. *Grundriss der Geschichte der neueren Philosophie in ihrer Beziehung zur Religion.* 1920.

Tulloch, John. *Rational Theology and Christian Philosophy in the Seventeenth Century.* 2 vols. 1874.

Wolf, A. (trans.). *Spinoza's Short Treatises on God, Man, and His Well-Being.* New York: Russell & Russell, 1963.

CHAPTER VI

THE FRENCH NATURALISTS

The term naturalism is used here in order to distinguish the French movement from the deistic movement in England. In many ways the two are the same. While more prominent English Deists like Toland and Tindal labored to relate natural religion to revealed religion, this endeavor was absent in France. French naturalism was not theological in character. This is easily explained. The France of Louis XIV was not Protestant, as was England, and in France it was the policy to use the official Roman Catholic church to hold the individual in the bondage of political absolutism. This produced a reaction against the Church among the French liberals. In England, where freedom of the press had prevailed since 1693 and where religious freedom was recognized in ever increasing degree, antipathy to traditional religion was not against the Church as such. In France the development drifted from the deism of Voltaire into the atheism and mechanical materialism of Lamettrie, Diderot, and von Holbach, until, with the idealism of Rousseau, a certain new element became engrafted upon the movement. The whole development issued in the French Revolution.

Several men may be mentioned as precursors of naturalism. Michel de Montaigne (d. 1592) was a skeptic whose fundamental thinking was expressed in two questions: "What do I know?" and "What does it matter?" He had observed the political exploitation of religion and pessimistically charged that religion incited controversies, wars, intolerance, and vice.

Pierre Charron (d. 1602) also sounded the note of a skepticism which found increasing acceptance among the cultured in France. At first this skepticism was negative. Gradually, however, it acquired some positive content from the English Deists and natural philosophy as well as through Voltaire.

Pierre Bayle (d. 1706), son of a Calvinist minister and author of the

Critical Dictionary, pointed to the impossibility of a religion established upon reason. This was directed against John Locke, who had insisted upon harmony between religion and reason. The objection of Bayle led the skeptics of his age to abandon revelation and to hold to reason. Voltaire thanked Bayle for having taught him the art of doubting. Bayle also raised the question: How can there be a good God and yet so much evil in the world? Rejecting the customary explanations as unsatisfactory, he suggested that the simplest solution would be in the Manichaean admission of a good and an evil God. If there is only one God we must deny either his goodness or his omnipotence. Leibnitz wrote against Bayle in his *Theodizee*. Bayle also insisted upon the absolute independence of morality from religion: Religion would adulterate the morality of the state. On this basis he demanded a separation of the Church from the state, and advocated that absolute tolerance be extended to include atheists.

Voltaire

Voltaire's real name was Francois Marie Arouet (1694-1788). "In Voltaire eighteenth-century France had its keenest wit. No philosopher, vain, self-seeking, but with genuine hatred of tyranny, especially of religious persecution, no one ever attacked religion with a more unsparing ridicule." [1] This does not mean that he was an atheist. In a letter to Diderot he insists upon recognizing "a great Intelligence," a "Workman infinitely able," who "has made everything that exists." [2] Against the materialistic Holbach he spoke of "a divine organizing intelligence." [3]

During a stay in England (1726-29) he became a deist. He believed in the existence of God and in a primitive natural religion of simple morality. He rejected all religion based on the authority of the Bible or of the Church. Like Locke, Voltaire insisted upon tolerance, but like Bayle, he differed from Locke in his views on the harmony between revelation and reason. Nonetheless, he could admire the wisdom of God who had constructed this universe. He believed in the so-called

[1] Williston Walker, *History of the Christian Church* (New York: Charles Scribner's Sons, 1959), p. 442.

[2] S. G. Tallentyre, *Voltaire in His Letters* (New York: G. P. Putnam's Sons, 1919), p. 81.

[3] Pellissier, *Voltaire Philosophe* (Paris, 1908), p. 172.

teleological proof of God's existence and combined the cosmological with it. Everything in this world has its cause in something else. He reasoned that this concatenation of causes must lead us back to a first cause, which is God.

Voltaire had his doubts on immortality, but later he recognized that immortality, along with the existence of God, was a belief necessary for the maintenance of order in society. He remarked that "If God did not exist, it would be necessary to invent him." At his home in Ferney, just inside the Swiss border, near France, he erected his own church with the inscription: "Voltaire erected this to God." In an article entitled "Theist," Voltaire gave expression to his faith. A theist, he said, is one who firmly believes in the existence of a supreme being who is good and powerful, "who punishes, without cruelty, all crimes, and recompenses with goodness all virtuous actions."[4] A theist, therefore, does not join a church or sect, for his religion does not consist of dogmas or ritual. For the theist, according to Voltaire, to worship is to do good; to submit to God is his creed.

His stay in England converted Voltaire to the natural philosophy which issued from the thinking of Newton and Clarke. From Locke he accepted the theory of knowledge. The main principles of his ethics were those of Shaftesbury. The English Deists in general gave him the critical method and his conception of a natural religion. He praised the moral life and taught that the voice of reason is absolutely reliable on virtues and vices. He rejoiced over the coming of the Age of Reason. To him, however, it was only for the well-bred; the common people, the shoemakers and servants, were to have no part in the glories of this condition. This is a frequently recurring remark in his voluminous writings. It was here that Rousseau differed fundamentally from Voltaire.

Voltaire stripped English deism of its religious and theological interests, and reduced religion to simple morality and rational metaphysics. He employed historical and ethnological material in his investigations to a greater degree than the English Deists had done. In this way he contributed effectively to the creation of a philosophy of history and a philosophy of religion. The rise of the positive religions is to be found in children and savages. Ignorance and fear of nature explain

[4] Durant, *op. cit.*, p. 265.

the rise of religious ideas. This line of thinking he applied to biblical history. It was in these investigations and criticisms that Voltaire made many frivolous statements which have earned him the reputation of having been an atheist. Voltaire was frivolous, but he was not an atheist. But with his frivolity he taught his age to mock at essential things in religion.

Voltaire's major arguments were: (1) The relativity of and analogies between the various religions; (2) the natural-pragmatic explanations of the Jewish-Christian religion in the interest of putting Christianity in a co-ordinate relation to the pagan religions and stripping the history of Christianity of its sacred character; (3) the inclination of ancient peoples to believe in miracles and the contemporary absence of miracles; (4) the extension of paganism as compared with the smallness of Judaism and Christianity; (5) the antiquity of the human race as compared with the newness of Christianity.

By engaging in these investigations Voltaire created a systematized theory of the history of religions. In the tribal god he saw the beginning of polytheism. Monotheistic Judaism produced the Christian and Mohammedan religions. Moses was a shrewd politician. The prophets were enthusiasts like the dervishes, or else epileptics. Jesus, to him, was a good man, but vain and enthusiastic, a visionary like George Fox. According to Voltaire, Jesus deceived his age by miracles. The disciples were deceived deceivers, falsifiers, and tricksters. The Christian religion received life only through its union with Platonism. The doctrinal controversies of the Church produced the barbarism of the Middle Ages and the shedding of blood that marked the Reformation and post-Reformation ages. Now the Age of Reason was opening the gates for a common morality which would bring peace and harmony to all.

In his younger years Voltaire was an optimist, although he took exception to the teaching of Leibnitz that this is the "best of worlds." The earthquake at Lisbon in 1755 led him into a bitter pessimism.[5]

[5] The earthquake occurred on All Saints Day when the churches were crowded with worshipers. About thirty thousand people perished. When the French clergy explained the disaster as a punishment for the sins of the people, Voltaire broke forth in a passionate poem: "The universe belies you, and your heart refutes a hundred times your mind's conceit" (quoted by Durant, *op. cit.*, p. 247).

THE TREND TOWARD MATERIALISM

Etienne de Condillac (d. 1780) was the philosopher of sensualism.[6] Locke had distinguished between outward and inner perceptions, between sensations and reflections. Condillac wanted to deduce all activity of the mind from outward perception. All life of the individual, even revelation, is deduced from sensation. He was not a materialist, but the drift was toward materialism.

Claude Helvetius (d. 1771) applied sensualism to the ethical sphere: We are trained by our environment. Egotism is the motive of all our action. The proper ambition is to be cultivated. Beside this idea religion is superfluous. True religion is identical with morality and knows no mysteries. The Church is criticized because it deals with private vices and ignores the interests of society.

Descartes, in his *Treatise on the Passions of the Soul,* had said that the limbs can be moved by the objects of the senses, and by the spirits without the aid of the soul.[7] Julien de Lamettrie (d. 1751) extended this concept to man. The mind is a function of the physical organism, a mere secretion of the brain. The only difference between the brain of man and the brain of an animal is development. There can be no immortality because the spirit (mind) perishes with the brain. Neither can we speak of a divine mind governing the universe, because the principle of life, movement, and sensation is in matter. But matter is animated; the universe is full of souls. At this point he admits that souls are more than machines.

Upon the foundation of this materialism Lamettrie erects a corresponding ethics. The purpose of life is happiness. He admits that there is a happiness of a higher and lower value, a happiness of a more lasting and of a passing sort. Nothing must interfere with that happiness. Repentance and pangs of conscience are to be rejected because they make man unhappy. Atheism is necesssary for the realization of this happiness. It must be kept in mind, of course, that this radicalism was a reaction against a persecuting church. The writings of Lamettrie have become a storehouse for all his successors in materialistic thought.

[6] Cf. his *Treatise on Sensations,* trans. Geraldine Carr (London: Favil Press, 1930).

[7] Cf. E. S. Haldane and G. R. T. Ross, translators, *The Philosophical Works of Descartes,* 2 vols. (New York, 1955).

Denis Diderot (d. 1783) was editor of the famous *Encyclopedie* or *Dictionnaire raisonne* (1751-66). He had d'Alembert as his chief assistant. They were assisted by such men as Voltaire, Rousseau, and von Holbach, known as the Encyclopedists. The writings of Diderot do not give us a unified philosophy because he passed through a development from theism and deism through skepticism and pantheism to materialism. The articles of the *Encyclopedie* dealing with religion and Christianity reflect a cautious, skeptical mind. Simon remarks: "Diderot kept himself from sinking into frivolity and cynicism by an ethical enthusiasm that stayed with him through life." [8]

Baron Dietrich von Holbach (1723-1789) was born in the Palatinate. He lived in Paris, where his home was the center of the radicals and liberals of his day. Here a materialistic psychology and ethics were cultivated. Moral theories, though derived from Hobbes and Hume, lost all connection with the position of English deism. All that exists, it was held, is matter. Holbach is without question the author of the *Systeme de la Nature* (1770) which was published in the name of Mirabeau. The contents of this volume may be summarized as follows: Among the primitives, religion arose from fear and hope, and from ignorance concerning the laws of nature. The different forms of religion were developed by designing social and political leaders who were prompted by egotism and ambition or led by morbidly enthusiastic minds. Systems of metaphysics and theology arose which were based upon an animalistic personification of the forces of the universe with constant suggestion of supernatural influences. With the English Deists and with Voltaire, Christianity is understood to be a transposition of Galilean teachings into Neo-Platonic metaphysics. This is why there is in the history of theology both an extreme anthropomorphism and an abstract metaphysics. Holbach dismissed the teleology of English deism and emphasized man's dependence upon the cold causality of the laws of nature. In connection with this mechanistic materialism he saw the essence of morality in the instinct of self-preservation on the part of race and individuals. In a bolder way than Bayle he said that ethics had become corrupted by religion.

[8] T. Simon, *Grundriss der Geschichte der neueren Philosophie in ihrer Beziehung zur Religion* (1920), p. 56.

The Naturalism of Rousseau

Jean Jacques Rousseau, born in Geneva (1712-1778), gave an altogether different turn to the English deism that Voltaire had imported into France. The constructive thought in his work of twenty-two volumes is contained chiefly in his *Emile* and in the *Social Contract*, both published in 1762. He turned away from Voltaire's emphasis upon the Enlightenment as an intellectual reform. Although he contributed articles to the *Encyclopedie*, he did not understand the comprehensive intellectual ambition of Diderot. He was fundamentally opposed to creating an intellectual aristocracy in which the common people were regarded as incapable of participating in the fruits of an age of reason. He would have nothing to do with the materialism of the Holbach circles. He could see nothing but a gloss over the degradation of society in the Enlightenment as cultivated by Voltaire and the Encyclopedists.

Salvation was to be sought in a return to nature. Human society had taken its beginning in a garden of nature where men lived as happy children. The "war of all against all" was not with the race at its beginning, but came with civilization, which developed the division of labor, the concept of property, and that brutal egotism which operated on the contrast between poor and rich, servants and masters. Man was good until civilization and art invaded his simplicity, corrupted his virtues, and transformed him into a suffering, sinful being.[9] In *Emile*, Rousseau proposed a program of education that would lead back to nature. Pedagogy is to proceed on the assumption of an innate virtue or moral sense which he distinguishes from acquired ideas. Force is to be avoided as much as possible so that nature may have a chance to develop.

The religion of Rousseau is established not upon dogmatic knowledge but upon a certain feeling which is not easy for the historian to describe. He means the feeling of the naive and disinterested understanding of the uncultured people. Troeltsch remarks: "With Rousseau natural religion takes on a new meaning. Nature is no longer universality or rationality in the cosmic order, in contrast to special

[9] Cf. the analysis of Rousseau's "Essay on the Origin of Languages" by Charles W. Hendel, *Jean-Jacques Rousseau: Moralist* ("Library of Liberal Arts" Series [New York: The Bobbs-Merrill Company, 1934]).

supernatural and positive phenomena, but inwardness, originality, and intuition in contrast to artificiality and reflection."[10] Although the system of Rousseau shows significant features of German idealism, it was irreconcilable with a religion of revelation in which sin and grace, law and gospel, occupy a central position.

In conclusion a quotation from Turner is in order: "If we except Rousseau, the representatives of the age of Enlightenment were men of meager or at most of mediocre intellectual ability, who failed to leave any lasting impression on the development of speculative thought. Indeed Voltaire, who certainly knew the age in which he lived, pronounced it to be an age of trivialities."[11] The French Naturalists, more than the English Deists, provided the radically irreligious minds of Europe in the eighteenth century and succeeding ages with the thoughts and ideas with which the Catholic and Protestant versions of the Christian faith were combatted and ridiculed. German rationalism was of a little later date. Notwithstanding its shallowness, German rationalism was far more religious in its points of emphasis and had its own history.

BIBLIOGRAPHY

BARTH, KARL. *From Rousseau to Ritschl.* London: SCM Press, 1959.

BESTERMAN, THEODORE (ed.). *Studies on Voltaire and the Eighteenth Century.* 16 vols. Geneva, 1955 ff.

GREEN, F. C. *Jean Jacques Rousseau: A Critical Study of His Life and Writings.* London: Cambridge University Press, 1955.

HIRSCH, EMANUEL. *Geschichte der neueren evangelischen Theologie* I, 1949, 63 ff., and 1951, 58 ff.

POMEAU, R. *La religion de Voltaire.* 1956.

ROLLAND, ROMAIN. *The Living Thoughts of Rousseau.* Toronto: Longmans, 1939.

TROELTSCH, ERNST. Articles on *Aufklärung* in *PRE,* II, 225 ff., and on *Deismus, PRE,* IV, 532 ff.

WADE, I. O. *The Search of a New Voltaire.* Philadelphia: American Philosophical Society, 1958.

WADINGER, R. *Voltaire, A Reformer in the Light of the French Revolution.* Geneva, 1959.

[10] *PRE,* IV, 557.

[11] William Turner, *History of Philosophy* (London: Ginn & Co., 1957), p. 505.

CHAPTER VII

GERMAN RATIONALISM

Theological rationalism can be observed in varying forms in the history of all religions. There was rationalism in the Church long before it appeared in the theology of the Enlightenment in the eighteenth century. One needs only to think of the Arianism of the ancient Church and of the Socinians during the Reformation.

All through the history of doctrine there has been the problem of properly relating reason and revelation. Both revelation and reason were accepted as sources of Christian truth. Catholic and Protestant theologians alike distinguished between articles of faith like the general belief in God and immortality, which have their source in both reason and revelation, and those articles which rest purely on revelation. The dividing line between these two sources, however, was never absolutely defined, and reason succeeded more and more in gaining ground as the foundation of Christian doctrine.

In Germany it was Gottfried Leibnitz (d. 1716) who sought to mediate between rational deism and the supernatural revelation of Christianity. He was of the opinion that the existence of an omnipotent and all-wise God can be positively proved by reason. This God created the best of all possible worlds.[1] The evil in this world is not positively bad, but is something negative, lacking in perfect good. Evil, then, was understood as an aid to the development of good. Leibnitz represents a positive optimism in his estimate of the world and man. This optimism blazed the trail for a fundamental trait of the modern age, especially of rationalism, and was in decided opposition to the pessimism produced by the conservative Protestant doctrine of sin. To Leibnitz the positive dogmas of Christianity appeared not as

[1] Leibnitz, *Theodicy,* trans. E. M. Huggard (London: Routledge & Kegan, 1952). Cf. H. W. B. Joseph, *Lectures on the Philosophy of Leibnitz* (Oxford: Clarendon Press, 1949).

contrary to reason, but rather as above reason. He aimed at mediating between rationalism and supernaturalism, and at creating a kind of super-rationalism.

Christian Wolff (d. 1754) popularized this line of thought. He was the real philosophical founder of early, pre-Kantian theological rationalism. It was Wolff who formulated the rational proofs for faith in a personal God and a personal immortality. He preached the necessity of a practical and humane morality to secure temporal and eternal happiness. Theoretically he did not deny a Christian revelation which was above reason, but he held that this revelation has to harmonize with natural religion and can be real only in so far as it does harmonize.

In the course of further development the strength of supernatural revelation was reduced to and identified with natural religion. In the so-called "Wolfenbüttel Fragments," published by Lessing, Hermann Reimarus (d. 1768) denied every special revelation and made natural religion the criterion of every historical religion, including Christianity. At the same time he sought critically to dissolve the historic foundation of Christianity as we have it in the Bible. Reimarus emphasized the late origin of the biblical books and called particular attention to inconsistencies and contradictions. He particularly pointed out inconsistencies, especially in the reports concerning the resurrection accounts and thereby called their credibility into queston.[2]

The ideas of the Enlightenment gained further momentum through the writings of G. E. Lessing (d. 1786), poet and literary critic who, next to Goethe and Schiller, ranks highest among the German classicists. Lessing agreed with the Deists and Rationalists that true religion is a religion of reason, but dissented from their view that religion reaches a rational stage only as the culmination of a long course of development. In the essay *Uber die Erziehung des Menschaeschlechts* Lessing asserts that revelation ought to be understood as education. As education gives nothing which an individual, in due time, could not discover by himself, so revelation gives nothing which reason, if left to itself, would not discover. Revelation simply expedites the process.

According to Lessing religion degenerated from an original monotheism to polytheism and idolatry. In order to correct this unhappy

[2] For a review of the controversy, cf. Albert Schweitzer, *Quest of the Historical Jesus* (London: A. & C. Black, 1931), pp. 13 ff.

development God chose Israel to educate the world for monotheism. He proceeded like a wise teacher. The Old Testament is a sort of a primer; it does not contain everything which an adult considers indispensable. For a long time the idea of divine transcendence remained unknown; likewise, the concept of immortality is not taught in the primer. A primer serves only the needs of a certain age. To make it acceptable to a growing mind one must read more into it than it actually contains. This was the task of the Jewish rabbis. Yet a more perfect teacher was necessary: Christ. He became the first dependable teacher of the doctrine of the immortality of the soul. His Apostles provided the world with the New Testament, the second primer. In the meantime the non-Jewish world had also matured. Monotheism and immortality were established as propositions of human reason. Lessing did not suggest dispensing with the New Testament and was opposed to the too hasty departure from the conventional forms of religion. They are still necessary for the vast multitude of people.

For Lessing, natural religion contains the whole truth of religion. All positive religions are conditioned by sociological factors. They are true to the extent that an agreement concerning nonessentials was necessary; they are false in so far as every convention involves a weakening and suppression of the essentials. The religion *of* Christ, the religion which He Himself practiced, is the true religion; the Christian religion is something quite different.

In the play *Nathan der Weise* (Nathan the Wise), Lessing took issue with orthodox Lutherans, particularly Pastor J. M. Goeze of Hamburg. In the play Lessing sought to impress upon orthodox Lutherans that they must verify their claim to be the true Church by moral excellence.

The influence of Immanuel Kant (d. 1804) deserves special attention. It is true that Kant, in his *Critique of Pure Reason*, upset the self-confidence of the Rationalists, especially their proofs of the existence of God and of immortality. On the other hand, through his *Critique of Practical Reason* he strengthened the confidence of the age in rationalistic moralism as the real essence of Christianity. Especially in his essay "Religion within the Limits of Pure Reason" (1793) he set himself the task of completely reconstructing religion according to the principles of rationalistic moralism. This essay became especially typical of the second stage of rationalism and exercised an influence far beyond Kant's own time. Its teachings had a lasting effect on the theological liberalism of the Continent and on modernism in the English-speaking world. The essay's basic thought presents a characteristic picture of rationalism.

The Theologians of Rationalism

Frequently all the theologians of this period have been thought of as being of one stripe. This is not quite correct. Two main schools of thought can be distinguished among them: the Supernaturalists and the Rationalists proper. The former exerted a kind of restraining influence in the earlier period of the Enlightenment; they marked the transition from Orthodoxy and pietism to rationalism. Among the supernaturalists were: S. J. Baumgarten at Halle (d. 1757); J. F. Buddeus at Halle and Jena (d. 1729); J. L. Mosheim at Helmstedt and Göttingen (d. 1755); C. M. Pfaff at Tübingen (d. 1760); J. G. Walch at Jena, editor of the works of Luther (d. 1775); and C. W. F. Walch at Jena and Göttingen (d. 1784). Relying on Kant's axiom that pure reason cannot establish religious truth, a second group of Supernaturalists emphasized that reason cannot deny the claims of Christianity. Among the proponents of this view were F. V. Reinhard at Wittenberg and Dresden (d. 1812) and G. C. Knapp at Halle (d. 1825). They labored to prove by rational means the possibility, necessity, and reality of the content of supernatural revelation. Truth was to be proved by Scripture. The idea was that Scripture, not reason, was to decide in matters of religion; but reason establishes what the teaching of Scripture is.

If rationalism reminds us of Socinianism, supernaturalism resembles Arminianism. The Trinity, the two natures of Christ, and the mystical union were not denied, but neither were they emphasized. Christ was the Redeemer, but he was subordinated to the Father. The fall of man was replaced by a mere inclination to evil and correspondingly there were Pelagian elements in the teachings about the way of salvation. There was variation in the teaching on the work of the Holy Spirit.[3]

The father of popular rationalism was Johann Salomo Semler. Edu-

[3] Cf. Hirsch, *op. cit.*, Vol. II; V, 70 ff.

cated at Halle in pietistic surroundings, and coming under the influence of Baumgarten, he became a leading figure of the new movement. As professor in Halle (from 1752) he soon was the recognized leader of the theological faculty until his death in 1791. In 1793 Eichhorn referred to him as a "Reformer of theology" and as the "greatest theologian of the century."[4] His position was mediating rather than radical. He wanted to restate the dogma of the Reformation by means of the new critical approach to Scripture and Church history.

A similar position was taken by Johann David Michaelis, who was born at Halle, 1717, and died at Göttingen in 1791. Notwithstanding his pietistic training, he applied his knowledge of Oriental languages to a comparative study of Old Testament Hebrew. His historico-grammatical approach gained momentum in the teaching of his pupil and colleague J. G. Eichhorn.[5] At Leipzig J. A. Ernesti (d. 1781), in his *Institutio interpretatis Novi Testamenti* (1761), laid down the principle that the New Testament, like any other book, has to be interpreted by the historico-grammatical method.

The study of Church history was put on a new basis by Johann Lorenz von Mosheim, professor and chancellor of the university of Göttingen (d. 1755). Influenced by Gottfried Arnold, Mosheim became the founder of the "pragmatic method," striving after objectivity rather than being motivated by confessional polemics. Theologically Mosheim vacillated between Orthodoxy, pietism, and the older rationalism.[6] After Mosheim the study of the history of doctrine developed as a separate theological discipline. Its object was to show that the dogma of the Church was a developing quantity. Dogma is not static and hence not absolute. Inevitably this new understanding of dogma called for a reinterpretation of confessional subscription to the Book of Concord by professors at the universities and pastors in general.[7] This understanding also had an influence on shaping the study of Christian symbolics. The outspoken humanistic trait of rationalism in its criticism of traditional orthodoxy made the savage method of discussing the differences between the churches of Christendom exceedingly distasteful. The new symbolics of J. Planck (1796), and soon after

[4] *Ibid.*, IV, 28 ff.
[5] *Ibid.*, IV, 32 ff.
[6] *Ibid.*, II, 354 ff.
[7] Hirsch discusses a controversy relating to this problem in *ibid.*, IV, 102 ff.

him Philip Marheineke, the special "father of comparative symbolics," laid the foundations for symbolics as a comparative science by which all the various traits of the churches and sects were examined. This examination was conducted along the lines of the historical approach of Marheinecke and under his dictum that the peace of history must be drawn over all critical discussion.[8]

The reconstruction of the Church's dogma according to the principles of rationalism was systematically carried out by J. F. Roehr of Weimar in his *Briefe über den Rationalismus* (1813) and later in his *Grund-und Glaubenssätze der evangelisch-protestantischen Kirche* (1832). Roehr declared that reason is the only principle out of which the religio-moral convictions must be developed. Reason is also the criterion for understanding and evaluating the alleged supernatural sources of traditional dogmatics. In short, he held that the Scriptures must be read critically and in the light of reason.

Next to reason, morality was looked upon as the determining and positively constructive principle. The one thing that is absolutely clear is the duty to lead a moral life. If so, then there must be a God, and our being must mean something for a future life. This idea had been expressed by the Deists in England and by most of the Naturalists in France.

Revelation is not special or supernatural; it is a matter of the universal, providential working of God. Under the heading "Divine Providence," Lutheran Orthodoxy distinguished between a "general concurrence of God" in all the actions and effects of the world and a "most special and extraordinary concurrence, peculiar to the holy writers of the Old and New Testaments." [9] In keeping with the spirit of the times, this distinction was entirely eliminated. Revelation is equated with the general manifestation of God in nature and the conscience of man. Christianity is a universal religion; it never should have become a positive religion. All supernatural traits of the Bible are dismissed as peculiar to biblical times. Stripped of what is local or temporary there is nothing of religious truth that the reason of man cannot find out for itself. In this connection attention must be called to the typical

[8] P. K. Marheinecke, *Konfessionskunde* (1810 ff.).

[9] Heinrich Schmid, *The Doctrinal Theology of the Evangelical Lutheran Church* (Minneapolis: Augsburg Publishing House, 1961), p. 185.

rationalistic exegete of the New Testament, H. E. G. Paulus, who, as a nonbeliever in miracles, worked miracles in his art of accommodating the tenets of rationalism to the text of the New Testament reports.[10]

The position of Christ in the dogmatics of rationalism is negatively formulated by Roehr. He says that Jesus is not the "object" of religion; he is only its "subject" in the double significance of teacher and ethical example. Roehr proceeds to attribute to Jesus a singular position in the history of religion: "Rationalism reveres in Jesus a man sent by God as a teacher of truth in the customary meaning of this expression. He was a man in whose life and mission Providence worked itself out in a select way." [11] "Jesus was a man in the fullest and most comprehensive meaning of that term, a natural product of his people and his age, but in regard to spirit, wisdom, virtue, and religion excelled by no mortal of the past or future, a hero of humanity in the highest sense." [12] "The historical elements of his life are not without value, but they are means to make the religious teachings real, comprehensible and interesting for the most common mind." [13]

Naturally this view of Christ left no room for the doctrine of the Trinity. As early as 1764 the Trinity was explicitly denied by W. A. Teller in his *Lehrbuch des christlichen Glaubens.* Semler, in his translation of Samuel Clarke's *The Scripture Doctrine of the Trinity* (1712), expressed in the preface a view bordering on Arianism. The Rationalists dismissed the idea of the vicarious significance of the death of Christ. It became customary to reject the Church's doctrine as sacrilegious. As the "waiting Father" God forgives without satisfaction made by an innocent one.[14] The biblical narrative of the devil and of demons was summarily dismissed in the same fashion by the Rationalists as an accommodation to the prevailing sentiment of the times. The "possessed" in the New Testament were simply mentally or emotionally deranged people.

For the Rationalists the Church is only a human institution, yet at the same time a distinct proof that Divine Providence intended to make the Master's ethical religion of reason accessible to man. The Church

[10] For a list of examples, cf. Schweitzer, *op. cit.,* pp. 51 ff.
[11] J. F. Roehr, *Briefe über den Rationalismus,* p. 16.
[12] *Ibid.,* p. 26.
[13] *Ibid.,* p. 33.
[14] J. G. Toellner, *Der thätige Gehorsam Jesu Christi,* 1768.

is essentially a society for the promotion of personal and civic virtues. The sacraments of the Church are only symbols; baptism is an act of initiation, while the Lord's Supper is a sentimental symbolical feast.[15] Confirmation, on the other hand, received much attention as a dedication to Christian virtues and as a commencement from grade school.

Summary

In one respect rationalism has been regarded as a reaction to the extreme intellectualism which prevailed in the orthodoxy of the seventeenth century and which was expressed in the theology of the Wittenberg theologians at the end of the syncretistic controversies. It cannot be denied that the detailed doctrinal definitions such as were voiced by Abraham Calovius in his *Consensus Repetitus* (1664), which went far beyond the Formula of Concord, were bound to result in a reaction. The Lutheran theology of the seventeenth century, particularly in its constant conflict with Calvinism, bled itself to death. The end result was a stagnant theology which could detect no new theological problems and was unable to employ historical methods.

The chief explanation for the rise of rationalism, however, lies in the rise of a modern philosophy which greatly stimulated humanistic thought. In theological language, this humanistic rationalism was undisguised Pelagianism, which held that man's nature is essentially good and that man is able to suppress evil and make himself acceptable to God.

The utilitarian and eudaemonistic character of this new philosophy was very conspicuous. Its central concern was for individual or social well-being and it often lost itself in the adulteration of hymns and absurdities in the pulpit. There was little interest in moral action as such; everything had to be done with a practical purpose in view. This called forth the criticism of Kant.

In Christology this rationalism was "Jesus-centric," not "Christocentric." The distinction between Christ, the God-Man, and Jesus, the ideal man, began to be discussed. Jesus was to be taken, not as the object, but as the subject of faith. The Church ceased to be a divine

[15] A pastor in Bavaria administered communion with the words: "Eat this bread! The Spirit of devotion rest on you with His rich blessing! Drink a little wine! Virtue does not lie in this wine; it lies in you, in the divine doctrine and in God." See H. Kurtz, *op. cit.,* III, par. 171, 4.

institution established for leading souls to salvation through the means of grace. It was converted into an ethical-religious school for the moral education of man.

Concerning the final disintegration of rationalism, Reinhold Seeberg says: "When tendencies and schools finally have achieved the much coveted dominion over their antagonist, then, as a rule, their days are numbered."[16] This was the case with the old rationalism. A development set in which spelled the defeat of rationalism all along the line. Kant, himself a contributor to a religion of reason restricted to ethical interests, demonstrated the inability of reason to deal with the problems which perennially confront the religious man. Among the philosophers it was chiefly Jacobi, who claimed to be "a pagan with his head, but with his heart a Christian," who labored to take religion out of the confines of pure reason and to discover it in the depth of the inner soul. In so doing Jacobi revived and stimulated what had been submerged under the prevailing system of rationalism. Even Lessing, who used seemingly anti-Christian language, simply wanted to make clear that the truth of Christianity does not depend upon external proofs, but must rest upon inner experience. Defective or incomplete as such a position was, it contributed to disestablishing the rationalism of pure reason. Ultimately it was a series of articles directed against Roehr in 1837 by the Church historian K. A. von Hase which is credited with having dealt the deathblow to popular rationalism.[17] But even before this time a revived pietism had sprung up in reaction to the religious barrenness of rationalism, and exercised a deep influence upon many, especially upon the younger theologians.

Postscript: Fools for Christ in the Age of Reason

Even though the Rationalists were dominant in the Church and theology, the old faith was not dead. It had a few outstanding representatives who dared be "fools for Christ."[18] The most remarkable of these was Johann Georg Hamann, a contemporary and fellow citizen of Kant in Königsberg (d. 1778). He used the skepticism of Hume

[16] *Die Kirche Deutschlands im neunzehnten Jahrhundert* (1903), p. 15.

[17] See "Anti-Roehr," K. A. von Hase, *Werke,* 12 vols. (Leipzig, 1890-93). VIII, sec. I, 35-414.

[18] The term is borrowed from Jaroslav Pelikan.

in order to combat the religious agnosticism of both Hume and Kant. Hume had questioned the validity of the causal law. Necessity, he wrote, "exists in the mind, not in the object." [19] Hamann turned the argument around: If the mind establishes the principle of necessity, no objective scientific argument can invalidate the biblical claim of supernatural revelation. Hume had honored the principle of belief.[20] Faith then is a personal decision, an existential commitment.[21]

Following his conversion in London in 1758, Hamann's whole thinking revolved around the Scriptures.[22] In the Bible he discovered that all self-knowledge is a descent into hell. He recognized not only his moral depravity but also the impotence of human reason. The Rationalists' preference for the abiding ideas of a universal religion was sheer paganism to him. The Hebrew mode of speech, he learned from Scripture, is concrete. The Word of the Lord is a thing to be seen (Jer. 2:31). According to the Rationalists, God "accommodated" himself to the crude concepts of the Hebrew people. But in the eyes of Hamann God "condescended" into the world of the Bible. We do not arrive at the truth by abstraction; rather, the truth is given us "in, with, and under" the words of the Bible. Nature and history are the two great commentaries on the divine Word, and the Word is the only key to unlock a knowledge of both.[23]

The difference between Judaism and Christianity is not in the so-called eternal truths and dogmas. The difference concerns historical truth: God in Christ. Hence Luther's *theologia crucis* became very dear to Hamann. All knowledge of God is indirect. Faith, not reason, is the hand by which fellowship with God is established.[24] The Rationalists regarded enlightened Jews as members of the Christian religion, for they too considered faith in God, virtue and immortality to be the

[19] Hume, *op. cit.*, p. 214.

[20] Cf. Hume's discussion of miracles, *ibid.*, pp. 114 ff. and Hamann's letter to Herder in Ronald Gregor Smith, *J. G. Hamann, A Study in Christian Existence* (London: Collins, 1960), p. 214.

[21] For Hamann's influence on Kierkegaard cf. Walter Lowrie, *J. G. Hamann, An Existentialist* (Princeton: Princeton University Press, 1950), p. 5, and Smith, *op. cit.*, pp. 18 ff.

[22] See "Thoughts about my Life," Smith, *op. cit.*, pp. 139 ff.

[23] *Ibid.*, p. 166.

[24] Fritz Blanke, *Hamann-Studien* (1956), p. 45. Blanke regards Hamann as a man who excelled all his contemporaries in his knowledge of Luther. *Ibid.*, pp. 61 ff.

very essence of true religion. In 1783 Moses Mendelsohn, the "German Plato" and friend of Lessing, published a book *Jerusalem*, in which he maintained that God had revealed to Israel not a new religion, but rather a new law. He therefore demands of man not faith, but moral action. Hamann replied with his *Golgotha und Scheblimini* (1784), which contains the most trenchant criticism of rationalism.[25] Christianity is not a system of morality; its core is "the promises, fulfillments and sacrifices which God has made and achieved for the benefit of men. This is the victory that overcomes the world" (I John 5:4).

We shall refer only briefly to three other men who bravely withstood the onslaught of rationalism. The first one is F. C. Oetinger (d. 1782). He was called the "Magus of the South," to distinguish him from Hamann as the "Magus of the North." His system is a strange blend of mysticism, pietism, and an admixture of rationalism.

The second one is J. C. Lavater (d. 1801), a Swiss theologian, and an eccentric mystic who contributed to the decline of rationalism. He is best remembered for his three-volume work, *Aussichten in die Ewigkeit* (1769 ff.). The book deals with the afterlife and the power of the soul to attain perfection in eternity.

Finally we mention Matthias Claudius (d. 1815). In contrast to the other two writers, he is the representative of a sober, nonmystical type of piety. Faith ought not to be rationalized; instead, reason should be spiritualized. As a Christian layman, he was undogmatic in his faith, yet he held to Jesus Christ as his stay in life and comforter in death. He was the first to write in a semi-devotional way for the German reading public. He was also the author of a number of hymns, among them the one which begins, "We plough the fields and scatter the good seed on the land."

BIBLIOGRAPHY

HAZARD, P. *Die Herrschaft der Vernunft: Das europäische Denken im 18. Jahrhundert.* 1949.

HIRSCH, EMANUEL. *Geschichte der neueren evangelischen Theologie*, Vol. IV, 1952.

HURST, J. F. *A History of Rationalism.* New York: Eaton & Mains, 1901.

[25] The title alludes to the crucified and exalted Lord (Ps. 110:1, "Sit thou at my right hand"—Hebrew: *scheblimini*). For an abridged English translation see Smith, *op. cit.*, pp. 224 ff.

LECKY, WILLIAM E. H. *A History of the Rise and Influence of the Spirit of Rationalism in Europe.* 2 vols. London: Longmans, Green & Co., 1865.

LOWRIE, WALTER. *J. G. Hamann, An Existentialist.* Princeton: University Press, 1950.

MAURER, WILHELM. *Aufklärung: Idealism und Restauration.* 2 vols. 1930.

NADLER, JOSEPH. *Johann Georg Hamann: Sämmtliche Werke.* 5 vols. Vienna, 1949 ff.

SMITH, RONALD G. *J. G. Hamann, A Study in Christian Existence.* London: William Collins Sons & Co., 1960.

WOLFE, H. M. *Die Weltanschauung der deutschen Aufklärung in geschichtlicher Entwicklung.* 1951.

CHAPTER VIII

THE SOCINIANS

In our first chapter we referred to that group of thinkers whom George H. Williams has called evangelical Rationalists. Their original home was in the Catholic countries of Southern Europe. They voiced a strong objection to the trinitarian dogma of the historic Church. There were also Anti-Trinitarians among the Spiritualists of the Reformation, for example, Hans Denck and Sebastian Franck, who either ignored or denied the Trinity. To these names may be added that of John Campanus of the Netherlands. A man who devoted himself entirely to teaching against the Trinity was the Spaniard Michael Servetus (d. 1557), who was burned at the stake under the regime of Calvin. He held that the doctrine of the Trinity is not biblical and that it is a negation of monotheism.

Fausto Sozzini (1539-1604), an Italian, is especially significant for having laid the doctrinal foundation of anti-trinitarianism. He had inherited anti-trinitarian views along with a number of unpublished manuscripts from his uncle, Lelio Sozzini (d. 1562). The movement which became known as Socinianism was based very largely on these writings.

During the sixteenth century many theologians who were persecuted because of their religious views fled to Poland for refuge. Among them were a number of Italians with anti-trinitarian convictions: Blandrata, Alciata, Gentilis, Ochino, Lismanini. The Inquisition had driven them from Italy and, failing to find safety in the congregation of refugees in Geneva at the time of Calvin, they went to Poland. There they found favor with the nobility and succeeded in disseminating their views, especially those regarding the Trinity. Conflict soon arose between the Socinians and Anabaptists who had also sought refuge in Poland. In view of this conflict and of the general political situation which prevailed in Poland, the government denied Socinians the right of permanent residence in 1564. But Socinian teachings had already taken root and attracted a considerable company of adherents.

The Socinian movement soon split up into factions. There were conservatives who insisted upon the pre-existence of Christ and advocated the worship of Jesus. There were radicals who refused all adoration of Jesus, basing their position upon the conviction of his absolute and exclusive humanity. There were also chiliasts who expected the millennium. The question of whether Christians should accept office in the state and be allowed to bear arms was debated. There was confusion over infant baptism. These last-mentioned topics reflect Anabaptist influence.

This was the situation which existed when Fausto Sozzini appeared in Poland after a stay in Transylvania, where he had been called by George Blandratra in the Davidis conflict. Sozzini gradually succeeded in eliminating the extremes from this disunited group in Poland. He opposed the pre-existence of Jesus, but taught, against Davidis, that Jesus must be the object of worship. Other differences were settled by diplomatic accommodation to existing conditions.

The most significant event in this period of organization in Poland was the publication of the Racovian Catechism in its final form in 1605, the year after the death of Sozzini.[1] This is the historical confessional document of the old Socinians. The preparatory and fundamental work had been done by Sozzini, and was finished by theologians who were in harmony with him. The introduction states that the Catechism has no intention of binding the conscience through confessional obligation; on the contrary, it seeks to present doctrinal opinions as aids by which to find the way to eternal life which is shown by God through Christ. The Catechism then discusses the Holy Scriptures, the way of salvation, the concept of God, the person of Christ in his three offices, and the Church.

Before proceeding to a review of the doctrinal characteristics of Socinianism brief mention must be made of the developments in Transylvania which, besides Poland, was really the first seat of historical Socinianism. In that day Transylvania was exposed to invasion

[1] Racov was the intellectual center of Socinianism in Poland. The Racovian Catechism and the writings of Sozzini are published in Vols. I and II of the *Bibliotheca fratrum Polonorum,* 1656 ff. An English translation was published in London in 1818 by Thomas Rees.

by Turkey, which justified its plans for conquering the West on religious grounds. The Turks claimed that the trinitarian dogma of historic Christianity was a cover for polytheism. This charge influenced the countries which were exposed to the danger of Moslem invasion to favor the unitarian concepts.

The Hungarian government had established the policy of tolerance for all doctrinal beliefs (1568). In 1600 the opponents of trinitarianism were recognized as Unitarians. This name was accepted later. Almost all Transylvanian Unitarians had come from the Reformed church. Their intellectual center was and continued to be the school at Klausenburg. Blandrata was the outstanding leader. He was opposed very persistently by Francis Davidis, Director at Klausenburg and a former Lutheran, who rejected not only the pre-existence of Jesus but insisted, logically, that He must not be addressed in prayer. This was the "non-adorant" faction among the early Unitarians. Sozzini and Blandrata were united in denying the pre-existence of Jesus, but they rejected, illogically, the non-adorant position of Davidis and his group. It is interesting to note that a Unitarian hymnbook published in Hungary in 1865 omitted adoration of Jesus.

Historical Socinianism

It must not be overlooked that the founders of Socinianism developed in opposition to the Roman Catholic church. Philosophically their roots can be traced back to the negative-rationalistic criticism of Duns Scotus and of Erasmian humanism. In addition to this they received impulses from the Reformation. In consequence, they represented a peculiar combination of supernaturalism and humanistic rationalism which came to embrace a complex of ideas and views which are foreign to historic Christianity. In the further evolution of Socinianism these ideas and views asserted themselves.

The founders of Socinianism and their followers up to about the middle of the seventeenth century were strict biblicists and supernaturalists. This biblicism treated the Old Testament with indifference, and the New Testament is taken as the only source of revelation. There is nothing of value in the Old Testament that is not better and more clearly taught in the New Testament. The idea of inspiration has reference only to the matters of special religious truth in

Scripture. The New Testament may contain something above reason, but it does not express anything against reason. Reasonableness, then, is a special criterion of truth in Scripture.

The Socinian concept of religion may be summarized in the following brief statements: (1) Only Christians and Jews can have religion because they alone have revelation. This indicates that the Socinians had not yet arrived at the teaching of the English Deists, namely that general natural religion is fundamental and essential religion. (2) Religion consists in the knowledge of saving doctrine. For the Socinians the Church was the gathering of those who hold and profess the saving doctrine. This statement reflects the intellectualism of the scholastic age. Harnack fittingly characterized these Socinians as a "theological academy."[2] (3) Only what can be proved by reason can be Christian truth. This "material principle" of Socinianism, which anticipated Kant's essay "Religion within the Bounds of Reason," led the Socinians to eliminate from the interest of religion such things as the incarnation, the two natures of Christ, and the Trinity. (4) Only what can be used for moral purposes is religion. In the stress upon this position, Socinianism presented itself as a movement in which rationalism and moralism enter into a very close and effective relation.

As far as the doctrine of God was concerned, Socinianism was primarily interested in the attribute of unity. The Racovian Catechism calls itself "the catechism of the churches which affirm that no one except the Father of our Lord Jesus Christ be the one God of Israel." The knowledge of God's unity is necessary for salvation.[3] The Holy Spirit is nothing but God's power and influence. Where Scripture speaks of Jesus as God it is simply giving recognition to His singular relation to God.

According to the Socinians, man was created in God's image and endowed with spirit and reason. It was this distinction that gave him dominion over the rest of creation. He was created in the condition of physical mortality. The fall of man is explained as follows: Original man possessed no such wisdom and knowledge as was taught by

[2] Adolph von Harnack, *History of Dogma,* trans. Neil Buchanan (New York: Russell & Russell, 1958), VII, 163.

[3] Racovian Catechism, Question 66.

conservative theology. His knowledge was imperfect and his will untried. Concupiscence, which was stimulated by the divine commandment, overpowered him. We hear nothing of an external temptation which would invite the charge that the Creator was the author of sin. Through the fall neither Adam nor his descendants lost their freedom to choose between good and evil. The Augustinian distinction of the conservative Reformation between civil righteousness and spiritual righteousness (i.e., the purely moral and the religious righteousness) is not made.

The insistence upon absolute freedom, Socinians taught, is a truth by which the admission of an "original sin" or an acquired depravity is to be tested. The Scriptures' admonition to repentance is interpreted to mean that man can repent and be converted if he wills. The work of the Holy Spirit as a creative, divine agent of grace in conversion is not needed. Pelagius had taught this before, and Kant espoused it later when he declared that man can do this because he ought to do it. The Socinians would say: There may be such a thing as a concupiscence and an inclination to sin, but it cannot be proved that such a condition is universal. If this could be proved, it would still be no evidence of the Adamic origin of this condition. Thus went the argument of Socinianism on the subject of original sin.

Harnack, in a brilliant comparative review of the differences between the Anabaptist and the Socinian groups of the Reformation era, says this about the Socinians: "The religious motive in the deepest sense is absent in these Italians." [4] That sin apart from any specific sinful act is a condition in man, and that divine grace is needed to remedy this condition is a fact to which the human spirit and the language of prayer, song, and piety bear eloquent and forceful witness.

Because the divinity of Christ is the root of the doctrine of the Trinity, the Socinians denied the doctrines of his pre-existence, incarnation, and divinity. For them Christ was an extraordinary and unique man, born of a virgin, upon whom God conferred infinite wisdom, power, and immortality. They explained Christ's uniqueness in this way. Although he was a man and in no sense divine, Christ was miraculously elevated into heaven, where God instructed him in the truths of Christianity by which immortality would be mediated to

[4] Harnack, *op. cit.*, 118 ff.

men. Thus, the Socinians affirmed a doctrine of one God and a created Christ. For them Christ was a man, not the pre-existent or incarnate Logos. He was the son of God only in the sense that among all the sons of God, he was *prōtotokos*, the most excellent and beloved. For this reason he was worthy of worship.[5]

The concept of the atonement as a satisfaction rendered to God by Jesus through his suffering and death was also criticized and rejected by the Socinians. They stressed the necessity of the death of Christ because it is through his resurrection that redemption takes place. His death was simply the seal upon His teaching. Among the objections which Socinianism raised against vicarious atonement were these: (1) A "wrath of God" from which mankind is to be delivered would be irreconcilable with his goodness. (2) If man can forgive a wrong without satisfaction, why cannot God so forgive? This argument overlooks the fact that God is "the wholly other." (3) Socinianism's main objection was that moral guilt is not transferable and that satisfaction can be rendered only by the offender himself.[6]

The Socinian soteriology was essentially Pelagian. The fall of man has left no effect of depravity in mind and will. Man learns of God's commandments and promises, accepts the truth, exercises confidence and obeys the divine commandments by his own natural powers. For the Socinians, justification was not a divine act declaring grace and forgiveness; instead, like Arminius and the German Rationalists, they regarded faith as expressing itself in obedience and as meritorious before God. Good works and earnest striving—though they may be imperfect—are the real factors of justification. Justification never consists in the imputation of Christ's righteousness which the Socinians called a human invention. Faith justifies insofar as it issues in obedience and "because it is a work worthy in itself."

In viewing the Socinian system on this point, however, the moral earnestness at the basis of those statements should not be overlooked. But the cleavage from the soteriology of the Reformation is fundamental.

[5] Racovian Catechism, Questions 239 ff.

[6] Cf. Fausto Sozzini, *De Jesu Christo Servatore.* The fact that Sozzini calls Jesus *Servator* ("Preserver") indicates the author's view of Christianity. Jesus did not come to save man from a fallen state, but rather to preserve him in his right relationship to God.

The sacraments meant very little to the Socinians. They are not means of grace. The arguments against infant baptism are essentially the same as those of Menno Simons: Scripture offers no example, infants are incapable of recognizing Christ and confessing him as Lord. Though meaningless, infant baptism is not a sin.[7] Baptism was held to have been meant only for the early times of Christianity in order to introduce the converts from Judaism and paganism into Christianity with a public profession. Still, it may be practiced as an old tradition, even in the case of infants. The Lord's Supper is simply a memorial of Christ's death. The Socinians therefore objected consistently to the term sacrament. Baptism and the Lord's Supper are mere rites or ceremonies.[8]

Eternal punishment for the unbelievers and godless was understood as annihilation. The varied language of Jesus on this subject was explained as an accommodation to the thought patterns of his day. Believing Christians, though not born with an immortal soul, have become immortal through union with the risen Christ.

There are several points in which the old Socinians had something in common with some of the Anabaptist groups: (1) Discipline was strict. They followed the Augustinian principle that Church discipline might be private where the sin was not public, but that it must be public where public offense was given. In the latter case social avoidance was the milder penalty, and formal excommunication the severest penalty. (2) Although they rejected interference in matters of Church discipline, the Socinians were loyal to the government under all circumstances. (3) They discouraged seeking redress of private grievances by appealing to the civil law; also the use of weapons. Nonetheless their position on these matters was flexible. Their general attitude forced them to consider the permissibility of holding public office. This very practical question threatened their organization with schism.

Unitarianism in England and America

Soon after the influence of Unitarianism had begun to be felt it became more or less blended with the general rise of liberalism in

[7] Racovian Catechism, Question 1.
[8] *Ibid.,* Questions 509 ff.

England before and after Coleridge. In New England Unitarianism arose and developed against a background of strict Calvinism.

A Latin copy of the Racovian Catechism which had been sent to James I in 1614 was publicly burned. Not until 1860 did the Socinians of the Continent come into formal and immediate negotiations with the Unitarians of England and America. The first organization of a Unitarian congregation in England took place in London in 1774. The leading spirit in this congregation was Theophilus Lindsey (d. 1808), who had resigned his position in the state church after unsuccessful efforts to abolish subscription to the Thirty-nine Articles as a condition of membership. But long before this liberal influences in England had been preparing the soil.

Among these influences were Arminianism and rational theology, movements which issued into latitudinarianism and English deism. A leader of the earlier English Unitarians was John Biddle (d. 1622). He emphasized the dignity of reason in interpreting Scripture. Joseph Priestley was an influential representative of Unitarianism in Birmingham, England. The work of Biddle and Priestley was continued by Thomas Belsham (d. 1829), Lant Carpenter (d. 1840), and others. In 1813, 1825, and 1844 statutes were enacted guaranteeing freedom of conscience and civil rights to all religious dissenters, including the Unitarians. In the meantime Unitarianism in England and America had developed doctrinal positions which, in many respects, were quite different from those of the old Socinians. The name "Arians" had come into use to describe their Christology. This term was not entirely unjustified for it was generally their position that Christ was more than just man.

In the first third of the nineteenth century America became the scene of interesting events. Priestley had emigrated to the vicinity of Boston, where he spent the last ten years of his life (d. 1804). There he devoted himself to a literary activity in which he produced 141 titles, which were published on both sides of the Atlantic.[9] In his writings he recognized the supernatural element to such an extent that, with some modifications, he was still a representative of the old historical Socinianism. But from now on, through men such as W. E.

[9] It is interesting to note that Priestley was the discoverer of oxygen. Another Anti-Trinitarian, Servetus, discovered the double circulation of the blood.

Channing, Theodore Parker, Ralph Waldo Emerson, and many others the whole development of Unitarianism took a different course.

The influences of historical Socinianism were noticeable in the Arminianism of Holland and of England. They are very clearly observable in German rationalism and in the succeeding forms of this movement. Thus the remark of Troeltsch is correct: "In stripping itself of the positivistic supernaturalism, Socinianism passed easily over into the rationalistic types of the modern enlightenment." [10]

BIBLIOGRAPHY

ALLEN, JOSEPH H. *Unitarians in the United States.* ("American Church History" Series.) New York: The Christian Literature Co., 1894.

CHADWICK, JOHN W. *Old and New Unitarian Belief.* Boston: G. H. Ellis, 1894.

CORY, D. M. *Faustus Socinus.* Boston: Beacon Press, 1932.

EMERTON, E. *Unitarian Thought.* New York: The Macmillan Company, 1911.

HARNACK, A. *History of Dogma.* Vol. VII. New York: Russell & Russell, 1958.

KOT, STANISLAW. *Socinianism in Poland.* Boston: Beacon Press, 1957.

MACLACHLAN, H. J. *Socinianism in 17th Century England.* London: Oxford University Press, 1951.

———. *The Unitarian Movement in the Religious Life of England.* Vol. I. London: George Allen & Unwin, Ltd., 1934.

———. *Essays and Addresses,* Manchester University, 1950.

MANNING, J. E. *The Religion and Theology of Unitarians.* 1911.

MARTINEAU, JAMES. *Unitarian Christianity.* 2nd ed. London: Association Press, 1881.

SANDUIS, C. (ed.). *Bibliotheca Antitrinitariorum.* 1694.

SOZZINI, FAUSTO. *Writings.* 1656 ff.

WILBUR, E. M. *A Bibliography of the Pioneers of the Socinian-Unitarian Movement in Modern Christianity in Italy, Switzerland, Germany, Holland.* Rome, 1950.

———. *A History of Unitarianism.* Vol. I: *Socinianism and Its Antecedents.* Cambridge: Harvard University Press, 1945. Vol. II: *A History of Unitarianism in Transylvania, England and America.* Cambridge: Harvard University Press, 1952.

[10] "Protestantisches Christentum und Kirche," *Kultur der Gegenwart,* I, No. 4 (1906), 275.

CHAPTER IX

ROMAN CATHOLICISM IN THE SEVENTEENTH AND EIGHTEENTH CENTURIES

The Council of Trent had cemented the forces of Roman Catholicism but it left the rift between Augustinian Thomism and the Pelagianizing tenets of Franciscan theology unresolved. The controversy between Curialism and Conciliarism was not settled either. Controversies, therefore, were bound to follow in the post-Tridentine period.

The Rejection of Augustinianism

Augustinianism reasserted itself in the teaching of Michael Bajus, professor at the university of Louvain. He defended a number of Augustinian theses, e.g., that the natural will of man is sinful without the help of God; that concupiscence is sin in the strictest sense of the term; that no human is without sin, not even the Holy Virgin. In 1567 Pope Pius V condemned seventy-nine theses of Bajus.[1]

Much more important was the attempt of Cornelius Jansen (d. 1638), Bishop of Ypres, to revitalize the influence of Augustine in the Roman communion. In his book *Augustinus,* published after his death, Jansen showed strong biblical, anti-scholastic, and anti-Jesuit tendencies and represented essentially the doctrine of Augustine. He was supported by the learning and piety of some of the noblest minds of France, clerical and lay, at the Cistercian convent Port-Royal des Champs, a few miles from Paris. He called forth two papal condemnations. In 1653, Pope Innocent X condemned five theses of

[1] See Carl Mirbt, *Quellen zur Geschichte des Papsttums* (4th ed., 1924), pp. 347-48.

Jansen, whose followers charged that Jansen had not actually said the things which the pope condemned.[2]

Among the friends of Jansen at Port-Royal was Blaise Pascal (1623-1662), mathematician, physicist, and Christian apologist. His masterpieces are the *Provinciales*, nineteen *petites lettres* in which he censured the moral code of the Jesuits (1656 f.); and the *Pensées*, fragments of Christian apologetics.[3] The *Pensées* reflect Luther's *theologia crucis* on the one hand, and anticipate Kierkegaard's Christian existentialism on the other. The God of Scripture is the *Deus absconditus*, revealed and yet hidden in the shame of the cross. Man without God is a monster and a miserable creature:

> The knowledge of God without that of man's misery causes pride. The knowledge of man's misery without that of God causes despair. The knowledge of Jesus Christ constitutes the middle course, because in him we find both God and our misery.[4]

The controversy was resumed and became more violent when Paschius Quesnel (d. 1719) renewed the position of Jansen. In his bull *Unigenitus* in 1713, Pope Clement XI condemned one hundred and one sentences extracted from Quesnel's *Moral Reflections on the New Testament* (1687). The condemned statements deal with the problem of the utter depravity of man, of irresistible grace, of faith as the primary grace of God and as the fountain of all other gifts (1-43). Sentences 44-71 stress the thought that love only corrects the human will. The remaining sentences deal with the Church as the company of the elect and that the reading of Scripture is for all its members (80).[5] The bull *Unigenitus*, with its renunciation of the precious inheritance from Augustine, is a landmark in the history of Catholicism.

While the Church of Rome rejected genuine Augustinianism, it took a progressively more lenient attitude toward Pelagian tendencies. An outstanding leader in this Pelagianizing movement was the Jesuit scholar Luis de Molina (1536-1600). In his *Concordia* he attempted to offer a logical explanation to the problem of grace and free will,

[2] *Ibid.*, pp. 383 f. Cf. Schaff, *op. cit.*, I, 103 f.

[3] Blaise Pascal, *Thoughts, Letters, and Minor Works* ("Harvard Classics" [Cambridge: Harvard University Press, 1910]).

[4] *Ibid.*, p. 334. Cf. Soren Kierkegaard, *Training in Christianity* (Princeton: Princeton University Press, 1952), especially pp. 71-72.

[5] See Mirbt, *op. cit.*, pp. 395 ff.; Schaff, *op. cit.*, I, 105 ff.

of foreknowledge, providence and predestination. Man is free, he maintained, in every state of life. In spite of original sin he possesses freedom "not only with reference to ethical good and evil in his natural actions, but also in his supernatural salutary works in which divine grace co-operates with his will."[6] In opposition to Pelagius he taught that God is the primary cause of salvation and that the free will of man is a secondary cause. In order to harmonize freedom of will with the eternal decrees he based the eternal decrees on the foreknowledge of God. The decrees, he maintained, presuppose a special knowledge in the light of which God infallibly foresees the attitude which man's will may assume. Guided by this foreknowledge, God determines what kind of grace He shall give to man. To be efficacious this grace must be congruous to the character and environment of the recipient.

Since the teaching of Molina was contrary to that of Thomas, which was regarded as authoritative, controversy was bound to follow. The chief leader of the Thomistic opposition was Dominicus Banez (1528-1604).[7] He maintained that the primary cause inevitably determines the secondary cause. God both creates and moves the will of man.[8]

Likewise, the lax Franciscan ethics gained new momentum in the teaching of the Jesuits. The papal decisions of 1659 and 1679 disapproved only the extreme consequences of the moral teachings of the Jesuits.[9] Casuistry and probabilism dominated their approach to Christian ethics.[10] The writings of Alphons Maria de Ligouri (d. 1787) became normative for the teachers of moral theology. He was canonized in 1839, raised to the position of a doctor of the church

[6] *Catholic Encyclopedia* (New York: The Universal Knowledge Foundation, Inc., 1911), X, 436 ff.

[7] Cf. Seeberg, *Lehrbuch der Dogmengeschichte,* IV, 844 ff.

[8] The whole controversy is a Catholic counterpart to the conflict between Calvinism and Arminianism in Protestant thought.

[9] Mirbt, *op. cit.,* pp. 387-88.

[10] The *Catholic Encyclopedia* (XII, 441) defines probabilism as follows: "Probabilism is the moral system which holds that, when there is a question solely of the lawfulness or unlawfulness of an action, it is permissible to follow a solidly probable opinion in favour of liberty even though the opposing view is more probable."

in 1871,[11] and to that of a patron of Catholic moralists and father confessors in 1950. Concerning the probabilistic controversy, he held a mediating position and developed the theory of "aequiprobabilism." [12] In fairness to the Jesuit order the fact should not be overlooked that some of its leaders vigorously protested the laxity of the order's moral teaching. The Church historian Ignatius Doellinger, who became a leader of the Old Catholic movement after 1870, referred to the writings of Ligouri as being replete with errors, lies, and poison to pervert the Catholic clergy.[13]

Papalism Contested

The second problem occupying the mind of the Roman Catholic church was the controversy between curialism and conciliarism. This controversy involved two problems: (a) the question of the divine rights of the bishops as independent from the pope and the conciliar rights as superior to the pope; (b) the question of Catholic tradition, whether the extent and content of tradition are to be determined by the principle of Vincent of Lérins or by papal decrees.[14]

When Pius IV sanctioned the decrees of Trent in the bull *Benedictus Deus*, July 26, 1564, he clearly showed his authority as being superior to that of the Council, for the decrees of a Council became valid only through confirmation by the pope. This was pointed out still more definitely in the so-called *Professio fidei Tridentini*, drawn up at Rome in the year 1564, which states the confessional oath of the Roman Catholic clergy in the following form: "I recognize the Catholic and Apostolic Church as the mother and teacher of all churches, and solemnly vow and swear faithful obedience to the pope at Rome, the successor of Peter, the blessed prince among the apostles, and the vicar of Jesus Christ." [15] Still more clearly defended

[11] Mirbt, *op. cit.*, pp. 468-69.

[12] "Aequiprobabilism maintains that, when the uncertainty concerns the existence of a law, it is lawful to follow the less safe opinion when it has equal or almost equal probability with the safe opinion but that, when there is a question of the cessation of a law, the less safe opinion cannot lawfully be followed, unless it is more probable than the safe view." *Catholic Encyclopedia, loc. cit.*

[13] Mirbt, *op. cit.*, p. 573.

[14] The criterion of Catholic and reliable tradition stated by Vincent of Lérins is what has been "believed everywhere, always, and by all."

[15] Mirbt, *op. cit.*, pp. 338 ff.

was the papal decision in the *Roman Catechism* of 1566 that although Christ is the invisible Lord of the church, "yet the visible one is he who as his legitimate successor occupies the Roman see of Peter, the prince among the apostles." The authority of the pope is independent of the authority of the councils, "for authority is granted to the pope not by any synod or other human institution, but by divine right." [16]

At the beginning of the seventeenth century the Jesuit Cardinal Bellarmin became the defender of the Tridentine Council, especially against the brilliant Protestant critic, Martin Chemnitz. A real champion of the papal claims, he formulated them in almost the same terms the Vatican Council (1870) accepted. In matters of faith and morals the pope can claim infallibility. Concerning the question of the relation of the pope to the bishops, Bellarmin held that the bishops do not derive their authority directly from Christ as successors of the Apostles, but through the pope. With respect to the secular claims of the church, Bellarmin held a mediating view. While he defended the right of the pope to depose governments which are contrary to the welfare of the Catholic church, he asserted not a direct, but indirect power of the papacy in temporal matters. This view, though at first rejected by Rome, was generally accepted by the curialist party.[17]

Not before the lapse of two full centuries, during which conciliarism successfully repelled curialism, could these opinions officially prevail as dogma. The criticism of the secular claims of the popes was especially outspoken in France, where royal power enlisted the support of the bishops in opposing papal authority. The Gallican Declaration of 1682 states in the first article: "To the holy Peter and his successors, to the Vicar of Christ, and to the Church itself God has granted authority in spiritual things pertaining to eternal life, not in civil and temporal affairs. The kings and princes are, therefore, by divine right subject to no authority of the Church in secular affairs. They can neither mediately nor immediately be deposed by the power of the keys held by the Church." The fourth article states: "The pope has also the highest authority in matters of faith, and his decrees apply to all churches and every church in particular; still, his decision

[16] *Ibid.*, p. 345.
[17] *Ibid.*, pp. 355 ff.

is not incapable of reform, unless the assent of the Church has been added."[18] These concepts became more generally widespread during the eighteenth century. It was then that the papacy and its chief support, the Jesuits, most declined. The main argument against the infallibility and universal episcopate of the pope was summarized by the suffragan Bishop Nicolas von Hontheim (d. 1790) in a book written under the assumed name Febronius. The book bears the title *De statu ecclesiae et legitima potestate Romani pontificis* (1763). On the basis of this book the four German archbishops declared at the Conference of Ems, in the so-called *Ems Agreement*, that in the past the bishops used their divinely ordained power, and that all authority which the Roman Curia had usurped on the basis of the forged *Pseudo-Isidorian Decretals* should be rejected. This position was defended at the Synod of Pistoja (1786) but was most emphatically rejected by the papacy.[19]

The Effect of the Enlightenment on Catholic Thought

In addition to the radicalism witnessed in France, opposition to the political and hierarchical schemes of the Jesuit Order became widespread. Pascal had ridiculed the Jesuits and other monastic orders were hostile to them. They were expelled from Portugal, Spain, Naples and other countries. In 1773 Pope Clement XIV dissolved the order in his bull *Dominus ac Redemptor noster*.[20]

The spirit of "Febronianism" also swept the countries of the Hapsburg dynasty. Joseph II (1780-90) extended toleration to the Lutheran, Reformed, and Uniat churches of his realm, 1781. The members of these churches obtained civil rights and freedom of worship under various restrictions.[21] A liberal, latitudinarian attitude asserted itself among the clergy and the rationalistic movement was firmly established for a while in some of the Catholic universities. Adam Weishaupt, professor of canon law in Ingolstadt, founded the secret Society of the Illuminati in 1776.[22] It was organized along lines similar to Freemasons for the promotion of a deistic religion and culture. I. A.

[18] *Ibid.*, pp. 387-88.
[19] *Ibid.*, pp. 414-15.
[20] *Ibid.*, pp. 404 ff.
[21] *Ibid.*, p. 413.
[22] Cf. *Catholic Encyclopedia*, VII, 661 ff.

Fessler, professor of Oriental languages and Old Testament, was converted to the Protestant faith and joined the Masonic order in 1791.[23] Catholic theology on the whole was at a very low ebb. France included, the spiritual decline was more serious in the Catholic world than in Protestantism.

BIBLIOGRAPHY

DENZIL, G. M. PATRICK. *Pascal and Kierkegaard.* 2 vols. London: Lutterworth Press, 1948.

MORTIMER, ERNEST. *Blaise Pascal.* London: Methuen, 1959.

SCHNEEMAN, G. *Entstehung und Entwicklung der thomistisch-molinistischen Kontroverse.* 1879-80.

SEEBERG, REINHOLD. *Lehrbuch der Dogmengeschichte.* Vol. IV. 1920.

[23] For this and similar incidents, see Kurtz, *op. cit.,* III, 94 ff.

Book Five

EUROPEAN THOUGHT SINCE THE NINETEENTH CENTURY

Introduction

At the beginning of the nineteenth century Germany regained philosophical and theological leadership in the West. Kant and Hegel were a universal phenomenon. The philosophy which was developed by these men contributed to the downfall of rationalism and to the religious and confessional revival of the first half of the century, represented by Schleiermacher and the Erlangen school. Kant and Hegel also contributed to the rise of a new liberal version of Christianity which was manifested in the Tübingen school, Albrecht Ritschl, and the historico-religious school. At the turn of the twentieth century, Continental theology was under the magnetic spell of Ritschl and Troeltsch. Then came the resurgence of the gospel under the aegis of the Luther and the Kierkegaard renaissance inaugurated by Karl Barth, the Lundensian school, and others.

British theology developed along similar lines. Scottish theologians showed a kind of predilection for the Kantian-Ritschlian aversion to metaphysics, while English theologians were enamoured of Hegelian immanentism. This trend affected high and low church people alike. The rediscovery of the biblical message in Britain may also be attributed to the dialectical theologians on the Continent. H. R. Mackintosh at Edinburgh was among the first scholars to write on Karl Barth in the English language.

In colonial America, Jonathan Edwards was a theologian of remarkable originality. Later the trends of German radical thought infiltrated the churches of the early English-speaking settlers to such an extent that by 1900 Congregationalism had practically lost its identity with the faith that had come over in the "Mayflower." Other denominations were also deeply disturbed by the modernist controversy. On the other hand, the confessional revival on the Continent resulted in the establishment of strictly conservative synods among the Lutheran immigrants. A similar conservative, biblicistic outlook gave rise to the fundamentalist movement, which was a sharp reaction against incipient modernism in the parent bodies of Calvinistic or Arminian Christianity.

In addition, the advance of science, technological development, and the rise of Marxism presented problems to all the countries of the West, and after 1918 these problems extended to the East. The churches were unprepared for these problems. Liberal theology tried to meet the challenge by accommodation, at times sacrificing the very essence of the gospel. Conservative theology, by and large, reacted negatively, either ignoring modern phenomena or condemning them as anti-Christian. The problems were not seriously dealt with until the resurgence of the gospel in Europe made itself felt on this side of the Atlantic.

The Roman communion, too, experienced a revival of its classical theology, for instance, that of Thomas, and also had to face the rise of a modernism peculiar to the structure of Catholicism.

BIBLIOGRAPHY

BARTH, KARL. *From Rousseau to Ritschl.* London: SCM Press, 1959.

ELERT, WERNER. *Der Kampf um das Christentum seit Schleiermacher und Hegel.* 1921.

FRANK, REINHOLD. *Geschichte und Kritik der neueren Theologie.* 1908.

HIRSCH, EMANUEL. *Geschichte der neueren evangelischen Theologie.* Vols. IV and V; 1952, 1954.

KATTENBUSCH, FERDINAND. *Die deutsche evangelische Theologie seit Schleiermacher.* 1926.

LICHTENBERGER, F. *History of German Theology.* Edinburgh: T. & T. Clark, 1889.

LUETGERT, WILHELM. *Die Religion des deutschen Idealismus und ihr Ende.* 4 vols. 1923 ff.

MACKINTOSH, HUGH R. *Types of Modern Theology.* London: Nisbet and Co., 1937.

MOORE, EDWARD C. *History of Christian Thought since Kant.* New York: C. Scribner's Sons, 1912.

PFLEIDERER, OTTO. *Development of Theology in Germany since Kant.* Translated by J. F. SMITH. 3rd ed.; New York: The Macmillan Company, 1909.

SEEBERG, REINHOLD. *Die Kirche Deutschlands im neunzehnten Jahrhundert.* 1903.

Section One

CONTINENTAL THOUGHT

CHAPTER I

IMMANUEL KANT

Immanuel Kant (1724-1804) is a landmark in the history of philosophy in general and in the philosophy of religion in particular. Differences notwithstanding, a common thread runs through the religious philosophy of Catholicism and Protestantism, of Spinoza and Locke. Both agree that religion is dependent upon metaphysics, and ethics dependent upon religion. But Kant divorced religion from metaphysics and made ethics an autonomous discipline.

Kant's concept of religion is intrinsically connected with his critical philosophy. Our discussion of Kant is based upon his *Critique of Pure Reason* (1781), *The Fundamental Principles of the Metaphysics of Morality* (1785), *Critique of Practical Reason* (1788), *Critique of Judgment* (1790), and *Religion within the Limits of Reason* (1798).

Kant's Theory of Knowledge

Kant distinguishes between a judgment or assertion *a priori* and a judgment *a posteriori*. He also distinguishes analytical judgment from synthetic judgment.

A judgment *a priori* is knowledge which is absolutely independent of experience. It is not related to anything empirical. A judgment *a posteriori* is knowledge derived from experience.

An analytical judgment or affirmation is one whose predicate is contained in the meaning of the subject. "If I say, for instance, All bodies are extended, this is an analytical judgment." [1] The term "body" implies extension because a body occupies space. The predicate "extended" adds nothing to the understanding of "body." But if I say, "All bodies are heavy, the predicate is something quite different from what I think as the mere concept of body. The addition of such a

[1] Immanuel Kant, *Critique of Pure Reason,* trans. N. K. Smith (London: Macmillan Co., 1956), pp. 41 ff.

predicate gives us a synthetic judgment." It is evident, then, that an analytical judgment does not enrich our knowledge of the subject of the sentence. In a synthetic judgment, however, our knowledge of the subject is amplified, for the predicate is not contained in the meaning of the subject.

Kant distinguishes three different faculties of the mind: sensibility, understanding, and reason. The empiricists were correct in their assertion that objective reality presents itself to man through the medium of sense experience, but they were wrong when they regarded the mind as a *tabula rasa.* In the act of knowledge the mind is not merely passive, for it contains the form in which experience is received and interpreted. There is some truth in the Rationalists' assertion of innate ideas. Yet these ideas are purely formal. Having perceived an external object, the mind begins to arrange the event according to space and time and to interpret the event by means of the categories of understanding. The most important category–so far as our presentation is concerned–is that of causality. Space and time, and the law of causality, therefore, are forms of apperception. They determine our knowledge of the objective world. Consequently, we do not know "the thing in itself" (*das Ding an sich*). The world of objects is only phenomenal; we see the world as it appears to us.

Kant has said that analytical judgments are valid *a priori,* and that synthetic judgments are valid *a posteriori.* Can synthetic judgments also be possible *a priori?* Kant says yes. For example he refers to the principles of mathematics. The human mind is convinced *a priori* that the maxims of mathematics and mathematical physics are always valid. Their maxims are not upset with each new generation, but continued advance is possible on the basis of propositions already established. Metaphysics, however, has failed in all its desperate endeavors to establish basic assertions securely. Reason has tempted men to make assertions about God as the *primary cause* of the world, and about the soul as immortal. Kant has shown that the law of causality is valid in the world of experience. But man cannot comprehend the world as a whole. The world is not just an aggregate of physical bodies that have already been experienced. The world includes at least two other attributes. It includes all the bodies that may be experienced in the future, and it implies that the bodies are not a disorderly medley of things, but belong to a single orderly system. Understood in this way, the world defies the experience of man.

Similar conclusions are reached in dealing with the idea of the soul. We may attribute existence to any particular sensation, volition, feeling, or the like occurring as a temporal event in our inner life and observable introspectively. That is part of human experience under the restrictions of time. But we cannot experience the soul as an independent substance, incorruptible and immortal.[2]

By denying to reason the possibility of establishing metaphysical truths, Kant shows the weakness of the traditional arguments for the existence of God. He concentrates on the ontological, cosmological, and physico-theological arguments.[3] The last-named argument points to the teleology observable in the world. This teleology is foreign to things themselves and belongs to them only contingently. Hence there must be a wise and beneficent cause behind the manifold things of the world. Kant says that this proof "will always deserve to be treated with respect." But the most that could be established by such a proof would be an architect of the world, not a creator. Actually this proof rests on the cosmological proof. Yet as stated earlier, man cannot comprehend the world as a whole. In fact, the world is not a "constitutive" category at all, only a "regulative" ideal. "World" symbolizes the attempt of the mind to arrange and perfect its understanding of a medley of external phenomena. The law of causality is of no use in this connection. Causality has meaning only in the world of sense.

The strength of the cosmological argument in turn rests on the ontological proof, which argues that God, as the most perfect being, must exist, for being is implied in the idea of perfection. Kant replies that the real does not contain more than the possible. "A hundred real dollars do not contain the least coin more than a hundred possible dollars."[4] Like the concepts of the world and the soul, the idea of God is merely a regulative principle or idea which unifies the external world and the internal soul. The objective reality of the idea of God cannot be proved, but neither can it be disproved by "merely specula-

[2] *Ibid.*, pp. 328 ff.
[3] *Ibid.*, pp. 495 ff.
[4] *Ibid.*, p. 505.

tive reason."[5] Kant therefore concludes that God cannot be an object of reason and remains unknown to pure speculative reason. Religious doctrines are not scientific propositions; they are merely moral postulates.

Religion as a Moral Postulate

Men observe wants and desires in their souls which motivate them to action. In themselves these desires are neither good nor bad; they are natural. Their ethical quality depends on that by which man is motivated. It would be immoral to be motivated by the pursuit of one's own happiness, for to do so would be to surrender one's rational character. Because man is basically a rational being, moral action is basically rational action.

In the field of theoretical reason Kant insists on universality and necessity. To be valid, a principle must be capable of unlimited generalization. Reason seeks a law which can be verified and exemplified in all events of the same type. Reason might also demand that the law never fail to prevail. Universality and necessity are united in the idea of law. "In all cases I must act in such a way that I can at the same time will that my maxim should become a universal law."[6] This "categorical imperative" represents an action as necessary of itself, without reference to another end, such as personal happiness.

The idea that the individual follows universally valid law leads to the idea of "a kingdom of ends," a union of rational beings in a system of common laws. Kant regards love and duty as essential to the attainment of such an end, and offers his own interpretation of the biblical injunction to love God above everything. Kant maintains that since God is not an object of our senses, he cannot, properly speaking, be loved. Kant says that to love God means to like to keep his commandments. The neighbor, of course, can be seen, but to love him means to "practice all duties towards him."[7] Duty, that "sublime and mighty name," is the real incentive to moral action. The moral person lives, not because he finds life pleasant, but rather because it is his duty![8]

[5] *Ibid.*, p. 531.
[6] John Watson, *Selections of Kant's Works* (1901), p. 230. Cf. T. M. Greene, *Selections of Kant's Works* (New York: Charles Scribner's Sons, 1929), p. 302
[7] T. M. Greene, *op. cit.*, p. 329.
[8] *Ibid.*, p. 333.

Can the good be realized by man? Kant answers confidently in the affirmative. The ideas of rationality, morality, and freedom of the will are inseparably intertwined. Every rational being has a will and an idea of freedom, "and acts entirely under this idea." [9] The moral injunction implies the ability to perform it: Thou canst for thou oughtst. "Two things inspire my mind with ever increasing admiration," Kant says, "the starry heavens above me and the moral law within me." [10]

This does not mean that Kant was blind to the forces of evil. He did not share the naive optimism of the German Rationalists and the French Naturalists that man is basically good. He spoke of the radical evil whose origin cannot be rationally explained. Human life is a conflict. Nevertheless, pure practical reason seeks the highest good. The antinomy between happiness and the good must be dissolved just as the antinomy between freedom and physical necessity must be dissolved. The moral law is holy; it cannot suffer defeat. In order to attain this end, Kant, in his *Critique of Practical Reason,* made the immortality of the soul and the existence of God postulates of practical reason. He transformed theology radically. Instead of being a metaphysical faith, Christianity became a morally grounded faith. Faith in God is not a scientific proposition, but an affirmation of the heart. Hence, practical reason is better equipped to probe the depth of life than theoretical reason.

In *Religion within the Limits of Reason,*[11] Kant gives a systematic presentation of the basic tenets of his religion. In religion, he says, we are confronted with an exclusively moral problem, namely the struggle between the good and the evil principle for dominion over man. The evil principle consists in allowing sensually selfish motives to undermine respect for the moral law. This evil principle has its roots in the will. The inclination of man toward evil, when there was an original and even a persevering disposition toward good, remains inexplicable. To Kant evil is a fact that needs no proof. He refuses to accept the Church's doctrine of original sin, but he does not charge

[9] T. M. Greene, *op. cit.,* p. 335.

[10] *Critique of Practical Reason* in Karl Vorlaender (ed.), *Kants Sämmtliche Werke* (1904 ff.), hereinafter referred to as *Werke,* II, 205.

[11] *Die Religion innerhalb der Grenzen der blossen Vernunft* in *Werke,* Vol. IV.

human depravity to the Creator.[12] Evil can be observed in man as soon as the use of freedom becomes manifest in him. Kant quotes Ephesians 6:12[13] and Romans 7:18,[14] 5:12,[15] and 14:23 with approval.[16] Human depravity is a weakness, but it is also a bent to wickedness and guilt. Through the incomprehensible freedom of reason by which the good and lawful are actualized, their opposite, the will for evil, can be actualized as well. These ideas of sin seem to be out of harmony with the other rationalistic tenets of Kant's religion. This is evident from his statement that a gradual reform will not suffice as a remedy for this condition, but that a remedy must be effected through a revolution of the mind, a kind of regeneration, and a putting on of the new man.[17] Judging by these statements, Kant's earlier pietistic training seems to have had a lingering effect.[18]

Kant also discussed the Church. Moral regeneration or the victory of the principle of good is to be realized, not merely in the individual man, but in human society. A kingdom of God or a society established upon moral laws is to arise. Although the visibly constituted Church repelled Kant, he regarded it as necessary, at least for the common people, for training men for the kingdom of God. Eventually the religion of reason was to prevail over the dogma of the Church.[19]

The biblical teaching of grace was also objectionable to Kant. He mocks the Christians who crave to be favored rather than to be good servants. They want the Lord to overlook something, and thus they discredit virtue. To put one's trust in grace is fanaticism; to rely on miracle is superstition; to wait for the revelation of supernatural mysteries is the delusive idea of one initiated into the mysteries of a cult; the attempt to influence the supernatural is magic. All these are an

[12] *Ibid.*, pp. 41 ff.
[13] *Ibid.*, p. 64.
[14] *Ibid.*, p. 29.
[15] *Ibid.*, p. 45.
[16] *Ibid.*, p. 31.
[17] *Ibid.*, IV, 51.
[18] Kant's mother belonged to a Pietist circle in Königsberg. In his youth he attended a preparatory school founded and managed by Halle Pietists.

Kant and his sovereign, Frederick the Great, are two tragic examples of misconceived Christian education. Both had been subjected to endless religious exercises day after day; both were repelled by the experience and turned against the Church—the king, indeed, against Christianity itself.
[19] Kant, *Werke,* IV, 183 ff.

aberration of a reason that wants to transcend its own limitations.[20]

Prayer as an inward divine service and means of grace is a superstitious illusion and cannot be required of the moral man who struggles on. At the same time, Kant defends churchgoing, baptism, and communion as practices of good citizenship which conform to good breeding and fine etiquette! After all, Kant did not want to be a revolutionary. He preferred to be known as a man who interprets the moral significance of Church life to the educated. Subjectively speaking religion is the knowledge of all our duties as divine commandments. For him religion is "pure rationalism,"[21] belief in reason as the infallible source and guide for morality. Moral conduct is the "strait gate" and the "narrow way" that leads to life; the Church is the "wide gate" and the "broad way" that leads to destruction. Kant adds that to rely on religious ceremonies as a substitute for morality is destructive.[22] Such divine service, so-called, is nothing but an illusion and a mock service.[23]

In 1788, Kant re-emphasized some of these ideas in his short volume *Der Streit der Fakultäten*.[24] Prior to the nineteenth century, the philosophical faculty in the German universities was called the lower faculty in contrast to the higher faculties of theology, jurisprudence, and medicine.[25] Kant objects to the arrogance of the theologians in calling philosophy the "handmaiden of theology." In his view philosophy is the apex of all sciences. The other three faculties train men for the welfare of society at the request of and under the supervision of the government. Their approach must be positive. They have to accept, not criticize, the premises of their respective fields of studies. The other faculties, especially the theological one, should learn to appreciate the service philosophy can render in separating the wheat from the chaff, the religion of reason from the dogma of the Church.

[20] *Ibid.*, p. 57.
[21] *Ibid.*, p. 180.
[22] *Ibid.*, p. 187.
[23] *Ibid.*, pp. 196-97. Vorlaender (*op. cit.*, X, 130) remarks that in an academic procession Kant regularly slipped out of the line and went home before the procession entered the church.
[24] *Werke*, Vol. V.
[25] In those days the doctor's degrees were reserved for graduates of the three higher faculties. Graduates of the philosophical faculty were awarded the degree of Master of Arts. Kant, therefore, was not a doctor of philosophy, but a master of arts.

Kant and Luther

Ritschl hailed Kant's work as a restoration of Protestantism. His appraisal was seconded by Julius Kaftan and Wilhelm Herrmann.[26] Indeed, some striking resemblances to Luther are evident. Like Kant, Luther voiced his protest against the proud attempt of human reason to reach God by speculation. In his Heidelberg Theses Luther rejected speculative theology as a theology of glory and called its advocates "miserable sophists." Like Kant, Luther did not presume to know God in Himself (*das Ding an sich*). All our knowledge of God depends on revelation. Like Kant, Luther considered man in his misery as the proper subject of theology. Pure reason cannot apprehend this. It can be apprehended only by an act of faith, just as Kant maintained that religion is a proposition of practical reason, a commitment to the holy will of God.

Nonetheless, there is a pronounced difference between Kant and Luther. Kant's religion is a thoroughgoing moralism, while Luther's is the religion of grace. Further, when Luther opposed speculation he was contrasting human speculation with divine revelation. Luther was not a historical positivist like the Neo-Kantian theologians. Natural religion was objectionable to him, but he regarded the dogma of the Church as a reliable exposition of the saving grace of God in Christ Jesus.

Post-Kantian Rationalism

After Kant, the older rationalism soon lost its hold on the minds of intellectual leaders. A few names deserve to be remembered by the historian. The Nestor of rational exegesis was H. E. G. Paulus (1761-1851) at Heidelberg, who was famous for his rational explanation of biblical miracles. The dogmatician of popular rationalism was J. A. L. Wegscheider (1771-1849), whose *Institutiones theologiae dogmaticae* went through eight editions. Post-Kantian rationalism was at its best in the field of historical and grammatical research. Wilhelm Gesenius' Hebrew-German dictionary (1810 ff.) and Hebrew grammar (1813) have had a wide circulation. Gesenius also started a critical thesaurus of Hebrew and Chaldean (1829 ff.).[27] The monumental *Corpus Refor-*

[26] For references see Kant, *Werke,* IV, lxii ff.

[27] Cf. E. F. Miller, *The Influence of Gesenius on Hebrew Lexicography* (New York: Columbia University Press, 1927).

matorum was founded by K. G. Bretschneider (1776-1848). By 1800, rationalism was seriously challenged by the emerging spirit of romanticism. The death blow to rationalism was dealt by the Church historian Karl von Hase and his book *Hutterus Redivivus* (1828). However, rationalism continued to exert an influence in Church life through rationalistically trained pastors till about 1870.

BIBLIOGRAPHY

BURTT, E. A. *Types of Religious Philosophy*. New York: Harper & Bros., 1951.

KANT, IMMANUEL. Selections. Translated by JOHN WATSON. 1901.

________. *Selections*. Edited by T. M. GREENE. New York: Charles Scribner's Sons, 1929.

________. *Critique of Pure Reason*. Translated by N. K. SMITH. London: Macmillan Co., 1956.

________. *Critique of Practical Reason*. Translated by L. W. BECK. New York: Liberal Arts Press, 1956.

VORLAENDER, KARL (ed.). *Kants Sämmtliche Werke*. 10 vols. 1904 ff.

CHAPTER II

FRIEDRICH SCHLEIERMACHER (1768-1834)

Like other great men of history, Schleiermacher had a forerunner. In his case it was Johann Gottfried Herder, critic, poet, and theologian.[1] Born in 1744, Herder died in 1803, as head of the Lutheran church in the Duchy of Saxe-Weimar. He was a friend of Hamann and Goethe. He was the first of the theologians to rebel against the abstract intellectualism and moralism of the Rationalists. Religion, he said, has its seat in feeling, which is not just one of the psychological faculties of the soul in addition to thinking and volition; it is rather the basic, vital function of life. From Hamann, Herder had learned to appreciate the simple, folklike mode of speech in the Bible. To understand the Old Testament, he maintained, one must become a contemporary of the ancient Hebrews. Revelation is inclusive and its purpose is the education of the human race. Creation and history are its two great commentaries. Sin and evil, in Herder's thought, lose their meaning as positive forces opposing the Holy God, and revelation is equated with the universal dynamic of life.

Herder rejected the trinitarian and christological dogmas of the ancient Church. The orthodox teaching of the atonement was repulsive to him. He anticipated Harnack by distinguishing between "the gospel of Jesus" and the "gospel about Jesus." He also anticipated the modern method of form-criticism when he insisted on "a gospel before the Gospels," that is, on a kerygma preceding its ultimate consolidation in the New Testament.

Factors Which Influenced Schleiermacher

The peculiarity of Schleiermacher lies in the many ideas that were

[1] Cf. Frank McEachran, *The Life and Philosophy of Johann Gottfried Herder* (Oxford: The Clarendon Press, 1939) and R. T. Clark, *Herder: His Life and Thought* (Berkeley: Univ. of California Press, 1955).

combined in him. It is not only interesting but necessary to trace the influences which contributed to his development.

Friedrich Daniel Ernst Schleiermacher came from a family of Reformed preachers. His grandfather, Daniel, was an adherent of the apocalyptic Ronsdorfer sect.[2] His father, Gottlieb, was a chaplain in the army of Frederick the Great. Sectarian influence confused Schleiermacher's father on matters of faith for a time; later, he returned to the Church through relationships with the Moravians at Herrnhut. Schleiermacher received his first higher education in the *paedagogium* of the Moravians at Niesky and, following this, in their seminary at Barby. Some of the fundamentals of faith troubled Schleiermacher and caused him to doubt. Neither his teachers nor his father had any understanding for his doubt and they were of no help to him.[3] His doubts were persistent. How can Christ, who calls himself the Son of man, be God? The idea of an atonement was objectionable to him. He related that at the age of ten he wondered whether the whole of ancient history might not be a fraudulent transmission. When he was eleven the question of eternal punishment troubled him. Criticism was his natural trait. His father allowed him to pursue his studies at Halle University (1787-89).

His descent from the Reformed church and the influence from the Moravians explain certain characteristics about him: The christocentric character of his theology, his warm subjectivism, his non-Lutheran outlook, and his stand for the union of Lutherans and Reformed.

Philosophical influences played a role in Schleiermacher's theological development. At Halle he studied the philosophy of Kant. Hegel, although a contemporary of Schleiermacher, had not yet attained sufficient prominence to influence Schleiermacher's thinking. Neither Kant nor Hegel held his continued interest. Of the Greek philosophers, he was drawn first to Aristotle, then to Plato. He translated Plato's writings into German. Later, he read Spinoza and Fichte.

[2] The founder of the sect was Elias Eller. He put away his first wife as a "reprobate Vashti" (cf. Esther 2:4). The child of his second wife, Anna, as "the Mother of Zion," was to be the Messiah (Rev. 12:1 ff.). Her first child, however, was a daughter; the second, the "Messiah," died in infancy. Daniel Schleiermacher was co-founder of this sect, but later separated from Eller. The "Mother of Zion" died in 1744. Following the death of Eller in 1750, the sect soon disintegrated. Cf. *PRE,* XVII, 131 ff.

[3] Cf. Wilhelm Dilthey, *Das Leben Schleiermachers* (1922), pp. 13 ff.

Romanticism made the deepest impression upon Schleiermacher. He became part of Berlin's circle of romantic liberals gathered about Moses Mendelssohn, where he met the kind of people – particularly women–to whom his own romantic nature was attracted. He became such a fast friend of Friedrich Schlegel, another member of the circle, that he even undertook to find points of truth and beauty in a questionable novel written by Schlegel. From this liberal circle Schleiermacher received impressions reflected later in his writings.

Luetgert has shown that in such circles as the one to which Schleiermacher became attached, the relationship between men and women often has encouraged dangerous combinations of spirit and flesh under the guise of freedom for the expression of genius.[4] Schleiermacher was not blind to this danger and warned against it in a catechism for women of noble birth.[5] In a book of sermons on marriage and the family, published in 1818, he spoke out against romantic approval of divorce.[6]

THE SPEECHES

In the year 1799, in the midst of his enthusiasm for romanticism, Schleiermacher anonymously published his famous *On Religion: Speeches to Its Cultured Despisers*.[7] These speeches were a symptom of the age in which he lived, when the spirit of classicism was spreading its wings in an atmosphere of a new culture. Many of these cultured spirits were groping for new forms to express religious ideas and attitudes. Schleiermacher, with a deep susceptibility for contemporary piety, stimulated by Greek classicism and modern romanticism, was fundamentally opposed to a tension between culture and religion, and was bent upon creating a "synthesis" between them. In the *Speeches*, as well as in later writings, he emphasized the need of a union of theology with the scientific spirit.

The first *Speech* is an introduction. In the second *Speech*, the most important of the five, Schleiermacher discusses the nature of religion. Succinctly stated, religion is intuition of the universe, a feeling of

[4] Wilhelm Luetgert, *Die Religion des deutschen Idealismus und ihr Ende* (1923 ff.), I, 254.

[5] In spite of such advice, Schleiermacher exposed himself to criticism because of his friendship with the wife of a Berlin pastor.

[6] See Schleiermacher, *Werke*, III, 181 ff.

[7] John Oman (trans.) (New York: Harper, 1958).

absolute dependence, an immediate awareness of ultimate reality as the unity in plurality, and as the Infinite revealed in the manifold experiences of life. For Schleiermacher "universe" is not identical with "world." The universe is the wholeness and unity of the spiritual and historical world. Religion is something independent of philosophy and ethics. It should not concern itself with the quest of truth and duty after the manner of the philosophy of transcendentalism, for the nature of religion is neither thinking nor acting; it is intuition and feeling. Religion submits, in childlike passivity, to be moved by the Universum. Philosophical speculation and ethics apart from religion smack of that human conceit which the gods have always opposed. Ethics is art and speculation is science, but religion is aptitude for the Infinite. The Universum is ever active and revealing itself at every moment. Religion is the acceptance of every single phenomenon as a part of the whole, and everything limited as a manifestation of the Infinite. True religion is all inclusive and therefore tolerant, for everyone whose eyes have been opened is a new priest, a new mediator, a new organ of divinity.

True religion has no quarrel with science. Miracle, for example, is merely the religious name for an ordinary event interpreted religiously. Revelation is every immediate awareness of the Universum. Inspiration is simply a religious name for the freedom to transmit one's own religious experience. All religious feelings are supernatural insofar as they reflect an immediate manifestation of the Universum. Immediacy is what counts. A holy book is merely a mausoleum of religion, a monument of a great spirit no longer at work. It is not the man who believes in a holy Bible who has religion, but rather the man who needs none, and could possibly write one himself.

Schleiermacher says that deity and immortality do not belong to the core of religion. In religion the idea of God is not as important as people often think. Truly religious people have never been fanatics about the existence of God. They have been tolerant of atheism, believing that there is something more irreligious than atheism. No one has ever denied that the Universum is always continuously active, begetting new life. The idea of God has nothing to do with the idea of a first cause or of a reward for good and evil. Man is a free moral being. He is autonomous and cannot be moved by another being.

The prevailing concept of immortality is contrary to the spirit of religion. Religion does not encourage man to preserve his individuality; rather does it challenge him to lose himself in the Infinite, as the Universum says, "He that loseth his life for my sake shall find it." Immortality is to be at one with the Infinite in the midst of finitude, and thus to be eternal in every moment.

In the third *Speech*, education for religion is discussed. All men have the religious aptitude from birth. The age of rationalism was not favorable to its development. Art and myths are better means of training in religion than the fanatical intellectualism and moralism displayed in rationalism. The truly religious person is always tinged with mysticism.

The fourth *Speech* deals with the social features of religion. Religion creates the most perfect forms of human society. The imperfections in the present empirical church have their root in the Church's connection with the state. The goal must be to have free associations of the pious with no hierarchy and with no dictation from the state. Schleiermacher then paints a picture of a truly spiritual service which is reminiscent of a Quaker meeting.

In his fifth *Speech*, Schleiermacher speaks of the relation of the so-called natural religion to the historical forms of religion. He observes that natural religion has "very little of the specific characteristics of the Christian religion," that religion must individualize itself as has been done in the specific positive religions. The real inner essence and life of the genus find expression in its species. His argument is a protest against English deism and German rationalism, which were rooted in the "general religion" of God, virtue, and immortality.

The individualization of religion is achieved through making the individual intuition of the universe the point in which everything is centered and to which everything is related. In the study of the specific religions this point is to be found. Through this emphasis Schleiermacher gave impetus to the comparative study of religions, a field in which he saw the unique root of theology.

It is not until the fifth *Speech* that Schleiermacher first expresses himself on Christianity and the person of Jesus. The relation between Christianity and Judaism, he says, is rather incidental, and is conditioned by a historical development; it is not essential. The religion of the Old Testament does not express the true genius of religion, for it is a book of laws and retributions. Its messianic expectation is political. In brief, Judaism lacks universality. But Christianity is a universal religion. Its central themes are sin and redemption, how the estrangement of the individual from God is overcome. Jesus' divinity lies in his perception of the fact that all men need the mediation of spiritual superiors in order to be united. He was aware that he possessed such an office of mediation, yet he never claimed that he was the only mediator. By the same token, Jesus' disciples did not attempt to circumscribe the activity of the Holy Spirit or to imprison him in a book. Furthermore, the Christian Bible does not deny divine inspiration to other writings.

IMPACT OF THE SPEECHES

It goes without saying that the Rationalists were repelled by the *Speeches*. Even the representatives of the new learning, men like Herder, Schiller, Goethe, Schelling, and Hegel, remained indifferent or critical. Only the Romanticists responded favorably. The poet Novalis felt that the *Speeches* were one with him in flesh and spirit. Later some of the theologians declared that the book had shown them the way to a new life. Claus Harms, in his autobiography, dated his beginning of a higher life from a reading of Schleiermacher's *Speeches*. Their real significance lies in their lasting effect on the theology of the nineteenth century.[8]

In order to do justice to the *Speeches*, one must keep in mind that their author did not intend to discuss the problem "What is Christianity?" as Harnack did a century later. Except in the closing pages, he speaks in the abstract about the nature of religion. His reserved attitude concerning God and immortality ought not be taken as corresponding fully to Schleiermacher's views at that time. The years 1798-99 were filled with tension. Fichte had been dismissed from his position in Jena by the government of the Duchy of Weimar with Goethe, as a minister of the cabinet, concurring in the charge of atheism against him. The case was reminiscent of the excommunication of Spinoza. Schleiermacher wanted to show that an atheist—if

[8] Cf. Hirsch, *Geschichte der neueren evangelischen Theologie,* IV, 538 ff. Concerning Claus Harms, see *PRE,* VII, 434-35.

there is one—is a man not wanting in reverence of life and therefore not unfit to be an educator in a university.[9]

The most serious defect of the *Speeches* lies in Schleiermacher's attempt to eliminate the quest of truth and morality from religion. Without truth, religion is an illusion; without an ethic, it is turned into aesthetics.

Schleiermacher's Concept of Theology

While composing his *Speeches,* Schleiermacher was the Reformed chaplain at the Charité, a large hospital in Berlin. In 1804 he accepted a call to Halle, but in 1807 he returned to Berlin, first as a preacher and soon as a professor at the new university which he helped to found.

His suggested method appeared in 1811 in *A Brief Outline of Theological Study*.[10] This writing shows the remarkable ability of Schleiermacher as a systematician. He was the first to conceive clearly the idea of a theological encyclopedia. Guided by the concept of Christian theology as an organism, he defined the relation of the individual branches of theology to the system as a whole.

Schleiermacher demanded a "philosophical theology" with starting points above and before Christianity.[11] This recalls the fifth *Speech,* in which he speaks of religious truth embodied in non-Christian religions, and says that Christianity must not assume an exclusive attitude toward such truth. In the language of today this would be called philosophy of religion. Apologetics and polemics especially are to be used as the channels for this discussion.[12] Independent of the Christian faith, entirely upon the basis of principles of its own, this "religious philosophy" or "philosophical theology" determines the content and truth in all the leading conceptions of Christianity and Church. The intra-theological disciplines, such as dogmatics and ethics, have nothing to

[9] For the charge against Fichte, cf. Hirsch, *op. cit.,* IV, 351 ff. It has been argued recently that Schleiermacher's sermons of this period are a more reliable source of information than his speeches. See, for example, Paul Seifert, *Die Theologie des jungen Schleiermacher.* The argument is not quite convincing. As other passages show, Schleiermacher was not averse to the principle of "accommodation." Cf. his discussion of the devil, *The Christian Faith,* trans. H. R. Mackintosh and J. S. Stewart (Edinburgh: T. & T. Clark, 1948), Pars. 44-45.

[10] William Farrer (trans.) *A Brief Outline of the Study of Theology* (Edinburgh: T. & T. Clark, 1850).

[11] *Ibid.,* Pars. 24, 33.

[12] *Ibid.,* Par. 67.

do with the finding of Christian truth except to report what religious philosophy has found.[13] By establishing the authority of such a philosophical theology, Schleiermacher prepared the way for the conversion of theology into a philosophy of religion in which the truth of Christianity is made dependent upon general speculations.

In his *Outline* Schleiermacher sees it as the purpose of theology to serve the Church. Theology is a positive, pragmatic science.[14] It should prepare the student for an effective discharge of his duty as a minister of a religious community. Apart from this practical purpose all branches of theology are parts of related studies. Exegesis, for example, is a part of general philology, Church history, a segment of the history of the Near East and of Western civilization. It is interesting to observe that Schleiermacher divided historical theology into four parts: exegesis, Church history, dogmatics, and statistics. Exegesis is a study of primitive Christianity. Dogmatics reports the specific understanding of the Christian faith at a given time in history or for a given denomination and includes ethics. Statistics is practically the same as what is presently called comparative symbolics. It describes the sociological structure of the Church during any period of history. As may be expected, Schleiermacher regards practical theology as the climax of the whole. All this is in keeping with what he says in the fifth *Speech*, that religion can exist only in a concrete sociological structure.

Schleiermacher's Dogmatics

The application of the program which has been discussed was made in Schleiermacher's work on dogmatics which appeared eleven years later: *The Christian Faith According to the Principles of the Evangelical Church, Presented under an Organizing Principle*. This work introduces a new method in the history of dogmatics. Seeberg writes: "This book was the teacher of theology to the church of the nineteenth century. All theologians have been influenced by it, and who could imagine the theology of today without it?"[15] By this Seeberg does not intend to recommend the work as a doctrinally reliable guide on the individual topics of dogmatics. His reference

[13] *Ibid.*, Par. 41.
[14] *Ibid.*, Pars. 5, 26.
[15] Reinhold Seeberg, *Die Kirche Deutschlands im 19. Jahrhundert* (1903), p. 84.

is to its organization, plan, and new method in the building of dogmatics as a system. Note the expression in the title: *Presented under an organizing principle.*

The type of dogmatic system that had prevailed since the Reformation was that of the *Loci.* Melanchthon gave us the first dogmatics of Protestantism in his *Loci communes rerum theologicarum* (1521). Guided by the "topics" (*Loci,* leading concepts) in Paul's Epistle to the Romans, Melanchthon sought the verification of these topics in the Scriptures. Chemnitz and the seventeenth-century theologians followed this method. They searched the Scriptures for *sedes doctrinae,* which they then grouped under the traditional headings: God, Trinity, soteriology, the means of grace, the Church, and eschatology —much like Melanchthon and like Calvin in his *Institutes.* With little variation this method prevailed up to the age of rationalism. Schleiermacher now created an all-around logical system erected upon a controlling, fundamental principle.

The actual forces of the religious life of the Christian fellowship must be studied in order to find what religion is and what is the content of religion. Such a development of dogmatics (1) upon the basis of a fundamental principle, (2) with the description of its content in terms of the life of the Church and, (3) in accordance with the demand that the dogmatician must express his own religious consciousness proved very fascinating to the theologians of the new age in Germany. Schleiermacher made the statement that the truth of the findings "must be approved by agreement with the evangelical confessions, and, in the absence of such, partly by the New Testament writings and partly by the connection of a doctrine with other already recognized doctrines." [16]

The most controversial topic is Schleiermacher's doctrine of God. Was he or was he not a pantheist? In his *Speeches,* Schleiermacher defines religion as "the feeling of absolute dependence," but he does not mention what it is upon which man is absolutely dependent. In *The Christian Faith* he writes that piety is "the consciousness of being absolutely dependent or, which is the same thing, of being in relation to God." [17] The question is, what kind of God? Because

[16] *The Christian Faith,* Par. 27.

[17] *Ibid.,* Par. 4.

Schleiermacher makes favorable mention of Spinoza in the second *Speech*, he has frequently been charged with teaching Spinoza's pantheism. In 1827, Schleiermacher denied that he had ever been a follower of Spinoza.[18] More recently, Erich Schaeder has charged Schleiermacher with an anthropocentric perversion of the theocentric faith of the Bible.[19] The same criticism has been voiced by Emil Brunner.[20] George Wobbermin, on the other hand, regards such criticism as unfair.[21] The difference between man's ordinary dependence and his religious dependence is qualitative, Wobbermin maintains against Schaeder, for it is dependence on God. Hirsch agrees that Schleiermacher's Universum has nothing in common with Spinoza's "God or Nature," except that both reject the idea of a personal, transcendent God.[22] True, Schleiermacher does not equate God with the mathematical structure of the universe. His Universum more closely resembles a spiritual life force. His is not pantheism in the sense that God and man are one. His teaching differs in this respect from that of the great philosophers of German Idealism. His religious philosophy cannot be comprehended as a special version of the philosophy of identity. Schleiermacher evidently rises above a pure immanentism, for in religion man is said to be absolutely dependent not on himself but on God. Yet Schleiermacher is not a theist either. He moves along the line of monism insofar as he identifies the will of God with the causal force of nature.[23] This equation has a telling effect on his understanding of sin and redemption.

Schleiermacher says that sin is the checking of the determinative power of the spirit, an antagonism of the flesh against the spirit.[24] Sin arrests the God-consciousness in man. However, the conscious-

[18] Cf. Hirsch, *op. cit.*, IV, 495.

[19] Erich Schaeder, *Theozentrische Theologie* (1925), Part I (1st ed.: Vol. I, 1909; Vol. II, 1915).

[20] Emil Brunner, *Die Mystik und das Wort,* 1924.

[21] Georg Wobbermin, *The Nature of Religion* (New York: Thomas Y. Crowell Co., 1933), pp. 81 ff. In a lecture at the University of Göttingen in 1929, the author recalls that Wobbermin said of Brunner's book: "Usually a book contains some correct statements; but in Brunner's book not a single sentence is reliable."

[22] Hirsch, *op. cit.*, IV, 503.

[23] *The Christian Faith,* Par. 46. In this paragraph Schleiermacher comes dangerously close to Spinoza's *Deus sive natura.*

[24] *Ibid.*, Par. 66.

ness of sin never exists in the soul of the Christian without the consciousness of the power of redemption. As we trace the annulment of sin by redemption to divine causality, so the existence of sin must in some sense be due to the divine causality.[25] God has ordained that the Christian recognize sin as the failure of the spirit over the dominion of the flesh. Insofar as God is the cause of redemption, he is also the cause of sin. His holiness is the cause of man's consciousness of sin. But is God also the author of sin itself? Schleiermacher argues that we fall into the Manichaean heresy of metaphysical dualism with respect to redemption if sin is not grounded in a divine volition. To maintain a monistic world-view, Schleiermacher is forced to originate sin in the divine will. Sin, then, is not actually guilt; it is a natural predicament of man. It manifests itself in the sensuous nature of man, in the lower faculties of the soul. It is a disturbance of the harmony between man's natural powers which hinder the ascendancy of the God-consciousness within him. In keeping with this, Schleiermacher dismisses the New Testament idea of the devil as an accommodation on the part of Jesus to the prevailing views of his time or as proverbial sayings which possess no dogmatic authority for the Christian theologian.[26]

The affinity of Schleiermacher with the theology of the Enlightenment and that of German Idealism is obvious. Schleiermacher's concept of redemption confirms this impression. Jesus is the ideal representative of religion. He is distinguished from us by "the constant potency of His God-consciousness."[27] He is the Archetype and Founder of Christianity, the Second Adam. In that sense he is indispensable for us; therefore, theology ought to be christocentric. Jesus is the first Christian. For Schleiermacher, to believe is not to believe *in* Christ but to believe *as* Christ.

Christ's uniqueness is a matter of his God-consciousness. Schleiermacher's theology is a theology not of the Logos but of the Spirit. The virgin birth is dismissed as poorly attested in the New Testament and as dogmatically meaningless.[28] Furthermore, Schleiermacher sees the Gospel narratives as rather unreliable, although this does not

[25] *Ibid.*, Par. 79.
[26] *Ibid.*, Par. 45.
[27] *Ibid.*, Par. 94.
[28] *Ibid.*, Pars. 97, 2.

detract from their religious value. In *Christmas Eve* (1806), Schleiermacher portrays a number of friends united in the religious celebration of Christmas.[29] One of the characters, Leonhardt, argues that Christmas has little, if anything, to do with the historical Jesus. Historically speaking, Jesus stands closer to John the Baptist than to Paul.

Concerning the atonement, Schleiermacher sets forth two principal thoughts: "The Redeemer receives believers into the power of His God-consciousness, and this is His redemptive activity." [30] "The Redeemer receives the believers into the fellowship of His undisturbed blessedness, and this is His reconciling activity." [31]

SCHLEIERMACHER'S ETHICS

From the beginning of his career, Schleiermacher had a deep interest in the study of ethics. As early as 1790, about the time of his examination as a candidate for the ministry, he wrote with penetrating insight on the problem of freedom and determination.[32] His sermons at that time show the moralistic trait in rationalistic fashion. The significance of Christianity is seen in its being the source of a higher morality. For six years, until 1802, Schleiermacher was a preacher in Berlin, where he published his *Speeches*, in 1800. His *Soliloquies* on the problems of general ethics, published in 1801, were later developed in *A Draft of a System of Ethics*, published after his death in 1838. His university lectures, *Christian Ethics*, were published in 1843.

Schleiermacher's strong interest in ethics indicates his ethical approach to Christianity as a religion. It is another symptom of the anthropocentric emphasis in theology of which Schleiermacher made himself the spokesman. In the inner soul of man he discovered that law of individuality which man is in duty bound to follow. This principle placed Schleiermacher's ethics on the side of Goethe and removed him from Kant.

Schleiermacher defines ethics as the development of the individual in loving union with humanity, especially in friendship and in the

[29] Translated by William Hastie (Edinburgh: T. & T. Clark, 1890).

[30] *The Christian Faith,* Par. 100.

[31] *Ibid.,* Par. 101.

[32] *Werke,* Vol. II, contains the first critical edition of the manuscripts on ethics in the Berlin archives.

married state. The whole tendency of Schleiermacher toward a union of theology with philosophy also colors his Christian ethics. The aim is a cultural ethic such as that developed by Richard Rothe.[33] Sin, redemption, and regeneration lose their Christian meaning. They are Platonized. Scheiermacher shows no appreciation of the fact that between the Church and the world there is not merely a difference, but an antithesis. The "Christian" ethics of Schleiermacher is strongly influenced by his conception of a generally humanistic ethics. The Christian and the truly human were identical to him. It must be kept in mind that his life came to a close before he could give his ethical writings the form which he desired for their publication.

Summary

Karl Barth has said that Schleiermacher's theology is Moravianism of the highest order.[34] Zinzendorf's theology was one of mediation and feeling; such also was the theology of Schleiermacher. He tried to synthesize God and the world, culture and religion, philosophy and theology, intuition and feeling, experience and history, Lutheranism and Calvinism. The formal principle and the material principle of his theology merge into one, for religious consciousness is both the means by which truth is apprehended and the very content of the truth. In his *Speeches*, Schleiermacher rejects the idea of a natural religion; yet he uses a concept of religion arrived at *a priori* to determine the nature of Christianity. In Zinzendorf's theology the idea of God practically vanishes before the impression emanating from the person of Jesus. Schleiermacher, too, is somewhat at a loss when he has to speak about God, but he is rather eloquent in extolling the religious significance of the Redeemer.

Schleiermacher laid the foundations for converting Christian dogmatics into a philosophy of religion. He set the example for the speculative theology of the nineteenth century.

Schleiermacher's strong emphasis on feeling and on the Christian's dependence upon God as the unifying principle of his *The Christian Faith* makes his theology a religious psychology. It may be admitted that it was through this act of positing the essence of theology in

[33] Cf. pp. 227 ff.

[34] Karl Barth, *Die protestantische Theologie im 19. Jahrhundert*, p. 332.

feeling, in the heart, instead of in the intellect or in the will, that he secured a province of its own for theology. Theology again became respected. The contempt in which it had been held is reflected in the treatment of Pastor Goeze by Lessing.[35] Practically all outstanding young theologians in the age of Schleiermacher turned from theology to philosophy, as did Fichte, Schelling, and Hegel. It was also upon this basis of psychological orientation that Schleiermacher brushed aside the theocentric interest in theology and replaced it with the anthropocentric.[36] Man's soul, instead of God and his work which had been the leading interest of the Reformation, becomes the center of theological thought. Schleiermacher committed dogmatics to the trend of modern philosophy since Descartes. This shows how Schleiermacher labored for a compromise between the traditional metaphysical and the historical components of Christianity and his own modernized world-view in which subjectivism and psychological orientation were stressed. Among the conservatives it was in the men of the "mediating school" that the principles of Schleiermacher found special appreciation.[37]

Pietistic and orthodox conservatives, while stimulated by Schleiermacher, refused to follow his interpretation of the Christian faith. They re-established the thought-categories of the Reformation. They were convinced that he had departed from the analogy of faith. Although many admired his method, they realized that he had bypassed the theology of the Reformation.

The most delicate point among the suggestions for reform from Schleiermacher's *The Christian Faith* is the practice of developing the contents of dogmatics out of the "pious self-consciousness" or out of Christian experience. A positive Christianity, however, cannot accept a theology which does not make the testimony of Scripture, God's revelation to us, the primary source of truth and its authority. There are pages—not many—in Schleiermacher's *The Christian Faith* where he refers to New Testament passages, but he uses them mostly as references or illustrations. He does not draw from them as real

[35] This was in connection with the controversy over the so-called "Wolfenbüttel Fragments." Cf. Albert Schweitzer, *Quest of the Historical Jesus*, trans. W. Montgomery (London: A. & C. Black, 1931), pp. 13 ff.

[36] *The Christian Faith*, Par. 30.

[37] Cf. pp. 224 ff.

sources. Yet he does use them as proofs.[38] Evidently Schleiermacher discovered that he could not apply his principle consistently. It is very interesting to observe that Schleiermacher put the confessions of the Evangelical church–i.e., of the Prussian Union, with its emphasis on the Augsburg Confession, Luther's Small Catechism, and the Heidelberg Catechism–before the Scriptures. This must not be taken, he said, as establishing precedence for these documents. They always appeal to Scripture, and an appeal to them always implies an indirect appeal to Scripture.[39] This was in keeping with his position that the confessions must be regarded as the Christian experience of the churches. It was upon this that Schleiermacher psychologically built his emphasis upon Christian experience as the primary source of dogmatic truth.

The significance of Scripture for dogmatics was ignored by Schleiermacher. Every new topic in his dogmatics is introduced by the statement of a principle. None of these begin with the Holy Scriptures. In Paragraph 15 he formulates the principle that Christian statements of faith are concepts of Christian religious affections exhibited in the form of speech. Wobbermin, a follower of Schleiermacher in many things, remarks that if Schleiermacher had added an answer to the question which of these conditions of the soul are Christian, it would have led him to the historical contents of the religious life, and from there to the relation of faith to the Holy Scriptures. True, Wobbermin adds, the Scriptures can be understood only by means of the individual experience of faith. On the other hand, the really Christian experience of faith must constantly orientate and validate itself on the Holy Scriptures as its real norm.[40]

One of the most remarkable theologians of history, Schleiermacher was a man of penetrating intellect; a philosopher and a theologian; a universal mind of remarkable insight into psychological facts; a creative genius; an organizer of thought, endowed with a wonderful ability to systematize his materials; a seminal mind; a prophet at the portals of a new age; inexhaustible in suggestions, even where his leading position is not acceptable. He was the father of modern

[38] *Ibid.,* Pars. 27, 1.
[39] *Ibid.,* Par. 27.
[40] Wobbermin in *Religion in Geschichte und Gegenwart* (2nd ed.), V, 174-75.

theology. At the news of his death, August Neander told his students that history would record the beginning of a new era in theology.[41] Yet theologians have been working with his thinking for more than a century.

BIBLIOGRAPHY

BECKMANN, K. M. *Der Begriff der Haeresie bei Schleiermacher.* 1959.

BRANDT, R. B. *The Philosophy of Schleiermacher.* New York: Harper & Bros., 1941.

CROSS, GEORGE. *The Theology of Schleiermacher.* Newton Center, Mass., 1911.

DILTHEY, WILHELM. *Das Leben Schleiermachers.* 1870. Re-edited by H. MULERT, 1922.

FLUEGIKER, F. *Philosophie und Theologie bei Schleiermacher.* 1947.

JOERGENSEN, P. H. *Die Ethik Schleiermachers.* 1959.

NIEBUHR, RICHARD R. *Schleiermacher on Christ and Religion.* New York: Charles Scribner's Sons, 1964.

SCHLEIERMACHER, F. D. *Sämmtliche Werke.* 31 vols. Berlin, 1835 ff.

SEIFERT, PAUL. *Die Theologie des jungen Schleiermacher.* 1960.

SELBIE, WILLIAM B. *Schleiermacher, a Critical and Historical Study.* London: Chapman & Hall, 1913.

[41] *PRE,* XVII, 615.

CHAPTER III

THE RELIGION AND THEOLOGY OF GERMAN IDEALISM

By the middle of the eighteenth century the crisis in theology began to affect the educated laity. The life and work of Goethe (1749-1832) is a classical example. Born into a respected family which took its Christian faith quite seriously and trained in Scripture and Luther's Catechism, he strayed from the faith of his youth. Nonetheless Goethe retained a kind of benevolent attitude toward Christianity. Emancipation from the authority of the confessions of the Reformation became an almost universal factor. This was the age of classicism followed by romanticism in German literature. The religion of these men, with very few exceptions, was no longer the Christian faith. They looked for a substitute and found it in German Idealism. Although a Rationalist in religion, Kant was the founder of the movement. Kant and his followers showed the cultured that this world, with man as its crown, is governed by spiritual laws, organized upon spiritual principles, and that for man there is a way of ascent into the world of ideas: God, freedom, virtue, and immortality. Briefly stated, this is what we understand by German Idealism.

It was a time for a remarkable originality of life. There was a new interest in the mysteries of origins and development, in the reason and purpose of all history. The impulses for this literary movement came from the philosophers Descartes, Leibnitz, and especially Kant, and later from Fichte, Schelling, and Hegel. Among the poets it was especially Schiller who idealized the thoughts and suggestions of Kant and Fichte. Schiller aimed at deepening the categorical imperative of duty into a free and joyful response to aesthetic ideals. According to him, man is not a dead entity but living, active, and responsible. Schiller went beyond Kant in trying to reconcile freedom for the use of the natural with an over-optimistic trust in man's nature, which was idealized after the fashion of Greek antiquity. This shows that the poets went creatively beyond the philosophers.

Fundamentally the goal was not a new religion but a new view of world and life. Idealism was a reaction against intellectualism and mechanization. The leaders of the movement were, as a rule, not churchmen, but poets and thinkers. Yet religious interests were everywhere included. The groping for a new religion was unconscious. There was aversion to all form in religion and, therefore, people turned away from traditional orthodoxy. Their need for unbounded freedom of thought, together with their worldliness, kept them from identifying themselves with movements such as pietism or Moravianism. Some interested themselves in religiously tinged forms of romanticism. The positively evangelical features of the Reformation were objectionable to them. They liked the ideas of "Protestantism" in religion, and on this ground they admired Luther! Kant, Lessing, Fichte, Schiller, and Goethe all thought that a proper interpretation would put Luther on their side. They felt that their new movement had to complete the Reformation by setting up new and independent fundamentals. But they and their followers in the field of theology soon discovered that the Lutheran Reformation was hopelessly against them.

This peculiar Idealism was characterized by a great variety of interests: ancient classicism, a new humanism, features of mysticism, and religious aestheticism. In addition to these interests of the poets there came the conflicting systems of the philosophers. Missing in all of those profound and brilliant views was a religious unity that would connect the movement with at least the leading ideas of historic Christianity. The Bible and Luther were misinterpreted or ignored. It soon became evident that Christianity had not been able to permeate this movement of national classicism. It is true that Lessing's criticism of traditional Christianity is to be explained by his conviction that the truth of the Christian religion is not proved by logical arguments. Goethe, who in his younger years[1] was open to pietistic influences, soon settled upon views concerning God which committed him to Spinozian pantheism. It furnished the basis for his philosophy

[1] Through the Moravian Fräulein von Klettenberg. See Hirsch, *op. cit.*, IV, 247 ff.

of nature. Spinoza wanted to understand nature; Goethe wanted to enjoy it. Goethe was a realist, and was opposed to Kant's idealism.[2] In *Faust* he speaks of Mephisto and of sin, but it lacks the depth of the Bible; for Goethe sin was nothing but a pantheistic principle. Redemption is self-redemption. The ethical principles held by Goethe were to some extent in harmony with the ethics which Schleiermacher expressed in his *Soliloquies*. Here again, Goethe was motivated by his intense naturalism. Schiller came close to historic Christianity, but he did not accept it.

Post-Kantian Idealism

The leaders of the new generation objected to Kant's teaching, *das Ding an sich*. They strove to arrive at a consistent idealism by dissolving all the phenomena into elements of consciousness, as necessary productions of the mind, as a system of reason. From this standpoint J. F. Fichte (d. 1814) declared that the truth is in the inner sanctity of our own being. The "I" is the point of certainty. All else is the "non-I" which is projected by the "I" which, through a reaction to the "non-I," arrives at certainties. This philosophy, as stated in the previous chapter, was the foundation of Schleiermacher's subjectivism in theology: The subject posits itself as object. In this way the subject receives impressions through its own object, which contributes to assuring the subject of truth. In this philosophy there was no room for a theistic conception of God. For Fichte God was merely the "moral law of the universe." When this gave rise to charges of atheism, he began to speak of God as "Absolute Being."[3]

F. W. Schelling (d. 1854) started out as a follower of Fichte's philosophy of the "I" but his study of Spinoza and his love of nature prompted him to attempt the vindication of the external world. In his philosophy of nature the external world is a preliminary stage of the Spirit. Nature is the unconscious side. Like Fichte, he regards the Absolute as activity, as a process, not as substance like Spinoza. This period of his teaching found its final expression in his system of identity: The two great divisions of nature and self, matter and spirit,

[2] Cf. his witty remark: "My child, I acted wisely, I never thought about thinking."

[3] Cf. Fichte, *Popular Works,* trans. William Smith (London: Trübner & Co., 1889).

real and ideal are only relative. Both are originally one; they are simply two different manifestations of the Infinite One.

After 1806 this rationalistic pantheism gradually gave way to a theistic interpretation of the universe. The creation of the world is a free act of a supernatural and personal God. The present sinful world has come into being by a mystical fall from the original identity in which it lived in the bosom of the Absolute and Divine Being. Schelling's lectures on *Mythologie und Offenbarung* reveal the influence of Boehme's thesosophy. While Schelling's philosophy of nature greatly appealed to Goethe, the philosophy of the second and third period contributed, to some extent, to the rise of the Erlangen theology. Likewise the mystic conception of the Lord's Supper held by some of the high churchmen of the nineteenth century has its root in Schelling's philosophy of nature.[4]

The movement reached its climax in the teaching of George Friedrich Wilhelm Hegel (d. 1831). Hegel identified being with thinking. In thinking we grasp reality to the extent of objectifying it. He does not mean that the thinking of an individual is necessarily identical with the objective being; its errancy and accidentality are admitted. But absolute thought, absolute reason, and objective reality are the same. It must be kept in mind that thinking is a part of absolute thought. In Hegel the "substance" of Spinoza becomes subject or mind and its reality consists in the participation of absolute thought. In contrast to Schleiermacher, Hegel stands for intellectualism in religion and theology.

God, the reality in the background or at the foundation of this thought, is objectively comprehensible by human thinking. Philosophy and theology have the same contents, namely God as the Absolute Mind. They differ in that religion and theology can see and comprehend God only symbolically and mythologically, as in the teachings of the Bible. The Church's dogma could not help but include matters contradictory to reason. Philosophy furnishes the intellectual and rational formulas in which those contradictions are

[4] See our article "High Church Tendencies in Nineteenth Century Lutheranism," *The Augustana Quarterly,* April, 1946, especially pp. 108-109. Extracts from Schelling's *System of Transcendental Idealism* (1800) were published in English in Benjamin Rand's "Modern Classical Library" (Boston: Houghton Mifflin Company, 1908).

harmonized and reduced to unified expression.

There is a difference between Spinoza and Hegel that qualifies the latter's concept of God. Spinoza conceived of God and world as "substance" at rest. In Oriental fashion, Absolute Being is thought of as the mass of waters in the ocean, the waves rising and receding eternally into that "substance," ever the same in eternal stagnation, an up-and-down movement; never in the manner of a flowing stream. Spinoza predicated real existence to substance only as that in which individual things are contained as modes. He did away with the individual life of personality. The Ego was no individual reality to him. According to Hegel, with his emphasis upon mind and the spiritual phenomena, we see God and world in a process of continuous development. It is in this development that reality must be seen. It is the doctrine that man is the end and aim of all expressions of life in the universe. The divine self-consciousness is unfolding itself from nonbeing to being, from something potential to something actual.

As Schelling had already pictured it in his philosophy of nature, the development of that absolute being in God and world begins with the appearance of life in nature and then moves through the realms of the mind. The actual movement is thus defined as a revelation upward, from art to religion, and from religion to philosophy. The method of this dialectical movement is indicated by the famous three stages: thesis (assertion of the idea), antithesis (its critique), synthesis (its harmonization)—an old thought, indicated by Empedocles and embodied in the "golden mean" of Aristotle. In the history of religion especially we behold that upward development in which God reveals himself with an ever clearer self-consciousness. In paganism, Judaism, and Christianity we have these progressing stages of development in the process of unfolding the divine. In Hegelian thought historical development is the constant representation of the Absolute. There is no permanency in this historical process. Indistinguishable from the phenomena, God Himself is in a constant process of change. He has no real existence. The Absolute is always on the way of becoming real, but it never reaches that end as a completed process.

Hegel's pantheism has greatly influenced the study of history. Before Hegel the historian saw only isolated historical facts which he succeeded in explaining by a so-called "pragmatism of individual motives." History was always written in this way: There once was a man who did thus and so. Hegel taught the historian to see in all historical development the rule of an objective and universal reason. This thought took hold of many theologians, as we shall see. The movements of individuals and groups were taken to be the acts of God as the Absolute which realizes itself through the action of individuals and groups. Religion is the self-consciousness of the Absolute Spirit. His life is the divine life in man. God and the world are interdependent. Without the world God is not God, as Eckhardt and Boehme had said. Grace is God's response to man; sacrifice is man's response to God.

Christianity is the highest, most perfect religion. God is spirit. As Spirit God thinks. In his thinking activity the Spirit distinguishes himself from the Other and returns to the Other. Hence, God is a triune God. The Divine Idea manifests itself first in the nonspatial world of infinity, God as he is in himself; secondly in the world as a phenomenon of divine perfection; thirdly in the Church as the symbol of the reunion of God and man.

Sin is man's separation from Being. In reconciliation man is re-united with God, who is no stranger to him. To be reconciled with God is the essence of the kingdom of God. The death of Christ is the death of death itself, the negation of negation, that is, God's negation of man's estrangement from God. Christ is essentially the Reconciler. To regard him merely as a martyr of the truth like Socrates is not the Christian point of view, nor that of true religion. However, the historic Christ is not the object of faith. The real object of faith is the Eternal Christ as manifest in the kingdom of God on earth. The truth of the Christian faith is to be validated not by history but rather by philosophy. The reconciliation of reason and religion is the ultimate goal of philosophy.

According to Hegel, then, there was no possibility of sinning in the purely natural world. In the spiritual world, among men who have come into an existence of being themselves, there is the possibility of independence and freedom. Man, as part of God, must decide for God. Then man is good. If he decides for himself and serves himself, he is evil. All men have to make this decision. The biblical record puts this experience of every individual at the beginning of man's history, and the Church explains the universality of sin through the doctrine of original sin. Hegel's idea of an absolute unity in the universe necessitated the rejection of a moral and rational dualism. For Hegel man's fall and sin in general became not only a necessary striving toward the higher, but even a needed impulse toward it. The fall in Christian "mythology" made man real. It was a fall upward. The dualistic conception disappears. The consciousness of his sinful condition made man long for reconciliation. He could not find that reconciliation if it did not already exist in the unity of the divine and the human. The mission of Christ as the God-Man was to be an objective, visible representation of the existing reconciliation. There is no real chasm to be bridged. In both of these concepts (sin and atonement) the biblical interpretation of sin as guilt and the uniqueness of Christ and his work are brushed aside. Christ is the Reconciler only in a symbolical and mythological sense.

Passing reference should be made to Hegel's concept of the relation between Church and state. He stressed the importance of the state as the goal of historical development. Here ethics and religion were to find their highest form. The Church is only a means of accomplishing it. This is an idea that has had such outspoken theological advocates as Strauss, Coleridge, Baur, Rothe, Dilthey, and Troeltsch.[5]

Hegel's significance for theology may be summarized as follows. First, Hegel paved the way for the reduction of historic religion to philosophical ideas and rational concepts. In this he was followed by a strong school of liberalistic theologians. Conservative theologians also made use of the Hegelian categories in order to present an orthodox system of theology in which the old conflict between "faith" and "knowledge" was thought to have been resolved.

Second, through Hegel the tendency in theology toward pantheism, which has been noted in connection with Schleiermacher, was greatly augmented.

Hegelian Influence

Hegelian influence upon theology can be clearly discerned in the Swiss Theologian A. E. Biedermann (1819-1885). The starting point

[5] The resumé of Hegel's thought is based on R. H. Gruetzmacher, *Textbuch zur systematischen Theologie* (1923), pp. 54 ff.

in his *Christliche Dogmatik* (1868) is the dogma of the Church. He seeks to exhibit the mythical character of the Church's historical foundations as well as the logical contradictions of its formulations. His own positive contribution consists in reducing the religious contents of the foundations of the dogma to philosophical formulas. The belief in God as person is rejected and replaced by Hegel's idea of the Absolute Mind. Individual immortality is held to be a matter of indifference; the truth of this teaching lies in the continuance of life in the universal mind which underlies all objective reality. The Christian idea of redemption is a representation of the ideal thought of redemption, which for the first time in history arrived at self-consciousness and realization in the person of Jesus.

The greatest response to Hegelian ideas is found among biblical scholars. From his standpoint of an evolution of the divine mind in history, Hegel could not admit the teaching of the English Deists that religion was originally pure and that it had become corrupted only gradually. David Hume had already taken the opposite position and taught a development from the imperfect toward the perfect. This had also been the teaching of Voltaire in France. Hegel accepted this thought and added the idea of an absolute progressive mind as the moving factor in this evolution. J. K. W. Vatke, pupil of Hegel and professor of Old Testament literature at the University of Berlin, published the first volume of his *Biblische Theologie* in 1835. For the first time Hegel's concept of evolution is applied to the history of the Old Testament. The Jahvistic monotheism of the Old Testament prophets is regarded as the result of a gradual evolution from the old, crude Semitic worship of nature to the purer concept of a personal God. Not much notice was taken of this book when it appeared, but here we have the teachings and principles of Wellhausen's school and its successors, all dominated by the Hegelian idea of evolution.

When Hegel died (1831), the left wing of his school, which comprised most of his followers (the so-called Young Hegelians), moved toward religious radicalism. The hope that Hegel's philosophy would be the basis for the union between faith and knowledge was soon shattered. The chief representative of the Hegelian left was David Frederick Strauss (d. 1874). He began as a teacher of theology at

Tübingen. Because of his radicalism he was removed from his theological position to one as teacher of classical subjects. Strauss refused this assignment and accepted a call to Zurich. Protests from the Church soon caused him to be pensioned, and he spent the rest of his life as a private scholar.

It was Strauss' book, *The Life of Jesus* (1835), which shattered the phantom of agreement between Hegelian philosophy and the faith of the Church. He began by denying the authenticity of the miracles of Jesus. Since the miracles are reported as historic in the Gospels of the New Testament, the Gospels cannot be accepted as history. The stories of Jesus must be legends which gradually came to be believed and which were woven about the Master by devoted disciples. These legends may be regarded as truth, but only in the sense that what the Gospels attribute to the individual can be claimed by humanity as a whole. Hegel had taught that in the God-Man Jesus we have an expression of the Universal Idea. Strauss concluded that the Idea does not exhaust its fullness in one individual, but distributes itself through the entire race. He argued that Christ can neither be the perfect revelation of the divine nature nor the perfect revelation of human nature. God can only be perfectly revealed by the entire kingdom of spirits; and the full Idea of man can only be perfectly revealed by the entire human race. The truth of the Gospel stories of Christ, according to Strauss, is simply that the human race lives, suffers, dies, is raised from the grave and ascends to heaven.

In the Gospels, then, we have myth and fiction. Strauss sees the starting point in stories of the Old Testament, occasionally also in legends of the pagan religions: the virgin birth of Christ in Isaiah 7:14; the star of Bethlehem in the star of Bileam (Numbers 24:17); the feeding of the five thousand in the wonderful feeding of the widow at Zarepta, and so on. According to earlier statements, these myths developed spontaneously, without intention, and were inspired by the powerful impression of Jesus upon his followers. In a fundamentally reconstructed "Life of Jesus for the German People" (*Leben Jesu für das Deutsche Volk*, 1864), Strauss maintained that these mythological representations were unconsciously created by the disciples for the purpose of presenting the life of Jesus in romances.

Strauss had gradually become very radical. In his *Christliche Glau-*

benslehre of 1840 he subjected the faith of the Church to a destructive criticism. He ridiculed the theistic conception of God as an impossible dualism. Man, the unity of the finite and the infinite, feels his limitations and produces God as a person over against himself. In clear thinking we must learn to conceive of God as the Infinite who arrives at personal representation in the finite spirits. In death, personality is lost and we return to the divine Unity. This was outright pantheism. There was no room in Strauss' system for the biblical and traditional faith of the Church.

In later writings, including the above-mentioned second *Life of Jesus* (1864), especially in his last book, "The Old and the New Faith" (*Der Alte und der Neue Glaube*, 1872), he moves on the downward grade as a theologian. He asks the question: "Are we still Christians?" His answer is negative. He characterizes Christianity as a modified Judaism. Christ's resurrection is mere "humbug." Our religion is seen in our relation to the universe in which there is order, law, reason, and kindness; but this universe is to him a blind mechanism without a purpose as far as Strauss is concerned. Ultimately he turned to materialism. There is no hope for a life to come. He praised Darwin's discoveries as the bible of a new religion without theology. The Church was to disappear. He recommended national classics as books of devotion, recommended the conversion of church buildings into concert halls, and advocated theatres as places of worship. As time went on Strauss' degeneration as theologian and as a Christian became more and more apparent. In his last years Strauss wrote a poem in which he mocked his own funeral. Instead of a church service, he wanted a burlesque to be performed with rotten eggs and some cats on hand.[6] This was the end of the David Frederick Strauss whose *Life of Jesus* succeeded in putting whole generations of theologians to work on the problems of Christology.

Another very remarkable representative of Hegelian philosophy in theology was F. C. Baur (1792-1862), the founder of the Tübingen school which included Zeller, Schwegler, Volkmar, Hilgenfeld, Holsten, and for a time Ritschl. Baur was a remarkable man. He is the only one in the first part of the nineteenth century who can be compared with Schleiermacher in mental endowment and in power

[6] Seeberg, *Die Kirche Deutschlands im 19. Jahrhundert*, p. 248.

of criticism. Schleiermacher had devoted himself chiefly to the dogmatic interests of the new century. Baur raised the historical questions: the problem of the history of dogma, the history of Christianity in the first centuries, and, subsidiary to all this, the history of the origin of the New Testament canon, to which he devoted his special attention. In his labors as a critic of history he showed a persevering diligence and a learning that was the marvel of the age. Lichtenberger describes him as reserved and detached from life. "He remained confined within the domain of intelligence. For him it is the world of thought and of science that alone exists, while the world of practical activity, of moral struggling and suffering, seemed closed to him. But purely as a scholar he was one of the most eminent representations of the intellectual nobility of Germany in the university of the world." [7]

Baur's research was based upon Hegelian ideas. Christianity is not a finished product expressed in the person of Christ and in the New Testament; but rather is it the expression of an idea in progressive development. On this basis Baur wanted to explain Protestantism as a functioning principle through the history of the Christian Church. For him the Reformation was beset with the transcendental limitations of Roman Catholicism, but the "Protestant idea" or "principle" constantly presses forward to spiritualization. The Anabaptists and Socinians did the pioneer work in this direction. The "new reformation" is said to have come with the age of rationalism as it was born of the new philosophy. Even in the most advanced religion of the present day, Baur said, there are still too many remnants of supernaturalism, irrationalism and mysticism, which must be overcome by a religion which is more humanized, rationalized, subjectified and spiritualized.

In order to discredit traditional religion and to furnish the foundations for the new religion, Baur reconstructed the whole history of doctrine upon the basis of Hegel's scheme for historical development. First, there is a period when in the form of a "thesis" a new, one-sidedly expressed idea is proposed in a comparatively crude and simple form. Against this elementary "idea" an antithesis arises

[7] F. Lichtenberger, *History of German Theology in the Nineteenth Century,* p. 380.

which contains corrective and supplementary elements, and promises greater perfection. But this antithesis is also one-sided because it carries the opposition too far. After a time of controversy between these two extremes a middle position, a "synthesis," is found, which represents clarified truth or at least is a compromise. Baur saw an illustration of such stages in the unfolding of the Idea in the history of doctrine. Among his works connected with it are a work on the difference between Catholicism and Protestantism,[8] a historical survey of the Christian philosophy of religion,[9] a work on Manichaeism,[10] a history of the doctrine of the atonement,[11] a history of the Trinity and incarnation,[12] and finally, a manual on the history of doctrine.[13]

Catholicism, Baur held, was succeeded by Old Protestantism, which was then followed by a New Protestantism. The field in which Baur and his followers concentrated was that of New Testament writings. His interest centered on the question whether the authorship of the New Testament writings entitle them to be standards of truth. Following the Hegelian scheme he finds the "thesis" in the period of Ebionitism, primitive or Judaeo-Christianity, or the Petrine Christianity, where the faith of the first Christians may be summed up in the single proposition: Jesus, the Messiah in whom the prophecies of the Old Testament are fulfilled. The representatives of this position are mostly Peter, James and "John." The literary documents are found in legendary narratives such as the Gospel of the Hebrews, of Peter, of the Ebionites, of the Egyptians; among the canonical books, the Gospel of Matthew and the Book of Revelation reflect the same tendency. In these writings Baur finds a narrow particularism which maintained itself with great tenacity in the early Christian Church. Against this "thesis" came the "antithesis" of Paul, who proposed "a new principle of life with a universal character, in open rupture with Judaism, the temple and the Mosaic Law."[14]

[8] *Über den Gegensatz des Protestantismus und des Catholicismus,* 1833.
[9] *Die christliche Gnosis oder die christliche Religionsphilosophie,* 1835.
[10] *Über den Manichaeismus,* 1836.
[11] *Geschicte der Lehre von der Versöhnung,* 1838.
[12] *Geschichte von der Dreieinigkeit und Menschwerdung Gottes,* 3 vols., 1841 ff.
[13] *Lehrbuch der Dogmengeschichte,* 1847; 3rd ed., 1867.
[14] Cf. *PRE,* II, 473.

The four great Epistles of Paul (Romans, Galatians, and both Corinthians), the only authentic ones, give evidence of Paul's struggle against Judaeo-Christianity. The conflict lasted beyond the lifetime of Paul into the middle of the second century. Then the inroads of Gnosticism and the persecutions of the Roman emperors made a union necessary and a compromise was reached. This event is reflected particularly in the "pseudo-Pauline" Epistles to the Thessalonians, Ephesians, Colossians, Philippians, Philemon, Timothy, Titus, and in Luke, with Mark in retouched form. Baur and his school decided that while the disciple of Christ was the author of the Apocalypse, he had not written the Gospel. They declared that the Fourth Gospel was written in the second century as high metaphysical speculation and related no actual history. The facts and acts attributed to Christ are only starting points, pretexts for his discourses, and attuned to the program contained in the prolog.

A few critical remarks on the "Tübingen Scheme" will suffice. Baur's fundamental mistake lay in the preconceived ideas of Hegelian categories. His criticism was directed by intuition, not by rational, historical reflection. His reconstruction of the history of primitive Christianity has gone up in smoke. Yet for a full generation his theory dominated the field of New Testament research to such an extent that all who refused to fall in line were branded as "unscientific." Seeberg remarks of Baur: "He gave work for two generations of theologians. One generation he forced to accept his views, the other he forced into the work of refuting them." [15] When we consider how completely the Tübingen school broke down, then we have an illustration of how thoroughly an age can be deluded by a "scientific" system. Lichtenberger characterizes Baur's book on the history of dogma as "an intellectual mechanism moved by a special force, a purely logical movement which receives no impulses from without and which notably remains without relation to the history of Christian life and morals." [16] Baur took the person of Christ too little into account. He wanted to explain the historical origin of Christianity, but he was unable to see anything of its supernatural character. For this reason he could not explain the resurrection of

[15] Seeberg, *Die Kirche Deutschlands im 19. Jahrhundert,* p. 145.

[16] Lichtenberger, *op. cit.,* pp. 380-81.

Christ and the conversion of Paul. Like Strauss, Baur discussed the question whether we are still Christians to the end of his life. He, too, arrived at a negative answer.

The crisis of theology occasioned by Hegel's philosophy is also apparent in Ludwig Feuerbach (1804-1872). Feuerbach was not a theologian but a philosopher and as such essentially an anti-theologue. Of his numerous writings the most important ones are *Das Wesen des Christentums* (1841) and *Das Wesen der Religion* (1851).[17] To Feuerbach, Hegel is still a theologian in disguise. Hegel is still a supernaturalist in that he postulates a divine Being in reason, separate from the individual. The abstract way of thinking in Hegel's system alienates man from his fellow man. Sense, experience, and love are better guides to reality and truth than pure thought. Where love is absent, truth is missing. Luther taught that God should be sought not in heaven but in the manger and in the elements of the Supper. This is a better way to know the truth than Hegel's speculative method. Nevertheless, Feuerbach believed that the decline of theology began precisely with Luther.[18] When the Reformer said, "As you believe in God, so you have him," he started a movement of which Schleiermacher and Hegel are the most conspicuous exponents: self-consciousness is God-consciousness. To be true, theology must become anthropology. In Feuerbach, man's consciousness of the Infinite becomes the infinity of consciousness. "God was my first thought, reason my second, man is my third and least thought."[19] The ascent of humanity will lead to the apotheosis of man. Religion has its origin in man's wish, it is a product of man's wishful thinking. As man's wishes are, so are his gods.

Feuerbach marks a turning point in the spiritual climate of Germany. He was soon superseded by Max Stirner (d. 1856), in whose eyes Feuerbach was still too religious because he believed in a supreme law for humanity. In *The Ego and His Own*, published in 1845,[20] Stirner proclaimed the Ego as the only law of life. All

[17] The former was translated into English by Marian Evans, *The Essence of Christianity*, 1853; reprinted with Introduction by Karl Barth and Foreword by H. Richard Niebuhr (New York: Harper, 1957).

[18] On Luther, see *Feuerbach, Sämmtliche Werke* (1903 ff.), Vol. VII. 311 ff.

[19] *Religion in Geschichte und Gegenwart* (2nd ed.), II, 571.

[20] Translated by S. T. Byington (New York: Bomi & Liveright, 1918).

restrictions on the individual are ridiculed as nonsense. Modern existentialism owes something to Feuerbach, for the "I," according to Feuerbach, fulfills its destiny only in relation to the "Thou." Feuerbach's criticism includes the whole range of theologians from Schleiermacher to Ritschl and Frank of Erlangen, for all of them wanted to base religious truth on the self-consciousness of man.

Bruno Bauer (1809-1882) disposed of the historicity of Jesus by making him a mere idea produced by the Graeco-Roman world in the closing years of the second century.[21] In proposing this view he gives an interesting anticipation of ideas which were later developed in more detail in the historico-religious school, where Christ appears, so to speak, as "a working hypothesis of God's character." Strauss' idea of the mythical character of the Gospels ultimately issued in the idea that Christ himself was a myth, as in the thought of Drews, von Schnehen, and Kalthoff.[22]

BIBLIOGRAPHY

FINDLAY, JOHN M. *Hegel: a Re-examination.* New York: The Macmillan Company, 1958.

HEGEL, G. W. F. *Early Theological Writings.* Translated by T. M. KNOX with an Introduction by RICHARD KRONER. Chicago: University of Chicago Press, 1948.

HOBHOUSE, L. T. *The Metaphysical Theory of the State.* London: George Allen & Unwin, Ltd., 1951.

HOOK, SIDNEY. *From Hegel to Marx.* New York: Humanities Press, 1950.

KNOX, T. M. (trans.). *Hegel's Early Theological Writings.* Chicago: University of Chicago Press, 1948.

KRONER, RICHARD. *Von Kant bis Hegel.* 1961.

MONTGOMERY, M. *Studies in the Age of Goethe.* London: Oxford University Press, 1931.

[21] Bruno Bauer, *Christus und die Caesaren. Der Ursprung des Christentums aus dem römischen Griechentum,* 1877.

[22] On the whole development from Strauss to Bauer, cf. Albert Schweitzer, *op. cit.,* pp. 68 ff., 314 ff.; Barth, *op. cit.,* pp. 355 ff.

CHAPTER IV

CONFESSIONAL THEOLOGY

During the first half of the nineteenth century there was a revival of religion throughout Germany. This religious movement was intimately connected with the romantic school in literature and the rebirth of German patriotism during the years of the Napoleonic oppression. The revival had a marked pietistic character in that it was primarily concerned with the salvation of the individual. Sin and grace were looked upon as the fundamental facts and experiences in the religious life. Although the tercentenary of the Reformation in 1817 brought with it only a very limited emphasis on the religious character of the Reformation, even as early as 1817 some individuals conscientiously turned back to the Reformation and united the subjective revival of the religious life with the objective content of Reformation theology. This was especially the case in the Ninety-five Theses of Claus Harms (1778-1855) with their uncompromising attack on rationalism and the Church union to be established in Prussia.[1] Harless and Thomasius, the founders of the Erlangen school, harked back to objective Lutheranism. They said: "We were Lutherans long before we knew it. We finally discovered that the content of our personal experience was also the content of the Lutheran Confessions." [2] The way was not from the objective confessions to religion but from a personal religious experience to the confessions of the sixteenth century. This new attitude toward the Reformation was not limited to the symbolical writings, but also included Luther's works,[3] the hymnals, the liturgical forms, and the Church orders of that period. The Lutheran church awoke to a new

[1] The Theses are given in English in *The Lutheran Cyclopedia* ed. H. E. Jacobs and J. A. W. Haas (New York: Charles Scribner's Sons, 1889).

[2] G. Thomasius, *Das Wiedererwachen des evangelischen Lebens in der lutherischen Kirche Bayerns* (1867), pp. 244-45.

[3] The Erlangen edition of Luther's works was begun in 1826.

life. The influence of Kliefoth of Mecklenburg was felt in the area of liturgies and Church order.[4] A new relationship to the state was sought which would give greater independence to the Church. The theological periodical of this revived Lutheranism was *Zeitschrift für Protestantismus und Kirche* ("Journal for Protestantism and the Church"). This title was explained as meaning: "We do not want Protestantism without the Church nor the Church without Protestantism."

Out of this religious revival and ecclesiastical re-organization there arose a Lutheran theology that sought to express its content in scientific form and which consisted of two main types: orthodox theology, which became known under the somewhat misleading term "theology of repristination," and the more progressive Erlangen theology.

The Theology of Repristination

This school sought not only to restore the treasures that had been cast aside by rationalism but also attempted to revive the scientific method of the Lutheran theology of the sixteenth and seventeenth centuries. A statement of its aim is found in *Die Theologie der Tatsachen wider die Theologie der Rhetorik*, published in 1856 by August Vilmar (1800-1868), professor at Marburg University. "Theology," he says, "must know that she has nothing new to say, nothing new to discover, but that her task is to preserve the spiritual treasure that has been given in Holy Scripture and received by the church, in such a form that it may be transmitted to future servants of the church undiminished, certain, and in its most useful form."[5] Vilmar's demands were, in fact, only the application of the program of literary romanticism to theology. Just as romanticism saw all perfection and light in the Middle Ages and reverted to them, so Lutheran theology was to return to the treasures inherited from the Fathers, to cherish and to transmit them to coming generations in the most practical form. The attempt was made to carry this out in all departments of theology.

First came the biblical disciplines with a series of Old Testament

[4] T. Kliefoth, *Liturgische Abhandlungen,* 8 vols., 1854 ff.

[5] August Vilmar, *Die Theologie der Tatsachen wider die Theologie der Rhetorik,* p. 16. Vilmar, an ardent student of German language and literature, was also the author of a remarkable *History of German Literature,* 1845.

studies by E. W. Hengstenberg (1802-1869) and a number of his students. He defended the genuineness of all the biblical writings according to the understanding of the churchly and rabbinical traditions. The Old Testament was looked upon as a prophecy that contained all the essential Christian doctrines.[6] Hengstenberg arrived at his conclusions on the basis of a markedly allegorical-spiritualizing exegesis. This method was also applied to the writings of the New Testament. The greatest stress was laid on the proof of the genuineness and authenticity of the biblical writings. He tried to read, the terminology of the later dogma back into the New Testament. As regards New Testament prophecy, Hengstenberg was an exponent of the so-called continuous-historical method.

C. P. Caspari, (1814-1892) a pupil of Hengstenberg, was born in Germany but held a theological chair in the University of Oslo, Norway, after 1847. Caspari used to refer to himself as a "hard-boiled Hengstenbergian." He wrote an Arabic grammar (1844 ff.) which was later translated into German (1859), English (1862), and French (1879-80). He was also a pioneer in the science of comparative symbolics.

A similar attitude towards Scripture became the basis for the dogmatic presentation of systematic theology. Its chief exponent was F. A. Philippi (1809-1882) of Dorpat and Rostock, who published the extensive and widely read *Kirchliche Glaubenslehre* (6 vols., 1854 ff.). This work seeks to present the ideas of the old Lutheran teachings together with a refutation of the attacks made on them in later times. Following the impetus given by Schleiermacher, Philippi regards "the experimental consciousness of the believers," as the source of systematic theology, but in practice systematic theology's only determining source is the logical use of the content of Scripture. "The source from which dogmatics must draw is the dogmatician's reason enlightened by revelation." [7] Consequently he begins his *Glaubenslehre* with a declaration concerning the inerrant, inspired Scriptures, in which he teaches an inspiration not of words but of the Word. "The Apostles, and Prophets, immersed in the Spirit of God,

[6] E. W. Hengstenberg, *Christology of the Old Testament* (Grand Rapids: Kregel Publications, 1956).

[7] F. A. Philippi, *Kirchliche Glaubenslehre* (3rd ed.), I, 125.

living and laboring under His impulses, could only speak with words filled with the Spirit." While claiming inspiration for the sacred writers, he explicitly denies verbal inspiration. "The single letters, syllables, and words, apart from their content and connection, are not to be regarded as something to be dictated from without, for Scripture is not the words but the Word of God; if it were, divine providence would not have permitted these sacred words to have been transmitted to us in variant readings." [8]

Philippi became involved in a vehement controversy with Hofmann of Erlangen over the orthodox Protestant statement of the doctrine of the atonement. "It is only because of reconciliation and justification, as taught in the Confessions, that I am a Lutheran theologian, a Lutheran Christian, or a Christian at all." He continues to argue that whoever belittles the comfort of faith in the atoning blood of Christ and in the imputation of Christ's righteousness, "robs me of Christianity itself." "Then I might as well have remained in the religion of him who was my father according to the flesh, Abraham." [9]

Although this school aimed at a complete return to the theology of the seventeenth century, influences emanating from the thought-world of the nineteenth century are discernible in its teaching. Theodor Kliefoth (1810-1895) in his first large work *Einleitung in die Dogmengeschichte* (1839), clearly portrays the influence of Schleiermacher and Hegel. The development of dogma is presented as divinely guided and as an actual, progressive incarnation of Christ. The development of dogma comes about as one doctrine after the other enters into the dogmatic consciousness. When one group of dogmas has been scientifically developed in all its aspects, another group demands consideration. This rationalistic and optimistic conception is corrected by Kliefoth himself through the recognition both of the supernatural and also the sinful element involved. In his work, *Acht Bücher von der Kirche* (1854), he speaks of the Church as a living organism, constituted by God, consisting of "articulated institutions and callings, offices and stations." [10] In regarding legal order as a part of the essence of the Church, Kliefoth has been accused of

[8] *Ibid.,* I, 251.
[9] Philippi, *Herrn Dr. von Hofmann gegenüber der lutherischen Versöhnungs- und Rechtfertigungslehre* (1856), p. 56.
[10] Gruetzmacher, *op. cit.,* p. 126.

Roman and Reformed tendencies. Vilmar held similar views, especially in his teaching of ordination as the means by which the office of the ministry is perpetuated. Another exponent of this high church conception was Wilhelm Loehe (1808-1872). Furthermore, the teaching of these men on the sacraments clearly marks a deviation from the traditional Lutheran conception. The office of the ministry, according to Kliefoth, safeguards the efficacy of the sacraments. While the Word, as Vilmar says, affects man, through the Spirit from above, the sacrament is a "physical action" of God with a gracious effect through matter, both on man's body and spirit.[11] The influence of Schelling's philosophy of nature is evident in a manner that cannot be mistaken. The teaching of these men forms an interesting parallel to that of the Oxford theologians of nineteenth-century England.

Vilmar also criticized the young Luther. "It is now admitted," he says, "that the book, *Address to the Christian Nobility*, is not properly speaking a Reformation writing, that Luther here overstepped his own appointed bounds."[12] Vilmar seeks to remove everything revolutionary from Luther. For Vilmar, Luther was essentially the preserver of a purer antiquity, and of the true Catholic Church from which the Roman church had strayed, especially at the close of the Middle Ages and later as defined in the Tridentine Council. In Vilmar's view Luther follows the pattern of a political conservative and of a citizen of a legitimate monarchical state. Consequently, Vilmar bitterly denounced the Prussian annexation of his native Hesse in 1866. In the same way, the Jewish convert, Julius Stahl (1802-1861), a jurist, regarded Lutheranism as a pillar for the support of a Christian monarchy. Consequently this school of theology had a close connection with the conservative and reactionary political movement in Germany during the time of Metternich, and most of its non-Prussian followers remained opposed to Bismarck even after the unification of Germany in 1871.

Erlangen Theology

This school is also rooted in the religious revival of the nineteenth century. In contrast to "repristination theology," it aimed at a

[11] Vilmar, *op. cit.*, p. 68.
[12] *Luther, Melanchthon und Zwingli* (posthumously edited in 1869), p. 51.

healthy synthesis of the Lutheran heritage with the new learning in order to teach the old truth in a new garb. Repristination theology interpreted the sixteenth century in the light of the seventeenth; the Erlangen school, on the other hand, wanted to make a careful distinction between Reformation and post-Reformation theologies, trying to uphold Luther and the confessions against the dogmaticians of the seventeenth century. To the men of the Erlangen school, the confessions were expressions of the religious experience of the Church in its conflict with error and in its search for truth. "Regarding the reproach of repristination," Thomasius said, "it is true that we have held fast faithfully to the Confessions of the church, and have defended them on many sides when they were assailed. But it is not true that they have ever been a mere external law or bond for us. We have confessed them from within because we found in them the expression of our own convictions and because we have been convinced of their scripturalness."[13] This distinction between the intentions of the confessions and their mere wording opened up a new vista before the eyes of the Church: Confessional theology must not be something static, but rather a dynamic force in the life of the Church. This new approach to the formulas of the past accounts for the original and progressive element in Erlangen theology. In the second place, this attitude explains the trend toward biblicism which is found in the Erlangen school. The Scriptures, the confessions, and religious experience are the three great principles upon which the Erlangen school established itself.

Erlangen theology also differed from Vilmar and Kliefoth in principle, and from Loehe with regard to the nature of the Church. Friedrich Hoefling, in his book, *Grundsätze evangelisch-lutherischer Kirchenverfassung* (1850) opposed the high church tendencies of his time.[14] He maintained that the external forms of Church life do not belong to the essence of the Church. The Church is a gathering of believers; its organization is a matter of historical expediency. While the ministry of the Word itself is a divine institution, the form, whether episcopal or congregational, cannot claim such dignity. This concept of Church and ministry was accepted not only by the other

[13] Thomasius, *op. cit.*

[14] For literature on the controversy see Francis Pieper, *Christian Dogmatics* (St. Louis: Concordia Publishing House, 1951-53), III, 445.

leading men of Erlangen—Harless, Hofmann, and Frank—but also by a number of teachers of Church law, particularly, in its extreme form, by Rudolf Sohm (d. 1917).[15]

The ethical peculiarity of the Erlangen theology is marked by the attempt to find a purely religious and Christian foundation for ethics. In contrast to the combination of theological with philosophical ethics in Neo-Protestantism, Hofmann declared: "How can the science of Christian morality be derived from the idea of morality in general or from man's ethical disposition, when for Christians the reality of ethical goodness is revealed only in Jesus Christ? There is no other starting point for theological ethics except one that at the very beginning is distinct from philosophical ethics." [16] As the source and motivation for Christian ethics Hofmann refers to justification, whereas Harless[17] and Frank[18] refer to regeneration. In regard to the relation of Christian ethics to the world, the Erlangen men hold a middle position. As Lutherans they value the world and its natural order as a gift of the Creator. On the other hand, they are convinced that sin has infected all creation and that communion with God surpasses all earthly values. As a result, a double asceticism is required of the Christian: he is to disregard all temporal goods as a means of attaining to the highest good, and he is to eliminate all influences of the world that might affect his personality. The immediate and paramount subject of ethics is the individual Christian. Since the individual is conditioned by his various social relationships, and he in turn is to influence others, the influence of Christian ethics must be extended into society.

The school's real founder and greatest genius was Johann Christian Konrad von Hofmann. He was born of poor parents in 1810. In 1827 he entered the university at Erlangen. Here he came in close contact with both Christian Krafft, pastor of the German Reformed congrega-

[15] Rudolf Sohm, *Kirchenrecht,* Vol. I (1892); Vol. II (1923). His position is classically expressed by the statement: "The Church of Christ is invisible. . . . There is no visible church. As a visible organization the church is a part of the world" (II, 135). The dangerous implications of this view became painfully evident in the struggle of the German churches against Hitler's effort to bring the churches in line with legal concepts of the state.

[16] *Zeitschrift für Protestantismus und Kirche,* 1863.

[17] Adolf von Harless, *Christliche Ethik,* 1842; 8th ed. 1893.

[18] Reinhold von Frank, *System der christlichen Sittlichkeit,* 1884 ff.

tion at Erlangen and professor at the university, and Karl von Raumer, a professor of natural sciences. Both were instrumental in Hofmann's conversion to a genuine evangelical piety. In 1829 Hofmann went to Berlin, where historian Leopold von Ranke attracted the young student far more than either Schleiermacher or Hengstenberg. In 1838 he established himself as an unsalaried lecturer at Erlangen. Four years later he went to Rostock in northern Germany. Returning to Erlangen in 1845, he held a leading position on the theological faculty until his death in 1877.

By following the idealistic interpretation of history, Hofmann effected a union of biblicism and Lutheranism with German Idealism. The approach of both Lutheran Orthodoxy and rationalism had been unhistorical. The former regarded a book (the Bible), the latter, human reason, as the medium of revelation. In the eyes of Hofmann history is revelatory. His theology is one of redemptive history. This is his chief significance for Christian theology. The idea of a history of redemption goes back to the "federal theology" of John Coccejus, represented in Erlangen by Christian Krafft, and to the Swabian Pietist, Bengel.

This close union of history and metaphysics is also found in the philosophy of Schelling, who exerted the most direct influence on Hofmann.[19]

This influence is most noticeable in Hofmann's treatment of prophecy and fulfillment in the Old and New Testament.[20] Prophecy is fulfilled in the first place not in words but in related facts, the significance of which is subsequently made clear by the word. The history of Israel is a related chain of actions which lead up to and prepare for Jesus Christ. "In the holy and blessed man Jesus the history of

[19] The influence of Coccejus and his school is also evident in the Reformed theologians Ebrard and Menken, as well as in Beck of Tübingen. This influence accounts for the biblicism in their theologies. For them the material and arrangement of dogmatics is subordinate to the content and historical development of the Scriptures. Their intense interest in the eschatological features of the Bible—world mission, conversion of Israel, the Anti-Christ, and the millennium—is also explained by this influence. Hofmann was first of all an exegete; Menken conscientiously followed the purely analytic method of preaching. Even Ritschl presented his theology in the form of a biblical study, *Rechtfertigung und Versöhnung*.

[20] *Weissagung und Erfüllung im Alten und im Neuen Testament,* Part I (1841; Part II (1844).

the relation of God and man has reached its preliminary consummation."[21] For Hofmann the history of Christ is the starting point of a further history which includes in itself another prophecy concerning the completion of communion between God and man. "In Christ's self-manifestation to the world we have both history and prophecy: history of the continued establishment of the communion between God and man, prophecy in the continual pointing to the final form of that communion."[22] The heathen religions are included in this prophetic view of history: "The heathen felt His presence in creation but did not differentiate between Him and created things, and they so mourned over Him when they mourned over the death of their religious heroes: Cadmilus and Dionysus and Adonis they call Him, and they wept over Him all too early, long before He died on the cross . . . The heathen knew of sons of God all too early, long before Jesus Christ, the Son of God, was exalted and made the Lord over all things."[23]

Hofmann made this so-called prophetic conception of history the basis of his second great work, a book on Scripture, *Der Schriftbeweis*.[24] Prior to any scientific investigation he says that Christianity has its independent existence first, in the experience of regeneration of the individual, second, in the history and fact of the Church, and third, in the Scriptures. The soundness of a man's theology is conditioned by its agreement with this threefold testimony of the Holy Spirit. Hofmann wrestles with two main problems in this book: the method of dogmatics and the form of scriptural proof.

The experience of regeneration makes the individual conscious of being a member of the Church. As there is but one faith, the Church's faith, the individual has his faith in common with all. Faith is the primary constituent factor of Christianity, which he defines as "a personal communion between God and man mediated through Christ Jesus."[25] Hofmann clearly distinguishes between faith and theology, which is the scientific interpretation of Christianity. In contrast to faith, a man's theology is conditioned by his own individ-

[21] *Ibid.*, I, 32.
[22] *Ibid.*, I, 40.
[23] *Ibid.*, I, 39.
[24] *Der Schriftbeweis*, 2 vols., 1852 ff.
[25] *Ibid.*, I, 7.

ual personality. In writing a book on theology, a theologian is really writing an autobiography. "I as a Christian am the primary object of my scientific investigation as a theologian." [26]

The emphasis of Erlangen theology on the psychological element is unquestionably due to the influence of Schleiermacher. However, the principal differences between Schleiermacher and Hofmann must not be overlooked. While Schleiermacher developed his dogmatics out of his religious self-consciousness, Hofmann intended to describe the divine fact in his life by which he was made a Christian. Schleiermacher's concept of God is conditioned by his monistic philosophy; Hofmann's is determined by the revelation of God embodied in Scripture. Schleiermacher was a religious intuitionist interested in the universal truth of religion; Hofmann was a confessional Lutheran with the Scriptures and confessions as his starting point. In brief, for Schleiermacher religious self-consciousness is the source of dogmatics; for Hofmann, it is the means by which he has become certain of the truth of the Bible.

As to the problem of scriptural proof, Hofmann rejects the kind of proof that was in use among the old dogmaticians and the writers of the Orthodox Lutheran revival. These men accumulated a mass of single passages without regard to their place in the history of redemption. He demands that proofs be derived from the whole of Scripture and that each single portion of the Bible be interpreted in the light of the whole. Above all, the historical events and the recorded facts are to furnish the proofs. "We have to receive everything in Scripture in its historic place and in the setting of its historic connection." [27]

The new understanding of revelation as "holy history" also had a bearing on Hofmann's teaching of the inspiration of Scripture. Hofmann took seriously the critical approach to Scripture by the Rationalists, Schleiermacher, and the Hegelians, and he was ready to learn from them. "As Christians we begin our study of Scripture with the certainty that it is the authoritative witness to saving truth." [28] Scrip-

[26] *Ibid.*, I, 10. Cf. also Hofmann, *Biblische Hermeneutik,* a course of lectures in 1860 published posthumously in 1880, translated by Christian Preuss as *Interpreting the Bible* (Minneapolis: Augsburg Publishing House, 1959), pp. 25 ff.

[27] *Der Schriftbeweis,* I, 25.

[28] *Interpreting the Bible,* p. 64.

ure is "Holy Scripture for us only as the authoritative witness of the things which are apprehended by faith." [29] Scripture bears witness to the purpose of God as ultimately realized in Christ." [30] The Bible is more than an errorless book, as the Orthodox theologians and modern fundamentalists are anxious to maintain. Things that belong to the created order are objects of natural knowledge and experience.[31] The Bible "is not an infallible book of cosmology, anthropology, psychology, etc., and the history recorded in the Bible is not to be understood as an errorless segment of a world history." [32] It is a misunderstanding of the nature of Scripture "to interpret Genesis according to the most recent investigation of natural science, or to interpret natural science according to Genesis." [33] When Joshua called upon the sun to stand still, "this has nothing to do with the Copernican system." [34] "It is also a serious error," Hofmann continues, "when expressions concerning the 'life' of man such as *ruach*, *nephesh*, *pneuma*, *psyche*, etc., are interpreted as if they were found in a textbook of psychology. They serve to express, by means of a common language, what has to be said concerning man's relationship to God and this world." [35] When *pneuma* and *psyche* are used with reference to God and man they are not designed "to communicate a special metaphysical knowledge concerning God, nor a special anthropological nor psychological knowledge concerning man." [36] To regard facts of history or cosmological and psychological statements, reported on the basis of common natural knowledge, as infallible simply because they are reported in the Bible is "the evil consequence of a merely rational doctrine of inspiration, and creates many conflicts with the actual world." [37]

[29] *Loc. cit.*

[30] *Ibid.*, p. 65.

[31] Hofmann anticipated Paul Tillich by almost a century when the latter says that things of the natural order which are unknown today, but which might possibly be known tomorrow are not a matter of the mystery of revelation. Cf. Paul Tillich, *Systematic Theology*, Vol. I (Chicago: University of Chicago Press, 1951), p. 109.

[32] *Interpreting the Bible*, p. 64.

[33] *Ibid.*, p. 65.

[34] *Ibid.*, p. 66.

[35] *Loc. cit.*

[36] *Loc. cit.*

[37] *Ibid.*, p. 67.

Moved by these insights into the nature of revelation, Hofmann began his gigantic commentary on the New Testament, *Die heilige Schrift neuen Testaments zusammenhängend untersucht* (1862 ff.), in which he posed two problems for solution: (1) to determine by a historical investigation whether and to what extent the Bible really is a source of the historic revelation of redemption; (2) to write a history of the testimony of the Church to the Scriptures. Death, however, did not permit Hofmann to carry out his second task.

In Christology, Hofmann accepted the kenotic theory.[38] What caused concern among confessional Lutherans was that he explicitly rejected the orthodox teaching that Christ suffered the punishment of our sins upon the cross. In his own words, "the Son was not the object of the Father's wrath, not even vicariously." Basically, Hofmann followed the Greek Fathers and Luther when he regarded the cross as the battleground between God and Satan. Christ's suffering was a physical evil, not a punishment, which befell him in the faithful pursuit of his calling. Preserving his personal fellowship with the Father, Jesus in his own person dissolved the contradiction between the eternal will of love and the sin of humanity. Reconciliation was made not *through* Jesus, but *in* Jesus, in whom fellowship is restored between God and man. Jesus is the Second Adam, the beginner of a new humanity.[39]

To sum up, Hofmann made a fourfold contribution to theology. (1) Revelation is not to be understood as an impartation of natural and supernatural knowledge but as a holy history which challenges man to make a personal decision for or against God. (2) This understanding of revelation enabled him to differentiate between form and subject matter in the Scriptures. Hebrew, Aramaic, Greek, and the cultural thought forms of the times, though biblical, are not divine; they are subject to critical investigation. On the other hand, the manifestation of God's saving purpose throughout Scripture is unalterable. (3) Because of his historical orientation, Hofmann discovered the significance of eschatology in the thought of Jesus and of the primitive Church long before Albert Schweitzer. But unlike Schweit-

[38] *Der Schriftbeweis,* II, Part 1, 1 ff.

[39] Cf. *Ibid.,* II, Part 1, 306 ff. See also Hofmann's *Schutzschriften für eine neue Weise alte Wahrheit zu lehren,* 4 vols., 1856 ff.

zer, he maintained that the eschatology of the New Testament is normative for the Church today. He discarded the continuous-historical interpretation of the Apocalypse, which Luther and the men of the seventeenth century had espoused. He rejected the older view that the pope is the Anti-Christ and that the millennium is to be sought in the past history of the Church. Both the Anti-Christ and the millennium are facts to be revealed in the future.[40] This view, as well as others, was followed by the leading theologians of the Erlangen school. (4) As the first confessional Lutheran Hofmann distinguished between Luther's theology and Lutheran theology, between the theology of the Reformer and that of seventeenth-century Orthodoxy. This distinction gave impetus to the Luther renaissance that was to come at the turn of the century.

Next to Hofmann, Franz Hermann Reinhold von Frank (1827-1894) stands out as the most original theologian of the Erlangen school. In 1857 he was called to Erlangen. Though in point of time Frank belongs to the second generation of Erlangen theologians, he developed most fully the subjective starting point of Erlangen theology. In contrast to Hofmann, Frank was not a historian. His chief interest lay in the psychological element of religion. He took the theme of his greatest and most independent work, *System of Christian Certainty*[41] from the characteristic attitude of the religious life of the Reformation, which, while it was bound by its conscience to God, broke with the authority of the Roman church. A second motive that influenced him in the method he followed in his writing was analogy to the methods of the natural sciences. When Frank published the first edition of his work in 1870, natural science was at the peak of its intellectual influence. The natural sciences are based on the principle of empiricism. They deal with facts, and the accurate observation of these facts is of fundamental importance. Natural science uses the principle of causality and by observing actions argues back to their efficient causes. Theology should pursue a similar method and from the facts of the new spiritual life seek to ascertain their causes. In the new methods of Hermann Helmholtz, professor of physiology and physics, that were used in the spectroscopic analy-

[40] *Der Schriftbeweis,* II, Part 2, 624 ff.

[41] Translated by M. J. Evans (2nd ed.; Edinburgh: T. & T. Clark, 1886).

sis of the sun, Frank saw a clue to the proper method for the theologian. If spectrum analysis has succeeded to a certain extent in determining the chemical composition of the sun by breaking up its light into its component parts, because the daylight that we see is the same as the rays that radiate from it, would it not be proper to discover in the spectrum of the regenerate human personality the nature of that Sun whose rays are reflected in it?

In his *System of Christian Certainty*, Frank begins with a universal, psychological definition of the nature of certainty: "Certainty is the becoming sensible of the harmony of the being with the notion, or of experience with knowledge."[42] Certainty is a condition of the subject which at the same time is related to an object. Christian certainty has the same formal character, but is distinguished in its content from ordinary certainty by the peculiar moral experience of regeneration and conversion. This experience produces a transformation of the moral life. A new ego asserts itself as the determining factor of a new ethical existence. In the language of dogmatics this moral transformation is called "regeneration" and "conversion." Regeneration is determined by external factors; conversion is the part which has been played by man in his own transformation.

From this fundamental experience of regeneration Frank deduces the certainty of all the important truths of Christianity as a religion of redemption. He distinguishes between three classes of such truths which he describes as immanent, transcendent, and transient. The "immanent" truths are the experience of regeneration, sin, righteousness, etc. From them he proceeds to the active factors which have produced them. The "transcendent" objects of faith are those whose nature and being lie beyond and outside the human subject. Because of their causal relationship, they do not remain transcendent but actively enter into the subject and become a part of his experience.[43] The objects of faith so classified include God and his personality, the Holy Trinity, and the God-Man and his work of redemption. The "transient" objects of faith are the channels through which the transcendent factors pass in order to effect their connection with the im-

[42] *Ibid.*, p. 74.
[43] *Ibid.*, p. 188.

mediate actions of the Christian life. Here the Church, the means of grace, and Scripture enter into the picture.

On the basis of Christian certainty, Frank carries on a controversy with the world-view that is opposed to Christianity. He maintains that an apologetic in the sense of an unprejudiced comparison of Christian and anti-Christian views is worthless. He wants to show that a Christian who is really a Christian is not disturbed by these contrasts and looks upon them as inevitable. He who experiences no miracle must be a rationalist; he who does not experience the powerful working of the Word of God must destroy that Word by criticism; and he who does not grasp the personal opposition between the Holy God and sin must, pantheistically, unite God with the world. Frank demonstrates, in principle, and in a certain sense historically, the necessity for the development of these opposing tides of rationalism, pantheism, criticism, and materialism. These, however, are unable to rob the Christian of his certainty.

Frank's system is a grandiose production which seeks to establish old truth by new methods. His opponents derisively said that he tried to deduce from Christian experience the whole theology of the Formula of Concord, which he had discussed in his first great work, *Die Theologie der Concordienformel* (1858 ff.). In spite of the subjective starting point in his system, Frank's subjectivism does not have a realistic character in the sense of those epistomologies and cosmologies which admit only a subjective knowledge and regard it as the final reality. His subjectivism is purely epistemological, beginning with the self-consciousness of the subject but proceeding from it to the perception of the object. From the standpoint of the old truth, little objection can be raised to the content of Frank's system, but the question must be raised as to whether the method pursued by him is correct and can prove what he attempted to prove.[44]

The Erlangen theology also made a contribution to Church history and the history of doctrines. Gottfried Thomasius (1802-1875) reflects Hegel's influence in his great work on the history of doctrine.[45]

[44] Cf. Ludwig Ihmels, *Die christliche Wahrheitsgewissheit* (1914), p. 165; also *Neue kirchliche Zeitschrift* (March, 1927), with articles on Frank by Seeberg, Ihmels, Bachmann, and Hofstaetter.

[45] G. Thomasius, *Die christliche Dogmengeschichte als Entwicklungsgeschichte des kirchlichen Lehrbegriffs*, 2 vols.; 1874, 1876.

He recognizes a distinct pattern in history. The first period of the Church was to develop the central dogmas of the Trinity and the two natures of Christ, since these dogmas are the basis for further progress. Next, it was the task of the Middle Ages to apply this material logically and to develop it further. Since the doctrinal content became distorted during this period, it was necessary for the third period, the Reformation, to purify the doctrinal tradition of its false accretions and to deepen the understanding of the ancient dogmas by relating them to the evangelical understanding of the Christian faith. Finally, it is left to our own time to arrive at a clearer understanding of the nature of the Church. Unlike Harnack, Thomasius regarded the doctrinal development from Nicea to the Formula of Concord as an adequate expression of the Christian faith.

In dogmatics, Thomasius followed Schleiermacher's christocentric method.[46] He also applied the speculative ideas of German Idealism to the treatment of dogma itself. He conceived of the Trinity as a volitional process within the Godhead. In the sphere of Christology he developed the speculative tendency in the doctrine of the kenosis. He referred the kenosis to the act of the incarnation itself, unlike the old Lutheran theologians, who referred it to the incarnate Christ. In his incarnation, Christ laid aside the so-called transcendent, divine attributes, namely, omnipotence, omniscience, and omnipresence, but he retained the so-called immanent attributes of absolute power, truth, holiness, and love. Thomasius regarded this far-reaching surrender—not to say transformation—of divinity as necessary for the union of the divine with the human in a real historical existence. With various modifications this kenotic theory was advocated by other theologians, especially by Frank, while in still other quarters it was vigorously assailed.

Erlangen theology was not limited to the university at Erlangen. For a time it was an influential factor also at the universities of Rostock, Dorpat, and especially in the theological faculty of Leipzig. At Dorpat its best-known representative was Theodosius von Harnack (1817-1891), the father of the great liberal, Adolf von Harnack of Berlin. While professor at Erlangen from 1853-1866 he wrote the

[46] *Christi Person und Werk: Darstellung der evangelisch lutherischen Dogmatik vom Mittelpunkt der Christologie aus,* 2 vols. (1852 ff.).

first volume of *Luther's Theologie* (1862).[47] It was a forerunner of the modern Luther renaissance. Johann Heinrich Kurtz (1809-1890), author of the widely used textbook on Church history, also taught at Dorpat.[48] As a biblical scholar, Kurtz held a mediating position between Hofmann and Hengstenberg. At Leipzig the Erlangen school was represented by Franz Delitzsch (1813-1890), F. A. Kahnis (1814-1888), and Ernst Luthardt (1823-1904). Delitzsch was a scholar of the Old Testament. His commentaries have been read widely. He also translated the New Testament into Hebrew. Kahnis was both a historian and a systematician. Though Luthardt was a student of Hofmann, the peculiarities of Hofmann are scarcely discernible in Luthardt's dogmatics, *Kompendium der Dogmatik*.[49] The greatest importance of Luthardt lies in the field of personal influence and practical work. He was the founder of the General Evangelical Lutheran Conference (1868) which helped to unify German Lutheranism against the encroachment of unionistic tendencies in German Protestantism. After World War I, the Conference, under the leadership of Bishop Ihmels, developed into the Lutheran World Convention, re-organized in 1947 as the Lutheran World Federation.

In conclusion, it must be said that the Erlangen theologians made a lasting contribution to Christian theology. They sought to find a place for theology independent of the other sciences. The Rationalists, the Kantians, and the Hegelians treated religion as a logical conclusion of reason, but in the eyes of the radicals religion was an illusion. Traditional apologists advanced the claim that the truth of the Bible can be vindicated by history, archeology, and natural science, but the number of scholars opposed to this view was impressive. A third group, exemplified by Goethe, held that the moral excellence of Christianity cannot be surpassed. Over against all these attempts to establish the validity of Christianity the Erlangen theologians, like Schleiermacher, regarded religion in general and Christianity in particularly as a phenomenon *sui generis*. The Christian com-

[47] The second volume was published in 1886. The whole work was re-edited in 1927 by W. F. Schmidt and Otto Greter.

[48] *Church History* (New York: Funk & Wagnalls, 1888 ff.).

[49] Cf. the 14th ed. (1937), edited by Robert Jelke, which includes references to British and American theology.

munity is a company of regenerate people. Unless a person is born again he "cannot see the kingdom of God" (John 3:3).[50]

Theological Trends in Scandinavia

Among the Danish Lutherans of the nineteenth century was the unique Nicolai Frederik Severin Grundtvig (1773-1872), theologian, poet, historian, and educator of his beloved people. He was a genuine son of the romantic movement and of Lutheran revival. His cousin, Henrik Steffens, in his lectures on Schelling and Fichte, led him to see Christ and to arrive at a deeper understanding of history. Grundtvig's position is marked by a close synthesis between Christianity and the nation. In his theology he at first accepted the Orthodox view with regard to the authority of Scripture. Later he substituted the authority of the "living Word" for that of the written Word, for in the pursuit of historical studies he arrived at a conviction that the written Word is not the original source and norm of the Christian faith. The gospel was spread by the living power of the Apostles and the Church independent of the written Word. The source and norm of Christianity is found in the life of the Church. Grundtvig set forth the idea that in the Apostles' Creed we have the earliest confession of faith, one which preceded the Bible and is Christ's own confession, imparted to the Apostles during the forty days after his resurrection. This view of the Apostles' Creed, which Grundtvig called his "discovery," remained basic and central for him during his long and influential career. To him, the importance of Scripture is only secondary; the Church, he claims, builds on history.

The living Word, Grundtvig teaches, is given to each successive generation in the sacraments. Baptism and the Lord's Supper are the "life fountains" of the Church in which we meet the living Christ. Consequently, he lays special emphasis on growth in faith instead of on conversion, and on the corporate conception of religion as against the extreme individualism of the Pietists and Kierkegaard. His concept of ethics bears an anti-nomistic stamp. Though fundamentally a Lutheran, Grundtvig shows a Romanizing tendency in his theology, because he sees tradition, not Scripture, as the basis of doctrine and

[50] Cf. Werner Elert, *Der Kampf um das Christentum seit Schleiermacher und Hegel* (1921), p. 497.

practice. In his earlier years Grundtvig was inclined toward the episcopate as the source of religious authority. Some years later, "he not only rejected this idea but took great efforts to make plain that his emphasis upon the historic church must not be identified with the emphasis upon the hierarchy and tradition which characterizes the Roman Catholic Church."[51] For Grundtvig the validity of the sacraments is not dependent on episcopal succession; instead, it is conditioned by the institution of Christ and the corporate life of the Church where Christ is present.

In his teaching on man Grundtvig placed great emphasis on the natural, created man and his corporate existence in the nation. The fundamental character of man is not contingent upon his religious experience but is inherent in creation. Grundtvig, therefore, stood opposed to both Orthodoxy and pietism in their narrow attitude toward secular life and, contrary to his great contemporary Kierkegaard, he defended the concept of a Christian, Protestant culture. Grundtvigianism represents a peculiar synthesis between sacramental Christianity and Danish nationalism. It took deep roots among the progressive and well-educated farm population. Biblical criticism and Marxist secularization of urban life caused a decline of the movement toward the turn of the century. Grundtvig's influence also extended to America. The Danish Evangelical Lutheran Church, since 1962 a part of the Lutheran Church in America, was basically Grundtvigian in its theology.[52]

Anti-nomistic tendencies were shared by another theological movement in the Scandinavian countries, namely, the theology of the Bornholmers. This was not an academic but a practical movement, which originated among the Pietists of Sweden about the year 1805. A few decades later, the movement gained momentum through the work of the Finnish theologian F. G. Hedberg. Its greatest genius was Karl Olaf Rosenius (1816-1868) of Stockholm. For a time it

[51] Johannes Knudson, *Danish Rebel* (Philadelphia: Muhlenberg Press, 1955). p. 187.

[52] Grundtvig's works are published in 10 vols., edited by Holger Begtrup, 1904 ff.

For further studies on Grundtvig in English see Noelle Davies, *Education for Life, a Danish Pioneer* (Liverpool: Williams & Norgate, 1931); Hal Koch, *Grundtvig,* trans. L. Jones (Yellow Springs, Ohio: Antioch College Press, 1952); P. G. Lindhardt, *Grundtvig: An Introduction* (London: SPCK, 1952).

had a foothold on the Danish island of Bornholm. The pioneering leader there was P. C. Trandberg, who later migrated to Chicago where he was on the faculty of the Chicago Theological Seminary of the Congregational Church until 1890. He then withdrew and founded the Evangelical Lutheran Free Church Seminary, Chicago. The theology of Rosenius and the Bornholmers is marked by a one-sided emphasis on the gospel of free grace. For them reconciliation and justification are practically identical. "The world is justified in Christ."[53] Since the death of Christ it is a sin to ask for forgiveness, for the sin of every man is forgiven through Christ before man comes to faith in him. Even the sins of the lost in hell are actually forgiven through the cross. Faith is the acknowledgement of the historical redemption. While the Bornholmers passionately set forth the riches of God's grace, they violently condemned the preaching of good works as detrimental to Christian piety. One of its representatives reportedly asserted: The drunkard in the gutter and the prostitute in her vice are just as close to the fatherly heart of God as the pious on his praying-chair! Nevertheless, in practice the Bornholmers were a pious group of people. While the Swedish followers of Rosenius remained within the established Church, the Danish group, influenced by Kierkegaard's severe criticism of the Church of Denmark, developed a rather hostile attitude toward the Establishment.[54]

During the second half of the last century the teaching of Paul Peter Waldenstroem (1838-1917), theologian and political leader, created much discussion among the followers of Rosenius. From 1873 on he attacked the orthodox conception of God and of the atonement. His theology bears a close resemblance to the teaching of Albrecht Ritschl. He is a striking example of the fact that a pietistic way of life and theological liberalism may go a long way together.

[53] The Lutheran Church—Missouri Synod's teaching of "objective justification" (see, for example, Pieper, *op. cit.,* II, 508 ff.) bears a close resemblance to this feature of the Bornholmer theology.

[54] The chief literary source is Karl Olaf Rosenius, *Geheimnisse in Gesetz und Evangelium,* 1870. A selection of his writings in English was made by A. Hult, *The Believer Free from the Law* (Rock Island: Augustana Book Concern, 1923) and by G. T. Rygh, *A Faithful Guide to Peace with God* (Minneapolis: Augsburg Publishing House, 1923). Both volumes include an introduction on the life and significance of Rosenius.

The movement created by Waldenstroem resulted in the organization of a new ecclesiastical group, the so-called Mission Covenant which has a branch also in our country, with a college and seminary in Chicago.

Last there was Soren Kierkegaard. Ignored, hated and ridiculed by the elite of Denmark, he gained wide acclaim after World War I. The "Socrates of the North" was born in Copenhagen in 1813. He inherited a deeply melancholic nature from his father. His early religious training centered exclusively on the cross of Jesus which the father one-sidedly held to be an expression of man's wickedness. In 1840 Kierkegaard became engaged to Regina Olson but soon broke the engagement; the mystery surrounding this decision has never been fully explained. Two more incidents added to the miseries of his life. Beginning with 1846 he became the target of the scurrilous weekly, *The Corsair*, which made life in Copenhagen very unpleasant for him. In 1854 Bishop Mynster died, and when Martensen, the great Hegelian theologian, Mynster's successor, preached a eulogy in which he called Mynster a "witness of truth," Kierkegaard began his bitter assault upon the hypocrisy of the Church of Denmark and "official" Christianity. This controversy lasted until his death in 1855.

Kierkegaard's writings must be seen and read in the light of his opposition to the objectivism of Hegel and of the older orthodoxy on the one hand, and to the aestheticism of the romantic movement on the other. The Hegelians were firm believers in a Christian civilization. Grundtvig emphasized the channelling of people into Christianity through the sacramental rites of the Church. Kierkegaard, however, said that to be a Christian means to become a contemporary of Christ in all his lowliness and to suffer for the truth. This New Testament Christianity, he complained, no longer exists when pastors are royal officials; for royal officials have no relation to Christianity. How, then, does one become a Christian? "Quite simply, and if you want that too, quite in a Lutheran way: only the consciousness of sin can force you into this dreadful situation—the power on the other side being grace. . . . Only through the consciousness of sin is there entrance to it and the wish to enter in by any other way is the crime of lèse-majesté against Christianity." [55] To be a Christian means total

[55] Kierkegaard, *Training in Christianity,* trans. Walter Lowrie (Princeton: Princeton University Press, 1952), p. 71.

surrender to Christ. Christianity must exist "existentially" before God. "Subjectivity is truth." By this statement Kierkegaard does not want to deny the metaphysical reality of God. What he objects to is the "thingification" of God in theological scholasticism and Hegelian philosophy. To know the Truth is to live the Truth. Christianity is not a philosophical doctrine, which desires to be intellectually grasped and speculatively understood. It is rather "an existential communication" to be realized in existence.[56] Kierkegaard does not deny that there is an intellectual element in Christianity. But the doctrinal element must be permeated by the consciousness that its meaning is existential. In this way Kierkegaard developed the concept of an "existential thinker" whose task it is to understand himself in his existence with its uncertainty, its risk, and its passion. Faith is a "leap" and has in every moment "the infinite dialectic of uncertainty present with it."[57]

Kierkegaard distinguishes three stages of life: the aesthetic, ethical, and religious. For the aesthete, pleasure is the aim of life. He lives for the moment and seeks momentary enjoyment. The ethical man has a sense of vocation in life. He lives with responsibility and duty, but both meet with disaster. For the religious man the profoundest thing in life is his relationship with God. For the Christian the aesthetical (the enjoyment of the moment) and the ethical (the universal moral principle) will find their proper place in life; but they will not be decisive. The Christian lives his life in relationship to eternity while the aesthete lives in the moment, and the ethical person in time. The aesthete cannot become an ethical man without a leap, nor can the ethical man become religious without a leap that changes his whole life.[58]

Rational truth can be taught. The succeeding generation may start with the findings of the preceding one. In Christianity "every generation has to begin all over again with Christ." Faith cannot be taught, it can only be experienced. How then can the truth be

[56] Kierkegaard, *Unscientific Postscript*, trans. D. F. Swenson and Walter Lowrie (Princeton: Princeton University Press, 1944), p. 330.

[57] *Ibid.*, p. 53.

[58] See Kierkegaard, *Either-Or* (Princeton: Princeton University Press, 1944).

learned?[59] Believing in divine immanence, Socrates obscured the qualitative difference between God and man. In Christianity the truth can be taught by none but God Himself. But man must be endowed by God with the capacity to understand the truth. God creates in man the consciousness of his sin. In response to God man is converted, becomes a new creature; he is born again. This is the "Moment before God," filled with the eternal. How can God be confronted as teacher and man as learner? The sinner cannot ascend to God; therefore, God descended to the sinner. God became man and assumed the form of a servant. Christ is the Absolute Paradox and an offense to reason. There is no offense in teaching that the human race is akin to God, as Hegel had taught; but that is ancient paganism. The offense lies in the Christian teaching that an individual man is God.[60] But when reason is set aside and man accepts the condition of understanding the eternal, then God and man happily encounter one another in the Moment. Each individual has to begin with this encounter. There is no secondhand disciple. "For whoever has what he has from God Himself clearly has it at first hand; and he who does not have it from God Himself is not a disciple."[61]

In *Fear and Trembling* Kierkegaard expresses a profound insight into the nature of Christian ethics. The story of the book is the event of Abraham's sacrifice of Isaac. Abraham finds himself in conflict between an ethical command which states that man must not kill, and a religious command which demands killing in obedience to God. This poses the problem of whether there is an absolute duty to God which can suspend an ethical law. The question is answered in the affirmative. With great acumen Kierkegaard distinguishes between the ethical and the religious "spheres of existence." Abraham's greatness is revealed when—against an unreasonable divine command—he retains faith in God. Christian ethics is not a set of immovable rules to be applied regardless of time and circumstances. The writer of Christian ethics can only point out the way to live under the Lordship of God.

Next to obedience, suffering is a distinguishing mark of the Chris-

[59] See Kierkegaard, *Philosophical Fragments,* trans. D. F. Swenson (Princeton: Princeton University Press, 1946), pp. 5 ff.
[60] *Training in Christianity,* p. 84.
[61] *Philosophical Fragments,* p. 89.

tian life.[62] True Christian suffering is independent of fortune or misfortune arising from external circumstances. It has its root in man's inward relation to God and is a pertinent feature of the religious life. The absence of suffering signifies the absence of the religious orientation of man. One is reminded at once of Luther's intense spiritual struggle in the monastery. In fact, Kierkegaard's understanding of Christianity is reminiscent of Luther at many points: both are averse to a speculative theology. Their interpretation of revelation, of the incarnation, of faith and the Christian life as *simul justus et peccator* is practically identical. A difference is observable in their respective attitudes toward the natural orders. While Luther's earlier asceticism gave way to a positive evaluation of marriage, Kierkegaard travelled in the opposite direction. Yet Kierkegaard realized that he was the irreplaceable individual, an exception to the rule.

Reformed Theology

A passing remark on Reformed theology during the period under discussion is in order. In Germany it almost passed out of existence during the nineteenth century. The few existing theological schools were suspended and most of the Reformed territories were swallowed up by the union movement. Virtually the only representatives of high Calvinism were the two brothers: Friedrich Adolf Krummacher (1767-1845) in Bremen, and Gottfried Daniel Krummacher (1774-1837) in Elberfeld. In Bremen there was also Gottfried Menken (1768-1834), a pupil of the lay theologian Samuel Collenbusch (1724-1803). Menken's concept of the atonement shows a striking similarity to that of Hofmann. In Erlangen the Reformed faith was represented by Christian Kraft and J. H. A. Ebrard (1818-1884). While Ebrard stressed the Calvinistic concept of Church order and worship, he openly opposed Calvin's teaching of a double predestination. At heart he was a mediating theologian. As a member of the consistory at Spires, Ebrard promoted the cause of Church union in the Palatinate. The same holds true of Heinrich Heppe (1820-1879) at Marburg, who was unrelenting in his opposition to Vilmar and the confessional move-

[62] Cf. Kierkegaard, *The Gospel of Suffering,* trans. D. F. and L. M. Swenson (Minneapolis: Augsburg Publishing House, 1947) and *Attack upon Christendom,* trans. Walter Lowrie (Boston: Beacon Press, 1957).

ment of Hesse. Heppe defended the theory that the German Reformed church is the genuine heir to original Protestantism as represented by Melanchthon, and doctrinally expressed in the *Altered Augsburg Confession* of 1540 as a reliable commentary on the Confession of 1530. Both Lutheranism and Calvinism, he said, deviated from the original position of the Reformation: Lutheranism, through its teaching of the Lord's Supper, Calvinism through its doctrine of a double predestination.[63]

Among the German-speaking Swiss Reformed, Hans von Orelli (1846-1912) deserves to be mentioned along with his commentaries on the Old Testament, and the French-Swiss scholar, Frederic Godet (1812-1900) for his work on the New Testament. In more recent times the Reformed confession had two able representatives in the theologians August Lang (d. 1945) of Halle, and Karl Mueller (d. 1940) of Erlangen. Lang wrote several volumes on Calvin and the Heidelberg Catechism. In 1920 he was made moderator of the *Reformierter Bund* in Germany. Mueller published, among other volumes, a *Symbolik* (1896) and *Die Bekenntnisschriften der Reformierten Kirche* (1903), until recently the standard collection of the Reformed confessions. In the Netherlands Abraham Kuyper (1837-1920) figured during the last generation as one of the most outstanding Reformed theologians. As a scholar he brought about a revival of historic Calvinism in Holland, and as a statesman he waged a determined battle against the revolutionary forces which threatened to undermine the Christian civilization of his country. He was a very prolific writer. In 1898 he delivered the Stone Lectures at Princeton, published under the title *Calvinism.* J. H. de Vries has translated a number of his best writings into English, *The Work of the Holy Spirit* (1900), and other works.

[63] Heppe defended his views in a number of writings, especially *Die Geschichte des deutschen Protestantismus, 1555-81,* 4 vols. (1st ed., 1852 ff.); (2nd ed., 1865 ff.).

BIBLIOGRAPHY

See pertinent chapters in the works cited in the introduction to Book Five.

CHAPTER V

THE MEDIATING THEOLOGY OF THE BIBLICISTS

Besides the confessional theology in the nineteenth century there was another form of Protestant faith, the so-called positive mediating theology. The men representing this school tried to preserve the new ideas of both Schleiermacher and Hegel. Though the two, as children of German Idealism, had disagreed in details they both regarded religion as necessary for attaining a truly spiritual interpretation of life. Both considered Christianity the means to overcome the cleavage between spirit and matter, God and the world. In working out their system, both felt free from the authority of the letter of the Bible and of the confessions of the Church.

Under the impact of the new awakening, the mediating theologians tried to make Schleiermacher and Hegel more acceptable to the Church. They polished the systems of their predecessors. They tried to remove the sting of monism from both Schleiermacher and Hegel. They sought to prevent a breach between the Church and secular culture. Hence they tried to counteract the radical biblical criticism of the Tübingen school. They tried to prove the authenticity of most of the New Testament writings, with the possible exception of the Pastoral Letters and II Peter. On the basis of this approach a number of "Lives of Jesus" were written in which most of the miracles and facts of redemption were regarded as credible.[1]

The mediating theologians were followers of the Union movement by conviction. Among the confessions of the Reformation, the Augsburg Confession was preferred, especially the altered version, while the Formula of Concord was rejected. Luther was interpreted *via* Melanchthon, and consequently misunderstood, while his uncompromising positions concerning the Supper and predestination were modi-

[1] Cf. Schweitzer, *op. cit.,* pp. 215 ff.

fied to suit the writer's taste. This position was especially maintained by Julius Koestlin (1826-1902) in *Luthers Theologie* (1862)[2] and in his biography of the Reformer, *Martin Luther, sein Leben und seine Schriften*, 1875. These theologians found sympathetic support for their program in the so-called "theistic philosophy." This was taught by a number of philosophers, like the younger Fichte (1797-1879), H. F. Chalybaeus (1796-1862), and Ch. H. Weisse (1801-1866). Having only a limited place in philosophy these men sought to make their influence felt in theology. They opposed the pantheistic tendencies of German Idealism and confessed a personal God who is independent of the world. They developed the doctrine of the Holy Trinity in a speculative way so that they assured the personal existence of God apart from the world. In this way they sought to provide theology with an assured philosophical foundation. Mediating theology accepted this philosophical foundation and believed that a harmonization of faith with knowledge had been achieved. The leading literary organ of mediating theology, the *Theologische Studien und Kritiken*, which appeared in 1828, formulated its program thus: "As little as there can be a true Christian theology without Christian faith, even so a theology that ignores the noble, divine gifts of reason and science, is a monstrosity. All true results in theology depend on the co-operation and intermingling of faith and knowledge."

Speculative Theologians

The Hegelian type is best represented by P. K. Marheineke (1780-1846) at Heidelberg and Berlin, and by Karl Daub (1765-1836) at Heidelberg. Karl Ullmann (1796-1865) at Heidelberg and August Twesten (1789-1876), successor to Schleiermacher in the chair of systematic theology at Berlin, on the other hand, leaned in the direction of Schleiermacher. In fact, Twesten represents the conservative Lutheran element among the followers of Schleiermacher. Karl Immanuel Nitzsch (1787-1868) lived and taught in Berlin. While Twesten believed in the confederate nature of the Prussian Union, Nitzsch was a staunch defender of its absorptive character. In 1846 Nitzsch proposed a new creed for subscription by theological can-

[2] *The Theology of Luther in Its Historical Development and Inner Harmony*, trans. Charles E. Hay (Philadelphia: Lutheran Publication Society, 1897).

didates at their ordination, containing, as it was claimed, all the basic truths of Christianity. No mention, however, was made of such doctrines as original sin, Christ's descent into hell, his ascension, the resurrection of the body, eternal life, or eternal condemnation. Nitzsch's opponents derisively called this creed, in distinction from the *Nicaenum* of the fourth century, the *Nitzschenum* of the nineteenth century.[3]

The greatest speculative genius of all was Isaak August Dorner (1809-1884), also at Berlin. In the introductory part of his *System der christlichen Glaubenslehre*[4] he discusses at length the quest for religious certainty. Man, he argues, puzzled by the historical in Christianity, will turn to purely timeless ideals for truth. These ideals cannot satisfy nor give real religious certainty. Man will arrive at such certainty, Dorner continues, only when he turns to Christianity, in which the ideal is united with the historical.[5] This theoretical approach is coupled, according to Dorner, with the ethical and practical, for the content of the gospel implies the self-condemnation of man and his justification through faith in Christ.

Dorner is remembered in the history of doctrine chiefly for his discussion of the christological problem. Dorner regards the union of God with man in Jesus as the ultimate goal and climax of the divine world order. The incarnation, he holds, was planned by God even apart from the fact of sin. For Dorner the Logos was merely a divine principle. In order for a real personal unity of life to be comprehensible in Jesus, it is said that the union of the two natures in Christ took place gradually during his earthly life. In conformity with the increasing receptivity of the human nature of Jesus to the divine, the Logos dwelt in him more and more, so that the process of the union between the divine and human was not completed until the end of the earthly life of Jesus.[6] This theory places alongside

[3] For orientation on the union in Prussia and other German states see J. L. Neve, *The Lutherans in the Movements for Church Union* (Philadelphia: United Lutheran Publication House, 1921), pp. 110 ff.

[4] *System of Christian Doctrine,* trans. Alfred Cave and J. S. Banks, 4 vols. (Edinburgh: T. & T. Clark, 1880 ff.).

[5] Isaak August Dorner, *System der christlichen Glaubenslehre* (2nd ed., 1886), I, 101.

[6] *Ibid.,* II, 412 ff. Dorner also published *Entwickelungsgeschichte der Lehre von der Person Christi* (2nd ed., 1845), which appeared in English as

the kenotic theory, which Dorner vigorously attacked, the most original speculative attempt to rationalize the God-manhood of Jesus that is found in nineteenth century theology.

The most original theologian of this school was Richard Rothe (1799-1867), a professor at Heidelberg. He was a speculative genius of first magnitude, wholly devoted to the effort of the mediating school to harmonize Christianity with philosophy. In his system he combines the formal principle of the Hegelian school, its dialectical method, with the theosophical tenets of Schelling and the peculiarities of Schleiermacher's theology. Rothe holds man to be a *microcosmos* who comprehends and recapitulates the whole universe in himself. Philosophical speculation, he says, must start from the consciousness of the ego, from the act of the thinking self; theological speculation, on the other hand, must start from the consciousness of God. God is to him the Absolute. Rejecting the Church's doctrine of the Trinity, Rothe holds to a threefold form of divine being: God's hidden nature, the I; matter, the non-I; and personality, in which God arrives at consciousness of himself. This fashioning of matter into the organ of the divine spirit Rothe regards as a continuous process of creation or, if viewed from the aspect of its goal, as the incarnation of God within the limits of material existence. He regarded Christianity as strictly supernatural, grounded in the "manifestation of God in history." From this divine manifestation he distinguishes "inspiration," that is, the immediate enlightenment of the biblical writers to receive and interpret the historical manifestation of God. Man is delivered from his abnormal sinful depravity by the Second Adam, who marks the beginning of man's normal development.

Jesus came into the world by a miraculous act of God: he was born of a woman though not begotten by a man. Jesus was not a divine being from the outset. The incarnation was, according to Rothe, a continuous process in which God became man and man became God. This process was completed in the resurrection and elevation of Jesus to the divine sovereignty of the world. At the end of time, Christ

Development of the Doctrine of the Person of Christ (1861 ff.). Cf. also A. M. Fairbairn, *The Place of Christ in Modern Theology* (New York: Charles Scribner's Sons, 1910), and P. T. Forsyth, *The Person and Place of Jesus Christ* (Boston: Beacon Press, 1909).

will visibly appear with all the saints. The pious will be clothed with a spiritual body while the wicked will be given over to complete annihilation. Finally, the terrestrial world will also be spiritualized and placed in communion with the heavenly spheres. Thus, the kingdom of earth becomes the kingdom of heaven. In keeping with this view, Rothe's interest centered in a "Christian civilization" which expresses the unity of nature and spirit. The Church can have only temporary significance because it is merely the means of bringing about a new order in which a general, humanized Church will be absorbed by a state (society) established upon the principles of general ethics.

Rothe's theology contains many contradictory elements. His conception of God, for example, is in part theistic while, at the same time, he holds to the Hegelian teaching that God arrives at consciousness of himself in man. In the same way, sin to him is an unavoidable passage in the development of man. Nevertheless, he also speaks of sin as guilt and considers the sinful depravity of man abnormal. Little wonder, that, on the one hand, Rothe's theology could appeal to such a scholar as Martin Kaehler, and that, on the other hand, liberals look to Rothe as a precursor of Neo-Protestantism in Germany.[7]

Another systematic theologian of the same school was Julius Mueller of Halle (1808-1878) who, in his work *The Doctrine of Sin*[8] set out to investigate the nature and origin of sin. According to him sin is selfishness and as such a freedom that destroys itself. Sin's origin is to be sought in a tragic misuse of freedom which had its beginning in the sphere of the extra-temporal. Mueller adopts the theory of a pre-mundane fall of man taught in the ancient Church by the Gnostics and Origen. However, Mueller is compelled to admit that evil in its essence is incomprehensible; it is the inescapable mystery of the world.

The attitude of this school regarding the relation of Christian ethics to human culture is best illustrated in the writings of the Danish

[7] His *magnum opus* is *Theologische Ethik*, 3 vols. (1845 ff.); 5 vols. (1867 ff.). Cf. the penetrating discussion on Rothe in James Hastings, *Encyclopedia of Religion and Ethics*, 13 vols. (New York: Charles Scribner's Sons, 1951), X, 858-63.

[8] Julius Mueller, *The Doctrine of Sin* (Edinburgh: T. & T. Clark, 1868).

professor and bishop, Hans Larsen Martensen (1808-1884). His *Den kristelige Dogmatik* (1849)[9] and *Den kristelige Ethik* (1878)[10] were widely read in both German and English translations. Martensen followed mainly the cultural ethics of Schleiermacher and Rothe. He also stood very close to Dorner. He saw in Christianity the means of purifying and completing all the intra-mundane accomplishments of human culture. This easygoing attitude aroused the resentment of Kierkegaard and his bitter attack on the Danish church.

Theology of Revival

While all these theologians were friends of a speculative development of Christian doctrine, there were two other men whose mediating theology bears a different stamp: August Neander of Berlin, and August Tholuck of Halle (1799-1877). The theology of both is rooted in the revival of religion during the earlier parts of the nineteenth century. Starting with Schleiermacher's theology of feeling, Neander developed it into what is called the "pectoral theology." It is the heart which makes the theologians. He was opposed to the speculative Hegelians as well as to the Orthodox Lutherans. His chief contribution lies in the field of historical studies. He also wrote a life of Christ (1837), in reply to the destructive work of Strauss. In Tholuck the strict pietism of his earlier days was later blended with certain latitudinarian tendencies.[11]

As has become evident, Lutherans and Calvinists, the followers of Schleiermacher and Hegel, Orthodox and Pietists, speculative theologians and the men who stressed religious experience, critical scholars and biblical literalists—all were invited to live a life of peaceful coexistence under the roof of the established Union Church of Prussia and of some of the smaller territories of Germany where the Union had been introduced, for example, Baden. Its strongholds were the Prussian universities of Berlin, Halle, and Bonn, and the University of Heidelberg in Baden.

[9] *Christian Dogmatics,* trans. William Urwick (Edinburgh, T. &. T. Clark, 1898).

[10] *Christian Ethics,* 3 vols. (New York: Charles Scribner's Sons, n.d.).

[11] Cf. G. N. Bonwetsch, *Aus August Tholucks Anfängen* (1921).

The Groningen School

Another type of mediating theology was taught by the Groningen school in the Reformed Church of Holland, with L. G. Pareau (1800-1866) and Petrus Hofstede de Groot (1802-1886) among its most prominent leaders. The Groningen theologians were pupils of P. W. van Heusde (1778-1823), philosopher and theologian at Utrecht. Tenets of Lessing, Herder, Schleiermacher, and the German mediating theology are traceable in the teaching of these men. They tended toward a humanistic interpretation of Christianity. Van Heusde regarded Christianity as the highest revelation of God, and history as the education of humanity for an understanding of the divine. The importance of sin was minimized and education took the place of regeneration. The Groningen theologians denied the Trinity and the deity of Jesus, though they maintained the supernatural in religion. In eschatology they taught the restoration of all things. They had a special fondness for Erasmus and took pride in calling themselves the "genuine" Dutch theologians over against the strict Calvinists. It was a theology "warmly pious"—after 1867 they were known as the Evangelicals—"frankly heterodox, but thoroughly supernaturalistic,"[12] showing a striking resemblance to the older type of Unitarians. In ecclesiastical politics they sided with the modernists, but in theological controversy they opposed the modernists as deniers of the supernatural in religion.

The Biblicists

This group rejected in principle every connection with any philosophy, whether of Kant or Hegel or Schelling, or of philosophical theism. The biblicists were averse to speculation as to the formation of a Christian world-view or, in the ethical field, to the creation of a Christian civilization. Nor did they care to consider the dogmatic development in so far as it goes beyond the Bible and is conditioned by philosophy. They regarded the contrast of the confessions of Lutheranism and Calvinism with indifference, and objected to Romanism only because of its insufficient biblical foundation. Finally, they rejected experience as a source of Christian knowledge in the sense of Schleiermacher and the Erlangen school. They held to the

[12] E. C. Vanderlaan, *Protestant Modernism in Holland* (Toronto: Oxford University Press, 1924), p. 16.

Bible as an objective norm rather than to subjectivism. In their positive tenets they were influenced by the same theological forces which are essential in Hofmann's theology of redemption, and they shared the intense interest of the Erlangen theologians in the eschatological teachings of the Bible.

The most original exponent of this school, Tobias Beck of Tübingen (1804-1874), has expressed the underlying principles most clearly. In his *Glaubenslehre* he states that "all true Christian knowledge is essentially conditioned by the fact that it has as its exclusive material the perfect and perfecting truth of doctrine laid down in Holy Scripture which constitutes the entire field of religious knowledge for the Christian and provides the positive content of doctrine for all Christian knowledge and science. Everything that is not given scripturally has no objective significance for Christian knowledge in the religious field."[13] Beck's concept of the Bible is essentially that of the seventeenth century: The Scriptures are regarded as identical with revelation. In exegesis he insisted on the "pneumatic" interpretation of the text. For him the real content of the Bible is the kingdom of heaven. This kingdom, however, does not designate an ideal condition of the Christian community, nor an ecclesiastical organization, nor any other historical product. On the contrary, the kingdom of God existed with God before the creation of the world as "an organized system of life."[14] It entered into history, particularly in Christ, to effect through him a regeneration, first, of the individual and, finally, of the whole universe. Christianity ushers in "a new type of life."[15] With this formula Beck expresses his moral concept of Christianity. The new life is imparted to the individual through justification. This establishes, as Beck says, "a righteous personal relationship to God in Christ which is at the same time a natural disposition for a corresponding righteous action."[16] Justification for Beck is not simply identical with moral regeneration; nevertheless, regeneration remains the real goal of justification. These views of Beck are not simply a reproduction of biblical ideas. On the contrary, they betray the influence of Jacob Boehme and such Swabian theo-

[13] Tobias Beck, *Glaubenslehre*, I, 583.
[14] *Ibid.*, I, 135.
[15] *Ibid.*, I, 398.
[16] *Ibid.*, II, 603.

sophists as Friedrich Christoph Oetinger and their insistence on a mystic, transcendental realism. In ethics Beck held that it is impossible to Christianize the world and its social forms. These are only "institutions of law and discipline for the regulation of life during the earthly development of mankind to serve as a protection against the destructive power and influence of sin."[17] Only eschatological transformation will bring the forms of society which conform to the Christian ideal. Beck, then, stands in pronounced opposition to the Neo-Protestant ideas of an intra-mundane ethical culture. This type of biblicism was also represented by Karl August Auberlen (1824-1864), professor at Basel, and by Robert Kuebel (1838-1894), who succeeded Beck at the University of Tübingen.

Another biblicist was Hermann Cremer of Greifswald (1834-1903). He likewise regarded justification as the content of biblical Christianity. In contrast to Beck, he understood that doctrine in its genuine Pauline sense: Justification is the utterly paradoxical imputation of righteousness to the sinner, in contrast to his moral condition, and without regard to the moral alteration in him. Cremer also bases the proof of religious certainty on this faith. As the natural man in his conscience experiences God as the Judge, Christianity confirms this impression, teaching men the paradox that they shall recognize the redeeming God in the condemning God.[18] In refutation of Harnack's *Essence of Christianity*, Cremer defined Christianity "not as the religion which Jesus Himself had taught, believed or practiced, but as the religion which establishes a personal relationship of the believer with Jesus, a religion which is communion with Jesus and through Him with God." The New Testament does not proclaim the religion of Christ, but the religion about Christ. "These two religions," he says, "are altogether different, contradicting and excluding each other, the one in which, as in the teaching of Jesus Himself, the forgiveness of sins is conditioned by His death and resurrection, the other in which man absolves himself."[19] With his *Biblisch-theologisches Wör-*

[17] Beck, *Christliche Ethik* (posthumously edited, 1882), p. 159.

[18] "Dogmatische Prinzipienlehre" in Otto Zoeckler, *Handbuch der theologischen Wissenschaften* (3rd ed., 1890), III, 61 ff.

[19] Hermann Cremer, *Das Wesen des Christentums* (1902). The book went through three editions in one year. The quotations are from the 3rd ed., pp. 220, 228.

terbuch zur neutestamentlichen Gräzitaet (1867), Cremer laid the foundation for a comparative study of the religious connotation of the New Testament Greek vocabulary. The work of Cremer was continued by Julius Koegel (1871-1928), who prepared the tenth (1910 ff.) and eleventh editions (1923) of this lexicon. The work of these two men in turn inspired Gerhard Kittel and his more than fifty co-laborers to start the publication of the gigantic *Wörterbuch zum Neuen Testament,* in the process of publication since 1932.

BIBLIOGRAPHY

See pertinent chapters in the works cited in the introduction to Book Five.

CHAPTER VI

NEO-KANTIANISM AND RITSCHLIAN THEOLOGY

The mid-nineteenth century was marked by a great spiritual revolution. Philosophical idealism was discredited and men no longer followed those theologians who tried to establish the metaphysical meaning of the world or even God's nature through speculation. The mystical experience of Schleiermacher's school was going out of fashion. The religious revival of the earlier part of the century had spent its force and practical religious life was declining. Popular interest was diverted from philosophy and religion to the natural sciences, sociology, and kindred subjects. Practical social and political movements came to the fore; socialism and communism gained ascendancy, and a materialistic philosophy seemed to satisfy every need. The idea of evolution, first a philosophical tenet, was taken over by the natural sciences, transformed into a mechanical operation, and made the basis of a monistic view of the world. Darwin, with true English caution, was slow in turning his theories into a philosophical system, but in Germany Ernst Haeckel (1834-1919) thought he could find in evolution an answer to all the riddles of the universe.[1] This monism soon passed into pure materialism. It has been pointed out earlier how Strauss and Feuerbach gradually turned to materialism, while the popular writings of Jacob Moleschott (1822-1893), Karl Vogt (1817-1895), and Ludwig Buechner (1824-1899) helped to diffuse the same ideas. Materialism soon became the socialistic philosophy of history and was made the explanation of the forces that motivated all religions, including Christianity.

With these changes in spiritual attitude, the theology of experience completely lost the props of an idealistic philosophy and the whole

[1] Ernst Haeckel, *The Riddle of the Universe* (New York: Harper & Bros., 1901).

speculative theology that had been tied up with it was carried along to destruction. Insofar as materialism even admitted the idea of religion, it was the religion of science. Then came a reaction in philosophic thought that seemed to offer new possibilities for religion and theology. Its cry was "Back to Kant," and that cry found a ready response. A Neo-Kantianism came into existence which interpreted Kant in a manner which theoretically rejects every form of metaphysics and denies the possibility of the knowledge of God. God is an entity with which neither philosophy nor science has anything to do. A philosophical view of God and the world is theoretically impossible. Besides this theoretical reason Neo-Kantianism recognizes the practical reason that deals with moral problems, the content of which is defined as Kant defined it: every human being has been endowed with the consciousness of a categorical imperative which demands unconditional performance of duty. This obligation of duty is universal, as the principles guiding the individual in his actions must be of the sort that are binding on all. Consequently, our duty has a double content: (1) that we assert our spiritual personality over against nature, and (2) that we unite in mutual regard with all other men in a spiritual kingdom. The individual is not only aware of this imperative, he also possesses the ability to realize its demands. In spite of natural limitations, man possesses free will and self-determination in moral action. Ethics, therefore, is autonomous, it has no need of religion. As with Kant, God and immortality are merely ethical postulates; their existence as metaphysical entities is left an open question. In the most extreme development of Neo-Kantianism, the religious concepts are treated as practical values, though theoretically they may be false. The University of Marburg became the center of the Neo-Kantian school with Hermann Cohen (1842-1918) and Paul Natorp (1851-1924) as its recognized leaders.

Albrecht Ritschl

Out of this spiritual and intellectual situation developed the Ritschlian theology. Its exact relation to Neo-Kantianism varied greatly and was less pronounced in the master himself than in some of his pupils.

Albrecht Benjamin Ritschl was born in Berlin in 1822. Educated at Bonn, Halle, Heidelberg, and Tübingen, he was at first a follower of Hegel and Baur. He early sensed the new trend in thought. His break with the Tübingen school became known when he published the second edition of his historical monograph, *Die altkatholische Kirche* in 1857, in which he refuted the Tübingen construction of the apostolic and post-apostolic Church. In 1864 he was called to Göttingen where he remained till his death in 1889. Here he wrote, among other books, his chief work, *Die christliche Lehre von der Rechtfertigung und Versöhnung*.[2]

Ritschl's position may be said to be a "negative" mediating theology. That is to say, Ritschl does not attempt to secure a place for religion and Christianity by pointing out the identity of reason and revelation, faith and knowledge; he insists instead on the otherness of faith and Christianity. If philosophy and the sciences move in the sphere of intellectual truths, religion has its place in the realm of practical values. Both religion and science can exist peacefully, side by side, if neither one oversteps its own limit. With Hegel the emphasis rests on synthesis; with Ritschl, on diastasis.[3] He expurgated the speculative and pietistic tenets from the older mediating theology.

Just as Ritschl tried to exclude the intellectual element from Christianity, so he strove to banish everything that was emotional and mystical. He severely criticized these elements in his *Geschichte des Pietismus* (3 vols., 1880 ff.), and even rejected such elements as the *unio mystica* which had found a place in all orthodox theology. While Schleiermacher had emphasized feeling in religion, Ritschl placed the emphasis entirely on the will. As a result he effected a moralizing of

[2] 3 vols., 1870 ff.; 3rd ed., 1888-89. The first volume was translated into English by John J. Black, *A Critical History of the Christian Doctrine of Justification and Reconciliation* (Edinburgh: Edmonston & Douglas, 1872); the third volume was edited by H. R. Mackintosh and A. B. Macauly, *The Christian Doctrine of Justification and Reconciliation* (Edinburgh: T. & T. Clark, 1900).

[3] Otto Pfleiderer discusses Ritschl under the heading "Elective Mediating Theologians," *op. cit.*, pp. 183 ff. Elert assigns Ritschl first place in the section "The Declaration of Theological Independence of Christianity," *Der Kampf um das Christentum* (1921), pp. 258 ff. There is something to be said for both arrangements. Ritschl's theology is mediating in that, in deference to the skeptical trend of his time, he rejected the metaphysical in the Church's doctrine. Yet in so doing, he was striving to put Christianity on its own basis; its right and verity are conditioned, in his judgment, by the practical values of religion. Cf. also Hirsch, *Geschichte der neueren evangelischen Theologie*, V, 557 ff.

Christianity according to the Kantian tradition. Christian theology, when limited to itself, has to describe the Christian idea of God and of man's salvation from a practical, ethical viewpoint. Consequently, all the elements of dogma that have no immediate significance of that sort are excluded. Theology is, as with Schleiermacher, a doctrine of salvation, not a science offering a comprehensive world-view.

In dealing with the metaphysical problem of theology, Ritschl distinguished between a merely intellectual statement about the existence of a thing (*Seinsurteil*), and an "emotional" statement about the existence of a thing (*Werturteil*), entirely eliminating the "judgments of being" from the scope of theology. By restricting theology to "judgments of value," Ritschl did not reject the metaphysical nature of God. He only denied to human reason the possibility of a theoretical knowledge of God. Ritschl's "judgments of value" stand in opposition not to the existential verity of the metaphysical world, but to a purely theoretical knowledge of the intellect concerning God.

Ritschl finds the sources for a genuine understanding of the Christian religion only in the biblical books which are closest to the time of the founding of Christianity. He was quite conservative about the genuineness of the New Testament sources. Ritschl's criterion of the canonicity of the New Testament Scriptures is their close connection with the Old Testament as contrasted with the post-apostolic writings, which already show the influence of pagan thought. Ritschl connects Christianity only with Judaism. He isolates Christianity from the general history of religion and from natural revelation far more completely than was the case in either Catholic or Protestant theology, to say nothing of the school of comparative religion. In principle Ritschl was a biblicist. Religion must draw from concrete facts. The theologian is not a speculative philosopher.

Ritschl's concept of God is strictly personalistic. From the nature of God he removes the concept of divine wrath, which he calls an "unrelated and formless theologumenon." [4] He also rejects the attribute of holiness. The only adequate concept of God is expressed in the concept of love. God's disposition has not been changed by man's sin, but as the loving Father he has always been ready to forgive unconditionally and to readmit man into His fellowship. When man

[4] *Rechtfertigung und Versöhnung*, 3rd ed., II, 155.

in his sin refuses to revere and trust God, he constructs a false picture of the holiness of Him whose wrath he fears. As a result, man no longer ventures to draw near to God. To remove this false idea and to impress man with his never-changing paternal love, God revealed himself in Christ. The revelation in Christ never intended to establish a new relationship between God and man, but only to reveal to man the never-changing attitude of divine love. At the same time, Christ appeared as the perfect moral man who, by his trust in God, overcame the world. Above all Christ preserved a moral fidelity to his mission. For Ritschl Christ is "the perfect Revealer of God and the Archetype of a spiritual dominion over the world." [5] The example of Jesus, he says, inspires men with a believing conviction of the love of God and of their forgiveness and justification by him. They give up their mistrust of God or, to put it in other words, they are reconciled to God.

Ritschl does not regard reconciliation as a prerequisite for justification but as its consequence. Justification is the forgiveness which, through the revelation made in Christ, is accessible to every believer; reconciliation is the subsequent conciliation between man and God.[6] Reconciliation expresses the idea that those who previously were in active opposition to God have been placed in accord with God.[7] The purpose of this divine forgiveness is to produce in the Church and individual the ethical life exemplified in Christ. Both the Church and the individual, through their communion with God, become lords over nature and its inherent limitations. The Christian exercises religious dominion over the world, which is the direct aim of reconciliation with God through Christ, through faith in the loving providence of God, through the virtues of humility and patience, and finally, through prayer.[8] According to Ritschl, the act of thanksgiving in prayer must predominate in the Church. Petitions are only a modification of the prayer of thanksgiving.[9] The individual Christian realizes this ethico-religious life in his worldly calling, the Church in close co-operation with the state. There is no room for the ascetic

[5] *Ibid.*, III, 367.
[6] *Ibid.*, III, 61 ff.
[7] *Ibid.*, III, 503 ff.
[8] *Ibid.*, III, 634.
[9] *Ibid.*, III, 608.

ideals of Catholicism and pietism in the ethics of Ritschl. For Ritschl the kingdom of God is mankind organized according to the principle of neighborly love. For him, as for Kant, the kingdom, stripped of its eschatological significance, is ethical through and through.[10] Ritschl's teaching of sin bears a sociological stamp. The Church's teaching of original sin was replaced by the corporate concept of a "kingdom of sin." [11]

Ritschl's Neo-Protestant concept of Christianity becomes quite apparent in the view of the Reformation given in his *Geschichte des Pietismus* and in his address commemorating the four-hundredth anniversary of Luther's birth. The assertion is made that the teaching of the Reformation remained essentially on a Roman Catholic level, so that the real meaning of the Reformation "is more concealed than revealed in the works of Luther and Melanchthon." [12] It was only in their ethical ideas that the Reformers offered something new. "If the Reformation of the sixteenth century did not display an ideal of a Christian life we would be in great embarrassment when trying to assign to it any epoch-making significance and a permanent place over against the Catholic concept of Christianity. In the ethical ideals of our Reformers, faith in God's providence, and prayer, and the valuation of a worldly calling, as the domain for the exercise of love towards our neighbor, all stand in mutual relationship." [13] In view of this appraisal of the Reformation it is quite understandable that Ritschl desired a new Protestant reformation and wanted to accomplish it through his teachings.

In spite of his biblical preliminary statement, Ritschl effected a marked alteration of historical Christianity into the form of an ethical Neo-Protestantism. His opposition to metaphysics converted Christ into an ideal man appointed by divine providence to be the perfect revealer of God's love, and the person of the Holy Spirit into an

[10] *Ibid.*, III, 12.
[11] *Ibid.*, III, 326.
[12] *Anniversary Address*, p. 14.
[13] *Geschichte des Pietismus* I, 41. The same concept of the Reformation is held by Harnack and Loofs in their respective histories of doctrine, and by such men as Theodor Brieger, *Der Glaube Luthers und seine Freiheit von menschlichen Autoritäten* (1892), Wilhelm Herrmann, *Der Verkehr des Christen mit Gott im Anschluss an Luther dargestellt* (1886), and other scholars.

impersonal power emanating from God and dwelling in the Church.[14] For faith in the reconciliation of a holy God through the work of Christ, Ritschl substituted trust in the divine, omnipresent paternal love revealed by Christ. In place of a specifically Christian faith in reconciliation came a general faith in divine providence. The chief purpose of Christianity is the realization of ethics in the Kantian sense. Frank of Erlangen and other conservative Lutherans charged Ritschl with "counterfeiting" Christianity. In fairness to Ritschl it must be said that some of these alternating tendencies were more of the kind of a hidden force than an open statement in his system. As for himself, he never denied the metaphysical sonship of Christ; he only claimed that it cannot be an object of theological inquiry.[15] Otto Ritschl tells us that as his father was dying, he requested him to recite the closing verses of Paul Gerhardt's famous hymn, "O Sacred Head, Now Wounded." These lines clearly express the idea of the vicarious nature of Christ's death.[16] This is all the more significant because of Ritschl's adverse criticism of this hymn in his *Geschichte des Pietismus*.[17]

Ritschlian Theologians

Among the followers of Ritschl, Wilhelm Herrmann (1846-1922) developed the anti-metaphysical and moralistic ideas of the master most drastically. Because of his magnetic personality and the opportunities afforded him by his long career as a professor at Marburg (after 1879), Herrmann exercised a widespread influence. He says of himself, "I have adopted the teaching of Kant in its separation of theoretical from ethical knowledge because I see in it the liberation of theology from the fetters of a philosophical world-view." [18] In his

[14] *Rechtfertigung und Versöhnung*, III, 444.

[15] Compare the very sound and reserved criticism of Ritschl by H. R. Mackintosh, *Types of Modern Theology* (London: Nisbet, 1937). The late Scottish theologian is right when he warns the student of Ritschl "to guard himself against the mistake of hastily identifying the 'theology of Ritschl' with what is known, more generally, as 'the Ritschlian theology' " (*op. cit.*, pp. 179 ff.). In his study of Ritschl, Mackintosh says, "We are confronted by the possibility of divergence between a writer's personal convictions and the logical implications of his actual words" (*ibid.*, p. 165).

[16] Ritschl, *Albrecht Ritschls Leben*, II, 524.

[17] II, 65.

[18] *Die Religion im Verhältnis zum Welterkennen und zur Sittlichkeit*, 1879, p. 14.

lectures on dogmatics he describes religion as a historical reality perceived by those who experience it.[19] Since evangelical Christianity cannot have dogmas in the old sense of the term, "religion means seeing the working of a God in the events of life."[20] Kant was wrong when he identified religion with ethics, although religion "is always bound up with morality."[21] "We possess it [religion] only when we come to the consciousness that God is working upon us in some particular situation as the Power which saves us."[22] This experience Herrmann calls "revelation," for the communication of religious forms and content of the past is no revelation at all, he says, "till religious conviction is created in ourselves; and only that which effects this in us ranks for us as revelation."[23] Obedience to the Scripture "should be required of no man as regards those passages in which he personally does not hear God speak to him."[24] In the person of Christ we find "what only God Himself can give" and he is to us "what only God Himself can be."[25] According to Herrmann, this is the meaning of his divinity. Christ's work was to open men's eyes to the goodness of God, not to effect a change in God's attitude to sinners.[26] For Herrmann, as for Ritschl, Christianity is still intrinsically bound up with the "historical Jesus." Since biblical criticism, however, has rendered the tradition about many details of Jesus' life quite uncertain, Herrmann wants to become independent of them in his appraisal of the Lord. Therefore, he singled out the "inner life of Jesus" as a plank unassailable by historical criticism, from which we may learn the ethico-religious significance of the Lord's earthly life. This inner life of Jesus is said to have as its essential content the universal ethical ideal of a spiritual personality and the founding of a spiritual brotherhood. When we unite our imperfect moral life with the moral life of Jesus, we receive the ability to do good. Herrmann has discussed these tenets of his theology more fully in his most

[19] *Systematic Theology*, trans. N. Micklem and K. A. Saunders (New York: The Macmillan Company, 1927), p. 18.
[20] *Ibid.*, p. 20.
[21] *Ibid.*, p. 27.
[22] *Ibid.*, p. 40.
[23] *Ibid.*, p. 39.
[24] *Ibid.*, p. 72.
[25] *Ibid.*, p. 138.
[26] *Ibid.*, pp. 121-22.

widely known book entitled *Der Verkehr des Christen mit Gott.*[27]

Thus Herrmann consistently reduced Christianity to a subjective system. The Scriptures mean less to him than to Ritschl. Emphasizing the psychological element in religion he has, in no small degree, altered the original Ritschlian theology by a retrogression to Schleiermacher. While Ritschl's thought revolves about the impersonal idea of the kingdom of God, Herrmann's religion, by a concentration upon and devotion to the person of Jesus, as he had learned it from his teacher Tholuck, is warmer because it is more personal.

The greatest historian of the Ritschlian school was Adolf von Harnack (1851-1930), who became a professor at Berlin in 1888. He published a great number of notable historical studies, especially in relation to the ancient Church and the New Testament. In his widely read book, *Das Wesen des Christentums,* he writes: "What is Christianity? We will seek to answer this question solely in a historical sense, that is, with the method of historical science and with the personal experience gained in life." [28] However, a dogmatic position lies concealed in this added personal experience which has been determinative for Harnack's historical conclusions. It is marked by a rationalistic religion of an ethical character. His rationalism is expressed, as it was in the case of Strauss, by the statement: "Miracles, of course, do not happen, but there is plenty that is marvellous and inexplicable." [29] He reduces the content of the gospel to the formula: faith in God the Father, his providence, the divine sonship of man, and the infinite value of the human soul.[30] This is practically the same as Ritschl's religion. On the negative side, von Harnack rejects the communion of Jesus with God in the metaphysical sense and affirms that "we can have the Easter faith without the Easter message." [31] In the first edition he said: "Not the Son but only the Father belongs in the Gospel that Jesus preached." [32] In his great *Lehrbuch der Dogmengeschichte,* Harnack follows the anti-meta-

[27] *The Communion of the Christian With God,* trans. J. S. Stanyon, rev. R. W. Stewart (London: Williams & Norgate, 1901).

[28] *What is Christianity?* trans. Thomas B. Sanders (London: Williams & Norgate, 1901), p. 4.

[29] *Ibid.,* p. 18.

[30] *Ibid.,* p. 44.

[31] *Ibid.,* p. 101.

[32] *Ibid.,* p. 19.

physical tendencies of Kant and Ritschl.[33] He fears that in the Church's dogma religious knowledge will supplant faith, and in his opinion, all forms of dogma contradict the very principles of Christianity and belong to a stage of development that has been or should be passed. On the other hand, he recognizes the fact that even with Jesus the gospel already possessed a clearly defined content which could not be formulated otherwise than in definite conceptions, that is, in dogmas. As a result von Harnack rejects the dogmas of the ancient Church because he believes that in them the Greek spirit was the determining factor. Thus he arrives at his famous definition: "Dogma in its conception and development is a work of the Greek spirit on the soil of the Gospel." [34] He has to admit that the Reformation not only permitted the dogma to continue but even filled the ancient formulas with a new religious significance for the Church. He therefore attributes a double character to the orthodox Protestant Reformation: "The Reformation, as it appears in the Christianity of Luther, is in many ways a catholic or more specifically, a medieval phenomenon, while judged by its religious essence, it is rather a revival of Pauline Christianity in the spirit of a new time." [35] Historically, Harnack prepared the way for a distinction between an Old and New Protestantism. He gave a popularized Ritschlian interpretation to the New Protestantism which became normative in wide circles.

Another historian of reputation was Friedrich Loofs (1858-1928) at Halle, whose writings are outstanding because of their abundant quotations from the original sources and their concise and factual presentation of the material.[36]

A combination along broad lines of Ritschlian theology with the philosophical ideas of Kant was undertaken by Julius Kaftan of Berlin (1849-1926). In his book *Philosophie des Protestantismus* (1917), he agrees with Ritschl that Kant's most important contribution to Protestantism lies in the limitation of the theoretical knowledge and

[33] Adolph von Harnack, *History of Dogma*, trans. Neil Buchanan, 7 vols. (Boston: Little Co., 1903-1907), translated from the third German edition.

[34] *Ibid.*, I, 17.

[35] Cf. *ibid.*, VII, 169.

[36] These writings include *Leitfaden zum Studium der Dogmengeschichte* (1889) and a great many monographs.

the exaltation of practical reason. In his *Dogmatik* (7th and 8th editions, 1920), Kaftan espouses in principle the positivistic concept of revelation held by Ritschl, but in fact, in many doctrines, e.g., the doctrine of God and the deity of Christ, he approaches the doctrinal statements of the Church so closely that it would not be fair to consider Kaftan an exponent of Neo-Protestantism.[37] The same is true of other exponents of the Ritschlian right wing like Theodor Haering (1848-1920), successor to Ritschl at Göttingen and later at Tübingen, Otto Kirn (1857-1911) at Leipzig, and Ferdinand Kattenbusch (1851-1936) at Halle. On the other hand, the radicals of the Ritschlian school, Ernst Troeltsch, for example, were in time attracted by the rising fame of the historico-religious school.

The literary organs of the Ritschlians were the *Theologische Literaturzeitung*, *Zeitschrift für Theologie und Kirche*, and *Die Christliche Welt*, the "Christian Century" of Germany, of which Martin Rade of Marburg was the editor for many years.

BIBLIOGRAPHY

BERNDT, B. *Die Bedeutung der Person und Verkündigung Jesu für die Vorstellung vom Reiche Gottes bei A. Ritschl.* 1959.

EDGHILL, E. A. *Faith and Fact, A Study of Ritschlianism.* London: Macmillan & Co., Ltd., 1910.

FRANK, R. *Ueber die kirchliche Bedeutung der Theologie Albrecht Ritschls.* 1891.

GARVIE, A. E. *The Ritschlian Theology: Critical and Constructive.* Edinburgh: T. & T. Clark, 1899.

LEMME, L. *Die Prinzipien der Ritschlschen Theologie.* 1891.

LIPSIUS, R. A. *Die Ritschlsche Theologie.* 1888.

MACKINTOSH, H. R. *Types of Modern Theology.* London: Nisbet Publishing House, 1937.

MACKINTOSH, ROBERT. *Albrecht Ritschl and His School.* London: Chapman & Hall, Ltd., 1915.

MOZLEY, J. K. *Ritschlianism.* London: Nisbet Publishing House, 1909.

ORR, JAMES. *The Ritschlian Theology and Evangelical Faith.* New York: Thomas Whittaker, 1898.

———. *Ritschlianism.* London: Hodder & Stoughton, 1903.

PFLEIDERER, O. *Die Ritschlsche Theologie.* 1891.

RITSCHL, O. *Über Werturteile.* 1895.

———. *Albrecht Ritschls Leben.* 2 vols. 1892–1896.

[37] Cf. Carl Stange, *Der dogmatische Ertrag der Ritschelschen Theologie nach Julius Kaftan* (1906).

WOELBER, H. O. *Dogma und Ethik, Christentum und Humanismus von Ritschl bis Troeltsch.* 1950.

WRZECIONKO, P. *Der Einfluss der Philosophie Kants auf die Theologie A. Ritschls.* 1953.

CHAPTER VII

FROM RITSCHL TO BARTH

When Ritschl died in 1889, Emperor Wilhelm II had just ascended the throne. When Karl Barth's famous commentary on Romans made its first appearance in the fall of 1918, the German Empire was doomed to destruction and with it was buried the nineteenth century's optimistic belief in progress and evolution.[1] Ritschl began as professor in Bonn and developed the final phase of his system at Göttingen. His school, therefore, is sometimes referred to as the Göttingen school. Karl Barth, on the other hand, began his academic career at Göttingen and concluded it, so far as Germany was concerned, at Bonn. The Ritschlian theology found its greatest rival and most formidable opponent in Karl Barth. Ritschl believed in a harmonious co-operation between Church and state, in a progressive Christianizing and ethicizing of society. He portrayed Jesus in accordance with the ethico-religious ideal of the middle-class society. While this cultural Protestantism continued to appeal to most of the Ritschlians as the great aim of Church and theology, some keen and honest thinkers soon discovered the injustice which the "historical Jesus" had suffered under the hands of Ritschl. Strange as it may seem, the reaction against the bourgeois Christ of Ritschl started within his own family. In 1892, Ritschl's son-in-law, Johannes Weiss (1863-1918), published his little volume *Die Predigt Jesu vom Reiche Gottes*. This publication has, in the words of Albert Schweitzer, "on its own lines, an importance equal to that of Strauss's first *Life of Jesus*."[2] In a consistent manner the author reveals the eschatological thought of Jesus which had been completely pushed into the background by Ritschl, thus opening up new vistas for theologians.

[1] In the Western Hemisphere the optimism of the nineteenth century extended into the early 1930's.

[2] *Op. cit.,* p. 237.

The Historico-Religious School

Theologians now began to emphasize the development of Christianity in the light of its historical and geographical environment. Ritschl had isolated Christianity and had recognized a connection only between Christianity and Judaism. Others before him, Schelling for example, had viewed the doctrinal content of Christianity in the light of the pagan religions of the ancient East. This emphasis on the general cultural background of Christianity received a new impetus in the work of Paul de Lagarde (1827-1891), a colleague of Ritschl in the university at Göttingen. De Lagarde insisted that theology is a historical, not a philosophical science; its field should be the comparative study of religion. The same demand was voiced by the philosopher Wilhelm Dilthey of Berlin (1833-1911). Equally important for the origin of the historico-religious school was the work of Otto Pfleiderer, who served as the connecting link between it and the older evolutionary (Hegelian) theology. A number of younger theologians were soon attracted to this new approach. A goodly number of classical scholars began to study the religious environment of the primitive Church. Among these scholars were Hermann Usener,[3] Richard Reitzenstein,[4] Eduard Meyer,[5] and others.

To some extent these German scholars were supported by the Dutch liberals. The Leyden school had kept abreast of the critical work in Germany. J. H. Scholten (1821-1892) leaned toward Hegelian monism, and C. W. Opzoomer was the leader of a new school in empiricism. In the Old Testament field Abraham Kuenen (1828-1891) was prominent. He was a pupil of K. H. Graf (1815-1869). Kuenen wrote a critical *Introduction into the Old Testament* (3 vols., 1861 ff.). The first compendium of comparative religion was written by Cornelius Petrus Tiele (1830-1902). This book was later revised by Nathan Söderblom and went through several editions. At Leyden there was also P. D. Chantepie de la Saussaye (1848-1920),

[3] *Religionsgeschichtliche Untersuchungen,* Vol. I, *Das Weihnachtsfest* (1889); Vol. II, *Christlicher Festbrauch* (1889); Vol. III, *Die Sintflutsagen* (1899).

[4] *Poimandres. Studien zur griechisch-ägyptischen und früh-christlichen Literatur* (1904), *Die hellenistischen Mysterienreligionen* (1910), *Weltuntergansvorstellungen* (1924), *Die Vorgeschichte der christlichen Taufe* (1929), and other works.

[5] *Ursprünge und Anfänge des Christentums,* 3 vols. (1921 ff.) and other works.

who published the first compendium of comparative religion in the German language (2 vols., 1887).[6]

Biblical Scholarship

The historico-religious method made its influence felt in the area of Old and New Testament study. In the Old Testament field Julius Wellhausen (1844-1918) and his school were most prominent. Wellhausen, the acknowledged leader of the higher criticism movement, tried to trace the evolutionary development of Israel's religion from an early and crude polytheism to a pure, ethical monotheism. Most startling was his bold assertion that, contrary to the traditional view, the great prophets of the Old Testament religion preceded the codification of the Mosaic law.[7]

The real explorer in the field of a historico-religious interpretation of the Old Testament was Hermann Gunkel (1862-1932). In his book, *Schöpfung und Chaos in Urzeit* (1895), he sets out to show that the biblical narrative of the beginning and end of time are based on extra-biblical legends of the Oriental peoples. Concerning the origin of Christianity, he asserts that Christianity is a syncretistic religion[8] and that the essentials of the Church's christological doctrine are not derived from the historical Jesus.[9]

Gunkel's view was developed further by Hugo Gressmann (1877-1927). He laid down the axiom of the historico-religious school in a book published in 1914: "There is in the world no material that does not have its history, no conception of thought without its connections with previous conceptions. This maxim holds true not only in the small and trivial things of life, but also concerning the prophetic religion of Israel and the origin of Christianity." [10] The study of history is conditioned by the axiom of development. He who rejects evolution can make no claim to scientific knowledge.[11] Evolution in

[6] See Vanderlaan, *op. cit.*

[7] *Geschichte Israels* (1878); 2nd ed. *Prolegomena zur Geschichte Israels* (1883); *Prolegomena to the History of Israel,* trans. J. Sutherland Black and Allan Menzies, with preface by W. Robertson Smith (Edinburgh, 1885).

[8] Hermann Gunkel, *Zum religionsgeschichtlichen Verständnis des Neuen Testaments,* p. 95.

[9] *Ibid.,* p. 64.

[10] Hugo Gressmann, *A. Eichhorn und die religions-geschichtliche Schule,* p. 35.

[11] *Ibid.,* p. 37.

the field of biblical studies is an established fact and has supplanted a biblical history based on supernatural forces. According to Gressmann, such prophetic elements as, for instance, the idea of the Messiah and eschatology are conditioned by similar extra-biblical concepts, not by supernatural revelation and inspiration.

Other scholars, for example, Wrede, Weinel, Heitmueller, and Bousset, applied this method to the study of the New Testament. According to Wilhelm Wrede (1859-1906), it was Paul and not Jesus who founded the Christian religion.[12] Jesus himself advanced no messianic claims. The impulse to give a messianic form to the earthly life of Jesus has arisen, according to Wrede, within certain circles of his followers among whom Mark, very likely, held a prominent place.[13] The supernatural tenets in the Gospels are dismissed by this school as accretions from the mystic religions of the ancient Orient which supplied the primitive Christian community with such ideas as the virgin birth, resurrection, and ascension of the Lord. The institution of the sacraments by Jesus is also denied. As to the origin of the sacraments, a distinction is usually made between a Jewish and a Hellenistic element as representing respectively the primary and secondary stage of development. The New Testament concept of baptism for repentance is said to be a Jewish notion; baptism as a washing of regeneration shows the influence of the mystic religions upon Christianity. The Lord's Supper was simply a farewell meal for Jesus. The Pauline interpretation of the Eucharist as a supper in which Christ gives the Church his body to eat and his blood to drink is identified with the mystery cults.[14] The "essence of Christianity" can be arrived at by stripping the New Testament of everything which might conceivably come out of the experience or reflection of the primitive Church. We would then be face-to-face with the "historical Jesus" whose features, broadly speaking, according to this school, are as follows: Jesus was the cheerful lad of a Galilean village.

[12] Wilhelm Wrede, *Paulus* (1905).

[13] Wrede, *Das Messiasgeheimnis in den Evangelien: Zugleich ein Beitrag zum Verständnis des Markusevangeliums* (1901), hereinafter referred to as *Messiasgeheimnis;* cf. Schweitzer, *op. cit.,* pp. 328 ff.

[14] A. Eichhorn, *Das Abendmahl im Neuen Testament* (1898); W. Heitmueller, *Taufe and Abendmahl bei Paulus* (1903); cf. also the article on *Abendmahl* in the first edition of *Die Religion in Geschichte und Gegenwart,* I, 20 ff.

Attracted by the message of John and being conscious of sin, he came to the Jordan for baptism by John. He then gathered a company of disciples and went about with them preaching the kingdom of God. His chief significance for faith lies in that he realized in his life the ideal of a universal religion, that is, belief in God, virtue, and immortality. What Jesus thought of himself, and what significance, if any, he attached to his death, we shall never know. It is likely that at some moments of his life he had visions of becoming the Messiah and the Son of man. By his criticism of Jewish legalism he attracted the suspicion and hostility of the Pharisees and scribes, who sought to ensnare and discredit him. When he showed himself in Jerusalem, he was arrested by the Jewish authorities. He remained passive and was condemned to death, the Roman government supporting the claims of the Jews.[15] The Jerusalem church, convinced that he was still alive after his crucifixion, envisaged this "Jesus of history" as the Messiah who would soon return in glory to inaugurate the final rule of God. This Judaistic Christology, it is said, underwent a further change in the Greek churches. The eschatological beliefs of the Jerusalem church gave way to the Hellenistic concept of Jesus as a divine *Kyrios*, the Lord of a mystery cult.[16]

The historico-religious school tried to explain the rise of Christianity by an intra-mundane evolutionary process of religion. It made theology a historical science and established itself upon the historical Jesus as its scholars saw him. Soon its leaders became painfully aware of the insufficiency of their religious foundation. Neither faith nor history could be satisfied with it. For the historian "the quest of the historical Jesus" seemed to be a hopeless undertaking since the documentary evidence in the New Testament seemed too scanty to provide a biography of Jesus. The scholars of this school held sharply conflicting views regarding the details of the life of Jesus. It was also felt that faith cannot live by a person of history. Because of its very nature faith seeks ties with an ever-present Reality. As a result, the historico-religious school underwent a great transformation. Turn-

[15] Wrede, *Messiasgeheimnis;* Wilhelm Bousset, *Jesus* (1904); Heitmueller, *Jesus* (1913).

[16] Bousset, *Kyrios Christos* (1913) and *Jesus der Herr* (1916); cf. our article "The Fifth Gospel: the Gospel according to Saint Paul," *The Lutheran Church Quarterly,* XIII, No. 3 (July, 1940), 223 ff.

ing from history and "the historical Jesus," it began to concentrate its efforts on the philosophy of religion and to replace the historical Jesus with a religious symbol rooted in human reason. This change of attitude was expressed by Wilhelm Bousset in a lecture at the Fifth Congress for Christianity and Religious Progress held at Berlin in 1910. The study of history, he said, points to something that lies beyond its own boundaries and forces us to look for another foundation of faith, that is, reason.[17] Continuing his argument, Bousset predicates a religious *a priori* in the soul of man. The great creative personalities of religion not only create religious symbols, but they are themselves symbols for their followers.[18] On account of this new attitude, the quest of the historical Jesus has lost its significance. We need not be alarmed, says Bousset, by the obvious failure of this quest, for we are concerned with Jesus as a religious symbol, not with the details of his life! For this reason, the Gospels, though they are a mixture of fiction and truth, will always have a greater appeal to man than the most exact reconstruction of the life of Jesus by a modern historian.[19]

While Bousset and others were indifferent to the details of the life of Jesus, some went a step further and flatly denied the historical existence of Jesus altogether. Albert Kalthoff was a pastor in Bremen, which for a time was the very hotbed of theological radicalism. According to Kalthoff, the origin of Christianity is rooted in a communistic movement in the Roman Empire. The crude social ferment at work in the Roman Empire amalgamated itself with the religious and philosophical forces of the time to form the new Christian social movement. In the late-Jewish literature, on the other hand, the principle of "personification" had long been at work. The early Christian writers made use of this principle and invented the historical person of Jesus. "From the socio-religious standpoint the figure of Christ is the sublimated religious expression for the sum of the social and ethical forces which were at work at a certain period."[20] A special sample of this view is the book published in 1906 by P. Jensen,

[17] Bousset, *Die Bedeutung der Person Jesu für den Glauben*, p. 10.
[18] *Ibid.*, p. 16.
[19] *Ibid.*, p. 17.
[20] For a critical review of the writings of Kalthoff, see Schweitzer, *op. cit.*, pp. 313 ff.

Das Gilgameschepos in der Weltliteratur, in which the author makes the whole life of Christ a Jewish version of a Babylonian epic. Adolph Deismann (1866-1937) must also be mentioned in this connection. By providence it became his task to liberate the New Testament from the strait jacket of a narrow concept of "biblical Greek" as being unique in vocabulary, inflexion, and style. He devoted all his efforts to interpret New Testament Greek in the light of life in the ancient East. His work was hailed by the scholars of the Anglo-Saxon world. Most of his writings were translated and he delivered many lectures in English and American institutions. This pupil of Herrmann, Wellhausen, and Cohen sought to explain the "essence of Christianity" in terms of a cult-worship and Christ mysticism.

Philosophers of Religion

In German thought there was a general shift in interest after 1900 from history to philosophy. The historico-religious school was transformed into a philosophico-religious school and its own greatest exponent, Ernst Troeltsch, was not a historian, but a systematic theologian.

Ernst Troeltsch (1865-1923), was a student of Ritschl. He held theological professorships at Göttingen, Bonn, and Heidelberg. In 1908 the theological faculty of the University of Berlin opposed his appointment as successor to Otto Pfleiderer. In 1914, however, he was called to Berlin as professor in the philosophy department. From 1919 to 1921 he held a position in the revolutionary government as secretary for church affairs.

At first Troeltsch synthesized Ritschl and Schleiermacher. He became dissatisfied with the isolation of religion in a special compartment. Realizing the need of a metaphysical foundation for religion, he went back to Hegel and the older liberal theology. Considering the structure of the human mind, he maintained that we are justified in speaking of a rational (though not intellectual) *a priori* of religion and of a "rational kernel of religion." With great mental acumen he began to investigate the absoluteness of Christianity. Christianity, he began, is a historical religion, yet it has always made the claim of offering religious absolutes. Can the historical nature of Christianity be reconciled with its claim of religious absoluteness? Troeltsch said no. History is an ever moving process involving change of form and thought. Whatever, therefore, is historical cannot be absolute. "To be historical and relative is identical."[21] Besides, everything historical is conditioned by the principle of causality. Consequently, Christianity as a historical phenomenon is subject to the principle of causality. There is no room in the modern mind for the supernatural origin of Christianity. The idea of the absoluteness of Christianity is dismissed. For the European-American mind Christianity represents the highest type of religion. "Christianity is indeed among the great religions the most potent and complete revelation of a personalistic religion."[22] What is the criterion for such an evaluation of the Christian religion? To answer this question Troeltsch appeals to the subjective, personal, yet unbiased and objectively minded conviction of the individual. In other words, Troeltsch admits that there is no objective-scientific criterion by which the question can be resolved. Not even the study of comparative religion can answer it. Religion is always a matter of personal conviction. Troeltsch does not follow a modern scientific method over against an antiquated dogmatic method of the Church. Rather is the theologian faced with two dogmatic principles, both of which are based on a preconceived axiom.

Troeltsch has discussed the "essence of Christianity" as follows:

> The Christian position is maintained when we are conscious of the Father of Jesus Christ as a living presence in our daily conflicts, labors, hopes, and sufferings, and when we arm ourselves, in the power of the Christian spirit, for the weightiest decision in the world, the final victory of all eternal and personal values of the soul.[23]
>
> The faith of the Christian religion is faith in the regeneration, the rebirth on a higher level, of a culture which in this world is alienated from God, by means of the knowledge of God in Christ, thus achieving the Kingdom of God by bringing culture into union with God.[24]
>
> Thus Christianity becomes the gospel of the attainment and preservation of the God-filled soul. . . . We do not ask: How can I obtain a gracious God? But rather: How can I find my soul again, how can I learn to love again?[25]

[21] Troeltsch, *Die Absolutheit des Christentums und die Religionsgeschichte,* rev. ed. (1912), p. 52.
[22] *Ibid.,* p. 86.
[23] *Zur religiösen Lage: Religionsphilosophie und Ethik* (1913), p. 440.
[24] *Ibid.,* p. 512.
[25] *Ibid.,* p. 522.

In brief, for the Christian faith in a divine Redeemer Troeltsch substituted belief in an evolutionistic development of human personality. The distinction between true and false, natural and revealed religion disappears. The attack of Troeltsch was directed mainly against Ritschl and his school because Ritschl declared the person of Jesus to be the sum total of redeeming truth, while the Ritschlians held the other religions to be burdened with so much error and uncertainty that without Jesus one would finally end up in atheism. The person of Jesus is not absolutely necessary for the religion of Troeltsch. In an address delivered in Aarau, Switzerland, in 1911, he declared that for sociological and psychological reasons it is desirable to maintain the person of Jesus as the focal point of worship and as the unifying factor in the community.[26]

Christianity, according to Troeltsch, has produced three distinctive social types: (1) the Church, inclusive, and possessing the indispensable and inalienable character of holiness by virtue of the means of grace administered by her, (2) the sect, an exclusive association of truly regenerate people, and (3) the religious mystic, interested only in the development of his own inner life. The Middle Ages did not end with the Reformation of the sixteenth century but rather with the Enlightenment in the eighteenth century, which issued into a Neo-Protestantism whose "symbolical books are God, freedom, and immortality and whose Christology is the earthly life of Jesus."[27] According to Troeltsch, the Lutheran church represents the most antiquated form of Protestantism, while Calvinism, by virtue of its alliance with humanism, is more modern and progressive. Still more progressive are the spiritualistic sects which have abandoned the supernatural and historical foundation of Christianity.

Christian ethics as well as dogma is relativized by Troeltsch. The ethical outlook of the primitive Church was purely ascetic and eschatological. The historic churches, in their pursuit of a Christian civilization, have rejected the ethical requirements of the New Testament. The pietistic sects, on the other hand, in trying to enforce the rigid otherworldliness of the New Testament, have forced themselves into

[26] "Die Bedeutung des Protestantismus für die Entstehung der modernen Welt."

[27] "Protestantisches Christentum und Kirche in der Neuzeit" in *Kultur der Gegenwart,* IV, 696 (2nd ed., 1909).

cultural inactivity. Troeltsch had no solution to offer with respect to the ethical duties of the present. The social work of the churches was highly problematic to him. Christian ethics in itself, he maintained, is unable to satisfy the needs of the time.[28] Little wonder that Troeltsch exchanged his theological professorship for a chair in the philosophical faculty. Karl Barth reportedly has called Troeltsch "the last of the romantic theologians." Troeltsch lived between the times. He was deeply conscious of the past failures of both orthodox and liberal theology, and he was groping for a new solution to be actualized in the future. He could no longer accept the idea of an external authority in religion. Expressing himself more radically than Harnack, he held that the Reformers had retained too many features of medieval Christianity. In his eyes, eighteenth-century rationalism was the beginning of the modern age, for it asserted the autonomy of man in religion. This freedom was to him the very core of a Neo-Protestantism as distinct from the older Protestantism of the sixteenth and seventeenth centuries. In fairness to Troeltsch it must be said that Neo-Protestantism is indeed an offspring of the Reformation. When Luther said at Worms that he would not recant unless convinced by Scripture and plain reason, because his conscience was captive to the Word, he upheld the right of the individual to interpret the Bible according to grammar and history, both of which evidently belong to the domain of human reason.

Philosophically speaking, Troeltsch was an eclectic. Starting with Kant and Ritschl, Troeltsch turned to Hegel and Idealism as interpreted by Wilhem Dilthey (d. 1911), and to Rudolf Eucken (d. 1926).[29] The problem of faith and history which confronted him is still a challenge to theology.[30]

Rudolph Otto (1869-1937) stands out as a man of many diverse

[28] Troeltsch, *The Social Teachings of the Churches,* trans. Olive Wyon, 2 vols. (London: Allen & Unwin, 1950).

[29] Facing an age of positivism and materialism, both Dilthey and Eucken maintained the priority of spirit over matter and nature, and regarded history as the manifestation of the divine spirit. Eucken's view of God is a kind of pantheism. As life itself, God is transcendent; but as the depth of being, God participates in all life. Cf. Rudolf Eucken, *Der Wahrheitsgehalt der Religion* (1927), p. 152.

[30] For the latest discussion of this problem see Gerhard Ebeling, *The Nature of Faith* (Philadelphia: Muhlenberg Press, 1961), especially pp. 19 ff., and *Word and Faith* (Philadelphia: Fortress Press, 1963), pp. 17 ff.

interests. Well versed in philosophy, the natural sciences, comparative religion, and theology, he tried to overcome the chasm between the individual and *das Ding an sich* by exploring feeling as an avenue to metaphysical truth, like Schleiermacher. Religion is not a purely introspective science; instead, it establishes fellowship with another, that is, with God. Out of Otto's religious-psychological and religious-historical investigation has come the widely read monograph *The Idea of the Holy*.[31] The concept that had been completely set aside by Ritschl appears here as the actual center of all religion. The Holy is the numinous, the mysterious, the "wholly other" which fills the soul of man with wonder and awe. On the other hand, the Holy possesses something fascinating and attractive which wins the confidence of man. It is composed of both super-rational and rational elements. Consequently, the doctrines of the Church contain both rational and super-rational statements. With this conception of the Holy, Otto helped to prepare the way for the Barthian reaction against the Ritschlian, Neo-Protestant version of Christianity.

In *The Life and Ministry of Jesus*[32] and *The Kingdom of God and the Son of Man*,[33] Otto interpreted the life of Jesus from the standpoint of the critical-eschatological school, while in *Die Gnadenreligion Indiens und das Christentum*[34] he paid special attention to the Hindu concept of grace.

On several occasions reference has been made to Albert Schweitzer (1875-1965), theologian, philosopher, physician, missionary, and musician. Following in the footsteps of Johannes Weiss, he has become the most consistent exponent of the eschatological interpretation of the life of Jesus. His endeavors to interpret the religion of Paul from a purely eschatological point of view have met with less success.[35] As to his world-view, Schweitzer does not share the naive, evolutionary optimism of the last century. A planned evolution can nowhere be discovered, he says. Good is always opposed by evil. He holds to the ethicizing concept of Christianity in Neo-Protestantism when he lays

[31] New York: Milford, 1928.
[32] Chicago: Open Court Publishing Co., 1908.
[33] London: Lutterworth Press, 1943.
[34] For an analysis see Emil Brunner, *Revelation and Reason* (Philadelphia: Westminster Press, 1946), p. 226.
[35] Cf. Schweitzer, *op. cit.,* and *The Mysticism of Paul the Apostle,* trans. William Montgomery (New York: Henry Holt & Co., 1931).

down the principle of "reverence for life" as an ethical imperative. "It is good to sustain and further life; it is evil to destroy and thwart life." He holds that this reverence for life is identical with the ethics of the Sermon on the Mount and therefore is the absolute ethic. To the extent we have the spirit of Jesus, Schweitzer says,[36] we have the true knowledge of him!

For the first time in modern German theology, the historico-religious school undertook to disseminate its ideas among a wider reading public. For this reason its scholars issued a series of semi-popular monographs;[37] a New Testament translation with commentary;[38] and an encyclopedia[39] written and edited exclusively from the standpoint of this school.

We must also say a word about Nathan Söderblom (1866-1931), the late Archbishop of Upsala and Primate of the Church of Sweden. By placing Söderblom at the end of this section, immediately preceding our discussion of the contributions made by conservative theologians, we indicate that Söderblom held a mediating position in his day. He was a liberal scholar but a conservative churchman. Prior to his appointment as primate of his church, he held the chair of comparative religion in Upsala and Leipzig. He had a pronounced leaning toward Luther. As scholar, churchman, and linguist he was of the first magnitude, and what is still more, he was a simple Christian with a heart of love for all mankind. He was the spiritual power behind the first ecumenical council of modern Christendom when it met in Stockholm in the summer of 1925 ("Life and Work"). His theological interest centered in the idea of "general revelation." "No religion is a product of culture, all religion depends on a revelation."[40] With an untiring effort he tried to demonstrate that God is active in nature, history, and in the consciousness of his prophets. According to Söderblom divine revelation is "continued revelation." It reached a climax in Christianity. Jesus is unique because he is the historical

[36] *Philosophy of Civilization* (1923 ff.).

[37] "Die religionsgeschichtlichen Volksbücher" Series.

[38] Johannes Weiss (ed.), *Die Schriften des Neuen Testaments, neu übersetzt und erklärt* (Göttingen: Vandenhoeck & Ruprecht, 1905 ff.).

[39] *Die Religion in Geschichte und Gegenwart* (1909 ff.).

[40] Nathan Söderblom, *The Nature of Revelation* (New York: Oxford University Press, 1933), p. 8.

revealer of God. In Jesus "the eternal reason and will of God, the Logos, became very flesh."[41] Söderblom quite definitely rejected the Ritschlian ethicizing of religion, "for the final question put to religion is not: How will you shape my life, what ought my life to be? It is rather this: How can you rescue my life and sustain it, so that I may not be engulfed in a meaningless existence or lost in despair?"[42] Religious experience was for him an experience of the infinite majesty and holiness of God coupled with an experience of "terror and anguish, of death and hell" as the natural reaction of the whole human personality, although he was willing to grant that "it is wrong and unpsychological to make the experience of the great hero of faith the standard for all."[43] The "otherness" of God and the *sola gratia* of Paul and Luther are foremost in his concept of Christianity. In this respect Söderblom was a genuine Lutheran. However, many Evangelical Christians will register their protest against his view of the *propter Christum* in the act of justification. He limits the incarnation to a personal embodiment of the character of God in the man Jesus, and the cross is regarded as "the strongest testimony that God has been seeking man."[44] Pupils of Paul and Luther will deplore the fact that Söderblom allowed Ritschl to obscure his understanding of the meaning of Christ.

Friedrich Heiler of Marburg was a great admirer of Söderblom. Reared and educated in the Roman church, he was early attracted to the principles of the Catholic modernists and Protestant liberals. In 1919 Heiler was received into the Lutheran communion by Söderblom without renouncing his membership in the Church of Rome. Heiler addressed himself to promoting the cause of an "evangelical catholicism" (a synthesis of the Catholic ideal of the Church and the Protestant emphasis on the *sola gratia* in piety). In his publications we discern the same comprehensive view of religion as in the writings of Söderblom. In the Anglo-Saxon world Heiler is best known by his book on *Prayer*.

[41] Söderblom, *The Living God* ("The Gifford Lectures" [New York: Oxford University Press, 1933]), p. 319.

[42] *The Nature of Revelation*, pp. 3-4.

[43] *Ibid.*, p. 93.

[44] *The Living God*, p. 344. Cf. also *The Mystery of the Cross*, trans. A. G. Hebert (Milwaukee: Morehouse Publishing Co., 1933).

In conclusion a word of criticism is in order. We do not wish to minimize the chasm that exists between such theologians as Ritschl and Söderblom. However, the chief concern of these scholars is not the *revelatio specialis* but "religion in general." They seek the "essence" of Christianity in the general history of thought and religion. The truth that breaks forth in the Gospel is not a new truth which did not exist before Jesus; it is a truth that always existed, the "immanent purpose" of the cosmological drama. This purpose was not clear until Jesus came. To these theologians, therefore, Christ is the Archetype (Schleiermacher), the Revealer, the Bearer of a moral idea, the founder of a religion in whom the ethico-religious ideal was realized for the first time. This is what they mean when they speak of the "uniqueness" of Christ. They regard his relation to Christianity as "factual and causal," but not as positive and absolutely necessary.[45] To believe is not to believe *in* Christ, but to have faith *like* Christ, who to them is not the object of faith, but rather an exemplification of faith and love.

The effect of Neo-Protestantism was destructive on the life of the churches in Germany. Church attendance dropped; theologians were swept up into the current of a general individualistic religiosity[46] or of a religious and political socialism.[47] They could not regain either the educated or the proletariat for Christ. The way for a restoration of biblical Christianity was prepared in the theologies of such men as Ihmels, Kaehler, Schlatter, and Schaeder, and accomplished in the Barthian and Neo-Lutheran revival of the next period.

Conservative Theologians

During these years when the historical and rational aspect of religion commanded the interest of theologians, German Protestantism did not lack men who not only exerted themselves to confess the

[45] Cf. Emil Brunner, *The Mediator* (Philadelphia: Westminster Press, 1947), p. 97.

[46] Cf. the position of Johannes Mueller, *Blätter zur Pflege persönlichen Lebens* and other works. Cf. also Karl Koenig, *Gott, warum wir bei ihm bleiben müssen* (1901); *Der moderne Mensch auf dem Wege zu Gott* (1904); and other works.

[47] Cf. F. Naumann, *Briefe über Religion* (1903).

creeds of evangelical Christianity,[48] but who with great scholarship and genuine piety waged a courageous fight for the faith of the Church.

In biblical studies, Theodor Zahn (1838-1933) stands out as the great authority on the New Testament and the literature of the ancient Church. He was both a student and successor of Hofmann in the chair of New Testament at Erlangen. Unhampered by the preconceived dogmatic theory of his teacher, Zahn endeavored to prove the authenticity of the early Christian tradition by a thorough historical investigation of all the extant literature of that period. With this in mind he wrote an *Introduction to the New Testament*.[49] We note also his *Forschungen zur Geschichte des neutestamentlichen Kanons* ("Research in the history of the New Testament canon"). At the advanced age of sixty-five he began his great commentary on the New Testament, to which he contributed the exposition of Matthew, Luke, John, Acts, Romans, Galatians, and Revelation.

The position of Zahn was, broadly speaking, shared by his collaborators in the commentary, Philip Bachmann (d. 1931), Gustaf Wohlenberg (d. 1917), Paul Ewald (d. 1911), the blind scholar Ernst Riggenbach (d. 1927), Paul Feine (d. 1933) of Halle University, and Adolf Schlatter; in the field of the Old Testament, by such men as Rudolf Kittel (d. 1929), Ernst Koenig (d. 1936), and Ernst Sellin (d. 1946). All these scholars give close attention to the literary and critical problems and to those of comparative religion. They do not regard the relatively late composition of a book as casting doubt upon its reliability. While rejecting the historico-religious school's evolutionary concept of Christianity, they follow the method of comparative religion not to destroy, but to disclose more clearly the unique character of biblical religion.

As to the origin of Protestantism, the conservatives look upon the Reformation of the sixteenth century as a revival of the biblical religion of redemption. They seek to understand and establish this Christianity as it is given in the Scripture, in the historic confessions,

[48] Alexander Schweitzer of Zurich is credited with saying that as the fathers once confessed their faith, so now theologians sometimes endeavor with might and main to believe in the confessions of their fathers. Cf. Ferdinand Kattenbusch, *Die deutsche evangelische Theologie seit Schleiermacher* (1926), p. 57.

[49] New York: Charles Scribner's Sons, 1917.

and in the living religious experience of the evangelical faith, with the scientific methods of the present, without permitting it to be destroyed in content by the so-called modern spirit. In 1883 the Weimar Edition of Luther's Works was begun. Prominent in the field of Luther research are Wilhelm Walther (d. 1924), Karl Holl (d. 1926), Heinrich Boehmer (d. 1927), *et al.*

In systematic theology, Ludwig Ihmels (1858-1933), professor at Erlangen and Leipzig, Bishop of Saxony, was the recognized leader of Lutheranism. He was a pupil of Frank, whose theology underwent a noteworthy modification along more conservative lines in his work. Ihmels agrees with Frank that the ultimate basis on which Christian certainty is founded is a subjective one.[50] Certainty can be arrived at only through a personal experience of salvation. The question arises whether a man can deduce the knowledge of objective Christianity from his subjective experience or whether this has to be given him in some other way. Ihmels' answer is the second of these alternatives. He says that the divine Word, when preached with its message of sin and grace, exercises its influence upon man. In this manner, he argues, man may become certain of divine realities. Religious experience is always secondary and arises from the objective knowledge of the Word. The way leads from the objective to the subjective, from history to psychology. A further difference between Frank and Ihmels lies in the definition of the fundamental religious experience. While Frank, in keeping with the age of Ritschl, interpreted religious experience ethically as regeneration, Ihmels designated this experience as justification. In fact, during the last twenty years of his life, Ihmels was a forceful preacher with the Fourth Article of the Augsburg Confession, on justification, as the basis of all his sermons.[51]

Another scholar who owes much of his theology to the Erlangen school is Ole Hallesby, professor at the Independent Theological Seminary, Oslo, Norway. In fact, Hallesby is the systematic theologian of evangelical pietism *par excellence*. He has become well known in America through personal contact and his translated writings.

[50] Ihmels, *Die christliche Wahrheitsgewissheit,* 1901, 3rd ed. 1914.

[51] Cf. his sermons, *Eins ist not* (2nd ed., 1907); *Aus der Zeit für die Zeit und Ewigkeit* (1921).

Reinhold Seeberg (1859-1935) held doctoral degrees in theology, philosophy, jurisprudence, and even medicine. He was a Baltic Lutheran. Frank of Erlangen influenced his thought considerably. Unlike Ihmels, Seeberg liberalized the Erlangen theology. He became known as a mediating theologian. His liberalizing tendencies prompted him to leave the historically Lutheran university of Erlangen and to accept a call to the Union University of Berlin. His main contributions lie in the field of historical and systematic theology, but he also was at home in higher biblical criticism. His scholarship is evident in his four large volumes on the history of Christian thought to which we make frequent reference. In the book *Die Kirche Deutschlands im 19. Jahrhundert* he stressed the need for a "modern positive theology" which would meet the spiritual need of the times. He sought to meet this need in a popular book, *Fundamental Truths of the Christian Religion*[52] and later in a more developed and different way in his *Christliche Dogmatik*. Here he describes the fundamental principle of his new dogmatic formulation as a "voluntaristic transcendentalism." In contrast to the "substantial" concepts of the divine and human being, he regards the will as the characteristic element in the human and divine being. The relationship between them, he maintains, must be described as a relationship of the will. The "essence of Christianity," according to Seeberg, is expressed in the two concepts of the redemptive supremacy of God and of faith, and of the kingdom of God and of love. This sovereignty of God is mediated by Jesus Christ. Christianity is the absolute religion "and all other religions are only religions in so far as their center is related to Christianity."[53] For Seeberg the source of Christian dogmatics is neither subjective experience nor the teaching of the Bible, but "the revelation that is believed."

In dealing with individual doctrines he adopts a more or less extensive modification of traditional dogmatics, especially in discussing the doctrines of the Trinity, Christology, and eschatology. Since the essence of a person is nothing but will, the Trinity consists of three wills in God: "The Father wills the world; the Son wills the church

[52] Trans. George E. Thomson and Clara Wallentin (New York: G. P. Putnam's Sons, 1908).

[53] *Christliche Dogmatik*, I, 195.

by overcoming the sinful antagonism of mankind; the Spirit wills myself as a member of the church and for labor within it."[54] Jesus had his origin as a man, with whom, at his baptism, the Logos or the Spirit united. This union was made perfect by Christ's resurrection.[55] Thus Jesus became the Son of God, the historical organ through whom God accomplished the redemption of mankind.[56] Seeberg framed anew the traditional eschatology with its many "open questions" on the basis of deeply devotional studies in Paul and John, and in 1915 published the result of his thought in a little volume under the title *Ewiges Leben* ("Eternal Life"). This book he dedicated to those who mourned loved ones fallen in World War I. This book, together with his other systematic studies, makes it very plain that some of the fundamental ideas of Christianity have been distorted by his leaning toward German Idealism. Little wonder that he held to an "analytical conception" of justification which involved purification of man in a "purgatory of grace."[57] In this connection his underestimation of God's wrath in the theology of Luther is highly significant. Yet Seeberg was far removed from modernism as a system. His heart was with the Lutheran church. In his work on dogmatics he does not stress the claim of science against the religion of faith, nor urge a naturalistic philosophy upon theology, nor does he deny the supernatural.

For a time it was believed that Seeberg would succeed in establishing a "modern-positive school." Even after it became evident that this could not materialize, men continued to speak of the "Seeberg circle," meaning that there was a group of mediating theologians, among them Karl Beth, R. H. Gruetzmacher and others, who attempted to steer between the old Erlangen theology on the one hand and theological liberalism on the other.

The most original of these scholars was Theodor Kaftan (1847-1932). In contrast to Seeberg's speculative idealism, Kaftan's modernism was conditioned by the Neo-Kantian opposition to metaphysics. He made a sharp distinction between faith and theology. The sub-

[54] *Ibid.*, I, 381.

[55] Seeberg made much of the "Spirit" of Christ as the *Kyrios* who had joined Himself to Jesus (referring to II Cor. 3:17, "Now the Lord is that Spirit").

[56] Cf. *Der Ursprung des Christusglaubens* (1914).

[57] *Christliche Dogmatik,* II, 568-69.

stance of faith cannot change; it must be the old faith or no Christian faith at all. Theology as the science of faith must develop according to the spiritual progress of mankind. Kaftan did not hold a theological chair but was the titular head of the Lutheran church of Schleswig. His heart was so much with the Lutheran church that even as emeritus he served a small independent Lutheran congregation in Baden.

The biblical tradition at its best was represented during this period by Martin Kähler (d. 1912), who was a pupil of Rothe, Tholuck, and Beck. He also shows the influence of Hofmann and thus combined a threefold heritage in his system: the pietistic, biblical, and churchly. Like the other great biblicists before him, Kähler made justification the center of Christianity. He even included this idea in the title of his great work, *Die Wissenschaft der christlichen Lehre von dem evangelischen Grundartikel aus im Abriss dargestellt.*[58] In this work Kähler presents a great wealth of biblical ideas which, as in Hofmann, are in the order of the history of redemption. In a somewhat limited way Kähler provides a place for the confessions of the Church,[59] but he strongly emphasizes the "proof of religious experience in the personal life." He goes beyond the bounds of a strict biblicism when he acknowledges value in the teaching of the Church, and in experience and speculation for the Christian recognition of the truth. It was Kähler in particular who furthered an understanding of the significance of the Bible. For him the central content of the Scriptures was the biblical Christ, and he contended for this content over against the popular "Lives" of Jesus and the "historical Jesus" type. This he did particularly in a book on the historical Jesus and the biblical Christ, originally published in 1892.[60] In the apostolic message concerning Christ the "super-historical" and the historical are inseparably intertwined. The whole biblical Christ is truly and deeply the historical Christ. We cannot go beyond the Gospels of the New Testament

[58] "An Epitome of Christian Doctrine written from the Standpoint of the Basic Article of Evangelical Faith" (1883). The book is not available in English.

[59] His concept of the Church is consistently nonconfessional. He taught at Bonn and Halle, both of which are universities of the Union.

[60] Martin Kähler, *Der sogenannte historische Jesus und der geschichtliche biblische Christus,* ed. E. Wolf (1953), available in English as *The So-Called Historical Jesus and the Historic Biblical Christ* (Philadelphia: Fortress Press, 1964). Our references are to the German edition cited.

in the search for the true Jesus. We can know Christ only through the mirror of the apostolic mind. The Christ as such cannot be the object of our scientific investigation. "The Risen Lord is not the historical Jesus underlying our Gospels, but the Christ of the Apostolic message, in fact, of the whole New Testament."[61] "Christ Himself is the source and author of the biblical picture."[62] Kähler must be credited with having shown the untenable nature of the Neo-Protestant picture of Christ.

Adolf Schlatter, a Swiss, was another representative of the biblical tradition. He taught at Bern, Greifswald, Berlin, and Tübingen. Although he resigned his chair in 1922, he continued his literary work till his death in 1938. Schlatter's method is empirical in the best sense of the word. "Learn how to see and how to hear." He strenuously opposed the "Greek" spirit which tries to master the world by means of ideas, the use of syllogism as a way to knowledge, and "pure reason" with its power of giving form to the thing perceived. True knowledge is "to see that which presents itself to us" by a "determined affirmation of the spiritual constitution given to us, and performance, in conformity with their inherent laws, of the functions implanted in us, performing them not only without reluctance but with concentrated will. Then we are no longer permitted to isolate our thinking from the objective reality that presents itself to our view, and every autonomous production of ideas becomes a sin for us. Over and above our self-made images there is now placed that which we have received, the process which we call 'seeing'."[63] In conformity with this theory of knowledge he defines the task of theology as the observation of man. "For we can arrive at a doctrine of God only by observing those events which transmit to us the knowledge of God, and these events occur within us. . . . In so far theology, especially when it seriously considers God, is anthropocentric because it has its place not above man but in man."[64]

Although he devotes the first 279 pages of his work on dogma to anthropology, he does not want to reproduce the scholastic teaching of a "natural theology," but rather to describe man as a creature of

[61] *Ibid.*, p. 64.
[62] *Ibid.*, p. 87.
[63] Quoted in Stange, *Religionswissenschaft*, I, 155.
[64] Adolf Schlatter, *Das christliche Dogma* (2nd ed., 1923), p. 14.

God, the Creator. Man in the state of sin is still the creature of God and capable of the knowledge of God. Schlatter's method marks a sharp deviation from the theological tradition of both Schleiermacher and Ritschl, who had reduced theology to a narrow soteriological doctrine. Schlatter rejected certain tenets of the Augustinian-Lutheran tradition, especially the axiom that man and nature are nothing but sin since the fall, an axiom he saw as a denial of the creative work of God. Man's condition, he asserts, is a "mixed" one; there is good and evil in him, and nature still reflects the glory of God. Against this background, Schlatter maintained a critical attitude toward the Reformation, claiming that Protestantism has never fully appropriated the whole message of the Bible. By its one-sided emphasis on the forgiveness of sins, Protestantism has failed to understand that man is called by Christ to serve God. The preaching of the churches has led the people to faith but seldom to new obedience and work.

Schlatter's greatest achievement lies in the field of New Testament studies, although he objected to being called a "biblicist." Pure biblicism is "senseless" in the eyes of Schlatter, for not only was God operative in the men of the Bible, but he still is active in history through his Spirit. "Theology dare never remain solely exposition, whereby the Scriptures are opened to our understanding, but the Church always has need of the dogmatician, especially at such times when she is shaken and confused and buffeted about by religious controversy." [65] Armed with an excellent knowledge of Palestinian Greek and rabbinical language and theology, he employed the method of comparative religion not to destroy but to establish the uniqueness of Christianity. He was decisively opposed to any attempt to establish a cleavage between Jesus and the Apostles. "The picture of Jesus," he says, "was not transmitted to the Church in a mechanical fashion, neither photographically nor stenographically. If we were to lament this, we should thereby prove that we had not yet comprehended that God is Spirit and Truth. Jesus speaks to humanity through His Apostles, and He does this by making His word and His picture the governing center of their life. To be sure, the Evangelists report things really heard and seen; but the seeing and hearing

[65] E. Stange, *op. cit.*, I, 156. Cf. also Schlatter, *Die Theologie des Neuen Testaments und die Dogmatik* (1909).

are by eyes and ears, and the reproduction of what eyes and ears have received is achieved by means of intellectual faculties by which the Evangelists give form to what they say. Thus the Evangelist, while he is showing us Jesus, simultaneously permits us to share his own innermost possession. The Gospel, therefore, reveals the Evangelist also, after the manner of an overtone which accompanies the principal tone and gives to the latter its peculiar coloring."[66]

In his commentaries on the Gospels, Schlatter proves with great clarity that both Matthew and John, as well as the "New Narrator" introduced by Luke, belong to the bilingual Palestinian circle, while Luke himself was a Hellenist employing a Greek diction that was current in Syria. Romans, Schlatter says, was not written to answer Luther's question, "How may I find a gracious God?" but sets forth the righteousness of God by which man is redeemed "to walk in the newness of life." In Corinthians, he maintains, Paul combats not Greek Gnosticism, but a perfectionism and enthusiasm rooted in erroneous Jewish ideas: "Onward and upward over that which is written" (I Cor. 4:6). The Letter of James, he says, is not a polemic against Paul, but the message of a Jewish sage who wrote as a Christian at a time when a mutual toleration between Christians and Jews still existed. The Pastorals, on whose Pauline authorship Schlatter had looked with suspicion in his earlier years, are accepted in 1936 as Pauline. In his *Ethics*, Schlatter insists with all the vehemence of the Reformed confessions on the application of the motives arising from religion to an active service in the Christian fellowship and in the secular calling.[67]

Erich Schaeder (1861-1936) also expressed his grievances against the theological trend of the nineteenth century. He complained that the whole theology of the previous century, not only of Schleiermacher, Ritschl, and the historico-religious school, but even of the Erlangen school, was too anthropocentric. All placed man and his need for salvation in the forefront and understood the love of God only as a means of attaining man's salvation. Against this Schaeder advocated a theocentric religion and theology in the work *Theozen-*

[66] Schlatter, *Gesunde Lehre* (1929), p. 201.

[67] Cf. W. Strunk, "The Theology of Adolf Schlatter," *The Lutheran Church Quarterly*, 1938, pp. 395-402.

trische Theologie. The majesty of God, which is revealed in nature and history as well as in Christ, occupies the center of his consideration. Our existence for God as serving instruments of divine governance is emphasized above God's work for us and his pardoning grace given in Christ. Schaeder himself admits that in such an orientation it is evident that certain teachings of Calvinism have been made fruitful for the Christian and the churchly teaching of faith.

BIBLIOGRAPHY

DAVIDSON, ROBERT F. *Rudolf Otto's Interpretation of Religion.* Princeton: Princeton University Press, 1947.

FUELLING, E. *Geschichte als Offenbarung: Studien zur Frage: Historismus und Glaube von Herder bis Troeltsch.* 1956.

HALLESBY, OLE. *Why Am I a Christian?* Minneapolis: Augsburg Publishing House, 1930.

———. *Prayer.* Minneapolis: Augsburg Publishing House, 1931.

———. *Conscience.* Minneapolis: Augsburg Publishing House, 1933.

———. *The Christian Life.* Minneapolis: Augsburg Publishing House, 1934.

———. *Religious or Christian?* Minneapolis: Augsburg Publishing House, 1939.

HODGES, H. A. *Wilhelm Dilthey, an Introduction.* London: Paul Trench & Trubner Co., 1944.

KAHLER, MARTIN. *The So-Called Historical Jesus and the Historic Biblical Christ.* Translated and edited by CARL E. BRAATEN. Philadelphia: Fortress Press, 1964.

NUELSEN, JOHN L. *Some Recent Phases of German Theology.* New York: Eaton and Mains, 1908.

OTTO, RUDOLPH. *The Idea of the Holy.* Fairlawn, N. J.: Oxford University Press, 1943.

RITZERT, G. *Die Religionsphilosophie Ernst Troeltschs.* 1924.

RUSSELL, LILIAN M. *The Path to Reconstruction.* New York: Henry Holt & Co., Inc., 1942.

SEAVER, GEORGE. *Albert Schweitzer, The Man and His Mind.* 4th ed.; Boston: Beacon Press, 1951.

SLEIGH, ROBERT S. *The Sufficiency of Christianity.* London: J. Clarke, 1923.

SODERBLOM, NATHAN. *The Mystery of the Cross.* Milwaukee: Morehouse, 1933.

VANDERLAAN, E. C. *Protestant Modernism in Holland.* Oxford University Press, 1924.

WOELBER, H. O. *Dogma und Ethos, Christentum und Humanismus von Ritschl bis Troeltsch.* 1950.

CHAPTER VIII

THEOLOGICAL THOUGHT SINCE WORLD WAR I

Introduction

The most striking feature during the decade following World War I was the resurgence of the gospel in academic theology. By the end of World War I, liberal thought had lost the props on which it was constructed. The great triumvirate of theological liberalism, Schleiermacher, Ritschl, and Troeltsch, fell into profound disrepute among German-speaking theologians, especially among the younger generation. This does not mean, however, that Continental scholars have abandoned liberalism as a methodological principle. They are far removed from the literalism of American fundamentalism. On the contrary, they endeavor to promote the cause of true evangelical religion through an unbiased, scientific approach to the problems of theology. With them theology must be strictly scientific as well as true to the essence of biblical religion. Consequently, the two classical periods of the Church, the period of the New Testament and of the Reformation, have attracted the special interest of these scholars. Through the Weimar Edition of Luther's Works, begun in 1883, theologians were offered a new opportunity to study the thinking of Luther and especially of the young Luther. To this must be added the startling discoveries of a number of manuscripts containing Luther's lectures on Romans, Hebrews, and some other material. All this tended to cause a revolution against the Ritschlian interpretation of Luther. As early as 1900 Johannes von Walter, in his book *Das Wesen der Religion nach Erasmus und Luther*, charged the Ritschlians with having established themselves not on Luther but on Erasmus. The honor of effecting a real turn of the tide belongs to

Carl Stange of Göttingen,[1] and Karl Holl of Berlin.[2] These scholars brought to light the theocentric character of Luther's theology. Luther is viewed as the great antagonist of ethical idealism with "the justification of the ungodly" at the center of his theology. This anti-idealistic concept of Christianity is also evident in many of the more recent New Testament studies. In Kittel's New Testament lexicon, the attempt is made to indicate and emphasize the unique character of the New Testament in comparison with Greek thought, the Old Testament, and contemporary Judaism (Josephus, Philo, and rabbinical studies).[3]

Interest is focused on the revival of conservative theology, but theological liberalism, though much discredited since World War I, is by no means a dead issue in the Continental churches. For a while liberalism gained new momentum in the theology of the German Christian Movement and of late it has made a comeback in a new garb in the theology of Bultmann and his followers.

Barthian Theology

Karl Barth, born in Basel, Switzerland, in 1886, was educated at Bern, where his father held a theological chair, Berlin, Tübingen, and Marburg. During World War I he was pastor of a church in Safenwil, Switzerland. In 1921 he was appointed professor of Reformed theology in the university at Göttingen. Afterwards he taught at Muenster and Bonn. In 1934 he was expelled from Germany and returned to Basel, where he taught at the university until his retirement in 1962. While a student at Berlin and Marburg he came under the influence of the two great Ritschlian scholars Harnack and Herrmann. Before entering the ministry he was for a short time (1908–

[1] *Die ältesten ethischen Disputationen Luthers,* 1904; *Die Heilsbedeutung des Gesetzes* (1904); *Studien zur Theologie Luthers* (1928). Stange has also contributed much to the discussion of philosophy, ethics, and general dogmatics. All his writings portray the author's keen mind and deep Lutheran piety.

[2] *Gesammelte Aufsätze zur Kirchengeschichte, Band I, Luther* (1922), and subsequent editions.

[3] In this connection reference should be made to H. C. Strack and Paul Billerbeck, *Kommentar zum Neuen Testament aus Talmud und Midrasch,* 4 vols. (1922 ff.), and to exegetical studies of C. Bornhaeuser, *Das Wirken des Christus* (1921); *Das Johannesevangelium, eine Missionsschrift für Israel* (1928); *Die Geburts-und Kindheitsgeschichte Jesu* (1930), and other works. Bornhaeuser is famous for his consistent approach to New Testament interpretation from the standpoint of contemporary Judaism.

1909) associate editor of the Ritschlian journal *Die christliche Welt.* "In Karl Barth liberal theology brought forth its own conqueror. He could overcome the liberal theology because he was bone of its bone and flesh of its flesh."[4] Barth's name will go down in history as the great conqueror of liberal theology, as a prophet of a new Christianity, because he interpreted the crisis of Western civilization in the light of the Word of God, proclaiming relentlessly the divine yes over against our human no, and the divine no over against our human yes.

Barth began his literary career with an article dealing with modern theology and the work of God's kingdom.[5] In this article Barth speaks of the predicament in which a theologian finds himself when he has been trained in religious individualism and historical relativism as taught in Marburg and Heidelberg. Nevertheless, as a faithful student of Herrmann, he defines religion as a strictly individual experience, and it is the task of the theologian, he maintains, to set forth this concept of religion in its scientific aspect with reference to the general human cultural consciousness. A change of outlook became noticeable in 1911 when Barth moved to Safenwil, where he became interested in the Swiss religio-social movement of Hermann Kutter and Leonhard Ragaz.[6] The effect of this movement on Barth is seen in a paper entitled "Der Glaube an den persönlichen Gott,"[7] in which he interpreted the kingdom in terms of God's lordship, and not in terms of human achievement and progress.

[4] Hermann Sasse, *Here We Stand,* trans. Theodore G. Tappert (Minneapolis: Augsburg Publishing House, 1938), p. 155.

[5] "Moderne Theologie und Reichsgottesarbeit," *Zeitschrift für Theologie und Kirche,* 1909, pp. 317-21.

[6] This radical movement owed much of its enthusiasm to the teaching of the Swabian pastor Christoph Blumhardt (1842-1919). Having been brought up in the biblical realism of his father, Johann Christoph (1805-1880), Blumhardt, in a manner not heard before, proclaimed the advent of the kingdom which he conceived as truly God's kingdom, not a product of human endeavors. To him Jesus was the Son of man, the Man of all men, the Savior of mankind, the Conqueror of all evil powers. He rejected the asceticism of the Swabian Pietists and associated himself with the political Social Democrats. He did not take this step because he equated Marxism with Christianity, but rather because he saw in Marxism a demonstration of the fact that God's love truly extends to all men. Cf. Eduard Thurneysen, *Christoph Blumhardt* (1926).

[7] *Zeitschrift für Theologie und Kirche,* 1914, pp. 21-32, 65-95; cf. Peter Haman Monsma, *Karl Barth's Idea of Revelation* (1937), pp. 44 ff.

The next step in Barth's development was in response to World War I. Seeing that socialism was unable to check the hostilities and cruelties of the war, he discarded religious socialism as well as the "bourgeois Christianity" of theological liberalism. He and his friends, as Thurneysen says in an article written in 1927,[8] learned to be more attentive to the Bible. Over against the concept of an immanent evolution, Barth began to lay stress on the transcendent dynamic principle in religion. A definite turn toward Reformation theology is noticeable. In an address delivered in 1916 he said: "His (God's) will is not a corrected continuation of our own. It approaches ours as a 'Wholly Other'." [9] In another lecture of 1916 on "The Strange World in the Bible," the idea of God as the wholly other is set forth with new emphasis. The thought of this period had its climax in the first edition of the *Römerbrief* in 1919. The divine, the wholly other, the eternal world, is a reality present in this life of ours.

The second edition of the *Römerbrief* in 1921 showed that Barth had again undergone a thorough metamorphosis. He now had reached that stage in his development which will be remembered in history as the "theology of the crisis." In the Preface to the revised edition he informs the reader that of the former structure "no stone is left upon another." As to the main factors that have influenced him, Barth mentions (1) a further study of Paul, (2) the teachings of Overbeck,[10] (3) a better understanding of Plato and Kant due to the work of his brother Heinrich, (4) an increased appreciation of Kierkegaard and

[8] *Zwischen den Zeiten,* 1927, pp. 513-522.

[9] Barth, *The Word of God and the Word of Man,* trans. Douglas Horton (Grand Rapids: Zondervan, 1928), p. 24.

[10] Franz Overbeck (1837-1905) was professor at Basel and an intimate friend of Friedrich Nietzsche. Like Albert Schweitzer, he held that primitive Christianity was an ascetic-eschatological movement. Because of its constant endeavors to arrive at a harmonious synthesis between Christianity and human culture, the Church's theology is, in his eyes, the "Satan of religion." Overbeck's thought revolves, according to Barth, around the two main ideas of primeval time and death. Primeval time is the super-temporal, the impenetrable beginning from which we come; death the supremely meaningful moment for which we are headed. Whatever lies between these two is the world, the historical, the relative. Christianity, as a historical religion, can hold no claims to religious absolutes. Christianity cannot be history; history cannot be Christianity. Overbeck had actually severed all ties with Christianity. He spoke merely as a historian. As a theologian he expected nothing but peaceful extinction of the Christian religion. Cf. Barth, *Zur inneren Lage des Christentums* (1924), p. 1-24.

Dostoevski,[11] and (5) the reception and criticism of the first edition by the reading public.

Barth's aim in the revised edition of the *Römerbrief* is to refute the theological relativism of the Harnack-Troeltsch era. The historico-religious school had fully discarded the historical foundations of religion. In this dilemma Wilhelm Herrmann had resorted to a psychological phenomenon, "the inner life of Jesus," as the staying principle in theology. The conservatives, in their apologetic endeavors, had usually arrived at some sort of a compromise between the results of biblical criticism and the religious finality of the Bible. Trained as a liberal, Barth could not accept the position of the fundamentalists. On the contrary, he set out to overcome the historism and psychologism in theology by holding to the theory that revelation and redemption are phenomena which lie beyond history and psychology. Under the influence of Kierkegaard, Barth had made use of the dialectical method before 1921; but in the revised edition his dialectics received an altogether new twist. Having found out that "Paul and Plato can go quite a ways together," dialectics now became an ontological verity over against the mere logical dialectics of the former period for Barth. A cosmic dualism underlies the religion of the revised *Römerbrief*. God and man, eternity and time, are viewed as metaphysical opposites. God is in heaven and man is on earth! God is known as the unknown God. The Absolute cannot be reached by man; the finite is not capable of the infinite.

A history of redemption is a *contradictio in adjecto*. History may be a predicate of revelation, but revelation can never be a predicate of history. Revelation is something super-historical and trans-historical, a moment between the times. Historical facts are nothing more than parables and demonstrations of the divine. The center of theology is the super-historical Christ, not Jesus the historical. Barth looks upon the fall of man not as a historical event but as super-historical verity. It is the realization of two metaphysical opposites, the cause

[11] Kierkegaard's disclosure of the "ultimate potentialities of the human soul" has been amply illustrated in the writings of the Russian novelist F. M. Dostoevski (1821-1881), who laid strong emphasis upon the otherness of God, the apocalyptic nature of the kingdom, the wickedness of the individual and society, the paradoxical character of forgiveness, and the new life by virtue of the resurrection. The quintessence of Dostoevski's thought is best set forth in the well-known story "The Grand Inquisitor."

of a distinction between the infinite and finite, time and eternity, God and creature. The teaching of supralapsarian predestination is the only key for an understanding of the universe. This concept of the fall involves the simultaneity of every individual! We are not separated from the fall by generations preceding us, but every moment of time stands in immediate relation to it. Consequently, the concept of sin receives a metaphysical twist. Time, creature, and sin, all belong to one and the same order of things. Likewise, the second coming is not a spectacular phenomenon at some distant future, but rather the super-historical, ever present annihilation of time.[12] Salvation is never realized on earth; we do not possess it; we can only hope for it. Whenever men take the law in their own hands they build not the kingdom but the tower of Babel. The problem of ethics is identical with that of dogmatics: *Soli Deo Gloria.* Man is not a divine instrument through which God achieves his purpose: the ethical life strives to honor God.

These are, in brief, the salient features of the theology of the crisis. A caustic critic, Wilhelm Schmidt, did not go amiss when he said: "The 'dialectic theologians' may well jot down their dogmatics on a scrap of paper: God is not man, revelation and redemption are not history, eternity is not time. Whatever else they may have to say, can only be a repetition of these sentences." [13] Barth remarked that his theology should not be regarded as a new system, but only as a marginal note, a pinch of spice in the food.[14] However, his revised *Römerbrief* is indeed a new system, a textbook of the theology of the crisis. Barthian theology had come into existence. As time went on, this fact became still more pronounced with the publication of Barth's *Dogmatik* in 1927 and 1932.

Barth styled the first edition of his dogmatics a prolegomena to "Christian" dogmatics. In the second edition the word "churchly" replaced the word Christian. This change is significant. Barth wanted to give new weight to his claim that theology is not a "free" science but "bound to the realm of the Church." In the revised edition he expressly states his refusal to grant philosophy any part in revelation.

[12] Cf. Barth's interpretation of the well-known passage Rom. 13:11-14.

[13] *Zeit und Ewigkeit* (1927), p. 285.

[14] Barth, *The Word of God and the Word of Man,* p. 198.

The Word is the only criterion of dogmatics. According to Barth the Word has a threefold form: the word spoken in the preaching of the Church, the written word of Scripture, and the revealed word to which the other two forms of the Word bear testimony. The content of the Word is Jesus Christ, the Immanuel; revelation is the speaking person of God (*Dei loquentis persona*). In the Logos the *Deus absconditus* becomes for us the *Deus revelatus*. In this fact Barth sees the root of the doctrine of the Trinity. Barth protests against the idea that in the act of recognizing the Word, it becomes a part of man. It is the Word only by a divine concurrence and as long as it is used divinely. The Bible is not an infallible book so far as scientific or historical data are concerned; it is not a document on a level entirely different from other religious literature. Higher criticism holds a legitimate place in theology. As to the epistemological problem, Barth rejects the Cartesian maxim "I think therefore I am," and holds on the contrary that knowledge of self is based on the knowledge of God: I am thought, therefore I am. As a believer, man is wholly the result of the object of faith, that is, of God. In faith, moreover, man is made to conform to the Word, adapted to hear God speaking.

On the supposition that God is revealed to us only in his Word, that is, God speaking to man, Barth rejected emphatically the Roman doctrine of a natural knowledge of God as well as the modern Protestant teaching of a religious *a priori*. This principle caused a painful breach in the ranks of his close friends and was the reason for his persistent opposition both to the Nazi German Christian Movement and to the confessional Lutherans who, on the basis of the Reformation doctrine of a general revelation, were prone to interpret the German national revival of 1933 as "the Lord's doing and marvelous in our eyes." [15]

Barth has given us a comprehensive exposition of the Christian faith in sixteen lectures on the Apostles' Creed delivered at the University of Utrecht in February and March, 1935, published under the title *Credo*. Most striking in these lectures is the absence of the

[15] The quarterly *Zwischen den Zeiten* was discontinued and Barth, assisted by Eduard Thurneysen, began to publish a series of pamphlets known as *Theologische Existenz heute*.

vehement eloquence of the Barthian language. If the caustic remark of Gerhard Heinzelmann was justified that Barth should have offered an apology in the revised *Römerbrief* for having so grossly misinstructed the reader about God and the world in the first edition of the *Römerbrief*,[16] the same remark is true with regard to the *Credo* in comparison with the revised *Römerbrief*. It is difficult to recognize the author of these two writings as the same man. The specific tenets of the crisis theology have disappeared. Whereas in 1921 Barth virtually heaped ridicule on those who look for a second coming at some distant future, he now speaks of Christ as our "future," our "hope." "The Second Coming of Christ is the restoration, but at the same time the universal and final revelation, of the direct presence of Jesus Christ as 'God-man,' for that was the content of the forty days after Easter." [17] The emphasis which Barth lays on the historical Jesus is in keeping with this temporal conception of the second coming. Pontius Pilate now holds a legitimate place in the Creed. While Barth formerly denounced the Church as the "annulment of the Gospel," he now writes that "the church is indeed the Kingdom of God in the interim period." [18] Only at one fundamental point did Barth remain the same: he still rejects each and every acknowledgement of a natural theology.

The rejection of a natural theology put Barth in a peculiar position when in 1935 he was invited by the Senate of the University of Aberdeen to deliver the Gifford Lectures on natural theology. In loyalty to his calling as a Reformed theologian, Barth felt that he could not do justice to the requirements of the Gifford Foundation, "to promote, advance, teach, and diffuse," the study of natural theology "among all classes of society," and "among the whole population of Scotland," in direct agreement with the intentions of the late Lord Gifford. He could make this task his own only indirectly, namely, "to confer on Natural Theology the loyal and real service of reminding it of its partner in the conversation." Barth delivered the lectures in 1937 and 1938. They are based on the articles of the Scottish Confession of 1560. The author is very frank about his

[16] See Schmidt, *op. cit.*, p. 14.

[17] *Credo* (New York: Charles Scribner's Sons, 1962), p. 121.

[18] *Ibid.*, p. 141.

rejection of any sort of natural theology. With regard to the general tenor of the lectures, the student who is wont to identify Barth with the theology of crisis will be as much surprised by these lectures as by the *Credo*. In direct opposition to his former emphasis on the "infinite difference between time and eternity," Barth says, "While it is beyond our comprehension that eternity should meet us in time, yet it is true because in Jesus Christ eternity has become time." [19] "Eternity is here (in the stable at Bethlehem and on the Cross on Calvary) in time." [20] His new emphasis on the reality of the Christian life and the divine mission of the empirical Church is agreement with this attitude toward the reality of God in time.

The condescension of God into space and time received special emphasis in Barth's *Dogmatics*[21] and especially in his essay on the *Humanity of God*.[22] In the former, Barth defends the doctrine of the virgin birth as the mode in which the Eternal was made man. The latter volume is a kind of self-criticism. Educated in the anthropocentric theology of the nineteenth century, Barth admits that in his earlier period he overstated the difference between God and man. His understanding of God at that time showed greater similarity to the God of the philosophers than to the God of Abraham, Isaac, and Jacob. A change of direction has taken place in his thinking. God's deity, rightly understood, includes his humanity. The incarnation gives dignity to man, human culture, and the Church.

Reading the later volumes of Barth's *Dogmatics*,[23] two features stand out: the christocentric orientation and the emphasis on the relevance of the gospel. Barth moves from the center to the periphery, from Christ to man. What this means can be illustrated by referring to Barth's understanding of predestination, of creation, of the law and of the state.

[19] Barth, *The Knowledge of God* (London: Hodder & Stoughton, 1938), p. 72.

[20] *Ibid.*, p. 78.

[21] *Church Dogmatics* (New York: Charles Scribner's Sons, 1957 ff.), IV, Part 1, 207.

[22] *The Humanity of God* (Richmond: John Knox Press, 1963), pp. 37 ff.

[23] To date 10 volumes have appeared and are being successively translated into English. Otto Weber has condensed Vols. I-III under the title *Barth's Dogmatics,* trans. A. C. Cochrane (Philadelphia: Westminster, 1953). Barth's postwar lectures given in Germany in 1946 are published under the title *Dogmatics in Outline* (New York: Philosophical Library, 1949).

Barth rejects point-blank the Calvinistic doctrine of an absolute decree. Election is that decree, he says, which has been executed by and through Jesus Christ, and is that which has happened to him. Jesus Christ is the "electing God" and "the elected man." John 1:1-2 shows that God's ways from the beginning have been his ways in Jesus Christ. Jesus is the electing God. The divine decree is a concrete decree, the object of which is man. Since the Logos became man, the man Jesus is the elected man and we are elected in him. No one is rejected in him. Faith in God's predestination is faith in man's non-rejection, not faith in his rejection.[24] The separation is not between the elect and the reprobate, but rather between the ungodly and the believers. Even believers are "potentially" rejected. They are elected only as believers in Christ.

Creation is grace, according to Barth. It is "the establishment of a place for the history of the covenant of grace." In the person of Jesus Christ God is disclosed to us as the Creator. This is true not only in the sense of knowing, but also ontologically, according to being, for Christ is truly the Word by which God accomplished his creation.[25]

Ethics, Barth says, explains the law as the form of the gospel. It is grounded in the knowledge of Jesus Christ who is both the sanctifying God and the sanctified man. In Christ God assumed responsibility for his creature. Barth therefore gives ethics a place in his doctrine of God.[26] In Barth's eyes the justification of the sinner through faith in Jesus Christ and the problem of justice and of human law are inseparable.[27] The state is a kind of an outer court of the divine sanctuary, for the Lordship of Jesus Christ cannot be limited to the inner life of man or to the Church. He is Lord over all principalities and powers. This understanding of the state in its relation to Christ made Karl Barth virtually an activist of first order during the Hitler regime. He became the backbone of the theological resistance movement in Germany. The "Barmen Declaration" with its

[24] "God's Gracious Election," *Church Dogmatics,* II, Part 2, 1-563. Cf. Weber, *op. cit.,* pp. 93-103.

[25] "The Work of Creation," *Church Dogmatics,* III, Part 1, 1-476. Cf. Weber, *op. cit.,* pp. 117-39.

[26] "God's Commandment," *Church Dogmatics,* II, Part 2, 564-875. Cf. Weber, *op. cit.,* pp. 104-116.

[27] *Church and State,* trans. G. Ronald Howe (London: SCM Press, 1939).

emphasis on Christ as the only word of God was mainly his work.[28] At the time of the Munich crisis in the fall of 1938 he wrote a letter to the Czech Christians saying that in fighting for "the righteous state" they were also indirectly fighting for the kingdom of God. He penned three similar letters addressed to the French Protestants in 1939 and 1940; in 1941 to the British Christians; followed by another document addressed to the Americans in 1942.[29] In the letter to the Americans he says that the present world-rending struggle is also fought for Christ's sake and in honor of him. Realizing, however, that the war is a struggle between two parties, neither of which is a spotless white sheep, American Christians should refrain from imagining the Allied cause a crusade in which the "just" are called to execute vengeance on the "unjust."

Following the collapse of Hitler and the rise of communism, Karl Barth has taken a different stand. He has refused to join the West in condemning communism.[30] He advised Christians in Hungary not to oppose the new regime or to lose their calm and sense of humor, but rather to be free and wait a little, for the Christian life is basically an affirmation of good, and only secondarily a condemnation of evil. When Emil Brunner, among others, expressed his disappointment, Barth replied that Brunner did not understand. No one in the West, except a few diehard Communists, he maintained, is tempted to deify Marxism as "German Christians" deified national socialism. Why should the Church go with the stream doing what Truman and the pope and a host of newspaper reporters are doing so effectively? The Church does not act "on principle," but judges spiritually and existentially in individual cases.[31]

In concluding our review of Barth, we are inclined to maintain that Barth stands before us as a modern "Church Father" who has labored both quantitatively and qualitatively more than all others.

[28] For an analysis, see Erwin Müller, "The Significance of the Barmen Declaration," *The Lutheran Church Quarterly,* XIX (1946), pp. 402 ff.

[29] The French and British letters have been published under the title *This Christian Cause* (New York: The Macmillan Company, 1941); the American document under the caption *The Church and the War* (New York: The Macmillan Company, 1944).

[30] *Against the Stream, Shorter Post-War Writings, 1946-52* (New York: Philosophical Library, 1954).

[31] *Ibid.,* pp. 106 ff.

However, both conservative and liberal scholars have taken exception to his theology. In the eyes of Cornelius Van Til and modern Evangelicals Barth's (and Brunner's) theology is just another kind of modernism.[32] Wilhelm Pauck, on the other hand, thinks the churches need a Harnack more than a Barth.[33] The most penetrating analysis of Barth's theology is given by Gustaf Wingren.[34] The frame of reference in Barth's theology, Wingren says, consists of three elements: (1) God as an unknown being until he reveals himself, and henceforth as known; (2) man without knowledge of God and directed to the place where God reveals himself; (3) the concept of revelation. All three elements are undoubtedly biblical elements: God, man, and revelation. Yet it is precisely this framework, Wingren maintains, that is questionable. This framework still reflects the Kantian-Ritschlian tradition in which Barth was educated. To be scriptural it ought to be replaced by a frame of reference constituted by three other elements: the works of God, the works of man, and justification. In Barth revelation stands in place of justification or forgiveness of sins. If justification stands in the center, it is assumed that man already knows something, that he is not without knowledge but rather without excuse. Before he is justified man knows of God and of his own sinful ways. Consequently man is guilty because as man he knows how he ought to order his life. In Barth, however, the framework God, man, and revelation is never broken. The chief significance of the incarnation is in giving man the proper knowledge of God. In Scripture the emphasis is on what God does in Christ, saving and justifying the sinner.

Early Co-workers of Karl Barth

In the twenties, the springtime of the dialectical movement, three other theologians worked with Karl Barth in ushering in a new day of theology: Eduard Thurneysen, Friedrich Gogarten, and Emil

[32] Van Til, *The New Modernism: An Appraisal of the Theology of Barth and Brunner* (Philadelphia: Presbyterian and Reformed Publishing Company, 1947).

[33] Pauck, *The Heritage of the Reformation* (Boston: Beacon Press, 1950), p. 358.

[34] Wingren, *Theology in Conflict* (Philadelphia: Muhlenberg Press, 1958), especially pp. 28 ff.

Brunner. These were the men behind the journal *Zwischen den Zeiten*.

Thurneysen (b. 1888) later became (1930) professor of practical theology at the university of Basel. He remained a lifelong friend of Barth. A serious rift between Barth on the one hand and Gogarten and Brunner on the other terminated the existence of *Zwischen den Zeiten* in 1932.

Gogarten (b. 1887) was the only German of the four, and the only Lutheran. His writings, therefore, have a Lutheran overtone. He opposes philosophical idealism on the basis of an existential understanding of human life. Historical existence to him is not an image of an eternal idea. The proper relationship between God and man is that of an I and Thou: God as Creator and man his creature. History is responsible living by faith in God the Creator. Though orthodox in doctrine, neither the priest nor the Levite had faith in God; the Samaritan on the other hand believed in God notwithstanding his heterodoxy.[35] When God entered history, he entered the realm of the secular. "Secularization" is a part of the Christian faith. It is the legitimate result of the gospel. "Secularism," on the other hand, issues into degeneration of life.[36]

In his *Politische Ethik* (1932), Gogarten follows essentially Luther's doctrine of the natural orders and puts heavy emphasis on the importance of the state. As he sees it, the state is the only effective check upon human selfishness. There is no such thing as a specifically Christian ethics. The things of this world are to be ordered according to the structure of the world. This view inevitably played into the hands of the rising Hitler movement. Gogarten joined those in the German Christian Movement not because, as he said, he agreed with their wild theological thinking, but because the Church can proclaim its message only in a given historical situation. He defended his attitude against both Karl Barth and Paul Althaus in a number of writings.

During the academic year 1957-58, Gogarten was a visiting professor in the graduate school of Drew University. The influence of both

[35] Gogarten, *Ich glaube an den dreieinigen Gott* (1926), p. 61. Cf. also his *Vom Glauben und Offenbarung* (1933).

[36] Cf. Gogarten, *Verhängnis und Hoffnung der Neuzeit* (1953).

Heidegger and Bultmann is quite evident in these lectures. Gogarten says theologians must not attempt to protect the Christian faith by asserting an "objectivity" as the basis of faith by claiming "historical factuality" for its message.[37] The Christian can meet the feeling of independence and subjectivism on the part of the modern man only by an understanding of faith as freedom for God. God gives to man along with the world as his inheritance the possibility of freedom for Him. The independence of a mature son toward his father is established. "The independence toward the world is based on the independence toward God. And the maturity of the heir toward the world has its measure in the maturity of the son before God, which is the filial freedom of man for God." [38]

The most internationally oriented of the three men under discussion is Emil Brunner (b. 1889), professor at Zurich since 1924. He has been a frequent lecturer in Great Britain, America, and even Japan. Brunner's breach with Barth became apparent with his publication of *Natur und Gnade* in 1932. In this treatise Brunner accused Barth of drawing unwarranted conclusions from the biblical doctrine *sola gratia:* the denial of the analogy of being between God and fallen man; the denial of a divine revelation in nature, conscience, and general history; the rejection of God's grace in the creation and preservation of the world; of the possibility of natural law, and of a point of contact, for the saving action of God.

Barth replied in an outburst of anger with a treatise *NO! Answer to Emil Brunner* (1934).[39] Barth set forth as his alternative a thoroughgoing biblical, christocentric theology. From Brunner's "natural theology," he said, only the church of the Anti-Christ could profit, although he admitted that even as a sinner man is man and not a tortoise. But he denied that the rationality of man makes him more suited to define the nature of God than anything else in the world. Since that time both disputants have on numerous occasions defined their respective views in much greater detail. In our eyes, Barth, by admitting the rationality of fallen man, has consistently refused to

[37] *The Reality of Faith* (Philadelphia: Westminster Press, 1959), p. 96.
[38] *Ibid.*, p. 107.

[39] Both Brunner's treatise *Nature and Grace* and Barth's reply have been translated by Peter Fraenkel and published in one volume, *Natural Theology* (London: G. Bles, 1946).

draw the necessary conclusions, while Brunner has spent much time and effort on exemplifying man's religious and moral responsibilities. Both anthropology and ethics have been a special field of his studies.[40] This does not mean that he has surrendered to "general religion." Brunner has always maintained the "once-for-allness" of the revelation in Jesus Christ.[41] He has always emphasized that the "old man" and with him the old view of God and of the self must be "put to death" in order that the "new man" may come into existence. This conflict, he says, must have its counterpart in theological reflection. The Christian must engage in discussion with the non-Christian about the proper knowledge of God and of good. This attempt Brunner prefers to call "theological eristics," a term which describes a combination of apologetics and polemics.[42] Here is a field which, in the eyes of Brunner, has been sadly neglected by Karl Barth and his followers.

In his *Dogmatics*, Brunner relies upon biblical criticism more than does Karl Barth. In the discussion of the person of Christ, Brunner maintains that the apostolic witness to the incarnation and the virgin birth is originally two separate accounts which are at odds with one another. The incarnation lies at the core of the New Testament message, while the teaching of the virgin birth is an attempt which lacks both conviction and historical accuracy to explain the divine mystery rationally. It finds no support in the New Testament apart from Matthew and Luke.[43]

Brunner persistently follows the nonliteralistic interpretation of the Bible proposed in his earlier writings,[44] in his book on eschatology, prepared originally for the meeting of the World Council of Churches at Evanston (1954).[45] The Church, he says, is faced with the task of formulating the New Testament hope of the future in such a way

[40] Emil Brunner, *Man in Revolt* (Philadelphia: Westminster Press, 1947); *Reason and Revelation* (Philadelphia: Westminster Press, 1946); *The Divine Imperative* (Philadelphia: Westminster Press, 1946); *Justice and the Social Order* (New York: Harper & Bros., 1945).

[41] *The Mediator* (Philadelphia: Westminster Press, 1947).

[42] Cf. *The Divine Imperative,* p. 61. The term "eristics" is derived from a Greek verb meaning "to wrangle."

[43] Brunner, *Dogmatics,* trans. Olive Wyon (London: Lutterworth Press, 1942-1962), II, 350 ff.

[44] Cf. *The Theology of Crisis* (New York: Charles Scribner's Sons, 1929) and *Our Faith* (New York: Charles Scribner's Sons, 1936).

[45] *Eternal Hope* (London: Lutterworth Press, 1954).

that justice is done to the reasonable demands of the existentialists and that the Christian hope is not brought into conflict with the modern scientific world-view. It is always the task of theology to shape the statements of faith "that faith is apprehended as a new understanding of life and a transformation of life."

Rudolf Bultmann

One of the prominent figures of the wider circle around Karl Barth in the twenties was Rudolf Bultmann (b. 1884), professor of New Testament theology at Marburg. In 1941 he published *Offenbarung und Heilsgeschehen*, containing two essays: "Die Frage der natürlichen Offenbarung" and "Neues Testament und Mythologie." [46] It was the second essay that gave rise to a vehement controversy over Bultmann's understanding of Christianity.[47]

Bultmann's essay opens with the challenging statement that the

[46] Republished in Rudolf Bultmann, *Kerygma and Myth* (London: SPCK, 1953).

[47] About twenty years before these works appeared, Martin Dibelius and Karl Ludwig Schmidt inaugurated the form-criticism method in the field of the New Testament studies. Both men worked independently, the former writing *Die Formgeschichte der Evangelien* (translated under the title *From Tradition to Gospel*, 1933), the latter *Der Rahmen der Geschichte Jesu.* In 1921, Bultmann followed suit with his *Die Geschichte der synoptischen Frage.* Here the interest is centered in such questions as, What took place between Jesus and the Gospels? What was the form of the Gospel stories before they received literary form? What were the motives which led to their selection and preservation? The exponents of this method regard the Gospels and the Book of Acts—and to some extent also the epistolary literature of the New Testament—as mosaics of tales, legends, sermons, and paradigms which became fixed by the preaching of the Church. These fragments were collected and loosely put together by the later evangelists. The framework, and in part also the stories of the Gospels, are altogether unhistorical; they are the result of the missionary zeal of the Church.

This method had its immediate precursor in Gunkel's and Gressmann's *gattungsgeschichtliche Forschung* of the Old Testament. These scholars claimed form (*Gattung*) is determined by a sociological factor, the *Sitz im Leben* or historical environment. The criterion by which a datum is identified as authentic, it is said, is "agreement with a known environment." According to Schmidt, the *Sitz im Leben* for the Gospels is the Christ-cult of the primitive Christian community. The Gospels, therefore, are not human biographies; rather, they reflect the central theme of the Church, the incarnation of the Logos, in a very great variety of fragments. It was against the background of this method that Dibelius wrote his little book *Jesus* (1939). In *A Fresh Approach to the New Testament and Early Christian Literature* (1941), Bultmann first applied this method to a wider field of research.

world-view of the New Testament is mythological. Its world is a three-story house with the earth as its center and with heaven above and hell below. The earth, however, is not only the place of natural human life; it is at the same time the plane where supernatural forces interfere. Man is not his own master. Demons may control him, but God and angels may also support him in his struggle against evil. The proclamation of the saving event is couched in equally mythological terms. A pre-existent divine being has appeared on earth and has suffered vicariously for the sins of the world. His resurrection marks the beginning of a cosmic catastrophe by which death will be annihilated. The risen and ascended One will return, the dead will rise, a final judgment will separate the good from the evildoers forever. Bultmann claims that this view is totally unintelligible to modern science, which will not permit of any intervention by so-called supernatural powers. Hence the New Testament must be demythologized. This is to be effected not by elimination, as the older liberal school tried to do, but rather by re-interpretation.

The New Testament is not a collection of religious and ethical truths, as liberalism held. The interpretation of liberal Christianity destroyed the very heart of the gospel. The New Testament is essentially a proclamation of an act of God for the salvation of the world. Must we then eliminate mythological expressions entirely? No, we must only eliminate the anthropomorphic presentation of transcendence which characterizes the New Testament. The gospel must be interpreted "existentially." On this point Bultmann is influenced quite consciously by Heidegger.[48] It is characteristic of man to ask the question of being in general and of understanding himself and ordering his life. In Heidegger's thought man finds himself in a predicament not knowing "whence he came nor whither he goes." This understanding is, to Bultmann, man's being apart from faith. Yet the gospel offers man a way of escape from nihilism. It proclaims the grace of God. To exist in faith means to exist eschatologically, to be related to the *eschaton* that is already present. What about the Christ event? Bultmann maintains that the New Testament reveals two lines of thought. On the one hand, the New Testament demythologizes its message because, in contradistinction to other religions,

[48] Martin Heidegger, *Being and Time* (New York: Harper & Bros., 1962).

its central figure is a historical person born and dying in time. On the other hand, it clothes Jesus in a mythological garb the texture of which was suggested to the disciples by Jewish apocalypticism and the mystery religions of late antiquity. It presents him as pre-existent, born of a virgin, and dying a vicarious death on the cross. What about the resurrection? Bultmann's answer is that it has no factual reality. The notion that a dead body can be reanimated is contrary to natural science. It constitutes an offense. It must be demythologized in order that the real offense of the gospel, that God freely forgives anyone who believes in him, may be proclaimed. The resurrection is simply an interpretation of the saving aspect of the cross, for according to a divine plan, the cross is a historic event, an event which affects the whole human race in its relation to God.[49] In addition to the cross, God through the disciples creates the kerygma, the message of the cross and the preaching of Christ crucified. The Christ event is the manifestation of the love of God which liberates man from the old self to a new self, to a life in faith and love. The difference between philosophy and the New Testament is that the New Testament interprets man's existence as an act of God which creates faith and love and gives a new dimension to life. The act of God is present in the kerygma, the Word. Stripped of its mythological dress, the New Testament bears witness to a divine act which occurred in time and space. In that sense, Christianity is unique even for Bultmann. When man is confronted with the preaching of the Word, he cannot ask any questions concerning its legitimacy; rather the Word asks hims whether he is willing to believe or not.

Bultmann has created a stir in the theological world. Opinions pro and con have not been withheld. Broadly speaking, three distinct positions are represented in the debate. First there are some who have allied themselves with Bultmann. Among these the most significant

[49] Bultmann makes a distinction between *historisch* and *geschichtlich*. The former expression, like the Engish "historical," refers to an event that has taken place in the past on the plane of history—for example, World War II. *Geschichtlich* corresponds to our "historic" and describes the lasting significance of an event which has not necessarily taken place at a given time. The creation of the world, for instance, is not a historical, but rather a historic event. Cf. L. Malevez, *The Christian Message and Myth* (London: SCM Press, 1958), pp. 73-74; cf. also Paul Althaus, *Fact and Faith in the Kerygma of Today* (Philadelphia: Muhlenberg Press, 1959), p. 21.

are Bultmann's longtime friends from the days of dialectical theology, Friedrich Gogarten with his book *Demythologizing and History* and Werner Bartsch, editor of the five-volume series, *Kerygma und Mythos*.

Second, there is the right-wing, including Karl Barth, Lutherans such as Paul Althaus, Gustaf Wingren, Ernst Kinder and others, Roman Catholics, and Giovanni Miegge, a Waldensian theologian. This group includes also several of the English-speaking contributors such as John Macquarrie of the University of Glasgow. These men insist that the Easter faith is indeed interested in the historical question, though Barth and Althaus, for example, do not intend to substitute historical knowledge for faith or to refurbish the doctrine that the risen Christ appeared for the eyes of a critical historian. Because he has reduced Christology to soteriology, Bultmann has abused the Lutheran dictum "to know Christ is to know his benefits." Because Bultmann is held captive by a phenomenological epistemology, he has allowed the Kantian-Ritschlian tradition to play havoc with the gospel. He is not as "modern" as he thinks he is. In modern physics nature is no longer regarded as a closed system; it contains "principles of uncertainty" which leave room for the biblical view of miracle.[50]

Finally there is a third point of view to the left of Bultmann's. The chief representatives are Fritz Buri and S. M. Ogden. A follower of Martin Werner, Buri rejects Bultmann's position as another attempt to evade the implications of the delayed parousia.[51] Both point to the structural inconsistency of Bultmann's position and call for a "dekerygmatizing" of theology. Bultmann emphasizes that the Christian faith is nothing but a proper understanding of the original possibility of authentic human existence—freedom from the past and openness for the future. Bultmann is just as insistent that it is solely because of the Christ event that man's historical existence is factually possible. Ogden replies that both of these propositions cannot be true; they involve a logical self-contradiction.[52] Ogden therefore

[50] Cf. Carl Heim, *The Transformation of the Scientific World View* (London: SCM Press, 1953).

[51] Fritz Buri, "Entmythologisierung oder Entkerygmatisierung der Theologie" in Bultmann, *Kerygma and Myth,* II, 85 ff.; see also S. M. Ogden, *Christ without Myth* (New York: Harper & Bros., 1961).

[52] Ogden, *op. cit.,* p. 117. For detailed literature, see the footnotes in this volume, pp. 193 ff.

prefers to return to the great liberal tradition of Schleiermacher and Hegel which remained content with the "idea of Christ" as the unity of God and man and with Jesus as the most prominent example of the religious possibilities of human nature.

The effect of existential thinking in dogmatics may best be seen in the writings of Gerhard Ebeling, successor to Brunner in Zurich. Ebeling has much to say about faith which is genuinely biblical. He is not concerned with "religion" which is to be discovered in the deepest recesses of the human soul. To be a Christian means to be a man of faith. Faith does not originate in the inner self. It comes from hearing the Word. Jesus is both the witness and the basis of faith, hence we must turn to him as he meets us in the kerygma of the Church. But Jesus is, properly speaking, not the object of faith. His earthly life was conditioned by the exigencies of history. His life does not constitute a holy history within general history, nor is the Bible a holy book different from other literature of antiquity. The alleged super-historical elements in the Bible are an offense to the modern world. Ebeling seems almost afraid to speak of God lest God be objectified as a "thing." God is rather a concept, a pointer to the radical questionableness of man's existence. He is the "whence" of faith and love, the activity which underlies man's passivity in his conception and death. The Holy Spirit is the "courage of faith." Faith has no encounter with a Thou that is wholly other, or even other. In Ebeling theology is in danger of becoming atheistic. The principle underlying this position is an aversion to metaphysics in the tradition of the Neo-Kantianism of the Marburg school. As for practical results, little difference can be discerned between this Kantian agnosticism and the immanental concept of God in Schleiermacher and Hegel. In all these teachings faith is a type of religious self-consciousness. Of course, God is not an object of investigation by the rational mind of man. But the terminology of Bultmann, Ebeling (and Tillich) is no less anthropomorphic than the biblical references to God as Father, Lord, and the like. A concept of God that does nothing to arouse in man the desire to worship him is irrelevant. A kerygma proclaiming God as unknown will never win man, not even modern man, to commit himself soul and body to serve God.[53]

Dietrich Bonhoeffer

Although a leader in the confessing Church and a personal friend of Barth, sharing Barth's aversion to a natural theology as expressed by the analogy of being concept, Bonhoeffer was not a "Barthian." [54] He did not share Barth's narrow christological approach. On the contrary, only when a person knows the Old Testament Name of God, Bonhoeffer says, can he speak properly of Jesus Christ.[55] Likewise, he conceived of the relation between Church and state not in Barth's but rather in Luther's understanding of the two kingdoms of God. The state is the kingdom of God insofar as it preserves the orders of marriage, family, and society which have their basis in the creative work of God; the Church, on the other hand, witnesses to the new creation of God.[56]

Bonhoeffer's thinking passed through three successive stages. The unifying element is in his Christology; but because Christ never exists without his body the Church, Christology includes ecclesiology. In the first period the revelational character of the Church was foremost in Bonhoeffer's mind. Revelation is concrete. It issued into the incarnation of the Logos and into the founding of the Church, which is "Christ as existing community." Man can come to a proper knowledge of himself and God neither through Kantian transcendentalism

[53] The review of Gerhard Ebeling is based on his *The Nature of Faith* (Philadelphia: Muhlenberg Press, 1961) and *Word and Faith* (Philadelphia: Fortress Press, 1963). For a criticism of the tendency toward an "atheistic theology" see Helmut Gollwitzer, *Die Existenz Gottes im Bekenntnis des Glaubens* (1963). Cf. also the article by A. C. Garnett, "Is Modern Theology Atheistic?" *The Christian Century,* May 31, 1961. John A. T. Robinson, *Honest to God* (London: SCM Press, 1963) is a classical example of this "atheistic theology."

[54] Cf. Dietrich Bonhoeffer, *Creation and Fall* (London: SCM Press, 1959), p. 37.

[55] *Prisoner for God* (New York: The Macmillan Company, 1954), p. 79. In a letter dated May 5, 1944, Bonhoeffer accused Barth of a "positivistic doctrine of revelation, which says in effect: Take it or leave it." The doctrine of the Trinity, of the virgin birth, and of anything else is regarded as equally important. Barth allows no degrees of significance or perception. The gift of Christ is turned into a law of faith. In the same letter, Bonhoeffer says that Bultmann's approach is basically the method of the liberals, that is, an abridgement of the gospel (*op. cit.,* pp. 125 ff.).

[56] Cf. Bonhoeffer's *Dein Reich komme* (1957). Cf. also J. D. Godsey, *The Theology of Dietrich Bonhoeffer* (Philadelphia: Westminster Press, 1960), p. 130, to which scholarly work we owe much for our orientation. Cf. also the symposium on *The Place of Bonhoeffer, Problems and Possibilities of His Thought* (New York: Association Press, 1962), edited by Martin E. Marty.

nor through Hegelian Idealism, for the former ends with a non-objective, unknowable God, while the latter identifies God and man. Limited to an act, faith loses its objectivity and continuity; understood as being, it becomes a doctrinal system or an institution. In Christianity personal faith and the Church must be brought into harmony. The believer must take his stand in the Christian community, but the confessions of the Church must be actualized by contemporary witnessing to Jesus Christ.[57]

In the second period Bonhoeffer was concerned with the fact that Jesus Christ is lord of the Church. Discipleship means commitment and involvement. It is a personal response to Jesus who calls and who demands obedience. Discipleship is not a law, not a set of principles, not a program, not an ideal. The deadly enemy of the Church is "cheap grace," grace understood as a doctrine, a principle, a system. The grace given to Luther was a "costly grace" which shattered his whole existence. His followers took up his doctrine and repeated it word for word, but they left out the obligation of discipleship. Justification for the sinner degenerated into the justification of sin and the world. Costly grace was turned into cheap grace.

Since the first Easter, the call of Jesus in his earthly life is extended through baptism. The sacrament is not an offer which man makes to God, but an offer made by Christ to man. Its nature is essentially passive: being baptized means to suffer the call of Jesus. By baptism we are made partakers in the death of Jesus. It is characterized by a certain finality. Christian baptism cannot be repeated, as was the case with John's baptism. Its unrepeatable character, therefore, puts certain restrictions on its use. Infant baptism is an abuse of the sacrament when it takes place apart from the Christian community.[58]

The danger of turning the gospel of grace into a new law is overcome in the third period with its profound exposition of the freedom that comes to those who are obedient to Christ, a freedom for a life of "worldly Christianity." Bonhoeffer ponders the question of how to speak of God without religion, how to speak of him in a secular

[57] These ideas are chiefly set forth in Bonhoeffer, *The Communion of Saints* (New York: Harper & Row, 1963), and *Act and Being* (New York: Harper & Bros., 1961). Cf. Godsey, *op. cit.*, pp. 27 ff.

[58] Bonhoeffer, *The Cost of Discipleship* (London: SCM Press, 1948). Cf. *Life Together* (New York: Harper & Bros., 1954).

fashion.[59] The problem is already present in Bonhoeffer's *Ethics*.[60] As Christians we are not to think in two spheres as if the sacred and the secular stood side by side. The religious and the secular, the supernatural and the natural, have their unity in Jesus Christ as the God-Man. The redeeming God has reaffirmed his creation in the incarnation. We cannot have the Christian without the natural. Christian ethics, therefore, is not an ethic of radicalism which hates the creation, nor is it an ethic of compromise which hates the *eschaton*. In the incarnation we recognize the love of God for His creature; in the cross, the judgment of God over all flesh; in the resurrection, the promise of a new world. It was Bonhoeffer's conviction that the world "had come of age," that the time for "religion" as a separate compartment of man's existence was over. We can no longer use God as a stopgap for our incomplete knowledge; rather, we must make room for him in the world. Worldly people at times may take God more seriously than religious people who are bent upon their inward life and detached from the world which God so loved that he gave his only begotten Son.[61]

Neo-Lutheranism in Germany

The age of Karl Barth also produced a number of scholars who, though sharing the general concern of Barth, wanted to continue the Lutheran tradition in German Protestantism. This includes such men as Werner Elert (1885-1954), Paul Althaus (b. 1888), Hermann Sasse (b. 1895), Ernst Sommerlath (b. 1889), Walter Kuenneth (b. 1901), Adolf Koeberle (b. 1898), and others. In keeping with the Luther renaissance the interest of this group is centered in a new and exhaustive study of Luther's works and the New Testament. They try to combat the theological liberalism of the Ritschlian-Harnackian era, and they reject the scholastic intellectualism in traditional Orthodoxy. In the mid-twenties, Elert, Althaus, and Sasse made Erlangen the academic center of Lutheranism once more. Of the three, Elert and Sasse represent an exclusive Lutheranism, laying stress on the difference between Lutheranism and Calvinism, whereas Althaus, as a

[59] *Prisoner for God*, pp. 121 ff.

[60] *Ethics* (New York: Harper & Bros., 1955), pp. 25 ff.

[61] Cf. *Die mündige Welt* (1955-1956); Bonhoeffer, *Gesammelte Schriften*, ed. Eberhard Bethge (1958 ff.). The work by Godsey contains an exhaustive German and English bibliography.

former student of Schlatter, followed a more mediating line. Elert's *Die Morphologie des Luthertums*[62] was a real incentive to a new appraisal of the Lutheran tradition. Opposing Troeltsch and Max Weber, Elert pointed out the constructive implications of Lutheran social ethics. His whole thought in both dogmatics and ethics revolves around the proper distinction between law and gospel. He was unrelenting in his criticism of Karl Barth.

Sasse's exclusiveness is well illustrated in his book *Here We Stand* and in his later writings on the Lord's Supper. Disappointed with what he regarded as a fateful confessional laxity on the part of leading churchmen, after the war he resigned his position in Erlangen to accept a call to the Lutheran seminary at Adelaide-Prospect, South Australia.

On the problem of epistemology the Neo-Lutherans follow, on the whole, the general trend toward existential thinking. Theology is not, as in Greek intellectualism, a study of the essence of God, nor an attempt to control the object of its investigation rationally. On the contrary, it should concern itself with the relation in which man stands to God, letting God give his understanding of man. Existential thinking is not limited to the human intellect; rather, it lays claim to the whole man. Consequently, faith is not an intellectual faculty of man but a personal decision, engaging man as a whole.

These scholars are not afraid to stress the "otherness" of the Bible, even at the risk of giving offense to the modern mind. Nor are their biblical studies apologetic in the old meaning of the term. To them the Bible is entirely divine and entirely human. With respect to introductory problems of the New Testament, they are far more critical than were Zahn and Schlatter.[63] Though it is evident from their biblical studies that the method of form-criticism has exerted some influence on their view of the Gospel narratives, the Neo-Lutherans feel that they cannot dismiss the question of the authenticity of the New Testament records so lightly as the Barthians. In keeping with the Lutheran maxim, *finitum capax infiniti*—or better, *infinitum capax finiti*, they reveal a deeper appreciation of the incarnation than

[62] 2 vols., 1931-1932. One volume has been translated as *The Structure of Lutheranism* by Walter Hansen (St. Louis: Concordia Publishing House, 1962).

[63] Cf. *Das Neue Testament Deutsch*, ed. Paul Althaus and J. Behm (1923 ff.), which is both truly evangelical and strictly critical.

do the Barthians, and they cling tenaciously to the great principle of Martin Kaehler that the whole biblical Christ is the historical Christ. They refuse to follow skepticism in its demands regarding the biblical records. They were unable to follow Barth in his radical opposition to the new German state, and took a mediating position. Althaus, for example, rejected both extremes: the illusion of the so-called German Christians, as if the Christian could hear in the voice of the people the very voice of God, as well as the nihilistic attitude which considers the state and the other orders of life so completely sinful that it attempts either to withdraw from the world or abandons all ethical judgment in the realm of the natural.[64]

With regard to the question of anthropology, the Neo-Lutherans seek to follow Luther's concept that the Pauline terms flesh and spirit are not psychological distinctions. They do not refer to a lower or higher quality in man, but rather have a theological connotation, "flesh" designating man in his state of opposition to God and "spirit" signifying man as a regenerated child of God.[65] Man as a whole, including his so-called higher nature, is under the curse of sin; likewise, redemption pertains to man as a whole, including the body. This has brought about a new interest in holiness of life. In conversion and regeneration the sinner is saved not only from the guilt of sin (justification) but also from the power of sin (sanctification). This rejection of an anthropological dualism implies a new emphasis on the biblical message of the resurrection of the dead over against the Platonic idea of immortality as an inherent quality of the human soul.[66]

[64] Cf. Althaus, *Theologie der Ordnungen* (1935), and Elert, *Karl Barth's Index der verbotenen Bücher* (1935).

[65] Carl Stange, *Luther und das sittliche Ideal* (1919); reprinted in *Studien zur Theologie Luthers* (1928), pp. 139-40.

[66] E. Stange, *Die Unsterblichkeit der Seele* (1925). Cf. also *Studien zur Theologie Luthers* (1928), pp. 287 ff.; *Luther und das fünfte Laterankonzil* (1928); a number of articles in *Zeitschrift für systematische Theologie;* and *Das Ende aller Dinge* (1930). In these studies, Stange has advanced the teaching of annihilation for the wicked. He also has tried to show that Luther rejected belief in the immortality of the soul. This was a matter of conflict between him and Althaus. The latter agrees with Stange in declining the Platonic concept of immortality, but the eternal "existence" of all men he sees warranted by the relationship with God as Creator in which all stand to God. From the relationship with God he distinguishes fellowship with God, which pertains only to the pious. Cf. "Die Unsterblichkeit der Seele bei Luther," *Zeitschrift für systematische Theologie,* III, 725 ff.; *Unsterblichkeit und ewiges Leben bei Luther* (1930); and *Die letzten Dinge* (4th ed. 1933), pp. 92 ff.

Althaus has voiced strong opposition to Barth's denial of a general revelation. With great emphasis he teaches that an original revelation precedes the divine revelation in Christ. The word "original," he says, must not be understood in the temporal sense. Christian dogmatics does not need to reconstruct the beginning and history of the human race. Instead it must interpret man's existence before God. God bears witness to Himself in the rational and volitional nature of man. Althaus quotes Calvin in the first paragraph of his *Institutes:* "No man can take a survey of himself but he must immediately turn to the contemplation of God in whom he 'lives and moves'." He says that Schleiermacher was right when he identified the feeling of absolute dependence with man's consciousness of God, but wrong when he ignored God's absolute claim on man.[67]

Althaus conceives of the special revelation of God in Christ as an act of divine kenosis. The divine kenosis does not materialize in history; history itself is an act of divine kenosis. Revelation of divine majesty and glory is unthinkable and impossible in the course of history. Consequently, Althaus rejects the Orthodox view that the supernatural character of the Bible can be demonstrated to reason. He rejects the idea that the Christian experience of regeneration carries weight to prove the truth of the Bible rationally to the unbelieving. A Word, demanding obedience, constitutes revelation. Through this Word, which was incarnate in Jesus, eternity reaches into time. The only human corollary to divine revelation is faith. In this way Althaus defines his theology as "a theology of faith."[68] History, death, and faith belong to one and the same order of things. Death is not a mere accident in historical life; it is a natural part of historical existence. The story of man's original state and of his fall does not mean a historical day of the human race; it is a reflection of human sin and guilt. The beginning and end of the universe as a physical entity is immaterial to a religious interpretation of life, Althaus holds. This attitude removes at once all friction between Christianity and natural science. The Church does not need to harmonize Genesis with modern science any longer. Althaus' conception of the end is in keeping with this view of the beginning of life. He

[67] Althaus, *Die christliche Wahrheit,* I (1947), 45 ff.
[68] *Ibid.,* p. 6.

regards the idea of the millennium as an idle fancy of pietistic Judaism. The kingdom of Jesus is never of this world, not even at the end. The apocalyptic material in the New Testament must be interpreted existentially as a word of comfort and warning to the Church at any time. It is given to us in order that every generation may derive from a spiritual interpretation of the past a true impression of the present in the light of the final judgment.

Under the impact of severe criticism from other Lutheran scholars, including Karl Heim, Ernst Sommerlath, Philip Bachmann, H. W. Schmidt, and especially Walter Kuenneth, Althaus has relinquished the radical dialectic conception of the second coming as a mere metaphysical antithesis to historical existence. In the fourth edition of his book on eschatology he writes: "The Second Coming marks the end of history. History moves in the course of time toward its end, and the end will come at its appointed time, day, and hour. In this respect the Second Coming is an historical-temporal occurrence. But the end of time is not to be identified with the Second Coming. The very nature of the Second Coming, the manifestation of glory, is impossible in history. The revelation of the Son of Man is not an event at the end of time but rather an event terminating time." [69] This means that Althaus now recognizes a march of time toward its appointed end, but he again reaffirms his view that history and eschatological manifestation of glory are metaphysical opposites.

By way of the exegetical findings of Schlatter and the existential thinking, which is interested more in the act than in the being of a thing, Althaus has also tried to modify the Lutheran concept of the Lord's Supper. In *Die lutherische Abendmahlslehre in der Gegenwart* (1931) he says that the teaching of a presence of the glorified body and blood of Christ in the sacrament has no foundation in the New Testament. The interpretative words over the bread and wine are not a definition of what the elements of the Supper are but of what Christ is doing. Body and blood in separate form signify a life which is given over to death. "You live by my death." The sacrament is a parable in action. The real presence is to be understood in the wider sense of divine revelation and the incarnation of the Logos

[69] *Die Letzten Dinge* (4th ed., 1933), pp. 242-43. Cf. also Folke Holmstroem, *Das eschatologische Denken der Gegenwart* (1936), pp. 279 ff.

which is perpetuated in his Church. Christ's presence, Althaus holds, is not confined to the sacramental elements; rather, the action of the Church warrants his real presence and his grace. This modification of the Lutheran view does not imply, however, that Althaus veers toward the Reformed concept of the Supper. He specifically rejects Calvin's view and insists on the Lutheran teaching of oral manducation and the manducation of the unworthy.

A similar view of the Supper is held by Carl Stange in his book, *Die Bedeutung der Sakramente* (2nd ed., 1927). According to Stange, not the elements, but the action of the Church, warrant the real presence of the Lord. In contrast to Althaus and Stange, Sommerlath has maintained the Lutheran view in a volume entitled *Der Sinn des Abendmahls nach Luthers Gedanken 1527–1529* (1930), and Sasse especially has taken sharp issue with his colleague's view in his book *Kirche und Herrenmahl* (1938), in the composite volume *Vom Sakrament des Altars* (1941), and in *This Is My Body* (1959),[70] defending staunchly the orthodox Lutheran position.

It may seem daring to classify Karl Heim (1874–1958) of Tübingen with the Neo-Lutherans. Some of the scholars named are his pupils, just as they are students of Stange. Heim, unlike Stange, did not altogether disown dialectics in theology and he kept unusually well abreast of the changing mood of thought in Germany after 1918. He always maintained the Reformation position which centers in the forgiveness of sins. Springing from the pietist tradition in his native Wuerttemberg, he was the "evangelist" among the academic theologians of Germany. Up to 1902 he served as one of the chief assistants of John R. Mott in the Student Christian Movement and he always sought to confront young men with the living Christ. The origin of faith, Heim holds, is completely independent of philosophical thought.[71] Nevertheless, he includes very elaborate epistemological propositions in his writings, but only for the purpose of meeting the modern man where he is and confronting him with the necessity of deciding for Christ. In the decade before World War I, the Ritschlian distinction between faith and reason held Heim's interest. He writes: "The all-comprehensive theme of dogmatics is the delineation of the

[70] Minneapolis: Augsburg Publishing House, 1959.

[71] Cf. his book *Glaubensgewissheit* (1916).

infinite misery of sin as it is removed by Christ."[72] After the war he turned to a critical investigation of problems suggested by Einstein and the existential philosophy of the Heidelberg school.

Heim's thinking is expressed in *Der Glaube und das evangelische Denken der Gegenwart* (1931 ff.). In the first volume Heim grapples with the question, "What does faith imply, when, in an age which is aware of the consequences of the Copernican revolution, it continues to speak of the Transcendence of God?"[73] In our day we know the world to be an infinite universe. The idea of the transcendence of God has lost its original "spatial" sense. Heim enters upon an elaborate discussion of the three-dimensional world of human experience: "my objective world" and "thy objective world;" the "I world" and the "It world," and the living "I World" and "Thou World." Each of these worlds is marked off from the other only in the "dimensional" mode, not by a "boundary of content." The question arises, Is the Beyondness of the omnipresent God to be compared with any of these intra-mundane forms of transcendence? The answer must be: No! for God is not an aspect of this world, accessible to our dimensional mode of cognition. If He were, then we would be forced either into idolatry, which is giving absolute value to something which has only relative reality, for example, race, blood, and soil; or into pantheism, "by deifying the infinite Whole of things." God simply transcends our thinking and observation. For a knowledge of God we are thrown back on his own revelation.

In the second volume of the work under discussion,[74] Heim supports the concept of Christ's work in the ancient Church as an overpowering of Satan. In the third volume, *Jesus der Weltvollender*,[75] he upholds the realistic eschatological drama of the New Testament over against the spiritualizing and explaining away of its importance in the thought of the liberals, and the purely axiological, Platonizing conception of eschatology in Barth's revised *Römerbrief*.

Emanuel Hirsch

Emanuel Hirsch (b. 1888), professor emeritus at Göttingen is a

[72] Karl Heim, *Leitfaden zur Dogmatik,* II, 20.
[73] *God Transcendent* (New York: Charles Scribner's Sons, 1936), p. 237.
[74] *Jesus is Lord* (Philadelphia: Muhlenberg Press, 1961).
[75] *Jesus the World's Perfecter* (Edinburgh: Oliver & Boyd, 1959).

truly tragic figure in recent German theology. As a pupil of Holl, he ranked in the twenties as one of the leading Luther and Kierkegaard students. But he could never overcome a pronounced leaning toward philosophical idealism, and this best explains his attraction to the so-called German Christian Movement of the Hitler era. In his studies on the Fourth Gospel[76] he proved to be a follower of F. C. von Baur and of the critical-mystical approach to religion demonstrated in the work of Söderblom, von Huegel, and Heiler. In his polemical writings[77] Hirsch tries to hold a middle ground. He does not deny that the Old Testament people "had dealings with the living God under the mantle of the Yahveh faith . . . a deeper (and that means also a more terrible) knowledge and experience of what it means to deal with the living God than other men in non-Christian religions, who also under their mantle had dealings with the living God." [78] But the Old Testament religion, he holds, is abrogated by the revelation of the New Testament. Hirsch wants to guard himself carefully against the deification of race, blood, and soil. The God in contemporary history is a hidden God to him, whereas in the New Testament we are face to face with God as revealed in Jesus Christ.

Totally blind since 1945, Hirsch nevertheless has published a five-volume work, entitled *Geschichte der neueren evangelischen Theologie* (1949 ff.). In keeping with his idealistic background, the author tries to show that the emancipation of the human mind from the authority of the Scriptures and the confessions of the Church, 1648–1848, has not destroyed man's real being *coram Deo,* but rather has provided man with knowledge of his real self. In his latest publication, Hirsch presents a kind of a theological testament. He expresses a passionate warning against an "institutionalistic" adulteration of the Christian faith. Dogmatic formulations, he holds, are out of place in the faith of the Reformation. The Reformation was trans-doctrinal in character. The Christian faith is pure subjectivity; it implies the

[76] *Das vierte Evangelium in seiner ursprünglichen Gestalt verdeutscht und erklärt* (1936); *Studien zum vierten Evangelium* (1936).

[77] *Deutsches Volkstum und evangelischer Glaube* (1934); *Die gegenwärtige geistige Lage* (1934); *Das Alte Testament und die Predigt des Evangeliums* (1936); *Der Weg der Theologie* (1937).

[78] The translation is that of Douglas Horton in *Contemporary Continental Theology* (1938), p. 121. See Schweitzer, *op. cit.,* pp. 307 ff.

immediacy of the individual before God. The Christian life is nothing but "the faith-bestowed wedding of human subjectivity with the Gospel." [79] In keeping with his theological pilgrimage Hirsch interprets Luther and the Reformation in categories derived partly from German Idealism, partly from Kierkegaard. The Reformation is dangerously modernized by Hirsch.

Lundensian Theology

Swedish theologians have always kept abreast of theological developments in Germany. Little wonder therefore that the new Luther research in Germany met with an enthusiastic response in Sweden. In the years prior to World War I Archbishop Söderblom took the lead. His first book dealt with Luther's religion (1894). The fruits of his lifelong study of Luther is contained in *Melankoli och humor och andra Luther-studier* (1919). The name of Einar Billing (1871–1939) looms large in Swedish thought as a pioneer in Luther studies. He wrote *Luthers laera om staten* (1901); *Ett bidrag till fragen on Luthers religioesa och teologiska utvecklingsgang* (1917). The fire which was kindled by these men at Uppsala was kept alive by Arvid Runestam, son-in-law of Söderblom, and by Torston Bohlin, and Tor Andrae, both disciples of Söderblom. Following World War I the University of Lund became the seat of a new theology, whose chief exponents were Gustav Aulén, Anders Nygren, Gustaf Ljungren, Ragnar Bring, and Hjalmar Lindroth.

"Lundensian thought," in the words of Ferre, "is best understood as the resurgence of historic Christianity, as a reaction to the indefiniteness of a confused liberalism which never won much more than the minds of its converts, and that only partially, as an affirmation of the absolute assurance of religion in the face of a bewildered relativism." [80] It is "a return from all relativism to the absolute assurance of religion, but not to the Biblical literalism of the past." [81] In other words, the Lundensians, like their contemporary German colleagues, endeavor to assert religious absolutes by means of modern scholarship. Religion and theology must be to them evangelical in content but

[79] *Das Wesen des reformatorischen Christentums* (1963), pp. 261 ff.

[80] Nels F. R. Ferre, *Swedish Contributions to Modern Theology* (New York: Harper & Bros., 1939), p. 23.

[81] *Ibid.*, p. 29.

strictly scientific in method. The Lundensians draw a sharp line of demarcation between the subjective nature of faith and the objective nature of science. Faith must be respected "in its claim to be an independent and unique category" supplying its own self-originated material as well as its own principle of interpretation. Religion as faith is never knowledge; it is alogical in nature. It is immedate commitment, a value judgment. The faith-state, they claim, is never devoid of intellectual content. In fact, something is comprehended in the faith-state. This nonlogical content of faith is transmitted in logical forms, for that which is comprehended is also capable of expression. For an illustration Nygren and Bring often refer to pain. As an experience, pain is far from logical in nature, but when it is comprehended by man, it may be expressed in logical categories.[82]

Theology in Conflict presents a lucid analysis of the earlier writings of Nygren which are not available in English.[83] In two works published in 1921, Nygren tried to define and solve the problem of a critical philosophy of religion.[84] Philosophy of religion, he argued, is bound to remain within the subjective consciousness of man and to find a basis on which it can differentiate between objectivity and subjectivity in a criterion immanent in man. Idealistic philosophy recognizes three fundamental values: the true, the good, and the beautiful. Religion can be incorporated into such a system of universal values. Religion deals with eternity, and eternity is the transcendent, fundamental category of religion without which other values lose their absoluteness. Thus defined, religion is an *a priori*, purely formal aspect for which the history of religion provides the content.

Since Christianity is rooted in history, it is the task of Christian theology to describe the nature of Christianity. Theology is descriptive, not normative. The content must be sought in the fundamental motif underlying the history of the Christian religion. This motif is Agape. The Lundensians therefore have developed what they call the motif analysis. In the analysis of dogma, they claim, the theologian must go beneath the outward form and dress of a given doctrine. He must penetrate through the outward form to the under-

[82] Cf. the chapter "Theological Methodology" in Ferre, *op. cit.*, pp. 34 ff.

[83] Gustaf Wingren, *Theology in Conflict,* trans. Eric H. Wahlstrom (Philadelphia: Muhlenberg Press, 1958).

[84] *Det religionsfilosofiska grundproblemet* and *Religioest a priori.*

lying motive. All basic motives are nothing more than "approximations," a "general notion" or "fundamental attitude." [85] For this very reason Aulén refuses to speak of the "idea" of God, but speaks in terms of the "picture" of God.[86] He stresses the same principle in *Die Dogmengeschichte im Lichte der Lutherforschung* (1932), maintaining that the history of doctrine must aim at understanding the inner history of Christianity. The Lundensians have applied this motif analysis mainly to four great dogmas of the church: Aulén to the concept of God and of the atonement, Nygren to the Christian idea of love, Folke Holmstroem to the teaching of eschatology.[87]

Aulén opens his dogmatics with the statement: "Systematic theology has as its object of study the Christian faith." [88] Its task is neither demonstrative nor normative, but analytical and critical. Faith, he says, is the only object of study, for God cannot be made the object of scientific investigation. "Systematic theology is concerned simply with investigating and clarifying a certain area of research." [89] Hence it is not confessional by nature. The nature of the Christian faith cannot be validated by an appeal to an infallible Bible.[90] Its entire content cannot with impunity be regarded as an equally normative word of God. The Old Testament prayers of vengeance, for example, are clearly contradictory to the gospel of the New Testament. Nor is a solution of our problem to be found in traditionalism, in either its legalistic form (Rome) or its evolutionary form (the confessional writings of Protestantism). The task can be "accomplished only by showing how the separate affirmations stand in an inner organic relation to this fundamental fact of Christian faith, the act of God in Christ." [91]

In *Den kristna gudsbilden* Aulén points to the fact that hitherto theology has failed to concentrate its efforts on the Christian concept

[85] Aulén, *Das christliche Gottesbild* (1930), p. 54.

[86] *Ibid.*, pp. 3-4.

[87] *Ibid.* Cf. also Aulén *Christus Victor* (London: SPCK, 1953); Nygren, *Agape and Eros* (rev. ed.; Philadelphia: Westminster Press, 1953); and Folke Holmstroem, *Det eskatologiska motivet i nutida teologi* (1933).

[88] *The Faith of the Christian Church,* trans. from the fourth Swedish edition (Philadelphia: Muhlenberg Press, 1948).

[89] *Ibid.*, p. 5.

[90] *Ibid.*, pp. 79 ff.

[91] *Ibid.*, p. 88.

of God. Theologians, in most cases, busied themselves with an investigation of single *loci* in dogmatics. Consequently, they failed to set forth the organic unity of the Christian faith, for every doctrine—for example, Christology—is ultimately a problem of one's "picture" of God. Aulén traces the "picture" of God through the course of history beginning with the biblical age, through the ancient Church, the Middle Ages, the Reformation, down to modern theology in Sweden, Germany, and England. Aulén arrives at the concept that God is sovereign love who condescended to men in Christ Jesus. There is only one way for man to God and that is God's way to man, never man's way to God.

In *Christus Victor*, Aulén points out the lack of understanding which modern theologians have shown of the atonement in the patristic age. He distinguishes among three main types of the atonement: the patristic, which he calls the "classical," the objective Anselmic, and the subjective Abelardian type. The negative attitude of modern scholars toward the classical type, Aulén claims, is a clear indication that they have failed to penetrate through the crude language of the Greek Fathers into the very motive by which the Fathers were guided. In the eyes of Aulén the classical teaching deserves the most careful attention. According to this view, the atonement is a cosmic drama in which "Christ—Christus Victor—battles and triumphs over the evil powers of the world, the 'tyrants' under which mankind is in bondage and suffering, and in Him God reconciles the world to Himself." The work of the atonement is, according to this view and according to this view only, what it must be, a continuous divine work from first to last. It is, moreover, the view espoused by the New Testament and by Luther, who always held that satisfaction is made by God, not merely to God. In criticism it must be said that Aulen's view tends to underrate the religious significance of the Anselmic doctrine of Christ's work as an expiation for human guilt. He likewise seems to miss the entire view of Luther. The Reformer did not one-sidedly follow the Greek Fathers. His own teaching is rather a synthesis of the best of the patristic age and the Middle Ages.

Nygren, in his *Agape and Eros*, strikes essentially the same note. To him the interpretation of Christianity in the whole Neo-Protestant school is altogether false. The Gospel does not, as Harnack claimed, deal with "the infinite value of the human soul." On the contrary, "when it is said that God loves man, this is not a judgment on what man is like, but on what God is like." Agape is altogether "spontaneous," "unmotivated," "indifferent to value," "creative." That which has no value in itself acquires worth by being the object of God's love. Agape is God's way to man initiating fellowship with God.[92] Having traced the meaning of Agape as seen in the Bible, Nygren discusses the Eros motif as it is found in Greek thought. The Platonic concept of love may be summed up in three points: Eros is the love of desire or acquisitive love; it is man's way to God; it is egocentric.[93]

From his stress on Agape, we must not infer that Nygren sees no value in the world of Eros, the world of man. A. G. Hebert, in an important translator's preface to the 1932 edition of Nygren's book, makes it clear that Nygren always endeavors to maintain a balance between creation and redemption: "It is fundamental to Christianity that God is both Creator and Redeemer. The God who created the world is the God of Agape. As Creator, He is the author of the natural world and of human life with its upward movement which Aristotle describes in terms of Eros, and in this natural world, and in the natural goodness of human life, God is present and His glory is manifested. It is only in redemption, that is, by Agape, that He is personally revealed, both in the incomplete revelation of Agape in the Old Testament, and in perfect manifestation in Christ."[94]

Undoubtedly Lundensian theology represents a serious attempt to return to Luther and the New Testament. It strikes at the humanistic perversion of the gospel in Neo-Protestantism. In the eyes of the Lundensians, moral idealism is an expression of man's rebellion against the religion of the incarnation. Lundensian thought is a great eulogy of the *sola gratia* and *sola fide*. Nevertheless, a younger Lundensian scholar, Gustaf Wingren, has severely criticized the approach of Nygren. Wingren's criticism in *Theology in Conflict* crystallizes into four propositions. First, he maintains, at least by implication,

[92] *Ibid.*, pp. 75 ff.
[93] *Ibid.*, pp. 175 ff.
[94] *Agape and Eros* (London: SPCK, 1932), I, xii.

that theology must be normative. Second, he charges Nygren with equating the authority of Paul and Luther, and insists that between the two there is the difference of the original biblical documents and their interpretation. Nygren, he maintains, undermines the uniqueness of the Scriptures by ignoring or correcting certain parts of the Bible.

Wingren's third complaint, which also includes the fourth, is that Nygren underrates the importance of the law. Agape must stand against the background of the law and of human sin. Agape means that God loves the sinner who in disobedience and rebellion has turned away from him. Wingren admits that this note is not missing in Nygren's treatment of Marcion, but says it has little, if any, meaning in the latter part of *Agape and Eros*, the section on Luther included. Wingren even feels justified to question whether Nygren's treatment of Marcion constitutes a critique of his own starting point in the first volume of 1930.

Wingren's *Theology in Conflict* is a declaration of war against the theologies of Nygren, Barth, and Bultmann. Dealing with the method of theology, it is more negative than positive. The positive side is discussed in two other writings of Wingren available in English: *The Living Word*[95] and *Creation and Law*.[96] In these books the main target of criticism is Karl Barth. The liberals' preoccupation with the *homo religiosus* was certainly a perversion of the biblical message. But neither can we arrive at the truth by inverting a lie. This is precisely what Barth has been doing by closing his eyes to God's gift in creation and by inverting the sequence of the Apostles' Creed. Being preoccupied with the knowledge of God, Barth has obscured the sequence of the acts of God: creation, the natural life, the fall, the law, Christ, the gospel, the Church, and the consummation of the world. Since man is created in the image of God and since Christ is the image of the Father, man is created "in Christ." Man is given life; he is not independent. God is actually working in creation, "speaking to man, and ordering and compelling him to goodness and to outgiving love."[97] Finally, the concern of Wingren as expressed in the first part of *Creation and Law* is that of Althaus and especially

[95] Philadelphia: Muhlenberg Press, 1960.

[96] Philadelphia: Muhlenberg Press, 1961.

[97] *Creation and Law*, p. 42.

of Schlatter: man's basic relation to God is to be found in creation. Though fallen, man is still a creature of God reflecting the nature of the Creator in his psychosomatic existence. To be true to the Bible means to begin with the First Article of the Creed.

In the second part of this book Wingren discusses the law. Though obsolete in Christ as "the Law of Moses," its underlying divine command has always been and still is operative in human life itself and is experienced by all men. Irenaeus and Luther saw the Decalog as written in the hearts of men and not primarily in the Bible. The law performs two functions. It is operative in the external world, regulating social life (the Lutheran concept of the first or political use of the law). The law also performs a function that is invisible in the world because it reveals man's condition *coram Deo* or in his conscience and puts him there as a captive and sinner "without excuse" (the second or theological use of the law).

In *The Living Word*, Wingren tries to overcome a false juncture between the objectivity and subjectivity of the Word as found in orthodox theology on the one hand, and in liberalism on the other. The saving deed of God is meaningless without man. In the kerygma the two are intertwined. Christ died and rose again for us. "Subjective preaching tends to cultivate the character of man; it tries to develop religious personalities. Objective preaching, on the contrary, tries to bring to men what they are lacking, superimposing supernatural knowledge on natural. It is difficult to integrate loyalty in one's vocation, for which man must be set free, in either of these views." [98] The antithesis between the natural and supernatural, God and man, remains unchanged for both the liberals and the anti-liberals. It is striking, Wingren says, that Karl Barth time and time again repeats his criticism of Luther's doctrine of the *communicatio idiomatum*, the unity of the human and divine in Christ. The cleavage between God and man remains unbridged for Barth, even in the incarnation.[99]

OTHER SCANDINAVIAN CONTRIBUTIONS

In Norway the rivalry between the Independent Theological Faculty founded in 1908 and the prevailing liberalism of the faculty at

[98] *The Living Word*, p. 30. Wingren's study *Luther on Vocation* (Philadelphia: Muhlenberg Press, 1957) should be read in the light of this statement.
[99] *The Living Word*, p. 31.

the state university has lost much of its original zeal. While conservative, the Independent Faculty was by no means fundamentalistic, and in the late Bishop Eivend Berggrav (d. 1959) the Church of Norway had a leader who was respected and loved by all. Berggrav was a student of Rudolf Otto and Friedrich Heiler and a number of his writings bear witness to his interest in psychology of religion. He will be remembered chiefly as the undaunted Church leader during the Nazi occupation of Norway, 1940-45. In his opposition to the Quisling government he discovered Luther as an ally in his struggle for the freedom of the gospel and for a state founded upon justice.[100] He was also very active in the ecumenical movement.

In the field of biblical studies Sigmund Mowinckel has received international recognition as an interpreter of the Old Testament. He holds that the Old Testament literature must be seen in the light of Israel's worship.

While the Kierkegaard renaissance is an interconfessional and international phenomenon, Danish theology shows signs of a new interest in the study of Grundtvig. This fact adds a singular note to Danish Luther research, considering Grundtvig's concern for the living Word and the Spirit as well as the high estimate which he put on the sacraments. This is evident in Regin Prenter's writings available in English: *Spiritus Creator*[101] and his three lectures on "Luther on Word and Sacrament." [102] This is still more evident in his dogmatics *Skabelse og Genloesning*. In the Preface to the German edition[103] Prenter states that the reader may be surprised to discover how little space is given to H. L. Martensen or Kierkegaard, while Grundtvig's basic concept of Christianity as God's covenant with his people, sealed in baptism, looms so large in this Danish dogmatics. In arranging his material, Prenter accepts the trinitarian pattern suggested by the Apostles' Creed and the Nicene Creed. He also uses the concept of the Trinity as his starting point for a critique of religious authority. According to a Lutheran understanding, the creeds, especially the Nicene Creed,

[100] Cf. Berggrav, *Man and State* (Philadelphia: Muhlenberg Press, 1951), especially the two supplements "Religion and Law" and "When the Driver is out of His Mind."

[101] Philadelphia: Muhlenberg Press, 1953.

[102] *Martin Luther Lectures* (Decorah: Luther College), II (1958), 65 ff.

[103] *Schöpfung und Erlösung* (1960).

establish the principle that, contrary to every form of a natural theology (Arianism and Spiritualism), God is to be known as the God of revelation in faith (*sola fide*) by means of the history of his covenant as proclaimed in the Holy Scriptures (*sola scriptura*). Prenter turns the prolegomena into an ecumenical dialogue with Rome and non-Lutheran Protestantism.

Prenter does not follow the Lundensians in conceiving of dogmatics as a purely descriptive discipline. According to him, dogmatics is a kind of "liaison officer" between biblical exegesis and homiletics.[104] This understanding assures the status of dogmatics as a science with a rightful place in the curriculum of a university, for science is an exercise of the human mind directed to a given object, objectively, thoroughly, and systematically pursued. Dogmatics is not proclamation, not preaching. The systematic theologian is not a prophet. Hence dogmatics does not belong to the pulpit. It is a study in a school of higher learning, enabling the future pastor to keep his proclamation pure of elements foreign to the gospel.

Theology in Finland

As elsewhere on the Continent, the Lutheran church of Finland went through a period of orthodoxy, pietism, and rationalism. Then came the religious revival of the nineteenth century with such men as Paavo Ruotsalainen (d. 1852), Henrik Renquist (d. 1866), F. G. Hedberg (d. 1893), whom we have mentioned in connection with the Bornholmers, and L. L. Laestadius (d. 1861) as leaders. Among the prominent scholars were F. L. Schauman (d. 1877), professor at Helsinki and Bishop of Borga, and A. W. Ingman (d. 1877), whose writings reflect the influence of Beck of Tübingen. G. G. Rosenquist wrote on Lotze and Ritschl. Current theological thought in Finland is characterized by a remarkable new vitality and productivity. The most influential of the twentieth century theologians is A. G. Pietilae (d. 1932), professor of dogmatics at Helsinki. He was the author of a three-volume *Christian Dogmatics* and a score of other doctrinal works. The richness and originality of his thought is explicable in part in terms of his Laestadian background. His successor at Helsinki, Eino Sormunen, is Finland's most outstanding representative of the

[104] *Ibid.*, pp. 172 ff.

new Luther-research. Two of his works have appeared in German, *Die Gnade Gottes* (1932) and *Die Eigenart der lutherischen Ethik* (1934). In these writings he made a close study of the Christian faith revealed in Luther's doctrine *simul justus et peccator.* Another theologian of note is Y. J. E. Alanen (d. 1960), known for his work on the relation between theology and cultural philosophy. Osmo Tiililae has shown much interest in the theology of pietism. The study of Luther, begun by Sormunen and Alanen, has its most outstanding representative today in Lennart Pinomaa. Writing chiefly in German, Pinomaa has become known in the English-speaking world through his book *Faith Victorious: An Introduction to Luther's Theology.*[105] Lauri Haikola is Alanen's successor at Helsinki. Aarne Siirala effects a healthy synthesis of theology and psychology in his work.[106] Uuras Saarnivaara, in his doctoral dissertation at the University of Chicago, *Luther Discovers the Gospel* (1951) challenged the widely accepted view that the crucial discovery of justification by faith was made prior to 1518.

Pietilae, Alanen, and Saarnivaara have been critical of the Lundensian school which finds its focus in the doctrine of salvation. The method of motif analysis was regarded as making theology a general science of religion. The Lundensians were criticized for their dependence on Kant as well as on Schleiermacher and Ritschl. It was feared that the Lundensian school would lead theology away from serving the Church and transform it into a purely methodological science and that the Ritschlian concentration on vocation in the secular realm would be detrimental to the spiritual nature of the Christian faith. In short, they argued that Finnish theology should remain loyal to the rich pietistic tradition of the past.[107]

BIBLIOGRAPHY

ALTHAUS, PAUL. *Fact and Faith in the Kerygma of Today.* Philadelphia: Muhlenberg Press, 1959.

BARTH, KARL. *Rudolf Bultmann; Ein Versuch, ihn zu verstehen.* 1953.

[105] Philadelphia: Fortress Press, 1963.

[106] *The Voice of Illness: A Study in Therapy and Prophecy* (Philadelphia: Fortress Press, 1963).

[107] This brief review is based chiefly on Geert Sentzke, *Finland: Its Church and Its People* (Helsinki, 1963) and Pinomaa (ed.), *Finnish Theology, Past and Present* (Helsinki, 1963).

BERDYAEV, NICHOLAS. *An Interpretation of Dostoevski.* New York: Meridian Press, 1936.

BERKOUWER, G. C. *The Triumph of Grace in the Theology of Karl Barth.* Grand Rapids: Wm. B. Eerdmans Publishing Co., 1956.

BULTMANN, RUDOLF. *Theology of the New Testament.* 2 vols. London: SCM Press, 1952, 1955.

CAIRNS, DAVID. *A Gospel Without Myth?* London: SCM, 1960.

COME, ARNOLD B. *An Introduction to Barth's Dogmatics for Preachers.* Philadelphia: Westminster, 1963.

FERRE, NELS F. R. *Swedish Contributions to Modern Theology.* New York: Harper & Bros., 1939.

HORTON, WALTER M. *Contemporary Continental Theology.* New York: Harper & Bros., 1938.

HOYLE, R. B. *The Teaching of Karl Barth.* London: SCM, 1930.

JOHNSON, ALEX. *Eivend Berggrav, God's Man of Suspense.* Minneapolis: Augsburg Publishing House, 1960.

JONES, G. V. *Christology and Myth in the New Testament.* New York: Harper & Bros., 1956.

MACQUARRIE, JOHN. *An Existentialist Theology.* London: SCM Press, 1955.

———. *The Scope of Demythologizing.* London: SCM Press, 1960.

MCCONNACHIE, JOHN. *The Significance of Karl Barth.* London: Hodder & Stoughton, 1931.

———. *The Barthian Theology.* New York: Harper & Bros., 1933.

MIEGGE, GIOVANNI. *Gospel and Myth in the Theology of Rudolf Bultmann.* Richmond: John Knox, 1960.

MONSMA, P. H. *Karl Barth's Idea of Revelation.* Somerville: Somerset Press, 1937.

MOWINCKEL, SIGMUND. *Prophecy and Tradition.* Oslo, 1946.

———. *He That Cometh.* Oxford: Blackwell, 1962.

———. *The Old Testament as the Word of God.* New York: Abingdon Press, 1959.

———. *The Psalms in Israel's Worship.* 2 vols. Oxford: Blackwell, 1962.

PAUCK, WILHELM. *Barth, Prophet of a New Christianity.* New York: Harper & Bros., 1931.

PINOMAA, LENNART (ed.). *Finnish Theology, Past and Present.* Helsinki, 1963.

PIPER, OTTO. *Recent Developments in German Protestantism.* London: SCM Press, 1934.

ROLSTON, HOLMES. *A Conservative Looks at Barth and Brunner.* Nashville: Cokesbury Press, 1933.

RUNIA, KLAAS. *Karl Barth's Doctrine of Holy Scripture.* Grand Rapids: Wm. B. Eerdmans Publishing Co., 1962.

SENTZKE, GEERT. *Finland: Its Church and Its People.* Helsinki, 1963.

THROCKMORTON, B. H. *The New Testament and Mythology.* Philadelphia: Westminster, 1959.

THURNEYSEN, EDWARD. *Dostoievski.* 1925.

TILLICH, PAUL. *The Religious Situation.* Translated by H. RICHARD NIEBUHR. New York: Meridian Books, 1932.

TORRANCE, T. F. *Karl Barth, An Introduction to His Early Theology, 1910–31.* London: SCM Press, 1962.

WINGREN, GUSTAF. *Theology in Conflict.* Philadelphia: Muhlenberg Press, 1959.

ZERBE, A. S. *The Karl Barth Theology.* Cleveland: Central Publishing House, 1930.

CHAPTER IX

CATHOLIC THOUGHT AND ACTION SINCE 1800

In the Age of Reason, the Catholic church passed through a series of crises which deprived it of material wealth and spiritual influence. The French Revolution and the Napoleonic Wars disproved the rationalists' belief in the innate goodness of man. Enthroned as a goddess, reason proved to be a source of terror and bloodshed. A reaction was inevitable. The first reaction against the Enlightenment was the romantic movement. The Romanticists were enamoured of the Catholic Middle Ages, the time of European unity. A typical example of this reaction is found in the essay by Novalis, "Christendom or Europe."[1] The Reformation had destroyed the medieval unity and thereby abolished Christianity. Luther misjudged its spirit, Novalis complained, and introduced a new religion, the religion of a book. The Congress of Vienna restored the papal states. Pope Pius VII, who had been taken captive by Napoleon in 1809 returned to Rome May 24, 1814 and immediately restored the Society of Jesus, August 7, 1814. Another movement which contributed to the resurgence of Roman Catholicism was ultramontanism, which believed that salvation must be sought on the other side of the Alps. In his book *Le Pape* (1819), the French Count de Maistre glorified the papacy as the only remedy for all the evils of the day.[2] Back to authority, submission to the papacy! No pope, no Christendom; no political or social stability.

[1] Friedrich von Hardenberg (Novalis) represents German Romanticism in a unique way. Cf. the penetrating discussion of Novalis by Barth, *From Rousseau to Ritschl* (London: SCM Press, 1959), pp. 225 ff.

[2] For an excerpt cf. Carl Mirbt, *Quellen zur Geschichte des Papsttums* (4th ed., 1924), pp. 433-34.

Papal Infallibility

The pontificate of Pius IX (1846-1878) marked a turning point in the history of the Roman church. The pope lost his worldly kingdom but gained a spiritual one. July 18, 1870 was a high day for the papacy. The First Vatican Council ratified the decree of papal infallibility. A few weeks later, September 28, the troops of Victor Immanuel entered the Holy City and the papal states came to an end. The way for papal infallibility had been prepared by the doctrine of the immaculate conception of Mary (1854) which the pope had raised to the status of dogma without the assent of a council. The dogma declared that Mary "at the first instant of her conception was preserved immaculate from all stain of original sin, by the singular grace and privilege granted her by Almighty God, through the merits of Christ Jesus, Saviour of mankind." [3] The dogma reasons that the sinlessness of Jesus depends upon the absence of sin which results from sexual intercourse. Mary could conceive immaculately because she, too, had been immaculately conceived.

On December 8 (Feast of the Immaculate Conception) 1864, the pope took another important step in his encyclical *Quanta cura* and in the *Syllabus of Errors* attached to it.[4] The encyclical condemns as insane the idea "that the liberty of conscience and of worship is the peculiar (or inalienable) right of every man, which should be proclaimed by law." The *Syllabus* contains eighty propositions, which condemn among other things, pantheism, naturalism, rationalism, indifference, socialism, communism, secret societies, Bible societies, opposition to the secular power of the papacy, public education, separation of Church and state, and freedom of worship for Protestants in Catholic countries. In the final statement the pope rejects the idea that the Roman Pontiff ought to reconcile himself and come to terms with progress, liberalism and modern civilization.

In 1869 Pius IX convened the First Vatican Council. The opening session of this Council, too, was held on December 8, the Feast of the Immaculate Conception. Out of 1037 (or 1050) prelates eligible to vote only 766 attended the council. Out of 541 from Europe, Italy,

[3] *Ibid.,* p. 447.

[4] *Ibid.,* p. 451. The English text is given in Anne Freemantle (ed.), *The Papal Encyclicals in Their Historical Setting* (New York: American Library, 1956), pp. 135 ff.

with a population of 27 million, was represented by no less than 276 prelates! The council dealt mainly with the Catholic faith and the constitution of the church. Natural revelation with all its implications was strongly emphasized. The real work of the council consisted of formulating the Constitution of the Church, which contains the doctrines of "the establishment, perpetuity, and nature of the sacred Apostolic primacy of Peter in the Roman Pontiff." To one prelate opposing the proposed dogma of infallibility Pius is reported to have uttered the now famous words "I am the Tradition."[5] A preliminary vote was taken on July 13 with 451 prelates voting affirmatively and 88 voting negatively. Of the remainder, 62 voted approval with certain amendments, while 70 abstained. Within the next five days the number in attendance dwindled to 555. Of these only two voted negatively on the fateful day of July 18, Bishop Edward Fitzgerald of Little Rock, Arkansas, and Bishop Luigi Riccio of Cajazzo, Sicily. Both men submitted to the decree as soon as it was passed. Among those opposed was one of the most prominent scholars, Ignaz von Doellinger. In 1871 his friends organized the Old Catholic Church.[6]

The decree states that it is a divinely revealed dogma "that the Roman Pontiff, when he speaks *ex cathedra,* that is, when in discharge of the office of pastor and doctor of all Christians, by virtue of his supreme Apostolic authority, he defines a doctrine regarding faith or morals to be held by the universal Church, by the divine assistance promised to him in blessed Peter, is possessed of that infallibility with which the divine Redeemer willed that his Church should be endowed for defining doctrine regarding faith or morals; and that therefore such definitions of the Roman Pontiff are irreformable of themselves, and not from the consent of the Church."[7] In order neither to underestimate nor to overestimate the importance of this decree the following must be considered: The point of importance lies in the

[5] Geddes MacGregor, *The Vatican Revolution* (Boston: Beacon Press, 1957), p. 50.

[6] At Bonn, Germany, in 1874, the Old Catholics formulated a doctrinal consensus with Greek and Anglo-Catholic theologians. See the Fourteen Theses in Schaff, *Creeds of Christendom,* II (1889), 545 ff.

[7] Mirbt, *op. cit.,* p. 473. For the full text of the Vatican Decrees in Latin and English see Schaff, *op. cit.,* II, 234 ff. and MacGregor, *op. cit.,* pp. 165 ff.

definite victory of curialism over conciliarism. The pope makes dogmatic decisions by virtue of his own power, not through the assent of the Church. The Council thereby lost every dogmatic importance in the sense of the ancient, medieval, and even of the Tridentine Council. An infallibility is transferred to the pope which the Roman church has always claimed. What really occurred within Catholicism was the shifting of the seat of infallibility from a group to an individual. The infallibility of the pope does not refer to his private person, to his personal thoughts and actions. It is rather limited by a number of stipulations: (1) The pope must function as the supreme teacher of all Christendom and make a decision valid for the entire Church, not just for a single diocese. (2) These decisions must relate to faith and morals, not to any practical questions of Church administration or to purely secular problems. (3) The decision must bear the character of *ex cathedra.* This limits the infallibility to such a decision which bears the marks given under No. 1 and No. 2. All these stipulations are so elastic that it is extremely difficult to determine when the pope exercises his power of infallibility.

Since 1870 only one papal decision has borne the character of infallibility: the proclamation of the bodily assumption of Mary into heaven, November 2, 1950. In the words of Pius XII, the assumption of Mary is a divinely revealed dogma which the pope pronounces "by the authority of our Lord Jesus Christ, of the blessed apostles, Peter and Paul, and by his own authority."[8] In the eyes of Catholic scholars, the two Marian dogmas leave the uniqueness of Christ unimpaired, for her immaculate conception and assumption are entirely dependent on the merits of Christ. Besides, she did not actively "ascend" into heaven, but was passively "assumed" (taken up) into heaven.

Scholasticism versus Modernism

Pius IX was succeeded by Leo XIII (1878-1903). The new pope (Count Joachim Pecci), and his brother Joseph had been educated in the tradition of Italian scholasticism. One of his first actions was to recommend to the world, in his encyclical *Aeterni Patris* (1879), the "precious wisdom of St. Thomas" and its propagation as a cure

[8] Freemantle, *op. cit.,* p. 288.

for the religious and social evils of the age. However, the then powerful historical and psychological approach to religion greatly disturbed the tranquility of the Roman church in the decades preceding World War One. The breakdown of nations and morals during the war gave new momentum to the Catholic cry: Back to authority! The prestige of the hierarchy was considerably enhanced by the shift of emphasis in the philosophical world from abstract Idealism and Monism to a new ontological Realism. Catholic schools such as the *Institute Superieur de Philosophie* at Louvain in Belgium, the *Institute Catholique* at Paris, and the universities at Freiburg, Switzerland and Innsbruck, Austria, became the leading centers of Thomistic studies. On the North American continent the Catholic universities at Washington, D. C., and Ottawa, and Laval University, now at Montreal, are promoting Neo-Thomism. The most accomplished scholars of the present are the French philosopher Jacques Maritain and the German Jesuit Erich Przywara at Munich.

As a scholastic, Maritain is unrelenting in his opposition to Luther, Descartes, and Kant. Luther's certainty of salvation, according to Maritain, has led to a metaphysical egotism which makes man, not Christ, the center of religion. He sees in the teachings of Thomas the specific antidote against all the evils resulting from the philosophies of Descartes and Kant, i.e., modern agnosticism, naturalism, and individualism.[9]

Over against the Barthian dislike of the intellectual element in religion, Erich Przywara stands out as a staunch defender of scholastic rationalism. God in Catholic thought, he says, is both like and unlike the world. He is in the world but also forever above the world. He is neither to be equated with the world nor is He the "Wholly Other." Catholic theology stands aloof from pure immanentism as well as from pure transcendentalism. It maintains that the way upward from man to God is closed to us, and that we shall never be able to reach a perfectly harmonious solution to our problems in this world. This doctrine revives the scholastic concept of an "analogy of being."[10]

[9] J. W. Evans and L. R. Ward (eds.), *The Social and Political Philosophy of Jacques Maritain* (London: G. Bles, 1956), may serve as guide to his thoughts and works.

[10] Among other books, Przywara wrote *Analogia Entis* (1932), which Barth calls "the theology of Anti-Christ." In English we have *Polarity: a German Catholic's Interpretation of Religion* (London: Oxford University Press, 1935).

Another philosopher of international reputation is Etienne Gilson (b. 1884). In addition to some French universities he has taught at Harvard and Toronto. At the latter city he founded the Institute of Medieval Studies. Gilson has shown special interest in the influence of Augustine on medieval thought. According to Gilson, the fundamental difference between Augustine and Thomas is that the Bishop of Hippo "who expected so much and received so little from the unaided reason, is especially struck by what it cannot give him. The Angelic Doctor, free as he was by walking in the light from the beginning of his life and sure of his way, could enjoy fully and fearlessly the magnificent spectacle of the wealth of truth that natural reason, even when lacking the illumination of faith, could reveal to pagans such as Aristotle." [11]

Opposition to curialism and scholasticism was by no means dead in the decades between the two Vatican councils. Its proponents resorted to a kind of sophistry: if the pope is said to be infallible when speaking *ex cathedra*, other papal announcements obviously are not binding. There is seemingly more freedom in Rome after 1870 than before! A galaxy of French theologians took the lead. The most prominent of them was Alfred Loisy (d. 1940). In Great Britain it was George Tyrell, in Germany, Hermann Schell. The new pope, Pius X (1903-1914) condemned the movement in the syllabus *Lamentabili sane*, July 3, and in the encyclical *Pascendi dominici gregis*, September 9, 1907.[12]

The modernists' main objective was to come to terms with Protestantism and modern thought. Religion must be interpreted in personal terms and dogma must be understood as an expression of religious experience. Their program included three principal points: (1) They accepted the most liberal results of New Testament criticism and applied them to a radical reconstruction of the Jesus of history. (2) Contending against the scholastic intellectualism in Catholic theology, they held to a dynamic conception of reality: God is a supreme life and immanent action, not an abstract being. They considered it wrong to isolate one moment in the divine process

[11] A. E. Peggis (ed.), *A Gilson Reader* (Garden City: Image Books, 1957), p. 79. The book will serve as a guide to Gilson's works.

[12] Mirbt, *op. cit.*, pp. 505 ff.; Freemantle, *op. cit.*, pp. 197 ff.

as possessing a unique significance for religion. The historicity of Jesus, his birth and resurrection, and the institution of the sacraments by him, are meaningless in comparison with the religious stimuli couched in these concepts. (3) They advocated a measurable amount of practical reform within the Roman communion.[13]

In the syllabus the pope condemns all who deny the plenary inspiration of the Bible. In the encyclical he maintains that the modernists are agnostics, followers of religious immanence; in other words, that they are too much swayed by the teachings of Schleiermacher, Kant and Hegel. In 1910 the pope took two more steps to eradicate the modernist heresy. On June 29, Pius issued a statement requiring all teachers of the Bible to take an oath submitting to all decisions of the Biblical Commission, both past and future.[14] Finally, in an edict of September 1, all priests, including professors in the universities, were required to take the so-called Anti-Modernists oath.[15] This includes acceptance of both papal pronouncements of 1907. Though the oath put a heavy burden on the conscience of many, in the end most of the clergy took the oath. That was the end of modernism in the Roman communion. The very pope that crushed the modernist movement was beatified (1951) and canonized in 1954. Yet strictly speaking modernism is not dead. A "new theology," a term coined by Pius XII (September 17, 1946) has again occasioned a certain amount of anxiety in the Roman communion. Its home is France with Henry de Lubac and Jean Danielou as its leaders. The theologians, they contend, must understand contemporary movements such as Marxism and existentialism. They should be at home in the world of Nietzsche, Kierkegaard, and Dostoevski. Different from the harsh attitude of Pius X, Pius XII limited himself to a kind of fatherly reproof of the new errors in the bull *Humani generis*, August 12, 1950.[16] On the positive side, the pope re-emphasized the traditional tenets of scholasticism that the existence of God and the external evidences of the Christian faith "can be brought home beyond question, even to the unaided light of reason." Negatively he states that

[13] Mirbt, *loc. cit.*
[14] Mirbt, *op. cit.*, p. 515.
[15] *Ibid.*, pp. 515 ff.
[16] Freemantle, *op. cit.*, pp. 283 ff. Cf. "The New Theology" in Walter von Loewenich, *Modern Catholicism* (London: Macmillan Co., 1959), pp. 240 ff.

existentialism is just as much a philosophy of error as idealism, immanentism, and pragmatism. The Church must uphold the view that all humanity has descended physically from Adam and that the story of the fall is an actual historical fact.

The Pontificate of John XXIII

Pius XII died October 9, 1958. He was succeeded by Angelo Giuseppe Roncalli who assumed the name John. The choice of the name was significant. Not counting the illegitimate pontificate of Balthasar Cossa, who called himself John XXIII and was deposed at Constance, 1415, no pope had chosen this name since John XXII (d. 1334). The brief reign of John XXIII (d. June 3, 1963) turned out to be a landmark in the history of Christendom. He proved himself the patron of the progressive party. He convened the Second Vatican Council (first session October 11 - December 8, 1962; second session September 29 - December 4, 1963). It was the first council called neither to combat heresies nor to promulgate a new dogma, nor to marshal the nations against the enemies of the Church. The pope seemed to favor a Thomism mitigated by modern thought. While it is still too early to pass judgment on the work of the council, which at this writing is still in session, the first session approved certain liturgical reforms. Among other things, the bishops were granted the right to decide for themselves whether they wish parts of the mass to be recited in the language of their own countries. This move opens the way for a further decentralization of Church government; gives the bishops a kind of infallibility in their own dioceses; and will let the Bible speak to the laity in the Church services. John's two most important public pronouncements are his bull *Mater et magistra,* dated May 15, but actually issued July 15, 1961, and *Pacem in terris,* 1963. The former commemorates the sixtieth anniversary of Leo III's encyclical *Rerum novarum,* May 15, 1891.[17] Leo's bull has rightly been regarded as the *magna charta* of the modern labor movement. John XXIII explained and extended the teachings of *Rerum novarum* to the present condition of the world. In *Pacem et terris*

[17] Freemantle, *op. cit.,* pp. 166 ff. Pius XI issued a bull *Quadragesimo anno* (May 15, 1931), in commemoration of the fortieth anniversary of Leo's "peerless encyclical," *Rerum novarum* (*ibid.,* pp. 228 ff.) Pius XII commemorated the fiftieth anniversary in a radio address on Pentecost Sunday, 1941.

the pope appealed to the leaders of both East and West to preserve the peace of the world.

Pope John also followed a new line in dealing with Eastern Orthodoxy and Protestantism. He referred to them as "separated brethren." Representatives from both groups participate in the council as official visitors. The common suffering under totalitarian governments had brought individual Christians and churches together. In the eyes of responsive Catholic theologians, Luther is no longer regarded as the lustful, immoral villain, but is respected as a man of the Bible and of prayer.[18] The Lutheran World Federation reciprocated by inviting representatives of Roman Catholicism as official visitors to its fourth general meeting at Helsinki, Finland, August, 1963. The Federation also established a permanent commission, The Lutheran Foundation for Interconfessional Research. Despite doctrinal differences, the two great branches of Christendom, Catholicism and Protestantism, have never been so close since the days of the Reformation as they are today. Hate and calumny have given way to respect and even love.

The Greek Orthodox Church

The disastrous aftermath of the two world wars has also brought the Eastern churches into the orbit of Western Christianity. Most of the national churches of the East now hold membership in the World Council of Churches. By approving such evangelical means of fostering spiritual life as preaching and Bible reading, the Orthodox churches seem to be revitalized in no small degree. Two of the most renowned contemporary scholars are the Russian lay theologian Nicholas Berdyaev (d. 1948) and his friend, Father S. N. Bulgakov (d. 1944). Both went through a spiritual metamorphosis which led them from Marx through Kant and the German Idealists to Christ and the Orthodox Church. Both were deeply influenced by the two great Russian writers Dostoevski and Vladimir Soloviev (1853-1900). Berdyaev's thought revolved mainly about God, man, and freedom. History he saw as the product of three factors: natural necessity, human freedom, and divine grace. He concurred with Oswald Spengler in the opinion that civilizations pass through "life-cycles." But unlike Spengler, he was not a fatalist. Civilization must not

[18] Cf. the chapter "Rome and the Reformation," Loewenich, *op. cit.*, pp. 265 ff.

inevitably revert to barbarism. It may be reborn and pass through a "religious transfiguration." Its ultimate meaning is not on the temporal but on the metaphysical plane.

Father Bulgakov's thought-world is much akin to that of Berdyaev. In a search for a metaphysical basis of human existence, he too turned to the biblical, or rather Orthodox-Platonic, view of man as created in the image of God. God is the ideal in whom all created things have their subsistence. "Theirs is an eternal humanity in God and eternal divinity in man." Like his teacher Soloviev, who later in life joined the Roman church, Bulgakov shows a keen interest in a real unity of a divided Christendom.

A third important figure on the ecumenical scene is George Florovsky. Born in Odessa, Russia, 1903, he later taught at the Orthodox Theological Institute in Paris. He came to America in 1948 and has taught at Union Theological Seminary and Harvard University. At ecumenical meetings he has been one of the prominent representatives of Eastern Orthodoxy. He is thoroughly convinced that the Eastern Church has no need to search for a "lost unity" because it is the *Una Sancta.* All Christian groups, including Rome, can recover their unity only by entering into the bosom of that church which has preserved its identity with the Church of the first Pentecost.[19]

BIBLIOGRAPHY

ADAM, KARL. *The Spirit of Catholicism.* New York: The Macmillan Company, 1957.

———. *One and Holy.* New York: Sheed & Ward, 1951.

ASMUSSEN, HANS (ed.). *Die Katholizität der Kirche.* 1957.

AULEN, GUSTAF. *Reformation and Catholicity.* Philadelphia: Muhlenberg Press, 1961.

BAUM, GREGORY. *That They May Be One.* Westminster: Newman Press, 1958.

———. *Progress and Perspective: the Catholic Quest for Unity.* New York: Sheed & Ward, 1962.

BERDYAEV, NICHOLAS. *The Realm of the Spirit.* New York: Harper & Bros., 1952.

———. *Truth and Revelation.* New York: Harper & Bros., 1953.

———. *The End of Our Time.* New York: Sheed & Ward, 1933.

[19] Cf. Paul S. Minear (ed.), *The Nature of the Unity We Seek* (Report of the North American Conference on Faith and Order; Oberlin, Ohio, 1957), pp. 159 ff.

________. *Freedom and The Spirit.* London: G. Bles, 1948.
________. *The Destiny of Man.* London: G. Bles, 1937.
________. *Slavery and Freedom.* London: G. Bles, 1944.
BULGAKOV, S. N. *The Orthodox Church.* New York: Morehouse-Gorham Co., 1936.
________. *The Wisdom of God.* New York: Paisley Press, 1937.
CARLEN, M. C. *A Guide to the Encyclicals of the Roman Pontiffs from Leo XIII, to the Present Day.* New York: H. W. Wilson, 1939.
________. *Guide to the Documents of Pius XII.* Westminster: Newman Press, 1951.
CULLMANN, OSCAR. *A Message to Catholics and Protestants.* Grand Rapids: Wm. B. Eerdmans Publishing Co., 1959.
DENZINGER, HENRY. *The Sources of Catholic Dogma.* St. Louis: Herder Book Co., 1957.
FREEMANTLE, ANNE (ed.). *The Papal Encyclicals in Their Historical Setting.* New York: American Library, 1956.
HEILER, FRIEDRICH. *Die katholische Kirche des Osten und Westen.* 1937.
HORTON, WALTER M. *Contemporary Continental Theology.* New York: Harper & Bros., 1938.
HUDSON, W. S. *Understanding Roman Catholicism.* Philadelphia: Westminster Press, 1959.
KUENG, HANS. *The Council, Reform, and Reunion.* New York: Sheed & Ward, 1961.
LILLY, A. L. *Modernism.* 1908.
LOEWENICH, WALTER, VON. *Modern Catholicism.* London: Macmillan Co., 1959.
LOSSKY, N. O. *A History of Russian Philosophy.* London: George Allen & Unwin, Ltd., 1952.
MACGREGOR, GEDDES. *The Vatican Revolution.* Boston: Beacon Press, 1957.
MIRBT, CARL. *Quellen zur Geschichte des Papsttums.* 4th ed.; 1924.
PELIKAN, JAROSLAV. *The Riddle of Roman Catholicism.* New York: Abingdon Press, 1959.
PETRE, M. D. *Modernism.* London: T. C. & E. C. Jack, Ltd., 1919.
________. *Autobiography and Life of George Tyrell.* New York: Longmans, Green & Co., 1912.
________. *Alfred Loisy: His Religious Significance.* Cambridge Univ. Press, 1944.
SKYDSGAARD, K. E. *One in Christ.* Philadelphia: Muhlenberg Press, 1957.
TYRELL, GEORGE. *An Autobiography and Life of George Tyrell.* 2 vols. New York: Longmans, Green & Co., 1912.
VALLON, M. A. *An Apostle of Freedom.* New York: Philosophical Library, 1960.
VIDLER, A. R. *The Modernist Movement in the Roman Church.* Cambridge University Press, 1934.
________. *Faith and Order Trends.* A quarterly publication of the National Council of the Churches of Christ in the U.S.A.

Section Two

THEOLOGICAL THOUGHT IN GREAT BRITAIN

CHAPTER I

INTRODUCTORY SURVEY

In the eighteenth century theological leadership passed from Germany to other countries of Western Europe. Holland and England took the lead during the Enlightenment. It was not till the end of the eighteenth century that Germany, through the work of Kant and Schleiermacher, regained the position which it had held during the time of the Reformation. During the greater part of the nineteenth century, especially since Kant, English thought was always a few decades behind the German in theological reconstruction. But if German theology has come to fruition more rapidly than English theology, it often tended toward the extreme in radical criticism and humanism. The conservatism of the English ultimately led to the triumph of a mediating theology in England. The genius of English theology is that it is liberal but not modernistic. "Adaptive traditionalism," in the phrase of Walter M. Horton,[1] is the chief characteristic of English thought. English theologians allow progress in theological thinking while maintaining the continuity of thought. They are liberal conservatives. Though the dogmatic formulation of the past may be questioned, English theologians try to preserve the great Christian truths.[2] On the other hand, it cannot be ignored that in our own century theological liberalism has made strong inroads into the Anglican communion.

Another characteristic of English theology is its emphasis on the Church. Anglicans view the Church largely as a unifying force in society. The apostolic succession, for example, is the force which unites the past and present generations. Since the days of Schleiermacher, German theology has tended toward individualism and the break-up of the corporate consciousness of the Christian religion,

[1] *Contemporary English Theology* (New York: Harper & Bros., 1936), p. 3.

[2] On the respective merits and demerits of English and German thought, compare, for example, Hugh R. Mackintosh, *Types of Modern Theology*, pp. 2 ff.

although such men of the nineteenth century as Stahl, Kliefoth, Loehe, and Vilmar were hardly less emphatic on the corporate nature of the Church than the English theologians. German pietism struck directly at the Church. It was not so in England. Even the pietistic, the evangelical, or the low churchman has an appreciation of the Church.

The third characteristic feature of English theology is its apologetic element. The irrationality of faith is thought of lightly while it is held that it is precisely the "business of theology" to show that the gospel is a reasonable thing.[3]

A fourth trait of English theology is its contradictory or compromising element.[4] This trait appears among the theologians who hold the highest views of the Church and the sacraments, yet at the same time accept the findings of critical biblical scholarship. For example, the late Charles Gore tried to bring the sacramentalism of the high church party into harmony with the results of biblical criticism. This apparent inconsistency is easily understood if we keep in mind the influence of Hegel in modern English thought.

A word ought to be said about the center of English theology. In German theology the atonement is the foremost problem. Lutheran theology considers the cross the center of its system. While the theology of the Nonconformists bears a resemblance to Lutheran theology in this respect, Anglican theology centers upon the incarnation. From this perspective Anglican thought discusses the inspiration of the Scriptures, the atonement, miracles, sacraments, and the Church. The incarnation, the sacraments, and tradition are the three great concerns of Anglican theology. The theology of the Nonconformists, on the other hand, revolves about such concepts as atonement, faith, and experience.[5]

Following the disintegration of eighteenth-century deism through the influence of Hume and Butler, there are three great movements that can be traced through a great part of the nineteenth century, the fruits of which extend right up to our day. These movements are the evangelical movement, the liberal or broad church movement,

[3] Cf. E. G. Selwyn, *The Approach to Christianity* (London: Longmans, Green & Co., 1925). See also L. Hodgson, *The Place of Reason in Christian Apologetic* (Oxford: Blackwell, 1945).

[4] Cf. W. Vollrath, *Theologie der Gegenwart in Grossbritanien,* pp. 24 ff.

[5] Cf. *ibid.*, pp. 259 ff.

and the high church movement. Of these the first was most influential early in the century; the other two may be regarded as more or less contemporary, though the period of the greatest activity of the second precedes that of the third. Of course, there are other movements that cannot be brought under any of the three, nor did any of the three act in isolation. We see action, reaction, and interaction under different circumstances, resulting in the complexity of the religious condition in which we find England today.

With respect to Scottish theology it may be said that theology in Scotland moved more slowly than in England. Calvinism remained the common creed of the country. However, the critical tendencies of the age were also strongly felt there which greatly disturbed the tranquility of Scottish Presbyterianism. W. R. Smith, the interpreter of Wellhausen in England, had to yield his position in the free church to his orthodox opponents. Still stronger inroads of modern ideas are found among the diverse groups of Nonconformists who had always been wavering between the legalistic pietism and critical rationalism via religious subjectivism.

The intellectual record of the nineteenth century presents a growing conviction that history offers a key to the right understanding of life. This century was above all historically minded. The historical method came into its own. The sciences of history of religion and comparative religion were born and opened a wide field for historical investigation. The historical method is genetic and organic. Scientifically speaking, it has no place for the supernatural. No event takes place in isolation. There are antecedents that make the flow of history possible. There is a growing tendency toward naturalism and away from a supernatural interpretation of history. Lessing and Herder in Germany, and Montesquieu in France were the fathers of the historical method. It was not until the latter part of the nineteenth century that this method came to be recognized in England.

In spite of the triumph of the historical method in the nineteenth century, the leading theologians are unhistorical to the core, e.g., Schleiermacher and Ritschl in Germany, Coleridge and the large train of his followers in England. Nineteenth-century theology is a search for an interpretation of the divine idea, the principle, and spiritual truth. Ritschl was in line with this tradition and interpreted Biblical history by a pre-conceived idea, i.e., the Kantian secularized conception of the kingdom of God. The three great religious postulates of Enlightenment theology, God, virtue, and immortality, were firmly rehabilitated at the close of the nineteenth century in the modern garb of the fatherhood of God, the brotherhood of man, and the supreme value of the human soul.[6]

Another spiritual force of the nineteenth century was romanticism, which arose as a protest against the overintellectualization of the preceding century. This movement gave England such geniuses as Burns, Shelley, Coleridge, Byron, Browning, and Tennyson. It formed the spiritual background of the Oxford Movement. Newman in the *Apologia*, when describing the sources of the Oxford Movement, speaks of a "spirit afloat" as the background of the religious revival.

The influence of the romantic movement was counteracted by a growing interest in the physical sciences in England which began to apply the principle of historical development in explaining the genetic growth of physical specimens in the natural world. In 1830 the first British association of scientists was founded. Science came to the fore in Charles Darwin, who more than any other man in England changed its thinking. All readers are familiar with the part science played from his time on through his two great disciples, Huxley and Spencer. Of all the new movements, the Darwinian theory of evolution is the one which materialism appropriated most readily, and to which it is most indebted.

The nineteenth century was further noted for a philosophical idealism which in Germany was closely allied with the romantic movement during the earlier part of this period. In England, theology as a whole did not feel the influence of German philosophy until after 1860. Nowhere has English insularity been more marked than in the philosophical outlook of the first half of the nineteenth century. The last eighty years, however, have seen German Idealism take hold of British thinking. Kant and Hegel have been earnestly studied and some of the very best interpreters of the two great philosophers are British: Thomas Hill Green, John Caird, and his younger brother Edward Caird.

[6] Cf. Aulén, *Das Christliche Gottesbild* (1930), pp. 285-86, 291, 323 ff.

During the whole period under discussion the social problem has played an important part in English life. England was the first country to experience the sweeping changes of the industrial revolution. Soon after 1800 English society witnessed the rise of a proletariat that was in utter want and despair. The broad church movement supplied England with farsighted and able men who aroused the English Christians to their social responsibility. F. D. Maurice became the leader of the Christian Socialists. In 1854 he founded a Working Men's College in London for the education of his neglected brethren. His ideas and endeavors were shared by many others, including Charles Kingsley. After 1889 the increasing sense of social responsibility led to the formation of Associations for Christian Social Service in all the denominations of the country. In 1924 these various Associations met at Birmingham to form a Conference for Christian Politics, Economics, and Civics. Through this joint effort of the established church and the Nonconformists the English churches have succeeded in taking the anti-religious sting out of the labor movement in England, while the Socialists of the Continent are much more pronounced in their opposition not only to the established churches but to religion and Christianity as such.

BIBLIOGRAPHY

BENN, A. W. *The History of English Rationalism in the Nineteenth Century*. 2 vols. London: Longmans, Green & Co., 1906.

BROWN, FORD K. *Fathers of the Victorians*. Cambridge University Press, 1961.

CARPENTER, S. C. *Church and People 1789–1889*. New York: The Macmillan Company, 1933.

DAVIES, HORTON. *Worship and Theology in England, 1690–1850*. Princeton: Princeton University Press, 1961.

ELLIOT-BINNS, L. E. *Religion in the Victorian Age*. Greenwich, Conn.: Seabury Press, 1953.

———. *The Story of England's Church*. London: SPCK, 1954.

———. *English Thought, 1860–1900: the Theological Aspect*. New York: Longmans, Green & Co., 1956.

HORTON, W. M. *Contemporary English Theology*. New York: Harper & Bros., 1936.

LLOYD, ROGER. *The Church of England in the Twentieth Century*. 2 vols. London: Longmans, Green & Co., 1946-47.

MOORE, EDWARD C. *History of Christian Thought since Kant*. New York: Charles Scribner's Sons, 1912.

PFLEIDERER, OTTO. *Development of Theology in Germany since Kant and Its Progress in Great Britain since 1825.* New York: The Macmillan Company, 1909.

SHELLHAAS, J. "English Theology since the Age of Deism." Unpublished S.T.M. thesis, Hamma Divinity School, Springfield, Ohio, 1931.

STEWART, HERBERT L. *A Century of Anglo-Catholicism.* London: J. M. Dent & Sons, 1929.

STORR, V. F. *Theological Development in Great Britain, 1800–1860.* London: Longmans, Green & Co., 1913.

TULLOCH, JOHN. *Movements of Religious Thought in Britain during the Nineteenth Century.* London: Longmans, Green & Co., 1896.

WARRE-CARNISH, FRANCIS. *The English Church in the Nineteenth Century.* 2 vols. London: Macmillan Co., 1910.

WEBB, C. C. J. *A Study of Religious Thought in England from 1850.* Oxford: The Clarendon Press, 1933.

CHAPTER II

THE EARLY EVANGELICALS AND THE EARLY ORTHODOX PARTY

EVANGELICALISM

The Anglican church might have retained the Methodists in its fold, for the early leaders of the Revival were loyal priests of the established church. But by and large the episcopate was not sympathetic to the Revival. The right of ordination was another issue. In the course of time the name Methodists was restricted to the seceders, while the others became known as the Evangelicals. The majority of the Methodists belonged to the lower classes of society. The evangelicals, on the other hand, appealed to the middle class of the country. The Methodists claimed the world as their parish and developed the itinerant system. The Evangelicals confined their pastoral activities to work in the parish.

The three main centers of Evangelical influence were London, Clapham, which in the eighteenth century was still separated from the City by a stretch of three miles of lovely meadows, and Cambridge. The Evangelicals had no real foothold in Oxford. In fact, as early as 1768 some undergraduates were expelled from the university as "frequenters of an illegal conventicle" and as "enthusiasts who talked of regeneration, inspiration, and drawing nigh to God." [1] Gradually the Evangelicals crept into the ranks of the episcopate. The first appointment was that of Henry Ryder to the see of Gloucester, 1815. In 1826 Charles Richard Sumner was consecrated as Bishop of Llandaff. As a curate he had been the domestic chaplain of George IV. Two years later his older brother, John Bird Sumner, became bishop of Chester. In 1846 he became Archbishop of Canterbury. Beilby Porteous, Bishop of London, 1787–1808, was also a friend of the Evan-

[1] For the story of the trial cf. G. R. Balleine, *A History of the Evangelical Party in the Church of England* (London: Longmans, Green & Co., 1933), pp. 124 ff.

gelicals. The literary organ of the party was *The Christian Observer*, first published in 1802.

One of the first Evangelicals in London was William Romaine (d. 1795). He was an accomplished scholar, author of a revised edition of Calasio's *Hebrew Concordance* (1748). His three best-known books—*The Life of Faith* (1763), *The Walk of Faith* (1771), and *The Triumph of Faith* (1795)—gained him wide recognition in all parts of England. Among his early sympathizers in London were two young clergymen: Thomas Jones (d. 1845)—"the seraphic Mr. Jones" as his admirers used to call him—and Henry Venn, who was curate at Clapham, 1754–1759. His son John was later rector of Clapham, 1792–1813. His congregation included a remarkable group of laymen, devoted to the cause of Evangelicalism: Henry Thornton, a banker and financier; Charles Grant, chairman of the East India Company; Zachary Macaulay, governor of Sierra Leone; William Wilberforce, and others. At Cambridge, Isaac Milner (d. 1820) and Charles Simeon (d. 1836) promoted the cause of the Evangelicals. Hannah More (d. 1833)—when she had "become serious"—was also attracted by the "Clapham Sect."

Though they were men of learning, the Evangelicals did not produce a new theology. They were Protestants by conviction and held to the doctrines of the Reformation: the doctrine of the Trinity, as opposed to the current semi-Socinianism of the older low church party, the doctrine of the depravity of the natural man, salvation by the merits of Christ, and the obligation of a life of holiness. The majority were moderate Calvinists, although a few held extreme Calvinistic (Romaine) or Arminian views (J. W. Fletcher). They loved the Church of England and subscribed wholeheartedly to the Thirty-nine Articles. The most influential book produced by the early Evangelicals is Wilberforce's *A Practical View of the Prevailing Religious Systems of Professed Christians in the Higher and Middle Classes contrasted with Real Christianity* (1797). The title is well chosen and reveals the religious concern of the Evangelicals. Over against the nominal Christianity of the day the author and his friends wanted to foster a piety which effected a real change of heart and life. To make this a reality, the Evangelicals, like the Methodists, gathered their converts into small societies. They introduced hymn-singing into the service. Romaine (1775), John Newton (1779), Joseph Milner (1780), John Venn (1785), and others published collections of hymns adapted to the trend of the Revival. In 1780 Robert Raikes, editor of the *Gloucester Journal*, started the first Sunday school. The next step was the founding of a number of societies for the propagation of the gospel on a national and international level. Some of these societies were the Church Missionary Society and the Religious Tract Society, both founded in 1799; the Bible Society (1804); and the London Society for Promoting Christianity among the Jews (1809). The greatest achievement was Wilberforce's struggle against the slave trade, a struggle which lasted from 1787 till 1807 when the slave trade was made illegal. In all these matters the Evangelicals co-operated with the various Nonconformist groups in the country, fostering an attitude that transcended the narrow confines of Anglicanism. On the other side of the ledger, we find the Evangelicals mainly responsible for the characteristic prudery of the Victorian era.

In comparing the Evangelical (and Methodist) movement with the Lutheran pietism of the eighteenth century, a significant difference is to be observed. Spener and his followers were opposed to an orthodoxy which carried theological definitions to the extreme. The Lutheran Pietists tried to curb the excesses of theological statements. In that sense they were un-orthodox. The Evangelicals and the Methodists, on the other hand, faced a church which ignored its doctrinal heritage. They had no cause to protest against an over-zealous orthodoxy. Bishops and ministers alike had surrendered in large numbers to the deistic and anti-trinitarian tendencies of the times. Consequently, the Evangelicals were immensely interested in a revival of biblical teaching. This union of a personal piety and biblical literalism became epoch-making for Anglo-Saxon Christianity.

The Early Orthodox Party

Side by side with the early Evangelical party in the first quarter of the nineteenth century was the early Orthodox party. This party deserves the name "orthodox" not so much with respect to its position on questions of biblical criticism but rather in regard to its highly conservative appreciation of the Church and of ecclesiastical tradition. It was composed of two elements: the "Church and state group" and the "spiritual high churchmen," who were the lineal ancestors of the Tractarians.

The father of this party was William Paley (d. 1805), theologian and philosopher. In his book *The Principle of Moral and Political Philosophy* (1785) he followed the utilitarianism of John Locke: Christian virtue is doing good to mankind, in obedience to the will of God, for the sake of everlasting happiness. His scholastic bent of mind is apparent in the title of two of his other larger writings: *View of the Evidences of Christianity* (1794) and *Natural Theology, or Evidences of the Existence and Attributes of the Deity collected from the Appearances of Nature* (1802). Next to him, Samuel Horsley (d. 1806) must be mentioned. With fire and fury he contended against both Unitarians and Methodists, the Rationalists and the Pietists of his day. Another theologian of renown was Herbert Marsh (d. 1838), Bishop of Llandaff and later of Peterborough. He had spent some years at Göttingen and knew German, a rare accomplishment for an Englishman of that time. While Professor of Divinity in Cambridge, he translated Michaelis' *Introduction to the New Testament*, adding a "Dissertation" of his own on the origin of the Synoptic Gospels. This was probably the first attempt to introduce German higher criticism into England, but it did not take root. Its publication caused a panic in circles which held to the infallible inspiration of Scripture. John Randolph (d. 1813), Regius Professor at Oxford, wrote, anonymously, *Remarks on Marsh's Hypothesis*, accusing Marsh of making the Evangelists "copiers of copyists." Marsh repudiated this accusation and defended the critical position of Michaelis. As bishop, Marsh was radical and resolved to drive the Evangelical party from the church.

Edward Maltby (d. 1859), Bishop of Durham, was a great Greek scholar and a theologian. George S. Faber (d. 1854) deserves special mention as one of the first writers on comparative mythology. In theology he was anti-Calvinistic, holding that there was no predestinarian theology among the Fathers. His work on prophecy[2] sets

[2] *A Dissertation on the Prophecies that have been fulfilled, are now fulfilling, or will hereafter be fulfilled relative to the Great period of 1620, the Papal and Mohammedan Apostasies and the Tyrannical Reign of the Antichrist or the Infidel Rome and the Restoration of the Jews* (1814).

forth the strictest Orthodox view on inspiration, and is an index to the state of the doctrine of inspiration in England at the beginning of the nineteenth century. His anti-Calvinistic feelings were fully shared by George Prettyman (d. 1827), Bishop of Lincoln and Winchester. To these may be added Charles Daubeny (d. 1827), Thomas Rennell (d. 1840), Alexander Knox (d. 1831), and William Cleaver (d. 1815), who rejected Evangelical theology and attributed regeneration, justification, and sanctification to the sacraments.

The theologians of the Orthodox party were the learned and cultured men of the early part of the nineteenth century. They had inherited a great creed, and they defended the creed rationally, though their theology was still shackled by eighteenth-century methods. Paley was their ideal. They held the following tenets: (1) The doctrine of the catholicity of the Church and of apostolic succession; (2) the sacramental conception of Christianity; (3) the stress on the unity of the Church. This party deplored schism and nonconformity. (4) Private judgment, they held, has no place in religion. (5) This party was on the whole anti-Calvinistic, though there were some Calvinists or at least moderate Calvinists among them.

BIBLIOGRAPHY

Balleine, G. R. *A History of the Evangelical Party in the Church of England.* London: Longmans, Green & Co., 1933.

Elliott-Binns, E. L. *The Early Evangelicals: A Religious and Social Study.* Greenwich, Conn.: Seabury Press, 1953.

CHAPTER III

COLERIDGE AND THE EARLY ORIEL SCHOOL

Modern English theology has its beginning with Samuel Taylor Coleridge (1772-1834), poet, lecturer, political and literary critic, philosopher, and theologian. His work must be judged along philosophical and spiritual lines. His interest was not centered in the Church's concept of a special revelation; on the contrary, he laid stress on the religious *a priori* in man. In many respects his work is comparable to that of Schleiermacher in Germany. He digressed from the religion of the Reformation, from theocentric thought to anthropocentric. His interest moved along three main lines: (1) the principles of religion, (2) biblical criticism, (3) the Church. His work was directed against the materialistic negation of his age on the one hand and against the Evangelicals on the other. Locke's philosophy led him to a materialism which denied the freedom of the will. The Evangelicals, in his eyes, had separated religion from life and made it a special compartment. Coleridge was averse to the materialism of the Locke school and sought to show that religion is not an isolated, purely supernatural matter, but written in the very heart of man and regulative in human life. Religion, he emphasized, is at home in the soul of man; it is native to his constitution. Coleridge postulated three assumptions: first, he held that there is a universal law of conscience; second, man has freedom of will; third, religion is native to man because he is made in the image of his Maker.

Like Kant, Coleridge distinguished between reason and understanding. Understanding has to do with outward facts that are conditional, while reason has to do with the necessary truths of life. The understanding is dependent upon sense experience and follows the mechanical law of nature. Not so with reason, which possesses freedom of will, orders its own world, and does not follow necessitarian lines.

"The Will," he says, "is ultimately self-determined, or it is no longer a Will under the law of perfect Freedom, but a Nature under the mechanism of Cause and Effect."[1] By this last fact man arrives at the great spiritual truths of life. It is a sort of intuition. Coleridge asserts that experience is the criterion for the truthfulness of religion, thus shifting the question of religious authority from an objective to a subjective basis. Because of this some have accused him of being a pantheist. He is precursor of the school of empiricism in religion in England that regards experience as the basis of religion and theology. Christian truth also is self-evidencing. "In all our creed," he says, "there can be nothing against reason. If Reason justly contradicts an article, it is not of the household of Faith."[2] "In no case can true Reason and a right Faith oppose each other."[3]

With respect to biblical criticism, Coleridge anticipated the modern concept that the Bible is both spiritual and rational. The Bible is divinely inspired because it plumbs the depth of the human heart. "In the Bible there is more that finds me than I have experienced in all other books put together. The words of the Bible find me at greater depth of my being; and whatever finds me brings with it an irresistible evidence of its having proceeded from the Holy Spirit."[4] Its divinity does not reside in a literally infallible text. Historical criticism is not to be rejected; rather it has exactly the same task with respect to the Bible as with respect to any other book of antiquity. The right interpretation of the Bible "must be determined by the industry and understanding of fallible, and alas! more or less prejudiced theologians."[5]

The Catholic emancipation movement prompted Coleridge to express his views on the nature of the Church.[6] Proceeding from the assumption that Church and state are not identical, he follows the Laudian and Non-Juror tradition in Anglican theology. He distinguishes between the Christian Church as such and any national church.

[1] *Aids to Reflection.*

[2] *Ibid.,* Aphorism CXIX.

[3] *Ibid.,* Aphorism CXXI.

[4] *Confessions of an Inquiring Spirit.* Cf. edition prepared by H. St. J. Hart (London: Adams and Charles Black, 1956).

[5] *Aids to Reflection.*

[6] *On the Constitution of Church and State* (1830).

The former is spiritual and universal, identical with the Church known only to the Father. It is the divine and Christian represented in every true church. A national church, on the other hand, is the embodiment of all the learning and culture in a country. Every nation, for the true well-being of its citizens, requires not only an agricultural, industrial, and commercial class, but also an educative class embracing all the spiritual forces of the nation and communicating to the citizenry a clear idea of its right and duties. The knowledge which this class, the "Clericy," has to cultivate and to diffuse is not only theology but also the liberal arts and sciences which constitute the civilization of a country.

Coleridge, who had visited Germany in 1798–1799, is in line with the Kant-Schleiermacher-Hegelian movement. His theology is really the apotheosis of man. As with Schleiermacher, he heterogeneous elements in his system were capable of development into both a conservative and a liberal school. His concept of the Church helped to promote the cause of the Oxford Movement, while his purely religious subjectivism became the starting point for a liberal school in English theology.

J. C. Hare (1795–1855) is one of the direct followers of Coleridge. Like his master, he was an ardent student of German philosophy and theology, particularly of Schleiermacher, Neander, and Tholuck. Two of his works are *Contest Against Rome,* published in 1842 against Cardinal Newman, and *Vindication of Luther* (1885), written against Sir William Hamilton, an exponent of the Scottish "Common Sense" philosophy.

From the year 1815 to the middle of the nineteenth century, Oxford was the center of two great theological movements, the earlier Oriel school and the later Oriel school. The first was a liberal movement, and the second was the great Tractarian movement. Let us first consider the early Oriel school. Edward Copleston, Provost of Oriel (1814–1848) and afterwards Bishop of Llandaff, was the father of this group. A brilliant group of scholars which included Whately, Hampden, and Baden-Powell came under the direction and influence of this magnetic teacher. With regard to the Church, Copleston "may be placed in the more liberal wing of the old high church or Orthodox part," [7] for he denied the necessity of the episcopacy and the sacramental character of the apostolic succession.

Edward Hawkins (1789–1882) followed Copleston as Provost at Oriel. He was a foe of the Tractarians, having dismissed Newman and Froude from Oriel. He elevated the view of the Church, holding that doctrines were not derived from Scripture but from the Church, while he viewed the Bible only as a witness which verifies the teaching of the Church.

Richard Whately (1787–1863) held an intermediate position between the high dogmatic school and the school of religious subjectivism. If it was the desire of Coleridge to test the doctrines of the Church by experience, Whately wanted to test the doctrines of the Church by historical criticism. He assailed "errors" on both sides, those of the Puritans as well as those of the Sacramentarians. It is noteworthy that he rejected the Calvinists' teaching on predestination as non-Pauline. He based justification on the moral renewal of man, rejecting the idea that the merits of Christ are imputed to the sinner. Apostolic succession, he held, cannot be proved from Scripture. The Lord's Day is not based on the legal command of the Old Testament.

R. D. Hampden (1793–1868) wrote an article on Thomas Aquinas and Scholastic philosophy for the *Encyclopedia Metropolitana*. It was an attack on the excessive development of dogma and an attempt to evaluate the dogmatic principle in the light of history. He insists upon the difference between the Christian faith and the mode of its expression. Religious experience comes first and is divine; theological terms are but symbols. Hampden's motto is "Back to the Scriptures; Scripture, not Tradition." "The difference between the New Testament and technical theology is that in the one you have divine truth, guaranteed by inspiration, in the other the human rendering of divine truth." [8] What then is the justification for dogmatic theology? First, dogmatics is to guard the original deposit of biblical revelation and see to it that the revelation is not eviscerated in theological development. Second, it seems to keep the religious community together as a social bond. Although Hampden heralded the cry, "Back to the

[7] V. F. Storr, *Development of English Theology in the Nineteenth Century, 1800–1860* (London: Longmans, Green & Co., 1913), p. 95.

[8] Storr, *op. cit.*, p. 102.

Scriptures," he did not do so in the interest of a pietistic evangelicalism. He intended to discredit the development of dogma, as had Harnack and other liberals in Germany. Two of his major writings are *Essay on the Philosophical Evidence of Christianity* (1827), and *Scholastic Philosophy Considered in Its Relation to Christian Theology* (1833).

Thomas Arnold (1795–1842) was a follower of Whately. To Arnold, Christianity was ethics. His idea of the Church pleased neither liberals nor the Orthodox party. He reproduced Hooker's theory of the identity of Church and state in a Christian commonwealth, but repudiated the idea of a priesthood and of apostolic succession.

Two other men who were not of the Oriel group shared its spirit: Bishop Thirlwall (d. 1875) and Henry Hart Milman (d. 1868). In these two men the historical spirit reached its height. Thirlwall knew the German language and German theology, and he breathed its critical spirit. Milman, in his work *History of the Jews* (1829), took the historical view of the Old Testament and interpreted sacred history on the same basis as profane history.

Robert Fellowes (1771–1847), known as a free-lance theologian, wrote two important books, *Religion without Cant* (1811) and *The Religion of the Universe* (1836). The first work was an attempt to defend the tenets of the Church of England against the misinterpretations of the Dissenters. He denies original sin and the doctrine of the Trinity. In his second work he is in open revolt against the traditions of the Church. He accepts an evolutionary creed and contends that religion is a matter of intellectual culture.

BIBLIOGRAPHY

ARNOLD, F. *Our Bishops and Deans.* Vol. I. London: Hurst, 1875.

CHAMBERS, E. K. *S. T. Coleridge: A Biographical Study.* Oxford: Clarendon Press, 1938.

COLMER, JOHN. *Coleridge: Critic of Society.* Oxford: Clarendon Press, 1959.

FITZPATRICK, WARREN J. *Memoirs of R. Whately.* 2 vols. London: R. Bentley, 1864.

GREEN, J. H. *Spiritual Philosophy, founded on the teachings of the late Samuel Taylor Coleridge.* 2 vols. London: Macmillan Co., 1865.

MARTINEAU, HARRIET. *Biographical Sketches.* London: Macmillan Co., 1870.

SANDERS, C. R. *Coleridge and the Broad Church Movement.* Durham: Duke University Press, 1942.

WILLEY, BASIL. *Nineteenth Century Studies.* New York: Columbia University Press, 1949.

WHATELY, E. J. *Life of Richard Whately.* 2 vols. London: Longmans, Green & Co., 1866.

WISE, J. T. *Bibliography of the Writings of Coleridge.* London: R. Clay and Son, 1913.

CHAPTER IV

THE OXFORD MOVEMENT

THE OXFORD MEN

Just as the English Reformation of the sixteenth and the seventeenth centuries was rooted more in a national protest against Rome than in a genuine religious appreciation of the Continental Reformation, so the political situation at the beginning of the nineteenth century was largely responsible for the inception of the Oxford Movement. The bloody revolution in France had made democracy obnoxious to the more aristocratic intellectuals. Political events, the rise of liberalism in politics and religion, and reaction against the French Revolution constituted a fertile soil for an aristocratic and conservative movement. The romanticism of Walter Scott, which looked to the past, could easily take root in a Church with a rich past. On two previous occasions Oxford had been the center of religious life in England. The university had produced Wyclif in the fourteenth century and the Wesleys in the eighteenth. Now in the nineteenth century it gave birth to a new religious movement which thoroughly changed the structure of the established church. The Anglican church, which had been preponderantly evangelical and Protestant at the beginning of the nineteenth century, became predominantly ritualistic and minimized its kinship to the Reformation by the close of the nineteenth century.[1]

The Oxford Movement was an ecclesiastical rather than a theological movement. Theology was of secondary consideration. Inspired by the religious zeal of the Evangelicals, the Oxford men applied the ecclesiasticism of the old high church party to the practical needs of the time. Also Coleridge, by way of his concept of the Church, exerted a considerable influence on the movement. The

[1] Cf. Edward C. Moore, *History of Christian Thought since Kant* (New York· Charles Scribner's Sons, 1912), p. 221.

first forerunner of the Oxford Movement was Hugh James Rose of Cambridge (1796–1838). Although he is more properly classified with the old high church party, he prepared the way for the new movement to some degree. In 1825 he delivered a series of lectures on *The State of Religion in Germany*, in which he drew a very dark picture of the admittedly ravaging influence of rationalism in that country. His action evoked a sharp reply from the pen of Pusey (who, at that time, was suspected of liberal tendencies), *Historical Inquiry into the Probable Causes of the Rationalist Character Lately Predominant in the Theology of Germany* (1828). The *British Magazine*, founded by Rose in 1832, soon became the chief literary organ of the Oxford Movement.

Another major forerunner of the Oxford Movement was the Irish lay theologian Alexander Knox (1757–1831), and his friend and pupil John Jebb, Bishop of Limerick. In Knox there was a fusion of the enthusiasm of the Evangelicals (after 1776 he corresponded frequently with John Wesley) and of the ecclesiastical principles of the old high church party. In his teaching he anticipated all that later became typical of the Oxford men: Anglicanism as a *via media*, apostolic succession, and the Anglican liturgy as the basic principle by which the catholicity and continuity of the Church is safeguarded.

The foremost leaders of the movement proper were Newman, Pusey, Keble, Froude, William Palmer, Perceval, and Ward. The most important men in this group were Newman and Pusey.

John Henry Newman (1801–1890) was brought up on the Calvinistic theology of William Romain, John Newton, and Thomas Scott. At the age of fifteen he underwent a religious crisis which he always regarded as his real conversion. From John Newton's *On the Prophecies* he came to regard Rome as the seat of the Anti-Christ. The romanticism of Walter Scott charmed his highly imaginative soul. In 1833 he became a fellow at Oriel College, where he was, for a time, under more liberal influences. Through his Oriel friends, Keble and Froude, his interest centered in patristic studies and the high churchmanship of Rose and his party. As the chief editor of the *Tracts* and through his *Parochial and Plain Sermons* (8 vols., 1837–1843) he soon became the recognized leader of the movement. As early as 1837 he began to express his outspoken dislike for Wesley.[2] Still more repugnant to him than Wesley was Luther.[3] Ignorance of Luther's language very likely helped to obscure Newman's historical vision of the ancient and medieval Church. Newman ranks foremost as a Christian preacher. As a poet and prose writer he commands the respect of the student of English literature. As a Catholic apologete he is an anti-intellectual voluntarist.

Next to Newman, Edward Pusey (1800–1882) was the most influential man of the Oxford Movement. His theology centers around a mystic-sacramental concept of the incarnation and the cross. When Newman converted to Rome, Pusey rallied the Anglo-Catholic forces and continued as their leader to the end of his long life in 1882.

John Keble (1792–1866), poet and theologian, provided the Anglican church with one of its most widely circulated devotional books, *The Christian Year* (1827). In these hymns, written in praise of the Church of his fathers, the author has given a Christian sacramental interpretation to the nature symbolism of the romantic school.

It was Richard Hurrell Froude, a pupil of Keble, who brought Newman and Keble together. Froude, who died at the age of thirty-three (1836), was strongly averse to the rationalist spirit for which he held the Reformers at fault, as well as Rome. Very likely Froude was the first of the Oriel friends to conceive of the idea of an Anglican *via media* which Newman later developed.

A. P. Perceval, divine counselor to George IV, William IV, and Victoria, was the spokesman of the Oxford Movement at the royal court. William George Ward became the leader of the radical faction of the Movement. Of changing temperament and devoid of any particular love for the Church of England, Ward was predisposed to Rome and to Jesuit teaching long before the famous *Roman Tract 90.*

In 1833 a Whig government was formed, and the new prime minister, Lord Grey, admonished the bishops to set their house in order. He meant that the bishops should remedy the gross abuses of nepotism, sinecures, pluralities and nonresidence which then were

[2] J. H. Newman, *Letters and Correspondence* (London: Longmans, Green & Co., 1898), II, 200.

[3] Newman, *Essays, Critical and Historical* (London: Longmans, Green & Co., 1895), I, 387. Cf. Rudolf Metz, *A Hundred Years of English Philosophy*, ed. J. H. Muirhead (New York: The Macmillan Company, 1938).

widely practiced in the Church of England.[4] Others took the words of the prime minister as a quotation from Isaiah's death message to King Hezekiah, "For thou shalt die, and not live." (II Kings 20:1.) The attitude of the government that the state is the supreme arbiter in affairs of the Church aroused the apprehension of the Oriel friends, and they resolved to act. The Oxford Movement began, in the eyes of its adherents, with Keble's sermon on National Apostasy Sunday, July 14, 1833. This was followed by a meeting at the Hadleigh rectory where Rose met with Froude, Perceval, and Palmer (July 25-29).

The Oxford Movement proper may be divided into three periods: (a) 1833–1835; (b) 1835–1839; (c) 1839–1846. During the first period the conservative and static element dominated. The main issue was the defense of the spiritual nature and independence of the Church. In the second period the specific characteristics of the movement became progressively more pronounced. Emphasis was laid on the awfulness of religion, the incarnation, mystic sacramentalism, and ethical asceticism. This period produced a vast new literature. The *Tracts,* which at first were rather brief, now became real dissertations. The Greek Fathers were translated and presented to the English-speaking public. In the third period, the progressive ideal of the Church received a wider recognition. The ascetic ideals became more pronounced. Both factors contributed to a deeper appreciation of Roman Catholicism. The crisis came when Newman's *Tract 90* undertook to prove the harmony between the Thirty-nine Articles and Tridentine Romanism. When Newman was converted to Roman Catholicism in October, 1845, he was followed by a group of the radical element.

Oxford Doctrines

In order to arrive at a clearer picture of the importance of this movement, it is necessary to set forth systematically the teachings of the Oxford men on some of the vital Christian doctrines such as the Church, the sacraments, justification, and practical piety.

[4] Cf. S. L. Ollard, *Short History of the Oxford Movement,* (London: A. R. Mowbray Co., 1915), pp.16 ff.

The Church

The Oxford men were inspired by the desire to uphold the spiritual and independent character of the Church. They made the doctrine of apostolic succession the cornerstone of their whole structure, presenting it in *Tract 1*, "Thoughts on the Ministerial Commission," written by Newman. Newman tried to prove succession as a historical fact in *Tract* 7, "The Episcopal Church Apostolical," while the proof from the Scriptures was advanced by Benjamin Harrison in *Tract 24*, "The Scripture View of the Apostolic Commission." As to the standard by which all doctrine should be judged, the maxim of Vincent of Lérins, "what has been believed always, everywhere, and by all," was given a new and vital application. The purest form of the Church was believed to be found in an earlier phase of the Anglican church and in the primitive Church of the Greek Fathers. Consequently, the Oxford men were both anti-Roman and anti-Protestant (*Tracts 15, 20*). Their ideal was the *via media* which would lead safely between the Scylla of Roman ecclesiastical infallibility and the Charybdis of Protestant individualism. While they were unanimous in rejecting the claims of Rome at this time, they varied considerably in their attitude toward the Reformation. Most outspoken in his criticism was Froude, who called the Reformation a limb badly set, that must be broken again and reset. Some members of the Oxford Movement saw the faith once delivered to the saints as the Apostles' Creed and the Nicene Creed, and them only. In comparison, all other creeds have but a secondary importance. The chief exponents of this static view of the Church, which rejects every development in doctrine, were Rose and Palmer, and later Pusey when it fell to him to rally the forces of the movement.

Beside this static view of the Church, Newman advocated a progressive view. In speaking of the prophetical tradition, he maintained that "Almighty God has placed in the church first Apostles, secondarily prophets. Apostles rule and preach, prophets expound. Prophets or doctors are the interpreters of the Revelation. Their teaching is a vast system pervading the church."[5] Besides, it is this prophetical tradition that imparts doctrine, while in Scripture we have only the

[5] See Yngve Brilioth, *The Anglican Revival* (London: Longmans, Green & Co., 1925), pp. 180 ff., 260 ff.

proof of it. It is evident that such a view of the Church can lead its advocates into the fold of the Roman church. In 1844 Newman published his *Essay on the Development of Christian Doctrine.* In addition, his genuine passion for an ascetic ideal of life based on obedience to authority served as a further incentive to accept the Church of Rome as the ideal of his life.

The Sacraments

The statements on the sacraments in the Thirty-nine Articles plainly attempt to harmonize Luther's view with Calvin's. In general, the Tractarians came closer to the historical meaning of the Articles than did their opponents, the Evangelicals, who had yielded to a Zwinglian conception of the sacraments. In *Tracts 67–69,* Pusey unreservedly pronounced baptism the means of regeneration. Post-baptismal sins are effaced by repentance and penance as a "plank after shipwreck." [6] As to the Eucharist, the Tractarians rejected the Roman teaching of transubstantiation as well as Luther's view of the presence of Christ's body under the bread. The Oxford men taught the virtual presence of Christ. In this they remained true to the Anglican tradition. However, they departed from it when Pusey, Palmer, and others taught the *manducatio indignorum.* To their way of thinking the efficacy of the sacraments does not depend upon the promise of Christ, as with Luther, but upon the priestly character imparted to the ministrant by the rite of ordination.[7]

Justification

According to Lutheran thinking, the doctrine of justification is the touchstone of a man's theology. The Church has produced three types of this doctrine: the prophetic or forensic, the mystic or sacramental, and the ethical. In Anglican theology the forensic and

[6] *Ibid.,* p. 312. Here Brilioth calls attention to the fact that Luther opposed the idea that sin could suspend the power of baptism (*WA,* VII, 529).

[7] *Tracts* 25-28, 81; cf. Pusey's sermons, "The Holy Eucharist a Comfort to the Penitent" (1843), "The Christian Life in Christ," and "Heaven the Christian's Home," *Sermons during the Seasons from Advent to Whitsuntide* (2 vols., 1848-53). For a complete orientation on the Anglican doctrine of the Eucharist see Darwell Stone, *A History of the Doctrine of the Holy Eucharist* (London: Longmans, Green & Co.), II (1909), pp. 107 ff. Cf. also O. E. James *et al., Doctrine in the Church of England* (New York: The Macmillan Company, 1938), pp. 120 ff.

sacramental views stand side by side. In the nineteenth century Joseph Milner, the Church historian, was an ardent defender of the Lutheran forensic view, while Alexander Knox opposed it and saw in justification "the acquisition of a condition of inward not merely outward and formal righteousness, a moral change." [8] To W. G. Ward the Lutheran view was "an abstract doctrine, which cannot, we verily believe, be held consistently even by the devils . . . more fundamentally at variance with our higher and better nature than Atheism itself." [9] Newman in his *Lectures on Justification* (1838) extolled the Anglican view as a *via media* between the Lutheran concept which, in his eyes, was false, and the Roman idea which, he claimed, was incomplete but had been complete in the teaching of Augustine. He argues for the idea of justification through baptism, not by faith as the "primary instrument" (as in the Lutheran view) without the exercise or even presence of love; nor by obedient works (the Roman view) alone, but by an acquittal of the sinner which results in actual holiness of life. According to Newman, justification becomes a quality, a substance, which changes man. It is the Christ in us who justifies. This indwelling of Christ is effected by the sacraments, first by baptism, then by the Eucharist, for "as Holy Communion conveys a more awful presence of God than Holy Baptism, so it must be the instrument of a higher justification." [10] In an ever-increasing measure man appropriates the nature of God. The incarnation of the Logos is perpetuated in all believers through the sacraments. In this inner mystic union Newman sees not only a bulwark against the Protestant conception of an outward imputation of divine righteousness, but also against the Roman teaching of a human merit. Like all advocates of the mystic sacramental conception of justification, Newman emphatically rejected the doctrine of "assurance." [11]

Practical Piety

To the Oxford men the realities of faith form a *mysterium tremendum*. "Awfulness," as the vivid feeling of the presence and

[8] Brilioth, *op. cit.*, p. 279.

[9] *Ideal of a Christian Church* (London: W. G. Ward, 1844), p. 305.

[10] Newman, *Lectures on Justification* (London: J. G. & F. J. Rivington, 1840), p. 169.

[11] Cf. Brilioth, *op. cit.*, pp. 274 ff.

majesty of God, is a catchword of their religion. The doctrines of the Trinity and the incarnation are specially dear to them. An earnest desire to strive daily after holiness of heart and life marks the piety of these men. Right belief must result in right action. Action is the criterion of faith. Religious discipline is highly praised, and the fast days as prescribed in the Prayer Book, were made a central point in the Oxford Movement. Through Pusey, whom Brilioth calls "the *doctor mysticus* in earlier Neo-Anglicanism,"[12] the mystic contemplation of the cross was introduced into Oxford piety. On the other hand, a piety with so strong an emphasis on ascetic ideals may easily lead to Pelagian tendencies. Froude, for instance, was actually in danger of reducing divine grace to a minimum in the process of sanctification.

The importance of the Oxford Movement lies in the realm of practical religion. In contrast to the older state Church concept of Hooker, this movement made the Church of England conscious of its spiritual foundation and commission. It further made that church mindful of its Catholic heritage. It gave new weight to the idea of a united Christian Church on the basis of the doctrinal consent of the first five centuries. The World Conference on Faith and Order was the legitimate offspring of the Oxford Movement. Through the interest of the Oxford men in the early Church, the Greek Fathers became living realities to the English public, and through the study of the Greek Fathers, English theology became oriented toward the incarnation as the center of Christian doctrine. As for scientific methods, the Oxford Movement was scholastic, pre-critical, and pre-scientific. It revived the sense of worship which bore such rich fruit in English pre-Raphaelite art. One of its finest features is the social passion which it infused into the life of the Church of England. The ritualistic movement of the later decades was not started by the early Oxford leaders. Although it received its impetus from the Oxford Movement, it was born outside the university.

The question whether the Oxford men were Protestants must be asked. As we see it, if the doctrine of justification is made the touchstone of all theology, it cannot be denied that these men definitely crossed the line from Protestantism into Catholicism. A theology

[12] *Ibid.*, p. 296.

which considers justification a process by which man is made whole by virtue of an infusion of a divine substance, and which makes the sacraments the main channels by which this divine medicine is infused, and which sees in the ordination of the ministrant the guarantee of the efficacy of the sacraments, has surrendered the historical meaning of the Thirty-nine Articles as well as the very principles of the Reformation.

BIBLIOGRAPHY

Brilioth, Yngve. *The Anglican Revival.* London: Longmans, Green & Co., 1925.

________. *Three Lectures on Evangelicalism and the Oxford Movement.* London: Oxford University Press, 1934.

Chadwick, Owen. *The Mind of the Oxford Movement.* Stanford, Cal.: Stanford University Press, 1960.

Church, R. W. *The Oxford Movement, 1833–1845.* London: Macmillan Co., 1891.

Fairweather, Eugene R. *The Oxford Movement.* New York: Oxford University Press, 1964.

Leslie, Shane. *The Oxford Movement.* London: Burns, Oates, & Washbourne, 1935.

Metz, Rudolf. *A Hundred Years of English Philosophy.* Edited by J. H. Muirhead. New York: The Macmillan Company, 1938.

Olland, S. L. *Short History of the Oxford Movement.* London: A. R. Mowbray Co., 1915.

Smith, B. A. *The Anglican Response to Newman.* London: Oxford Univ. Press, 1958.

Voll, Dieter. *Catholic Evangelicalism: The Acceptance of Evangelical Traditions by the Oxford Movement during the Second Half of the Nineteenth Century.* Translated by Veronica Ruffler. London: Faith Press, 1963.

Webb, C. C. J. *Religious Thought in the Oxford Movement.* New York: The Macmillan Company, 1928.

CHAPTER V

THE CONSOLIDATION OF LIBERAL FORCES

Nineteenth-century latitudinarianism is usually included under the rather vague term "broad church." The expression broad church was first used by Arthur P. Stanley, Dean of Westminster, in an article in the *Edinburgh Review* in July, 1850, in connection with the Gorham controversy. Gorham, a minister of the established church who had denied the doctrine of baptismal regeneration, was refused installation in a parish of the Exeter diocese. The decision of the Bishop was reversed by the Judicial Commission of the Privy Council. As a result the archdeacons Manning and R. I. Wilberforce, with other clergy and laymen, seceded from the Anglican church and went over to Rome. In his article Stanley pleaded for a liberal Church polity, for the Church of England was, as he said, "by the very condition of its being neither High nor Low, but Broad." The term was used by him not in any partisan sense, but as a characterization of the nature of the Church of England. A few years later in an article published in the same periodical by J. J. Conybeare, "the name was distinctly applied in a party sense as denoting a succession of liberal no less than Anglo-Catholic and Evangelical teachers, which have always prevailed in the Church."[1] The broad church really began with Coleridge. It was given impetus by the liberal school at Oriel. This party sought to preserve the ethical postulates of Christianity and to give room for broad thinking. It is through this school that the social implications of Christianity were brought to the fore.

As to ecclesiastical polity, A. M. Fairbairn says that the broad church was as civil in its basis as the old high church party. In comparing its polity with that of the Oxford men, he remarks: "The

[1] John Tulloch, *Movements of Religious Thought in Britain during the Nineteenth Century* (London: Longmans, Green & Co., 1896), p. 261.

modern Broad Church is a theory as to how the old connection of the civil and ecclesiastical states may be maintained under a democracy; the modern High Church is a theory as to how the church may, while living within and under a democracy, yet be independent of it. What occasioned the rise of the two were the same events differently regarded; love of the liberalism which had gained the ascendancy in the state made the Broad Church, fear of it created the High." [2]

F. D. Maurice

The first broad churchman to whom we direct our attention is Frederick Denison Maurice (1805–1872). Originally a Unitarian, he was a friend of John Sterling and an an admiring student of Coleridge. He was also influenced by the writings of Erskine. He says, "I was led to ask myself what a gospel to mankind must be; whether it must not have some other ground than the fall of Adam, and the sinful nature of man. I was helped much in finding an answer to the question by Mr. Erskine's books . . . and by the sermons of Mr. Campbell. The English Church I thought was the witness for that universal redemption which the Scotch Presbyterians had declared incompatible with their confessions." [3] Three years later, in January, 1834, he became a minister of the Church of England.

The thinking of Maurice is based on two fundamental principles. The first is that every man is in Christ. Maurice begins with the divine capacity of man, not with man's fall. Man, as a creature of God, is a child of God through Christ. He does not need to become a child of God either by baptism (high church) or by conversion (Evangelicals). [4]

The second principle for which Maurice contended was the idea of Christian unity. Like him, his mother and his three sisters left the Unitarians; they embraced the theology of the Anglican and Baptist churches. What kept the family apart? Not the affirmatives of their religion, he argued. If men could only forget their negatives and stop quarreling about things divisive they could unite around essentials. Maurice shared this desire for unity with Newman and the

[2] Fairbairn, *The Place of Christ in Modern Theology* (New York: Charles Scribner's Sons, 1916), pp. 177-78.

[3] F. Maurice, *Life of F. D. Maurice* (New York: Charles Scribner's Sons, 1884).

[4] In a letter to his mother, *ibid.,* I, 155-56.

other leaders of the Oxford Movement. Unlike them, he did not seek unity in dogma and ritual, but rather in the fundamental positive principles which underlie the Christian faith. This note runs through both of his notable works, *The Religions of the World* (1847) and *Moral and Metaphysical Philosophy* (1861). As to the doctrine of the atonement, he denied the idea of an "artificial substitution." "Christ satisfied the Father by presenting the image of His own holiness and love." "He bore the sins of the world in the sense that he felt them with that anguish with which only a perfectly pure and holy being, which is also a perfectly sympathizing and gracious being, can feel the sins of others." [5] This view is essentially in harmony with Abelard's view of the moral influence concept of the atonement. In 1853 Maurice was expelled from his professorship in King's College at London because of a dispute over eternal condemnation. Following Erskine, he interpreted the Greek word *aionios* ("eternal") as denoting quality rather than duration. According to Maurice, the word applies to God and to things extra-temporal.[6]

Maurice's *Kingdom of Christ* (1838) is a grand eulogy of the Anglican communion as a spiritual and genuinely catholic church because of its mediating character. Within this communion, he says, a churchman may best serve his country not by allying himself with any of the existing parties but by striving to transcend the theological, social, and national limitations of them all.

The characteristic traits of Maurice's teaching must be understood in the light of the idealistic philosophy of Plato. All reality, according to Maurice's view, is recapitulated under one head: Christ is the divine idea of humanity. By his incarnation he became the historical Savior, Jesus. Apart from him, no one has an independent existence. The difference between a believer and an unbeliever is that the unbeliever does not know or acknowledge the truth. Consequently, the atonement cannot involve the idea of substitution, for Christ and humanity are one. Christ only helps man to overcome his separation from God by revealing the love of the Father.[7]

[5] F. D. Maurice, *Theological Essays* (1853); *The Doctrine of Sacrifice* (1854).

[6] Cf. his *The Word "Eternal"* (1863).

[7] A two-volume edition of Maurice's *Kingdom of Christ,* based on the 2nd ed., 1842, was prepared by A. C. Vidler (London: SCM Press, 1958).

It was Maurice's *Kingdom of Christ*[8] that brought him and Charles Kingsley (1810–1875) together, and it was the social note of the gospel that cemented their friendship. In his historical novel *Hypatia*, Kingsley implies a veiled warning against the fanaticism and intolerance of the Oxford men. His repeated attacks upon the insincerity of Roman Catholic writers in general, and upon Newman in particular, prompted Newman to publish his *Apologia* (1864).

Other Broad Theologians

F. W. Robertson (1819–1875) was keenly alive to the needs of his day. He was a great preacher, and in his sermons we have a very penetrating analysis of the meaning of the gospel as he saw it.[9] Robertson did not reject the dogma and creeds of the Church. However, he was not concerned with the historical meaning of the formulas, but tried to penetrate the "underlying truth" which they express. In his view no dogma can adequately express the whole divine verity. The content of his theology clearly bears a humanistic stamp. God is Father because he is the Creator! Neither baptism nor faith makes God our Father, he says. The paternity of God is authoritatively declared by baptism and personally apprehended by faith.

Other theologians who were "broad" in their thinking were Dean Stanley (1815–1888), who was in full sympathy with Thomas Arnold's view of the identity of Church and state, and Bishop Alexander Ewing, to whom the undogmatic approach to history and life was truly congenial.[10]

Looking back over the period we see five forces at work: the Evangelical party; the early Orthodox party; liberalism and latitudinarianism, which were converging into a broad church party, the Tractarian movement, and a naturalistic movement which had its basis in empirical philosophy.[11] The climax of all these forces came

[8] Cf. Pfleiderer, *op. cit.*, pp. 373 ff. Cf. also R. S. Franks, *A History of the Doctrine of the Work of Christ* (London: Hodder & Stoughton, 1918), II, 387 ff., and the study by Claude Jenkins, *Frederick Denison Maurice and the New Reformation* (New York: The Macmillan Company, 1938).

[9] Frederick W. Robertson, *Sermons*, 5 vols. (London: K. Paul, Trench, Trübner, Co. Ltd., 1902–1904).

[10] Cf. Tulloch, *Movements of Religious Thought . . .*, p. 322.

[11] The reference is to James (d. 1836) and John Stuart Mill (d. 1873), Matthew Arnold (d. 1888), and Herbert Spencer (d. 1903). Arnold, for ex-

in *Essays and Reviews.* Pfleiderer[12] likens the years 1860, in which *Essays and Reviews* appeared, to the year 1835 in German theology. He compares the storm this collection of theological essays evoked in England with the indignation in Germany over Strauss' *Life of Jesus.* The initiator of this series of essays was Henry Briston Wilson. The seven authors of the essays, however, wrote independently. The purpose of the essays, according to the Preface, was "to illustrate the advantage derivable to the cause of moral and religious truth, from a free handling, in a becoming spirit, of subjects peculiarly liable to suffer by the repetition of conventional language, and from traditional methods of treatment." The publication of these essays was a milestone in English theological liberalism.

The collection opens with the essay of Frederick Temple, "The Education of the World." Temple maintains that three stages can be distinguished in the development of the human race, corresponding to childhood, youth, and maturity. Education during the respective stages is provided by rules (the law), example (the Son of man), and principle (the Spirit). Today we must study the Bible not as children but as men. There is a certain ambiguity of terminology about the historicity of the miracles and the implication of scriptural authority.

The second essay, "Bunsen's Biblical Research" by Rowland Williams, is more aggressive. Baron von Bunsen, a sincere Christian and lay theologian, had been Prussian minister to the Vatican and to London (1841–1854). He welcomed the results of the biblical criticism of Ewald at Göttingen without relinquishing the essentials of the Christian faith. In this essay the distinction between a natural and revealed religion is obscured. On the whole, the author adopts the results of the so-called higher criticism. The Pentateuch is a gradual growth, not the work of one man; Chapters 41 to 66 of Isaiah are not Isaiah's work; the narrative of Jonah contains late legend founded on a misconception; Daniel was written in the second century before

ample, substituted an impersonal ethical ideal for the Christian concept of God. In a similar way Thomas Carlyle (d. 1881) spoke of God as Eternities, Immensities, Veracities, as is the case in Spinoza, German Idealism and Goethe. Francis Newman (d. 1897), brother of John Henry Newman, identified himself with the skeptical movement. Both Newman brothers left the Anglican communion, the one to become in time a Roman cardinal, the other, vice-president of the Unitarian Association.

[12] Pfleiderer, *op. cit.,* p. 387.

Christ; the Letter to the Hebrews is not Pauline, but was probably written by Apollos; and the Second Letter of Peter is not Petrine.

Baden-Powell, the author of "The Study of Evidences of Christianity," was a professor of astronomy at Oxford who believed wholeheartedly in evolution. He hailed Darwin's *The Origin of Species* as the dawn of a new day in the study of mankind. With regard to the supernatural in history, this essay was the most destructive of all.

The fourth essay, "The National Church" by Wilson himself, pleads for a liberalization of doctrine and discipline in the Church of England. Subscription to the Thirty-nine Articles should not be required. His reference to "the dark patches of human passion and error which form a partial crust upon it [the Bible], and the bright center of spiritual truth within,"[13] caused much resentment.

C. W. Goodwin, a layman, wrote "The Mosaic Cosmogony," contending that the scientific concepts of the author of Genesis cannot be reconciled with scientific facts. Mark Pattison, the rector of Lincoln College, Oxford, contributed the essay "Tendencies of Religious Thought in England, 1688–1750." He pointed out the continuity of religious thought and the need for revision of former beliefs.

In the last essay, "The Interpretation of Scripture," Benjamin Jowett asserts that the Bible should be interpreted like any other book. The actual nature of the Bible, which is not inerrant with respect to historical and scientific facts, should determine our idea of inspiration. Historical understanding is required of the interpreter, who must be cautious not to make dogmatic development in the Church the measure by which the Bible should be judged. Though interpreted like any other book, Jowett believed that the Bible would "still remain unlike any other book."[14]

Essays and Reviews created no small sensation in England. Low churchmen and high churchmen alike united in a common attack upon its authors. After a lengthy trial the collection was condemned by both Houses of Convocation. Critics contended that the spirit of the volume was subversive to the very essence of the faith. As a matter of fact, *Essays and Reviews* caught the Anglican communion wholly unprepared for a critical study of the Bible.

[13] *Essays and Reviews* (London: Longmans, Green & Co., 1861), p. 177.
[14] *Ibid.*, p. 375.

BIBLIOGRAPHY

HIGHAM, FLORENCE. *F. D. Maurice.* London: SCM Press, 1947.

JENKINS, CLAUDE. *F. D. Maurice and the New Reformation.* New York: The Macmillan Company, 1938.

KENDELL, GUY. *Charles Kingsley and His Ideas.* London: Hutchinson, 1947.

POPE-HENNESEY, UNA. *Canon Charles Kingsley.* New York: The Macmillan Company, 1948.

RAMSEY, A. M. *F. D. Maurice and the Conflicts of Modern Theology.* Cambridge: Cambridge University Press, 1951.

STUBBS, C. W. *Charles Kingsley and the Christian Social Movement.* London: Blackie and Son, 1899.

VIDLER, A. R. *The Theology of F. D. Maurice.* 1948.

WOOD, H. G. *F. D. Maurice.* Cambridge: Cambridge University Press, 1950.

CHAPTER VI

SCOTTISH THEOLOGY

Scottish theology has always moved more slowly than English theology. While Scotland contends assiduously for "the faith once delivered to the saints," it has also produced naturalists whose philosophical implications defy religion. Tulloch, who was Scottish himself, called it a superficial judgment to suppose that the Calvinistic creed of the country remained unshaken under all its intellectual progress: "There has always, from the days of Hume, survived in Scotland a vein of naturalistic speculation."[1] Sir John Leslie and Thomas Brown might be cited as naturalists in the earlier part of the nineteenth century. The writers in the *Edinburgh Review* were naturalistically inclined. In the early nineteenth century no one represented this type of thought so ably as did George Combe. In 1825 his *System of Phrenology* appeared, and in 1828 *The Constitution of Man*. In line with him were William and Robert Chambers. Combe sought to combine a theism with views that would lead to materialism. The circulation of his *Phrenology* in England caused great unrest among the Evangelicals. Those early days are spoken of in the *Christian Instructor*, the literary organ of Scottish orthodoxy, as an age of "modern heresies." The most conspicuous leaders of these "heresies" were Erskine and Campbell.

Thomas Erskine (1788–1880) was not a professional theologian, but a jurist. His major writings are *Internal Evidence of the Truth of Revealed Religion* (1820), *The Unconditional Freeness of the Gospel* (1828), and *The Brazen Serpent* (1831). In these works his theological thinking revolves around two main concepts: (1) He is concerned almost exclusively with the internal aspect of religion. Christianity is not a matter of conventional or historical forms, creeds, dogma, and history. The question concerning the historical veracity of the Gos-

[1] Tulloch, *Movements of Religious Thought* . . ., p. 127.

pel narratives is of minor importance in comparison with man's inward spiritual experience of God. (2) Salvation, according to Erskine, is universal. Because forgiveness is already obtained for every sinner in the mission and death of Christ, the love of God will not rest until the lost are found and he has united all things in Christ. Christ came as the head of a new humanity. His sufferings manifested the character of God and of man's rebellion. The cross is an open vindication of the holiness and truth of God. God was pleased with the sufferings of Christ because they exhibited the triumph over the powers of evil. The gospel is the declaration of the truth that the human race is pardoned in Christ.

The influence of Erskine and Coleridge upon John McLeod Campbell (1800–1872) was very pronounced. In 1831 he was removed from office in the Church of Scotland for his heretical concept of the atonement. Campbell went beyond a moral view of the cross and regarded Christ's death as an expiatory confession of the sin of mankind. This Campbell calls the "retrospective" aspect of the atonement. He also lays great stress on the "prospective" aspect of the work of Christ. Just as Christ is the "revealer of the Father," so is he the "revealer of man," disclosing the "inestimable preciousness which was hidden in humanity" and imparting to it that same attitude, the holiness and love of God, which was realized in his own sacrifice.[2]

In its "prospective" aspect the fundamental agreement of Campbell's view with the theories of Schleiermacher and Ritschl is very obvious, while in its "retrospective" aspect it offers a point of contact with Jonathan Edwards, who had advanced the thought that a perfect repentance on man's part would have sufficed to satisfy for sin. Christ's work is that of vicarious penitence, not of vicarious punishment. Later this line of thought was further developed by R. C. Moberly.

The General Assembly of 1831 not only deposed Campbell but also took action against the eschatological fancies of Edward Irving (1792–1834). Irving was never a real thinker, but is remembered as the founder and one of the "angels" of the Catholic-Apostolic church.

[2] J. M. Campbell, *Nature of the Atonement* (2nd ed.; New York: The Macmillan Company, 1867), pp. 135, 160.

At the time of the liberal movement a fresh evangelical life began to make itself felt in the Church of Scotland. Thomas Chalmers (1780–1847), a great churchman, worked along ecclesiastical rather than theological lines. He was a great orator of the Evangelical school. He shared many of the views of his friend Erskine. Chalmers was instrumental in regaining for the Evangelicals the leadership and prestige which had been lost to the moderate wing which was led by F. W. Robertson and Principal Hill. In 1813 Chalmers published a well-known paper on Christianity in the *Edinburgh Encyclopedia* in which he denounced the ability of natural reason to judge the revelation given in Christianity. Reason might have a say about external evidences of Christianity, but not about internal evidences. The article was severely criticized by Duncan Mearns of Aberdeen, who replied that religion must meet the rational needs of man before it can be accepted as divine.[3]

Chalmers is remembered chiefly as the father of modern social missions. In Glasgow he reorganized the parochial system in order to reclaim the destitute and social outcasts. Placing emphasis on the responsibility of the Christian community, he circumvented the idea of the welfare state. He carried out an extensive program of Church extension on a voluntary principle. When in 1843 the government refused to endorse the veto law, opposing the legal exercise of patronage, Chalmers withdrew from the Establishment, followed by some two hundred ministers, and founded the Free Church of Scotland.[4]

The true interpreter of the mind of Scotland as well as of the differences between the new and the old theology was Andrew Thompson (1779–1831). He was a most zealous defender of traditional orthodoxy in the Scottish church.

A book that brought unrest into the orthodoxy of Scottish Cavinism was *The True Plan of a Living Temple* published in 1830. It was anti-Calvinistic and stressed the inherent goodness in the world and the individual. The function of Christianity, it affirmed, is to reinforce the good against the evil, displacing the rule of evil with a divine kingdom and extending the happiness of men. When it was

[3] Cf. Tulloch, *Movements of Religious Thought . . .*, p. 135.

[4] Chalmer's *Works* were edited in 25 vols. in 1848 ff.; *Posthumous Works,* 9 vols. in 1847 ff.; and *The Memoirs of Thomas Chalmers,* 4 vols., in 1849 ff.

learned that Thomas Wright was its author, he was removed from his parish at Borthwick.[5]

The next decade, 1840–1850, was a momentous age for Scottish Presbyterianism. Opposition to the exercise of patronage led to the organization of the Free Church of Scotland in 1843. In May, 1841, the United Presbyterian Church was formed. This church body originated out of a merger between the United Secession Church of 1733 and the Relief Church of 1752. During this age Carlyle and John Stuart Mill were at the zenith of their influence.

The Burnett Lectures of Andrew Thompson and John Tulloch on theism appeared in 1855. Thompson's lectures set forth the compatibility of a progressive theory of creation with theism from the scientific standpoint. There is a connection between this and the famous work on *The Vestiges of Creation* (1844) by Robert Chambers. Thompson thought much remained to be done before a theory of development could be "applied to living beings." He did not know that Darwin's *The Origin of Species* woud appear in 1859.

William Robertson Smith published his article on the Bible in the *Encyclopedia Britannica* in 1876. He endorsed the position of Wellhausen and as a result was removed from his professorship in the free church college at Aberdeen (1881). Smith's attempt to introduce Wellhausen to the English-speaking world prompted statesmen, bishops, professors, and moderators to speak out against him.[6]

The greatest apologist of the times was Alexander B. Bruce (1831–1899). In 1874 this Glasgow theologian wrote *The Humiliation of Christ in Its Physical, Ethical, and Soteriological Aspects.* Bruce accepts the view of the Erlangen theologian Hofmann that when Christ became man he felt in himself the effects of the divine wrath though he, because of His relation to God, was not the object of that wrath. The value of the sacrifice of Christ was equal to his divine dignity and multiplied by his perfect obedience, his boundless love, and his sufferings. Later Bruce wrote his great work *Apologetics* (1902). *The Training of the Twelve* (1871) is also significant and has gone through several editions.

At the close of the nineteenth century John Tulloch (1823–1886),

[5] For details, cf. Tulloch, *Movements of Religious Thought . . .*, pp. 163 ff.
[6] Cf. Vollrath, *op. cit.*, pp. 48 ff.

John Cunningham (1819–1893), George Matheson (1842–1906), and Robert Flint (1838–1910) held the leadership of thought in the established Church of Scotland and contributed to a liberalization of Scottish Calvinism. The principal work of Tulloch is *Rational Theology and Christian Philosophy in England in the Seventeenth Century* (2 vols., 1872). Matheson wrote *Studies on the Portrait of Christ* (2 vols., 1899–1900), of which 11,000 copies were sold within one year. Flint, who wrote *Theism and Antitheistic Theories* (1877) and *Agnosticism* (1903), opposed the prevailing agnostic interpretation of Kant, holding that agnosticism is not a corollary of Kantian criticism.

In 1894 Otto Pfleiderer, the liberal Hegelian and persistent critic of agnostic tendencies in Ritschlianism, delivered the Gifford Lectures on *Philosophy and Development of Religion*, in which he eliminated the supernatural from Christianity. These lectures met with the protest of three of the free church theologians: Robert Rainy, James Orr, and Marcus Dods. Orr also stated that Ritschlian theology was radically unsound.[7]

Some independent theological influence developed outside the three great Presbyterian bodies. Chief among these was the Arminian Evangelical Union under the leadership of John Morison. Scottish Congregationalism was ably presented by such men as Ralph Wardlaw and W. L. Alexander.

BIBLIOGRAPHY

CAMPBELL, J. M. *The Nature of the Atonement.* 4th ed. Edited by E. P. DICKIE. London: J. Clarke, 1959.

OLIPHANT, M. O. *Thomas Chalmers, Preacher, Philosopher, and Statesman.* Boston: Houghton Miffiin Co., 1893.

ORR, JAMES. *The Ritschlian Theology and the Evangelical Faith.* New York: Whittaker, 1898.

RAINY, ROBERT, *et al. The Supernatural in Religion.* Edinburgh: T. & T. Clark, 1894.

WATT, HUGH. *Thomas Chalmers and the Disruption.* Edinburgh: T. Nelson & Sons, 1943.

[7] James Orr, *Ritschlianism, Expository and Critical Essays* (London: Hodder & Stoughton, 1903), p. vii.

CHAPTER VII

NONCONFORMIST THEOLOGY

Congregational Theology

Congregationalist theologians have not been cloistered academics but pastors with a wide knowledge of human nature. Their emphasis on subjective experience made them more receptive to the new learning than either Anglicans or Presbyterians. This is true of the other Nonconformist groups.

The first Congregational theologian to teach a purely governmental view of the atonement was Edward Williams (1750–1813). He was minister of Carr's Lane Church, Birmingham, and afterwards tutor at Rotherham College. His work on *The Cross of Christ*, published in 1792, was the first attempt to reconcile the Calvinistic doctrine of the absoluteness of the divine decrees with divine justice. He also made it plain that God does not will evil when He elects man to reprobation.

The rigid Calvinism of the Scottish church prompted Ralph Wardlaw (1779–1853) to join the Congregational church. He influenced thought on both sides, in Scotland as well as Engand. His work *The Extent of the Atonement and Universal Pardon* (1830) was along the same lines as that of Edward Williams. His view of the atonement was also governmental, and he too retained the view of election to reprobation and the decrees of God.

The first significant voice raised against Calvinism in Scotland was that of John Kirk, Congregational minister of Hamilton. In 1842 he published *The Way of Life Made Plain*, in which he maintained the thesis that Jesus Christ died for every man, and that the Spirit of God is inclusive not exclusive. The saved are those who yield to God, and the unsaved are those who do not yield. This caused much trouble, and a number of ministers were expelled from the Congregational Union. Under the leadership of James Morison, they united to form the Evangelical Union.

In 1818 John Pye Smith (1774-1851), tutor at Homerton College, published *The Scripture Testimony to the Messiah* (4 vols.), in which he undertook to defend the divinity of Jesus against the English Unitarians and the German Rationalists. He had a sound knowledge of natural science. In 1839 he delivered a series of lectures in which he attempted to effect a compromise between the Scriptures and science.

Among the older generation of English Congregationalists in whom latitudinarian tendencies were more manifest were such men as George Payne, Henry Rogers, a friend of Whately who was equally opposed to the Tractarians as well as to the rising tide of skepticism, and James B. Brown. Samuel Davidson (1807–1898) was more outspoken in his liberal views on the inspiration of Scripture. This cost him his position in Lancashire College. The greatest figure among Congregational preachers at that time was Robert William Dale (1829–1895). His contribution to theology is his anti-Calvinistic volume on *The Atonement* (1875). Dale was not satisfied with the moral influence interpretation of the atonement, but he stopped short of penal substitution. Dale held that it was God himself who suffered in the agonies of Christ.

The outstanding Congregational scholar in the nineteenth century was Andrew Martin Fairbairn (1838–1912). Schooled at Edinburgh under Morison, he later studied in Germany, where the scholarship, especially the mediating theology of Dorner, was more to his liking. He was principal of Manchester College, Oxford, from 1886 to 1909.

Fairbairn's position is essentially christocentric. At a time when German theology was almost completely occupied in the quest of the historical Jesus, Fairbairn and other English scholars were at work restating christological dogma. Like most of his contemporaries in England and Germany, Fairbairn held to the kenotic view. He also combined the speculative and the ethical. For him the trinitarian dogma represents the highest achievement of speculative intuition. The Deity as God is an object of natural knowledge; the Deity as the Godhead is the subject of supernatural revelation.

Unitarian Theology

English Unitarians differed considerably from their more radical American brethren. The biblical tenets of Socinianism were still very pronounced. The founder of the Unitarian Society (1791) was Thomas Belsham (d. 1829). In his view of Jesus he had moved from Arianism to Socinianism. The *Inquirer* was the literary organ of the Society. In its early years the Society was influenced by Joseph Priestly (d. 1804) as well as by Belsham. These men represent the first stage of Unitarian theology. Its fundamental tenets were: belief in the unipersonality of God, human determinism, utilitarian ethics, and the religious authority of the Bible. These older Unitarians meant to teach the doctrine of the New Testament. They would have been Trinitarians if they could have found any trinitarian doctrine in the New Testament. They believed in the inspiration of the Scriptures, miracles, and in the resurrection of Jesus. The second stage of Unitarian theology, under the influence of William Ellery Channing, proclaimed human freedom with the zeal of the Evangelicals. During this stage Unitarian theologians stressed the ethical side of religion rather than the iron necessities of nature. The third stage was ushered in by the greatest Unitarian scholar, James Martineau, and in this stage we have the religion of the human spirit.

James Martineau's (1805–1900) thinking was influenced by Locke, Hartley, Collins, Edwards, Priestly, Bentham, and Mill until 1834. He clashed with utilitarianism and began to emphasize the importance of motive rather than of consequences. This was brought about not by reading but by reflection on his own inner experience. He came to believe in the freedom of the will and in the intuitive faculties of the soul. Like Kant, he found the significance of the religious life in the conscience, and duty was a divine concept for him. Will rather than intellect was the basic element of his theology. He taught a philosophical theism. God is eternal will and the sole cause of the universe. In Christology, Martineau drifted from Arianism to complete humanitarianism. Jesus is but one of the many explorers of religious truth. There is no supernatural divine revelation. Revelation is from within and not from without. Man is a rational, moral, and spiritual being, and free to choose the good. Martineau accepted the critical conclusions of the Tübingen school on the New Testament canon. His main works are *A Study of Spinoza* (1882), *Types of Ethical Theory* (1885), *Study of Religion* (1888), *Seat of Authority in Religion* (1890), and *Essayes, Reviews, and Addresses* (1890 ff.).

Moore calls attention to a striking parallel between Martineau and Newman. Both busied themselves with the question of religious authority, and since criticism was fatal to both concerning the view of the Scriptures, Newman turned to find that authority in an infallible Church, while Martineau embraced the principle of an inward authority of the religious personality.[1]

METHODIST THEOLOGY

The Methodist theologians remained true to their semi-Augustinian heritage during the greater part of the nineteenth century. The first great scholar of this period was Richard Watson (1781–1833), who edited *The Liverpool Courier* (1808) and wrote *Remarks on the Eternal Sonship of Christ* (1818) against Adam Clarke. He published his *Theological Institutes* in 1823. For many years this was the standard work of Wesleyan theology. Watson was an exponent of a strictly supernatural rationalism. He distinguished between external and internal evidence. The former was primary in his thinking and he appealed to miracles and prophecy as the absolute evidence of divine revelation. Internal evidence is a mere impression of truth and therefore cannot be distinguished from any other discovery of the human intellect. Internal evidence can have no authority.

William Burt Pope (1822–1903) was the first to write from the standpoint of modern theological science. In 1867 he became professor of systematic theology at Didsbury College, Manchester. His *Compendium of Christian Theology* (3 vols., 1875 ff.) is a scholarly exposition of Christian doctrine from the Methodist point of view. Though he gave a larger place to the self-evidencing power of experience than Watson, his viewpoint also was essentially rational.

Other names of renown are those of Thomas Coke, Henry Moore, Joseph Benson, Robert Newton, William Arthur, John Telford, and John Shaw Barks.[2]

BAPTIST THEOLOGY

Baptist theology in the nineteenth century was represented by John Foster (1770–1843). Although a predestinarian at heart, he contended

[1] Moore, *op. cit.*, p. 235.

[2] For orientation see Dean Knudson's article on Methodist theology in the *Methodist Review*, March, 1925.

against the teaching of eternal punishment. Arian tendencies are noticeable in his Christology. The tenets of Coleridge are likewise manifest. John Howard Hinton (d. 1863) was an Evangelical but receptive to broad church influences. His writings include *Harmony of Religious Truth and Human Reason.* Under John Clifford (1836–1923), doctrinal tolerance gained a foothold in the Baptist Union. When Clifford succeeded in keeping the Union from commitment on such doctrines as the infallibility of inspiration, vicarious atonement, and eternal punishment for the unconverted, Spurgeon, along with his followers, withdrew from the Union. Outstanding among the leaders of the liberal wing were Thomas W. Davies, John T. Marshall, and Newton H. Marshall.

BIBLIOGRAPHY

ARMSTRONG, R. A. *Martineau's Study of Religion.* London: J. Clarke & Co., 1900.

CARPENTER, J. E. *James Martineau.* London: P. Green, 1905.

CLIFFORD, JOHN. *The Gospel of Gladness.* Edinburgh: T. & T. Clark, 1912.

FAIRBAIRN, A. M. *Studies in the Philosophy of Religion and History.* New York: Lovell, Adam, Wesson, 1876.

———. *The Place of Christ in Modern Theology.* London: Hodder & Stoughton, 1902.

———. *The Philosophy of the Christian Religion.* New York: The Macmillan Company, 1910.

SELBIE, W. B. *Congregationalism.* London: Methuen, 1927.

———. *The Life of A. M. Fairbairn.* London: Hodder & Stoughton, 1914.

CHAPTER VIII

THEOLOGICAL DEVELOPMENT IN THE ANGLICAN CHURCH 1860-1900

After 1860 the Oxford Movement went under the name of ritualism. The ritualistic aspect almost inevitably grew out of the teachings, of the Oxford Movement, although Pusey was never in favor of it. Samuel Wilberforce stressed the sacrificial aspect of the Eucharist, and Keble, in his book *on Eucharistical Adoration*, published in 1857, defended the adoration of Christ in the sacramental elements. Pusey taught sacramental confession and others followed him as is witnessed by the book *The Priest in Absolution*, published anonymously in 1877.

The leading men of the Oxford party at this time were Pusey, Mozley, Church, and Liddon. James B. Mozley (1813–1878) agreed with the predestinarianism of Augustine, and was at odds with his party concerning the doctrine of baptismal regeneration, which he did not accept. He wrote *Augustinian Doctrine of Predestination* (1855) and *Essays Historical and Theological* (1859). Richard William Church (1815–1890) is the classic historian of the Oxford Movement. Henry Perry Liddon's (1829–1890) influence was due to his oratory and pulpit eloquence. His conservatism is evident in his defense of the continued use of the Athanasian Creed.

Apart from the Oxford men there was another group of scholars who, though they were loyal to the Anglican church, showed little interest in the characteristic traits of the Oxford theology. This group included such biblical scholars as F. B. Westcott (1825–1901), T. B. Lightfoot (1828–1889), and F. J. R. Hort (1828–1892). All three served on the committee for the revision of the King James Bible. Hort and Lightfoot, with I. E. B. Major, founded the *Journal of Classical and Sacred Philology* in 1854. Lightfoot's commentaries in the field of New Testament interpretation are well known. Westcott and Hort gained international recognition for their edition of the Greek New Testament.

In 1889 *Lux Mundi* was published. This volume is a landmark in Anglican theology. It was a sober attempt to reconcile the conservative element that came from Newman through Church and the liberal stream that came from Coleridge and Maurice through Westcott and Hort. The twelve essays of the volume move somewhat along the line of the older Erlangen school in that they seek to teach the old truth in a new garb and to harmonize the new learning with the faith of the fathers. Unlike the authors of *Essays and Reviews,* these writers had a dogmatic basis and displayed a genuine appreciation of the historic creeds of the church. *Lux Mundi* has more or less affected every Anglican treatise written since 1889. When the book appeared it caused even more comment than *Essays and Reviews,* for it was written at the very center where Froude, Newman, and Pusey had reigned.

The essay that startled the Anglican world most was the one written by the editor, Charles Gore, "The Holy Spirit and Inspiration." Gore makes revelation a historical process. The biblical records, though they are broadly correct, lack historical preciseness in detail. The Pentateuch, for example, contains much material which is post-Mosaic. The books of Jonah and Daniel are dramatic compositions presented as history. Our Lord's reference to Jonah and his apparent assumption of the Davidic authorship of Psalm 110 should not be regarded as a scientific solution to the literary problem. Because he held the kenotic theory of the incarnation, Gore believed that the historical Jesus was not omniscient in things temporal. To draw the line between the human and the divine in the Bible, the author distinguishes what God revealed from what God used:

> He [Jesus] revealed God, His mind, His character, His claim, and within certain limits His Threefold Being. He revealed man, his sinfulness, his need, his capacity. He revealed His purpose of redemption and founded His church as a home in which man was to be through all ages reconciled to God in knowledge and love. All this He revealed, but through and under conditions of a true human nature. Thus He

used human nature, its relation to God, its condition of experience, its growth in knowledge, its limitation of knowledge.[1]

The development of the broad church party up to the twentieth century can be sketched briefly. Benjamin Jowett (1817–1893) took the lead in Great Britain in the field of biblical criticism. In 1855 he published *The Epistles of St. Paul to the Thessalonians, Galatians, and Romans, with Critical Notes and Dissertations.* In this volume Jowett introduced the critical views of Baur to the English reading public. Jowett himself took a mediating position. While Baur had seen a complete disharmony between Paul and the older Church, Jowett held that while there was not complete harmony, neither was there an absolute antagonism between the two.

Among the leading biblical scholars were Samuel R. Driver (1846–1914) and Thomas K. Cheyne (1841–1915) in the field of the Old Testament; and William Sanday (1843–1920), and Frederick C. Conybeare (1856–1924) in the area of New Testament literature and criticism. Cheyne gained renown as editor of Armenian texts. The two theologians Edwin Hatch (1835–1889) and Henry A. Redpatch (1848–1908), authors of the famous *Concordance to the Septuagint* (1891 ff.), deserve special mention. The initiative of this group of scholars produced *The International Critical Commentary*.

That biblical criticism was coming to its own in the English church is shown in the case of John W. Colenso (1814–1883), missionary bishop in Natal. In his book entitled *The Pentateuch and the Book of Joshua Critically Examined* (1862), Colenso showed the composite character of these writings, questioned the historical and scientific accuracy of the biblical narrative, and also questioned the Mosaic authorship of the Pentateuch. He was condemned by both Houses of Convocation of the Province of Canterbury, although the condemnation was nullified in 1865 by action of the secular court, the Privy Council.

In 1874 the three-volume work *Supernatural Religion*, appeared, a book against the supernatural and miraculous in Christianity. Miracle is explained on psychological grounds and on the ground of the unreliability of human testimony. The apostolic authorship of the canonical Gospels is denied. Acts is held to be a legendary composi-

[1] Charles Gore *et al., Lux Mundi* (London: John Murray, 1904), pp. 300 ff.

tion of late date. In short, *Supernatural Religion* was a historical criticism of Christianity followed by an attempt to prove that it has no better foundation than any other religion. "Never before had such a systematic attack, based upon solid learning, been made in English upon the external evidences of the Christian religion, which still continue to hold a foremost place, not merely in the popular, but also in the theological apologetics of England (Mansel, Newman, Mozley)." [2]

Another outstanding force in the theological world in the last quarter of the nineteenth century was Frederick William Farrar (1831–1903). Through the influence of Maurice he was led to study Coleridge, whose writings profoundly influenced his faith and opinions. As a theologian he occupied a mediating position between the broad church party and the Evangelical party. He gained his place in the theological world through two volumes, *Eternal Hope* (1878) and *Mercy and Judgment* (1881), in which he contended that, though there may be an endless hell for some because they resist the grace of God beyond the grave, there is no hell of material fire, and through God's mercy and Christ's sacrifice, a complete purification and salvation will be obtained for the great majority.

The Evangelical party made no great theological contribution except the work of Handley C. G. Moule (1841–1921), professor of divinity at Cambridge and Bishop of Durham. His devotional and expository writings, *The Epistle of Paul to the Romans* (1894), *Ephesian Studies* (1900), and *Christus Consolator* (1915), reflect the position of the Evangelical party of this period.

BIBLIOGRAPHY

GORE, CHARLES, *et al. Lux Mundi.* London: John Murray, 1904.

[2] Pfleiderer, *op. cit.*, p. 397.

CHAPTER IX

THEOLOGICAL MOVEMENTS IN THE TWENTIETH CENTURY IN THE LIBERAL, PROTESTANT, AND CATHOLIC TRADITIONS

With the beginning of the twentieth century there was a gradual dissolution of theological schools and parties in Great Britain, as well as in Germany. The scholars of the conservative wing learned to respect and utilize many of the historico-critical tenets of the liberal schools, and—due to the disastrous results of World War I—many of the liberal theologians, turning against the naive and optimistic evolutionism and immanentism of pre-war theology, recaptured a deeper appreciation of the religious values of biblical Christianity.

It is best to disregard completely the old party labels such as high, low, and broad, for a twentieth-century high churchman may be a liberal with respect to his method, his views on inspiration, and his views on the beginnings of Christianity, while in turn a liberal may have a genuine understanding of the sinfulness of man and his need for redemption. With the exception of the Unitarians, theological liberalism in England never crystallized into a real party or denomination. The liberals had always been theological free lances. They tilted their shafts against each other as often as against their high or low church opponents. A much clearer conception of the present-day situation in England can be gained by tracing the Catholic, Protestant, and liberal traditions in English theology.

In this process of rethinking and restating religion and theology, the moderation of the English again stands out in contrast to the radicalism of German and even of American theology. English liberalism is less radical than the naturalistic theology of Germany and

America, and the postwar reaction against liberalism is likewise less radical than Continental Barthianism. The Socinian emphasis on the historical in Christianity exercised a check on some of the modernists. Such radicals as Major and Cadoux have a higher regard for the person of Jesus than Troeltsch and his school on the Continent.

What is true of England also applies to Scotland. Traditionalism and liberalism both have contributed to mold the thought of the younger theologians in the Presbyterian church which, with the exception of the small dissenting minority, became reunited in 1929.

English Liberalism

On the one hand liberalism in England grew out of eighteenth-century deism and moralism, crystallizing in Unitarianism; on the other hand, it is an offshoot of that broad or liberal church group beginning with Coleridge and the authors of *Essays and Reviews*. The difference between the broad church basis and the present movement is admirably expressed by Major in these words:

> The tendency of the older English Broad Churchmanship or Liberalism was to be rationalistic and *a priori*, individualistic and negative, unemotional and undevotional, unsacramental and anti-ecclesiastical, Erastian and academic. It regarded Christianity as a religion of illumination and good conduct. Its approach to Christianity was philosophical or ethical rather than religious and mystical. The tendency of Modernism is scientific and historical; its ideal of religion is mystical and social.[1]

The last two adjectives aptly indicate the point on which the English modernism differs from the German. In Germany, modernism was academic, intellectual and individualistic, for such men as Naumann, Geyer, and Rittelmeyer were theological outsiders. Prior to World War I the modernist controversy in Great Britain revolved about the concept of God and issued in a reaffirmation of divine transcendence. After 1918 the conflict was chiefly concerned with the problem of evil and issued in a new emphasis on the suffering love of God.

At the beginning of our century six Oxford scholars jointly produced the volume known as *Contentio Veritatis*.[2] In this volume we find a broad or liberal church theology again at home in Oxford.

[1] H. D. A. Major, *English Modernism* (Cambridge: Harvard Univ. Press, 1927), p. 37.

[2] William R. Inge *et al.*, *Contentio Veritatis* (London, 1902).

Outstanding among the various contributions are the two essays by Dean Inge on the person of Christ and on the sacraments. In 1905 H. B. Swete published a volume of fourteen essays of which he said:

> The purpose of the book will have been gained if, taken as a whole, it is judged to have set forward what is perhaps the most important work that lies before the theology of the twentieth century; if it has helped to assimilate the new views of truth suggested by modern knowledge without sacrificing any part of the primitive message, and to state in terms adapted to the needs of a new century the truths which the Ancient Church expressed in those which were appropriate for its own times.[3]

The tenor of the book is that of a mediating theology. Among the contributors we find the names of F. R. Tennant and F. J. Foakes-Jackson, whose essay "Christ in the Church: The Testimony of History" repudiates the narrow christocentric and anti-metaphysical theology of Ritschl and Harnack.

In the *London Theological Studies* each of the six theological schools of the University of London is represented and each of the principal parts of theological curriculum has some share of attention. Outstanding among the essays are the discussions of the christological problem by H. T. Andrews and P. T. Forsyth. The latter states, in opposition to the Ritschlian tendencies of that age, that "we do not continue to get the Christian ethic or the Christian philanthropy without the Christian creed."[4] Andrews tries to distinguish between the transitory and the permanent in the eschatological sayings of Jesus. The Lord, due to the kenotic implications of the incarnation, "did not possess the necessary historical perspective to predict a continuous event, spread over many centuries, in the history of the church."[5] "No Parousia happened or will happen in the manner in which Jesus foretold it; yet, says he, the parousia utterances retain their significance for the modern mind: "They illustrate the indestructibility of the Christian hope. . . . They imply a transcendental conception of the Person of Christ by portraying Him as Lord of the future, seated

[3] H. B. Swete, *Essays on Some Theological Questions of the Day by Members of the University of Cambridge* (New York: The Macmillan Company, 1905), p. x.

[4] *London Theological Studies* (London: 1911), p. 137.

[5] *Ibid.*, p. 87.

at the right hand of God and swaying the destinies of the human race. And finally, they teach us that the Kingdom of God must come from God and cannot be evolved from man." [6]

In 1912 B. H. Streeter (d. 1937), in co-operation with Oxford scholars Brook, Moberly, Parsons, Rawlinson, Talbot, and Temple, published the volume *Foundations: a Statement of Christian Belief in Terms of Modern Thought*. The book holds to a mediating theology. The writers take a psychological approach. Dismissing as untenable the idea both of an infallible Book and of an infallible Church, they base religious authority on the corporate experience of the Church. The writers, especially Moberly, were aware that the current idealistic liberalism was too naively optimistic; but Moberly defended the view of God as the Absolute as philosophically irrefutable and as the most religious view of God that had ever been devised. Yet in 1926, Streeter, in his volume *Reality*, recanted absolute idealism, conceiving of God as a personal life force. His interest in the Oxford Movement is reflected in his volume, *The God Who Speaks* (1936), in which he argues that under certain conditioning circumstances, the voice within can be regarded as authentic communication from God.

Strictly speaking, all four of these composite volumes are critical rather than liberal. The uniqueness of the Christian message remains unabated; all writers hold to a theistic or supernatural interpretation of Christianity. The dissensus of opinion from the older theology is pronounced chiefly in the field of biblical criticism and on those concepts which have a bearing on the origin and evolution of man.

The liberal tendency of the early years of the twentieth century found its climax in the modernist controversy which stirred the minds of Protestant and Roman Catholic theologians alike. Its most significant Protestant exponent was the then Congregational theologian, R. J. Campbell. At that time Campbell held to views of absolute idealism and extreme immanentism. To him evil was nonbeing; the devil, a vacuum; sin, a mistake which is in itself a quest for God, albeit a blundering quest. He was expelled from the National Free Church Council. As time went on, Campbell underwent a thorough spiritual transformation. His optimistic belief in immanence and progress received a severe shock from the extreme and radical position revealed

[6] *Ibid.*, pp. 91, 94 ff.

in the christological controversy over Tyrell's posthumous work, *Christianity at the Cross Roads* (1910). Influenced by von Huegel's strong vein of transcendentalism and by the sympathetic attitude of Bishop Gore expressed in his *The New Theology and the Old Religion* (1907), Campbell joined the Church of England and was reordained to the priesthood in 1916.

The years of World War I are the landmark which separate us from the nineteenth century. Immanentism and evolution are really nineteenth-century problems. The war shattered the optimism of most thinking men. Men asked how the horrors and injustice of war could be reconciled with the idea of human progress and of an all-loving and almighty God. The religious concern of the postwar period centered in the problems of evil and of the suffering love of God.

G. A. Studdert-Kennedy (1877–1929) addressed himself to this problem. His message is couched in unconventional language. Evil, he said, is the most insoluble problem; it is "not rational and cannot be explained. God did not will it, that we are certain of, and our business is not to explain it but to destroy it." [7] He disliked the concept of God as an oriental despot "upon a throne, calm, serene, and passionless, ruling the world with a wave of the hand." [8] To him such a God was the devil in disguise, an "Almighty Cat":

> Almighty Cat, it sits on the throne of the world,
> With paw outstretched, grinning at us, the mice
> Who play our trivial games of virtue and vice
> and pray—to that which sits on the throne of
> the world.[9]

Kennedy took refuge from the trials of life in the thought that upon the cross there is revealed the "suffering" of God, not only God's "sympathies." [10] It was the mission of Jesus to blend the agelong creative discord of the universe into the unity of a new creation by revealing "a perpetually creative God travailing to bring to birth a

[7] *The New Man in Christ* (London: Hodder & Stoughton, 1932), p. 72.

[8] *The Hardest Part* (London: Hodder & Stoughton, 1918), p. 149.

[9] *The Warrior, the Woman, and the Christ* (Garden City: Doubleday, Doran, 1929), p. 194.

[10] Cf. *The Sorrows of God, and Other Poems* (New York: George H. Doran, 1924).

new heaven and a new earth." [11] The eternal God became the "comrade God" and Kennedy, amidst the great agony of life, became a "rebel for God," and not, like others, a rebel against God.[12]

According to Horton, "Next to the World War, von Huegel's influence is the greatest single cause to which the decline of pre-war immanentism can be ascribed." [13] Friedrich von Huegel (1852–1925), a German baron who spent most of his life in England, was perhaps the most prominent Roman lay theologian of recent times. As a student of Oxford theologians W. G. Ward and J. H. Newman, and of such German critical scholars as Gustav Bickell, an Orientalist and convert to Roman Catholicism, and H. J. Holtzmann, an adherent of the Tübingen school, von Huegel exercised a great influence not only on the Catholic modernists in England and France, but also on such men as Söderblom, Troeltsch, and Heiler. Heiler calls von Huegel's theology a "classical example of Catholic universality, synthesis and balance." [14] Von Huegel's thought revolved around three main ideas: The transcendence of God, the insufficiency of all dogmatic formulas to define the Absolute, and the incarnation as the process in which the Eternal and Infinite descends into finite space, time and history, and into the institutional and sacramental. His works include *Eternal Life* (1912), *Essays and Addresses on the Philosophy of Religion* (2 vols., 1921, 1926), and others.

The pioneer work in the revival of mysticism had been done by J. R. Illingworth (d. 19155) and W. R. Inge, who later became known as the "Gloomy Dean." Influenced perhaps by William James's *Varieties of Religious Experience* (1892), they tried to reconcile the traditional Anglican consciousness of religious growth with the Evangelical emphasis on conversion.

In 1899 when Inge delivered the Bampton Lectures he chose as his subject Christian mysticism. For a long time no Anglican scholar had seriously explored the field of mysticism. Inge presented an incarnational religion that could use the presence of the eternal Word in the man Jesus as a key to unlock the mystery not only of religion but also of human personality and of the universe. Due to Inge's bold

[11] *The Warrior . . .*, p. 124.
[12] *Ibid.*, p. 194.
[13] Horton, *op. cit.*, p. 44.
[14] *Religion in Geschichte und Gegenwart* (2nd ed.), II, 2034.

step, the mystic writers, both ancient and medieval, have received considerable attention from Anglicanism. The Anglican writer *par excellence* on mysticism was Evelyn Underhill (d. 1941). Her writings attracted the attention of many. Her book *Mysticism, a Study in the Nature and Development of Man's Spiritual Consciousness,* first published in 1911, went through many subsequent editions. Although the utilitarian and pragmatic interpretation of English life and thought at the turn of the century was hostile to the revival of mysticism, mysticism had a strong ally in philosophical idealism. As a matter of fact, Inge preferred to be known as a "Christian Platonist." The tragedy of our age is not belief in the objective world of science, but disbelief in the objective reality of ideal values. The constructive task which lies before us, Inge says, is "to spiritualize science." "The vision of God should appear to us as a triple star of truth, beauty and goodness. These are the three objects of all human aspiration; and our hearts will never be at peace till all three alike rest in God." [15]

In sharp contrast to the mystic approach to reality, F. R. Tennant (d. 1957) represents the scientific type of liberalism. Tennant worked out an elaborate epistomological theory in the first volume of his *magnum opus Philosophical Theology,* subtitled *The Soul and Its Faculties* (1928). Not only must theology conform with the results of science; its method, too, must be reasonable. Theology is the pursuit of a "once-born" person. There is no such thing as a "religious sixth sense," as mysticism claims, by which man arrives at extraordinary knowledge. As physical science can be expounded "atheously" so must the theological order of recognition be interpreted.[16] It may be reinterpreted theistically only when the theistic world view has been established. Of all theories of knowledge, phenomenalism corresponds most clearly to psychological facts. But Kant's phenomenalism needs correction, since he held that the mind shapes the cosmos by imposing its categories on the formless matter perceived by the senses. According to Tennant, the thing in itself must be credited with far more responsibility. Though the *sensum* or percept is not identical with the thing in itself, and though we have acquaintance

[15] William R. Inge, *Christian Mysticism* (New York: Charles Scribner's Sons), pp. 322 ff.

[16] F. R. Tennant, *Philosophical Theology* (Cambridge: Cambridge University Press, 1956), I, 328.

only with the sensible or phenomenal, "we are having rapport with, and phenomenal knowledge of or about, the noumenal." [17] Scientific theology is a rational science. Tennant evidently enters into the heritage of eighteenth-century natural theology. Horton calls his theory of knowledge a kind of modernized version of Locke's *Essay on Human Understanding*, influenced by the skepticism of Hume and the criticism of Kant, and deeply indebted to the psychological principles of James Ward.[18]

In the second volume, subtitled *The World, the Soul, and God*, Tennant enters upon a discussion of the conclusions which emerge from his principles. He admits that knowledge of God is not given directly like knowledge of the world and self. The idea of God is needed only when it can be shown that nature and man cannot be explained without it. Nature is suggestive of design. The world-ground is characterized by moral intelligence. It is the teleological argument which, in the eyes of Tennant, has the most persuasion. The inter-adaptiveness of all the facts of the cosmos, including the moral life of man, presents an overwhelming weight for the probability of theism. The power and love of God is limited by human freedom which may thwart the divine purpose. This theism may disown knowledge of Christ's being of one substance with the Father, but it may consider him the unique revealer of God in that he possessed the fullest insight into the divine purpose of the world. If reverence for Christ's person and acceptance of His teaching deserve the name of Christianity, "then Christianity may be said to be the climax of the historical development of natural religion, and the crown of natural theology." [19]

H. D. A. Major holds that unlike most American modernists, the English modernist sees the need of dogma but holds that dogma is developing. Experience comes first; doctrinal formulation second. The formulation of dogma must change its method of expression as new categories of thinking emerge. Spiritual dogmas like, God is love, light, truth, spirit; Jesus is the reflection of the invisible Father, the Word of God in human history, are "of supreme importance." [20]

[17] *Ibid.*, I, 247.
[18] Horton, *op. cit.*, p. 87.
[19] Tennant, *op. cit.*, II, 240.
[20] Major, *op. cit.*, p. 83.

Major goes on to speak of the historical dogmas and says, "Such dogmas as that Jesus was born of the Virgin Mary, was crucified, dead, and buried, etc., that He rose from the dead on the third day, these dogmas are of less importance to the Christian Religion than the first class of dogmas. The Christian Religion may survive without them." [21]

In general, it can be said that the English modernist proposes the following: (1) Concerning God, he combines the ideas of immanence and transcendence, and the doctrine of the Trinity, though it "is liable to be perverted into Tritheism," is "preferable to the old Unitarian doctrine." [22] (2) His attitude toward original sin is negative. Children should be baptized because they belong to God and have no original sin. (3) The idea of propitiatory sacrifice is thrown aside as a pagan doctrine. The English modernist accepts the moral influence theory of the atonement. (4) Belief in miracles is dismissed as a survival of a prescientific age. (5) As to eschatology, the Second Coming is rejected along with all the catastrophic elements of biblical eschatology. (6) The English modernist does not believe in everlasting punishment. (7) He rejects the infallibility of the Bible. The truth of the Bible is dependent on whether it meets the need of the human soul. (8) Revelation is not supernatural in the sense that it is extraordinary; but revelation comes because man's mind is naturally religious.[23]

English modernism lays down the following axioms about Jesus: (1) Christianity is Jesuanity. (2) The virgin birth is not necessary for the incarnation. (3) The incarnation is a higher form of divine immanence. (4) The incarnation and indwelling of the divine Logos in Jesus Christ and in us is a difference not of kind but of degree.[24]

The English modernist places a high value on the sacraments. "He interprets them both dramatically and mystically. Their reverent use in his experience unites him with past generations of fellow churchmen, and also provides him with an ideal means of communion with the spiritual world." [25]

[21] *Ibid.*, p. 85.
[22] *Ibid.*, p. 105.
[23] *Ibid.*, pp. 106 ff.
[24] *Ibid.*, pp. 139 ff.
[25] *Ibid.*, p. 35.

The position of Major is shared by Cecil John Cadoux in all the essentials, in his study, *The Case for Evangelical Modernism.*[26] The author is fully aware of the disfavor into which theological liberalism has fallen during his own time. He emphatically renounces all allegiance to any kind of a rational humanism. Liberal modernism means to him "that attitude to Christian doctrine which, taking due account of the occasional conflict between truth and tradition, rejects the customary identification of tradition and orthodoxy and sees the real test of orthodoxy (i.e., right belief) in truth." [27] "Whatever validity the traditional Christian doctrines possess they owe ultimately, not to their antiquity, nor to their ubiquity, nor even to their scripturality, but to their capacity to vindicate themselves to Christian hearts and minds as true." [28] In other words, Cadoux looks to reason and experience as the final test of religious truth. Over against a non-christocentric humanism, Barthianism, and traditionalism – which he calls the "three blind alleys" in contemporary theological thought–Cadoux believes that we draw nearer to the truth by keeping close to the gospel of the historical Jesus.

A modern historical picture of the Lord would, "in all probability," he says, be as follows: Jesus was the legally born son of Joseph and Mary, born at Nazareth, not at Bethlehem. He was not conscious of his being pre-existent with the Father, nor was he exempt from "unintentional imperfections." [29] He was not omniscient, nor did he "claim to forgive sins in His own right." The alleged nature miracles are ill attested, probably unhistorical. His physical body did not leave the grave, "nor can we think of it as having ascended into the sky." [30] On the other hand, we can be "historically sure that Jesus lived a life of unbroken, growing and intimate fellowship with God and of unstinted love for man. His ministry was shaped primarily with an eye to the moral and spiritual needs of Israel and the world at the particular junction in human history; but in being so perfectly adapted to them, it displayed then, and for all time will display, the universal

[26] Cecil John Cadoux, *The Case for Evangelical Modernism* (London: Hodder & Stoughton, 1939).

[27] *Ibid.*, p. 10.

[28] *Ibid.*, p. 16.

[29] *Ibid.*, p. 145.

[30] *Ibid.*, p. 154.

sweep of God's love and the eternal meaning of His will." [31] Jesus' divinity, Cadoux says, is to be explained by belief in "the divinity of the human race, as proclaimed by Him and in which He shared, by virtue of his moral excellence, in a unique way." Cadoux says that such a Jesus can still be the object of our worship. Worship is nothing but reverence for worth. "All that is worthy of our reverence, our adoration, our obedience, either is, or in some way embodies and represents, God." [32] To this picture of Jesus he adds the defiant statement: "And if anyone shall have said that to rest content with such a formula as this is virtually to deny our Lord's divinity and to abandon the Christian gospel, let him be anathema!" [33]

The foregoing liberalism in all its essentials is also shared by Canon Charles E. Raven of Cambridge. Raven, a theologian and trained scientist, is a monist. He contends, pantheistically, that God is revealed as much in creation and the secular realm of life as in the Scriptures and the Church.[34] After the World War II Raven reaffirmed his liberalism in his Gifford Lectures on *Natural Religion and Christian Theology*. He welcomes the revolution which is taking place in the realm of the physical sciences. Albert Einstein, Max Planck, Niels Bohr, and others have shown us that nature is not a closed system. This insight opens up new and unforeseen opportunities for a new dialogue between science and theology. Unfortunately, Raven says, the great theologians of our time have blocked the road to a mutual understanding. Barth, Aulén, Nygren, Maritain, Gilson, and Berdyaev, he maintains, have confined themselves to a re-examination and reaffirmation of the chief types of earlier evangelical theology.[35] A revival of "the ideas of the third or thirteenth or sixteenth centuries is hardly relevant to the scale and character of the changes demanded in the twentieth. Salvation can come only by applying the truth of the great liberal theologians such as Coleridge and Maurice in England or Rauschenbusch and Shailer Mathews in America. Creation ought

[31] *Ibid.*, p. 156.
[32] *Ibid.*, p. 161.
[33] *Ibid.*, p. 167.
[34] Cf. his writings *Jesus and the Gospel of Love* (New York: Henry Holt & Co., Inc., 1931), *Christian Socialism* (New York: The Macmillan Company, 1936) and *The Gospel and the Church* (London: Hodder & Stoughton, 1940).
[35] *Natural Religion and Christian Theology* (Cambridge: Cambridge University Press, 1951), I, 201.

to be understood not as an act but as a continuing evolution from atom and molecule to mammal and man. The Incarnation is to be understood as the continuous indwelling of the Spirit in the cosmic process, of which Christ is the true symbol and the perfect manifestation, because the Cross reveals the highest human values, i.e. suffering and redemptive love." [36]

Through Christ the Spirit produces universal *koinonia* in humanity and the Church. Reconciliation between Christianity and communism should be the most urgent concern of the Christian.[37] Raven is seconded by John MacMurray[38] of Edinburgh. A passionate communism, he says, is closer to God than an indolent Church, and God is revealed as much in the social passion of atheistic Marxism as in the dogma and ritual of the established church. The proper subject of religion is fellowship and community. The category of transcendence applies equally to God and man. To apply transcendence exclusively to God is a mistake, for the union of transcendence and immanence is characteristic of all personality.[39]

In *Honest to God* John A. T. Robinson has challenged what he believes ambiguous in the teaching of MacMurray. The category of transcendence ought to be dismissed. God is neither "up there" nor "out there." The category of depth defines the nature of God much better. God is the "ground of being" (Tillich). The necessity for retaining the name "God" lies in the fact that our being has a depth which naturalism cannot or will not recognize. In addition to Tillich, Robinson leans heavily on Bultmann and Bonhoeffer, especially on Bonhoeffer's statement that the truth of the gospel does not depend on a peculiar "religious" disposition of man. The world has come of age. It thinks it can get along perfectly well without "religion." "Ecstatic naturalism" (Tillich) is the only form in which the gospel can be understood by the modern man.

[36] *Ibid.*, I, 157.

[37] *Ibid.*, II, 167 ff. Cf. also C. E. Raven, *A Wanderer's Way* (London: M. Hopkinson & Son, Ltd., 1928), pp. 202 ff.

[38] Cf. MacMurray's writings on Marxism: *The Philosophy of Communism* (London: Faber & Faber, Ltd., 1933) and *Creative Society* (New York: Association Press, 1936).

[39] Cf. *The Structure of Religious Experience* (New Haven: Yale University Press, 1936); *The Self as Agent* (London: Faber & Faber, Ltd., 1951); *Persons in Relations* (New York: Harper & Bros., 1961).

Protestant Theology

The Keswick Movement,[40] as well as some able Evangelical Anglican, Nonconformist, and Scottish theologians, proves not only that the Protestant tradition is still alive, but that it occupies a dominant position in the life of the churches. Contemporary English Protestantism is a blend of the Evangelical and Nonconformist tradition. It is represented today by men of the low church tradition, by the Council of the Free Churches, and by the Presbyterian theologians of Scotland. While the orthodox Evangelicals of the nineteenth century contributed little to theological thought in England, a kind of liberal Evangelicalism which displays a keen interest in theology as a science is evident in our century. The same may be said of the theology of the Dissenters. Presbyterians or Congregationalists who still hold without qualification to the "Five Points of Calvinism" are rather exceptional. Among the Dissenters the gulf between Calvinism and Arminianism has been closing. Protestant forces have been drawn together in a common defense against the irreligious sentiment of our age and the bold inventions of the Anglo-Catholics.

Evangelical Anglicans

Among the prominent leaders of the Evangelical group in the Anglican communion are such theologians as V. F. Storr (d. 1940) and W. R. Matthews, the successor of Inge as Dean of St. Paul's. In co-operation with the Baptist scholar H. Wheeler Robinson (d. 1945), he edited a series of theological monographs, *The Library of Constructive Theology*. The literary productivity of this group has been commendable. The contributors include C. H. Dodd, O. C. Quick, H. R. Mackintosh, H. H. Farmer, and Evelyn Underhill. O. C. Quick's *The Christian Sacraments* shows how a theologian who is "low" as a churchman, "critical" in the study of the Bible, and "liberal" as to the metaphysical in Christianity approaches the problem of the sacramental in religion. The real presence is constituted by the efficacious relation of the glorified Lord to the sacramental elements. For "whatever is the organ of Christ's activity is, so far, His body."[41] Quick is

[40] Steven Barabas, *So Great Salvation: The History and Message of the Keswick Convention* (London: Marshal, Morgan, & Scott, 1952).

[41] O. C. Quick, *The Christian Sacraments* (New York: Harper & Bros., 1927), p. 209.

even willing to "accept the statement that the bread and wine are changed so as to become the Body and Blood of Christ, if it be understood that the terms body and blood denote, not material things as such, but outward things as they are in relation to a spiritual activity which operates and expresses itself through them." [42]

To W. R. Matthews religion is "one of the ways of 'coming to terms' with the Other by means of a special mode of interpretation." [43] "The main function of theology is to act as an intermediary between philosophy and religion." [44] The Christian doctrine of the Trinity, "springs from the Christian experience of God." [45] As to the person of Christ, there can be no doubt that for Paul "Christ has 'the value' of God." [45] In Christian experience man lays hold of metaphysical reality.[46]

In 1923 twelve Anglican scholars issued *Essays in Liberal Evangelicalism*, a theological manifesto by the younger Evangelicals. In the Preface they declare that the Bible "still stands in its unique position." But, they add, "it is the mind of Christ, not the letter of Holy Scripture, which is authoritative." [47] The Bible is "the record of God's self-revelation to mankind." [48] With regard to the atonement, R. T. Howard's essay "The Work of Christ" bears a decidedly Ritschlian stamp. The cross was necessary, he says, "because nothing short of the Cross could make man sure that God was of such a nature," i.e., loving and ready to forgive. In Jesus God "identified Himself completely with man in order that by the power of His personal influence He might bring him back to Himself." [49] As Evangelicals these writers are proud to be called heirs of the Reformation[50] and they are not sympathetic with the trend toward medievalism in the Anglican church. E. W. Barnes says: "We need at the present time not a modified but a new Catholicism, a true synthesis of the Gospel and modern knowledge." [51]

[42] *Ibid.*, p. 226.
[43] *God in Christian Experience* (New York: Harper & Bros., 1930), p. 11.
[44] *Ibid.*, p. 97.
[45] *Ibid.*, p. 184.
[46] *Ibid.*, p. 190.
[47] *Essays in Liberal Evangelicalism* (Garden City: George H. Doran Co. 1923), p. vi.
[48] *Ibid.*, p. 80.
[49] *Ibid.*, p. 129.
[50] *Ibid.*, p. 291.
[51] *Ibid.*, p. 293.

Free Church Theology

Next to Fairbairn's *Philosophy of the Christian Religion*, P. T. Forsyth's work *The Person and Place of Christ* (1911) is the one outstanding contribution of the Congregationalists during the first quarter of the twentieth century. Forsyth (1842–1921) was a Scot who also studied in Germany. He was considerably influenced by the practical emphasis of the Ritschlian theologians. To him Christianity is not a philosophy of the Absolute. Evangelical faith is personal and predominantly ethical. Forsyth also applies the ethical approach to his discussion of the christological dogma. "It is the work of Christ that gives us the key to the nature of Christ."[52] Jesus is not a genius. "Geniuses are repeated, but Christ never, the Son never."[53] Forsyth accepts the kenotic theory of the incarnation, discarding the view that Christ renounced some of his attributes; he retained them all, but in a new mode of being. The possibility of kenosis is found in the divine infinitude. "If the infinite God was so constituted that He could not live also as a finite man then He was not infinite."[54] Implicit in the kenosis is the *plerosis*, the self-fulfillment of Christ, i.e., in Christ's historic person God offered himself in his saving fullness by identifying himself with humanity. Later Forsyth seems to have accepted the favorite christological formula of Seeberg when he says that Christ's "person came back to be the Holy Spirit of all He had done."[55] In his doctrine of the atonement he preserved the penal idea, yet he insisted strongly on the initiative of God's love.[56] Over against the critical tendencies of our age, Forsyth, like Kähler, contended that the whole biblical Christ is truly and deeply the historic Christ.

Another Congregational theologian of repute was Alfred Ernest Garvie (1861–1945). Born in the Russian part of Poland, educated at Edinburgh, Glasgow, and Mansfield College of Oxford, he became a prominent leader of the Congregational churches of Great Britain.

[52] P. T. Forsyth, *The Person and Place of Jesus Christ* (Boston: Beacon Press, 1909, p. 346.

[53] *Ibid.*, p. 285.

[54] *Ibid.*, p. 315.

[55] *This Life and the Next* (New York: The Macmillan Company, 1918), p. 108.

[56] *The Work of Christ* (London: Hodder & Stoughton, 1911).

At heart he was a liberal Evangelical with a pronounced interest in the social implications of the gospel.[57] Though not a Ritschlian himself, so he said, he contributed much to interpret Ritschl to Anglo-Saxon scholars.[58] He regarded Ritschl's reduction of Christ's deity to a mere judgment of value as unsatisfactory; nevertheless, he agreed with Ritschl concerning the place experience holds in religion, and with Herrmann concerning the importance of the "inner life of Jesus." In brief, his theology was christocentric, with emphasis on the person of Jesus as the manifestation of God.

The volume of Presbyterian John Wood Oman (1860–1939), *Grace and Personality* (1918), is a theological classic. With his Calvinistic background and German training in Kant, Schleiermacher, and Ritschl, Oman revived Augustine and Calvin by making one important alteration in their teaching: He substituted "persuasive" grace for "irresistible" grace. While the *sola gratia* of Paul and Augustine remains uncurtailed, the old antinomy of religion and morality, grace and works, finds its solution in the higher synthesis of God and human personality. Absolute moral independence and absolute religious dependence are not opposites "but necessarily one and indivisible." [59] "Grace has always a convex side towards God, and a concave side towards man. Taken separately, they are contradictory and opposite, but, united, they are perfectly one as the convex and concave sides in one line." [60] Oman had treated the same problem earlier from the historical point of view in *The Problem of Faith and Freedom in the Last Two Centuries* (1907).

Oman denies that there is no way to reality except that of the natural sciences. The total richness of life, he holds, is not discovered by scientific empiricism; it discloses itself only to the intuitive faculties of man. All monistic concepts of religion and of mysticism are rejected. Only in monotheistic religion, he asserts, does the natural world remain real, and man is inspired with zeal and hope to conquer

[57] Cf. Alfred E. Garvie, *The Christian Ideal for Human Society* (London: Hodder & Stoughton, 1930); *Can Christ Save Society?* (London: Hodder & Stoughton, 1933); *Christian Moral Conduct* (London: J. Heritage, 1938).

[58] Garvie, *The Ritschlian Theology* (Edinburgh: T. & T. Clark, 1899).

[59] John Wood Oman, *Grace and Personality* (London: Macmillan Co., 1918), p. 22.

[60] *Ibid.*, p. 182.

the evil inherent in the natural order.[61] His book *Honest Religion*[62] (published posthumously in 1941) represents a type of matured Ritschlianism.

The Methodists have also produced a number of prominent scholars. Leslie Weatherhead and Eric S. Waterhouse have sought to relate the Christian dogma and ethics to psychology. Their writings in this area are widely read. Gordon Rupp and Philip S. Watson have made noteworthy contributions to modern Luther research. Watson's book *Let God be God* (1949) is a remarkable interpretation of some of the major themes of the Reformer's theology.

The most eminent scholar among the Baptists was H. Wheeler Robinson. His emphasis was also upon experience. Though critical of the traditional terminology, he was anxious to retain the religious values embodied in the terminology of the past—values he called vital to Christian experience. In *The Christian Doctrine of Man* (1911),[63] he stressed the religious and moral concept of man as against the rational and aesthetic view of man inherent in Greek thought. His *The Christian Experience of the Holy Spirit*,[64] while critical of the doctrine in its conservative form, nevertheless rejects the purely immanental aspect of the Spirit as taught by Schleiermacher and Ritschl. In *Redemption and Revelation in the Actuality of History*[65] Robinson treats of the doctrine of redemption.

Scottish Theological Thought

In twentieth-century Scottish theology there is a great array of notable scholars. Standing at the head of this list is James Denney (1856–1917). At first critical of Ritschlian theology, Denney later became known as a semi-Ritschlian. In his theology he also shows similarities to Adolf Schlatter. His method is modern and progressive. All religious knowledge is based on experience. This experience is found only in the historical revelation of God in Christ. The Scriptures, which record the experience of the early Church, are the

[61] Oman, *The Natural and Supernatural* (Cambridge: Cambridge University Press, 1931).

[62] Cambridge: Cambridge University Press, 1941.

[63] Edinburgh: T. & T. Clark, 1911.

[64] London: Nisbet & Co., 1928.

[65] New York: Harper & Bros., 1942.

records of that divine revelation. *In Jesus and the Gospel*[66] Denney argued that there are not two gospels in the New Testament, but one, and that the Church at all times has rightly regarded Christ as an object of faith. Christianity is a religion of mediation, the blessings of which are dependent on the work of Christ.

Denney insists that in the substance of Christianity there is not merely an experience of forgiveness that comes to us through Christ, but a doctrine of an objective atonement. Christ not only accomplished a subjective influence over the minds of men, but he did a work. The reconciliation of man to God is based on the atonement wrought by Christ. "Even if no man should ever say, 'Thou, O Christ, art all I want, more than all in Thee I find,' God says it. Christ and His work have this absolute value for the Father whatever this or that individual may think of them."[67] In his laborious search for a satisfactory theory of the *modus operandi* of Christ's sacrifice, Denney ended by proclaiming that no theory offered so deep a spiritual insight as that of MacLeod Campbell.

Another outstanding Scottish theologian was Hugh Ross Mackintosh (1870–1936). His translation of Schleiermacher and Ritschl helped materially to acquaint English theologians with masterpieces of German scholarship. As a theologian Mackintosh held a mediating position. Through him the anti-metaphysical tenets of Ritschl, which held little appeal for an English world saturated with philosophical idealism, received a hearing in Scotland. But Mackintosh was far from being a full-fledged Ritschlian. What appealed most to him was not the pragmatism and moralism in Ritschl but the quite un-Ritschlian, Tholuckian trend in Herrmann, i.e., the emphasis on the mystical experience of the forgiveness of sin mediated through the person of Jesus.[68] Mackintosh was untiring in his emphasis upon the "essential" deity of Christ and in so doing was very close to the Erlangen concept of the incarnation. He followed Thomasius in accepting the kenotic view, but rejected the theory that Christ relinquished his external divine attributes in the act of his incarnation.

[66] London: Hodder & Stoughton, 1918.

[67] *The Christian Doctrine of Reconciliation* (London: Hodder & Stoughton, 1918), p. 234.

[68] See his note on "The Theology of Herrmann," in *The Christian Experience of Forgiveness* (London: Nisbet & Co., 1927), pp. 44 ff.

Like Forsyth, Mackintosh preferred to speak of a "transposition of attributes." The historic Christ was very dear to him, and he disowned speculative rationalism in deference to the concrete and historical in Christianity.

Two prominent figures in the postwar world were Donald M. Baillie (d. 1954) and John Baillie (d. 1960). The two brothers studied at Edinburgh, Marburg, Heidelberg (Donald) and Jena (John). Both were very active in the ecumenical movement. While teaching at Edinburgh, Donald gradually moved from philosophy of religion to dogmatics. His best-known works, *God was in Christ*[69] and *The Theology of the Sacraments*,[70] reveal a mind at home in the Evangelical tradition of the Reformed faith. John, on the contrary, was preoccupied throughout his life with the nature of religion, revelation, and man's knowledge of God. This theme runs through his books.

For John Baillie religion and morality grow from the same root: they embody values that are not really ours at all; they belong rather to a wider order of reality of which we are privileged to partake. Human discovery and divine revelation are complementary and come from the selfsame fact of human experience.[71] The immediacy of God is mediated not *through* the world but *with* the world. The universe is sacramental. "Nature is not an argument for God, but it is a sacrament of Him."[72] The presence of the triune God is given "in, with and under" the whole corporeal world. More eminently than in nature the footprints of God are revealed in human nature as moral personalities.[73] The Deity is pre-eminently revealed in the person of Jesus. If we want to know what God is like we must turn to "the man Christ Jesus." Jesus is the greatest and best of men but also God's greatest gift to men. He is both the summit of human attainment and the climax of the divine self-disclosure.[74] The gospel is a story "not only of great faith but also of great grace."[75] Written

[69] London: Faber & Faber, 1948.
[70] New York: Charles Scribner's Sons, 1957.
[71] *The Interpretation of Religion* (New York: Charles Scribner's Sons, 1928), p. 458.
[72] *Our Knowledge of God* (New York: Charles Scribner's Sons, 1939), p. 178.
[73] *Interpretation of Religion,* p. 461.
[74] *Ibid.,* p. 467.
[75] *The Place of Jesus Christ in Modern Christianity* (New York: Charles Scribner's Sons, 1929), p. 109.

in 1928 and 1929, these statements reflect the tendency of a semi-Ritschlian to come to terms with the ancient and Reformation doctrine of the person of Jesus. Influenced later by the new theology of the Continent, the Reformation insight into the person and life of Jesus prevailed over the humanism of the earlier period.

In his posthumous publication, *The Sense of the Presence of God*, Baillie has a concise statement about the biblical message of the saving name of Jesus, on the eternal truth of the incarnation and the atonement. The Good News is not only that God was incarnate in a man, but that the kind of man in which he was incarnate constitutes the gospel: in a baby in a horse's stall and in a man hanging on a gallows tree. Here Baillie has stated in terse language the *scandalon* of Luther's theology of the cross.[76]

Baillie sides with those who hold that the Bible is not revelation but a witness to revelation. The medium of revelation, in the narrower sense, is redemptive history. It is an event. The Bible is the record of what God has done in the act of revelation and of the response of men contemporary with the divine event. The prophetic interpretation of God's dealings with Israel is authenticated to the believer through the internal testimony of the Holy Spirit. Divine revelation is completed by the interchange of event and interpretation. Scripture is inspired because the same Holy Spirit who enlightened the prophets and Apostles also guided them in their efforts to convey the message of salvation to those whom their words, whether oral or written, would reach.[77] In expressing these views Baillie is in agreement with Barth, Tillich, and other modern theologians. He also agrees with Tillich that much religious language is symbolical. But he does not go all the way with Tillich and others who say that all religious language must be symbolical, with the single exception that "God is being itself." To affirm that God is personal is to make just as intelligible an assertion as it is to attribute personality to man. Personality is not a symbol that points beyond itself: rather divine person-

[76] John Baillie, *The Sense of the Presence of God* (New York: Charles Scribner's Sons, 1962), p. 210.

[77] Baillie, *The Idea of Revelation* (New York: Columbia University Press, 1956), pp. 110 ff.

ality is perfect personality, just as human personality is imperfect personality.[78]

Barth's influence on Scottish theology is found in George S. Hendry's short book, *God the Creator* (1937), the Hastie Lectures of 1935. The book voices an ardent plea to Scottish theologians to turn from the current theology of England and America, engaged in rationalizing religion by the empirical method of science, and to go back to Luther for theological food.

In *Calvin's Doctrine of Man*[79] Thomas F. Torrance (d. 1913) has tried to disentangle the Reformer from the web of a static orthodoxy. Like Luther, Calvin must not be equated with the later Orthodox theology that goes under his name.[80] Torrance has also taken an active part in the ecumenical movement.

The Catholic Tradition

Modern Anglo-Catholicism is characterized by a blend of high church principles and a critical approach to the Scriptures. Charles Gore (1835–1932) is an example of this critical approach. His article on "The Holy Spirit and Inspiration" in *Lux Mundi* had caused more tumult than any other article in that volume. In the field of Old Testament criticism Gore generally accepted the views of modern critical scholarship, but his views on the New Testament were more conservative.[81] Nonetheless he proved to be a staunch defender of a supernatural and sacramentarian theology. He wholeheartedly accepted the biblical concept of the virgin birth and bodily resurrection of Jesus. He defended the theological language of the ancient councils and was suspicious about the motives of their modern critics. Gore also showed an intense interest in the social problems of his country. One of his books, *The Body of Christ*,[82] contains a constructive discussion of the doctrine of the Eucharist.

A literary manifesto of modern Anglo-Catholicism is found in the

[78] Baillie, *The Sense of the Presence of God* (New York: Charles Scribner's Sons, 1962), p. 118.

[79] Grand Rapids: Wm. B. Eerdmans Publishing Co., 1957.

[80] Cf. also Torrance, *Kingdom and Church, a Study in the Theology of the Reformation* (Edinburgh: Oliver & Boyd, 1956).

[81] Cf. Charles Gore, *The Doctrine of the Infallible Book* (London: SCM Press, 1924).

[82] New York: Charles Scribner's Sons, 1901.

volume entitled *Essays Catholic and Critical.*[83] A very intense supernaturalism and the highest criticism are represented in this book. Oliver E. James's essay, "The Emergence of Religion," attempts to make the incarnation a climax of the evolution of all primitive faiths. A. E. Taylor's essay, "The Vindication of Religion," upholds religious experience as the source of evidence. A. E. J. Rawlinson's essay deals with authority as a ground of belief. Wilfred L. Knox's contribution on the authority of the Church holds that authority is not to be vested in an infallible Bible nor in individual experience, but in the corporate experience of the Church. The authority of the Church is neither "oracular nor infallible," but must at all times vindicate its claims "at the threefold bar of history, reason, and spiritual experience."[84] The essay "The Christ of the Synoptic Gospels," by Sir Edwyn Clement Hoskyns, is a masterpiece of constructive biblical criticism. He rejects the prevalent liberal theory that the Christ of the Church was the product of "the gradual apotheosis of a Jewish prophet under the influence of Greek-Christian belief and worship" as historically unsound.[85] "The contrast is not between the Jesus of history and the Christ returning to glory; the two being held together by the title Son of Man, which suggests both."[86] In the last four essays the authors set forth the Catholic interpretation of such disputed doctrines as ecclesiology, the Spirit and the Church in history, the Reformation, the origins of the sacraments, and the Eucharist. The appraisal of the Reformation is not too liberal. The number of the sacraments is fixed at four. "It is, however, possible," says N. P. Williams, "to simplify the subject matter . . . for Penitence, Baptism, and Confirmation are in primitive Catholicism not three distinct sacraments, but rather parts of, or moments in, one great cleansing, regenerating, and Spirit-imparting rite. . . . This single original rite of entrance to Christianity we will designate by the word 'Initiation.' "[87] He interprets the Last Supper as "but a 'shadow' Eucharist—a typical object-lesson, not the mystic and glorious reality which could only be consummated in the 'Kingdom of God' (i.e., the new Christian

[83] E. G. Selwyn, ed. (London: Macmillan Co., 1926).
[84] *Ibid.*, p. 95.
[85] *Ibid.*, p. 157.
[86] *Ibid.*, p. 176.
[87] *Ibid.*, p. 376.

dispensation) which His death was to inaugurate." [88] On the question of eucharistic sacrifice the last writer, W. Spens, remarks that "the Last Supper and the Eucharist are not separate sacrifices from that of Calvary, but supply a necessary element in the sacrifice of Calvary, by expressly investing our Lord's death before God and man with its sacrificial significance." [89] "The immolation once made can never be repeated. But equally necessary in its bearing upon the salvation of the world is the rite by which down the long succession of ages our Lord makes His death to be our sacrifice and enables us to appropriate the blessings thus secured." [90]

The Roman influence in the Anglo-Catholic group was very pronounced during the time of the Conversations of Malines (1921-26) which were carried on between representatives of the Anglo-Catholics and Cardinal Mercier, Primate of Belgium, with a view toward the possible reunion of the Church of England with Rome. The publication of these proceedings was received with much indignation in England. When the pope made it known that union meant subjection to Rome, the majority of the Anglo-Catholics returned to the *via media* of their fathers. During the next two years the English Parliament gave forceful expression to the Protestant sentiment of the country when the Lower House rejected the Romanized revised edition of the Book of Common Prayer. (While the Evangelicals lean on the theology of the Thirty-nine Articles, the Catholic group shows a decided preference for the Prayer Book.) All these things helped to bring a so-called "Central Party" into prominence. Under the leadership of this party the established church has succeeded in making Canterbury a Western patriarchate equal in rank with and superior in influence to the ancient sees of the East. Full communion has been extended, and partially established, both with the Eastern Orthodox churches and with the Lutherans of Sweden, who have preserved the historic episcopate. The Anglican church has even approached the Dissenters in England and its appeal has met with a very cordial response from that group.

The Catholic tendencies of the Anglicans crystallized in the World

[88] *Ibid.*, p. 423.
[89] *Ibid.*, p. 436.
[90] *Ibid.*, p. 439.

Conference on Faith and Order. The movement itself goes back to the initiative of Charles Brent, a bishop of the Protestant Episcopal Church of America. The Conference sponsored two important international meetings at Lausanne in 1927 and at Edinburgh in 1937.[91] That the Church of England has approached the problem of Church unity from the standpoint of the Central Party and of a mediating theology is evident from the report of the committee on christian doctrine appointed by the Archbishop of Canterbury, published under the title *Doctrine in the Church of England*.[92] In the introduction it is stated that the Anglican churches "are heirs of the Reformation as well as of Catholic tradition."[93] The claim of catholicity "does not depend on mere numbers or on the extension of a belief at any one time, but on continuance through the ages and the extent to which the consensus is genuinely free."[94] In other words, the Commission upheld only the first part of the Vincentian maxim that what is Catholic has been accepted always, everywhere, and by all. Though all hierarchical claims are denied, the Report stresses the Episcopate, *jure divino*, as a guarantee of continuity and an identity of teaching.[95] The Church is defined not as a communion of believers, but as "the whole company of those who share in the regenerate life."[96]

The Scriptures are viewed as the first but not as the sole source of authority, for "Scripture and the Church alike bear witness" to the revelation of God in history.[97] The tradition of the inerrancy of the Bible, it is said, "cannot be maintained in the light of the knowledge now at our disposal."[98] The actual teaching of Jesus was "called forth by particular occasions and was conditioned by the thought-forms and circumstances of the time," and its record in the Gospels "cannot be accepted as always reproducing the *ipsissima verba* of our

[91] In 1948 at Amsterdam, the World Conference on Faith and Order merged with the Universal Conference for Life and Work (which was organized in Stockholm, 1925) to form the World Council of Churches. The work of the Conference on Faith and Order is carried on as a branch of the World Council under the name the Commission on Faith and Order.
[92] London: SPCK, 1938.
[93] *Ibid.*, p. 25.
[94] *Ibid.*, p. 35.
[95] *Ibid.*, p. 115.
[96] *Ibid.*, p. 106.
[97] *Ibid.*, p. 27.
[98] *Ibid.*, p. 29.

Lord."[99] In keeping with this view of the Bible is the Commission's attitude toward the Anglican Formularies. The language of the Formularies is not final but subject to modifications in accordance with fresh knowledge or fresh attitudes.[100] God is defined as "the perfect Truth or ultimate Existence," and the causal ground of the world.[101] The Commission's concept of sin borders on Pelagianism.[102] In its view of grace it has remained close to the theology of the East by defining grace both as *favor Dei* and *gratia infusa.*[103] As to the earthly beginnings of Jesus, it is stated that some members of the Commission believe that the incarnation is "integrally bound up with belief in the Virgin Birth," while others hold that "a full belief in the historical Incarnation is more consistent with the supposition that our Lord's birth took place under the normal conditions of human generation."[104] These critical scholars are likewise inclined to the belief that "the connection made in the New Testament between the emptiness of a tomb and the appearances of the Risen Lord belongs rather to the sphere of religious symbolism than to that of historical fact."[105]

This type of Central theology shaped the thinking of the late Archbishop William Temple (d. 1944). In fact, Temple was a member of the Commission from its inception in 1922, and served as chairman after the death of Bishop Burge in 1925. He saw the solution to our problems in a return to the healthy objectivism of the medieval mind, combined with the sincerity of the modern mind. Temple's argument proceeds from a scientific materialism to an immanent theism and to a supernatural, divine personality who in turn descends into this world. He is very emphatic in maintaining the reality of general revelation in nature and history. As God is the ground of all, so all existence is a revelation of God.[106] Only upon this basis is

[99] *Ibid.*, p. 32.
[100] *Ibid.*, p. 37.
[101] *Ibid.*, p. 41.
[102] *Ibid.*, p. 56.
[103] *Ibid.*, p. 52.
[104] *Ibid.*, p. 82.
[105] *Ibid.*, p. 86.
[106] Temple, who once held a philosophical lectureship at Oxford, was influenced by Alfred North Whitehead's metaphysics with its view of a divine evolutionary process. According to Whitehead, it is true to say that God is

the expectation of a particular revelation well grounded. The nature of special revelation, according to Temple, is not to be seen in dictated words or sacred books, nor in an "organized society." Rather it is the faith of Christendom, "that in the Gospel there is given an unalterable revelation of the eternal God, not in the form of doctrinal propositions which once and for all have been drawn up for the acceptance of men of every age, but in the form of a Person and a human Life to which all the doctrinal formulations point." [107] The gospel is unchanging, though the world in which it appears is changing. Therefore, theology must always be changing.[108] The possibility of miracles is not altogether denied. They are, he writes, "if they occur, a manifestation of the God immanent in the same way as in the ordinary process of nature," [109] for God has not left "nature as a closed system into which he periodically intervenes from outside." [110]

The fundamental sacrament, Temple says, is the universe. It became a sacrament only by virtue of the incarnation "which is the perfect sacrament intensively," because the incarnation is a momentary perfect expression of the will of God. The Church, which is the "Spirit-bearing Body," results from the incarnation. The sacramental nature of the Church remains incomplete, as long as its members "are not utterly surrendered to the spirit within it." Sacred rites of the Church, commonly called sacraments, are nothing but a part of this body of Christ.[111] We ought not to think of the real presence in the term of transubstantiation, i.e., as a change of matter, but should conceive of it as a "transvaluation" or "convaluation" of the blessed element[112] and valuation, he holds, is fundamental to reality.

both one and many, transcending and creating the world as well as being transcended and created by the world. Cf. Whitehead, *Process and Reality* (Cambridge: Cambridge University Press, 1929). For interpretation see Wolfe Mays, *The Philosophy of Whitehead* (New York: The Macmillan Company, 1959), pp. 62 ff.

[107] William Temple, *The Church and Its Teaching Today* (London: Macmillan Co., 1935), p. 36.

[108] *Ibid.*, p. 34.

[109] Temple, *Nature, Man, and God* (London: Macmillan Co., 1933), p. 295.

[110] *Ibid.*, p. 46.

[111] Temple, *Christ the Truth* (New York: The Macmillan Company, 1924), p. 279.

[112] *Ibid.*, p. 295.

"Everything exists as far as it is good." [113] The "thing signified" is neither the human body of Christ in its physico-chemical substance, nor the risen and glorified body. In addition to the New Testament use of the term "body" as signifying both the fleshly body of the Lord and the Church, there is a third use of the term: the eucharistic body. "That Bread is not itself the Glorified Body of the Lord, but it is the Body of the Glorified Lord—the Body of Christ who is known to us as crucified, risen, ascended, glorified." [114] As his body, the bread is the "instrument" by which the Lord gives himself to us.[115] It is the means by which Christ is accessible; but, he continues, "the accessibility is spiritual, not material or local, and Christ is actually only present to the soul of those who make right use of the means of access afforded." [116] Furthermore, the kingdom is not to be equated with any economic order. It is in the world, but its consummation is not conceivable in the conditions of this mortal life.[117]

Anglican theology has continued to move with its customary moderation and complexity. Alan Richardson's *Christian Apologetics*[118] is an analysis of the sense in which theology can be a science. Science is a study of observable facts and their systematic classification according to the nature of the things observed, whether historical or natural. Each branch of science has not only its limited field of investigation, but also its categories or principles of investigation. The task of examining the validity of the categories is the work of the metaphysician. He must select a key-category by which to interpret our experience as a whole. Theology, too, is an empirical science. It deals with the data provided by the existence of the Christian community. As the metaphysician may ask questions about the ultimate nature of physical objects, so the philosopher may ask questions about the ultimate nature of the Christian faith.

According to Richardson, the basic affirmation of the Christian faith is the resurrection of Jesus. Despite the cross and the shattering effect of the crucifixion on the disciples, the eleven came together

[113] *Ibid.*, p. 16.
[114] *Ibid.*, p. 299.
[115] *Ibid.*, p. 285.
[116] *Ibid.*, p. 287.
[117] Temple, *The Church and Its Teaching Today*, pp. 21-22.
[118] London: SCM Press, 1947.

almost immediately, and within a few weeks they boldly proclaimed that God had raised this Jesus and made him Christ and Lord. Such behavior, Richardson says, can only be explained on the ground that the disciples had had a tremendous experience. It compelled them to bear witness to what they had heard and seen and what they had received as a commission from the risen Lord. As a result, the Church came into being. There can be no question of these facts upon historical grounds. But the historian cannot answer the question: How can we know that these people were not victims of a hallucination? This question carries us beyond the scope of historical science. "There is no logical compulsion to accept the testimony of other people concerning what they have seen and heard. Christian faith involves the acceptance of the Apostolic testimony, and hence it remains faith and never becomes proof." [119] Of course, the personal disposition of the investigator enters into his conclusions; thus, the faith or non-faith of the historian necessarily conditions the acceptance of the crucified Jesus as the living Lord. What transpired on Good Friday is historical, but the Easter event is a meta-historical fact and beyond the scope of historical science.[120]

The growing emphasis on biblical studies in Anglican theology is also reflected in the writings of such scholars as Sir Edwin C. Hoskyns (d. 1937), A. G. Hebert, L. S. Thornton, and Michael Ramsey. These writers concentrate on Christ and the Church as a divine-human mystery. Hoskyns, in co-operation with Noel Davey, edited *The Riddle of the New Testament* which, like Richardson's work, is both exegetical and apologetic. The historian can outline the figure of Jesus as presented in the New Testament. He can demonstrate that the life and death of this man became the occasion "of quite a remarkable outburst of faith in the living God." But he is unable to decide between faith and unbelief. The historian is faced by the problem of theology just as the unbeliever is faced by the problem of faith.[121]

Anglicanism seems to have been predestined to become a leading force in the ecumenical movement, which in turn has received much

[119] *Ibid.*, pp. 40 ff.

[120] Cf. in Richardson, *Science, History and Faith* (London: Oxford University Press, 1950), pp. 55 ff., the discussion, "Did Jesus really arise from the dead?"

[121] Edwin C. Hoskyns and Noel Davey (eds.), *The Riddle of the New Testament* (3rd ed.; London: Faber & Faber, 1949), pp. 179 ff.

inspiration from the Second Vatican Council. An ecumenical theology has been in the making for quite some time. This theology seeks Christian unity not so much in doctrinal agreement as in a diversity of theological traditions and in the sharing of divergent views of worship. With the modernists almost silenced by the sobering effects of World War II, a moderately conservative theology, including Neo-Orthodoxy, has been much more influential in the forming of an ecumenical theology than the older liberal type. This reflects the genius of Anglicanism.

BIBLIOGRAPHY

BARABAS, STEVEN. *So Great Salvation: The History and Message of the Keswick Convention.* London: Marshall, Morgan, & Scott, 1952.

BELL, G. K. A. *Christian Unity and the Anglican Position.* London: Hodder & Stoughton, 1948.

———. (ed.). *Documents on Christian Unity.* New York: Oxford University Press, 1924, 1930, 1948.

COCK, ALBERT A. *A Critical Examination of von Huegel's Philosophy of Religion.* London: H. Rees, 1955.

DAKIN, A. H. *Von Huegel and The Supernatural.* New York: The Macmillan Company, 1934.

DENNEY, JAMES. *Studies in Theology.* London: Hodder & Stoughton, 1894.

FLETCHER, JOSEPH. *William Temple, Twentieth Century Christian.* New York: Seabury Press, Inc., 1963.

GARVIE, ALFRED E. *The Christian Doctrine of the Godhead.* New York: George H. Doran Co., 1925.

———. *Revelation Through History and Experience.* London: I. Nicholson & Watson, Ltd., 1934.

———. *The Christian Faith.* London: Duckworth Press, 1936.

———. *Memories and Meanings of My Life.* London. George Allen & Unwin, 1938.

GORE, CHARLES. *The New Theology and the New Religion.* London: J. Murray, 1907.

———. *Work and the Church.* London: A. R. Mowbray Co., 1916.

———. *The Reconstruction of Belief.* London: J. Murray, 1926.

HIGGINS, A. J. B. (ed.). *New Testament Essays, Studies in the Memory of Thomas Walter Manson.* Manchester: Manchester University Press, 1959.

HORTON, WALTER M. *Contemporary English Theology.* New York: Harper & Bros., 1936.

ILLINGWORTH, JOHN R. *Personality, Human and Divine.* New York: The Macmillan Company, 1894.

———. *Divine Immanence.* New York: The Macmillan Company, 1898.

———. *Divine Transcendence.* London: Macmillan Co., 1911.

INGE, WILLIAM R. *Christian Mysticism.* New York: Charles Scribner's Sons, 1899.

IREMONGER, F. A. *William Temple, Archbishop of Canterbury: His Life and Letters.* 2 vols. London: Oxford University Press, 1948.

MACKINTOSH, HUGH R. *The Doctrine of the Person of Jesus Christ.* Edinburgh: T. & T. Clark, 1912.

———. *Christianity and Sin.* New York: Charles Scribner's Sons, 1913.

———. *Immortality and the Future.* London: Hodder & Stoughton, 1917.

———. *The Originality of the Christian Message.* New York: Charles Scribner's Sons, 1920.

———. *The Christian Experience of Forgiveness.* London: Nisbet & Co., 1927.

———. *Types of Modern Theology.* London: Nisbet and Co., 1937.

MACQUARRIE, JOHN. *Twentieth Century Religious Thought.* New York: Harper & Bros., 1963.

MAJOR, H. D. A. *English Modernism.* Cambridge: Harvard University Press, 1927.

MOZLEY, JOHN KENNETH. *Tendencies in British Theology from the Time of the Publication of Lux Mundi to the Present Day.* London: SPCK, 1951.

NEDONCELLE, MAURICE. *Baron Friedrich von Huegel: A Study of His Life and Thought.* New York: Green & Co., 1937.

OMAN, JOHN WOOD. *The Natural and Supernatural.* Cambridge: Cambridge University Press, 1931.

———. *Honest Religion.* Cambridge: Cambridge University Press, 1941.

RAMSEY, A. M. *From Gore to Temple.* London: Longmans, Green & Co., 1960.

RAVEN, CHARLES E. *Jesus and the Gospel of Love.* New York: Henry Holt & Co., Inc., 1931.

———. *Christian Socialism.* New York: The Macmillan Company, 1936.

———. *The Gospel and the Church.* London: Hodder & Stoughton, 1940.

ROBINSON, H. WHEELER. *The Religious Ideas of the Old Testament.* Revised by L. H. BROCKINGTON. 2nd ed.; London: Duckworth Press, 1956.

STREETER, B. H. *Reality.* New York: The Macmillan Company, 1926.

———. *The God Who Speaks.* New York: The Macmillan Company, 1936.

STUDDERT-KENNEDY, G. A. *I Believe: Sermons on the Apostles' Creed.* New York: George H. Doran, 1921.

———. *The Wicket Gate: Sermons on the Lord's Prayer.* London: Hodder & Stoughton, 1923.

THOMAS, OWEN C. *William Temple's Philosophy of Religion.* New York: Seabury Press, Inc., 1962.

TORRANCE, THOMAS F. *Conflict and Agreement in the Church.* 2 vols. London: Lutterworth Press, 1959-60.

Book Six

THEOLOGICAL THOUGHT IN AMERICA

CHAPTER I

FACTS AND FORCES IN AMERICAN THEOLOGY

Calvinism was the creed of New England. The Pilgrims at Plymouth were radical Separatists who rejected a static concept of the Reformation. When leaving for America, John Robinson remarked, "Luther and Calvin were great and shining lights in their times, yet they penetrated not into the whole counsel of God. I beseech you, remember this—'tis an article of your church covenant—that you be ready to receive whatever truth shall be made known to you from the written word of God." The Pilgrims established their separatist principles in the New World. They held that membership in the Church should be restricted to the "saints," and that the local church is autonomous. Besides, joining the Church meant entering into a covenant, not subscription to a creed. As Dissenters they were more interested in conduct than in dogma. Original Calvinism underwent a strong modification in their teaching.[1]

The Puritans who later settled at and around Boston were potential Presbyterians and no friends of separatism. However, the two factions soon amalgamated into one harmonious group. In 1629 the Puritans accepted the Plymouth model of Church administration, while the whole body of Congregational churches expressed belief in the principles of the Westminster Confession, first, by adopting the Cambridge Platform in 1648 and, later, the Savoy Confession[2] in 1680. Since religious liberty was restricted to the Congregational churches

[1] Thomas C. Hall rejects the view that Calvinism had a hold over the English Dissenters. Dissent, he says, was not a product of Calvinism, but had its beginning with Wyclif and the Lollards in the Middle Ages; *The Religious Background of American Culture* (Boston: Little, Brown & Co., 1930).

[2] A Synod assembled at Cambridge, Massachusetts, in June, 1648, gave assent to the Westminster Confession except for some statements pertaining to Church government and discipline. The Cambridge Platform anticipated the Savoy Confession by ten years. See the introductory discussion and the text in Philip Schaff, *Creeds of Christendom* (New York: Harper & Bros., 1877), I, 836; III, 707 ff.

and the holding of civil offices was made dependent on Church membership, the New England churches came close to abandoning their dissenting views in favor of a new Establishment.

In the eighteenth century the modified Calvinism of the Puritans underwent a further modification because of Anabaptist, Spiritualist, Socinian, and Arminian influences. When Puritanic Calvinism clashed with the Anabaptists and Quakers, these radicals were banished, tortured, or put to death by the civil magistrates. Gradually, however, the Calvinism of New England drifted into eighteenth-century deism. New England proved to be an even more fertile soil for deistic optimism than England, because of its unlimited natural resources and greater freedom from the conventions and social forms of the past. The clash between Arminian and predestinarian views, on the other hand, gave rise to a long and trenchant literary controversy crystallizing in a new and modified concept of predestination and of man's moral ability in the New England theology of Jonathan Edwards and his school.

In the course of time the free church principle proved to be a strong factor in favor of religious individualism and toleration. Rhode Island and Pennsylvania especially became havens for religious radicals from New England and Europe. This trend toward individualism and toleration was strengthened in the eighteenth century by the prevailing political theories from French philosophy. The American Constitution declared Church and state mutually independent. The states followed suit. Shortly after the adoption of the Constitution in 1789 the Anglican Establishment in the southern colonies was repealed. The New England states were slower in moving. It was not till the first decades of the nineteenth century, 1816 in Connecticut and 1833 in Massachusetts, that the special privileges of the Congregational churches were discontinued. Within a single century there was a change in the whole structure of American society which has no parallel elsewhere: in politics, a complete change from state-supported churches to complete religious toleration; in philosophy, a turning from the supernatural to scientific empiricism; and in religion, a shift of emphasis from revelation to reason. This change is marked by the life and work of three men: Thomas Jefferson, Benjamin Franklin, and Ethan Allen.

Conditions in the New World compelled the churches to adopt new methods of work. In European countries where state churches existed, Church membership was general. In the New World the actual membership of churches was comparatively small. Even in New England only a few out of the total population belonged to the Church. There was a greater number of unchurched people in New England than in any country of Europe. This situation gave impetus to the development of a new technique to win the unchurched. This new method was revivalism. The Awakening of 1735 and 1740 was only the beginning of other revival movements which are characteristic of American Christianity. The religious camp meetings and the Methodist circuit riders are genuine products of American frontier life.[3]

The missionary character of the American churches also put the stamp of adaptability and practicability on the Church life and theology of our country. There is no such thing as a rift between the Church and theology as a science. American theology is preachable. The really great American theologians have been the great preachers of their day, e.g., Edwards, Channing, Finney, Parker, and Walther. Some of the great sermons have carried the weight of important theological manifestoes, e.g., Channing's Baltimore sermon on Unitarian Christianity. This feature of American theology, though it may have its parallel in England, is quite different from conditions as they existed in Germany. The style of German theological books used to be ponderous, written with an eye only to the expert. Ordination was not a requirement for holding a theological professorship, and consequently some of the German professors would never officiate in the services of the Church.

Another feature of American Christianity is its schismatic character. Schisms in American churches have been due mainly to two causes. The first cause is religious. On the one hand, the radical application of the dogmatic and confessional principle has caused endless friction in American Christianity. This trend was not without precedence in the Calvinistic countries of Europe, for the literalism, legalistic, and spiritualistic tendencies in Calvinism breed dissent. Even the Lutheran

[3] Cf. William W. Sweet, *Religion in Colonial America* (New York: Charles Scribner's Sons, 1942), pp. 7-8.

church became subject to this development in America when a specific theological interpretation of the Lutheran confessions was made the prerequisite of altar and pulpit fellowship. On the other hand, the number of denominations was unduly multiplied by immature attempts at Church union as represented, for example, by the Disciples of Christ, the United Church of Canada, and the so-called Federated or Community Churches.

The other cause is political and economic. The problems of slavery and the Civil War seriously hampered the unity of the churches. The disruption in the Lutheran church caused by the Civil War was not healed until 1918; the Methodists reunited as late as 1939, while some of the other denominations are still divided into Northern and Southern groups. Today, dogmatic problems have also perpetuated these schisms. The Southern Baptists, for instance, are far more conservative than the Northern Baptists.

America was called a "melting pot" by Israel Zangwill; others, more correctly, have said "mixing pot."[4] Since so many nationalities have contributed to the making of America, it is somewhat presumptuous to speak of an American church or of American theology. A single Church has never been formed; rather, churches with various backgrounds and theologies have arisen. A discussion of American theology, therefore, should not be limited to the English tradition in American life. Continental Lutheranism and Calvinism, even Roman Catholicism, can claim a just share in building the spiritual forces of the North American continent. In Quebec, for example, a French-Catholic culture is very much alive today.

Since the American population, its culture and civilization, is but a scion of European peoples, American theology cannot expect to be something peculiar. The general trend of thought and religion in Europe has inevitably been felt on this side of the Atlantic. As English, French, and German philosophy has found a response in America, so the development in European Calvinism and Lutheranism has acted and re-acted on American theology. This does not mean that European thought has not undergone strong modification in the new environment. This has been especially true in the case of German and Scandinavian Lutheranism, which had to be integrated into a free,

[4] *Literary Digest*, October 13, 1926.

pluralistic society employing the English language. But the differences from the mother countries are largely confined to matters of Church polity. They have not produced a theological tradition characteristic of America. As Ahlstrom correctly observes, not even the social gospel so often regarded as typically American is an exception to this statement. It is deeply indebted to German thought and has its parallel movements on the Continent and in Great Britain.[5]

The Civil War is a landmark in American history. Until 1870 America was chiefly an agricultural country and traditional Christianity held sway in American life. Since the Civil War, industrialization has made rapid headway and its consequent evils, e.g., the disintegration of family life and the depersonalization of the individual, have become an ever greater problem to the Christian character of America. The clash between traditional Christianity and the new learning has created great unrest in many churches. The conflict between fundamentalists and modernists was especially bitter in the decade after World War I.

Viewed from the broader aspect of European-American solidarity, five main currents that have contributed to theological thought in America are discernible: (1) seventeenth-century Orthodoxy; (2) the eighteenth-century theology of the inner light and of reason; (3) the spiritual tenets of German Idealism (Kant, Schleiermacher, Hegel, and Ritschl); (4) the revival of Lutheran confessionalism in the nineteenth century; (5) the rise of modern science. At present a powerful radical liberalism exists side by side with an influential prescientific view of religion. American theology tends toward either extreme liberalism or extreme conservatism. The modern spiritual crisis is accentuated in America by an unhistorical, rational mind according to which historical tradition counts for little, utility for almost everything.[6] American theology, therefore, is either dogmatic or speculative and critical. Dogmatic treatises with a mark of originality have been

[5] See Sidney E. Ahlstrom, "Theology in America: A Historical Survey," in J. W. Smith and A. L. Jamison, *Religion in America* (Princeton: Princeton University Press), I (1961), 232 ff., especially the concluding statements on p. 321.

[6] "The American mind is an empirical mind. It is less conscious of dependence upon the past than any other type of mind in Christendom"; C. C. Morrison, "Oxford, Edinburgh, and the American Mind," *Christendom*, Autumn, 1937, pp. 582 ff.

produced, but they often lack a biblical and historical basis. American conservatives and fundamentalists are traditionalists. Their weakness lies in their neglect of a fresh analysis of faith in the light of advanced linguistic and historical studies of the Scriptures. The modernists are really religious philosophers more than Christian theologians. Until recently there was little interest in Luther and the Reformation. Before World War II even the Lutheran churches were more oriented toward post-Reformation theology than toward Luther himself. They did not envision a comprehensive translation of Luther's writings until a decade ago.

BIBLIOGRAPHY

BRAUER, JERALD C. *Protestantism in America: A Narrative History*. Philadelphia: Westminster Press, 1953.

BROWN, WILLIAM A. *The Church in America: A Study of the Present Condition and Future Prospects of American Protestantism.* New York: The Macmillan Company, 1922.

GREENE, EVARTS B. *Religion and the State in America.* New York: New York University Press, 1942.

HALL, THOMAS C. *The Religious Background of American Culture.* Boston: Little, Brown & Co., 1930.

HUDSON, W. S. *The Great Tradition of American Churches.* New York: Harper & Bros., 1953.

———. *American Protestantism.* Chicago: Chicago University Press, 1961.

HUMPHRY, EDWARD F. *Nationalism and Religion in America, 1774–1789.* Boston: Chipman Law Publishing Co., 1924.

LATOURETTE, KENNETH S. *The Great Century in Europe and the United States, A.D. 1800–1914.* ("The History of the Expansion of Christianity," Vol. IV.) New York: Harper & Bros., 1941.

MEAD, SIDNEY E. *The Lively Experiment.* New York: Harper & Row, 1963.

NIEBUHR, H. RICHARD. *The Kingdom of God in America.* Chicago: Willet, Clark & Co., 1937.

OLMSTEAD, C. E. *History of Religion in The United States.* Englewood Cliffs, N. J.: Prentice-Hall, 1960.

ROWE, HENRY K. *The History of Religion in the United States.* New York: The Macmillan Company, 1924.

SMITH, J. W. and JAMISON, A. L. (ed.). *Religion in American Life.* 4 vols. Princeton: Princeton University Press, 1961.

SWEET, WILLIAM W. *The Story of Religion in America.* New York: Harper & Bros., 1939.

———. *Religion in Colonial America.* New York: Charles Scribner's Sons, 1942.

———. *Religion in the Development of American Culture, 1765–1840.* New York: Charles Scribner's Sons, 1952.

THOMPSON, CHARLES L. *The Religious Foundations of America.* New York: Fleming H. Revell Co., 1917.

CHAPTER II

NEW ENGLAND THEOLOGY

Religious Conditions in New England

The religion of the Pilgrims and Puritans was the modified Calvinism of the English Dissenters. To them the Scriptures were all-sufficient, the final authority in all matters of faith and life. They argued that the Bible was a law book, not only of religion but also of civil affairs. A quotation from the Bible—regardless of its historical content and meaning—settled any question. God was looked upon as the sovereign Ruler of the universe. His will was supreme, his decrees unchangeable. Along with this idea of God went the concept of man's utter inability to contribute anything to his own salvation. Thomas Shepard said, "Oh thou mayest wish and desire to come out sometime, but canst not put strength to the desire, nor indure to do it. Thou mayest hang down thy head like a Bulrush for sin, but thou canst not repent of sin." [1]

Having turned against the formalism of the Roman and Anglican form of worship, their religious life was marked by the most minute and rigorous introspection. A hundred years before Hopkins, Thomas Hooker promulgated the doctrine of "unconditional resignation" and willingness to be eternally condemned if God's will required it. They also had a very vivid feeling of the machinations of the devil. His trails and footprints were believed to infest all the narrow roads through the primeval forests of New England. In 1648 a woman was executed in Hartford for alleged communion with the devil. In the years 1692 and 1693 more than a hundred women were arrested on that same charge, and twenty of them were executed or died from torture.[2] In short, the religious life of New England was marked by

[1] Thomas Shepard, *Sincere Convert* (1646).

[2] Cf. Charles W. Upham, *Salem Witchcraft* (New York: F. Ungar Publishing Co., 1959).

that awfulness in religion which leaves the sinner alone in the very presence of Almighty God.

Calvinistic theology was preached in New England by such men as Thomas Shepard, the radical Thomas Hooker (d. 1647), the learned John Cotton, who wrote *The Keys of the Kingdom of Heaven* (1644), and a catechism: *Milk for Babes* (1646); and the members of the noble Mather dynasty: Richard (1596-1669), who advocated the Half-Way Covenant; Increase (1639-1723); Cotton (1662/63-1727/28); and Samuel (1700-1785).

The proper background of New England theology is seen in the general decline of religion and morals which began with the second generation of the Pilgrims. The great emphasis which was laid on the divine sovereignty and man's moral inability by the preaching of New England clergy reduced the number of conversions and depleted Church membership. The decline of piety was increased by the spread of Arminian literature in New England. Tillotson, Whitby, Taylor, and Clarke, and subsequently the Socinian writings of Thomas Emlyn were studied widely.[3] A change for the better came with a succession of revival movements in 1735 and the Great Awakening in 1740. The revival began with a series of sermons preached by Jonathan Edwards, pastor at Northampton, Massachusetts.

Jonathan Edwards

Jonathan Edwards was born in 1703. Having graduated from Yale in 1720, he was installed at Northampton in 1727 as the colleague of his grandfather, Solomon Stoddard. The attempt to revert to the stricter disciplinary principles of the earlier period led to his dismissal by the congregation in 1750. For a number of years he was active in missionary work among the Indians. In 1758 he was called as president of Princeton College but he died in the same year.[4] Among

[3] *An Humble Inquiry into the Scripture Account of Jesus Christ, or a Short Argument Concerning His Deity and Glory, According to the Gospel.*

[4] There is no complete edition of his works. The most inclusive is the one by S. E. Dwight in ten large volumes, *The Works of President Edwards* (New York, 1829-30), hereinafter referred to as *DE.* Of recent editions we mention: *Freedom of the Will,* ed. Paul Ramsay (New Haven: Yale University Press, 1957). *Jonathan Edwards on Evangelism,* ed. Carl J. C. Wolf (Grand Rapids: Wm. B. Eerdmans Publishing Co., 1958). Jonathan Edwards, *Religious Affections,* ed. John E. Smith (New Haven: Yale University Press).

his writings are *The Distinguishing Marks of a Work of the Spirit of God* (1741), *Thoughts on the Revival* (1742), *Religious Affections* (1746), *Qualifications for Full Communion* (1749), *Freedom of the Will* (1754), and *Original Sin* (1758). Among works published posthumously are *History of Redemption* (1774), *Nature of Virtue* (1788), *God's Last End in Creation* (1788), and *Essay on the Trinity* (1903).

Edwards was "profoundly attached to the Calvinistic system, and his first instinct was to restore it to its high place of influence." But the great originality of his mind and the wide range of his studies did not permit him "to remain where his fathers had been."[5] While a sophomore at Yale he read Locke's *Essay on Human Understanding*. The book made a profound impression on him. He put the Calvinistic theology which he had inherited from his progenitors on the new basis of an empirical piety. Yet he did not accept Locke's view of the mind as a blank sheet of paper to be written upon by experience. He combined the empiricism of Locke with a metaphysical realism. With him "God and real existence are the same." Created spirits are "immanations" and "communications" of God's being.

There were two spirits in Edwards. On the one hand, he spoke of the excellency of God in the glowing language of an ardent mystic. When he read the First Epistle of Paul to Timothy, there came over him, according to his own narrative, "a sweet delight in God and divine things." He often experienced, when "sweetly conversing with Christ," being "wrapt and swallowed up in God."[6] Edwards was never satisfied with a moralistic concept of piety. Religion was not morality but affection, emotion, "a gracious experience of the reality of God," and a "feeling of divine joy and happiness." On the other hand, in a truly Calvinistic fashion, God was for him the sovereign Lord possessed of awful wrath who holds the unconverted sinner over the pit of hell, "much as we hold a spider, or some loathsome insect over the fire."[7] In keeping with this is the stress which Edwards sometimes placed on man's complete dependence "on God's arbitrary

[5] Frank H. Foster, *A Genetic History of the New England Theology* (Chicago: University of Chicago Press, 1907).

[6] S. Hopkins, *Life and Character of J. Edwards* (1765), p. 26.

[7] See the sermon "Sinners in the Hands of an Angry God," *DE,* VII, 163 ff.

and sovereign good pleasure,"[8] and at other times on the principle of mystical illumination by the Supernatural.[9]

Foster, in his discussion of the New England theology, has presented the teachings of Edwards in their relation to his psychology of the will, and criticized them as they do or do not measure up to the psychology of Foster himself. "This is unfortunate," as Haroutunian remarks, "because the chief aim of the Edwardian theology was not to formulate a theory of the will; it was inspired by a piety which sought to glorify God and His sovereignty over man. On the other hand, it asserted human responsibility, and sought to reconcile it with its theocentric piety."[10] In other words, Edward's chief concern was to harmonize Calvinistic predestinarianism with a proper emphasis on man's moral responsibility. Over against Arminianism he held to the necessarian view. He worked out his concept of freedom in the famous treatise *Freedom of Will.*[11] He divides the "mind" into the "faculties" of "understanding" and "will." Following John Locke, he defines the will as "that by which the mind chooses anything."[12] The mind perceives. That which is perceives is a "motive." When confronted with several alternatives, the mind will follow that "which, as it stands in view of the mind, is the strongest."[13] This is the determining factor over the will. As to the "abilities" of man, Edwards distinguishes between "natural ability" or "inability," i.e., "whatever a nature does or does not allow," and "moral inability" which consists, as he says, "in the opposition or want of inclination."[14] A man has the natural ability "to hold his hand from striking," or "to show his neighbor kindness," or "to keep the cup (of intoxicating liquor) from his mouth."[15] Inasmuch as man is under no physical compulsion to do or not to do these things, he is said to be free. This is man's only liberty. What man lacks is "moral ability." Edwards says, "moral inability, which consists in disinclinaton, never can

[8] See the sermon "God Glorified in Man's Dependence," *DE,* VII, 149 ff.

[9] See his sermon "The Reality of Spiritual Light," *DE,* VI, 171 ff.

[10] Joseph Haroutunian, *Piety versus Moralism: The Passing of The New England Theology* (New York: Henry Holt & Co., 1932), p. xxiii.

[11] *DE,* II, 9 ff.

[12] *Ibid.,* p. 16.

[13] *Ibid.,* p. 19.

[14] *Ibid.,* p. 35.

[15] *Ibid.,* p. 37.

excuse any person in disobedience, or want of conformity to a command."[16]

Although Edwards was an ardent supporter and defender of the revival, he proved to be very sober and circumspect concerning the development of the movement. He was no friend of Enthusiasts, for he did not look to personal experience or immediate inspiration as the authority of religion. He includes among the "erroneous principles" the notion "that it is God's manner in these days, to guide His saints, at least some that are more imminent, by inspiration, or immediate revelation." "By such a notion," he says, "the devil has a great door opened for him."[17] The Bible is the only infallible guide of both doctrine and conduct. Edwards made a careful distinction between inspiration and illumination. Whereas he defined inspiration as "suggesting new truths or doctrines to the mind, independent of any antecedent revelations . . . either in word or writing," illumination, he said, "reveals no new doctrine, . . . but only gives a due apprehension of those things that are taught in the word of God."[18] Nevertheless, Edwards was close to Zwingli when he stressed the Reformed conception that the divine light is given immediately and that the word of God is not the proper cause of this effect.

His view on the ministry was rather "high." He looked askance upon itinerant ministers who trespassed established parochial boundaries. The ordaining of a person spiritually qualified for the ministry but lacking in proper education is "a greater calamity than missing such persons in the work of the ministry." The admission of unlearned men to the ministry might easily lead to "impulses, vain imaginations, superstitions, indiscreet zeal, and such like extremes." Lay exhorters "ought not to clothe themselves with the like authority with that which is proper for ministers"; if they do, "they invade the office of a minister."[19]

Like Zwingli, Edwards viewed baptism as a "sign" and "sacred badge" of Christian people. He upheld the practice of infant baptism but wanted to extend it only to the children of parents themselves in a state of sanctifying grace. Likewise, Church membership should be

[16] *Ibid.*, p. 163.

[17] *DE,* IV, 198.

[18] *DE,* VI, 171 ff.

[19] See his "Thoughts on the Revival," *DE,* IV, 77 ff.

restricted to those who are "visibly gracious Christians" and professors of godliness, while those who are merely moral in their living, who only confess the common virtues should be excluded from the visible Church. In other words, Edwards sought to restore the original ideal of the Pilgrims, and advocated the abrogation of the Half-Way Covenant. The Church is the communion of Christians professing "a saving grace," not merely "religion and virtue that is the result of common grace, or moral sincerity." In New England this view helped to widen the gap between Church and state and to prepare the Congregational churches for the principle of separation of Church and state. After Edwards, the old Calvinistic antithesis of "elect" and "non-elect" lost its significance in New England and was replaced by the spiritualistic alternative of "converted" and "unconverted."

In keeping with this view of the Church was his concept of the Lord's Supper. He regarded the Eucharist as a confessing, not a converting ordinance. "There is in the Lord's Supper a mutual solemn profession of the two parties transacting the covenant of grace, and visibly united in that covenant; the Lord Christ by His minister, on the one hand, and the communicants (who are professing believers), on the other." For who else but a person who is in the state of sanctifying grace is qualified, while he takes, eats and drinks those things "which represent Christ," to profess: "I take this crucified Jesus as my Saviour, my sweetest food, my chief portion, and the life of my soul. . . .?" [20]

Concerning the origin of evil, Edwards adhered to the supralapsarian view of the Fall, although he had no liking for the idea that God willed man to fall. He introduced a new element into the discussion of original sin.[21] By divine disposition, he says, the human race is one person and is guilty of the transgression of Adam. God "dealt with Adam as a *public person*—as the head of the human species—and had respect to his posterity, as included in him." [22] The imputation of the first transgression, therefore, is mediate, not immediate. This conception reflects the metaphysical realism of Edwards. Original sin,

[20] "Qualifications for Communion," *DE*, IV, 281 ff

[21] *DE*, II, 301 ff.

[22] *Ibid.*, p. 438. This teaching of Edwards' reflects the influence of the French theological school of Saumur. Cf. Charles Hodge, *Systematic Theology* (New York: Scribner, Armstrong & Co., 1874), II, 205 ff.

is not a positive taint. When God made man, he says, "He implanted in him two kinds of principles. There was an inferior kind, which may be called the natural, being the principles of mere human nature," and the "superior principles, the spiritual, holy, and divine," which may be called the supernatural. Edwards desires the reader to observe that the words "natural and supernatural" are not used here "as epithets of distinction between that which is concreated or connate, and that which is extraordinarily introduced afterwards . . . but as distinguishing between what belongs to, or flows from, that nature which man has, merely as man, and those things which are above this which is not essential to the constitution of nature."[23] He comes very close to the Scholastic conception of man when he defines the effect of the fall as the loss of the supernatural gifts.[24]

As to the order of salvation, Edwards sided with the spiritualistic trend in Protestantism. He stressed the Spirit's immediate operation on man's soul. There is no such thing as a gradual, quiet growth into the kingdom. Conversion, he says, "is a great and glorious work of God's power, *at once* [italics ours] changing the heart, and infusing life into the dead soul." He admitted, however, that as for fixing the precise time of conversion, "there is a great deal of difference in different persons."[25]

Justification, Edwards says, is "manifestly a forensic term."[26] He vitally modified the forensic view when he termed faith a spiritual qualification which renders man, if not deserving, yet "fit" and "meet" to be justified. "God justifies a believer . . . because He sees something in this qualification that . . . renders it a fit thing that such should be justified."[27] In the act of justification God and man are placed almost on the same level when Edwards says, "God sees it fit, that in order to a union being established between two intelligent active beings or persons, so as they should be looked upon as one, there should be the mutual act of both, that each should receive the other, as actively joining themselves one to another. . . . And if there be any act or

[23] *DE,* II, 536.

[24] Cf. A. V. G. Allen, *Jonathan Edwards* (Boston: Houghton Mifflin Company, 1889), pp. 65-66, on Edwards' distinction between the "natural and supernatural."

[25] "A Faithful Narrative of Surprising Conversions," *DE,* IV, 3 ff.

[26] "Justification by Faith Alone," *DE,* V, 351 ff.

[27] *Ibid.,* p. 358.

qualification in believers of that uniting nature, that it is meet on that account the judge should look upon them and accept them as one, no wonder that upon the the account of the same act or qualification, he should accept the satisfaction and merits of one for the other, as if these were their own satisfaction and merits." [28] Evidently, Edwards shared the view of pietism which looks upon faith as a virtuous quality in man. Such thinking of necessity leads to a synergistic and moralistic concept of salvation; and while this remained latent in Edwards, it became an open fact in the theology of his successors.

Virtue, according to Edwards, is the highest spiritual beauty. Its nature is benevolence. It is love to the entire society of intelligent beings in proportion to the amount of "being" which they possess. Virtue is absolute love to God and limited love to other beings, for he who "has the greatest share of universal existence, has proportionately the greatest share of virtuous benevolence." [29] In contradistinction to this, sin is defined as selfishness.

Man was created for an ever increasing union with and closeness to God. The creation of the world has its cause in a "disposition in God . . . to an emanation of His own fullness." He makes Himself His end. From this it is evident that Edwards was, philosophically, a monist. All reality is subsumed in God.[30]

The Edwardian School

Jonathan Edwards had coadjutors and followers capable of refuting Arminianism and arousing the old school of Calvinism out of its lethargy. But gradually the initial emphasis of Edwards on the glory of God as the last end in creation gave way to a utilitarian aspect of religion. While in the opinion of Calvin and Edwards man lives to worship God, in the theology of Edwards' successors God lives to serve human happiness.[31]

Joseph Bellamy (1719-1790) opposed the Half-Way Covenant. He agreed with Edwards that man has the ability to repent, and that every minister is under solemn obligation to call his hearers to repentance. God is not a capricious being, but a being of infinite benevo-

[28] *Ibid.*, p. 364.
[29] "The Nature of True Virtue," *DE*, III, 93 ff.
[30] "God's Last End in Creation," *DE*, III, 5 ff.
[31] Cf. Haroutunian, *op. cit.*, p. 145.

lence. The eternal decrees rest in the love of God. The origin of sin is limited to divine permission. On the basis of Leibnitz's optimism he declared that sin is the necessary means to the greatest good. He laid emphasis on the use of the means of grace in the act of conversion.[32]

In Samuel Hopkins' teaching (1721-1803) the theology of Edwards underwent a further modification. He also based the divine eternal decrees on the love of God and took great pains to uphold the optimistic belief in the loving government of God. As to the question of evil and human freedom, he said that the divine decrees include freedom for man, for God saves man through man's volition. All is included in the divine decrees and nothing is done by man independent of God.

Like Bellamy, Hopkins maintained that sin is the necessary means of the greatest good. It is a free act. Strictly speaking, all sin is voluntary sin. There is no imputation of the first transgression. "If the sinfulness of all the posterity of Adam was certainly connected with his sinning, this does not make them sinners, before they actually are sinners. . . . The children of Adam are not answerable for his sin."[33] Man has not lost any of his natural powers, he has only lost his inclination to serve and to obey God. This is the meaning of his teaching of "divine efficiency" even in the sinful choices of man. Since Hopkins, the imputation of the sin of Adam was discarded from the New England theology.

For Hopkins, regeneration is an act of God. It consists of illumination.[34] Man reacts to the regenerative work of God by conversion. A supporter of revivalism, Hopkins says that regeneration is "instantaneous, wrought not gradually, but at once."[35] Justification is a moral union which takes place between the sinner and the Saviour.[36] God treats the sinner "as if he had never sinned" for Christ's sake.[37]

[32] "The Wisdom of God in the Permission of Sin" (1758) *Complete Works,* Vol. II (1852). According to the standards of Reformed theology there are three distinct means of grace: the Word, sacraments, and prayer. Lutherans do not conceive of prayer as a means of grace. They apply the term only to those means by which God reaches out for man.

Cf. Aulén, *Faith of the Christian Church,* pp. 401 ff.

[33] Samuel Hopkins, *Works* (1852), I, 233, 235.

[34] *Ibid.,* p. 399.

[35] *Ibid.,* p. 368.

[36] *Ibid.,* p. 463.

[37] *Ibid.,* p. 458.

Hopkins rejects the idea of imputation of Christ's righteousness.[38] The effect of the atonement is universal. The essence of sin is self-love. Virtue is disinterested benevolence. Man should love himself not as a self but only as a part of universal Being. If God requires it, man should consent unconditionally to be cast off eternally.[39] Through his book *System of Doctrines*, published in 1793, Hopkins had a direct influence on the founders of Andover Theological Seminary.

Jonathan Edwards, Jr. (1745-1801), and Nathanael Emmons (1745-1840) were in substantial agreement with Hopkins. Edwards made his principal contribution to theological thought in his discussion of the atonement. Emmons further atomized the concept of sin. Sin is no natural state. Sin, like holiness, consists in "free voluntary affections and exercises." Man is not merely passive but active in regeneration. Justification is the pardoning act of God. His sins forgiven, man may live a godly life and by his good works win a reward, the blessed life of heaven.[40]

The influence of Hopkinsianism in New England theology was perpetuated at Andover Seminary through the teaching of Leonard Woods (1774-1854), while Timothy Dwight (1752-1817), president of Yale and grandson of Jonathan Edwards, Sr., was the most distinguished representative of that school of Edwardians which was opposed to Hopkinsian peculiarities. Dwight was a moderate Calvinist. For Dwight divine foreknowledge and the decrees are coetaneous. Sin exists by divine permission; its essence is selfishness. "Virtue is founded in Utility," for it tends to promote the happiness of the universe.[41]

New Haven Theology

The chief exponent of the New Haven theology was Nathaniel W. Taylor (1786-1858). He modified the older New England doctrines of man's depravity and responsibility, the divine permission of sin and regeneration. Like Hopkins, he denied original sin. The universality of sin is due to the present condition of man and the circumstance of

[38] *Ibid.*, p. 477.

[39] Cf. *ibid.*, p. 389.

[40] J. Ide (ed.), *The Works of Emmons with Memoir of His Life by E. A. Park* (6 vols.; Boston, 1860 ff.).

[41] Timothy Dwight, *Theology Explained and Defended,* posthumously edited (1818 ff.).

his life. But he rejected Hopkins' doctrine which reduces sin to individual acts of the will. Sin is a permanent state of the will. He also opposed the doctrine that sin is the necessary means to the greatest good. To avoid the least semblance of fatalism, Taylor introduced "the power of contrary choice" into the discussion of human ability. He met the Pelagian implication of this concept by asserting the prior certainty of all moral choices. There is the certainty, he held, that all men will persist in sinning until they are converted under the power of divine grace. He distinguishes between selfishness and self-love, the natural desire for happiness. Self-love is a neutral state of the soul which is neither good nor evil. In this state, man is capable of obeying the gospel call regardless of grace.

Chauncy A. Goodrich (1790-1860) and Eleazar T. Fitch (1791-1871) defended Taylor's teachings. Taylor's most prominent opponents were Joseph Harvey, Leonard Woods, and Bennet Tyler. The opposition was so pronounced in Connecticut that it led to the establishment of a new theological institution, which was first located at East Windsor, but later removed to Hartford.

The New Divinity

The Pelagian tendencies in the New Divinity are manifest in the revivalistic theology of Oberlin College. The two most prominent leaders of Oberlin Theology were Charles G. Finney (1792-1875) and Asa Mahan (1799-1889). Their theology centers in the preaching of total consecration and sinless perfection. Finney rejects the Edwardian distinction between natural and moral ability.[42] His view of the will is wholly Pelagian: man is free to choose. To the doctrine of natural ability the Oberlin theologians added that of the simplicity of moral action. This doctrine was first proclaimed by William Cochran, a member of the graduating class of 1839. Since a moral action is not of a mixed character, and the will is competent to make but one choice at a time, whenever a man makes a right choice he is perfect at that moment and continues to be perfect as long as right choices prevail. According to Finney regeneration is a turning to God. The preacher should use the force of persuasion to convert the

[42] Charles G. Finney, *Lectures on Systematic Theology,* ed. J. H. Fairchild (Grand Rapids: Wm. B. Eerdmans Publishing House, 1957), pp. 320 ff.

sinner. Perfect sanctification is attained by the baptism of the Holy Ghost, who is indispensable to the "appropriate happiness and befitting characteristics of the children of God." [43]

The teaching of the Oberlin men left a permanent mark on American church life in that it gave impetus to the establishment of Holiness and Pentecostal churches. Prominently identified with this movement are W. E. Boardman (1810-1886), A. B. Simpson (1843-1919), and A. M. Hills (1848-1935). Though differing on many points of doctrine and practice, e.g., baptism with the Holy Ghost, gift of tongues, divine healing, footwashing, etc., they all agree on an Arminian view of man and on the Wesleyan teaching of entire sanctification.

The last outstanding representatives of the New England Theology were Fairchild and Park. James Harris Fairchild (1817-1902), the successor of Finney at Oberlin, represents the same fundamental principles in his teaching which Finney had taught. Edwards Amasa Park (1808-1900) was a pupil of Woods and even more of Taylor. At one time he was considered to be the greatest dogmatic genius of America. In general, Park followed the modified Calvinism of Edwards and Taylor. God is all-cooperative, but his decrees are based on his love. Park uses the Scholastic method of proving biblical truth on rational grounds. He was one of the founders and the first editor of the *Bibliotheca Sacra.*

The discussion of the atonement attracted much interest in the New Divinity, but it did not come into prominence until the liberal movement singled out this doctrine for attack. The New England theologians tried to define their teaching so as to reject a limited atonement as well as to give greater emphasis to the grace and mercy of God in the conversion of the sinner. Their doctrine, commonly called the governmental, or benevolence theory of the atonement, united certain tenets of the Grotian and Arminian concepts of the atonement with the Calvinistic doctrine of divine sovereignty. The chief contributors to this theory were Bellamy[44] and Jonathan Edwards, Jr.[45] According to this theory, God made his own Son suffer on the cross in order to demonstrate that his law had not changed. The heinousness of

[43] *Ibid.*, pp. 402 ff.

[44] Joseph Bellamy, "The True Religion Delineated," (1750), *Complete Works* (3 vols.; Boston, 1850).

[45] Jonathan Edwards, Jr., *Three Sermons on the Atonement,* 1785.

man's sin demanded God's action. The sufferings of Christ were not punishment, for the law had no claim on him: they were an adequate exhibition of God's wrath against sin. The moral government has been maintained, and God will forgive him who turns from evil to good. The work of Christ has not changed God's attitude to man, but wants to effect a change in man's disposition toward God.[46]

Conclusion

The New Divinity sought a happy medium by which to bridge the chasm between stark Calvinism and Pelagian Arminianism. The New England theological controversy, like the Arminian dispute, was a Protestant counterpart to the Semi-Pelagian controversy in the ancient Church of the West. While the Arminians placed emphasis on the human side in the work of salvation, the New Divinity stood closer to the divine. The exalted place which reason had in the Arminian system found no favor with Edwards. He was a mystic. Illumination comes to man as a divine gift. Edwardian theology is Semi-Calvinism, shading off, in Hopkins and Taylor, into Semi-Pelagianism.

Trained in a religion that was marked by rigid self-introspection, the New England theologians undertook a minute analysis of the psychological faculties of man. Stephen West's *Essay on Moral Agency* (1772), and Asa Burton's *Essays on Some of the First Principles of Metaphysics, Ethics, and Theology* (1824) are, along with the contributions of other leading figures of the movement, classics of the New Divinity.[47] Against the background of Calvinistic determinism, the unique contribution of the New England theology to the development of theological thought lies in these minute psychological studies.

As a *via media* between Puritan Calvinism and eighteenth century Arminianism the New Divinity aroused the antagonism of the genuine Calvinists and lost the support of the progressives when the latter attempted to reconstruct theological thought in the light of the natural sciences. The New Divinity proved too narrow and supernaturalistic for the progressives; for the genuine Calvinists, it conceded too much to human ability. They felt that the Calvinism represented by the New Divinity was nothing but "the faith of the fathers ruined by the

[46] Cf. George N. Boardman, *A History of New England Theology,* pp. 221 ff.

[47] Cf., "The Theory of Will" in Foster, *op. cit.,* pp. 224 ff.

faith of their children" [48] because theological interest was focused in man, in his ability, and happiness. The grand concept of Edwards, "affection for being in general" became love for all intelligent beings. In short, Christianity, stripped of the metaphysical and supernatural, became a humanitarian creed. "And thus New England theology perished from the earth." [49]

The opposition to the New Divinity branched off into two directions: the liberal movement, which struck at the supernatural element retained in the system of the Edwardians, and the conservative reaction, which attempted to restore Calvinism to its own.

BIBLIOGRAPHY

ALLEN, A. V. G. *Jonathan Edwards.* New York: Houghton Mifflin Co., 1889.

BOARDMAN, GEORGE N. *A History of New England Theology.* New York: A. D. F. Randolf Co., 1899.

BYINGTON, EZRA H. *The Puritan as a Colonist and Reformer.* Boston: Little, Brown & Co., 1899.

CUNNINGHAM, CHARLES E. *Timothy Dwight: A Biography.* New York: The Macmillan Company, 1942.

DWIGHT, S. E. ed. *The Works of President Edwards.* 10 vols. New York, 1829-30.

FISHER, GEORGE PARK. *History of Christian Doctrine.* New York: Charles Scribner's Sons, 1906.

GERSTNER, JOHN H. *Steps to Salvation: The Evangelistic Message of Jonathan Edwards.* Philadelphia: Westminster Press, 1959.

GOEN, C. C. *Revivalism and Separatism in New England, 1740–1800.* New Haven: Yale University Press, 1962.

HAROUTUNIAN, JOSEPH. *Piety versus Moralism: The Passing of the New England Theology.* New York: Henry Holt & Co., 1932.

MILLER, PERRY. *The New England Mind: From Colony to Province.* New York: The Macmillan Company, 1939.

SCHNEIDER, HERBERT W. *The Puritan Mind.* New York: Henry Holt & Co., 1930.

SIMPSON, ALAN. *Puritanism in Old and New England.* Chicago: University of Chicago Press, 1955.

WERTENBAKER, T. J. *The Puritan Oligarchy.* New York: Charles Scribner's Sons, 1947.

WILLIAMS, DANIEL D. *The Andover Liberals.* New York: Kings Crown Press, 1941.

WINSLOW, OLA E. *Jonathan Edwards, 1703–1758.* New York: The Macmillan Company, 1940.

[48] Haroutunian, *op. cit.,* p. 281.
[49] Foster, *op. cit.,* p. 552.

CHAPTER III

THE LIBERAL MOVEMENT IN AMERICAN THEOLOGY

In America rationalism and liberalism were a reaction to the Calvinistic use of the Bible as a book of laws and as a textbook on nature. The liberal movement had its root in English Arminianism, latitudinarianism, Socinianism, and Unitarianism. Theological unrest was intensified by the spread of French infidelity, "the legacy of French co-operation in the War of the Revolution." [1] In time, the religious individualism inherent in Puritanism and its concept of Christianity as a covenant proved to be a strong factor in liberalizing the substance of faith. Calvinism lost the famous Puritan pulpits in Boston and its vicinity to Unitarianism. There is some truth in the saying that the seeds of American Unitarianism came to this country in the "Mayflower" and were planted here by the Pilgrims. The change of the colonial charters in 1692 served as another stimulus to growing liberalism in America. As a result, liberal books and other literature were brought into the colonies from England. During the eighteenth century the growth of liberalism became progressively more apparent. Among those who exercised a great influence on the liberal side of Puritanism was Ebenezer Gay (1696-1787) of Hingham, Massachusetts, who has been called the father of American Unitarianism, and John Wise (1652-1725) of Ipswich, Massachusetts, called the "Father of American democracy," whose book *Vindication of the New England Churches* (1717) is a remarkable exposition of the principles of civil government.

Liberalism in America was primarily a humanitarian movement which emphasized the ethical and social aspects of Christianity. The controversy over the atonement was rooted in the humanitarian protest against Calvinism. The dispute over the Trinity, which became

[1] Foster, *op. cit.*, p. 273.

the issue between the Unitarians and the orthodox, "merely crystallized the growing estrangement between Calvinism and the spirit of the new age, and brought it to a head."[2] The difference between the Unitarians and the Universalists was a difference only in degree. With the Universalists the main stress was on the concept of a general atonement; with the Unitarians the stress was on the unity of God. For the Universalists God is too good to damn man; for the Unitarians, man is too good to be damned.

In *The Meritorious Price of Our Redemption* (1650), William Pynchon held to the idea of a limited atonement, but protested against the teaching that Christ on the cross had suffered the pains of hell of the condemned and against the doctrine of imputed righteousness. It was still premature for a man to deny a fundamental principle of Calvinism openly. Pynchon's book was to be burned and the author returned to England a few years later.[3]

Universalism

Universalism was introduced into America by John Murray, who arrived in New Jersey in 1770.[4] He had been brought up as a strict Calvinist and had been a co-worker of Wesley and Whitefield till he became attracted to the teaching of James Relly, an exponent of Universalist doctrine in its grossest form in England.[5] Relly taught that the human race was so united to Christ that this union "renders His condition theirs in every state which He passes through."[6] The next great leader of the movement was Elhanan Winchester (1751-1797). He was a Trinitarian.[7] He taught a universal restoration and contended that there must be adequate but not eternal punishment. His influence was soon superseded by that of Hosea Ballou (1771-1852), who became the recognized leader of the movement. Ballou effected the shift of Universalism from a trinitarianism to a unitarianism. He was a

[2] Haroutunian, *op. cit.,* p. 180.

[3] Cf. Boardman, *op. cit.,* pp. 221 ff.

[4] Cf. C. R. Skinner–A. L. Cole, *Hell's Ramparts Fell. The Biography of John Murray* (Boston: Universalist Publishing House, 1941).

[5] James Relly, *Union; or a Treatise of the Consanguinity and Affinity between Christ and His Church* (1759).

[6] Cf. Foster, *op. cit.,* p. 190.

[7] Elhanan Winchester, *The Divinity of Christ Proved from the Scriptures,* undated.

determinist; for, if the will of God to save all is carried out, the will of man must be denied the power of resistance. The effect of the atonement is universal; its purpose is universal holiness, i.e., the happiness of mankind. The human race, which originated in God, must finally be united with the fountain from which it sprang. He argued that everlasting punishment for some members would interfere with the happiness of the whole race.[8] Ballou's lack of a scriptural basis for his doctrine was corrected by Walter Balfour in his book, published a decade later, *An Inquiry Into the Scriptural Import of the Words Sheol, Hades, Tartarus, and Gehenna, All Translated Hell in the Common English Version* (1824). In this treatise Balfour analyzes the scriptural teaching of eternal condemnation. He concludes that since none of the words under investigation designates an eternal condition, there is no such thing in the Bible as eternal punishment.

The most formidable opponent of Universalism was Moses Stuart, professor at Andover. He tried to refute Balfour in his book entitled *Exegetical Essays on Several Words Relating to the Future Punishment* (1830). Stuart upheld the orthodox view of eternal punishment. Thomas Whittenmore, himself a Universalist, rejected the tenets of Balfour's exegesis in his own *Plain Guide to Universalism* (1830). In a statement of faith issued in 1935, the Universalists avowed their faith "in God as Eternal and All-Conquering Love, in the spiritual leadership of Jesus . . . and in the power of men of good will and sacrificial spirit to overcome all evil and progressively establish the kingdom of God."[9]

Unitarianism

Of far greater significance than the Universalist movement is the rise of Unitarianism in America. James Freeman and his congregation of King's Chapel Episcopal Church, Boston, became the first church in New England to embrace Unitarianism openly. Soon Harvard became a hotbed of Unitarianism. In 1805 Henry Ware (1764-1845), an outspoken liberal, was elected to the Hollis Chair of Divinity at Harvard. Intellectual and liberal theology was cultivated through the Anthology Club and through *The Monthly Anthology*, *The Christian*

[8] Hosea Ballou, *A Treatise on the Atonement* (1804).

[9] Frank S. Mead, *Handbook of Denominations in the United States* (New York: Abingdon Press, 1956), pp. 206-207. In 1961, the Unitarians and Universalists merged to become the Unitarian Universalist Association.

Monitor (after 1806), and the aggressive *General Repository and Review* (after 1812). New England Congregationalism began to split into a conservative and a liberal wing. The conservatives founded Andover Seminary in 1808 to train a clergy which would be free from the taint of the Unitarian heresy. The formation of a new denomination out of the liberal wing, however, was a very slow and gradual progress. The separation of the two wings was not complete until 1833, by which time the liberal movement had passed through its first radical transformation. Whatever headway the movement made in America at the beginning of the nineteenth century, it remained for Channing, Emerson, and Parker to crystallize Unitarian principles.

William Ellery Channing was born at Newport, Rhode Island in 1780, of stern Calvinistic parents. At Harvard he became a pupil of Samuel Hopkins. In 1803 he became pastor of Brattle Street Church in Boston, where he remained till his death in 1842. In 1819 he delivered his epoch-making Baltimore sermon, "Unitarian Christianity," at the installation of Jared Sparks. In the introduction of this sermon Channing exalts reason as capable of perceiving revelation and expounding the Scriptures. He went on to reject the trinitarian doctrine, the Church's doctrine of Christ's twofold nature, and the orthodox view of the atonement. Salvation is obtained by the exercise of man's moral faculties. The sermon furnished the Unitarians, who hitherto were in disagreement among themselves on every doctrine save the Trinity, with something which they could regard as a platform. In the later years of his life Channing became a champion of the Abolitionist movement. The keynote of Channing's theology is his supreme faith in man. Reason is the ultimate source of authority. Man is endowed with a knowledge of right and with the power to do right. To deny man the exercise of a free will would make the sentiment of duty illusory. God is the Infinite Being, the Parent Mind, the Universal Father, and the Father of our spirits. He is substantially immanent. Man experiences the fact of revelation in his own conscience. A special revelation can supplement the laws of nature, not contradict them.

Of Jesus Channing says in his Baltimore sermon, "We believe that Jesus is one mind, one soul, one being, as truly one as we are, and equally distinct from the one God." At another place (*Imitableness of Christ's Character*) he says of Jesus, "I believe Him to be a more than human being," continuing, however, a little later, "For though so far above us, He is still one of us, and is only an illustration of the capacities which we all possess. . . . All minds are of one family." According to Channing, Christ is a pre-existent rational creature of God. This is a crude and unphilosophical sort of Arianism "which strikingly indicates the transitorial character of Channing's type of theology." [10] God's justice, according to Channing, is in perfect harmony with his mercy. God "desires strongly the happiness of the guilty; but only through their penitence." There is no place in Channing's theology for a doctrine of vicarious atonement. Christ's mission is "the recovery of man to virtue." "We regard Him a Saviour," he said in his Baltimore sermon, "chiefly as He is the light, physician, and guide of the dark, diseased and wandering mind." Channing revived the old Socinian arguments in his objections to the doctrines of the Trinity and the double nature of Christ. His piety was of a highly emotional and spiritual quality, thus refuting the concept current among his contemporaries that a liberal theology is of necessity cold and dull. Channing was not interested in denominational lines; he even disliked being called a Unitarian.[11]

Next to Channing, Ralph Waldo Emerson's magnetic personality stands out as one of the greatest leaders of the liberal movement. Emerson was born in 1803 at Boston. Educated at Harvard, he was ordained to the Congregational ministry in 1829. After three years of service at the Second Church, Boston, he resigned his charge because the congregation was unwilling to discontinue, or, at least, radically change the communion service. Upon his resignation he continued to speak to an ever growing audience as philosopher and poet, till his death in 1882.

In Emerson's world of thought three different currents meet: the skeptical or empirical, the ethical, and the mystical. While the skeptical vein is regarded as merely methodological, the ethical is the basis, and the mystical the subcurrent, of all his thought. His view of God

[10] George P. Fisher, *History of Christian Doctrine* (New York: Charles Scribner's Sons, 1906), p. 431.

[11] Channing's works have been collected into three volumes and edited by the Unitarian Association (1848 and subsequent editions).

borders on pantheism. Consequently, evil is denied ontological reality. While he does not deny the immortality of the individual, his emphasis is on the ethical import of immortality. God incarnates himself in every man as he did in Jesus. Under the impact of the Church's theology, Christianity has become a *mythos*, and Jesus, the friend of man, has been made the injurer of man. The word miracle, as pronounced by the churches, is a monster. Revelation is progressive; it comes from within. If a man exchanges his own knowledge of God for a secondary knowledge, e.g., for that of Paul or of George Fox or of Swedenborg, "you get wide from God with every year this secondary form lasts." [12] While the older Unitarians wanted to uphold the truth of the Scriptures against the historical creeds of the Church, Emerson's theology is as un-scriptural as it is non-creedal. The ultimate authority of religion rests in the law of reason and of right as it stands revealed in the mental and moral constitution of man. Emerson became the foremost exponent of American transcendentalism, which sought to comprehend the transcendental verities by the intuition of the soul.[13]

In Emerson an important change in the thinking of American scholars is manifest. His theology struck not only at the fundamentals of Congregationalism but also at the foundation of Unitarianism of the Channing type. The Emersonian teaching made the question as to the place of the supernatural and the concept of God a pointed issue. The age of Emerson was the time when German philosophical and theological thought was first introduced into the English-speaking world by Coleridge, Carlyle, and others. The wealth of German thought began to open up new vistas to the Anglo-Saxons. American students crossed the ocean in great numbers to study at German universities. The question of miracles was much discussed by German scholars. German theology was just emerging from rationalism and was under the influence of Kant, Schleiermacher, and Hegel. This new thought completed the critical work of eighteenth-century Eng-

[12] "The Divinity School Address," July 15, 1838. Printed by the American Unitarian Association as *Tract C* (1935), p. 18.

[13] Cf. the centenary edition of *The Complete Works of Ralph Waldo Emerson* (12 vols.; Boston: Houghton Mifflin Co., 1903-1904); *The Journals of Ralph Waldo Emerson,* edited by E. W. Emerson and W. E. Forbes (10 vols.; New York: Houghton Mifflin Co., 1909 ff.); *The Letters of Ralph Waldo Emerson,* edited by R. L. Rusk (New York: Columbia University Press, 1939).

lish deism and French naturalism. The supernatural and miraculous foundation of Christianity was being discarded. The rationalists had given a rational interpretation to the miracles related in the Bible; the new school interpreted them mythologically or symbolically.

Equally harassing was the new concept of God. With Spinoza, God was substance; with Hegel, thought. For Kant religion was an ethic, for Schleiermacher feeling, and for Hegel, was thinking. Emerson's "Divinity Address" clearly reflects this new trend in religious thinking. The beginning of Unitarianism goes back to a Socinianism resembling the dynamistic monarchianism of the ancient Church: the one personal God. This was still the view of Channing. In Emerson we see the Spinozian concept, which was soon replaced by Hegelian pantheism, beginning to take hold of liberal thinkers.

The transcendental principle expressed by Emerson was applied more concretely by Theodore Parker (1810-1860). While a student at Harvard, Parker acquainted himself with the writings of such German rationalists as de Wette, Eichhorn, Ammon, Paulus, and Wegscheider. He also studied Spinoza, Descartes, Leibnitz, Lessing, and Herder. In 1843, while on a visit to Europe, he came into personal contact with Schelling, Vatke, Tholuck, Ewald, Bauer, and de Wette. In 1836 he translated de Wette's *Introduction to the Old Testament* into English. Parker's sermon "The Transient and Permanent in Christianity," preached at South Boston in 1841, is a landmark in the development of American Unitarianism. Parker takes the stand that Christianity is nothing but "absolute pure morality, absolute pure religion—the love of man; the love of God acting without let or hindrance."[14] The authority of Jesus does not rest on his divine nature but on the truth of his words. These words need no miraculous confirmation. Even "if it could be proved—as it cannot . . . that the Gospels were the fabrication of designing and artful men, that Jesus of Nazareth had never lived, still Christianity would stand firm, and fear no evil."[15] Likewise, the "idolatry of the Old Testament" must cease in the church. As with the eighteenth-century rationalists, the idea of God, the moral law, and the immortality of the soul are the great axioms of Parker's theology. In his views about God he

[14] Published by the American Unitarian Society as *Tract D* (1935).
[15] *Ibid.*

wavers between the concepts of theism and pantheism. Special revelation has no place in his system. Christianity is a purely natural product. Miracles are myths. The fall of man is as inevitable as the fall of a child who learns to walk. By stumbling the child learns to walk. Each fall is a fall upward.[16]

Parker's innovations in theology caused great concern to the more conservative Unitarians. His chief antagonist was Andrews Norton (1786-1853), a professor at Harvard. Unitarian scholars friendly to Channing were Orville Dewey (1794-1882) and Ezra Stiles Gannett (1801-1872). For half a century the Unitarians were divided into two warring factions. In order to check the growing radicalism, the conservatives were constantly struggling to obtain a creedal statement in the constitution of the Unitarian denomination, but they never succeeded. By the end of the Civil War the interest in miracles diminished. The question of "whether a religious organization is primarily to be formed about a belief or about a purpose, a common point of view or a common end of action" was decided in 1894 in favor of the latter interpretation.[17] Unitarianism today is religious pragmatism.

During the latter decades of the nineteenth century the radical wing was represented by such scholars as Octavius Brooks Frothingham (1882-1895), author of *Life of Theodore Parker* (1874), James Freeman Clarke (1810-1888), who wrote *Ten Great Religions* (1873-1883) and *Essentials and Non-Essentials in Religion* (1878), and Joseph Henry Allen (1820-1898), the historian of the Unitarian Movement, who wrote *Our Liberal Movement in Theology* (1882) and *Historical Sketch of the Unitarian Movement since the Reformation* (1894).

Congregational Theology

By the middle of the nineteenth century the liberalizing influence of German thought was also beginning to influence Congregational theologians. The anthropological problems which had been discussed by the Edwardians were receding into the background. Naturalism, supernaturalism, and the questions of scriptural authority, of the person of Christ, and of the atonement were the topics that attracted

[16] *The Religious Demands of the Age; a reprint of the preface to the London edition of the collected works of Theodore Parker,* ed. F. P. Cobbe (Boston: Walker, Wise, & Co., 1863).

[17] Wilbur, *Our Unitarian Heritage,* p. 23.

the interest of the younger generation. The "later New Haven theology" is best exemplified in the life and work of Horace Bushnell (1802-1876). Bushnell was primarily a preacher, not a technical scholar. He was a conscientious theologian, and left his mark upon the Congregational theology of the last century.

In his two volumes entitled *God in Christ* (1849) and *Christ in Theology* (1851), Bushnell undertook to solve the doctrine of the Trinity on a Sabellian hypothesis. Father, Son, and Holy Spirit are three different modes through which the Ineffable One disclosed himself to man. The Trinity is a Trinity of revelation, an instrumental Trinity. The language of the historical creeds should not be pressed to the letter "for the very sufficient reason that the letter is never true. They can never be regarded as proximate representations, and should therefore be accepted not as laws over belief or opinion, but more as badges of consent and good understanding." [18] His aversion to the creeds at this time was due to a lack of proper historical studies, for he later admitted that upon a new and more thorough investigation of the Nicene Creed, its language appealed much more to him. In an article, "The Christian Trinity, a Practical Truth," published in the *New Englander* in November, 1854, he made a striking advance toward Athanasian theology. "He (God) is eternally three-ing himself, or generating three persons," he wrote. "By a certain inward necessity (God) is being accommodated in His action to the categories of finite apprehension." "Here is a certain real immanence of the Trinity," as Fisher rightly remarks, but it is an immanence "conditioned on relativity." [19] According to Athanasian theology, God is triune, independent of his relation to the world.

In his reconstruction of the christological doctrine, Bushnell stressed the divine in Christ. The human element in Christ he held to be of little or no account. Though he did not exactly deny the human soul of Christ as Apollinaris did, yet over against the Nestorianizing form of christological dogma, he denied what he called the "distinct subsistence (of the soul) so as to live, think, learn, worship, and suffer by itself." [20] In his view of the atonement, Bushnell anticipated Ritschl, whom he very likely did not know. Christ came into this

[18] Horace Bushnell, *God in Christ* (Hartford: Brown & Parsons, 1849), p. 81.
[19] Fisher, *op. cit.,* p. 441.
[20] Bushnell, *op. cit.,* p. 154.

world, he held, to renovate the character of man. He did this by demonstrating in his life and death the pity, forbearance, and yearning love of God. As in his studies on the Trinity, Bushnell, in a later treatise on the atonement entitled *Forgiveness and Law* (1874), expressed himself more favorably toward the traditional orthodox view. He admitted that God entered upon a self-sacrifice and self-propitiation in the atoning work of Christ. By the agony on the cross God appeased his just indignation at the sin of mankind.[21] Bushnell also dealt a heavy blow to the revival method of New England theologians in his *Christian Nurture* (1846). The spasmodic excitement and sporadic conversions, he pleaded, should give way to a systematic method of Christian nurture in the home. In this way he became instrumental in inaugurating the modern era of religious education. When Bushnell's view became known, the criticism was made that he was discounting the agency of the Holy Spirit in man's salvation by an appeal to the congenital origin and progressive growth of character by the law of heredity on the plane of naturalism. He struck the same note in a later volume entitled *Nature and the Supernatural* (1858). Both the natural and the spiritual, reason and revelation are parts of one system. Bushnell arrived at a concept of religious authority which, like the mystics, he held to be innate in human reason.[22]

Another representative of this school of thought was Samuel Harris (1814-1899). He holds a transitional position in New England theology. Kant has an established place in his system and, like Hegel, Harris conceived of God as Absolute Reason progressively revealing himself. His principal works are *Philosophical Basis of Theism* (1883), *The Self-Revelation of God* (1887), and *God, the Creator and Lord of All* (1896).

The greatest stumbling block to the liberals was the Calvinist doctrine of the eternal decrees, the concept of a limited atonement, and eternal punishment for the reprobate. With the rise of evolution, the liberals attempted to interpret Christianity in terms of Hegel's concept

[21] According to A. H. Strong, *Systematic Theology* (Philadelphia: Judson Press, 1907), pp. 739-40, Bushnell recanted this moral influence theory of the atonement on his deathbed.

[22] Thornton T. Munger, *Horace Bushnell* (Boston: Houghton Mifflin Co., 1899). Cf. also Foster, *op. cit.*, pp. 401 ff.

of divine immanence and the progressive unfolding of divine truth. Hegelian idealism was just being introduced into English-speaking countries by the Cairds in England and by Royce in America. In addition, Otto Pfleiderer, whose lectures were attended by students from both countries, greatly aided the cause of Hegelianism in the Anglo-Saxon world. Under the influence of Hegel's concept of God as the ever immanent power and the organizing and rationalizing principle of the universe, the supernatural and miraculous revelation of God in Christ and the Scriptures was in danger of being eliminated from Christianity. The seat of religious authority was transferred from the Bible or the Church to human experience in which, according to Hegel, the Infinite becomes self-conscious.

Though Darwinism was branded as atheism by Charles Hodge of Princeton in *What Is Darwinism?* published in 1874, Henry Ward Beecher, in *Evolution and Religion*, 1885, and Lyman Abbott, *Theology of An Evolutionist*, 1897 decidedly cast the lot of Congregational theology with evolution. Bushnell's interpretation of the Trinity was given further consideration by James M. Whiton in *Gloria Patri*, 1892. He conceived of the Sonship of Jesus as a divinity of moral attributes. Lyman Abbott's volume, *The Evolution of Christianity*, published in the same year, strikes the same note, and after 1892 liberal theology was largely Unitarian. Eschatological questions received special attention at Andover, where Egbert Smyth, co-editor of *Progressive Orthodoxy* (1885), and his colleagues shared the view of a continued probation after death for those who had not known God in Christ during their earthly life. This view created a great deal of resentment among the rank and file of the conservatives in those days.

Theodore T. Munger wanted to reconstruct Christianity on reasonableness. He transferred the seat of religious authority from the Bible to individual experience. To George A. Gordon divine revelation and human discovery were reciprocal, and the distinction between natural and revealed religion was an "unholy distinction." [23] He interpreted the doctrine of the Trinity socially. As man is a social being, so there is in the Godhead a social prototype of man's social personality. The work of Newman Smyth, who was one of the first to catch the signifi-

[23] *Harvard Theological Review,* I, No. 2, p. 145.

cance of biology for the spiritual order and to conduct his theological research in scientific laboratories, was epoch-making. The result of such investigation is evidenced in three volumes: *The Place of Death in Evolution* (1897), *Through Science to Faith* (1902), and *Constructive Natural Theology* (1913). A still more consistent liberalism is manifest in Levi L. Paine's *The Evolution of Trinitarianism*, 1901, and *The Ethnic Trinities*, 1902; and of Frank Hugh Foster during the later part of his life. As the nineteenth century drew to its close, theological liberalism in the Congregational church had, broadly speaking, arrived at the following position: (1) The principle of evolution was generally accepted and applied to the field of historical investigation; (2) biblical criticism was recognized in principle and in some of its results; (3) belief in a metaphysical Trinity and Christology was widely shaken; (4) the nature of the atonement was generally conceived of in agreement with Bushnell; (5) eternal condemnation was rejected; and (6) such topics as predestination and original sin were eliminated from serious consideration in theology.

LATITUDINARIANISM

The liberalizing and humanizing process in theology was not confined to the Congregational church. While it was a slowly evolving movement in the latter denomination, it proceeded with revolutionary force in the Episcopal and Presbyterian churches. Evidences of a "broad" theology in the Episcopal church are found in the lives and works of such men as Frederick D. Huntingdon (1819-1904), William R. Huntingdon (1838-1910), Alexander M. G. Allen, Charles C. Tiffany, the historian of the Episcopal church in America, Phillips Brooks (1835-1895), and Richard H. Newton.

Outstanding among the liberal scholars of the Presbyterian church were Charles W. Shields, and Henry M. Baird, who was an authority on the Huguenot movement in France. Other prominent liberal theologians were Willis J. Beecher, James F. McCurdy, Robert E. Thompson, and Francis Brown.

Latitudinarian theology was represented among the Methodists by William F. Warren; Milton S. Terry, the author of a number of Old Testament commentaries; John F. Hurst; Henry C. Sheldon; Robert W. Rogers; Wilbur F. Tillett; John J. Tigert; Gross Alexander; Hinkley G. Mitchell, and Olin A. Curtis.

Though the Baptists were rather slow at first in accepting the new learning, an extreme type of radicalism made great headway among them. One of their first liberal thinkers was Ezekiel G. Robinson (1815-1894). In 1879 Crawford H. Toy was suspended from Southern Baptist Seminary for his liberal views. Under the presidency of William Rainy Harper (1856-1906) the University of Chicago became a center of liberal learning. One of the most radical Baptist scholars was George B. Foster (1858-1918), of the University of Chicago. He was a student of Ritschl and Harnack. In many respects his development was similar to that of Troeltsch. He finally discarded the name of a Christian altogether and called himself an "ethical culturist." In 1909 his name was removed from the Baptist Ministers' Conference of Chicago.[24] Other Baptist liberals were George Washington Northup and Augustus H. Strong (1836-1921), President of the Rochester Theological Seminary, 1872-1912.

Religious Outsiders

Along with these rational and critical tenets in theology there is a current of philosophical and religious idealism in American thought which is fundamentally at variance with the orthodox belief in the Bible as the sole authority of faith. This current is manifested in such organizations as the Quakers, the Mormons, Christian Science, and Theosophical Societies. Nothwithstanding the great difference among these groups as to the positive tenets of their faith, all of them are religious intuitionists. The theology of the inner light and new revelations claimed by their members counter the authority of the written Word. Against the background of philosophical idealism, matter counts little with them. True reality is metaphysical; man is a spiritual intelligence. The doctrines of pre-existence and reincarnation are cherished ideas. Christ is pre-eminently the Teacher, not the Savior.

BIBLIOGRAPHY

Allen, J. H. *Historical Sketch of the Unitarian Movement Since the Reformation.* ("American Church History" series, Vol. X.) New York: The Christian Literature Co., 1894.

[24] Cf. D. C. Macintosh, *The Problem of Religious Knowledge* (New York: Harper & Bros., 1940), pp. 97 ff.

BUCKHAM, JOHN W. *Progressive Religious Thought in America.* Boston: Houghton Mifflin Co., 1919.

DIRKS, J. E. *The Critical Theology of Theodore Parker.* New York: Columbia University Press, 1948.

EDDY, RICHARD. *Universalists in the United States.* ("American Church History" series, Vol. X.) New York: The Christian Literature Co., 1894.

ELIOT, SAMUEL A. (ed.). *Heralds of the Liberal Faith.* 3 vols. 1910.

EMERTON, E. *Unitarian Thought.* New York: The Macmillan Company, 1925.

FOSTER, FRANK H. *The Modern Movement in American Theology.* New York: Fleming H. Revell Co., 1939.

HUTCHISON, W. R. *Transcendentalist Ministers: Church Reform in the New England Renaissance.* New Haven: Yale University Press, 1959.

MANNING, I. E. *The Religion and Theology of the Unitarians.* 1906.

MILLER, P. *The Transcendentalist.* Cambridge: Harvard University Press, 1950.

MUNGER, T. T. *Horace Bushnell.* Boston: Houghton Mifflin Co., 1899.

RUSK, R. L. *The Life of R. W. Emerson.* New York: Charles Scribner's Sons, 1949.

SCHOLEFIELD, H. B. (ed.). *Pocket Guide to Unitarianism.* Boston: Beacon Press, 1954.

WHICHER, S. E. *Freedom and Fate: An Inner Life of R. W. Emerson.* Philadelphia: University of Pennsylvania Press, 1953.

WILBUR, E. M. *Our Unitarian Heritage.* Boston: Beacon Press, 1925.

———. *A History of Unitarianism: Vol. I, Socinianism and Its Antecedents.* Cambridge: Harvard University Press, 1945.

———. *A History of Unitarianism: Vol. II, In Transylvania, England, and America.* Cambridge: Harvard University Press, 1952.

WILLIAMS, DANIEL D. *The Andover Liberals.* New York: Kings Crown Press, 1941.

WRIGHT, CONRAD. *The Beginnings of Unitarianism in America.* Boston: Beacon Press, 1955.

CHAPTER IV

CONSERVATIVE FORCES IN NINETEENTH-CENTURY ANGLO-AMERICAN THEOLOGY

While English Puritanism controlled theological thought in the Northeastern states, Scottish-English Calvinism gained a strong foothold in the Middle Atlantic states. Both schools of thought had the Calvinism of Geneva and Dort in common and both were divided into conservative and progressive wings. While the liberals far outnumbered the conservatives in New England during the second half of the nineteenth century, the doctrinal grounding of Presbyterianism exerted a much stronger check on the rise of a liberal party. For more than a century Princeton remained a stronghold of a conservative theology. To a large extent the story of liberal theology is the story of Congregational theology, and the story of conservative theology is predominantly the story of Presbyterian theology. While the modernization of theological thought was an evolutionary process among the Congregational churches, it proceeded with the force of a revolution in the Presbyterian denomination.

Old School Presbyterians

The first notable theologian of the American Presbyterian church was Jonathan Dickinson (1688-1747). He was the first president of the College of New Jersey. He undertook to defend the five points of high Calvinism: supralapsarian predestination, limited atonement, total depravity, irresistible grace, and the perseverance of the saints. These five points he regarded as a "golden chain which extends from everlasting to everlasting and connects a past and future eternity, which takes its rise in God's foreknowledge and eternal purpose of grace to the elect and reaches through their vocation and justification on earth into their eternal glorification in heaven."[1]

The founding of Princeton Seminary in 1812 ushered in a new epoch in the history of Presbyterianism. This seminary, through its illustrious teachers, exercised a strong influence for a long time not only on the Presbyterians but on American Protestantism as a whole. The first professor in the chair of systematic theology was Archibald Alexander (1772-1851). He was the father of what after 1832 was called "the Princeton theology." The Reformed theologian Philip Schaff defines the Princeton theology as a "scholarly, logical, luminous and warmhearted reproduction of the Calvinism of the seventeenth century as laid down in the Westminster standards of 1647, and revised in America, 1788."[2]

The chief exponent of the Princeton school to be considered here is Charles Hodge (1797-1878). Upon his election to the professorship he spent two years at the university in Halle, where he became intimately acquainted with Tholuck. He was the founder and the first editor of the *Princeton Theological Review.* He wrote several commentaries on Paul's letters and a history of the Presbyterian church. His *Systematic Theology* appeared in three elaborate volumes.[3] He was influenced by Francois Turretin of Geneva (1623-1687) and the Helvetic Consensus Formula (1675) in his teaching of "immediate imputation" and of verbal inspiration. Hodge also made the federal theology of Coccejus a consistent part of his theology. According to this theology, God entered into a covenant with Adam as the head and representative of the whole race. Consequently, everything promised or granted to Adam, or threatened against him, has a bearing upon the whole race. The soul of each child is created by the immediate agency of God and the sin of Adam is immediately imputed to all. The plan of salvation is conceived of as a covenant. Hodge

[1] Dickinson, *The True Scripture-doctrine Concerning Some Important Points of Christian Faith* (1741). It is significant that later, during the nineteenth century, no leading Presbyterian subscribed to these points without qualification. On the contrary, the teaching of double predestination was openly repudiated by the leaders of the Princeton and Mercersburg schools.

[2] Philip Schaff, *Theological Propedeutic* (2nd ed.; New York: Charles Scribner's Sons, 1894), p. 390.

[3] Charles Hodge, *Systematic Theology* (New York: Scribner, Armstrong & Co., 1874).

distinguishes between a covenant of grace and a covenant of redemption. The former between God and his people is universal, for "God offers to all men eternal life on condition of faith in Jesus Christ." [4] Since this covenant of grace is founded on the covenant of redemption between the Father and the Son, grace becomes efficacious only in the elect who are given to the Son by the Father. In unmistakable terms Hodge rejects all the special tenets of New England theology.

In some important doctrinal matters, Hodge's theology marks a real advance over the older Calvinism: (1) He allows more room for the human element in the composition of the Bible. True, he teaches plenary inspiration and holds that all the books of the Bible are equally inspired. "Inspiration," he says, "extends to everything which any sacred writer asserts to be true," including "incidental circumstances, or facts of apparently minor importance, as e.g., that Satan tempted our first parents in the form of a serpent." [5] However, he wants the theologian to distinguish "between what the sacred writers themselves thought or believed, and what they teach. They may have believed that the sun moves around the earth, but they do not so teach." [6] (2) His theology is less polemical. He freely gives credit to the Roman Catholic church wherever she has preserved the truth of Scripture. He opposed the old school General Assembly when in 1845 it declared Catholic baptism invalid. (3) As for the doctrine of predestination, he taught infralapsarianism. God permitted the fall of man, he is not the cause of it.[7] (4) Most significant is the fact that Hodge holds a more liberal view concerning the number of the saved. Siding with the humanistic trend in Calvinism, he teaches that all who die in infancy are saved.[8] In the closing paragraph of the whole work he makes the remarkable statement: "We have reason to believe . . . that the number of the finally lost in comparison with the whole number of the saved will be very inconsiderable." [9] Essentially the same position was held by his son, Archibald Alexander Hodge (1823-1886).

[4] Hodge, *op. cit.*, II, 363.
[5] *Ibid.*, I, 163.
[6] *Ibid.*, I, 170.
[7] *Ibid.*, II, 313.
[8] *Ibid.*, I, 26.
[9] *Ibid.*, III, p. 879.

William G. T. Shedd (1820-1894), professor at Andover and later at Union Theological Seminary, elaborated a similar system of Calvinism. In matters of anthropology there is a real difference between Shedd and Charles Hodge. While Hodge held to the view of philosophical nominalism, Shedd, on the basis of philosophical realism, distinguished between the generic human nature and the individual. According to him, humanity is numerically one and the same substance in Adam and in all his posterity. Adam's sin was the sin of all mankind. Imputation is mediate, not immediate, and traducianism is the only logical view of the propagation of original sin.[10]

Other prominent old school theologians of the nineteenth century were Ashbel Green, Robert J. Breckenridge, Robert L. Dabney, Francis L. Patton, Benjamin B. Warfield. Warfield (1851-1920), successor to A. A. Hodge at Princeton, held firmly to the doctrine of plenary inspiration and of original sin. However, he confined scriptural inerrancy to the nonexistent autographs.[11]

The New School Theology

The new school theology held a mediating position between Princeton theology and New England Congregationalism. A number of its distinguished leaders such as Lyman Beecher and H. B. Smith were New Englanders. There always had been a frequent intermingling between Presbyterians and Congregationalists. In 1836 the two denominations combined their efforts to establish Union Theological Seminary, New York. The new school theology wanted to unite the progressive thought of the New England theology with the teachings of the Westminster Confession. The factional spirit in the Presbyterian church led to a schism in 1838 which lasted until 1869. The points of controversy were mediate or immediate imputation, and the extent of the atonement. Other problems of a more practical nature entered into consideration, e.g., conflicting views as to the authority

[10] Cf. Wm. G. T. Shedd, *Dogmatic Theology* (3 vols.; New York: Charles Scribner's Sons, 1888-94).

[11] See his book, *An Introduction to the Textual Criticism of the New Testament* (New York: T. Whittaker, 1886). The distinction between "inerrant autographs" and "errant copies," set forth in the seventeenth century by the Catholic scholar Richard Simon, has also played a part in the discussion of Lutheran theologians. The former American Lutheran Church was officially committed to this theory in its constitution of 1930.

of the General Assembly, the plan of union with the Congregationalists, the slavery question, and moral reforms.[12] In the second part of the nineteenth century controversy centered about the questions of biblical infallibility and eschatology.

The older generation of the new school theology was represented by James Richards (1767-1843), who presided over the Auburn Convention in 1837; Baxter Dickinson (1794-1876), author of the Auburn Declaration;[13] Lyman Beecher (1775-1863), the famous antagonist of Unitarianism; Albert Barnes (1798-1876), author of a number of commentaries on the Bible; and Thomas H. Skinner (1791-1871). The most outstanding theologian of this school was Henry B. Smith (1815-1876). He was a pupil of Leonard Woods at Andover and of Enoch Pond at Bangor. While in Europe he came into contact with Tholuck, Fichte, and Hegel. His German studies did not essentially modify his thought. He remained a New Englander, holding in general to the doctrine of mediate imputation and to the governmental theory of the atonement. His chief contribution to theology lies in his systematic effort to "make Christ the central point of all important religious truth and doctrine."[14] His *System of Christian Theology*[15] was edited posthumously.

The christocentric principle was carried out with still greater consistency by Lewis E. Stearns. His training under Hodge, Smith, Dorner, Kahnis, and Luthardt reflects the breadth of his theology. In Christology he accepted the kenotic theory and progressive incarnation. His main concern was to formulate a consistent doctrine of predestination which would be Calvinistic in its assertion of the divine sovereignty and at the same time do justice to the truth to which Arminianism bears witness, i.e., human responsibility. Stearns became the interpreter of the Erlangen theology to American scholars. Like Frank, he believed in the apologetic value of Christian experience for the defense of the fundamental doctrines of Christianity.

[12] Schaff, *Theological Propedeutic,* p. 396.

[13] The old school charged the new school with sixteen Pelagian and Arminian errors. Representatives of the new school met at Auburn, New York, in August, 1837. Hence the document refuting the charges of the old school is called the Auburn Declaration. Cf. Schaff, *Creeds of Christendom,* I, 809-810; III, 771.

[14] Quoted by Schaff, *Theological Propedeutic,* p. 398.

[15] New York, A. C. Armstrong, 1884.

Mercersburg Theology

Simultaneously with the old and new school theology in the Presbyterian church, another school of thought developed in the German Reformed Synod, the Mercersburg theology. As its name indicates, it began at the Mercersburg institutions of the German Reformed church, Marshall College and the theological seminary. The outstanding leaders of the movement were F. A. Rauch, J. N. Nevin, and Philip Schaff.

Frederick A. Rauch's labor was frustrated by his premature death in 1841. John W. Nevin (1803-1886) held the chair of theology in the theological seminary. His chief contribution to the Mercersburg theology lies in his discussion of the nature of the Church and the sacraments. The greatest genius of this school was Philip Schaff. He was born in Switzerland in 1819. Receiving his theological education at Tübingen, Halle, and Berlin, he came in close contact with such theologians as Ferdinand Christian Baur, Tholuck, and Neander. He emigrated to the United States in 1843, and for twenty years held a professorship at Mercersburg. In 1870 he was made professor in Union Theological Seminary, a position he held till death in 1893. Through his connection with the Presbyterian church, he became a powerful leader among the English branch of the Reformed church, and the new school theology may claim him as well as the Mercersburg school. In fact, his influence far transcended both his own denomination and his adopted country.

As a co-founder of the Evangelical Alliance,[16] Schaff was president of its American branch. He was also president of the American Committee of Bible Revision. He joined in the formation of the Alliance of the Reformed Churches and delivered the opening address at its first council held in Edinburgh, 1877. In his teaching career he was obligated to teach all the various theological disciplines, though his chief interest was in the field of Church history. His background and position eminently fitted him to act as a mediator between American and European thought. Schaff was a voluminous writer.

Mercersburg theology stemmed from the contact of German Evangelical thought with Anglo-American church life. It attempted to

[16] The Evangelical Alliance, a precursor of the ecumenical movement, was founded in London in 1846. Its nine doctrinal articles are given by Schaff, *Creeds of Christendom,* III, 827-28.

combine personal, Evangelical piety with a Catholic outlook on the Church. It opposed the teaching of double predestination and the Arminian emphasis on free will. It was strictly christocentric. In fact, it produced the first thoroughgoing christocentric system in American Calvinism. It conceived of Jesus Christ, the incarnate Son of God, as the federal head of the human race. All believers, born by the Spirit, are Christ's members, constituting a mystical body with him. This is the holy, catholic, and apostolic Church which is one through all the ages and never changes though the form of its life and doctrine may change. Hence no doctrinal statement is necessarily final. The Church may modify its teachings as it progresses in Christian knowledge. Christ perpetuates his mediatorial work through chosen men who, by the rite of ordination, are duly invested with divine authority to preach the word, to administer the sacraments, and to rule over Christ's flock. The sacraments are not empty symbols but significant signs and seals of God's covenant with man. The Mercersburg theologians also advocated a return to the liturgical principles of the past. Since their views on the ministry, the sacraments, and the liturgy were a novelty among their own constituency, the Mercersburg teachers were subject to three heresy trials held in 1845 and subsequent years. In each case they were acquitted almost unanimously. Their opponents charged them with Romanizing tendencies and intending to substitue the teaching of redemption through a substantial conveyance of a regenerated humanity for the doctrine of salvation by faith in the atonement, in and by the incarnation of Christ, through outward channels such as the Church and the sacraments.[17]

The significance of the Mercersburg school is that it constituted a Reformed counterpart to the Oxford Movement in England and nineteenth-century Neo-Lutheranism in Germany. Under the impact of philosophical transcendentalism, all three movements developed the sentiment of high churchism and of mystical sacramentarianism.

Episcopal Theology

The Oxford Movement began to exert a considerable influence in the Episcopal church about 1850. The outstanding representative of

[17] Cf. James H. Nichols, *Romanticism in American Theology: Nevin and Schaff at Mercersburg* (Chicago: University of Chicago Press, 1961.).

the old high church party was Bishop Seabury (d. 1796), and later John H. Hobart. Other prominent high churchmen were George Washington Doane, Morgan Dix, Samuel H. Turner, William H. Odenheimer, and Arthur C. Coxe, remembered especially as editor of the American edition of *Ante-Nicene Fathers* (1885 ff.).[18]

The father of the Evangelical party was Bishop William White (d. 1836). Besides White there were Stephen H. Tyng, William Meade, and Alexander V. Griswold. William Augustus Muhlenberg (1796-1877) was a theologian of no ordinary ability. He combined a great love for the episcopal form of the Church with a deep mysticism and a genuine social passion. An eminent writer also was Charles P. McIlvaine. As in the Lutheran church, the discussion of denominational principles occupied much of the time and energy of conservative Episcopalians. This fact explains the isolation of Episcopal theology.

Methodism

Conservative theology among the Methodists was represented by Nathan Bangs, Daniel D. Whedon, and G. R. Crooks. Other prominent figures were Daniel Steele, Matthew Simpson, Daniel Dorchester, and John McClintock.

Baptist Scholarship

Conservative Baptist theologians made a real contribution to biblical studies: Horatio B. Hackett, John A. Broadus, Asahel Kendrick, and Howard Osgood were all great linguists and biblical scholars. Other noteworthy writers were William C. Wilkinson, Elijah H. Johnson, Alvah Novey, Thomas Jefferson Conaut, Henry C. Vedder, Calvin Goodspeed, Edgar Y. Mullins, and Edwin C. Dargan.

Another force in American theology which stresses "believers' baptism" is represented by the Disciples of Christ. This denomination originated with Thomas Campbell (1763-1854) and his son Alexander (1788-1866). Its basis is a Puritanic biblicism and thoroughgoing unionism: No creeds, but Christ! The theology of the Disciples was more a simple lay theology than a scholarly exposition of Christianity. The later disruption in this group, caused by the inroad of

[18] Cf. G. E. DeMille, *The Catholic Movement in the American Episcopal Church* (Philadelphia: The Church Historical Society, 1941).

theological liberalism, is a striking example of the fact that a vague appeal to the Bible and Christian experience is no safeguard against theological modernism.

BIBLIOGRAPHY

DEMILLE, GEORGE E. *The Catholic Movement in the American Episcopal Church*. Philadelphia: The Church Historical Society, 1941.

SCHNECK, B. S. *Mercersburg Theology Inconsistent with Protestant and Reformed Doctrine*. Philadelphia, 1874.

CHAPTER V

LUTHERAN THEOLOGY

INTRODUCTION

Lutheranism in America has had to struggle under the disadvantage of two major handicaps. The first of these was the general disinclination on the part of the established churches in the European homelands to provide for the spiritual needs of emigrants to the New World. The establishment of Lutheran church bodies in America, therefore, fell to devout laymen and pioneering pastors in a land of pioneers.

The second handicap was that of language. Lutherans came from non-English speaking lands. In America they were confronted with the English language and with the problem of preserving their Lutheran identity. For many of these immigrants it seemed that the only way to preserve their Lutheran faith was to preserve the mother tongue. Others, however, particularly among the second generation, insisted upon the necessity of using English. The language question became a serious problem over the years and gave rise to the charge—not always without foundation—that the use of the English language cut Lutherans off from their doctrinal heritage and opened the door to Puritanizing and revivalistic influences. The language question occasioned much internal strife and was intensified by the nineteenth-century immigrations which were influenced by the confessional revival abroad. It also had the effect of establishing Lutheran bodies as nationality groups reflecting movements and trends in the homeland. The result was that Lutherans were not only alienated from the mainstream of American religious thought, the language of which was English, but were also isolated from each other by nationality. Nonetheless, transition to English was inevitable and continuous, and today English is the language of Lutheran theology and of virtually all of the congregations.

Early American Lutheranism

The chief work of the pioneer pastors was practical. Their contribution to American theological thought was insignificant, save for the confessional principle on which they established the Lutheran church in America. Henry Melchior Muhlenberg (1711-1787) was a loyal son of the Lutheran Reformation. The pietism of Halle University gave a certain color to his Lutheranism but did not displace it. Luther's Small Catechism was the textbook of religious instruction. The constitutions of both the Ministerium of Pennsylvania and that of New York obligated the ministry to confessional loyalty in unequivocal terms.

After the death of Muhlenberg the Lutheran church passed into a period characterized by a deterioration of its confessional life. Unionism and Socinianism threatened to undermine its very existence. In 1792 the Ministerium of Pennsylvania removed all references to the symbolical books from its constitution. The New York Ministerium considered a union with the Episcopal church, and the Ministerium of Pennsylvania contemplated a union with the German Reformed Synod. Many union churches were built which housed Lutheran and Reformed congregations. Lutheran and Reformed churches engaged in co-operative educational work (Franklin College at Lancaster, Pennsylvania); a union hymnal with frank concessions to Socinianism was published in 1817; and the *Evangelisches Magazin*, established by the Ministerium of Pennsylvania in 1811, was frequently circulated among the Reformed and the Moravian Brethren. In 1807 F. H. Quitmann, who had been a student of Semler at Halle and who held the doctor of divinity degree from Harvard, was elected to the presidency of the Ministerium of New York, a position he held for twenty-one years. He published an *Evangelical Catechism* in 1814 in which he openly denied the supernatural teachings of the Lutheran confessions. A similar rationalistic catechism, *The North Carolina Catechism,* had been prepared as early as 1787 by J. C. Velthusen. The year 1818 marked the appearance of a little book bearing the title *The History, Doctrine and Discipline of the Evangelical Lutheran Church,* by G. Lochman. Its translation of the Augsburg Confession was significant for its numerous omissions, especially the condemnatory clauses and Articles XXII and XXVIII. Rationality was made the test of the doctrine of the Trinity. Lochman rejected the teaching of the imputation of original sin. The doctrines of baptismal regeneration and of the real presence were eliminated. The Formula of Concord was particularly in disfavor because of its anti-Calvinistic attitude. Four years later Lochman expressed this same anti-confessional sentiment in a catechism which he prepared. The knowledge of Luther's theology at this time was not very wide. His works were not easily obtainable, and when he was studied, the theologians did not hesitate to interpret him according to their own preconceived ideas.

It was against this background of confessional laxity that the General Synod, the first general Lutheran church body, was established in 1820. The constitution of this body contained no reference to the Lutheran confessions. The theology of the leading men in the General Synod was that of an American Lutheranism modified by Puritanism and revivalism. In the eyes of many this "American Lutheranism" was a legitimate modification of "Old Lutheranism" and was justified by the theological development of the eighteenth century and by the new American environment.

The Gettysburg School

Ernest L. Hazelius, of Moravian descent and education, and professor first at Hartwick (1815), later in Gettysburg (1830), and from 1834 till his death (1853) in the seminary of the Synod of South Carolina, followed the general tenor which prevailed in his synod. The historical Lutheran concepts of both the Eucharist and baptism were untenable to him.

Benjamin Kurtz (1795-1865) was editor of *The Lutheran Observer*, in which he discussed the question, "Why are you a Lutheran?" in a series of articles. According to him, the great fundamental principle of the Lutheran church is belief in the sole authority of the Bible "without note or comment." His teaching on the Eucharist uses the language of the Reformed churches. In an elaborate treatise on baptism, he makes no mention of the Lutheran position.[1]

[1] See his *Arguments Derived from Sacred Scripture and Sound Reason, Exhibiting the Necessity and Advantages of Infant Baptism, and Proving Sprinkling or Affusion to be the Most Scriptural and Appropriate Mode of Administering It: Together with a Number of Essays Connected with Baptism* (1840).

THE CONTROVERSY OVER "AMERICAN LUTHERANISM"

The dominant figure in the General Synod at this time was Samuel Simon Schmucker (1799-1873). He received his theological training at Princeton. When the Lutheran Seminary was established at Gettysburg, he became the first professor in this institution. While still a student at Princeton, he envisaged a return to the Augsburg Confession, and with his election to the professorship at Gettysburg, we find the first official reference to the Lutheran symbols in any declaration of the General Synod. His subscription to the Augsburg Confession was conditional. He had a pronounced dislike for liturgical worship. He viewed the rise of confessionalism in Europe and among the new Lutheran immigrants with deep distrust, and was one of the founders and leading spirits of the Evangelical Alliance. In a paper read before the Synod of Western Pennsylvania in October, 1840, "Portraiture of Lutheranism,"[2] the author pointed out six features of the Lutheran church which needed improvement: (1) the church should commit itself to the Bible, the whole Bible, and nothing but the Bible; (2) the teaching of the presence of the glorified human body of Christ in the Eucharist has become obsolete, "bread and wine are merely symbolic representations of the Saviour's absent body"; (3) the practice of confession as preparation for Holy Communion should be rejected; (4) a new adjustment of the doctrines of the Lutheran church is needed; (5) the advisory power of the General Synod should be changed in favor of a more rigid system of church government; (6) all that should be required of ministers is a subscription to the Bible and to the belief that the fundamental doctrines of the Bible are taught in a *substantially* correct manner in the Augsburg Confession.

In 1855 Schmucker, together with Kurtz and Sprecher, printed and distributed a pamphlet entitled *Definite Synodical Platform*. The pamphlet advanced a new doctrinal basis for the General Synod which would safeguard "American Lutheranism." The chief importance of the document lies in its attitude toward the Augsburg Confession. While the remaining Lutheran symbols are flatly rejected, the Augs-

[2] Published in *The American Lutheran Church. Historically, Doctrinally, and Practically Delineated, in Several Occasional Discourses* (5th ed., 1852), pp. 41-89.

burg Confession is presented in a new, abridged recension in which the authors omit Articles XI, XXII, and XXVIII, nearly all the condemnatory clauses and such passages, discarded as "errors." Five points in the Augsburg Confession are thus classified: (1) the sanction of the ceremonies of the "mass," i.e., the communion service as drafted by Luther (Art. XXIV); (2) the commendation of private confession (Art. XI); (3) the denial of the divine obligation of the Sabbath (Art. XXVIII); (4) the doctrine of baptismal regeneration (Art. II); (5) the doctrine of the real presence. In Article VIII the phrase that "it is lawful to use the sacraments administered by evil men" is omitted.[3]

This platform was rejected, and this marked a turning point toward a better appreciation of the confessional heritage of the Lutheran church. In spite of his failure and the rejection of his leadership, Schmucker should not be belittled or underestimated. He was a warm-hearted Christian, a devoted teacher, a prolific writer, and an ecumenical churchman. Schmucker's brother-in-law, Samuel Sprecher, president of Wittenberg College, Springfield, Ohio, from 1849 to 1884, died in 1906 at the advanced age of ninety-six years, having lived long enough to witness the complete collapse of the cause for which he and Schmucker had labored. To a large extent he had recanted his former position. His greatest contribution to theology is *The Groundwork of a System of Evangelical Lutheran Theology*.[4] The central idea in this *System* is the personal assurance of salvation, the Christian certainty and decision, which, he holds, are indispensable to the purity of the Church.

The ambiguity of the doctrinal position of the General Synod continued to make it a hotbed of theological unrest. The secession of several member synods in 1866, which issued in the formation of the General Council, was by no means a clear cleavage between the confessional and nonconfessional theologians. A mediating party dominated with the motto, "The Augsburg Confession, nothing more, nothing less." Gettysburg Seminary was the chief theological school of this Neo-Melanchthonian theology. Prominent among its expo-

[3] The text of Schmucker's recension is reprinted by Vergilius Ferm, *The Crisis in American Lutheran Theology* (New York: Century Press, 1927), pp. 351 ff.

[4] Philadelphia: Lutheran Publication Society, 1879.

nents was Milton Valentine (1825-1906), an original thinker,[5] and J. W. Richard (1843-1909). Both of these theologians promoted accommodation to the Melanchthonian point of view. According to Valentine, the Scriptures are a supernatural revelation from God presenting "themselves before us as rationally capacitated to discern their credentials and meet our responsibility in relation to them." [6] In baptism "regeneration is fully provided for," he says, "but the actuality can come only in the time and order of the ongoing process." [7] The Eucharist is a means by which Christ "through a real, special, definitive Presence . . . gives Himself to believers as the ever-living Saviour." [8] Richard rejected the Lutheran teaching of the oral reception of the body of Christ by worthy and unworthy communicants alike.

John H. W. Stuckenberg (1835-1903) was a scholar of no ordinary ability. He was pastor of the interdenominational American Church in Berlin, Germany. He distinguished himself as an author by widely read articles on European thought and as a pioneer in the field of sociological studies. He was in sympathy with the Evangelical Alliance and the General Synod. He looked with misgiving upon the growing friendliness between the General Synod and the General Council because this involved a conservative trend. He communicated his views through a number of pamphlets and articles.

Pietism versus Confessionalism

The issue of pietism versus confessionalism caused considerable division among the Norwegian Lutherans in America. In the nineteenth century, from 1825 on, Norwegian immigrants began to come in a steady stream. Norway had been under the cloud of rationalism for a century, but underwent a revival through the efforts of H. N. Hauge, a layman. One of his ablest followers, Elling Eielsen (1804-1883) came to America in 1839 and straightway began to preach to his countrymen who were scattered in small settlements throughout the Midwest. Like Hauge, Eielsen had been persecuted and imprisoned in Norway for having preached without ordination. Even after

[5] Milton Valentine, *Christian Theology* (2 vols.; Philadelphia: Lutheran Publication Society, 1906).

[6] *Ibid.*, I, 60.

[7] *Ibid.*, II, 330.

[8] *Ibid.*, II, 358.

his ordination in 1843, Eielsen distrusted the university-trained pastors who were coming over to America, and always feared contagion by the formalism and rationalism of the state church tradition and heritage.

In 1846 Eielsen and his friends organized the "Evangelical Lutheran Church of America," known as the Eielsen Synod. A constitution was drawn up and put into final form in 1850. This so-called Old Constitution recognized "God's Word in the Holy Scriptures in conjunction with the Apostolic and Augsburg Articles of Faith" as the rule of Church order. According to paragraph two, only the converted or nearly converted could be accepted as a member of synod. In paragraph six the Constitution rejected "popish authority and also the common ministerial garb" of the Norwegian clergy. Likewise, the Lutheran practice of absolution is rejected in several pronouncements. Though Eielsen stood in sharp opposition to the theology of Grundtvig, his opponents assailed the Constitution as Grundtvigian in character because in paragraph one the Apostles' Creed is put on virtually the same level as the Scriptures. Opponents also objected to the view of the Church set forth in paragraph two as Donatistic in character.[9]

Prominently identified with Eielsen was P. A. Rasmussen (1829-1898). He made it his task to defend the peculiarities of Eielsen against the attacks of the orthodox pastors of the Norwegian Synod, which was founded in 1853. In later years, however, he retracted his Donatistic view of the Church and joined with the Norwegian Synod.

George Sverdrup was the most distinguished leader of pietistic Lutheranism among the Norwegians. He was born in Norway in 1848 and studied theology and Semitic languages in the universities of Oslo, Erlangen, and Paris. In 1874 he was called to Augsburg Seminary at Minneapolis, Minnesota, where he taught theology for thirty-four years till his death in 1907. He conceived of the Church as an unorganized federation of separate societies edified by lay preachers. This was contrary to the view of the Norwegian Synod, which laid stress on the unity of organization and in doctrine. He stressed the autonomy of the local congregation. He wished, as his biographer says, "that the separate congregation should take seriously its tasks

[9] The text of the Constitution is given in an English translation in E. C. Nelson and E. L. Fevold, *The Lutheran Church among Norwegian-Americans*, I, 337 ff.

of representing the 'Body of Christ.' "[10] His view on the origin and history of Christianity was conservative, although he did not hold to the teaching of plenary inspiration. In his concept of the Christian life he emphasized a personal religious experience. He opposed the teaching of predestination, the Lutheran practice of absolution, and the distinctive Lutheran elements in baptism and the Supper. The dogmatic exclusiveness, as it developed among the confessionalists, was repugnant to him. When the majority of the Norwegian-Danish Conference merged with two other bodies to form the Norwegian United Church in 1890, he and his friends withdrew and in 1897 founded the Norwegian Lutheran Free Church in order to perpetuate a pietistic Lutheranism.[11]

Lutherans in Union with Calvinism

The unionistic tendencies of Lutheranism, which the majority of Lutheran church bodies in America rejected, found a home in the theology and polity of the former German Evangelical Synod of North America, which was organized about 1840. Andrew Irion (1823-1870) and Carl Emil Otto (1837-1916) were the Synod's early outstanding leaders. Irion represented the pietistic theology of his synod, while Otto was more a critical scholar.

In 1934 this synod united with the Reformed Church, also of German background, to form the Evangelical and Reformed Church. In its constitution it cited the Holy Scriptures as the ultimate rule of Christian faith and practice and the Heidelberg Catechism, Luther's Catechism, and the Augsburg Confession "as an authoritative interpretation of the essential truth taught in Holy Scripture." In points where these confessional writings differ, ministers and congregations may avail themselves of the liberty of conscience inherent in the gospel. In 1944 the Evangelical and Reformed Church proposed steps leading to a merger with the Congregational and Christian Churches, a group which had been organized in 1931. The United Church of Christ, as the four merged denominations are known today,

[10] John O. Evjen in *Augsburg Seminary and the Lutheran Free Church,* ed. L. Lillehei (Minneapolis, 1928), p. 7.

[11] A similar spirit is characteristic of the very small group of the Lutheran Brethren and of the Apostolic Lutherans.

became a reality in 1958 and is the first American merger to unite the Continental Reformation with English Nonconformity.

The Confessional Revival

The confessional revival had two distinctive centers in America. In the East it was sponsored by a confessional party in the old Muhlenberg synods, and in the West by the new immigration of Germans and Scandinavians. The leader in the East was Charles Porterfield Krauth (1823-1883). He was prominent in the General Council, which was founded in 1867 by the synods which had withdrawn from the General Synod. His most noteworthy contribution is the book entitled *The Conservative Reformation and Its Theology* (1871).[12] Other scholars of distinction were B. M. Schmucker, who became one of the finest liturgical scholars of the Lutheran church; W. J. Mann; G. F. Krotel; A. Spaeth; and R. F. Weidner.

Among the conservatives of the General Synod there were E. J. Wolf of Gettysburg and the faculty of Hamma Divinity School: S. A. Ort, L. A. Gotwald, and S. F. Breckenridge, who combined their influence with the theologians of the General Council. E. J. Wolf (d. 1905), colleague of Valentine and Richard, exercised a great influence upon his students and upon many men influential throughout the whole Lutheran church and thereby contributed greatly to turning the tide in the old General Synod from Melanchthonianism to Lutheranism. Soon the General Synod, the General Council, and the United Synod of the South appointed a standing committee to create a common liturgy and forms for ministerial acts for the three bodies.

In the Western synods Carl Ferdinand Wilhelm Walther (1811-1887) was the leader of the Missouri Synod Lutherans. His co-laborers were F. C. D. Wyneken, Wilhelm Sihler and quite a number of other university-trained pastors from Germany who helped to shape the theology of the Missouri Synod. The brothers Gottfried (d. 1899) and Siegmund (d. 1900) Fritschel, together with John Deindoerfer (d. 1907) distinguished themselves as leaders of the Iowa Synod. After its rupture from the Missouri Synod the Ohio Synod was led by Matthias Loy (d. 1915) and F. W. Stellhorn (d. 1919).

The pioneer theologian among the Swedes was L. P. Esbjorn (1808-

[12] Reprinted by the Augsburg Publishing House (Minneapolis, 1963).

1870), who did valuable work both as pastor and professor. From the beginning of his teaching in Springfield, Illinois, he stressed the confessional basis of Lutheranism. It is not without significance that both the Synod and the Seminary, established at Chicago in 1860, bore the name *Augustana.* In the developing years strict orthodoxy was represented by Eric Norelius (1833-1916). He was a prolific writer in Swedish. The schoolman of the first half of the Augustana Synod's history was T. N. Hasselquist (1816-1891). He was very efficient as an expositor of the Bible.

The leaders of the Norwegian Synod were at first handicapped by the division which Grundtvigianism caused among their ranks. J. W. C. Dietrichson (1815-1883) was thoroughly committed to the teachings of this great Danish theologian. Similar tendencies are seen in C. L. Clausen (1820-1892), and H. A. Stub (1822-1907). The ascending tide of anti-Grundtvigianism, on the other hand, was represented by H. A. Preus (1825-1894), N. O. Brandt (1824-1921), and G. F. Dietrichson (1813-1886), all students of Gisle Johnson of Oslo University.

Later Theological Controversies

It was in these synods that a peculiar confessional Lutheran theology was developed. Though all synods subscribed unreservedly to the whole Book of Concord, they nevertheless became involved in a number of trenchant controversies. The dominant figure throughout the whole period was Carl Ferdinand Wilhelm Walther, professor at Concordia Seminary in St. Louis, Missouri. His theological labors were marked by a persistent attempt to purge American Lutheranism of all alien principles and to restore the theology of the Reformation and post-Reformation period. The theological controversies centered mainly about the following five problems: (1) the doctrine of the Church and the ministry; (2) open questions; (3) eschatology; (4) Sunday observance; (5) predestination.

(1) J. A. A. Grabau, a leader of the band of Lutherans who had left Prussia in protest against the Union of 1817 and who had settled in and near Buffalo, New York, and Milwaukee, Wisconsin, espoused a high view of the Church and the ministry in a pastoral letter in December, 1840. This letter gave offense to the Lutherans of the Missouri Synod. Walther, insisting that the Church is essentially invisi-

ble, developed what has become known as the "transference theory," which holds that inasmuch as every Christian is a priest of God, he has the right to function as a minister. But in the interest of order and by divine command, the many Christian priests choose one among them as pastor who, as the representative of the congregation, performs the ministerial rites. The ministerial office is the spiritual priesthood of all believers transferred to an individual. This transfer takes place by virtue of the call of a congregation; the act of ordination is merely an ecclesiastical usage.[13]

This conflict also involved the theologians of the Iowa Synod. Wilhelm Loehe of Neuendettelsau, the spiritual father of this synod, rejected any hierarchical claims of the ministry, but he held to the view that the ministerial office has been committed to the Church as a whole. The individual Christian cannot transfer his personal share, but the Church as an entity transmits the office to the pastor in the rite of ordination.

(2) Under the influence of historically progressive Erlangen theology, the Iowa theologians considered certain tenets of pre-millennialism as matters on which Lutheran theologians should be given freedom of interpretation, provided that their teaching be in harmony with the "analogy of faith" (Rom. 12:7). The expectation of a personal Anti-Christ to be revealed in the future belonged in this category. Luther's reference to the pope as "the very Anti-Christ" in the Smalcald Articles was looked upon by Iowa and its predecessors in Germany as more or less an incidental remark, not intended to be a confessional expression. The Missourians, on the other hand, pointing to II Thessalonians 2:2 ff., insisted that Luther's reference must not be so interpreted. In regard to the fulfillment of the "thousand years" in Revelation 20, the Iowa theologians were inclined to allow the right of different interpretation of this passage, while to the Missourians, the teaching of chiliasm in any form was incompatible with the language of Article XVII of the Augsburg Confession.

(3) The Iowa theologians held that unity in the essentials of faith is sufficient to establish Church fellowship, but that doctrinal issues which do not affect the essentials of faith must not interfere with

[13] Cf. Theodore Engelder (ed.), *Walther and the Church* (St. Louis: Concordia Publishing House, 1938).

Church fellowship. Walther and the other Missourians rejected such a distinction and insisted on complete agreement concerning every scriptural doctrine.

(4) As to the question of Sunday observance, the Augsburg Confession says that those "greatly err" who believe that the observance of Sunday rests on a divine institution (Art. XXVIII). In the seventeenth century the dogmatician Gerhard had taught that, nevertheless, the Church is under divine obligation to set apart one day in seven. Both the Missourians and Iowans were firmly established on Article XXVIII of the Augsburg Confession. However, the Missourians wanted to exclude those who accepted Gerhard's views from Church fellowship, while the theologians of Iowa tolerated Gerhard's view.

Prior to the controversy between Walther and the Iowa Synod, the question of Sunday observance had caused some division among the Norwegians. C. L. Clausen upheld the view that the Third Commandment imposes a divine obligation. Clausen later retracted this view.[14]

(5) The most important controversy revolved about the question of eternal predestination. In this long-protracted and caustic controversy, the Missourians sought to safeguard the free efficiency of divine grace to the exclusion of any resemblance to synergism in the doctrine of salvation. Their opponents, the theologians of the Norwegians,[15] Ohio, and Iowa synods, sought to establish election as an organic part of the whole order of salvation in order to avoid the danger of fatalism and despair. For the Missourians predestination was a theological problem; for their opponents it was a psychological question. Iowa followed seventeenth-century teaching: election takes place *intuitu fidei* ("in view of faith"). Walther and his school objected to this, claiming that such a definition is unwarranted by the Scriptures and

[14] J. M. Rohne, *Norwegian-American Lutheranism up to 1872* (New York: The Macmillan Company, 1926), pp. 223 ff.

[15] The Norwegian Synod had close ties to the Missouri Synod. In 1859 a Norwegian professorship was established in Concordia Seminary, St. Louis, with L. Larsen (1833-1915) as its first incumbent. In 1872 the Norwegian Synod took part in the organization of the Synodical Conference. F. A. Schmidt, a Norwegian who had been on the Concordia faculty 1872-1876, attacked Walther's teaching of predestination set forth in the presidential reports of the Missouri Synod, 1877 and 1879.

the confessions. Election, according to them, is not *intuitu fidei* but *ad fidem* ("to faith"). The question why God elected some men before others, they held, must remain an unfathomable mystery. Salvation depends exclusively on this divine election; condemnation, however, will result from man's own willful resistance. Though the Missourians at times came close to the Calvinistic teaching of a double predestination, they expressly rejected this view. Walther also rejected the Reformed teaching of final perseverance, that no true believer can totally fall from grace. Walther believed that a Christian may fall totally from grace through mortal sin and that the elect must repent of his sin, but added that an elect Christian will inevitably repent before his death, otherwise he could not be elect.[16]

The predestination controversy divided the Norwegian Synod into two opposing factions.[17] In order to prevent a schism, this body withdrew from the Synodical Conference in 1883. Nonetheless, in 1887, Schmidt and his followers withdrew from the Synod and organized the Anti-Missouri Brotherhood. A reunion of the two groups was effected through the mergers of 1890 and 1917.

The Ohio and Iowa Synods made a serious attempt to meet the view of the Missourians through the Chicago Theses of 1929. The Norwegians advanced the view of predestination expressed by the Danish Pietist theologian Pontopiddan (1698-1764) in his *Explanation of Luther's Catechism.* According to this view, "God has predestined all those unto eternal life, whom He from eternity has foreknown as willing to accept the proffered grace, believe in Christ, and in this belief remain true to the end." [18]

Related to the problem of predestination was the controversy over the meaning of justification and absolution. The Missourians as well as the men of the Norwegian Synod came very close to the view of Rosenius and his followers[19] who attempted to equate justification

[16] C. F. W. Walther, *The Proper Distinction Between Law and Gospel,* trans. W. H. T. Dau (St. Louis: Concordia Publishing House, 1929), p. 323.

[17] Cf. F. W. Stellhorn, F. A. Schmidt, *et al., The Error of Missouri* (1897). Missouri's position is treated exhaustively by Francis Pieper, *Conversion and Election* (St. Louis: Concordia Publishing House, 1913).

[18] *Dr. Martin Luther's Small Catechism,* trans. by E. Eielsen in 1841, reproduced and edited by O. M. Norlie (Minneapolis: Augsburg Publishing House, 1925).

[19] Cf. p. 217.

with reconciliation. According to this view, the forgiveness of sins is imparted in absolution to all to whom it is proclaimed whether they believe it or not and even though it is not accepted by all. Their opponents, both in the Iowa Synod and among the pietistic-minded Norwegians, adopted the view that absolution imparts no forgiveness to unbelievers. Over the years these disputes have spent their force. While they still exist on paper, they are no longer living issues.[20]

It was through these controversies that the theology of C. F. W. Walther, sanctioned by the Missouri Synod, became a powerful factor in American Lutheranism. Walther's *The Proper Distinction between Law and Gospel* is a real theological classic. Although his orthodoxy was strict, it possessed a sincere evangelical piety. Walther took an active part in preparing the St. Louis edition of Luther's works which is based on the Walch edition. In his theology he unreservedly taught the theory of vicarious atonement. He conscientiously rejected such idealistic tenets of nineteenth-century Neo-Lutheranism as the high church view of the ministry; the concept of the Lord's Supper as the implanting in man of the seed of immortality; the doctrine of a future probation after death; and chiliasm. On the other hand, the Iowa theologians distinguished themselves by their appreciation of the genetic growth of the Christian dogma. Walther's use of Scripture in his polemical writings is at times artificial and inconclusive. Likewise, the nominalistic trend inherent in Protestant thought is very pronounced in his concept of the Church.

Lutheranism since World War I

World War I had a profound effect on the Lutheran churches in America. A narrow, provincial outlook gave way to broader, more tolerant outlooks. The era of "splendid isolation" was at an end. The responsibility of providing theological leadership and the necessary funds for the orphaned German missions fell to Lutheran synods in America. To meet the needs of its members in the armed forces, the National Lutheran Commission was organized in October, 1917. This organization became the parent body of the National Lutheran Council, formed in September, 1918. The various Lutheran bodies, except the members of the Synodical Conference (Missouri Synod, Wisconsin

[20] Cf. Rohne, *op. cit.*, pp. 226 ff.

Synod, *et al.*) co-operated. After the war the National Lutheran Council continued its efforts to assist the churches ravaged by the war. This work of charity established a close personal relationship between American and European churchmen and when the Lutheran World Convention was organized in 1923, John Alfred Morehead (d. 1936), an American, was elected as its first president.[21] In America the spirit of co-operation produced a number of significant mergers. In 1916 there were no fewer than six different Norwegian Lutheran synods. Three of these, the Hauge Synod, the Norwegian Synod, and the United Church, merged in 1917 to form the Norwegian Lutheran Church. The next year the General Synod, the General Council, and the United Synod of the South merged and formed the United Lutheran Church in America. The Synods of Buffalo, Ohio, and Iowa formed the American Lutheran Church in 1930. Each of these mergers followed a cultural pattern. Whether of German or Scandinavian origin, like united with like. The two great mergers of our own decade, however, transcend all cultural lines. In 1961 the American Lutheran Church (German in background) united with the Norwegian Lutheran Church and the United Danish Evangelical Lutheran Church, representing the pietistic tradition, to form the American Lutheran Church (ALC). The following year the United Lutheran Church, the descendant of Muhlenberg, merged with the once Swedish Augustana Synod, the American Evangelical Lutheran Church of Danish background and Grundtvigian leanings, and the (Finnish) Suomi Synod to form the Lutheran Church in America (LCA).

Theologically, the ALC is closer to traditional Lutheran orthodoxy than the LCA. A fundamentalistic view of Scripture is set forth in the constitution of the ALC. There it is stated that the church accepts the Scriptures "as a whole, and in all their parts . . . [as] the divinely inspired, revealed, and inerrant Word of God . . ." [22] The constitution of the LCA, on the other hand, makes a clear distinction between the historical revelation of God consummated in Jesus Christ and the Scriptures as "the divinely inspired record of God's redemptive act in Christ." [23] The strictly orthodox Synodical Conference, organized

[21] This body was re-organized in Lund, 1947, as the Lutheran World Federation.

[22] Art. IV.

[23] Art. II.

in 1872, which had embraced the Missouri and Wisconsin Synods as well as the very small Synod of Evangelical Lutheran Churches and a splinter group of the Norwegian Synod, dissolved in 1963. Charges of "unionism" and "liberalism" were brought against the Missouri Synod, especially by the Wisconsin Synod.

In the period between the two world wars there were some skirmishes over the issues of predestination, verbal inspiration, and the theological categories of seventeenth-century orthodoxy still dominated in the systematic writings of such men as Henry Eyster Jacobs (d. 1932),[24] C. E. Lindberg (d. 1930),[25] J. A. Singmaster (d. 1926),[26] and Francis Pieper (d. 1931).[27] But a new spirit began to exert its influence on the younger generation. The Stockholm Conference, 1925, initiated a lively dialog between Continental, British, and American churchmen. British theologians like Philip S. Watson and Gordon Rupp, and American Lutherans began to translate Scandinavian works and to interpret the Lutheran theology of Scandinavia for American Protestantism.[28] Two outstanding German publications were presented in an English garb to American Protestants. Theodore G. Tappert translated Herman Sasse's *Was heisst lutherisch?*[29] and John C. Mattes translated Köberle's penetrating study on justification and sanctification.[30] In recent years a great many European works, among them, those of Elert, Althaus, Heim, Aulén, Pinomaa, Ebeling, Wingren, Thielicke, *et al.* have been translated into English. Original studies in English which reveal the new appreciation of Luther as

[24] *A Summary of the Christian Faith* (Philadelphia: Lutheran Publication House, 1905).

[25] *Enchiridion in Dogmatics* (Rock Island, Ill.: Augustana Book Concern, 1922).

[26] *Handbook of Christian Theology* (Philadelphia: United Lutheran Publication House, 1927).

[27] *Christliche Dogmatik* (3 vols., 1917 ff.) trans. as *Christian Dogmatics* (3 vols.; St. Louis: Concordia Publishing House, 1950 ff.).

[28] Among these works are: Gustaf Aulén, *The Faith of the Christian Church,* trans. Eric H. Wahlstrom and G. Everett Arden (Philadelphia: Muhlenberg Press, 1948); Anders Nygren, *Commentary on Romans,* trans. Carl C. Rasmussen (Philadelphia: Muhlenberg Press, 1949); Eivend J. Bergrav, *Man and State,* trans. George Aus (Philadelphia: Muhlenberg Press, 1951); Regin Prenter, *Spiritus Creator,* trans. John M. Jensen (Philadelphia: Muhlenberg Press, 1953); Gustaf Wingren, *Luther on Vocation,* trans. Carl C. Rasmussen (Philadelphia: Muhlenberg Press, 1957).

[29] *Here We Stand* (Minneapolis: Augsburg Publishing House, 1938).

[30] *Quest for Holiness* (New York: Harper & Bros., 1936).

distinct from that of seventeenth-century Lutheran orthodoxy are evident in the works of Edgar M. Carlson, Herman A. Preus, Joseph Sittler and others. These men received many stimuli from the late John O. Evjen (d. 1942). Educated in America and abroad, Evjen's numerous writings in English, Norwegian, Danish, and German reveal a wide range of interest. They are also indebted to the Reformation research of Roland H. Bainton[31] and of Wilhelm Pauck.[32]

Johannes Knudsen has discussed the life and thought of Kierkegaard's great antagonist, N. F. S. Grundtvig, in *Danish Rebel*,[33] while in *The Moment before God*[34] by Martin Heinecken the thought of Kierkegaard and that of the author seem to be inseparably interwoven.

A. D. Mattson grappled with the social responsibility of the churches. His book *Christian Social Consciousness*[35] is an introduction to Christian sociology. The author does not present a static set of rules. He does not propose programs or techniques. He enunciates the basic principles of Christian ethics. George W. Forell, on the other hand, limited himself to a discussion of Luther's social ethics.[36] Since much of the study of the Reformer's social views in the English-speaking world is characterized by a dependence on secondary sources, especially on Ernest Troeltsch, the author tries to make Luther speak for himself in this volume. Forell undertook a similar task in the field of Christian doctrine. In *The Protestant Faith*[37] he emphasizes the great central religious assertions and the essential unity of classical Protestantism. Against the background of the revival of theology in America, T. A. Kantonen discusses the basic truths and perennial relevance of the Christian message in *The Resurgence of the Gospel*.[38] Jerald C. Brauer of the Divinity School of the University of Chicago presents a bird's-eye view of the whole history of Protestant thought and life in *Protestantism in America*.[39] Martin E. Marty has issued a call for a cultural ethic for American Protestantism. A radical Protes-

[31] *Here I Stand: A Life of Martin Luther* (New York-Nashville: Abingdon-Cokesbury Press, 1950).
[32] *The Heritage of the Reformation* (Glencoe: Free Press, 1961).
[33] Philadelphia: Muhlenberg Press, 1955.
[34] Philadelphia: Muhlenberg Press, 1956.
[35] Rock Island, Ill.: Augustana Book Concern, 1953.
[36] *Faith Active in Love* (New York: The American Press, 1954).
[37] Englewood Cliffs, N. J.: Prentice-Hall, Inc., 1960.
[38] Philadelphia: Muhlenberg Press, 1948.
[39] Philadelphia: Westminster Press, 1953.

tantism, in his eyes, is truly evangelical Catholic and is the only means of leading a Christian life in a secular culture.[40] E. G. Schwiebert, student of Preserved Smith, has tried to reorientate the study of Luther with particular emphasis on the theological, philosophical and sociographical factors that contributed to the moulding of the Reformer's thought.[41] The many-sided interest in Luther and the Reformation is gathered up in *The Martin Luther Lectures*[42] delivered under the auspices of Luther College, Decorah, Iowa.

The most versatile writer of the younger generation is Jaroslav Pelikan, formerly at Chicago, now at Yale University. He has published a number of works on the Greek Fathers, and on Luther. His interest in the ecumenical movement has been evidenced in *The Riddle of Roman Catholicism*[43] and in *Obedient Rebel: Catholic Substance and Protestant Principle in Luther's Reformation.*[44]

The organ of the Neo-Lutherans is *Dialog*, a quarterly published since 1962 in Minneapolis, Minnesota. Its many contributors represent a formidable array of scholars both American and European.

The most outstanding monument to the Luther renaissance in America, however, is the translation of *Luther's Works* in fifty-five volumes, published jointly by Fortress Press (formerly Muhlenberg Press), Philadelphia, and the Concordia Publishing House at St. Louis, with H. T. Lehmann and Jaroslav Pelikan as editors-in-chief.

BIBLIOGRAPHY

Anstadt, P. *The Life and Times of Dr. Schmucker.* York, Pa.: P. Anstadt & Sons, 1896.

Evjen, John O. *The Life of J. H. W. Stuckenberg.* Minneapolis: Lutheran Free Church Pub. Co., 1938.

Ferm, Vergilius. *The Crisis in American Lutheran Theology.* New York: Century Press, 1927.

———. ed.). *What Is Lutheranism?* New York: The Macmillan Company, 1930.

[40] *The New Shape of American Religion* (New York: Harper & Bros., 1958); *Second Chance for American Protestants* (*ibid.*, 1963).

[41] *Luther and His Times* (St. Louis: Concordia Publishing House, 1950).

[42] *Martin Luther Lectures* (4 vols.; Decorah, Iowa: Luther College Press, 1957 ff.).

[43] New York-Nashville: Abingdon-Cokesbury Press, 1959.

[44] New York: Harper & Row, 1964.

HAZELIUS, ERNEST L. *A History of the American Lutheran Church.* Zanesville, Ohio: E. C. Church Press, 1846.
MANN, WILLIAM J. *The Life and Times of Henry Melchior Muhlenberg.* Philadelphia: G. W. Frederick, 1887.
NELSON, E. C. and FEVOLD, E. L. *The Lutheran Church among Norwegian Lutherans.* 2 vols. Minneapolis: Augsburg Publishing House, 1960.
NEVE, J. L. and ALLBECK, W. D. *History of the Lutheran Church in America.* Burlington, Iowa: Lutheran Literary Board, 1934.
NYHOLM, PAUL C. *The Americanization of the Danish Lutheran Churches.* Minneapolis: Augsburg Publishing House, 1963.
QUALBEN, LARS P. *The Lutheran Church in Colonial America.* New York: T. Nelson & Son, 1940.
RICHARD, J. W. *The Confessional History of the Lutheran Church.* Philadelphia: Lutheran Publication Society, 1909.
SPAUDE, PAUL W. *The Lutheran Church under American Influence.* Burlington, Iowa: Lutheran Literary Board, 1943.
TAPPERT, THEODORE G., and DOBERSTEIN, JOHN W. (eds.). *The Journals of Henry M. Muhlenberg.* 3 vols. Philadelphia: Muhlenberg Press, 1942 ff.
WENTZ, ABDEL ROSS. *Basic History of Lutheranism in America.* Philadelphia: Muhlenberg Press, 1955. Rev. ed., 1964.
———. *History of the Gettysburg Theological Seminary.* Harrisburg, 1926.

CHAPTER VI

THE TWENTIETH CENTURY

With the beginning of the twentieth century the change from the authoritarian medieval mind to the scientific modern mind began to exert an ever stronger influence on the theological thinking of the American ministry and educated laity. The modern mind is empirical. It regards itself as autonomous, even in the realm of religion. It is opposed to the idea of religious absolutes. In order not to surrender God and religion in deference to science, theology thought that it was forced to discover a new plank on which its claim might rest. To accomplish this aim, two different possibilities seemed to offer themselves. Theology might try to overcome the limitations of sense-experience, rest religious authority in a broadened concept of experience, and surrender the doctrinal implications of religion as of little or no importance. This leaves the theologian in a dualistic position, i.e., the theologian may be a heathen in his thinking but a Christian in his feeling. Over against this dualism, Troeltsch and others resorted to a new rational defense of religion. Postulating a religious *a priori,* they claim that religion does not lie beyond the reach of human reason. A third vital factor in modern thinking is the principle of utility. Theologians pointed to the ethical tenets of Christianity in order to secure for it a place in modern society. The individual is taught that it pays to be good and society is taught that it cannot progress without the altruistic teachings embodied in historic Christianity. Experience, reason, and utility became the pivotal factors around which theology revolved, whereas the authority of the Bible was to be found only in the religious spirit which the Bible breathes.

Theology in Transition

At the opening of our century the semi-modernistic Ritschlian theology had reached America. Ritschlianism was a connecting link between the old and the new theology. Although it abandoned the metaphysical implications of the Church's teaching in favor of the prevailing agnosticism of the Neo-Kantian school, it maintained belief in a unique revelation of God which reached its climax in Christ and was recorded in the Bible. It should be remembered that the rise of this theology in America coincided with the rise of William James' pragmatism. The quest for the historical Jesus, the historical beginnings of Christianity, and the response to the practical implications of religion commanded the interest of theologians. Among the theologians who turned from a study of dogma to the Bible was Charles A. Briggs who, suspended in 1893 by the Presbyterian General Assembly,[1] was received into the Episcopal church.

The historical, anti-metaphysical trend is fully evident in the teaching of Henry Churchill King (d. 1934) at Oberlin College. In reconstructing theology he sided with Kant, Lotze, Ritschl, Herrmann, Harnack, and Julius Kaftan. He restricted theology to a study of phenomena and experience. Statements about Christ's divinity were not to be regarded as metaphysical propositions; they must be an outcome of man's personal experience with Christ. They must be "value judgments." A concept of the sonship of Christ in terms of substance or essence is wholly unsatisfactory.[2]

William N. Clarke (d. 1912) and William A. Brown (d. 1943) were two of the many liberal theologians who took full cognizance of this new trend in theology. Influences from Schleiermacher and Hegel were also at work in these two men. Clarke was a Baptist teaching at Colgate Seminary. Among his many students was Harry Emerson Fosdick. His most important accomplishment is the *Outline of Christian Theology* (1898). It virtually became the textbook of American liberalism. The influences from Schleiermacher and Ritschl are apparent from the opening pages of the book. "Religion is natural to man." In religion man recognizes his dependence on a Power above him. Theology is the science of religion, Christian and non-Christian alike. It is a historical study. All the great religions contain some truth. Christianity is the true religion because it correctly sets forth the real

[1] See Edwin H. Rian, *The Presbyterian Conflict* (Grand Rapids: Wm. B. Eerdmans Publishing House, 1940).

[2] Cf. King's two most important works: *Reconstruction of Theology* (New York: The Macmillan Company, 1901) and *Theology and the Social Consciousness* (New York: The Macmillan Company, 1902).

God and rightly interprets man's relation to him. The sources of theology are the universe as interpreted by natural science, philosophy, history, the various religions of the world, and man as seen in the light of psychology, but above all by God's self-revelation in life and action as preserved in the Scriptures. The divinity of Christ is a matter of religious experience. The *Outline* is a typical product of liberal individualism. The sacraments and the ministry are not discussed at all. In a brief review the church is defined as "a comprehensive name for the Christian people," and "as the sum of those organizations which have been formed to serve as organs of Christ, for the expression and promotion of his religion." [3]

The Presbyterian scholar William A. Brown (d. 1943) was more thoroughly trained in theology than William N. Clarke. As a student at Union Theological Seminary he had been exposed to both the old school (William G. T. Shedd) and the new school (Philip Schaff, C. A. Briggs and Francis Brown) Presbyterians. In Berlin he was a student of Harnack. He also learned to appreciate Schleiermacher and Troeltsch. The ethical in Christianity, he later held, must be tempered with the mystical and rational. Belief in the Absolute must be combined with the experience of progress. With a keen mind he faced the issue of science and its effect upon Christianity. The technique of science is also applicable to the religious problems. The final test of the truth or falsehood of any view, he says, is its ability "to unify and interpret our experience as a whole." Both faith and reason have a legitimate place in theology. The historic creeds, according to him, are affirmations concerning a great reality, but they are "couched in a language taken from the thought of a bygone age." To be intelligible to the modern man they need constant restatement and redefinition in the light of the present age. He worked out his views in *The Essence of Christianity*,[4] *Christian Theology in Outline*,[5] *Beliefs That Matter*,[6] and *Pathways to Certainty*.[7]

Of the historic churches, Brown said that the Roman church is

[3] William N. Clarke, *Outline of Christian Theology* (New York: Charles Scribner's Sons, 1899), p. 381.

[4] New York: Charles Scribner's Sons, 1902.

[5] New York: Charles Scribner's Sons, 1906.

[6] New York: Charles Scribner's Sons, 1928.

[7] New York: Charles Scribner's Sons, 1930.

pre-eminently a religion of authority while Protestantism, as he conceives it, is the religion of individualistic faith. To combine the superior qualities of both forms of Christianity, he suggested a third form, which he calls "democratic religion." By "democracy" he means "the conviction that since God speaks to every man directly according to his capacity each personality is to be respected by every other." He developed these ideas in *Imperialistic Religion and the Religion of Democracy*,[8] and in *A Creed for Free Men*.[9] The former was intended as a contribution to better understanding between Protestants and Catholics in America.[10]

The Rise of Modernism

The most influential exponents of Hegel's philosophy in America were Josiah Royce (d. 1916) at Harvard, and George T. Ladd (d. 1921) at Yale. While Royce was a romanticist with a strong poetic imagination, Ladd, who had been a Congregational minister, systematized philosophical thought. His monistic idealism verges on personalism. He also introduced the study of psychology from Germany.

The main representative of personalism was Borden P. Bowne (d. 1910). Personalism is a system of philosophy which views personality as the active ground of the universe. It linked itself with voluntarism and metaphysical individualism. It is theistic; but the divine being is said to exist in, and not apart from, his activity. Personalism combines Kant's emphasis on the personal self with Hegelian metaphysics. It is quantitatively pluralistic; but qualitatively monistic. The universe is a society of personal selves. The Supreme Self is immanent in the human self. There are six characteristics of personalism: (1) it is metaphysical; (2) ethical; (3) as a social philosophy it stresses "the free co-operation of different distinct individual persons in a common purpose"; (4) it is rational; (5) mystical; and (6) it infers the immortality of the human persons. With its stress on the personality of God and the sanctity of human life, it regards itself as the Christian philos-

[8] New York: Charles Scribner's Sons, 1923.

[9] New York: Charles Scribner's Sons, 1941.

[10] Cf. Brown's autobiographical sketch in Vergilius Ferm (ed.), *Contemporary American Theology* (New York: Round Table Press, 1932), II, 63 ff.

ophy *par excellence.*[11] Bowne never pretended to be a theologian. He held a chair in the philosophy department of Boston University. Nevertheless his influence on students of theology was great, along with that of Albert C. Knudson (d. 1953) and Edgar S. Brightman (d. 1953) and other men in Methodist institutions such as Ralph T. Flewelling and Francis J. McConnell.

Knudson conceived of God as an absolute, metaphysical and personal Being who is, at the same time, the immanent and causal ground of the world. He rejected both the imputation of the sin of Adam as well as that of the righteousness of Christ. Every individual begins his life on a non-moral plane and is redeemed only by a personal moral transformation.[12] Brightman, too, holds that all reality is personal, and that religion is essentially metaphysical. Experience reveals a world with good and evil in perpetual conflict. The good is confronted with real obstacles besides those of man's own making. The choice, Brightman says, is between metaphysical dualism or a "finite God" who is limited by what Brightman calls "The Given," i.e., the eternal, uncreated restraints in God's own nature. This fact accounts for the tragic suffering in the world. God is no more responsible for it than man is for his biological heredity; but like man, God is responsible for ultimate meaning of life.[13]

The Social Gospel

The emphasis on the practical implications of the divine immanence issued into what is usually called the social gospel. Tendencies which had been latent in American thought—the Puritan belief in social discipline and a thoroughly Christianized society, the optimistic moralism of the Deists, the humanization of God in revivalism and the emphasis which the revivalists laid on works as an evidence of salvation—together with the influence of science, evolution, sociology, and the pragmatic bent in the philosophies of the humanists, were the forces

[11] Cf. B. P. Bowne, *Personalism* (New York: Houghton Mifflin Co., 1908); also A. C. Knudson, *The Philosophy of Personalism* (New York: Abingdon Press, 1927).

[12] A. C. Knudson, *The Doctrine of God* (New York: Abingdon Press, 1930) and *The Doctrine of Redemption* (New York: Abingdon Press, 1933). Cf. Ferm, *op. cit.*, I, 219 ff.

[13] Cf. *ibid.*, I, 53 ff.

which created the social gospel. Christian activism came to be looked upon as a typically American form of religion.[14]

The stress on the social meaning of the gospel can be discerned in the work of Horace Bushnell, J. W. H. Stuckenberg, and later in that of Washington Gladden, Francis G. Peabody, Wilbur J. Tucker, and others. But it was Walter Rauschenbusch (1861-1918) of the Rochester Theological Seminary who became the outstanding spokesman for the social gospel. Kant, Hegel, Darwin, Karl Marx, Pfleiderer, Ritschl, and Dewey supplied Rauschenbusch with the necessary tools. The social gospel, he maintained, is a divine agent for continuing what the Reformation began. Historic Calvinism fails to deal adequately with a man "who appears before the judgment seat of Christ with $50,000,000 and its human corollaries to his credit, and then pleads a free pardon through faith in the atoning sacrifice." The concept of God must be democratized; it must be purged of all accretions of despotism so as to reflect the human values of freedom, solidarity and justice. The sinful mind is the unsocial and anti-social mind. The kingdom of God is a new society, humanity organized according to the principle of love. Both sin and salvation are super-individual, collective realities. Individual immortality is not essential to religious faith.[15] On other occasions he said that a perfect religious hope should include both eternal life for the individual and the Kingdom of God for humanity.[16]

Stanley Jones in his book entitled *Christ's Alternative to Communism*[17] was no less challenging and optimistic than Rauschenbusch. The alternative to revolution is the "Lord's Year of Jubilee." If men would only live according to the law of Christ, the latent power of Christianity would burst into a flame. The kingdom may be nearer than men suppose!

Under the impact of these teachings the so-called *Social Creed of the Churches* was drawn up by Frank Mason North and published

[14] Cf. W. A. Visser 't Hooft, *The Background of the Social Gospel* (New York: Oxford University Press, 1928).

[15] Rauschenbusch developed these ideas in *A Theology for the Social Gospel* (New York: The Macmillan Company, 1918).

[16] Rauschenbusch, *Christianity and the Social Crisis* (New York: The Macmillan Company, 1910), pp. 106-107.

[17] New York: Abingdon Press, 1935.

by the Federal Council of the Churches of Christ in America in 1908. It was revised in 1912 and again in 1932.

The weakness of the social gospel is now quite evident. It subjected the truth of religion to an external test. The objective validity of Christianity, according to the social gospel, is dependent on its social utility. The sovereignty of God is lost in the emphasis upon the democratic. The otherness of God is also lost. Man is regarded as essentially good, and his shortcomings are attributed to the influences of an unwholesome environment. Consequently, the social gospel is not only anti-individual, but also anti-ascetic and anti-eschatological. Inasmuch as Rauschenbusch leaned toward identifying reason and revelation, he confused the natural and spiritual orders. The kingdom is not the supernatural reign of God in which God will destroy sin, death, and devil and change the whole cosmic order; it is the spiritual reign of reason, liberty, and justice. It is immanent and will be established by the process of historical evolution. Rauschenbusch was not a Marxist. He believed that his portrait of the future state was a legitimate re-coinage of biblical ideas. Many "social gospelers" shared the naïve and sentimental optimism that an adequate mechanism of social justice would automatically create individuals disciplined to give according to their ability and take according to their need.

John C. Bennett, in his volume *Christian Ethics and Social Policy*[18] mentions three major characteristics which have been carried over from the social gospel to play a large part in the social thinking of most churches. The first is the emphasis on social responsibility. Unlike many in other years, very few today would try to claim that the soul is an entity completely independent of the body and of environment. Christ came to save both soul and body, as his miracles and the resurrection demonstrate. A second characteristic is the fact that the status quo is not necessarily ordained of God. The social and political orders are constantly changing. The third point is that the Christian West has been awakened to its responsibility to the classes and races that have been most oppressed in the past.

Empirical Theology

At the turn of the century American philosophy drew upon the empirical and idealistic traditions emanating from Kant and Hegel.

[18] New York: Charles Scribner's Sons, 1946.

With Charles S. Peirce (d. 1914) pragmatism was a logical method of clarifying metaphysics. In deciding on the rival theories of free will and fatalism, the practical effects that the object of our conception may have must be considered.[19] In John Dewey pragmatism degenerated into a useful tool of action. His faith is that of a humanist. He dismissed religion (faith in a distinct personal Being) as a survival of outgrown cultures. Supernaturalism, he asserted, separates man from nature and considers it accursed or negligible. But militant atheism is also affected by a lack of reverence for nature. A religious attitude preserves the dependence of man on the enveloping world. Such words as "God" or "divine" may convey the union of what is and what ought to be and may protect man from a sense of loneliness and from despair or defiance.[20] William James wanted to mediate between empirical materialism and the *a priori* concept of reality. Though truths emerge from facts, truth itself is greater than experience, which is always limited. He purposed to meet the needs of the individual and to uphold his independence of matter.[21]

The empirical theologians attempted to answer materialism and humanism on the common ground of human experience and scientific knowledge. They viewed their task on a broad scale which included both the development of the historical-critical approach to the Bible and a systematic reconstruction of the Church's teachings. They also expressed concern for the ethical teaching of the gospel in the search for social justice. They demythologized the New Testament long before Bultmann by reinterpreting theological symbols in a new intellectual situation. While Bultmann's emphasis is on grace and redemption they, like Harnack, found "the essence of Christianity" in the ethical teachings of Jesus.

This theology under discussion was especially promoted at the University of Chicago, though its impact was felt at other schools too. While Shirley Jackson Case (d. 1947) distinguished himself in the

[19] Cf. Justus Buchler, *Charles Peirce's Empiricism* (New York: Harcourt, Brace & Co., 1939).

[20] Cf. John Dewey, *A Common Faith* (New Haven: Yale University Press, 1934).

[21] H. W. Schneider, *A History of American Philosophy* (New York: Columbia Univesity Press, 1946), pp. 511 ff. E. D. Moore discusses the entire movement in *American Pragmatism: Peirce, James, and Dewey* (New York: Columbia University Press, 1961).

field of higher criticism, Shailer Mathews (d. 1941) and Henry Nelson Wieman tried to systematize the thoughts of the religious empiricists.

According to Mathews, theology is a study of religion as actual human behavior. Its dogmatic symbols are "patterns" which can be properly understood only through discovery of their origin and function in social experience. Dogmas are determined by a sociological factor, the *Sitz im Leben*, i.e., they reflect the cultural environment of their origin. "Father," "Lord," "King," "Judge" are cultural symbols and patterns by which a religious group expresses its experience. The idea of God symbolizes the objective and ontological, but God is not a metaphysical Being. God signifies "the conception of those personality producing activities of the universe with which men are organically connected and with which they can set up personal relations." [22] God is a term for the reality on which man ultimately depends. Jesus is the pattern of the good life, for in the Christian religion the thrust is toward the good life "in which the worth of others as persons is fully recognized." [23] Since "justification" is an element of a juridical and political pattern, it no longer demands consideration and is replaced by faith, which is a readiness to make Jesus' example and central teaching regulative in one's moral life. The Christian Church is the social expression of men's response to the values expressed in the life of Jesus.

Mathews defined his position as "conceptual theism," by virtue of which, he says, man is brought into personal relation with the personality-creating, personally responsive, and personally conceived activities of the cosmos. Unlike the humanists, he did not look upon God as "retired." Yet the willingness to regard all religious termini, including that of God, as symbols rooted in the relativities of human experience, actually undermines the objectivity of God.[24]

The content of the Christian faith suffered further loss through Edward S. Ames (d. 1958), the former dean of the Disciples' Divinity House at Chicago. Like Dewey, he conceived of God symbolically, in terms of life's function in the world. The word God signifies certain proportions of life in its ideal aspect. God is Reality idealized

[22] Shailer Mathews, *New Faith for Old* (New York: The Macmillan Company, 1936), p. 285.
[23] See Ferm, *op. cit.*, II, 187.
[24] *Ibid.*, II, 163 ff.

and personified, or expressed more simply, "God is life as you love it." "God is life, actual and potential, a process ever becoming, changing and permanent, novel and familiar." "God is the power which makes for righteousness."[25] We must strive to discover all religious values in experience. The only parts of the Apostles' Creed he would care to subscribe to, Ames said, are the statements of fact and experience that Jesus Christ suffered under Pontius Pilate, was crucified, dead and buried. One may also believe in the communion of saints and in the forgiveness of sins, he adds, provided an individual is granted the right to his own interpretation. All other statements are beyond the realm of verifiable facts.[26]

Henry N. Wieman distinguished himself in his endeavor to check the extreme religious subjectivism of the humanists by establishing an objective criterion for the apprehension of divine truth. Under the stimulus of the metaphysics of Whitehead and the empiricism of John Dewey, Wieman sought a doctrine of God which would express man's immediate relationship with God, and yet would also furnish a rational and experiential check upon all human concepts of God. God is the source of values disclosed in experience. The structure of progressing values has objective validity. It is not created by man; it is an order by which man is continually tested. This is meant when Wieman says that religion must be theocentric.[27]

The source of all human good, Wieman says, is a creative process which is always and everywhere operative in nature. This process has its own structure and can therefore be cognatively apprehended as any other structure of reality can be known. Knowledge of the creative process does not rest upon speculative reflection or upon faith but upon empirical evidence. It is not reasonable nor necessary to look beyond this process to God; the process itself is God. God is not Creator but rather creativity. The creative process must be distinguished from all other goods it has created such as family, an ordered society, peace, art, the United Nations, and the like. All

[25] Edward S. Ames, "Liberalism Confirmed," *The Christian Century,* March 22, 1939.

[26] Ferm, *op. cit.,* II, 13.

[27] In addition to his earlier writings Wieman has set forth his views in *The Source of Human Good* (Chicago: University of Chicago Press, 1946). He has reaffirmed his position in *Intellectual Foundation of Faith* (New York: Philosophical Library, 1961).

these are subject to change. No form of society is absolute. No form ought to be deified. The creative process alone demands man's highest devotion.[28] On this basis Wieman challenges the naturalist view that man is the creator of values. Man does not create values, but rather co-operates with the creative process. Wieman also challenges traditional Christianity. God is not a person; he is more than personal. Wieman incorporates the Christian ideology into his system, not as truth but as a myth provided by the creative process. Concerning morals, a theologian may interpret revolutionary communism as an expression of the creative process with which he is bound to co-operate. The conventional forms of sex life are not static. That which demands man's devotion is not monogamous marriage but rather sexuality as an expression of the creative process.

Charles C. Morrison, the late editor of *The Christian Century*, has given an excellent criticism of empirical theology.[29] To say that God is more than personal is sheer verbalism. "Does God know what He is doing? If He does, He transcends all His works." The treatment of sexuality is distinctly slanted in the direction of sensuality. To worship a creative process man must worship a God who is less than himself. The difference between Wieman and Dewey, for example, is minimal, for the humanist or naturalist must also admit that he is conditioned by the objectively given facts of nature. For the naturalist life depends on the objective fact of sexuality no less than for Wieman.

Douglas C. Macintosh (1877-1951) is another protagonist of religious realism. A Canadian-born Baptist, he experienced a conversion at the age of ten which gave him, he says, the comfortable conviction that he was "saved and in no further danger of hell-fire." [30] He later engaged in evangelistic work. His interest in philosophy led him to a point where he could no longer maintain his earlier evangelical concept of Christianity. In 1909 he was called to teach at Yale where he became a leader in the circles of the Neo-Realists.[31] Though theology is an empirical science, it cannot dispense with the task of meta-

[28] Cf. Ferm, *op. cit.*, I, 339 ff.

[29] *The Christian Century,* November 13, 1946, and January 29, 1947.

[30] Cf. Ferm, *op. cit.*, II, 275 ff.

[31] Cf. Douglas C. Macintosh (ed.), *Religious Realism* (New York: The Macmillan Company, 1931) and *The Problem of Religious Knowledge* (New York: Harper & Bros., 1940).

physics. Macintosh called his theory of religious knowledge critical monism, critical monistic realism, or critical realistic monism. The biblical doctrine of man's fall, he says, "has passed through the stages of being believed, denied, and ridiculed, and is now almost forgotten." [32] To him the essence of Christianity is a sort of moral optimism. "God the Father is the God of moral optimism, and He is not a different God from God the Holy Spirit, the God of the religious experience of moral salvation." It is this one God who "indwelt in such a fullness the life of the historic Jesus and gave Him so divine a value and function in human history and experience that He is rightly regarded as the divine man, the historic revelation of God." This, according to his view, is the "religious kernel or essence of Trinitarian Christianity," and constitutes what he calls "the new Christian orthodoxy." [33]

Another prominent theologian who aims at grounding theology in the combined evidence of experience and reason is Walter M. Horton of Oberlin College. In his earlier writings his thought revolved about a scientific natural theology and his interest centered in the person of God, the reality of evil, and the ethical implications of religion.[34] His book *Realistic Theology* (1934) which asserted that liberalism is dead as a theological system, marked a turning point in his development. Since that time he has been drawing closer to a biblical understanding of Christianity. He has lost faith in science as a guide through the perplexing problems of our time and, as he wrote in *The Christian Century:* "I look for concrete light and guidance, above all, to the biblical revelation of God in the series of mighty acts leading up to the incarnation of Christ, and all that has resulted from the incarnation in subsequent history." [35] Horton has expressed these ideas in a number of valuable studies.[36]

[32] *The Reasonableness of Christianity* (New York: Charles Scribner's Sons, 1925), p. 94.

[33] *Ibid.*, pp. 154-55.

[34] Cf. his *Theism and the Modern Mind* (New York: Harper & Bros., 1930); *A Psychological Approach to Religion* (New York: Harper & Bros.' 1931) and *Theism and the Scientific Spirit* (New York: Harper & Bros., 1932).

[35] May 17, 1939.

[36] Among these studies are: *Our Christian Faith* (Boston: The Pilgrim Press, 1945); *God, Jesus, and Man* (New York: Association Press, 1953); and *Christian Theology* (New York: Harper & Bros., 1955).

Conservative Reaction

Even during the twenties the Church did not lack men who combined faith in the gospel with scholarly attainment. Among these were John Alfred Faulkner, a Methodist (d. 1931) and J. Gresham Machen (d. 1937), a Presbyterian. In *Modernism and the Christian Faith* Faulkner committed himself unreservedly to "the metaphysical Christ." Though somewhat in sympathy with Ritschl's protest against the intellectualization of faith, Faulkner says that theology cannot be satisfied with mere value judgments. "You cannot save men with a Unitarian God." [37]

Machen was very pronounced in his opposition to Neo-Kantian agnosticism. The issue in theology, he said, is not between two varieties of the same faith, but between two essentially different types of thought and life. The faith of which the Church speaks is not the faith which Jesus had in God, it is faith in Jesus himself.[38]

A popular reaction of conservative forces against modernism arose in the so-called fundamentalist movement. Through numerical strength the modernists succeeded in gaining responsible and influential positions in their respective denominations. They seemed to aim at a gradual metamorphosis of the theology of their churches. It was this situation that awakened the warning cries of the fundamentalists. The inception of this movement dates back to the year 1909, when a group of devout believers united in a common effort to preserve the gospel of their fathers. In twelve volumes entitled *The Fundamentals,* they set forth the supernatural character of Christianity as they understood it. The publication of these volumes was made possible largely through the generosity of two wealthy laymen, Lyman and Molton Stewart, who founded a Bible institute in Los Angeles and established the Stewart Evangelistic Fund for promoting orthodox faith. The paganizing influences of World War I and the militant spirit which it instilled into the American public gave fresh impetus to the movement. In 1918 The World's Christian Fundamentals As-

[37] John Alfred Faulkner, *Modernism and the Christian Faith* (Nashville, 1921), p. 224.

[38] Machen voiced his views in *Christianity versus Liberalism* (New York: The Macmillan Company, 1923); *What Is Faith?* (New York: The Macmillan Company, 1925); *The Virgin Birth* (New York: Harper & Bros., 1930). Cf. Ferm, *op. cit.*, I, 245 ff.

sociation was founded. The Baptist weekly, *The Watchman Examiner*[39] marshalled all men "who mean to do battle royal for the fundamentals." Thus the conservatives became the fundamentalists.

The fundamentalists pursued two objectives: (1) to restore the primacy of the biblical gospel in the American churches, (2) to check all anti-Christian tendencies in the secular life and culture of our nation. To obtain their first objective they engaged in such positive constructive endeavors as evangelistic work by preaching and printed literature in order to win the unchurched (Christian Fund Association). Next, they tried to gather the "saved" into Bible conferences and spiritual retreats. Finally, they aimed at training spiritual leaders in Bible schools and such orthodox colleges as Moody Bible Institute, Wheaton College, Dallas Theological Seminary. Side by side with these constructive measures the fundamentalists engaged in a very lively crusade against every kind of modernism in the Church. Their polemical attacks upon theological liberalism created a serious friction in all the major churches of the Reformed camp. The conflict was especially bitter among the Baptists and the Disciples of Christ, who had hitherto objected to any creedal statement binding upon all members, and in the Methodist church, which had always put a vital experience of Christ above subscription to its Twenty-five Articles. The spirited rift created by this conflict became evident in the duplication of such church parties as the Methodist League for Faith and Life; the National Church League, the Churchmen's Alliance, and the Modern Churchmen's Union, representing respectively the Protestant, Catholic, and latitudinarian tradition in the Episcopal church. There was a duplication of church papers (*The Essentialist*, perpetuating *The Call to the Colors* of the Methodist fundamentalists; *The Christian Standard*, to check the liberalizing influence of *The Christian Century*, and *The Christian Evangelist*, among the Disciples), and of theological seminaries (the Northern Baptist Theological Seminary to counteract the influence of the Divinity School in Chicago; the Eastern Baptist Seminary to offset the teachings of Crozier Theological Seminary; and the Westminster Theological Seminary in opposition to Princeton). The fundamentalists resorted to the extreme measure of schism only in two cases:

[39] July 1, 1920.

the Baptist fundamentalists organized the Baptist Bible Union of North America in 1923, under the leadership of J. Frank Norris, William B. Riley, and T. T. Shields. This group continued to function till 1930, and remained, as its name indicates, loyal to the historical tenets of the Baptist church. In the second instance, a group of fundamentalists, at the urging of M. S. Kirkland, established an independent new denomination on a principle that cuts across all sectarian lines by founding the American Conference of Undenominational Churches.

In order to check the paganizing tendencies in public life and to achieve their second goal, the fundamentalists attempted to halt the teaching of evolution in tax-supported schools. The fundamentalist reaction against science became identified with the name and life of William Jennings Bryan (1860-1925), and reached its climax in the famous Scopes trial at Dayton, Tennessee, in 1925. In more recent years the fundamentalists have engaged in warfare against alleged Communist influences in the churches. These influences, fundamentalists claim, are strengthened by the National Council of Churches and by inter-religious groups and movements. The conflict between the modernists and the fundamentalists revolves chiefly about those doctrines that are especially open to rational attack: literal infallibility of the Bible, special creation; the possibility of miracles, the virgin birth and complete deity of Jesus, his atoning death for the sins of the world, his bodily resurrection and return in bodily form to the earth. Concerning all these problems the fundamentalists have been zealous in defending their strict view of orthodoxy.

The mentality of fundamentalism is prescientific. They want to defend and to prove biblical truth on the basis of a prescientific theology. But historical facts and scientific data cannot be discredited by an appeal to belief in the super-rationality of Christian dogma; therefore, the fundamentalist cause is lost. The apparent inability to distinguish properly between revelation and its historical setting in the Scriptures is the chief mistake in the theology of fundamentalism. The object of the Christian faith is the Christ, the Son of God. The man Jesus of Nazareth is certainly not immaterial to faith for "in Him dwelleth all the fulness of the Godhead bodily." But like the prophets before him and the Apostles after him, Jesus was a representative of an ancient civilization of Western Asia. The Church is not obligated to continue this ancient civilization; it is commanded to preach the saving revelation of God. The fundamentalists bitterly resent all findings of biblical criticism, for these findings seem to be aimed at the very foundation of the faith. But Christianity is not a set of rational doctrines concerning scriptural infallibility, the Trinity, virgin birth, the two natures of Christ, etc., important as such concepts may be; the gospel is a *dynamis*, a power, to save a sinful world through faith in the Crucified and Risen Christ.[40]

A peculiar tenet of fundamentalism is the doctrine of dispensationalism. According to a definition in the Scofield Reference Bible (in a note to Gen. 1:27), "a dispensation is a period of time during which man is tested in respect to some specific revelation of the will of God." Scofield distinguishes seven such dispensations: (1) innocence in the garden of Eden; (2) conscience, which began with the expulsion of Adam and Eve from Eden; (3) human government, embracing the period from the Flood to the call of Abraham, when man was put under civil authority; (4) promise, covering the lives of the patriarchs; (5) the law, extending from the Exodus to the crucifixion of Jesus; (6) grace, the time of the Church, and (7) the kingdom.

A similar outline of history is given by W. E. Blackstone in his widely read book *Jesus Is Coming*. On the basis of Ephesians 3:11 he presents the following plan of the aeons.[41] Eden, the aeon (i.e., age) of innocence; (2) the Antediluvian aeon of freedom when conscience was the only restraint; (3) the postdiluvian aeon of government, when man was put under civil authority, terminating with the destruction of Sodom; (4) the patriarchal or pilgrim aeon; (5) the Israelitish aeon, terminating with the destruction of Jerusalem in A.D. 70; (6) the "aeon of Mystery," the time of the Church; and (7) the millennium, the "aeon of Manifestation" (Rom. 8:19). Blackstone, who holds that the second coming will occur at the beginning of the millennium, asserts that the eschatological drama includes the first resurrection, when the saints meet Christ in the air. The Church thereby escapes

[40] For further information on the fundamentalist conflict, see especially Stewart G. Cole, *The History of Fundamentalism* (New York: R. R. Smith, Inc., 1931). Cf. also Smith-Jamison, *op. cit.*, IV, 1097 ff.

[41] W. E. Blackstone, *Jesus Is Coming* (New York: Fleming H. Revell Co., 1908), p. 225.

the seven-year period of tribulation. At the commencement of this period, the Jews who have returned to Palestine in unbelief will enter into a seven-year covenant with the Anti-Christ. At the end of three-and-one-half years the Anti-Christ will be revealed as the man of sin. Under the power of the devil and his angels the Anti-Christ will bring unparalleled persecution upon all who have not received his mark. "A third part [i.e., one-third] of the Jews in the land are brought through this time of trouble and are gathered by the Lord in Jerusalem to be purged of their dross." Upon an attack by the nations Jerusalem is taken and half of its people are carried into captivity. But the Lord will go forth for the destruction of his enemies and the deliverance of his people, and establish the millennial kingdom. At the close of the thousand years Satan is loosed for a "little season" to marshal the nations for a final battle against the Lord, but fire from God will destroy them. Then will follow the "resurrection of damnation" and the last judgment.

It is evident that in contrast to liberal theology, the fundamentalists have maintained the divine agency in the establishment of the kingdom. The eschatological hope is based not on philosophical speculation but on the promises of the Bible. Yet their interpretation of Scripture is thoroughly literalistic and atomistic, and the materialistic conception of the reign of Christ bears all the earmarks of Judaism. It is significant that with the exception of the older Erlangen school, Lutheran theology has been consistent in rejecting chiliasm as a "Judaistic opinion."[42] Modern dispensationalism is the result of the imposition of Darby's theology upon that of Augustine and of John Cocceius.[43]

NEO-ORTHODOXY

The rise of dictatorships in Europe and the expansionistic policy of Japan nullified the idea that World War I had been "a war to end all wars." By 1930 the United States was in the grip of a disastrous economic depression. The moral optimism of many liberals was severely tested. Perhaps the kingdom was not just around the corner. Some of the writings of Karl Barth were already available in English. But American theologians did not know what to think of him. In the

[42] Article XVII of the Augsburg Confession.

[43] Cf. the excursus in H. L. Strack-Paul Billerbeck, *Kommentar zum Neuen Testament aus Talmud und Midrasch*, IV, Part II (1928), 977 ff.

eyes of the fundamentalists, Barth was just another liberal, though more sophisticated, while the liberals and modernists were inclined to dismiss him as a strange survival of Protestant orthodoxy. In 1932 Walter Lowrie, who later became known as a translator of Kierkegaard, called upon Americans to heed the "crisis theology" which was calling into question virtually every proposition of Amercian liberal thought.[44] In the same year H. Richard Niebuhr introduced Paul Tillich to Americans by translating *The Religious Situation.* Reinhold Niebuhr, Richard's brother, attacked individualistic and utopian social thinking in his book *Moral Man and Immoral Society*. In 1934, Reinhold Niebuhr berated the pathetic inability of our senile social systems to amend the error of their ways in *The End of an Era,* and made the biblical roots of his protest more articulate in his Rauschenbusch Lectures published under the title *An Interpretation of Christian Ethics.* In the same year Walter Marshall Horton deserted the Macintosh-Wieman axis with his volume *Realistic Theology,* and the Methodist scholar Edwin Lewis caused no small sensation with the publication of his *Christian Manifesto.*

The clearest call to repent was voiced by George W. Richardson of the Mercersburg seminary in his book *Beyond Fundamentalism and Modernism: The Gospel of God,* published in 1934.[45] Aiming his criticism at both extremes, Richardson wrote that it is a serious mistake to assume that the gospel is in conflict with modern science, pyschology or social reform as the fundamentalists hold. It is an equally serious error to assume that the scientist, statesman and social reformer has no need of the gospel, as the modernists think.

When *The Christian Century*, beginning with the issue of January 18, 1939, published the spiritual autobiographies of twenty-nine scholars under the caption "How My Mind has Changed," it became evident that a new theological outlook had emerged. The liberalism which had been the common presupposition of Christian scholars had been seriously challenged for the first time. The optimistic belief in an evolutionary process as a means of ushering in the kingdom of God was viewed as superficial and unwarranted. The New Testament and

[44] Cf. Walter Lowrie, *Our Concern with the Theology of Crisis* (Boston: Meador Publishing Co., 1932).

[45] George W. Richardson, *Beyond Fundamentalism: The Gospel of God* (New York: Charles Scribner's Sons, 1934).

Reformation theology presented themselves in a new light. T. A. Kantonen was right when a decade later he spoke of a broad and many-sided "resurgence of the Gospel." [46]

Though the transition was a collective phenomenon, Reinhold (b. 1892) and H. Richard (1894-1962) Niebuhr have probably contributed more to American thought than anyone else by their incisive thinking and active participation in the life of the churches. Both of them were deeply conscious that the Church was in bondage to the social situation, to national, ethnic, and class ideologies, and both lamented that Christianity had so identified itself with the bourgeois ideals of Western capitalism that it had failed to understand the depth of the social crisis.

It is commonly held that Reinhold Niebuhr is not a systematic theologian. At Union Seminary he holds the chair of "applied Christianity." If systematic thinking means to think from a center and to relate all findings to this center, Niebuhr certainly qualifies as a systematic theologian. In his two-volume work, *The Nature and Destiny of Man*, Niebuhr discusses virtually all the leading concepts of Christian dogmatics except the doctrine of the sacraments. Though often concealed, Christology is the *leitmotif* of his thinking. In his theology he seeks to set forth the significance for contemporary man of the *Christ for us* and the *Christ in us*. "The issue of biblical religion is not primarily the problem of how finite man can know God but how sinful man is to be reconciled to God and how history is to overcome the tragic consequences of its 'false eternals,' its proud and premature efforts to escape finiteness." [47]

In passing from theological liberalism and a predilection for Marxist social theories, Niebuhr has often obscured the change in his mind by retaining the diction of the previous period. The title of his book *Moral Man and Immoral Society*, for example, is certainly misleading. The adjectives used suggest an orthodox Marxist as author. The title of the book should have been, as Niebuhr is reported to have said jokingly, "Immoral Man and Even More Immoral Society," for the

[46] T. A. Kantonen, *The Resurgence of the Gospel* (Philadelphia: Muhlenberg Press, 1948).

[47] Reinhold Niebuhr, *The Nature and Destiny of Man* (New York: Charles Scribner's Sons), I (1943), 147.

book's thesis is that the individual is the primary sinner though his sins grow in collective society.[48]

Niebuhr says of himself that he is a "supernaturalist" [49] in the sense that he believes that faith discerns the freedom of the divine or of the human person above the ontological and epistemological categories of philosophy, which Tillich regards as ultimate.[50]

Niebuhr's neo-orthodoxy is closer to Brunner than to Barth. In the nature of man Niebuhr discerns "points of contact" with God. He takes man as a creature of God, including fallen man, very seriously. The "image of God" is a relational term. "The self is a creature which is in constant dialogue with itself, with its neighbours and with God." [51] But the doctrine of original sin is no excuse for ethical indolence. The goodness of God's grace represents both God's forgiveness and overpowering of man. Rejecting ethical perfectionism as an idle dream, Niebuhr preserves the perfectionist element in Christianity in his view of Christian love. His ethic is an ethic of justification through grace by faith. Christian ethics cannot be expressed in static terms. Living responsively means making decisions in response to the vicissitudes of history where the believer's failures are covered by the grace of God. Because of the inherent sinfulness of man, including the believer, the kingdom of God cannot be materialized in the complexity and moral ambiguity of history. With these insights into the nature of life Niebuhr seems to contradict himself in his analysis of social and political issues. Classified as a radical, the older Niebuhr, in the eyes of many, seems to veer toward conservatism. Actually this apparent change was theologically conditioned and relates to an increasing appreciation of the created, organic factors in life in contrast to the tendencies which, stemming from the Enlightenment, treat social life and the instruments of order and justice as if they were merely artifacts. The freedom of the self to transcend rational categories cast a shadow of relativity over the rational recon-

[48] June Bingham, *Courage to Change: an Introduction to the Life and Thought of Reinhold Niebuhr* (New York: Charles Scribner's Sons, 1961), p. 161.

[49] Charles W. Kegley and Robert W. Bretall (eds.), *Reinhold Niebuhr: His Religious, Social and Political Thought* (New York: The Macmillan Company, 1956), p. 433.

[50] *Ibid.*, p. 434.

[51] Reinhold Niebuhr, *The Self and the Drama of History* (New York: Charles Scribner's Sons, 1955), p. 4.

structure of life. It is this indictment of relativity against the false assumption of reason that constitutes Niebuhr's attack on capitalistic liberalism as well as on collective socialism.[52]

In comparison with Reinhold, H. Richard Niebuhr was not as absorbed in the analysis of the ethical and social situation of our times. In the Preface to *The Meaning of Revelation*, which appeared in 1941, he appealed to Ernst Troeltsch and Karl Barth as his teachers. The theocentric orientation of Karl Barth is quite evident in Richard Niebuhr's emphasis on Christian ethics as God-centered, not sin-centered.[53] The influence of Troeltsch is more formal, affecting the method of theological inquiry. In dealing with the intricate problem of faith and history, Troeltsch postulated a religious *a priori* as an irreducible element in the noumenal self. The actual content of religion, on the other hand, is always embedded in historical particularity. No historical form of religion, Christianity included, is absolute. Without surrendering the absoluteness of the Christian faith, Richard Niebuhr was inspired by Troeltsch to investigate the cultural and ethical expressions in the American churches. The same concern also made him a leader in the field of theological education.

The Theology of Paul Tillich

There is an unusual breadth in the thought world of Paul Tillich. Born in Germany (1886) he came to America in 1933, along with other intellectuals dismissed or expelled by Hitler. In his earlier days he was close to the Barthian movement, but Barth and Tillich are actually as different as day and night. "If Barth is the Tertullian of our day, abjuring ontological speculations for fear that they may obscure or blunt the *kerygma* of the Gospel," Reinhold Niebuhr says, "Tillich is the Origen of our period, seeking to relate the Gospel message to the disciplines of our culture and to the complete history of culture." [54] Philosophy science, and history are all integrated into Tillich's system. His theology also breathes the spirit of true ecu-

[52] Cf. Theodore Minnema, *The Social Ethics of Reinhold Niebuhr* (Grand Rapids: Wm. B. Eerdmans Publishing Co., 1958), especially the Summary Observations, pp. 117 ff.

[53] See Paul Ramsay (ed.), *Faith and Ethics: The Theology of H. Richard Niebuhr* (New York: Harper & Bros., 1957), p. 140.

[54] Charles W. Kegley and Robert W. Bretall (eds.), *The Theology of Paul Tillich* (New York: The Macmillan Company, 1956), p. 217.

menism. Catholic theology needs the prophetic voice of Protestantism, while Protestantism needs the sacramental principle of Catholicism. Without Catholicism's insistence upon the "holiness of being," Protestantism's concern for the "holiness that ought to be" would wither away.[55] But Tillich does not share the Catholic predilection for natural revelation and a natural theology. Revelation is never natural, he says; it is always an ecstatic experience. Against Barth, on the other hand, Tillich is sincerely interested in nature and history as media of revelation.

The object of theology is that which concerns man ultimately, Tillich states.[56] The word "concern" points to the existential character of religious experience. We cannot argue about religion in detached objectivity. As the object of total surrender, religion also demands the surrender of our subjectivity. It is a matter of "infinite passion and interest." Because religion is a matter of ultimate concern, we must not confuse religion with scientific, historical, political or other problems which deal with our relation to the world of our existence. The first criterion of theology, Tillich maintains, is the question: what is the content of our ultimate concern? Since the first criterion must remain formal and general, the content cannot be a special object, not even God. The second formal criterion of theology is that which concerns us ultimately, that which determines our being or not being.

The basic source of systematic theology, Tillich says, is Scripture, for it contains the original witness of those who participated in the redemptive events of God. The Bible is both original event and original document. However, the Bible is not the only source of dogmatics. Its message could not be understood and could not have been received had there been no preparation for it in human religion and culture. According to Tillich the Word of God cannot be limited to a book. "The biblical message embraces more (and less) than the biblical books."[57] Properly speaking, religious experience is not a source of Christian dogmatics, for the event on which the Christian

[55] *Ibid.*, pp. 41-42. Cf. Tillich, *The Protestant Era* (Chicago: University of Chicago Press, 1948).

[56] Paul Tillich, *Systematic Theology* (3 vols.; Chicago: University of Chicago Press, 1950, 1957, 1963). Vol. I, p. 11 ff.

[57] *Ibid.*, I, 35.

faith builds is not derived from experience; it is given in history.[58] Rather is experience a medium of revelation.

Another important term used by Tillich in this connection is that of correlation. This term designates the interdependence of questions and answers, of philosophy and theology, of God and man. The questions are rooted in our human situation; the answers are derived from divine revelation. The analysis of the situation is the task of philosophy. In this analysis the theologian works as a philosopher. In keeping with this method of correlation, Tillich presents the whole content of the Christian faith in five parts. In each part he tries to correlate questions implicit in human existence with answers implicit in divine revelation: (1) reason and revelation; (2) being and God; (3) existence and the Christ; (4) life and the Spirit; (5) history and the kingdom of God.

The following are a few of the basic assertions of Tillich: (1) The content of revelation, says Tillich, is that which concerns man ultimately. Formally speaking, revelation is a "special and extraordinary manifestation which removes the veil from something which is hidden in a special and extraordinary way."[59] The hiddenness or mystery appears objectively as a miracle and is subjectively received in a state of ecstasy. Ecstasy is not a negation of reason; it is a state in which reason is beyond itself, beyond its subject-object structure. Reason could not receive any thing irrational or anti-rational without destroying itself. Likewise, miracle is not an event contrary to the rational structure of the universe. God is not split within himself. He is not a sorcerer of the cause of possession. A miracle is a sign-event. It consists of a special constellation of elements of reality in correlation to a special constellation of the elements of the mind. In short, reason and revelation are the two foci of a theological epistomology.[60] (2) The world is a structured whole, and every being participates in the structure of being. In religion God is the answer to the question implied in being. He is "being-itself" or "the ground of being." This is the only non-symbolic statement we can make about God. All other designations of God are symbolical, including the expression "personal God." Since a symbol participates in the reality it sym-

[58] *Ibid.*, I, 42.
[59] *Ibid.*, I, 108.
[60] *Ibid.*, I, 106.

bolizes, God may symbolically be called Person, Father, etc., for he participates in personhood, fatherhood, etc. But God is neither a Person nor a Father. "God is not God without universal participation."[61]

(3) Tillich's description of creation and man's fall is reminiscent of Origen. Creation, he says, does not describe an event. "It points to the situation of creatureliness and to its correlate, the divine activity."[62] It marks the transition from the eternal to the temporal. The creature is finite. Man does exist, and his existence is different from his being. With respect to his essence, the creature is "inside" the divine life; as to his existence, he is "outside." Man is separated from God and stands upon himself. Adam was in a state of "dreaming innocence, a stage of infancy before contest and decision."[63] Strictly speaking, the verb "was" is inadequate here since it presupposes actualization in time. This cannot be asserted of a state transcending potentiality and actuality. Thus "innocence" means a state of potentiality. Fully developed creatureliness is fallen creatureliness.[64]

Salvation lies in the actualization of the New Being which "is essential being under the condition of existence, conquering the gap between essence and existence."[65] The New Being appeared in a personal life, in Jesus as the Christ, whose life and mission were the conquest of the estrangement between being and existence, God and man. The paradox of the gospel is that essential manhood has appeared under the conditions of existence in one personal life without being conquered by the exigencies of finitude.[66] Christ is the Immanuel, the God for us. He also is the incarnation of the Logos, i.e., the personal manifestation of the intelligible foundation of the world.[67] This makes it possible for the Christian faith to enter into a dialog with culture.[68] But the Christ-symbol had its beginning before the appearance of Jesus. It began the moment man began to realize his historical estrangement and the question of the New Being. Likewise, the symbolical

[61] *Ibid.*, I, 235.
[62] *Ibid.*, I, 252.
[63] *Ibid.*, I, 259.
[64] *Ibid.*, I, 255.
[65] *Ibid.*, II, 118.
[66] *Ibid.*, II, 94.
[67] *Ibid.*, II, 95.
[68] Cf. Tillich's volume, *Theology of Culture,* ed. Robert C. Kimball (New York: Oxford University Press, 1959).

significance of Christ may come to an end in case of a complete transformation of historical mankind. Christ is only the center as long as our historical continuum last.[69] The Christ-symbol also has spatial limitations. Realizing the infinitely small part of the universe which man and his history constitute, the possibility of other worlds in which divine self-manifestation may appear and be received cannot be denied.[70]

(4) Life is actualized by self-integration. But self-integration is continually threatened by disintegration: health by disease, and the like. All forms of life, culture, morality, and religion, bear the marks of ambiguity. The divine answer to man's dilemma is seen in the manifestation of the Spirit of God which creates a new and spiritual community, the Church, and incorporates the individual into this spiritual community in which the individual participates in the New Being. Luther's dictum of *simul justus et peccator* best describes the paradoxical nature of this experience.[71] Participation in the New Being remains incomplete. Neither the individual nor the Church can wholly escape the ambiguities of historical existence. The riddle of life will be solved in the consummation of the world. (5) To the historical churches the answer is the kingdom of God, which is the end of history and the final conquest of the ambiguities of life. This end, which is the transcendent side of the Kingdom of God, is permamently present.

The doctrine of a twofold eternal destiny contradicts the biblical assertation that the creation of the finite is "very good" (Gen. 1:31). The doctrine of double predestination is demonic. The individual's participation in eternal life is expressed by the two symbols of "immortality" and "resurrection." By immortality Tillich means a quality that transcends temporality. If so used, no objection can be made to this term. However, the expression "resurrection" is preferred, for it is a token of the prophetic faith in the goodness of creation. Resurrection means that the kingdom of God includes all dimensions of being.[72] All life will be taken up into God, and God will be all in all.

Tillich's dogmatics constitutes an impressive system. Many feel that

[69] Tillich, *Systematic Theology,* II, 100-101.
[70] *Ibid.,* II, 95.
[71] *Ibid.,* III, 226.
[72] *Ibid.,* III, 412.

he has provided our age with a monumental tool for confronting the "cultured among the despisers of religion" with the truth of the gospel. Many regard him as the Origen or Schleiermacher of the twentieth century. In one respect he has transcended Schleiermacher. Unlike Schleiermacher, Tillich does not conceive of revelation as springing from the depth of the human mind. Revelation does not come *from* man, rather it comes *to* man. In Tillich man asks questions about the ultimate meaning of life. But in the Bible God addressed the first question to man and is continually asking and challenging man. Tillich's God is an abstract Personality Itself. In his little volume *Biblical Religion and the Search for Ultimate Reality*, Tillich maintains, against Pascal, that the God of Abraham, Isaac and Jacob is the same God as that of the philosophers. "He is a person and the negation of himself as a person." [73] He is abstract Personality Itself. Consequently, the assertion that in Jesus "God has become man," Tillich says, is a "nonsensical statement." [74] Jesus is the Son of God symbolically, for in him the Ground of Being became fully transparent, and in that sense Jesus is the final revelation in the continuum of human history. On the cross he subjected himself to the ultimate "negativities" of existence, to finitude and its categories, without losing himself.[75] Furthermore, for Tillich sin is implicit in finite existence; it is not actually guilt. Salvation means acceptance into the New Being. The edge of a final judgment is dulled, for every man will experience the "pains of hell" in being purged of non-being and be accepted into the "bliss of heaven," i.e., be reunited with the Ground of Being. Ideologically speaking, Tillich's theology is a theology "between the times," between the Reformation and German Idealism.

The Theology of Otto Piper

Otto Piper (b. 1891) is another theologian who came to America from abroad. In philosophy he holds to a realistic interpretation of reality. The prevalent nominalistic view, in his opinion, has not only made Protestant theology incapable of coping with the materialistic and biologic realism of modern science, it also has impoverished theol-

[73] *Biblical Religion and the Search for Ultimate Reality* (Chicago: University Press, 1955), p. 85.
[74] Tillich, *Systematic Theology,* II, 94.
[75] *Ibid.*, II, 158 ff.

ogy itself. As evidence of this Piper cites the fact that the concepts of angels and of Satan were dropped in modern theology or else given an insignificant place. In theology he rejects the static conception of God as the Absolute and stresses the dynamic aspect in religion: God is a personal God with unlimited power. Consequently, in the field of ethics, it is not possible for the Church to offer a so-called Christian program to the world; rather ought the Church make known the power of God in every concrete situation of life.

Conclusion

The Barthian reaction against liberalism was occasioned by a new understanding of the Bible. Kittel's monumental *Wörterbuch zum Neuen Testament* and the interest of theologians in the Dead Sea Scrolls bear witness to this. Biblical scholarship, especially in the field of the Old Testament and the biblical languages, is held in new esteem. Furthermore, the ecumenical movement has brought the churches into a dialog never before witnessed. The doctrinal interest of the ecumenical movement centers in the concept of the Church and the nature of the ministry. But is Neo-Orthodoxy (a term invented by its opponents) disintegrating? As previously mentioned, George W. Richards in 1934 pointed to a position "beyond fundamentalism and modernism." Fifteen years later Nels F. S. Ferre described his position as "beyond liberalism and Neo-Orthodoxy." [76] Neo-Orthodoxy, he felt, expresses a mood of irrationalism and despair. The Christian faith should make the fullest use of reason, thereby freeing theology from rationalization, but at the same time giving it a perspective from which the problems of contemporary life can be increasingly answered. Ferre makes a bold attempt to give a philosophical rationale to the Christian faith. Influenced by Whitehead, he wants to keep the aspect of process in his view of God and yet affirm that in God there is a higher order of being which is not subject to the limitations of existential processes. Love is ultimate being for which non-being is the condition and the occasion. Ferre's view of reality is an ultimate monism, involving a dynamic dualism, including also a distinct pluralism, wherein nature, time, and man are real, according to the nature

[76] Beyond Liberalism and Neo-Orthodoxy," *The Christian Century,* March 23, 1949.

of their being.[77] God is love and that means he is continually creative. He combines the ideal and the actual. God is also absolutely sovereign, and in the end will save all things. God has no permanent problem children.[78] In this way Ferre thinks he can hold together the struggle between good and evil and the idea that God transcends all limitations. Whereas Tillich speaks in guarded language about the historical limitations of the man Jesus,[79] Ferre ascribes moral imperfection to Jesus. Ferre's thought lacks the balance, discernment and circumspection which is so characteristic of Tillich's "system."

In 1959 the Westminster Press published three volumes intended to provide a clear statement of three contemporary theological viewpoints: *The Case for Orthodox Theology*, by Edward John Carnell; *The Case for Theology in Liberal Perspecive*, by L. Harold DeWolf; and *The Case for a New Reformation Theology*, by William Hordern.

Hordern pleads his case chiefly from the perspective of the Kierkegaard-Barth axis. DeWolf does not want to defend every tenet of theological liberalism but feels that a thankless generation has distorted such faithful Christian thinkers as W. N. Clarke, Walter Rauschenbusch, William A. Brown, Albert C. Knudson, *et al.* "Liberal" means to him a free, unbound inquiry into the nature of Christianity. His focus of attention is on the divine revelation preserved in the Christian community. He is anxious to show the importance of a natural revelation, which is so repugnant to the Barthians. Carnell is careful to distinguish between conservatism and fundamentalism. He holds to the principle of progressive revelation and admits that problems of authorship and preservation of the biblical text are a matter of historical criticism. This concession in no way interferes, Carnell holds, with the doctrine of plenary inspiration. Both Carnell and Hordern understand the incarnation as the personal indwelling of the Son of God in human flesh; DeWolf defines the union of God and man in Jesus in dynamic terms. All three writers have a different approach to the doctrine of the atonement. Hordern favors the *Christus Victor* idea as set forth by Aulén.[80] DeWolf sees in the cross

[77] Ferre, *The Christian Understanding of God* (New York: Harper & Bros., 1951), p. 18.
[78] *Ibid.*, p. 229.
[79] Tillich, *Systematic Theology*, II, 125 ff.
[80] William Hordern, *The Case for a New Reformation Theology* (Philadelphia: Westminster Press, 1959), pp. 142 ff.

the climax of the life and teachings of Jesus, adding that faith in the cross can release men for righteous living.[81] This interpretation clearly resembles that of Abelard and Ritschl. Carnell reiterates his faith in the satisfaction theory.[82] To a certain degree, though not entirely, these three scholars are perhaps representative of theological thought in contemporary America.

Henry P. Van Dusen, too, wants to remain an adherent of the liberal tradition, albeit a chastened one. Such gains of liberal theology as the historical critical approach to the Bible, its openness to science and social reform, and the like, he maintains, should not be lightly dismissed. In these matters the liberals may count on the support of the Neo-Orthodox theologians, but the latter will continue in their opposition to the liberal portrayal of Jesus by Ritschl and Harnack.[83]

Likewise, fundamentalism, whose mentality and tactics are severely reprimanded by Carnell, has experienced a rebirth that cannot be ignored.[84] Preferring to be known as "Evangelicals," the men identified with *Christianity Today*, published fortnightly since 1956, reveal thought which is abreast of contemporary philosophy and theology. They try to restore the "old-time religion" to intellectual and social respectability. Several factors have contributed to the rise of this movement: the "return to religion" in the Eisenhower era; the emphasis on the fact that American life is rooted in the Protestant tradition; the American penchant for direct, uncomplicated answers to complex problems; and the intense desire for evangelical warmth and simplicity manifested in the response to Billy Graham. Though not wavering in their insistence on the inerrancy of the Bible, they admit that we are confronted with phenomena which present difficulties that cannot be dismissed lightly. But they assert that revelation consists of acts and words. The writing of the inspired Scriptures is an essential part in the revelatory activity of God. Hence, "propositional truth" is an

[81] L. Harold DeWolf, *The Case for Theology in Liberal Perspective* (Philadelphia: Westminster Press, 1959), p. 75.

[82] Edward John Carnell, *The Case for Orthodox Theology* (Philadelphia: Westminster Press, 1959), p. 68.

[83] Henry P. Van Dusen, *The Vindication of Liberal Theology* (New York: Charles Scribner's Sons, 1963). Cf. also the re-affirmation of liberalism in Vergilius Ferm (ed.), *The Protestant Credo* (New York: Philosophical Library, 1953).

[84] Cf. Arnold W. Hearn, "Fundamentalist Renascence," *The Christian Century*, April 30, 1958.

indispensable element in revelation. By and large, their criticism of Neo-Orthodox theologians misses the point. The Neo-Orthodox do not maintain that Scripture is the human, and therefore fallible, response to revelation. The response to Jesus as the Christ and Son of God has never been a matter of the human mind. Whenever a man responds in faith he is moved by the Spirit of God. The ecumenical creeds are no less inspired than Scripture, but Scripture is the original response, whereas all other creedal or devotional statements are a dependent response, according to Tillich. This makes the Bible unique in its witness to Jesus as the Christ and Son of God and the criterion of all later doctrinal statements.[85]

BIBLIOGRAPHY

Aubrey, Edwin E. *Present Theological Tendencies.* New York: Harper & Bros., 1936.

Bass, Clarence B. *Backgrounds to Dispensationalism.* Grand Rapids: Wm. B. Eerdmans Publishing Co., 1960.

Braden, Charles S. *Varieties of American Religion.* New York: Willett, Clark & Co., 1936.

Burggraff, W. *The Rise of Liberal Theology in America.* Grand Rapids: Wm. B. Eerdmans Publishing Co., 1930.

Carnell, E. J. *The Theology of Reinhold Niebuhr.* Grand Rapids: Wm. B. Eerdmans Publishing Co., 1960.

Carter, Paul A. *The Decline and Revival of the Social Gospel, 1920-1940.* Ithaca, N. Y.: Cornell University Press, 1956.

Cauthen, Kenneth. *The Impact of American Liberalism.* New York: Harper & Row, 1962.

Cobb, John B. *Living Options in Protestant Theology.* Philadelphia: Westminster Press, 1962.

Coffin, Henry S. *Religion Yesterday and Today.* Nashville: Cokesbury Press, 1940.

Conger, George P. *The Ideologies of Religion.* New York: Round Table Press, 1940.

DeWolf, L. Harold. *Present Trends in Christian Thought.* New York: Association Press, 1960.

Eckhardt, Arthur Roy. *The Surge of Piety in America.* New York: Association Press, 1958.

Ferm, Vergilius (ed.). *Contemporary American Theology.* 2 vols. New York: Round Table Press, 1932-33.

Ferre, Nels F. S. *Searchlights on Contemporary Theology.* New York: Harper & Bros., 1961.

[85] Cf. Carl F. H. Henry (ed.), *Revelation and the Bible: Contemporary Evangelical Thought* (Grand Rapids: Baker Book House, 1958).

FOSTER, FRANK H. *The Modern Movement in American Theology.* New York: Fleming H. Revell Co., 1939.

HAMILTON, KENNETH. *The System and the Gospel.* New York: The Macmillan Co., 1963.

HARLAND, GORDON. *The Thought of Reinhold Niebuhr.* New York: Oxford University Press, 1960.

HOMRIGHAUSEN, E. G. *Christianity in America.* New York: Abingdon Press, 1936.

HORSCH, JOHN. *Modern Religious Liberalism.* Chicago: Chicago Bible Instistute, 1938.

HUGLEY, J. N. *Trends in Protestant Social Idealism.* New York: Kings Crown Press, 1948.

KELLER, ADOLPH. *Dynamis.* 1924.

———. *Karl Barth and Christian Unity.* New York: The Macmillan Company, 1933.

KEPLER, THOMAS S. (ed.). *Contemporary Religious Thought.* New York: Abingdon-Cokesbury Press, 1941.

KNUDSON, ALBERT C. *Present Tendencies in Religious Thought.* New York: Abingdon Press, 1927.

KRAUS, CLYDE W. *Dispensationalism in America.* Richmond: John Knox Press, 1958.

LEIBRECHT, WALTER (ed.). *Religion and Culture: Essays in Honor of Paul Tillich.* New York: Harper & Bros., 1959.

MACFARLAND, CHARLES S. *Contemporary Christian Thought.* New York: Fleming H. Revell Co., 1936.

———. *Trends of Christian Thinking.* New York: Fleming H. Revell Co., 1937.

———. *The Christian Faith in a Day of Crisis.* New York: Fleming H. Revell Co., 1939.

———. *Current Religious Thought.* New York: Fleming H. Revell Co., 1941.

MARTY, MARTIN E. *The New Shape of American Religion.* New York: Harper & Bros., 1958.

PIPER, OTTO. *God in History.* 2 vols. New York: The Macmillan Company, 1939.

SMITH, GERALD B. (ed.). *Religious Thought in the Last Quarter Century.* Chicago: University of Chicago Press, 1927.

———. *Current Christian Thinking.* Chicago: University of Chicago Press, 1928.

TAVARD, GEORGE H. *Paul Tillich and the Christian Message.* New York: Charles Scribner's Sons, 1962.

THOMAS, J. H. *Paul Tillich: an Appraisal.* Philadelphia: Westminster Press, 1963.

WIEMAN, HENRY N. and MELAND, BERNARD E. *American Philosophies of Religion.* Chicago: Willett, Clark & Co., 1936.

WILLIAMS, DANIEL D. *What Present-Day Theologians Are Thinking.* New York: Harper & Bros., 1959.

EPILOGUE

The international ecumenical movement has had a profound effect upon the churches. None of the churches can afford to exist in isolation. The constant interchange of theological thought through theological conferences and the printed word is expediting mutual understanding among the various branches of Christendom. This factor has contributed to a new appreciation of the great theological tradition of the past. Dialectical theology and the Luther renaissance are a part of this phenomenon. In view of the catastrophic events of the last half century, the optimism of nineteenth-century liberalism has been weighed and found false. The scholars, including Bultmann and his followers, have learned to listen anew to the gospel of sin and grace. However, Bultmannites are not as far removed from the nineteenth century as they may think. Kantian agnosticism and the idealism of Schleiermacher and Hegel restricted the task of theology to the description of subjective faith. The result has been that men lost sight of the redemptive acts of the living God. For this reason, Ebeling and his friends may easily undo the work which Barth, Brunner, and a host of others began during the dark days following World War I. The new so-called Evangelicals cannot change the course of events. Consistently applied, their theology would only widen the gap between the gospel and modern man. Christian theology must be a theology of the Word, not of a biblicism which makes the Book an infallible authority in every field of knowledge.

INDEXES

TOPICAL INDEX

INDEX OF NAMES

Type, 10 on 13, 9 on 11, and 9 on 10 Janson
Display, Garamond
Paper, Spring Grove E. F. with Titanium